# Working Words in Spelling

## Teacher's Edition

Grade 5

G. Willard Woodruff and George N. Moore
with Robert G. Forest, Richard A. Talbot,
Ann R. Talbot

**Great Source Education Group**
A Houghton Mifflin Company
Wilmington, Massachusetts

# Contents

Printed in the United States of America

*Great Source* ® is a registered trademark of Houghton Mifflin Company.

International Standard Book Number: 0-669-45954-2

3 4 5 6 7 8 9 10 - VHP - 04 03 02

# About Working Words in Spelling

**It works.**

- 100% spelling
- 100% effective
- Promotes student independence and spelling success.
- Easy to manage—just 10–15 minutes daily!

| Level | A | B | C | D | E | F | G | H |
|---|---|---|---|---|---|---|---|---|
| Grade | 1 | 2 | 3 | 4 | 5 | 6 | 7 | 8 |
| Student's Text/Hardcover | | ■ | ■ | ■ | ■ | ■ | ■ | ■ |
| Student's Text/Softcover | ■ | ■ | ■ | ■ | ■ | ■ | ■ | ■ |
| Teacher's Edition | ■ | ■ | ■ | ■ | ■ | ■ | ■ | ■ |
| Teacher's Resource Book | ■ | ■ | ■ | ■ | ■ | ■ | ■ | ■ |
| Wordfinder | ■ | ■ | ■ | ■ | ■ | ■ | ■ | ■ |

# Student's Text

**All the right words...all the right spelling skills... crisp, easy-to-follow directions...and a motivating variety of exercises that are fun to do.**

**EACH LESSON BEGINS WITH A SELF-CORRECTED PRETEST** following the test-study-test method.

**VISUAL WARM-UP** helps students form a correct visual image of the whole word.

**EASY-TO-FOLLOW DIRECTIONS** lead students to spelling independence.

## 26

**A. Pretest and Proofreading**

**B. Spelling Words and Phrases**

| | |
|---|---|
| **1. eighteen** | eighteen students |
| **2. eighty** | eighty days |
| **3. weigh** | to weigh and measure |
| **4. neighborhood** | a friendly neighborhood |
| **5. plain** | plain wrapper |
| **6. raise** | had to raise it higher |
| **7. maintain** | to maintain order |
| **8. ashes** | burned to ashes |
| **9. badge** | showed your badge |
| **10. flashlight** | the dimming flashlight |
| **11. edge** | at the edge of the wharf |
| **12. else** | nothing else to do |
| **13. kettle** | heated the kettle |
| **14. settle** | to settle in the town |
| **15. freckles** | covered with freckles |
| **16. quest** | their quest for gold |
| **17. question** | asked another question |
| **18. mention** | the mention of my name |
| **19. western** | wore western clothes |
| **20. cherries** | a basket of cherries |

*Other Word Forms*

| | |
|---|---|
| eighteenth | flashlights |
| eightieth | edges, edging, edgy |
| weight, weighed | kettles |
| neighbor, neighboring, neighborly | settler, settled |
| plainly, plainer, plainest | freckled |
| raises, raised, raising | questing |
| maintained, maintenance | questions |
| ash | mentioned, mentioning |
| badges | west, westerly |
| | cherry |

**C. Visual Warm-up** Write each word in its correct shape.

a.
b.
c.
d.
e.
f.
g.
h.
i.
j.
k.
l.
m.
n.
o.
p.
q.
r.
s.
t.



**D. Word Search** Find each of the spelling words in the grid below. The words appear across and down. Circle and write the words.

| | | | | | | | | | | | |
|---|---|---|---|---|---|---|---|---|---|---|---|
| q | u | e | s | t | i | o | n | a | t | n | e |
| v | j | s | w | e | s | t | e | r | n | a | r |
| l | o | r | a | i | s | e | i | r | l | j | m |
| f | l | a | s | h | l | i | g | h | t | k | e |
| r | e | v | m | e | i | g | h | t | e | e | n |
| e | t | l | e | d | b | o | b | y | v | m | t |
| c | w | e | i | g | h | a | o | p | s | a | i |
| k | p | l | g | e | v | s | r | l | e | i | o |
| l | r | s | h | w | m | h | h | a | t | n | n |
| e | k | e | t | t | l | e | o | i | t | t | d |
| s | j | s | y | v | m | s | o | n | l | a | t |
| q | u | e | s | t | b | a | d | g | e | i | d |
| c | h | e | r | r | i | e | s | t | i | n | d |

Across

1. ________
2. ________
3. ________
4. ________
5. ________
6. ________
7. ________
8. ________
9. ________
10. ________

Down

11. ________
12. ________
13. ________
14. ________
15. ________
16. ________
17. ________
18. ________
19. ________
20. ________

**E. Build a Word** Write the four spelling words that use *eigh* to make the long *a* sound.

1. ________
2. ________
3. ________
4. ________



**OTHER WORD FORMS**—a unique feature—extends word knowledge by presenting the related forms of spelling words.

**ACTIVITIES PROVIDE MOTIVATION THROUGH VARIETY.** Students write each word more times per lesson than in any other spelling program.

# Review Lessons

**Every five lessons, a Review Lesson reinforces all the spelling words from the five previous lessons, emphasizing their Other Word Forms.**

# Spelling Dictionary/WORDFINDER

**This useful dictionary toward the back of each student's text defines all the basic spelling words and lists appropriate Other Word Forms at the end of each entry.**

# Yellow Pages

**This self-help resource at the end of every student's text is a guide to better spelling. It provides proofreading tips, spelling rules, spelling strategies, and word lists to support spelling independence.**

**CHALLENGE WORD** exercises accommodate your higher-ability spellers.

**OTHER WORD FORMS** of the spelling words are practiced in every lesson.

**Spelling Words**

| | | | |
|---|---|---|---|
| eighteen | eighty | weigh | neighborhood |
| plain | raise | maintain | ashes |
| badge | flashlight | edge | else |
| kettle | settle | freckles | quest |
| question | mention | western | cherries |

**F. Generally Speaking** Write a spelling word for the group it best fits.

1. logs, fireplace, ________
2. lantern, lamp, ________
3. grapes, apples, ________
4. pot, pan, ________
5. medal, pin, ________
6. ordinary, simple, ________
7. keep, continue, ________

**G. Missing Vowel** The following words from the list are missing the same vowel. Write the words.

1. __ ls __ ________
2. s __ ttl __ ________
3. qu __ st ________
4. fr __ ckl __ s ________
5. __ dg __ ________
6. m __ ntion ________
7. w __ st __ rn ________
8. qu __ stion ________
9. rais __ ________

**H. Using Other Word Forms** Write the Other Word Form that fits each clue.

Base Words: maintain(ed) neighbor(ly) edge(y) raise(ing) eighteen(th)

1. follows the seventeenth ________
2. friendly with the people next door ________
3. kept in proper working condition ________
4. lifting up ________
5. nervous or uptight ________

**I. Challenge Words** Write the Challenge Word that fits each clue.

**understanding projector protection reflected refreshments**

1. This turns reels of film. ________
2. A seatbelt provides this. ________
3. You buy these snacks at the movies. ________
4. This image is given back by a mirror. ________
5. This is knowledge. ________

**J. Spelling and Writing** Use as many Spelling Words, Other Word Forms, and Challenge Words as you can to write *two* or more answers to each question. A few words are suggested. Proofread your work.

1. What could you do to start a safety-education program in your area?
   neighborhood – maintain – flashlight – badge – protection – understanding
2. What advice would you give to someone who wanted to capture a beautiful sunset on videotape?
   western – mention – quest – question – reflected – projector
3. What suggestions do you have for putting out a campfire?
   settle – edge – ashes – kettle – raise – else

106 Lesson 26

Working Words in Spelling 107

**A WRITING EXERCISE IN EVERY LESSON** promotes the transfer of spelling words into daily writing.

# Teacher's Edition

## Clear, Clean, Easy-to-Use

**OBJECTIVES** and **SUMMARY OF SKILLS** state the goals and the language arts skills contexts in which spelling is practiced for every lesson.

**OPTIONAL TEACHING PLAN** provides an alternative teaching plan for those wishing to emphasize sound/symbol relationships in spelling.

**PRETEST AND PROOFREADING** features a procedure for giving students the pretest and having them correct their own tests using the Corrected-test Procedure.

**WORD GROUPS** box classifies the spelling list by sound/symbol relationships.

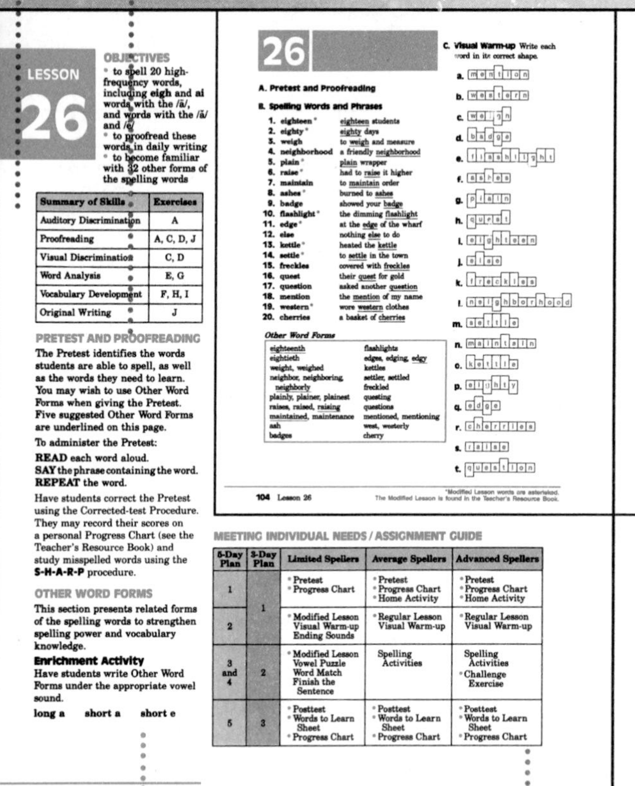

LESSON 26

OBJECTIVES
- to spell 20 high-frequency words, including eigh and ai words with the /ā/, and words with the /ă/ and /ĕ/
- to proofread these words in daily writing
- to become familiar with 32 other forms of the spelling words

| Summary of Skills | Exercises |
|---|---|
| Auditory Discrimination | A |
| Proofreading | A, C, D, J |
| Visual Discrimination | C, D |
| Word Analysis | E, G |
| Vocabulary Development | F, H, I |
| Original Writing | J |

PRETEST AND PROOFREADING

The Pretest identifies the words students are able to spell, as well as the words they need to learn. You may wish to use Other Word Forms when giving the Pretest. Five suggested Other Word Forms are underlined on this page.

To administer the Pretest:

**READ** each word aloud.
**SAY** the phrase containing the word.
**REPEAT** the word.

Have students correct the Pretest using the Corrected-test Procedure. They may record their scores on a personal Progress Chart (see the Teacher's Resource Book) and study misspelled words using the **S-H-A-R-P** procedure.

OTHER WORD FORMS

This section presents related forms of the spelling words to strengthen spelling power and vocabulary knowledge.

**Enrichment Activity**
Have students write Other Word Forms under the appropriate vowel sound.

**long a** **short a** **short e**

104 Lesson 26

26

**A. Pretest and Proofreading**

**B. Spelling Words and Phrases**

1. eighteen* — eighteen students
2. eighty* — eighty days
3. weigh — to weigh and measure
4. neighborhood — a friendly neighborhood
5. plain* — plain wrapper
6. raise* — had to raise it higher
7. maintain — to maintain order
8. ashes* — burned to ashes
9. badge — showed your badge
10. flashlight* — the dimming flashlight
11. edge* — at the edge of the wharf
12. else — nothing else to do
13. kettle* — heated the kettle
14. settle* — to settle in the town
15. freckles — covered with freckles
16. quest — their quest for gold
17. question — asked another question
18. mention — the mention of my name
19. western* — wore western clothes
20. cherries — a basket of cherries

*Other Word Forms*

| | |
|---|---|
| eighteenth | flashlights |
| eightieth | edges, edging, edgy |
| weight, weighed | kettles |
| neighbor, neighboring, neighborly | settler, settled |
| plainly, plainer, plainest | freckled |
| raises, raised, raising | questing |
| maintained, maintenance | questions |
| ash | mentioned, mentioning |
| badges | west, westerly |
| | cherry |

**C. Visual Warm-up** Write each word in its correct shape.

a. mention b. western c. weigh d. badge e. flashlight f. ashes g. plain h. quest i. eighteen j. else k. freckles l. neighborhood m. settle n. maintain o. kettle p. eighty q. edge r. cherries s. raise t. question

104 Lesson 26 — *Modified Lesson words are asterisked. The Modified Lesson is found in the Teacher's Resource Book.

MEETING INDIVIDUAL NEEDS / ASSIGNMENT GUIDE

| 5-Day Plan | 3-Day Plan | Limited Spellers | Average Spellers | Advanced Spellers |
|---|---|---|---|---|
| 1 | 1 | Pretest; Progress Chart | Pretest; Progress Chart; Home Activity | Pretest; Progress Chart; Home Activity |
| 2 | | Modified Lesson Visual Warm-up Ending Sounds | Regular Lesson Visual Warm-up | Regular Lesson Visual Warm-up |
| 3 and 4 | 2 | Modified Lesson Vowel Puzzle Word Match Finish the Sentence | Spelling Activities | Spelling Activities; Challenge Exercise |
| 5 | 3 | Posttest; Words to Learn Sheet; Progress Chart | Posttest; Words to Learn Sheet; Progress Chart | Posttest; Words to Learn Sheet; Progress Chart |

**D. Word Search** Find each of the spelling words in the grid below. The words appear across and down. Circle and write the words.

Across
1. question
2. western
3. raise
4. flashlight
5. eighteen
6. weigh
7. kettle
8. quest
9. badge
10. cherries

Down
11. freckles
12. else
13. eighty
14. edge
15. ashes
16. neighborhood
17. plain
18. settle
19. maintain
20. mention

**E. Build a Word** Write the four spelling words that use *eigh* to make the long a sound.

1. eighteen
2. eighty
3. weigh
4. neighborhood

Working Words in Spelling 105

OPTIONAL TEACHING PLAN

Write the four Word Group headings on the chalkboard. Ask the students to name the four spelling words with the long a sound that are spelled with eigh. Write the words as the students say them. Continue identifying the other Word Groups. Note that the long a sound is spelled with **eigh** in some words and with **ai** in other words. Point out the **dge** ending in **badge** and **edge**.

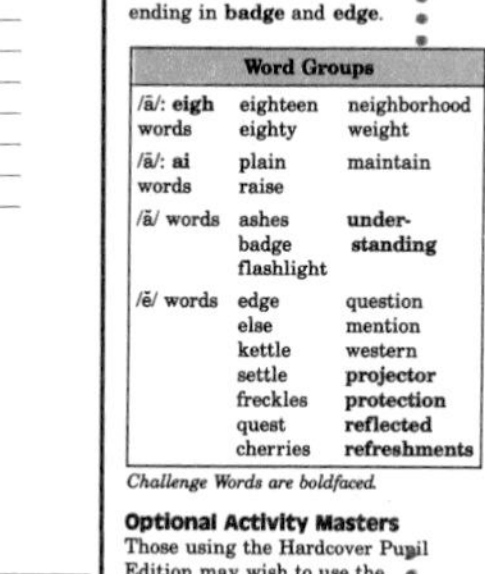

| Word Groups | | |
|---|---|---|
| /ā/: eigh words | eighteen, eighty | neighborhood, weight |
| /ā/: ai words | plain, raise | maintain |
| /ă/ words | ashes, badge, flashlight | **under-standing** |
| /ĕ/ words | edge, else, kettle, settle, freckles, quest, cherries | question, mention, western, **projector**, **protection**, **reflected**, **refreshments** |

*Challenge Words are boldfaced.*

**Optional Activity Masters**
Those using the Hardcover Pupil Edition may wish to use the Optional Activity Masters in the Teacher's Resource Book for Exercises C, D, and G.

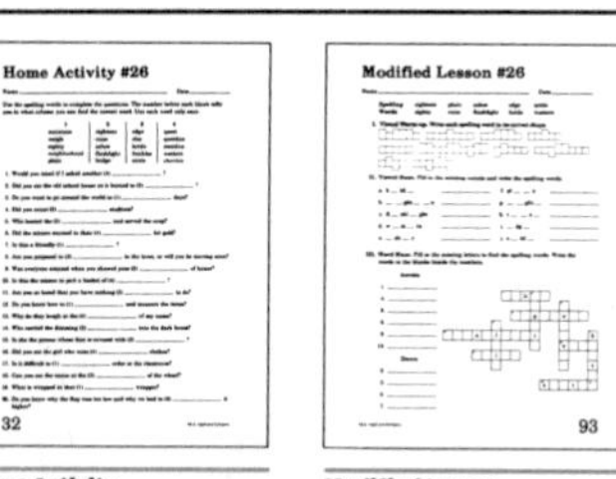

Home Activity #26 — 32
Modified Lesson #26 — 93
Modified Lesson #26 (continued) — 94

**Home Activity**
A weekly homework assignment

**Modified Lesson**
An alternative lesson for limited spellers

*(The Answer Key can be found in the Teacher's Resource Book.)*

Working Words in Spelling 105

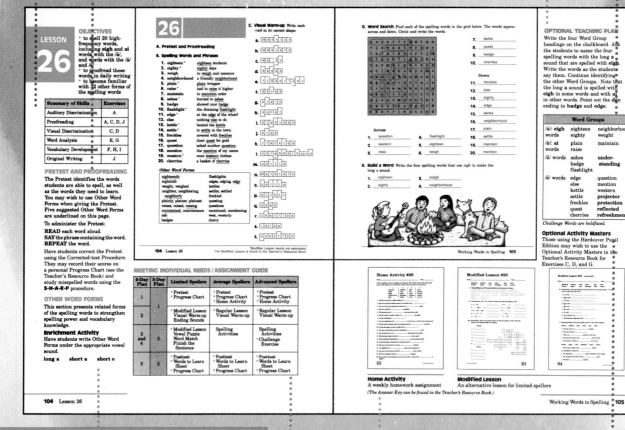

**OTHER WORD FORMS** suggests an activity for using these related forms.

**OPTIONAL ACTIVITY MASTERS** reference alternative blackline copymasters for selected hardcover exercises.

**MEETING INDIVIDUAL NEEDS/ASSIGNMENT GUIDE** helps plan your lessons, providing for three levels of spelling ability.

**HOME ACTIVITY** copymaster and **MODIFIED LESSON** copymasters reference optional support material for each lesson.

# Resources

**The Resources section at the back of this Teacher's Edition provides a wealth of program information and teaching support. See page 193 for a list of contents.**

**CHALLENGE EXERCISE** copymaster references additional activities for advanced spellers.

**USING OTHER WORD FORMS** focuses on using and understanding the other forms of the spelling words, highlighting the appropriate useful spelling generalizations.

LESSON 26 CONTINUED

Challenge Exercise #26

136

**Challenge Exercise**
Additional activities for advanced spellers

**Spelling Words**

| | | | |
|---|---|---|---|
| eighteen | eighty | weigh | neighborhood |
| plain | raise | maintain | ashes |
| badge | flashlight | edge | else |
| kettle | settle | freckles | quest |
| question | mention | western | cherries |

**F. Generally Speaking** Write a spelling word for the group it best fits.

1. logs, fireplace, ashes
2. lantern, lamp, flashlight
3. grapes, apples, cherries
4. pot, pan, kettle
5. medal, pin, badge
6. ordinary, simple, plain
7. keep, continue, maintain

**G. Missing Vowel** The following words from the list are missing the same vowel. Write the words.

1. _e_ ls _e_ — else
2. s _e_ ttl _e_ — settle
3. qu _e_ st — quest
4. fr _e_ ckl _e_ s — freckles
5. _e_ dg _e_ — edge
6. m _e_ ntion — mention
7. w _e_ st _e_ rn — western
8. qu _e_ stion — question
9. rais _e_ — raise

106 Lesson 26

**H. Using Other Word Forms** Write the Other Word Form that fits each clue.

Base Words: maintain(ed) neighbor(ly) edge(y) raise(ing) eighteen(th)

1. follows the seventeenth — eighteenth
2. friendly with the people next door — neighborly
3. kept in proper working condition — maintained
4. lifting up — raising
5. nervous or uptight — edgy

**I. Challenge Words** Write the Challenge Word that fits each clue.

**understanding projector protection reflected refreshments**

1. This turns reels of film. — projector
2. A seatbelt provides this. — protection
3. You buy these snacks at the movies. — refreshments
4. This image is given back by a mirror. — reflected
5. This is knowledge. — understanding

**J. Spelling and Writing** Use as many Spelling Words, Other Word Forms, and Challenge Words as you can to write *two* or more answers to each question. A few words are suggested. Proofread your work.

1. What could you do to start a safety-education program in your area?
   neighborhood – maintain – flashlight – badge – protection – understanding
2. What advice would you give to someone who wanted to capture a beautiful sunset on videotape?
   western – mention – quest – question – reflected – projector
3. What suggestions do you have for putting out a campfire?
   settle – edge – ashes – kettle – raise – else

Working Words in Spelling 107

**USING OTHER WORD FORMS**

**Vocabulary is expanded through the use of other forms of basic spelling words. Emphasis is on the relationship of syntax to suffix choices. The following generalization applies to the Other Word Forms used in Exercise H.**

**Spelling Rule**

Adding suffixes to words ending in silent **e**

**When adding a suffix that begins with a vowel to words that end with silent e, drop the final e.**
**(raise, raising)**

**POSTTEST AND PROOFREADING**

**Follow the same testing procedures used in the Pretest, although you may wish to correct the tests yourself. Have students write any misspelled words on the Words to Learn Sheet and record spelling success on the Progress Chart.**

**CONTROLLED DICTATION (Optional)**

These dictation sentences provide maintenance for spelling words previously taught and practice for words currently being studied. Dictation should be administered on Day 4. The teacher or another student may dictate the sentences. Be sure to dictate all marks of punctuation. Challenge Word sentences are preceded by an asterisk.

1. **Eighty neighborhood** centers make up the **western** city.
2. In her **quest** to earn a **badge**, the troop member answers one **question** about camping.
3. Did anyone **else mention** the **freckles** on your face?
4. Place the **ashes** inside the **kettle** to **weigh** them.
5. They will **settle** near the **edge** of the village and **raise** potatoes.
6. He is putting the **cherries** on a **plain** white cake.
7. Each of the **eighteen** campers needed a **flashlight** to **maintain** order at night.

*8. Keep the **refreshments** under **protection** so no animals will eat them.
*9. My **understanding** about light being **reflected** from a **projector** is wrong.

**THE SPELLING-WRITING LINK**

**Purpose** This activity helps students retain the correct spelling of words and transfer the words to their daily writing. Students use lesson words to answer questions promoting higher-order thinking skills.

**Procedure** Read the first question and write the suggested words on the chalkboard: **neighborhood, maintain, flashlight, badge, protection, understanding.** Have students list some Other Word Forms of the lesson words. Brainstorm with the class possible answers to question 1. Remind students to look at all the lesson words for ideas. Write the answers on the chalkboard, noting any lesson words.

**Practice** Tell students to finish the activity by writing two or more answers to each question. Remind them to proofread their work.

106 Lesson 26

Working Words in Spelling 107

Optional **CONTROLLED DICTATION** can serve as a testing alternative, as additional practice, and as maintenance of previously learned spellings. A separate, expanded version, *Daily Spelling,* is also available.

The **SPELLING-WRITING LINK** provides suggestions to link the Spelling and Writing activity in each lesson to the larger process of writing.

**POSTTEST AND PROOFREADING** completes the test-study-test procedure, reinforcing students' ability to proofread for their *own* spelling errors.

# Teacher's Resource Book

## This book of blackline copymasters provides optional resources for meeting individual needs and promoting the transfer of good spelling habits to personal writing.

### Three Levels of Practice

**HOME ACTIVITIES.** Introduces parents to the weekly spelling list and provides students with practice using the spelling words in context.

**MODIFIED LESSONS.** Two-page alternative lessons designed for less able spellers practice half of the weekly spelling list.

**CHALLENGE EXERCISES.** Provides more challenge for your advanced spellers.

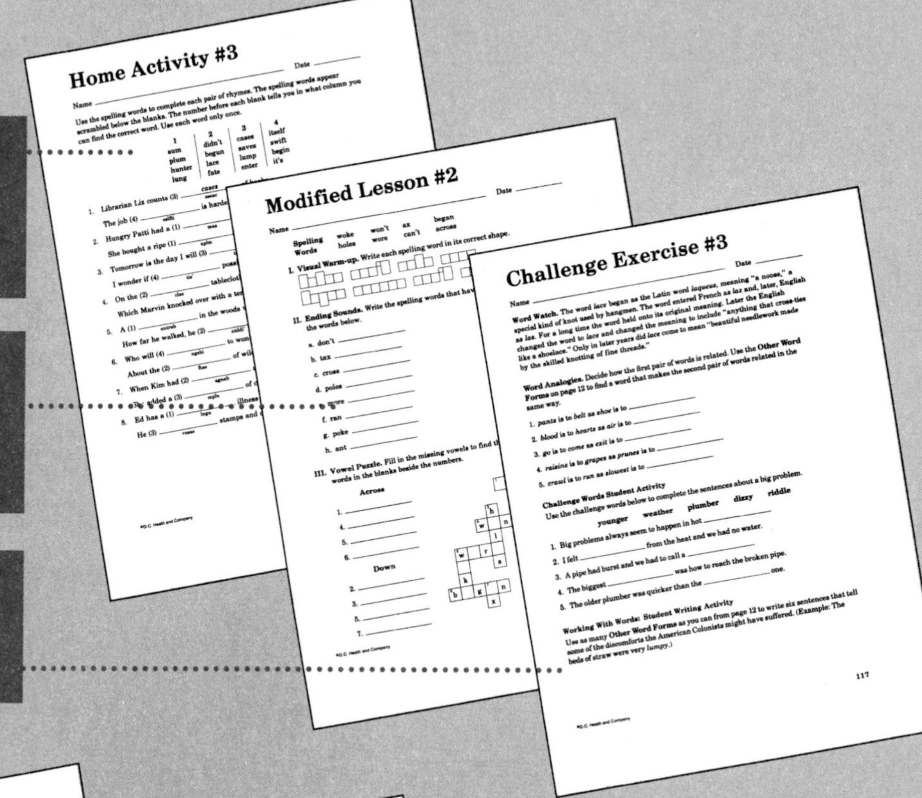

Home Activity #3

Name ____ Date ____

Use the spelling words to complete each pair of rhymes. The spelling words appear scrambled below the blanks. The number before each blank tells you in what column you can find the correct word. Use each word only once.

Modified Lesson #2

Name ____ Date ____

Spelling Words: woke, holes, won't, wore, ax, can't, began, across

I. Visual Warm-up. Write each spelling word in its correct shape.

II. Ending Sounds.

III. Vowel Puzzle.

Challenge Exercise #3

Name ____ Date ____

**Word Watch.** The word *lace* began as the Latin word *laqueus*, meaning "a noose," a special kind of knot used by hangmen. The word entered French as *laz* and, later, English as *las*. For a long time the word held onto its original meaning. Later the English changed the word to *lace* and changed the meaning to include "anything that cross-ties like a shoelace." Only in later years did *lace* come to mean "beautiful needlework made by the skilled knotting of fine threads."

**Word Analogies.** Decide how the first pair of words is related. Use the **Other Word Forms** on page 12 to find a word that makes the second pair of words related in the same way.

1. *pants* is to *belt* as *shoe* is to ____
2. *blood* is to *hearts* as *air* is to ____
3. *go* is to *come* as *exit* is to ____
4. *raisins* is to *grapes* as *prunes* is to ____
5. *crawl* is to *run* as *slowest* is to ____

**Challenge Words Student Activity**

Use the challenge words below to complete the sentences about a big problem.

**younger weather plumber dizzy riddle**

1. Big problems always seem to happen in hot ____.
2. I felt ____ from the heat and we had no water.
3. A pipe had burst and we had to call a ____.
4. The biggest ____ was how to reach the broken pipe.
5. The older plumber was quicker than the ____ one.

**Working With Words: Student Writing Activity**

Use as many **Other Word Forms** as you can from page 12 to write six sentences that tell some of the discomforts the American Colonists might have suffered. (Example: The beds of straw were very *lumpy*.)

117

©D.C. Heath and Company

Proofreading Exercise Lesson #12

Name ____ Date ____

**Proofreading the Spelling of Others**

Justin made a list of things to buy. He made some spelling errors. Circle the misspelled words. Write the correct words on the lines. (Some items on the list will contain no errors. Leave those lines blank.)

**Justin's List**

1. one thick brush to skrub walls
2. one bag of frash apples
3. blue and yelow flowers for the table
4. new outfits for the twins
5. one wooden picture fraim
6. soap for the shouer
7. a lace gowne for Carla's doll
8. two notbooks for history class
9. nails to build the dog house
10. peanuts for the klub meeting
11. toy bloks for the baby
12. thin paper to traice pictures
13. a power drille to make holes in wood
14. a book about the sky and spase
15. a toy swored for the school play
16. a mild soap for dirty hands
17. cookies for hungary football players
18. a book about lions and mighty animals
19. a sharp tool to skraip off old paint
20. a stoking hat for grandmother

146

Review Test: Lesson #12

Name ____ Date ____

**Directions:** Read each sentence. Select the word with the correct spelling to complete each sentence. Fill in the correct letter in the answer column.

1. Where's the ____ of cloth? A. skrap B. scrap C. scrape D. scrapp
2. It was ____ in the closet. A. haung B. hugn C. hunge D. hung
3. They will ____ their teeth. A. brushe B. brush C. braush D. brosh
4. It's almost three ____. A. o'clock B. oclock C. oc'lock D. oclok
5. We are not ____ ready. A. kwite B. kwit C. quite D. quit
6. Try not to ____ out. A. strike B. strik C. sterike D. stricke
7. I cashed a ____. A. chek B. check C. cheke D. checke
8. She wore a ____ ribbon. A. yello B. yallow C. yellow D. yelow
9. If you ____, I'll be there. A. wate B. wait C. weight D. waight
10. What can be ____ and thin? A. thicke B. thic C. thik D. thick
11. We learned a new ____. A. skil B. skile C. skell D. skill
12. They need new camping ____. A. outfitts B. owtfits C. outfits D. outfets
13. I tried to ____ the plate. A. scrape B. scraip C. skrap D. scrap
14. It's a white wedding ____. A. gowne B. gawn C. gown D. goun
15. Who took a cold ____? A. chower B. shower C. shouer D. showere
16. The kicker has a ____ toe. A. soer B. sore C. soar D. soor
17. Whenever they ____, they fall. A. clim B. clime C. klime D. climb
18. The lion has a ____ roar. A. mity B. migty C. mighty D. myty
19. We played some ____ of game. A. sorte B. sawt C. sort D. sot
20. I've nothing to ____ about. A. wory B. worry C. wurry D. werry

155

©D.C. Heath and Company

### More Practice

**STANDARDIZED-FORMAT TESTS.** Presents alternative formats for review tests, half-year tests, and end-of-year tests.

**PROOFREADING EXERCISES.** Extends the self-correction proofreading techniques learned in the program to proofreading the work of others.

# Instructional Support

**TEST FORM.** For students to record the pretest and posttest and to identify correct and misspelled words.

**PROGRESS CHART.** For students to track their pretest and posttest results and to monitor their progress.

**WORDS TO LEARN SHEET.** For students to record words they misspell on the weekly tests.

**OPTIONAL ACTIVITY MASTERS.** For hardcover users who wish the convenience of a copymaster format for selected activities.

**ANSWER KEY.** For all practice copymasters that appear in the Teacher's Resource Book.

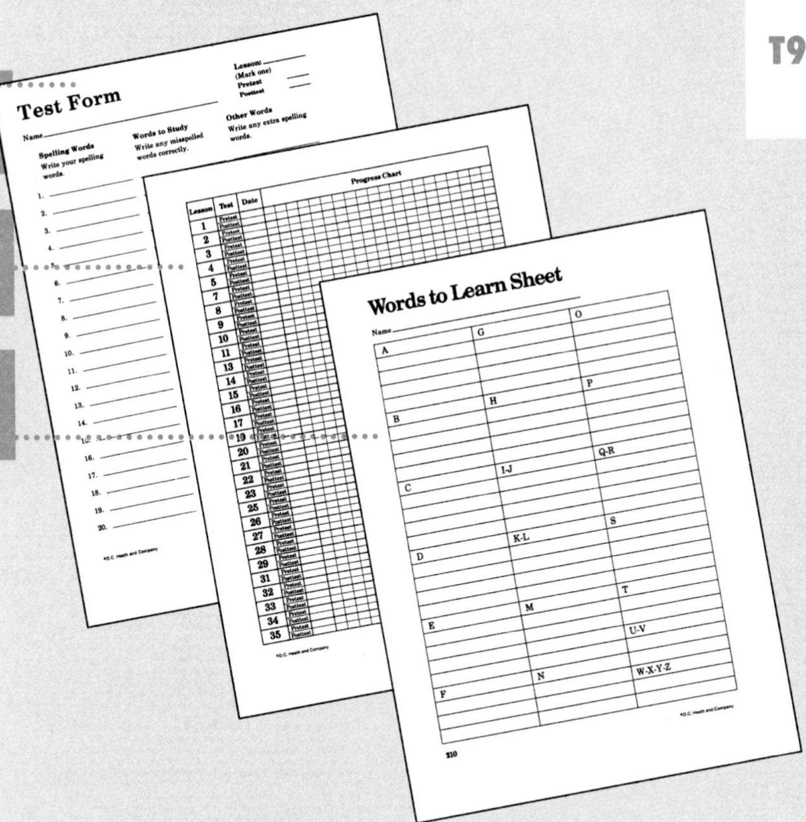

Test Form

Name

Lesson: (Mark one) Pretest Posttest

Spelling Words Write your spelling words.

Words to Study Write any misspelled words correctly.

Other Words Write any extra spelling words.

Progress Chart

Lesson Test Date

Words to Learn Sheet

Name

A B C D E F G H I-J K-L M N O P Q-R S T U-V W-X-Y-Z

©D.C. Heath and Company

# Personal Spelling–Writing Link Folder

**Four forms in the Teacher's Resource Book are designed to be copied and kept for reference in the student's writing folder as constant support for good spelling in personal writing.**

**PROOFREADING TIPS.** A duplicate of the Tips provided in the student text Yellow Pages, this sheet is a collection of techniques for proofreading final writing.

**STORY WRITING** and **SUBJECT WRITING.** These forms provide frameworks for writing narratives (Story Writing) and informational essays (Subject Writing) in which students can use their personal words to express themselves.

**PERSONAL SPELLING DICTIONARY.** Using multiple copies of this form, students can organize their personal words alphabetically for easy access when writing.

# The Research Basis

**Activities and approaches in the student and teacher materials are based on** confirmed **and** independent **research.**

| | Research Principle | Working Words in Spelling |
|---|---|---|
| 1 | **Spelling words should be high-frequency writing words that are well-established in students' reading, speaking, and listening vocabularies.** | This program teaches over 99% of the words children and adults need in their daily writing. |
| 2 | **The single most important factor in learning to spell words occurs when students correct their own spelling tests, with the teacher's help.** | The Corrected-test Procedure, an essential part of all levels of the program, is a self-corrected test procedure that involves the visual, auditory, and kinesthetic modalities. |
| 3 | **Spelling words should be initially presented in a list and later studied in the context of a phrase or sentence.** | All spelling words are introduced first in list form, and then in the context of a meaningful phrase or sentence. |
| 4 | **Premarking hard spots in words or identifying hard words for study are not useful practices. Hard spots in words or hard words are never identified.** | Students find their own hard spots and difficult words through the Corrected-test Procedure. |
| 5 | **To learn to spell, a student must form a correct visual image of the whole word.** | The S-H-A-R-P Word Study Procedure, Visual Warm-ups, and practice exercises stress formation of correct visual images of whole words. |
| 6 | **The most effective time allotment for the study of spelling is 60–75 minutes per week.** | Lesson materials promote brisk, motivating sessions of 12–15 minutes daily. |

| Research Principle | Working Words in Spelling |
|---|---|
| 7 / **The test-study-test method of instruction is superior to the study-test method.** | The test-study-test format is the conceptual framework for the lessons in this program. |
| 8 / **A systematic word-study procedure involving visual, auditory, and kinesthetic modalities should be established for studying spelling words.** | The S-H-A-R-P Word Study Procedure, which utilizes visual, auditory, and kinesthetic modalities, is employed through all levels of the program. |
| 9 / **Students completing word-study exercises using words already mastered will transfer up to five times as many words into their own writing as students who do not complete the practice exercises.** | Students who do well on the pretest are still asked to complete all word-study exercises. This additional practice promotes the transfer of spelling words into daily writing. |
| 10 / **Student interest plays a critical role in learning to spell.** | Known language arts activities, as well as crossword puzzles, word searches, and codes, stimulate and sustain student interest. |
| 11 / **The only spelling rules that should be taught are those that apply to a large number of words and have few exceptions.** | Only high-utility generalizations are taught in this program. Students arrive at useful generalizations inductively through the study of the words. |
| 12 / **Spelling becomes relevant only when the weekly spelling words are mastered and used regularly in daily writing.** | To increase transfer, only high-frequency words and their derivatives—those words most likely to be used regularly in student writing—are studied. Maximum reinforcement is achieved through the practice exercises as well as consistent opportunities for original writing and proofreading. |

# Getting Started

**The "About *Working Words in Spelling*" section and the "Resources" section in the back of this Teacher's Edition contain all the information you will need to make full use of the program. However, if you don't have time to review them thoroughly, you can immediately introduce the program in the classroom by following these five steps.**

1. Take ten minutes to familiarize yourself with the features of the Student's Text (T4–T5) and the Teacher's Edition (T6–T7). Every 4-page weekly lesson in *Working Words in Spelling* follows the same approach. Once you are familiar with the set-up of these four pages, you know the basics.

2. Select the Teaching Options from page T15 that best fit your classroom.

3. Preview the Student's Text with your students, focusing on the S-H-A-R-P Word Study Procedure on page 3, the four-page lesson, and the Yellow Pages beginning on page 177.

4. Turn to Lesson 1 on page 3 of this *Teacher's Edition* and get started. Use the Lesson 1 pretest to teach students the Corrected-test Procedure (T14).

5. Send the students home with copies of the Parent Letter found toward the back of the *Teacher's Resource Book*.

## *Now That You've Begun . . .*

**Once the students are actively involved in the program, you can familiarize yourself with the complete *Working Words in Spelling* program and adjust your approach to meet the needs of your students.**

6. Review your teaching options (T15) and the students' assignments. Individualize the program to meet specific needs. See
   - the *Teacher's Resource Book* practice options (T8),
   - Personalizing the Spelling Program (T16), and
   - the Meeting Individual Needs/Assignment Guide at the beginning of every lesson.

7. Become familiar with the Resources at the back of this *Teacher's Edition.*
   - Scope and Sequence and skills summaries lay out the foundations of the program.
   - Various research-based word lists provide a rich source of alternatives for benchmarking student achievement or expanding the regular spelling list.
   - Games can be used to augment practice as well as to provide a change of pace.

8. Celebrate good spelling in everyday writing assignments!

# Placement Test

## Testing the Students

*(Optional)*

**The optional Placement Test given at the beginning of the year can help determine the level of support and particular materials each student needs. Other sources include student records, standardized tests, conferences with previous teachers, and simply observing students' achievement during their first few weeks in the program. Ask students to number their papers from 1–20. Use the Level E Placement Test. The Level D Placement Test has also been provided for students who need additional testing at the next-lower grade level.**

### *Administering the Test*

**Dictate the words by using the following format: Say the word—Say the phrase—Repeat the Word. After giving Level E Placement Test, explain the Corrected-test Procedure (page T14) to students. (Students will use the procedure throughout the program to correct their own tests.)**

## Student Placement Levels

### Advanced Level

- Number Correct on grade-level test: 18–20
- Assign student to grade-level program.
- Allow student to work independently.
- Use Challenge Exercises from the Teacher's Resource Book.
- Expand the spelling list. (See T16.)

### Directed Instruction Level

- Number correct on grade-level test: 8–17
- Assign student to grade-level program.
- Provide Challenge Exercises for student at upper end of level.
- Allow opportunity to work independently.

### Limited Proficiency Level

- Number correct on grade level test 0–7
- Consider administering the Level D Placement Test.
- Assign student to grade-level program, but use the Modified Lesson instead of the regular weekly assignment.

### Level E Placement Test

| | |
|---|---|
| invent | to **invent** the wheel |
| company | **company** for dinner |
| depend | to **depend** on others |
| eighty | **eighty** days |
| record | played the new **record** |
| ninth | the **ninth** inning |
| downstairs | dashed **downstairs** |
| married | were **married** today |
| mountain | a **mountain** trail |
| canyon | a deep, narrow **canyon** |
| worse | **worse** than before |
| listen | will stop, look, and **listen** |
| settle | to **settle** in the town |
| perhaps | will do it later **perhaps** |
| square | each corner of the **square** |
| flashlight | the dimming **flashlight** |
| grasp | a tight **grasp** |
| doesn't | **doesn't** have to go |
| smooth | will **smooth** the bedspread |
| apron | a red-checked **apron** |

### Level D Placement Test
*(Optional)*

| | |
|---|---|
| print | large, even **print** |
| another | to one **another** |
| earth | the rotation of the **earth** |
| hunter | **hunter** in the woods |
| lesson | next **lesson** |
| dream | unusual **dream** |
| homesick | **homesick** camper |
| rolled | **rolled** across the floor |
| means | whatever it **means** |
| sort | some **sort** of game |
| busy | should be **busy** |
| o'clock | almost three **o'clock** |
| meeting | attended the **meeting** |
| slide | long, steep **slide** |
| pound | 89¢ a **pound** |
| itself | the job **itself** |
| packed | **packed** too tightly |
| tend | **tend** to wait too long |
| already | **already** there |
| wore | **wore** old clothes |

# Corrected-test and S-H-A-R-P

**Two special features of *Working Words in Spelling* should become second nature to your students: the Corrected-test Procedure and the S-H-A-R-P Word Study Procedure. These research-based strategies have proven to be the single most important factors in spelling success.**

## Corrected-test Procedure

The Corrected-test Procedure is a multi-modality procedure that employs the visual, auditory, and kinesthetic modalities. It helps students identify their *own* problem areas by focusing on the individual letters of each word, an essential practice in building spelling and proofreading effectiveness.

Students should use the Corrected-test Procedure after the pretest given on the first day and to correct every spelling test thereafter.

### Administering the Pretest

- Read each word aloud.
- Say the phrase containing the word.
- Repeat the word.

### Using the Corrected-test Procedure

The teacher will:

Spell each word slowly and clearly and write it on the chalkboard.

The student will:

- Touch each letter as the word is spelled. (The teacher may wish each student to put a dot with his or her pencil under each letter after it has been touched.)
- Circle any misspelled part.
- Rewrite the entire word correctly beside the misspelled word.

## S-H-A-R-P Word Study Procedure

The S-H-A-R-P Word Study Procedure appears at the front of each student text. This systematic procedure is a powerful instructional tool that involves the visual, auditory, and kinesthetic modalities. It helps students become more independent, more purposeful spellers. On the basis of the Pretest, students may adjust their own instruction by using the S-H-A-R-P Word Study Procedure to study the words with which they had particular difficulty.

### S-H-A-R-P Word Study Procedure

**S**ee the word.
- Look at the word.
- Think about the letters that spell the word.

**H**ear the word.
- Say the word.
- Listen to the consonant and vowel sounds.

**A**dopt the word.
- Close your eyes.
- See the word in your mind's eye.
- Think about how it looks and sounds.

**R**ecord the word.
- Cover the word.
- Write the word.

**P**roofread the word.
- Correct the word.
- Touch each letter.
- Think about the word again.

# Teaching Options

*Working Words in Spelling* suggests a 12–15 minute time frame for each session, a total of 60–75 minutes per week. These brief, frequent sessions keep interest high while allowing time for maximum spelling growth.

The program is flexible and can easily be adapted to fit your own classroom needs. Two possible teaching plans are modeled below.

| 5 Day Plan | 3 Day Plan | Teacher | Students |
|---|---|---|---|
| 1 | 1 | • gives Pretest<br>• reads spelling of words as students correct their own tests<br>• reviews S-H-A-R-P steps<br>• assigns Home Activity | • take Pretest<br>• correct their own tests<br>• record spelling success on Progress Chart<br>• complete Home Activity |
| 2 | | • selects instructional material from sources in the teaching notes to introduce the spelling words and Other Word Forms<br>• assigns Warm-up activity | • learn more about the phonetic and structural patterns of the spelling words and Other Word Forms<br>• complete Warm-up activity |
| 3/4 | 2 | • monitors students' work on word-study exercises<br>• assigns optional Challenge Exercises<br>• gives optional Controlled Dictation | • work on word-study exercises independently<br>• work on Challenge Exercises if applicable<br>• write Dictation Sentences if test is given |
| 5 | 3 | • give Posttest<br>• reads spelling of words as students correct their own tests | • take Posttest<br>• correct their own tests<br>• record test results on Progress Chart<br>• record misspelled words on Words to Learn Sheet |

# Personalizing the Spelling Program

**Any formal spelling program must have two primary goals:**

1. **to help students learn the correct spellings of a core writing vocabulary, and**
2. **to promote the transfer of these spellings and of effective spelling strategies to personal writing.**

***Working Words in Spelling*** **develops automatic spelling of a core writing vocabulary—the 4000 base words and over 13,000 related forms (Other Word Forms) that comprise 99% of the most commonly used words in both children's and adults' writing. True transfer of correct spellings into daily writing requires classroom strategies that strengthen the link between formal spelling instruction and students' writing. Following are five selected strategies for personalizing the spelling program to make good spelling part of students' writing.**

**1 EXPAND SPELLING LISTS.** Students need to be able to spell words related to topics they care about or are learning about. Each week, add five to ten words to the basic *Working Words in Spelling* word list. The additional words may come from commonly misspelled words in students' writing, from words brainstormed around a writing topic, or from a content area subject currently under study. (A list of grade-appropriate content area words appears in the Resources section at the back of this Teacher's Edition.) Include the new words in the regular pretest and end-of-week spelling test.

**2 PERSONALIZE SPELLING LISTS.** To increase responsibility and independence, ask students themselves to expand their own spelling lists, adding difficult words from their Words to Learn lists, interesting words related to their writing, or challenging words that are simply fun to spell. Have students select one to five personal words after the pretest, allowing students who make the fewest mistakes (and thus need to study the fewest words) to add the most personal words to their lists. After the group spelling test at the end of the week, let pairs of students take turns testing each other on their personal words.

**3 MAKE PROOFREADING FOR SPELLING A REGULAR PART OF DAILY WRITING.** Students should always proofread and correct the spellings in final published writing. Sometimes, notes and drafts that will be referred to later may also be proofread and corrected. The Proofreading Tips in the Yellow Pages of the Student's Text provide a variety of strategies for checking and correcting spelling. They should be part of every student's writing folder.

**4 PROMOTE PERSONAL WORD LISTS.** Help students develop the habit of keeping personal word lists. The Spelling Strategies section of the Yellow Pages and the Personal Spelling-Writing Link section in the *Teacher's Resource Book* support the use of personal words lists.

**5 NURTURE CONFIDENT SPELLERS.** Since students' reading, listening, and speaking vocabularies are far greater than their spelling vocabularies, it is likely that any developing writer will want to use words that he or she cannot confidently spell with complete accuracy. Encourage students when drafting to use their knowledge of spelling rules, word patterns, and visual configurations to "approximate" (See the Approximation strategy in the Yellow Pages) correct spellings, returning later to proofread for and correct the spelling. This approximation-and-correction technique teaches two critical lessons:

- Writing fluency and using rich words are important in drafting.
- Correct spelling is important in final written work.

# WORKING WORDS IN Spelling

G. Willard Woodruff and George N. Moore
with Robert G. Forest, Richard A. Talbot, Ann R. Talbot

# E

GREAT SOURCE EDUCATION GROUP
A Houghton Mifflin Company
Wilmington, Massachusetts

# Contents



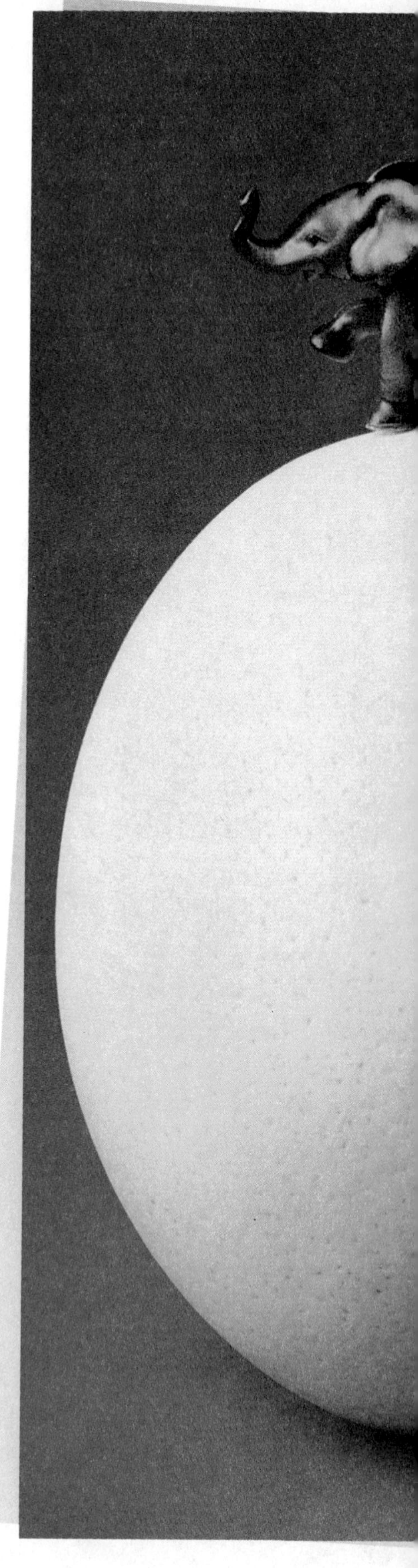

Art and design credits appear on page 192.



Printed in the United States of America

*Great Source* is a trademark of Houghton Mifflin Company.

International Standard Book Number: 0-669-45938-0

1 2 3 4 5 6 7 8 9 10 - BA - 04 03 02 01 00 99 98 97

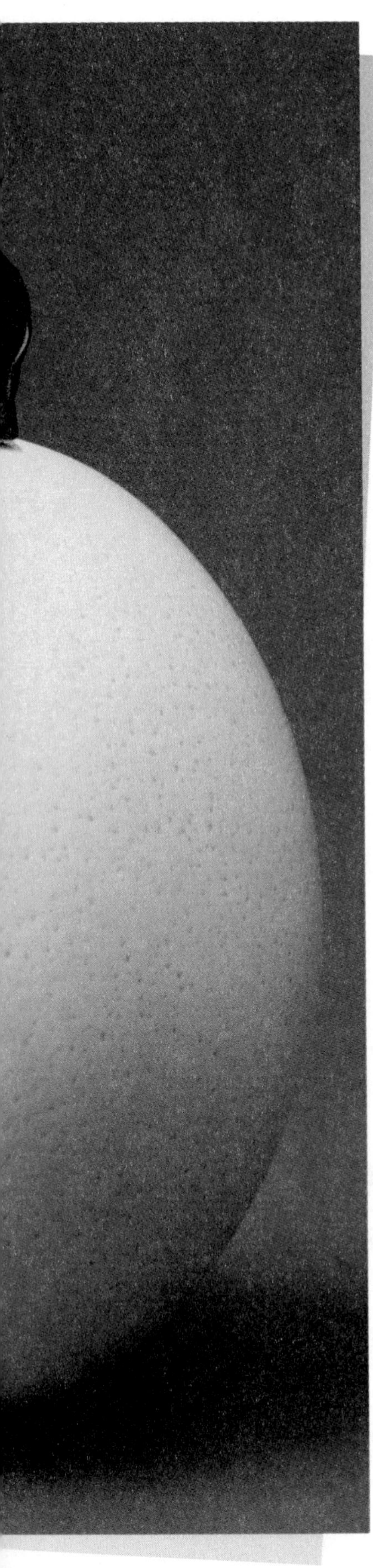

# Become a SHARP speller

## See the word.

- Look at the word.
- Think about the letters that spell the word.

## Hear the word.

- Say the word.
- Listen to the consonant and vowel sounds.

## Adopt the word.

- Close your eyes.
- See the word in your mind's eye.
- Think how it looks and sounds.

## Record the word.

- Cover the word.
- Write the word.

## Proofread the word.

- Correct the word.
- Touch each letter.
- Think about the word again.

# LESSON 1

## OBJECTIVES

- to spell 20 high-frequency words with the /ā/ and /âr/
- to proofread these words in daily writing
- to become familiar with 41 other forms of the spelling words

| Summary of Skills | Exercises |
|---|---|
| Auditory Discrimination | A |
| Proofreading | A, C, I |
| Visual Discrimination | C |
| Vocabulary Development | D, E, H |
| Context Usage | F |
| Word Analysis | G |
| Original Writing | I |

## PRETEST AND PROOFREADING

The Pretest identifies the words students are able to spell, as well as the words they need to learn. You may wish to use Other Word Forms when giving the Pretest. Five suggested Other Word Forms are underlined on this page.

To administer the Pretest:

**READ** each word aloud.
**SAY** the phrase containing the word.
**REPEAT** the word.

Have students correct the Pretest using the Corrected-test Procedure. They may record their scores on a personal Progress Chart (see the Teacher's Resource Book) and study misspelled words using the **S-H-A-R-P** procedure.

## OTHER WORD FORMS

This section presents related forms of the spelling words to strengthen spelling power and vocabulary knowledge.

### Enrichment Activity

Have students write sentences that include these Other Word Forms.

1. **mistakes – comparing**
2. **operates – safest**
3. **escaped – rarely**
4. **scary – whaler**

**A. Pretest and Proofreading**

**B. Spelling Words and Phrases**

| | |
|---|---|
| **1. grace*** | moves with grace |
| **2. graze** | to graze in the meadow |
| **3. whale*** | protecting the whale |
| **4. brake** | tightened the brake |
| **5. operate** | to operate the machines |
| **6. mistake*** | without a mistake |
| **7. escape** | to escape from danger |
| **8. grapes*** | a bunch of grapes |
| **9. safely** | drove safely |
| **10. crazy*** | a crazy day |
| **11. break*** | to break a dish |
| **12. greatest*** | the greatest animal |
| **13. fare** | paid a full fare |
| **14. bare*** | running in bare feet |
| **15. rare** | an extremely rare gem |
| **16. scare*** | wouldn't scare me |
| **17. square*** | each corner of the square |
| **18. compare** | to compare prices |
| **19. preparing** | preparing a meal |
| **20. scarce** | a scarce supply |

*Other Word Forms*

| | |
|---|---|
| graces, graceful | broke, breaking |
| grazes, grazing | great, greatly |
| whaling, whaler | fares, faring |
| braking | barely, barest |
| operates, operating | rarer, rarest, rarely |
| mistakes, mistaken, mistaking | scared, scaring, scary |
| escaped, escaping | squarest, squarely |
| grape | comparing, comparison |
| safe, safest | prepare, preparation |
| craziest, crazily | scarcest, scarcely |

**C. Visual Warm-up** Write each word in its correct shape.

a. fare
b. bare
c. operate
d. grace
e. graze
f. compare
g. rare
h. safely
i. preparing
j. whale
k. greatest
l. crazy
m. scare
n. brake
o. escape
p. square
q. grapes
r. break
s. scarce
t. mistake



*Modified Lesson words are asterisked.
The Modified Lesson is found in the Teacher's Resource Book.

## MEETING INDIVIDUAL NEEDS / ASSIGNMENT GUIDE

| 5-Day Plan | 3-Day Plan | Limited Spellers | Average Spellers | Advanced Spellers |
|---|---|---|---|---|
| 1 | 1 | • Pretest • Progress Chart | • Pretest • Progress Chart • Home Activity | • Pretest • Progress Chart • Home Activity |
| 2 | 1 | • Modified Lesson Visual Warm-up Ending Sounds | • Regular Lesson Visual Warm-up | • Regular Lesson Visual Warm-up |
| 3 and 4 | 2 | • Modified Lesson Vowel Puzzle Word Match Finish the Sentence | Spelling Activities | Spelling Activities • Challenge Exercise |
| 5 | 3 | • Posttest • Words to Learn Sheet • Progress Chart | • Posttest • Words to Learn Sheet • Progress Chart | • Posttest • Words to Learn Sheet • Progress Chart |

**D. Hidden Words** Find the spelling word in each larger word below. Write the word.

1. mngracefol grace
2. scarceing scarce
3. toscrazy crazy
4. sbrakeng brake
5. bareion bare
6. unmistakem mistake
7. grapesing grapes
8. docomparek compare
9. whaleable whale
10. tescapedom escape
11. safelyot safely
12. propreparingst preparing
13. sgrazet graze
14. nonbreakiner break
15. forsquaret square
16. zagreatester greatest
17. rares rare
18. wonscare scare
19. donoperated operate
20. faret fare

**E.** Write a spelling word for the group it best fits. You may wish to use the **Spelling Dictionary** to look up the meaning of *rare* and *scarce.*

1. frighten, terrify, scare
2. walrus, porpoise, whale
3. circle, rectangle, square
4. oranges, apples, grapes
5. poise, manners, grace
6. cautiously, carefully, safely
7. error, misprint, mistake
8. dwindling, few, scarce
9. making, cooking, preparing
10. best, biggest, greatest
11. unusual, unique, rare
12. insane, foolish, crazy
13. getaway, exit, escape
14. match, study, compare
15. smash, crack, break
16. control, run, operate

## OPTIONAL TEACHING PLAN

Write the four Word Group headings on the chalkboard. Ask the students to name the nine spelling words with the long **a** sound that follow the **a-e** pattern. Continue identifying the other Word Groups. Note that the long **a** sound is spelled with the **a-e** pattern in words such as **grace** and with **ea** in words such as **break.**

| Word Groups | | |
|---|---|---|
| /ā/: **a-e** pattern | grace | graze |
| | whale | brake |
| | operate | mistake |
| | escape | grapes |
| | safely | **related** |
| /ā/: **a** words | crazy | **reputation** |
| | **relaxation** | |
| /ā/: **ea** words | break | greatest |
| /âr/ words | fare | bare |
| | rare | scare |
| | square | compare |
| | preparing | scare |
| | **canary** | **rarely** |

*Challenge Words are boldfaced.*

### Optional Activity Masters

Those using the Hardcover Pupil Edition may wish to use the Optional Activity Masters in the Teacher's Resource Book for Exercises C and D.

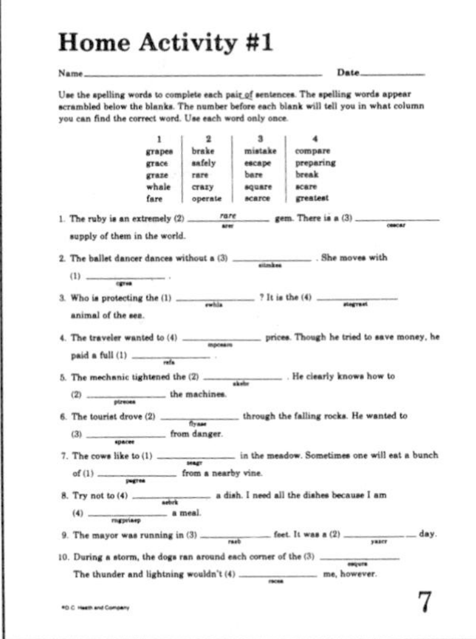

**Home Activity #1**

7

**Modified Lesson #1**

43

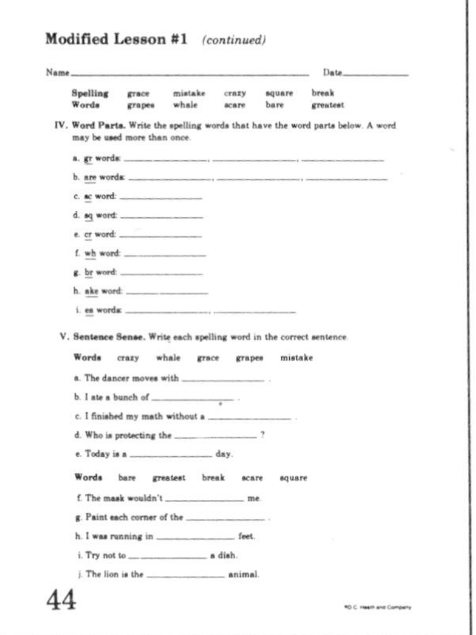

**Modified Lesson #1** *(continued)*

44

### Home Activity

A weekly homework assignment

### Modified Lesson

An alternative lesson for limited spellers

*(The Answer Key can be found in the Teacher's Resource Book.)*

**LESSON 1 CONTINUED**

### Challenge Exercise #1

Name____________________ Date__________

**Word Watch.** Five hundred years ago in England, the word *crazy* meant "full of cracks." People then spoke of crazy bowls and crazy ships that were liable to break apart or fall to pieces. The word originated from the French word *ecraser*, meaning "to shatter into pieces." Today when one speaks of a crazy idea, one speaks of something that is foolish. In a very broad sense, something foolish may still be considered full of cracks.

**Word Analogies.** Decide on the relationship that exists between the first pair of words. Using the Other Word Forms on page 4, find a word that completes the second pair of words and establishes the same relationship.

1. *prune* is to *plum* as *raisin* is to __________
2. *slowly* is to *rapidly* as *sanely* is to __________
3. *winds* is to *breezes* as *errors* is to __________
4. *taken* is to *given* as *caught* is to __________
5. *making* is to *building* as *cracking* is to __________

**Challenge Words Student Activity**

Use the challenge words below to complete the paragraph.

**canary rarely reputation relaxation related**

Many people keep a __________ or a parakeet as a pet. A parakeet is __________ to a parrot. Most owners __________ let their birds out of their cages. However, some let them fly freely, despite their __________ for messiness. Pets of any kind are good company and increase a person's sense of __________.

**Working With Words: Student Writing Activity**

Choose any six of the Other Word Forms from the list on page 4. Use the six words in a letter to a friend who has moved to another state. Tell your friend about sighting a UFO.



115

**Challenge Exercise**
Additional activities for advanced spellers

### Spelling Words

| | | | | |
|---|---|---|---|---|
| grace | graze | whale | brake | operate |
| mistake | escape | grapes | safely | crazy |
| break | greatest | fare | bare | rare |
| scare | square | compare | preparing | scarce |

**F. Context Clues** Using only words on the spelling list, solve the word mysteries. Write the words. If you need help, use the **Spelling Dictionary**.

1. These gems are expensive. They must be rare *or* scarce.
2. You must pay a fee to ride the bus. You must pay a fare.
3. The baby is unclothed. He is bare.
4. He worked all morning. He was entitled to a break.
5. Jumping from a high place could be frightening. It may scare you.
6. The prisoner cannot be found. Did he escape?
7. I shouldn't have opened the letter. That was my mistake.
8. Some mammals live in the sea. One of them is the whale.
9. These cows need a large meadow. They must graze.
10. They're used for making raisins. They must be grapes.
11. This rectangle has equal sides. It must be a square.
12. Use the floor pedal to stop the car. Use the brake.
13. The skater glides smoothly over the ice. She has grace.
14. The doctor is going to remove my appendix. She must operate.
15. Be careful crossing the street. Please walk safely.
16. My spaniel chases his tail. Sometimes I think my dog is crazy.
17. The chef enjoys cooking. What is he preparing now?
18. There are many great wonders in the world. The pyramids in Egypt are the greatest.
19. The twins are different in many ways. Why do people compare them?
20. There are only a few of these birds around. They are rare *or* scarce.



## CONTROLLED DICTATION (Optional)

These dictation sentences provide maintenance for spelling words previously taught and practice for words currently being studied. Dictation should be administered on Day 4. The teacher or another student may dictate the sentences. Be sure to dictate all marks of punctuation. Challenge Word sentences are preceded by an asterisk.

1. The **brake** on the car did not **operate**.
2. The farmer is **preparing** the field for cows to **graze safely**.
3. My **greatest scare** is the **crazy** driver.
4. You must **break** the small **square** door to escape.
5. The **rare** white **whale** swims with **grace**.
6. Walking in **bare** feet was a **mistake**.
7. No bus **fare** can **compare** with our prices.
8. **Grapes** and oranges are **scarce** this year.

*9. I **rarely** have enough time for **relaxation**.

*10. That company has a good **reputation** for delivery on time.

*11. He is **related** to the boy who bought your **canary**.

**G. Using Other Word Forms** Write the Other Word Form that completes each series.

Base Words: rare(est) scarce(est) safe(est) crazy(est) bare(est)

1. safe, safer, ________
2. crazy, crazier, ________
3. rare, rarer, ________
4. bare, barer, ________
5. scarce, scarcer, ________

**H. Challenge Words** Write the Challenge Word that fits each group of words.

| canary | rarely | related | relaxation | reputation |
|---|---|---|---|---|

1. sparrow, finch, ________
2. rest, comfort, ________
3. alike, connected, ________
4. seldom, hardly ever, ________
5. character, fame, ________

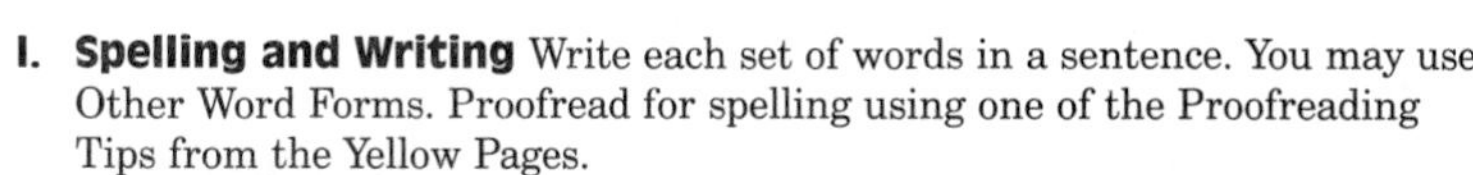

**I. Spelling and Writing** Write each set of words in a sentence. You may use Other Word Forms. Proofread for spelling using one of the Proofreading Tips from the Yellow Pages.

Example: square, operate, crazy
Operating a bicycle with square wheels is a crazy idea.

1. greatest, grapes, compare
2. whale, scare, escape
3. brake, mistake, safely
4. bare, graze, crazy
5. preparing, square, operate
6. rare, grace, scarce
7. break, fare, greatest
8. canary, related, relaxation
9. reputation, rarely, safely
10. realize, ideally, beaming



## USING OTHER WORD FORMS

Vocabulary is expanded through the use of other forms of basic spelling words. Emphasis is on the relationship of syntax to suffix choices. The following generalizations apply to the Other Word Forms used in Exercise G.

### Spelling Rule

Adding suffixes to words ending in silent **e**

When adding a suffix that begins with a vowel to words that end with silent **e**, drop the final **e**.
(**fade, fading**)

Adding suffixes to words ending in **y**

When adding a suffix to words ending with consonant-**y**, change the **y** to **i**, unless the suffix begins with **i**.
(**crazy, craziest**)

## POSTTEST AND PROOFREADING

Follow the same testing procedures used in the Pretest, although you may wish to correct the tests yourself. Have students write any misspelled words on the Words to Learn Sheet and record spelling success on the Progress Chart.

## THE SPELLING-WRITING LINK

**Purpose** This activity helps students effectively transfer lesson words into their daily writing. Students (a) determine a relationship among three given words and (b) write a complete sentence.

**Procedure** On the chalkboard, write the three words from the Example: **square, operate, crazy,** and the Other Word Forms: **squarely, operating, craziest.** Have students read the sample answer and create additional sentences using some of their own ideas.

**Practice** Tell students to write original sentences using the word sets and to proofread their work. You may want them to circle the lesson words.

# LESSON 2

## OBJECTIVES

- to spell 20 high-frequency words, including words with the /ē/ and two contractions
- to proofread these words in daily writing
- to become familiar with 29 other forms of the spelling words

| Summary of Skills | Exercises |
|---|---|
| Auditory Discrimination | A |
| Proofreading | A, C, E, H |
| Visual Discrimination | C, E |
| Word Analysis | D |
| Context Usage | F |
| Vocabulary Development | G |
| Original Writing | H |

## PRETEST AND PROOFREADING

The Pretest identifies the words students are able to spell, as well as the words they need to learn. You may wish to use Other Word Forms when giving the Pretest. Five suggested Other Word Forms are underlined on this page.

To administer the Pretest:

**READ** each word aloud.
**SAY** the phrase containing the word.
**REPEAT** the word.

Have students correct the Pretest using the Corrected-test Procedure. They may record their scores on a personal Progress Chart (see the Teacher's Resource Book) and study misspelled words using the **S-H-A-R-P** procedure.

## OTHER WORD FORMS

This section presents related forms of the spelling words to strengthen spelling power and vocabulary knowledge.

### Enrichment Activity

Have students write synonyms or related phrases for these Other Word Forms. Be sure they write the Other Word Form with its synonym next to it.

**beating, sealed, easiest, realize**

# 2

**A. Pretest and Proofreading**

**B. Spelling Words and Phrases**

| | |
|---|---|
| **1. beam*** | a beam of light |
| **2. seal*** | will seal the envelope |
| **3. heap*** | a heap of trash |
| **4. cheat** | caught the cheat |
| **5. peace*** | a lasting peace |
| **6. preach*** | heard you preach |
| **7. reason** | one good reason |
| **8. ideal** | an ideal day |
| **9. easy*** | easy to use |
| **10. dealing** | dealing the cards |
| **11. reaches*** | reaches the top |
| **12. reached*** | reached the prize |
| **13. eastern** | on the eastern slope |
| **14. really** | if it really matters |
| **15. beaten** | the beaten team |
| **16. meantime*** | in the meantime |
| **17. meanwhile*** | in the meanwhile |
| **18. seashore** | walked along the seashore |
| **19. we've** | whatever we've done |
| **20. we're** | if we're going |

*Other Word Forms*

| | |
|---|---|
| beamed, beaming | easier, easiest |
| sealed, sealing | deal, dealt, <u>dealer</u> |
| heaped | reach, <u>reaching</u> |
| cheated, <u>cheater</u> | east, <u>Easterner</u> |
| peaceful | real, realize |
| preaches, preaching | beat, beating, beater |
| reasoned, <u>reasonable</u> | seashores |
| ideals, ideally | |

**C. Visual Warm-up** Write each word in its correct shape.

a. we've
b. we're
c. preach
d. really
e. reached
f. easy
g. seal
h. beaten
i. dealing
j. peace
k. meantime
l. reaches
m. reason
n. meanwhile
o. ideal
p. beam
q. heap
r. eastern
s. seashore
t. cheat



*Modified Lesson words are asterisked.
The Modified Lesson is found in the Teacher's Resource Book.

## MEETING INDIVIDUAL NEEDS / ASSIGNMENT GUIDE

| 5-Day Plan | 3-Day Plan | Limited Spellers | Average Spellers | Advanced Spellers |
|---|---|---|---|---|
| 1 | 1 | • Pretest • Progress Chart | • Pretest • Progress Chart • Home Activity | • Pretest • Progress Chart • Home Activity |
| 2 | 1 | • Modified Lesson Visual Warm-up Ending Sounds | • Regular Lesson Visual Warm-up | • Regular Lesson Visual Warm-up |
| 3 and 4 | 2 | • Modified Lesson Vowel Puzzle Word Match Finish the Sentence | Spelling Activities | Spelling Activities • Challenge Exercise |
| 5 | 3 | • Posttest • Words to Learn Sheet • Progress Chart | • Posttest • Words to Learn Sheet • Progress Chart | • Posttest • Words to Learn Sheet • Progress Chart |

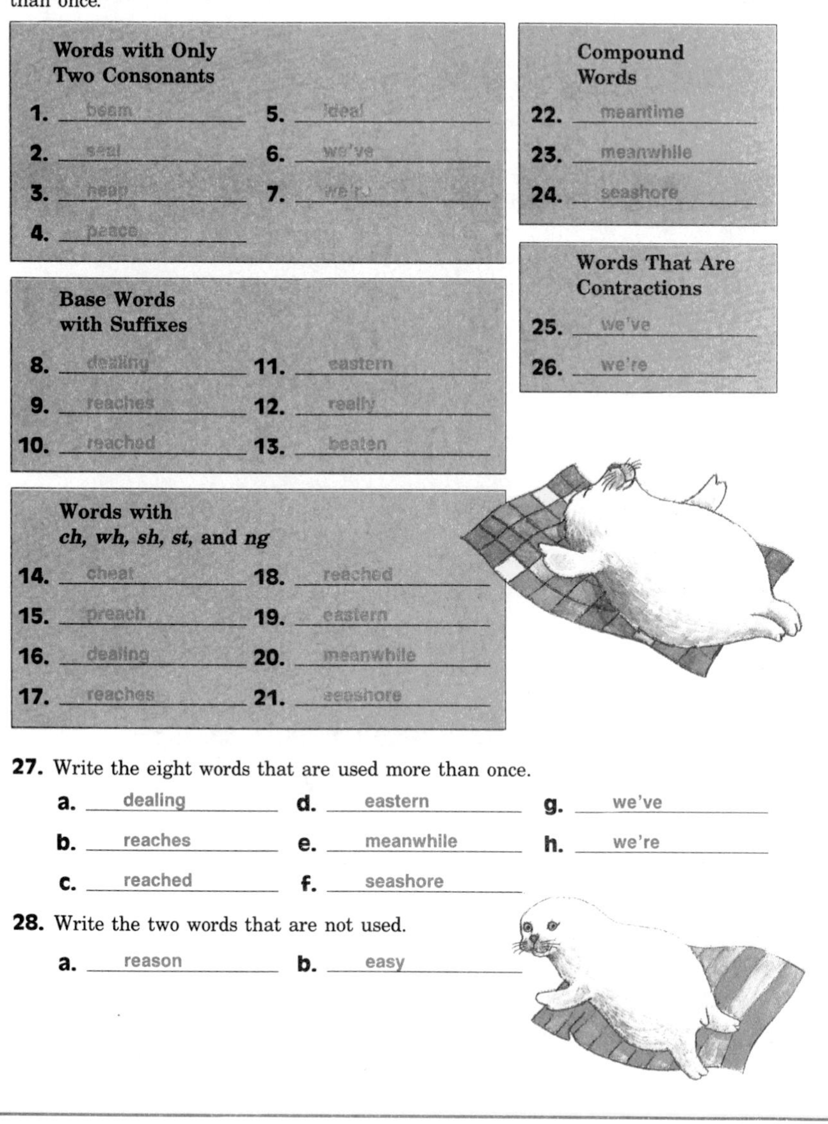

**D. Recycle** Write each of the spelling words where it belongs. A word may be used more than once.

**Words with Only Two Consonants**

1. beam
2. seal
3. heap
4. peace
5. ideal
6. we've
7. we're

**Compound Words**

22. meantime
23. meanwhile
24. seashore

**Base Words with Suffixes**

8. dealing
9. reaches
10. reached
11. eastern
12. really
13. beaten

**Words That Are Contractions**

25. we've
26. we're

**Words with *ch, wh, sh, st,* and *ng***

14. cheat
15. preach
16. dealing
17. reaches
18. reached
19. eastern
20. meanwhile
21. seashore

27. Write the eight words that are used more than once.

a. dealing d. eastern g. we've
b. reaches e. meanwhile h. we're
c. reached f. seashore

28. Write the two words that are not used.

a. reason b. easy

Working Words in Spelling 9

## OPTIONAL TEACHING PLAN

Write the four Word Group headings on the chalkboard. Ask the students to name the fifteen spelling words with the long **e** sound that are spelled with **ea** and are not compound words. Continue identifying the other Word Groups. Note that the long **e** words are spelled with **ea**. Compare the sound of these words with the **ea** words of Lesson 1 (**break, greatest**).

| Word Groups | | |
|---|---|---|
| /ē/ words | beam | seal |
| | heap | cheat |
| | peace | preach |
| | reason | ideal |
| | easy | dealing |
| | reaches | reached |
| | eastern | really |
| | beaten | **agreeable** |
| | **easier** | **meaningful** |
| | **decrease** | **peacefully** |
| /ē/: **ea** compound words | meantime | meanwhile |
| | seashore | |
| /ē/: contraction | | we've |
| er: contraction | | we're |

*Challenge Words are boldfaced.*

## Optional Activity Masters

Those using the Hardcover Pupil Edition may wish to use the Optional Activity Masters in the Teacher's Resource Book for Exercises C and E.

**Home Activity #2**

Name________ Date________

The spelling words in Lesson 2 appear in the phrases below. Write each phrase in a sentence and circle the spelling word.

| Phrases | Sentences |
|---|---|
| 1. a beam of light | 1. I saw a (beam) of light. |
| 2. will seal the envelope | 2. |
| 3. easy to use | 3. |
| 4. a heap of trash | 4. |
| 5. caught the cheat | 5. |
| 6. reaches the top | 6. |
| 7. a lasting peace | 7. |
| 8. heard you preach | 8. |
| 9. dealing the cards | 9. |
| 10. reached the prize | 10. |
| 11. one good reason | 11. |
| 12. in the meanwhile | 12. |
| 13. the beaten team | 13. |
| 14. an ideal day | 14. |
| 15. on the eastern slope | 15. |
| 16. walked along the seashore | 16. |
| 17. if it really matters | 17. |
| 18. in the meantime | 18. |
| 19. if we're going | 19. |
| 20. whatever we've done | 20. |

8

**Modified Lesson #2**

Name________ Date________

Spelling Words: beam, seal, heap, easy, peace, preach, reaches, reached, meantime, meanwhile

I. Visual Warm-up. Write each spelling word in its correct shape.

II. Vowel Hunt. Fill in the missing vowels and write the spelling words.

III. Word Maze. Fill in the missing letters to find the spelling words. Write the words in the blanks beside the numbers.

Across Down

45

**Modified Lesson #2** *(continued)*

Name________ Date________

Spelling Words: beam, seal, heap, easy, peace, preach, reaches, reached, meantime, meanwhile

IV. Word Parts. Write the spelling words that have the word parts below. A word may be used more than once.

a. ch words:
b. wh word:
c. pr word:
d. ea words of one syllable:
e. word beginning with ea:
f. Write the two compound words.

V. Sentence Sense. Write each spelling word in the correct sentence.

Words: easy, beam, seal, peace, meantime

a. I saw a ______ of light.
b. Who will ______ the envelope?
c. In the ______, I will work for you.
d. The oven is ______ to use.
e. We hope for a lasting ______.

Words: heap, preach, meanwhile, reached, reaches

f. We heard you ______ about safety.
g. I raced across the line and ______ the prize.
h. I hope the hiker ______ the top of the mountain.
i. You clean the room; in the ______, I will cook the dinner.
j. A ______ of trash blocked the gate.

46

## Home Activity

A weekly homework assignment

## Modified Lesson

An alternative lesson for limited spellers

*(The Answer Key can be found in the Teacher's Resource Book.)*

# LESSON 2 CONTINUED

## Challenge Exercise #2

Name________________________________ Date__________

**Word Watch.** Under medieval laws, there were many ways a lord could lose title to his land. Properties with questionable titles were called *escheats* and were often turned over to the king. Kings, eager to gain land, employed special agents to look after these escheats. The *escheators*, as they were called, worked for a commission and made money only when they seized property; so, they worked around the law. Because of this dishonest practice, a person who today uses questionable methods to gain what he or she wants is known as a cheat.

**Word Analogies.** Decide on the relationship that exists between the first pair of words. Using the Other Word Forms on page 8, find a word that completes the second pair of words and establishes the same relationship.

1. *big* is to *large* as *perfectly* is to ____________
2. *door* is to *closed* as *envelope* is to ____________
3. *noisy* is to *loud* as *quiet* is to ____________
4. *north* is to *south* as *west* is to ____________
5. *potato* is to *masher* as *egg* is to ____________

**Challenge Words Student Activity**

Use the challenge words below to complete the partial outline.

**easier agreeable decrease meaningful peacefully**

I. Things Most People Want Out of Life
   A. Friends who are ____________
   B. A country where one can live ____________
   C. Machines that make work ____________
   D. A relationship that is ____________
   E. Medicines that will ____________ illness

**Working With Words: Student Writing Activity**

Choose six words from the Other Word Forms on page 8. Use the words to write a suggestion for improving your school. This suggestion might be placed in a principal's suggestion box.

116



### Challenge Exercise

Additional activities for advanced spellers

### Spelling Words

| | | | | |
|---|---|---|---|---|
| beam | seal | heap | cheat | peace |
| preach | reason | ideal | easy | dealing |
| reaches | reached | eastern | really | beaten |
| meantime | meanwhile | seashore | we've | we're |

**E. Word Search** The spelling words and some Other Word Forms (p. 8) can be found in the word puzzle. The words appear across, down, and diagonally. Circle and write the words.

p e a c e r e a l l y b e o
v m w e r e n s e a l e d p
i d e a l e a s t e r n n e
d d e a l o d e a l i n g a
h e a p n r e a c h e d b c
p e i c h w c b e a t h e e
r e a s o n h b e a m e a f
e e a s y l e i w e r a t u
a w e v e x a a l l e p e l
c r c h e a t e r e a e n e
h s e a s h o r e m l d r a
i s e a l m e a n t i m e s
n n o r t r e a c h i n g t
g r e a c h e s p r e a c h

**Spelling Words**

**Across**

1. peace
2. really
3. we're
4. ideal
5. eastern
6. dealing
7. heap
8. reached
9. reason
10. beam
11. easy
12. we've
13. seashore
14. seal
15. meantime
16. reaches
17. preach

**Down**

18. cheat
19. beaten

**Diagonally**

20. meanwhile

**Other Word Forms**

**Across**

21. sealed
22. deal
23. beat
24. cheater
25. reaching

**Down**

26. preaching
27. real
28. heaped
29. peaceful
30. east



## CONTROLLED DICTATION (Optional)

These dictation sentences provide maintenance for spelling words previously taught and practice for words currently being studied. Dictation should be administered on Day 4. The teacher or another student may dictate the sentences. Be sure to dictate all marks of punctuation. Challenge Word sentences are preceded by an asterisk.

1. It's not **easy** to **cheat** when another child is **dealing**.
2. In the **meantime**, put the broken **beam** on the wood **heap**.
3. The **eastern seashore** is **ideal** because it **reaches** far into the water.
4. **Meanwhile**, the **reason we've** been **beaten** is that **we're** in need of a coach
5. She **reached** up and got a **seal** for the package.
6. He **really** did **preach** about **peace**.

*7. Our being **agreeable** made the meeting **easier** and more **meaningful**.

*8. We will **peacefully decrease** our arms.

**F. Using Other Word Forms** Write the Other Word Form that completes each sentence.

Base Words: reach(ing) reason(able) cheat(er) Eastern(er) deal(er)

1. A person who cheats is a ________________ .
2. A person who deals is a ________________ .
3. A person who is from the East is an ________________ .
4. A person who uses reason is ________________ .
5. A person who is stretching is ________________ .

**G. Challenge Words** Write the Challenge Word that fits each analogy.

| agreeable | easier | decrease | meaningful | peacefully |
|---|---|---|---|---|

1. **grow** is to **shrink** as **enlarge** is to ________________
2. **care** is to **carefully** as **peace** is to ________________
3. **heavier** is to **lighter** as **harder** is to ________________
4. **sad** is to **happy** as **unpleasant** is to ________________
5. **wonder** is to **wonderful** as **meaning** is to ________________

**H. Spelling and Writing** Write two or more questions about each statement. Use as many Spelling Words, Other Word Forms, and Challenge Words as you can. A few words are suggested. Proofread for spelling using one of the Proofreading Tips from the Yellow Pages.

> Example: The beach was comfortable on a summer's day.
> ideal seashore peace reason beat
>
> Did the sun beat down on the seashore on that ideal day?

1. Sometimes it is difficult to wait for an important event.
   really meanwhile we're we've reason agreeable
2. Early explorers had many reasons for going to new lands.
   reached eastern preach heaped seal ideal seashore
3. Playing games can be fun on a rainy day.
   easy meantime beam beaten reaches cheat peacefully



## USING OTHER WORD FORMS

Vocabulary is expanded through the use of other forms of basic spelling words. Emphasis is on the relationship of syntax to suffix choices.

## POSTTEST AND PROOFREADING

Follow the same testing procedures used in the Pretest, although you may wish to correct the tests yourself. Have students write any misspelled words on the Words to Learn Sheet and record spelling success on the Progress Chart.

## THE SPELLING-WRITING LINK

**Purpose** This activity helps students to retain the correct spelling of words and transfer the words to their daily writing. Students use lesson words to create questions, which promotes inquiry and research skills.

**Procedure** Read the Example and write the suggested words on the chalkboard: **ideal, seashore, peace, reason, beat.** Read the sample questions and brainstorm additional ones. Remind students to look at all the lesson words for ideas, not just the suggested words. Write the questions on the chalkboard, noting any lesson words.

**Practice** Tell students to finish the activity by writing two or more questions about each statement. Remind them to proofread their work for spelling.

# LESSON 3

## OBJECTIVES

- to spell 20 high-frequency words, including words with the /ī/ and five contractions
- to proofread these words in daily writing
- to become familiar with 39 other forms of the spelling words

| Summary of Skills | Exercises |
|---|---|
| Auditory Discrimination | A |
| Proofreading | A, C, D, J |
| Visual Discrimination | C, D |
| Context Usage | D, E, I |
| Dictionary Skills | F |
| Word Analysis | G, H |
| Original Writing | J |

## PRETEST AND PROOFREADING

The Pretest identifies the words students are able to spell, as well as the words they need to learn. You may wish to use Other Word Forms when giving the Pretest. Five suggested Other Word Forms are underlined on this page.

To administer the Pretest:

**READ** each word aloud.
**SAY** the phrase containing the word.
**REPEAT** the word.

Have students correct the Pretest using the Corrected-test Procedure. They may record their scores on a personal Progress Chart (see the Teacher's Resource Book) and study misspelled words using the **S-H-A-R-P** procedure.

## OTHER WORD FORMS

This section presents related forms of the spelling words to strengthen spelling power and vocabulary knowledge.

### Enrichment Activity

Have students write Other Word Forms under the appropriate ending.

**-ing** **-ed** **-er** **-est**

# 3

**A. Pretest and Proofreading**

**B. Spelling Words and Phrases**

| | Word | Phrase |
|---|---|---|
| 1. | rise* | saw the balloon rise |
| 2. | guide | will guide the way |
| 3. | invite* | wanted to invite |
| 4. | decide | will decide on a color |
| 5. | divide | to divide by seven |
| 6. | finest* | the finest piece of work |
| 7. | ninth* | the ninth inning |
| 8. | lining | the lining of my jacket |
| 9. | filing | filing the letters |
| 10. | knives | sharpened the knives |
| 11. | lively* | a lively game |
| 12. | item | counted each item |
| 13. | final | the final race |
| 14. | dried | a box of dried fruit |
| 15. | tied* | tied the ribbon |
| 16. | I'd | if I'd tried |
| 17. | I'll* | because I'll be there |
| 18. | I've* | since I've started |
| 19. | hadn't* | hadn't gone |
| 20. | doesn't* | doesn't have to go |

*Other Word Forms*

| | |
|---|---|
| rises, rose, rising, risen | file, filed |
| guided, guiding | knife, knifed |
| invites, invited, inviting | live, livelier, liveliest |
| decides, decided, deciding | items, itemize |
| divides, divided, dividing | finally, finalist |
| fine, finer | dry, dries, drying, drier |
| nine | tie, ties, tying |
| line, lines, lined | |

**C. Visual Warm-up** Write each word in its correct shape.

a. rise
b. filing
c. guide
d. hadn't
e. knives
f. I'll
g. final
h. decide
i. item
j. tied
k. ninth
l. invite
m. dried
n. lining
o. I'd
p. doesn't
q. lively
r. finest
s. I've
t. divide

12 Lesson 3

*Modified Lesson words are asterisked.
The Modified Lesson is found in the Teacher's Resource Book.

## MEETING INDIVIDUAL NEEDS / ASSIGNMENT GUIDE

| 5-Day Plan | 3-Day Plan | Limited Spellers | Average Spellers | Advanced Spellers |
|---|---|---|---|---|
| 1 | 1 | • Pretest<br>• Progress Chart | • Pretest<br>• Progress Chart<br>• Home Activity | • Pretest<br>• Progress Chart<br>• Home Activity |
| 2 | | • Modified Lesson<br>Visual Warm-up<br>Ending Sounds | • Regular Lesson<br>Visual Warm-up | • Regular Lesson<br>Visual Warm-up |
| 3 and 4 | 2 | • Modified Lesson<br>Vowel Puzzle<br>Word Match<br>Finish the Sentence | Spelling Activities | Spelling Activities<br>• Challenge Exercise |
| 5 | 3 | • Posttest<br>• Words to Learn Sheet<br>• Progress Chart | • Posttest<br>• Words to Learn Sheet<br>• Progress Chart | • Posttest<br>• Words to Learn Sheet<br>• Progress Chart |

**D. Be a Sentence Detective** Unscramble the scrambled word to find the spelling word that completes the sentence. Write the word.

1. Who will decide (dicdee) where to go?
2. I passed the final (lafin) exam.
3. Every tour is led by a guide (digue).
4. Divide (diveid) the crayons among the children.
5. The laundry dried (deidr) rapidly.
6. This rope is tied (deit) too tightly.
7. Use both forks and knives (knevis).
8. I enjoy lively (vyllie), fun-loving people.
9. Invite (vintie) your friends to the party.
10. Does the sun rise (esir) in the east?
11. Each item (temi) must be priced for the sale.
12. Give the teacher only your finest (stifen) work.
13. She placed ninth (thinn) in the marathon.
14. The tailor sewed the lining (ingnil) of his coat.
15. The secretary enjoys filing (lingif) and typing.

**E. Let's Talk** Complete the conversation below by using the correct contractions from the spelling list. Write the contractions.

Arthur: **(1.)** I've (I have) seen that person before.

Police officer: He **(2.)** doesn't (does not) match the description of the jewel thief. **(3.)** Hadn't (Had not) you better take a closer look?

Arthur: **(4.)** I'd (I had) better.

Police officer: **(5.)** I'll (I will) bring him down to the station for questioning.



## OPTIONAL TEACHING PLAN

Write the four Word Group headings on the chalkboard. Ask the students to name the eleven spelling words with the long **i** sound that follow the **i-e** pattern. Continue identifying the other Word Groups. Note that the long **i** sound is spelled with the **i-e** pattern in words such as **rise**, with **i** in words such at **item**, and with **ie** in words such as **dried**.

| Word Groups | | |
|---|---|---|
| /ī/: **i-e** pattern | rise | guide |
| | invite | decide |
| | divide | finest |
| | ninth | lining |
| | filing | knives |
| | lively | **advised** |
| /ī/: **i** words | item | final |
| | **bridle** | **guidance** |
| | **identify** | **miser** |
| /ī/: **ied** words | dried | tied |
| Contractions | I'd | I'll |
| | I've | doesn't |
| | hadn't | |

*Challenge Words are boldfaced.*

### Optional Activity Masters

Those using the Hardcover Pupil Edition may wish to use the Optional Activity Masters in the Teacher's Resource Book for Exercises C and H.

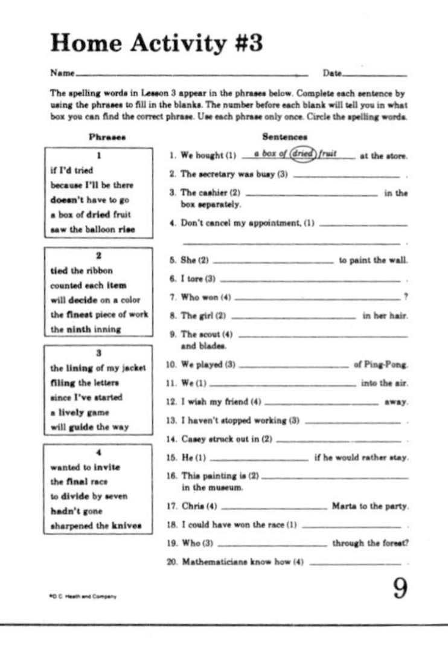

# Home Activity #3

Name________ Date________

The spelling words in Lesson 3 appear in the phrases below. Complete each sentence by using the phrases to fill in the blanks. The number before each blank will tell you in what box you can find the correct phrase. Use each phrase only once. Circle the spelling words.

**Phrases**

**1**
if **I'd** tried
because **I'll** be there
**doesn't** have to go
a box of **dried** fruit
saw the balloon **rise**

**2**
**tied** the ribbon
counted each **item**
will **decide** on a color
the **finest** piece of work
the **ninth** inning

**3**
the **lining** of my jacket
**filing** the letters
since **I've** started
a **lively** game
will **guide** the way

**4**
wanted to **invite**
the **final** race
to **divide** by seven
**hadn't** gone
sharpened the **knives**

**Sentences**

1. We bought (1) *a box of dried fruit* at the store.
2. The secretary was busy (3) ________ .
3. The cashier (2) ________ in the box separately.
4. Don't cancel my appointment, (1) ________ .
5. She (2) ________ to paint the wall.
6. I tore (3) ________ .
7. Who won (4) ________ ?
8. The girl (2) ________ in her hair.
9. The scout (4) ________ and blades.
10. We played (3) ________ of Ping-Pong.
11. We (1) ________ into the air.
12. I wish my friend (4) ________ away.
13. I haven't stopped working (3) ________ .
14. Casey struck out in (2) ________ .
15. He (1) ________ if he would rather stay.
16. This painting is (2) ________ in the museum.
17. Chris (4) ________ Marta to the party.
18. I could have won the race (1) ________ .
19. Who (3) ________ through the forest?
20. Mathematicians know how (4) ________ .



9

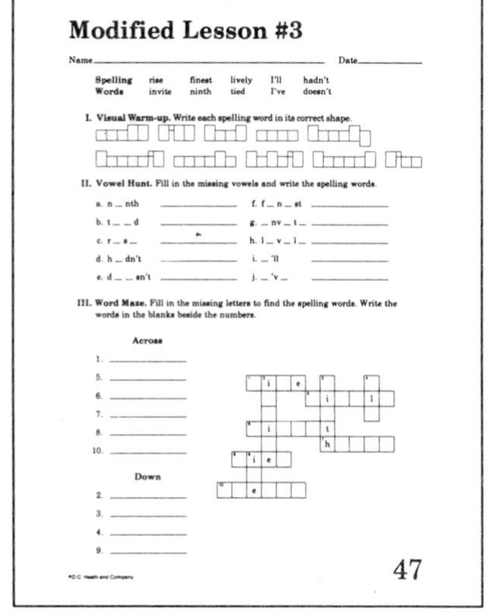

# Modified Lesson #3

Name________ Date________

**Spelling Words** rise invite finest ninth lively tied I'll I've hadn't doesn't

**I. Visual Warm-up.** Write each spelling word in its correct shape.

**II. Vowel Hunt.** Fill in the missing vowels and write the spelling words.

a. n _ nth ________ f. f _ n _ st ________
b. t _ _ d ________ g. _ nv _ t _ ________
c. r _ s _ ________ h. l _ v _ l _ ________
d. h _ dn't ________ i. _ 'll ________
e. d _ _ sn't ________ j. _ 'v _ ________

**III. Word Maze.** Fill in the missing letters to find the spelling words. Write the words in the blanks beside the numbers.

**Across**
1. ________
5. ________
6. ________
7. ________
8. ________
10. ________

**Down**
2. ________
3. ________
4. ________
9. ________



47

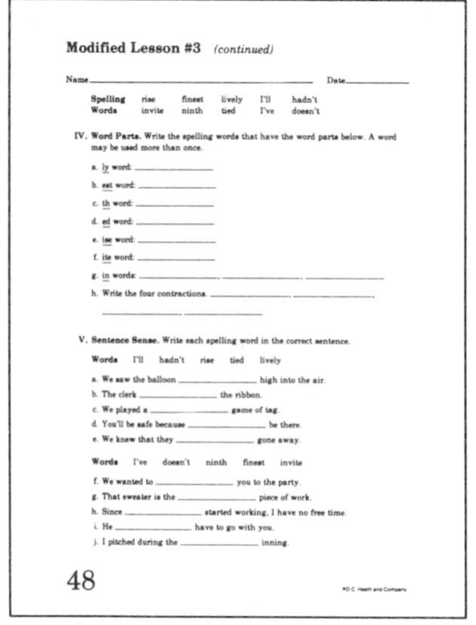

**Modified Lesson #3** *(continued)*

Name________ Date________

**Spelling Words** rise invite finest ninth lively tied I'll I've hadn't doesn't

**IV. Word Parts.** Write the spelling words that have the word parts below. A word may be used more than once.

a. ly word: ________
b. est word: ________
c. th word: ________
d. ed word: ________
e. ise word: ________
f. ite word: ________
g. in words: ________, ________, ________
h. Write the four contractions. ________, ________, ________, ________

**V. Sentence Sense.** Write each spelling word in the correct sentence.

**Words** I'll hadn't rise tied lively

a. We saw the balloon ________ high into the air.
b. The clerk ________ the ribbon.
c. We played a ________ game of tag.
d. You'll be safe because ________ be there.
e. We knew that they ________ gone away.

**Words** I've doesn't ninth finest invite

f. We wanted to ________ you to the party.
g. That sweater is the ________ piece of work.
h. Since ________ started working, I have no free time.
i. He ________ have to go with you.
j. I pitched during the ________ inning.

48



### Home Activity
A weekly homework assignment

### Modified Lesson
An alternative lesson for limited spellers

*(The Answer Key can be found in the Teacher's Resource Book.)*

# LESSON 3 CONTINUED

## Challenge Exercise #3

Name__________ Date__________

**Word Watch.** As long as people have been using utensils, there probably has been a word for *knife* in their language. Our word *knife* derives from the Old English word *cnif*. One interesting story about knives tells how table knives came to have rounded ends. In the early 1600's, Cardinal Richelieu of France grew annoyed when a dinner guest picked his teeth with the pointed end of a table knife. The next day, Richelieu directed his steward to file the points from the table knives. From this beginning, the idea of rounded knives caught on and spread to other countries.

**Word Analogies.** Decide on the relationship that exists between the first pair of words. Using the Other Word Forms on page 12, find a word that completes the second pair of words and establishes the same relationship.

1. *slow* is to *fast* as *wet* is to ________
2. *adds* is to *subtracts* as *multiplies* is to ________
3. *one* is to *three* as *three* is to ________
4. *shaving* is to *razor* as *cutting* is to ________
5. *songs* is to *singing* as *knots* is to ________

**Challenge Words Student Activity**

Use the challenge words below to complete the definitions.

**miser guidance bridle advised identify**

1. ________: suggested what should be done
2. teacher: a person who gives children ________
3. ________: someone who stores away money
4. stranger: a person one cannot easily ________
5. ________: part of a horse's harness

**Working With Words: Student Writing Activity**

Use as many Other Word Forms as you can from page 12 to write a list of things you must do to get ready for a big family party. (Example: finish *inviting* the guests)





**Challenge Exercise**

Additional activities for advanced spellers

### Spelling Words

| | | | | |
|---|---|---|---|---|
| rise | guide | invite | decide | divide |
| finest | ninth | lining | filing | knives |
| lively | item | final | dried | tied |
| I'd | I'll | I've | hadn't | doesn't |

**F. All in a Row** Write the twenty spelling words in alphabetical order. Then join the boxed letters and write four hidden words.

1. decide
2. divide
3. doesn't
4. dried
5. filing
6. Hidden Word: dividing
7. final
8. finest
9. guide
10. hadn't
11. I'd
12. Hidden Word: intend
13. I'll
14. invite
15. item
16. I've
17. knives
18. Hidden Word: limes
19. lining
20. lively
21. ninth
22. rise
23. tied
24. Hidden Word: invited

**G. Arrange and Change** Put the words together to write the five contractions from the spelling list.

I / had / will / have / does / not

| | Two Words | | | | Contractions |
|---|---|---|---|---|---|
| 1. | I | + | had | = | I'd |
| 2. | I | + | will | = | I'll |
| 3. | I | + | have | = | I've |
| 4. | had | + | not | = | hadn't |
| 5. | does | + | not | = | doesn't |



## CONTROLLED DICTATION (Optional)

These dictation sentences provide maintenance for spelling words previously taught and practice for words currently being studied. Dictation should be administered on Day 4. The teacher or another student may dictate the sentences. Be sure to dictate all marks of punctuation. Challenge Word sentences are preceded by an asterisk.

1. We may **decide** to **divide** the work.
2. Do they use **knives** to cut **dried** grapes?
3. The **finest** cloud **doesn't** have a silver **lining**.
4. **I've** seen the **ninth** and **final** game.
5. **I'd** known that the cost for **filing** each **item** would **rise**.
6. **I'll invite lively** children to my party.
7. The **guide hadn't tied** the rope.

*8. Without any **guidance**, he was able to **identify** the stolen **bridle**.
*9. The **miser advised** everyone to give nothing.

**H. Using Other Word Forms** Write the Other Word Form that completes each series.

Base Words: tie(ing) divide(ing) rise(ing) dry(ing) guide(ing)

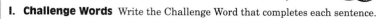

1. rises, rose, ____________
2. guides, guided, ____________
3. divides, divided, ____________
4. dries, dried, ____________
5. ties, tied, ____________

**I. Challenge Words** Write the Challenge Word that completes each sentence.

| bridle | guidance | identify | advised | miser |
|---|---|---|---|---|

1. A witness might ____________ the suspect.
2. A hoarder of gold might be a ____________.
3. An expert might have ____________ the president.
4. A rodeo rider might check the horse's ____________.
5. A counselor might provide ____________ to a student.

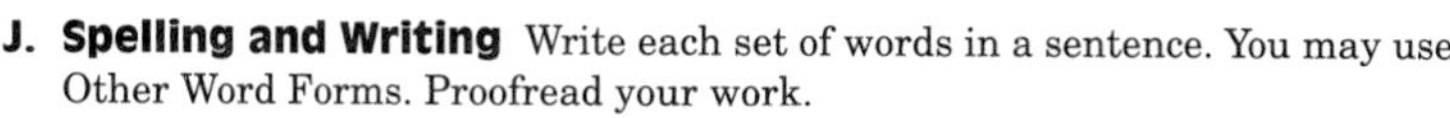

**J. Spelling and Writing** Write each set of words in a sentence. You may use Other Word Forms. Proofread your work.

Example: rise – lining – finest—*Light from the rising sun shone on the lining of her fine coat.*

1. final – ninth – tied
2. knives – I've – finest
3. invite – hadn't – lively
4. dried – guide – I'll
5. decide – filing – I'd
6. doesn't – divide – item
7. advised – miser – rise
8. identify – finer – bridle
9. guidance – decided – lining

## USING OTHER WORD FORMS

Vocabulary is expanded through the use of other forms of basic spelling words. Emphasis is on the relationship of syntax to suffix choices. The following generalizations apply to the Other Word Forms used in Exercise H.

### Spelling Rule

Adding suffixes to words ending in silent **e**

When adding a suffix that begins with a vowel to words that end with silent **e**, drop the final **e**.
(**rise, rising**)

Adding suffixes to words ending in **y**

When adding a suffix to words ending with consonant-**y**, change the **y** to **i**, unless the suffix begins with **i**.
(**dry, drying**)

## POSTTEST AND PROOFREADING

Follow the same testing procedures used in the Pretest, although you may wish to correct the tests yourself. Have students write any misspelled words on the Words to Learn Sheet and record spelling success on the Progress Chart.

## THE SPELLING-WRITING LINK

**Purpose** This activity helps students effectively transfer lesson words into their daily writing. Students (a) determine a relationship among three given words and (b) write a complete sentence.

**Procedure** On the chalkboard, write the three words from the example (**rise, lining, finest**) and the Other Word Forms (**rises, rose, rising, risen, line, lines, lined, fine, finer**). Have students read the example answer and note the lesson words. Then have students think of other ways the three words might be related. Have them think of things or people the words suggest. Ask students to create sentences using some of their ideas.

**Practice** Tell students to write original sentences using the word sets and to proofread their work. You may want them to circle the lesson words.

## OBJECTIVES

- to spell 20 high-frequency words with the /ō/ and /ôr/
- to proofread these words in daily writing
- to become familiar with 36 other forms of the spelling words

| Summary of Skills | Exercises |
|---|---|
| Auditory Discrimination | A |
| Proofreading | A, C, I |
| Visual Discrimination | C |
| Word Analysis | D |
| Context Usage | E, G |
| Dictionary Skills | F |
| Vocabulary Development | F, H |
| Original Writing | I |

## PRETEST AND PROOFREADING

The Pretest identifies the words students are able to spell, as well as the words they need to learn. You may wish to use Other Word Forms when giving the Pretest. Five suggested Other Word Forms are underlined on this page.

To administer the Pretest:

**READ** each word aloud.
**SAY** the phrase containing the word.
**REPEAT** the word.

Have students correct the Pretest using the Corrected-test Procedure. They may record their scores on a personal Progress Chart (see the Teacher's Resource Book) and study misspelled words using the **S-H-A-R-P** procedure.

## OTHER WORD FORMS

This section presents related forms of the spelling words to strengthen spelling power and vocabulary knowledge.

### Enrichment Activity

Have students write Other Word Forms under the appropriate ending.

-ing    -ed    -s    -er

**A. Pretest and Proofreading**

**B. Spelling Words and Phrases**

| | |
|---|---|
| **1. hose*** | the garden hose |
| **2. whole*** | ate it whole |
| **3. jokes*** | tells jokes |
| **4. tones** | tones of the bells |
| **5. votes*** | votes for the mayor |
| **6. chosen** | had chosen the ripe melon |
| **7. frozen*** | a frozen lake |
| **8. lonely*** | a lonely task |
| **9. lonesome** | lonesome and homesick |
| **10. don't*** | if we don't care |
| **11. ore** | mined the ore |
| **12. bore*** | to bore through the plank |
| **13. border** | around the border |
| **14. forbid** | to forbid talking |
| **15. scorn** | will scorn and reject |
| **16. northern** | a northern state |
| **17. formed*** | formed a straight line |
| **18. ordered** | ordered them to stop |
| **19. orchard** | a peach orchard |
| **20. forward*** | looking forward |

*Other Word Forms*

| | |
|---|---|
| hoses, hosed, hosing | bores, bored, boring |
| wholly | bordered |
| joke, joker, joking | forbidden |
| tone, toned, toning | scorned, scornful |
| voter, voting | Northerner |
| choose, chose, choosing | forming, formal |
| freeze, freezes, freezing, froze | order |
| lone, lonelier, loneliest | orchards |
| ores | forwardness |

**C. Visual Warm-up** Write each word in its correct shape.

a. hose
b. scorn
c. forbid
d. tones
e. votes
f. formed
g. ore
h. whole
i. jokes
j. frozen
k. chosen
l. lonely
m. lonesome
n. bore
o. northern
p. ordered
q. border
r. orchard
s. forward
t. don't



*Modified Lesson words are asterisked. The Modified Lesson is found in the Teacher's Resource Book.

## MEETING INDIVIDUAL NEEDS / ASSIGNMENT GUIDE

| 5-Day Plan | 3-Day Plan | Limited Spellers | Average Spellers | Advanced Spellers |
|---|---|---|---|---|
| 1 | 1 | • Pretest<br>• Progress Chart | • Pretest<br>• Progress Chart<br>• Home Activity | • Pretest<br>• Progress Chart<br>• Home Activity |
| 2 | | • Modified Lesson Visual Warm-up Ending Sounds | • Regular Lesson Visual Warm-up | • Regular Lesson Visual Warm-up |
| 3 and 4 | 2 | • Modified Lesson Vowel Puzzle Word Match Finish the Sentence | Spelling Activities | Spelling Activities<br>• Challenge Exercise |
| 5 | 3 | • Posttest<br>• Words to Learn Sheet<br>• Progress Chart | • Posttest<br>• Words to Learn Sheet<br>• Progress Chart | • Posttest<br>• Words to Learn Sheet<br>• Progress Chart |

**D. Find the Right List** Write each spelling word where it belongs.

| *r*-controlled *o* One Syllable | *r*-controlled *o* Two Syllables | Long *o* with *e* Plus an Ending |
|---|---|---|
| 1. ore | 5. border | 11. jokes |
| 2. bore | 6. forbid | 12. tones |
| 3. scorn | 7. northern | 13. votes |
| 4. formed | 8. ordered | 14. chosen |
| | 9. orchard | 15. frozen |
| | 10. forward | 16. lonely |
| | | 17. lonesome |

| Long *o* with Silent *e* Ending | |
|---|---|
| 18. hose | 19. whole |

| A Contraction with Long *o* |
|---|
| 20. don't |

**E. Drawing Conclusions** Complete each conclusion with a word from the spelling list. Write the word. If you need help, use the **Spelling Dictionary**.

1. Amy watered the garden. Most likely she used a hose.
2. Senator Gray was reelected. She received the most votes.
3. The ice cubes had hardened. No doubt they were frozen.
4. Dogs and cats are different. Dogs bark. Cats don't.
5. I traveled solo. The trip was a lonely *or* lonesome one.
6. Rust and tan are similar colors. They are brown tones.
7. The camper was homesick. He was lonely *or* lonesome for his parents.
8. The comedian caused much laughter. Perhaps he told many jokes.
9. We each ate half of the pie. The whole pie was eaten.
10. Gail was elected class president. Gail was chosen.



## OPTIONAL TEACHING PLAN

Write the three Word Group headings on the chalkboard. Ask the students to name the nine spelling words with the long **o** sound that follow the **o-e** pattern. Continue identifying the other Word Groups. Compare the sounds of the long **o** words with the /ôr/ words. Note the consonant digraphs in **whole** (**wh**), **chosen** (**ch**), and **northern** (**th**).

| Word Groups | | |
|---|---|---|
| /ō/ words | hose | whole |
| | jokes | tones |
| | votes | chosen |
| | frozen | lonely |
| | lonesome | **whole-sale** |
| | **polar** | **rodent** |
| | **post office** | **unknown** |
| /ō/: contraction | don't | |
| /ôr/ words | ore | bore |
| | border | forbid |
| | scorn | northern |
| | formed | ordered |
| | orchard | forward |

*Challenge Words are boldfaced.*

### Optional Activity Masters

Those using the Hardcover Pupil Edition may wish to use the Optional Activity Masters in the Teacher's Resource Book for Exercise C.

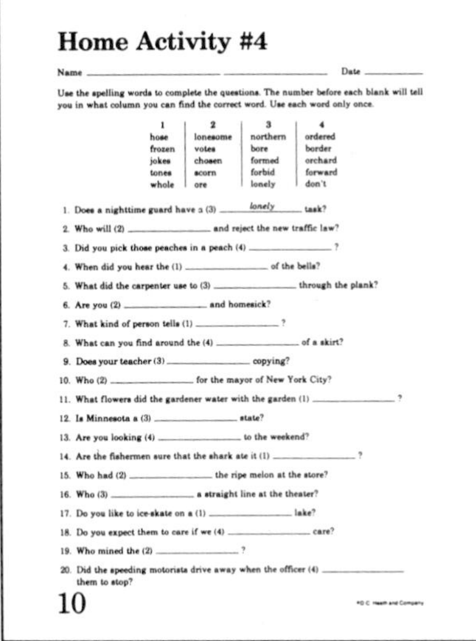

**Home Activity #4**

Name ______ Date ______

Use the spelling words to complete the questions. The number before each blank will tell you in what column you can find the correct word. Use each word only once.

| 1 | 2 | 3 | 4 |
|---|---|---|---|
| hose | lonesome | northern | ordered |
| frozen | votes | bore | border |
| jokes | chosen | formed | orchard |
| tones | scorn | forbid | forward |
| whole | ore | lonely | don't |

1. Does a nighttime guard have a (3) *lonely* task?
2. Who will (2) ______ and reject the new traffic law?
3. Did you pick those peaches in a peach (4) ______ ?
4. When did you hear the (1) ______ of the bells?
5. What did the carpenter use to (3) ______ through the plank?
6. Are you (2) ______ and homesick?
7. What kind of person tells (1) ______ ?
8. What can you find around the (4) ______ of a skirt?
9. Does your teacher (3) ______ copying?
10. Who (2) ______ for the mayor of New York City?
11. What flowers did the gardener water with the garden (1) ______ ?
12. Is Minnesota a (3) ______ state?
13. Are you looking (4) ______ to the weekend?
14. Are the fishermen sure that the shark ate it (1) ______ ?
15. Who had (2) ______ the ripe melon at the store?
16. Who (3) ______ a straight line at the theater?
17. Do you like to ice-skate on a (1) ______ lake?
18. Do you expect them to care if we (4) ______ care?
19. Who mined the (2) ______ ?
20. Did the speeding motorists drive away when the officer (4) ______ them to stop?

10



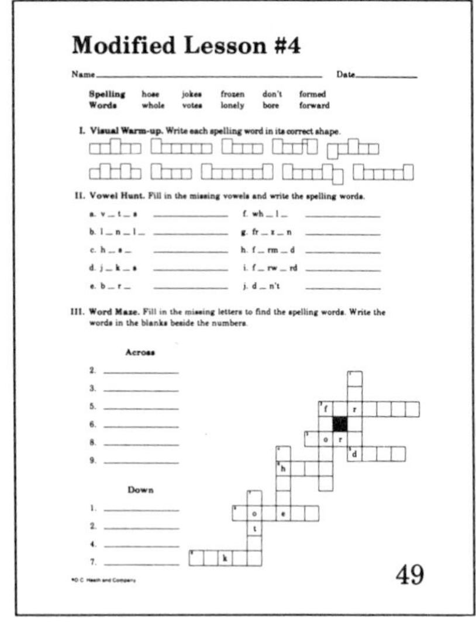

**Modified Lesson #4**

Name ______ Date ______

**Spelling Words** hose jokes frozen don't formed whole votes lonely bore forward

I. **Visual Warm-up.** Write each spelling word in its correct shape.

II. **Vowel Hunt.** Fill in the missing vowels and write the spelling words.

a. v _ t _ s ______
b. l _ n _ l _ ______
c. h _ s _ ______
d. j _ k _ s ______
e. b _ r _ ______
f. wh _ l _ ______
g. fr _ z _ n ______
h. f _ rm _ d ______
i. f _ rw _ rd ______
j. d _ n't ______

III. **Word Maze.** Fill in the missing letters to find the spelling words. Write the words in the blanks beside the numbers.

Across

2. ______
3. ______
5. ______
6. ______
8. ______
9. ______

Down

1. ______
2. ______
4. ______
7. ______

49



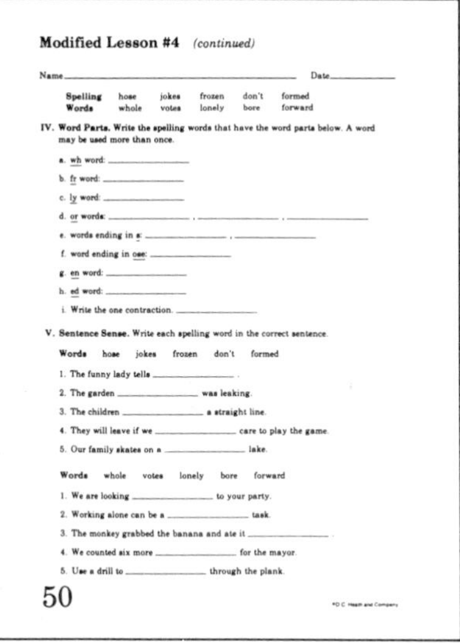

**Modified Lesson #4** *(continued)*

Name ______ Date ______

**Spelling Words** hose jokes frozen don't formed whole votes lonely bore forward

IV. **Word Parts.** Write the spelling words that have the word parts below. A word may be used more than once.

a. wh word: ______
b. fr word: ______
c. ly word: ______
d. or words: ______ , ______ , ______
e. words ending in s: ______ , ______
f. word ending in ose: ______
g. en word: ______
h. ed word: ______
i. Write the one contraction. ______

V. **Sentence Sense.** Write each spelling word in the correct sentence.

**Words** hose jokes frozen don't formed

1. The funny lady tells ______ .
2. The garden ______ was leaking.
3. The children ______ a straight line.
4. They will leave if we ______ care to play the game.
5. Our family skates on a ______ lake.

**Words** whole votes lonely bore forward

1. We are looking ______ to your party.
2. Working alone can be a ______ task.
3. The monkey grabbed the banana and ate it ______ .
4. We counted six more ______ for the mayor.
5. Use a drill to ______ through the plank.

50



### Home Activity

A weekly homework assignment

### Modified Lesson

An alternative lesson for limited spellers

*(The Answer Key can be found in the Teacher's Resource Book.)*

# LESSON 4 CONTINUED

## Challenge Exercise #4

Name____________________ Date__________

**Word Watch.** The word *orchard* refers to a cultivated area where a group of fruit or nut trees are grown. Hundreds of years ago, the English word for *orchard* was *ortgeard*, meaning a "garden yard," the place where herbs and fruit trees were grown. In a sense, the well-kept orchard of today is truly a beautiful garden yard.

**Word Analogies.** Decide on the relationship that exists between the first pair of words. Using the Other Word Forms on page 16, find a word that completes the second pair of words and establishes the same relationship.

1. *oranges* is to *groves* as *apples* is to __________
2. *Westerner* is to *Easterner* as *Southerner* is to __________
3. *steam* is to *boils* as *ice* is to __________
4. *electricity* is to *wires* as *water* is to __________
5. *many* is to *several* as *single* is to __________

**Challenge Words Student Activity**

Use the challenge words below to complete the comparisons.

**unknown** **polar** **wholesale** **rodent** **post office**

1. It's never very warm, so it could be a __________ climate.
2. It's not a cat eating cheese, so it must be a __________.
3. It's not known by anyone, so it must be __________.
4. It's not in the mailbox, so it could be at the __________.
5. It's not the retail price, so it could be the __________ price.

**Working With Words: Student Writing Activity**

Use as many Other Word Forms as you can from page 16 to write silly definitions for animals. (Example: The hyena is the only animal that will laugh at a *boring joke*.)

118



### Challenge Exercise

Additional activities for advanced spellers

### Spelling Words

| | | | | |
|---|---|---|---|---|
| hose | whole | jokes | tones | votes |
| chosen | frozen | lonely | lonesome | don't |
| ore | bore | border | forbid | scorn |
| northern | formed | ordered | orchard | forward |

**F. Compare and Contrast** Use each of the spelling words in one of the phrases below. Write the words.

1. not ballots, but votes
2. not entertain, but bore
3. not ordered, but asked
4. not the center, but the border
5. not shaped, but formed
6. not frozen, but melted
7. not admire, but scorn
8. not polished metal, but ore
9. not half, but whole
10. not sociable, but lonely *or* lonesome
11. not forbid, but allow
12. not forward, but backward
13. not orchard, but forest
14. not happy, but lonely *or* lonesome
15. not northern, but southern
16. not jokes, but riddles
17. not squawks, but pleasant tones
18. not do, but don't
19. not with a sprinkler, but with a hose
20. not rejected, but chosen



## CONTROLLED DICTATION (Optional)

These dictation sentences provide maintenance for spelling words previously taught and practice for words currently being studied. Dictation should be administered on Day 4. The teacher or another student may dictate the sentences. Be sure to dictate all marks of punctuation. Challenge Word sentences are preceded by an asterisk.

1. **Lonely** children need love, not **scorn**.
2. The singer **jokes** about our poor **tones**.
3. The guide **ordered** us **forward** to the **northern border**.
4. **Don't** you feel **lonesome** working alone?
5. Meanwhile, the diggers will **bore** for **ore**.
6. We found the **frozen hose** in the **orchard**.
7. Who will **forbid** the club to be **formed**.
8. If the **whole** class **votes**, you will be **chosen**.

*9. The **wholesale** items are to be picked up at the **post office**.
*10. It was **unknown** if the **rodent** was caught.
*11. She explored the **polar** region last year.

**G. Using Other Word Forms** Write the Other Word Form that completes each sentence.

Base Words: choose(ing) Northern(er) joke(er) lonely(est) vote(er)

1. A person who tells jokes is a joker.
2. A person who is the most lonely is the loneliest.
3. A person from the North is a Northerner.
4. A person who votes is a voter.
5. A person who is selecting an item is choosing it.

**H. Challenge Words** Write the Challenge Word that fits each group of words.

| polar | post office | rodent | unknown | wholesale |
|---|---|---|---|---|

1. mysterious, strange, alien, unknown
2. products, purchase, discount, wholesale
3. animal, small, mouse, rodent
4. cold, arctic, bears, polar
5. mail, stamp, building post office

**I. Spelling and Writing** Use each phrase in a sentence. You may want to use the words in a different order or use Other Word Forms. Proofread for spelling using one of the Proofreading Tips from the Yellow Pages.

Example: a lonely road
We drove down the lonely country road.

1. whole numbers
2. tells funny jokes
3. chosen by six votes
4. ordered frozen food
5. a lonely apple orchard
6. a lonesome northern trail
7. but don't shout
8. iron ore
9. can bore the audience
10. a border of lace
11. forbid me to go forward
12. scorn for cowards



## USING OTHER WORD FORMS

Vocabulary is expanded through the use of other forms of basic spelling words. Emphasis is on the relationship of syntax to suffix choices. The following generalizations apply to the Other Word Forms used in Exercise G.

### Spelling Rule

Adding suffixes to words ending in silent **e**

When adding a suffix that begins with a vowel to words that end with silent **e**, drop the final **e**.
**(joke, joker)**

Adding suffixes to words ending in **y**

When adding a suffix to words ending with consonant-**y**, change the **y** to **i**, unless the suffix begins with **i**.
**(lonely, loneliest)**

## POSTTEST AND PROOFREADING

Follow the same testing procedures used in the Pretest, although you may wish to correct the tests yourself. Have students write any misspelled words on the Words to Learn Sheet and record spelling success on the Progress Chart.

## THE SPELLING-WRITING LINK

**Purpose** This activity helps students transfer lesson words into their daily writing. Students write complete sentences using the listed phrases.

**Procedure** On the chalkboard write the phrase from the Example: **a lonely road.** Have the students read the phrase and note how it has been used in the sentence: **We drove down the lonely country road.** Have them think about things or people the phrase suggests for their own sentence.

**Practice** Tell the students to write original sentences using all the phrases. Remind them they can use Other Word Forms or change the phrases around if it will improve the sentences.

# LESSON 5

## OBJECTIVES

- to spell 20 high-frequency words, including words with the /yo͞o/, /o͞o/, /o͝o/, /yo͝or/, /o͝or/, and /är/
- to proofread these words in daily writing
- to become familiar with 36 other forms of the spelling words

| Summary of Skills | Exercises |
|---|---|
| Auditory Discrimination | A |
| Proofreading | A, C, I |
| Visual Discrimination | C |
| Dictionary Skills | D |
| Word Analysis | E |
| Vocabulary Development | F, G |
| Context Usage | H |
| Original Writing | I |

## PRETEST AND PROOFREADING

The Pretest identifies the words students are able to spell, as well as the words they need to learn. You may wish to use Other Word Forms when giving the Pretest. Five suggested Other Word Forms are underlined on this page.

To administer the Pretest:

**READ** each word aloud.
**SAY** the phrase containing the word.
**REPEAT** the word.

Have students correct the Pretest using the Corrected-test Procedure. They may record their scores on a personal Progress Chart (see the Teacher's Resource Book) and study misspelled words using the **S-H-A-R-P** procedure.

## OTHER WORD FORMS

This section presents related forms of the spelling words to strengthen spelling power and vocabulary knowledge.

### Enrichment Activity

Have students write variations of the same sentence using each of the Other Word Forms for a spelling word.

The college student will **choose** his profession soon.
**chose, choosing**

**A. Pretest and Proofreading**

**B. Spelling Words and Phrases**

| | |
|---|---|
| **1. cute*** | cute baby |
| **2. amuse*** | to amuse with stories |
| **3. excuse*** | made no excuse |
| **4. usually** | usually done on time |
| **5. uniform** | wore a uniform |
| **6. unit*** | a small unit |
| **7. pupil** | one for each pupil |
| **8. choose** | will choose my own |
| **9. stoop** | had to stoop down low |
| **10. troop** | will troop down the hall |
| **11. foolish*** | seemed rather foolish |
| **12. loose** | some loose change |
| **13. spoon*** | stirred with a spoon |
| **14. smooth*** | will smooth the bedspread |
| **15. mood*** | in a bad mood |
| **16. junior** | a junior in college |
| **17. juicy*** | too juicy for a fork |
| **18. secure** | will secure with a lock |
| **19. surely** | if we surely must |
| **20. aren't*** | if we aren't ready |

***Other Word Forms***

| | |
|---|---|
| cuter, cutest | fool, foolishly |
| amused, amusing | looser, loosely, loosen |
| excuses, excused, excusing | spooned |
| usual | smoothly, smoother, smoothness, smoothed |
| uniformly | moody |
| units, unity | juniors |
| pupils | juice, juicier, juiciest |
| chose, choosing | secured, securing |
| stooped | sure, surer |
| troops, trooped, | |

**C. Visual Warm-up** Write each word in its correct shape.

a. unit
b. mood
c. excuse
d. secure
e. stoop
f. cute
g. uniform
h. foolish
i. troop
j. surely
k. junior
l. aren't
m. juicy
n. spoon
o. pupil
p. loose
q. choose
r. smooth
s. usually
t. amuse



*Modified Lesson words are asterisked.
The Modified Lesson is found in the Teacher's Resource Book.

## MEETING INDIVIDUAL NEEDS / ASSIGNMENT GUIDE

| 5-Day Plan | 3-Day Plan | Limited Spellers | Average Spellers | Advanced Spellers |
|---|---|---|---|---|
| 1 | 1 | • Pretest<br>• Progress Chart | • Pretest<br>• Progress Chart<br>• Home Activity | • Pretest<br>• Progress Chart<br>• Home Activity |
| 2 | | • Modified Lesson<br>Visual Warm-up<br>Ending Sounds | • Regular Lesson<br>Visual Warm-up | • Regular Lesson<br>Visual Warm-up |
| 3 and 4 | 2 | • Modified Lesson<br>Vowel Puzzle<br>Word Match<br>Finish the Sentence | Spelling Activities | Spelling Activities<br>• Challenge Exercise |
| 5 | 3 | • Posttest<br>• Words to Learn Sheet<br>• Progress Chart | • Posttest<br>• Words to Learn Sheet<br>• Progress Chart | • Posttest<br>• Words to Learn Sheet<br>• Progress Chart |

**D. Finding Words** The words in the spelling list appear in the beginning (A-H), middle (I-Q), or end (R-Z) of the **Spelling Dictionary**. Write each word.

| Beginning A-H | | Middle I-Q | | End R-Z | |
|---|---|---|---|---|---|
| 1. | cute | 7. | pupil | 12. | usually |
| 2. | amuse | 8. | loose | 13. | uniform |
| 3. | excuse | 9. | mood | 14. | unit |
| 4. | choose | 10. | junior | 15. | stoop |
| 5. | foolish | 11. | juicy | 16. | troop |
| 6. | aren't | | | 17. | spoon |
| | | | | 18. | smooth |
| | | | | 19. | secure |
| | | | | 20. | surely |

**E. Word Parts** Using the letters below, write the eight oo words from the spelling list.

1. spoon
2. smooth
3. mood
4. loose
5. foolish
6. troop
7. stoop
8. choose



## OPTIONAL TEACHING PLAN

Write the five Word Group headings on the chalkboard. Ask the students to name the seven spelling words with the /yo͞o/ sound. Continue identifying the other Word Groups. Note the /yo͞o/ sound of **u** in words such as **cute** and the /o͞o/ sound of **u** in words such as **junior**. Explain that **excuse** is a homograph and can be pronounced in two ways.

| Word Groups | | |
|---|---|---|
| /yo͞o/: **u** words | cute | amuse |
| | excuse | usually |
| | uniform | unit |
| | pupil | **unusual** |
| /o͞o/ and /o͝o/ words | choose | stoop |
| | troop | foolish |
| | loose | spoon |
| | smooth | mood |
| | **scooter** | **wolves** |
| /o͞o/: **u** and **ou** words | junior | juicy |
| | **you've** | |
| /yo͝or/ and /o͝or/ words | secure | surely |
| | **purely** | |
| /är/: contraction | aren't | |

*Challenge Words are boldfaced.*

### Optional Activity Masters

Those using the Hardcover Pupil Edition may wish to use the Optional Activity Masters in the Teacher's Resource Book for Exercises C and F.

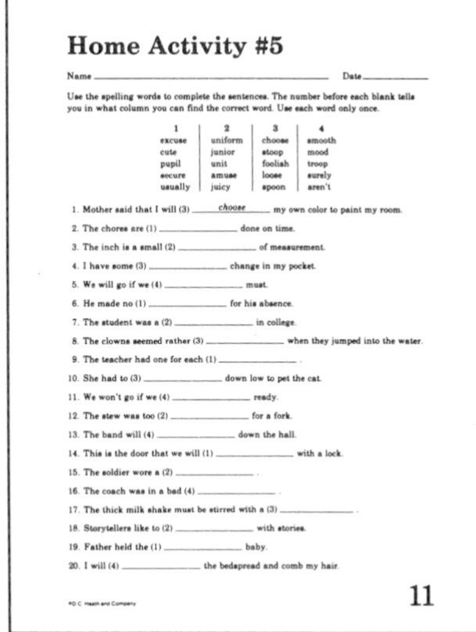

**Home Activity #5**

Name ________ Date ________

Use the spelling words to complete the sentences. The number before each blank tells you in what column you can find the correct word. Use each word only once.

| 1 | 2 | 3 | 4 |
|---|---|---|---|
| excuse | uniform | choose | smooth |
| cute | junior | stoop | mood |
| pupil | unit | foolish | troop |
| secure | amuse | loose | surely |
| usually | juicy | spoon | aren't |

1. Mother said that I will (3) <u>choose</u> my own color to paint my room.
2. The chores are (1) ________ done on time.
3. The inch is a small (2) ________ of measurement.
4. I have some (3) ________ change in my pocket.
5. We will go if we (4) ________ must.
6. He made no (1) ________ for his absence.
7. The student was a (2) ________ in college.
8. The clowns seemed rather (3) ________ when they jumped into the water.
9. The teacher had one for each (1) ________ .
10. She had to (3) ________ down low to pet the cat.
11. We won't go if we (4) ________ ready.
12. The stew was too (2) ________ for a fork.
13. The band will (4) ________ down the hall.
14. This is the door that we will (1) ________ with a lock.
15. The soldier wore a (2) ________ .
16. The coach was in a bad (4) ________ .
17. The thick milk shake must be stirred with a (3) ________ .
18. Storytellers like to (2) ________ with stories.
19. Father held the (1) ________ baby.
20. I will (4) ________ the bedspread and comb my hair.

©D.C. Heath and Company 11

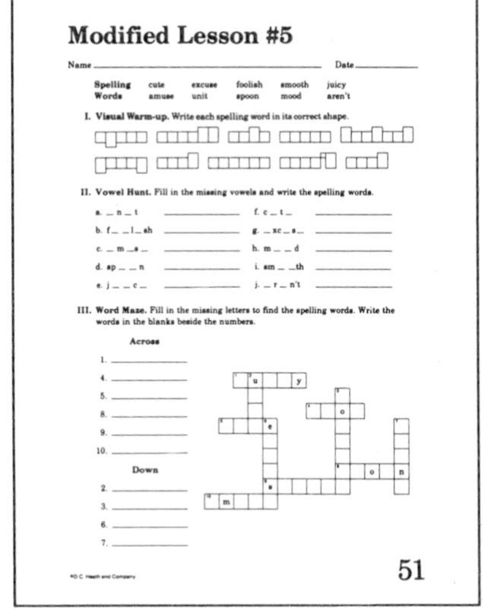

**Modified Lesson #5**

Name ________ Date ________

**Spelling Words** cute amuse excuse unit foolish spoon smooth mood juicy aren't

**I. Visual Warm-up.** Write each spelling word in its correct shape.

**II. Vowel Hunt.** Fill in the missing vowels and write the spelling words.

a. _ n _ t ________ f. c _ t _ ________
b. f _ _ l _ sh ________ g. _ xc _ s _ ________
c. _ m _ s _ ________ h. m _ _ d ________
d. sp _ _ n ________ i. sm _ _ th ________
e. j _ _ c _ ________ j. _ r _ n't ________

**III. Word Maze.** Fill in the missing letters to find the spelling words. Write the words in the blanks beside the numbers.

Across
1. ________
4. ________
5. ________
8. ________
9. ________
10. ________

Down
2. ________
3. ________
6. ________
7. ________

©D.C. Heath and Company 51

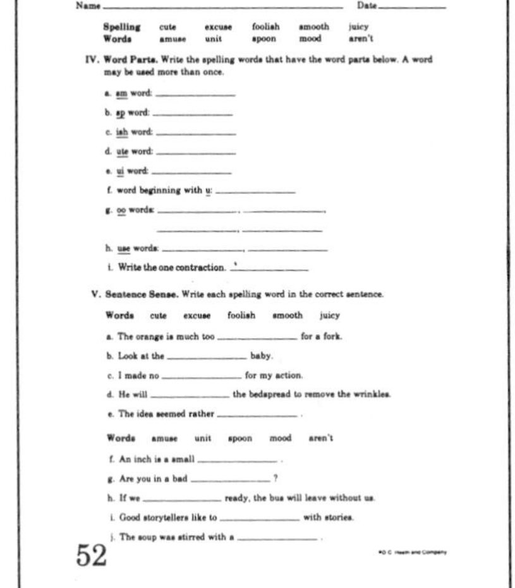

**Modified Lesson #5** *(continued)*

Name ________ Date ________

**Spelling Words** cute amuse excuse unit foolish spoon smooth mood juicy aren't

**IV. Word Parts.** Write the spelling words that have the word parts below. A word may be used more than once.

a. sm word: ________
b. sp word: ________
c. ish word: ________
d. ute word: ________
e. ui word: ________
f. word beginning with u: ________
g. oo words: ________, ________, ________, ________
h. use words: ________, ________
i. Write the one contraction. ________

**V. Sentence Sense.** Write each spelling word in the correct sentence.

**Words** cute excuse foolish smooth juicy

a. The orange is much too ________ for a fork.
b. Look at the ________ baby.
c. I made no ________ for my action.
d. He will ________ the bedspread to remove the wrinkles.
e. The idea seemed rather ________ .

**Words** amuse unit spoon mood aren't

f. An inch is a small ________ .
g. Are you in a bad ________ ?
h. If we ________ ready, the bus will leave without us.
i. Good storytellers like to ________ with stories.
j. The soup was stirred with a ________ .

52 ©D.C. Heath and Company

### Home Activity

A weekly homework assignment

### Modified Lesson

An alternative lesson for limited spellers

*(The Answer Key can be found in the Teacher's Resource Book.)*

# LESSON 5 CONTINUED

**Challenge Exercise #5**

Name ______________________ Date __________

**Word Watch.** In old France the word *amuser* meant "to be put in a stupid state." When the word entered the English language, it meant "to deceive or mislead." So, in 14th-century England, if you amused someone, you deceived the person. Soldiers of that period spoke of amusing the enemy. Today the word *amuse* means "to entertain," and no soldier today would ever set out to entertain the enemy.

**Word Analogies.** Decide on the relationship that exists between the first pair of words. Using the Other Word Forms on page 20, find a word that completes the second pair of words and establishes the same relationship.

1. *cows* is to *herds* as *soldiers* is to __________
2. *doctor* is to *patients* as *teacher* is to __________
3. *sad* is to *sorrowfully* as *funny* is to __________
4. *sophomores* is to *freshmen* as *seniors* is to __________
5. *steering* is to *guiding* as *electing* is to __________

**Challenge Words Student Activity**

Use the challenge words below to solve the problems.

**purely you've wolves scooter unusual**

1. One word becomes a verb when the suffix is dropped: __________
2. One wo. is a singular form that ends with *f*: __________
3. One word can take the suffix *ly*: __________
4. One word is made from two words: __________
5. One word becomes an adjective when the suffix is dropped: __________

**Working With Words: Student Writing Activity**

Use as many Other Word Forms as you can from page 20 to write sentences about the things you do for daily exercise. (Example: To *loosen* up, I will be *choosing* the stretching exercises.)



119

## Challenge Exercise

Additional activities for advanced spellers

**Spelling Words**

| | | | | |
|---|---|---|---|---|
| cute | amuse | excuse | usually | uniform |
| unit | pupil | choose | stoop | troop |
| foolish | loose | spoon | smooth | mood |
| junior | juicy | secure | surely | aren't |

**F. Crossword Puzzle** Solve the puzzle by using all the words from the spelling list. Write the words. Check your answers in the **Spelling Dictionary.**

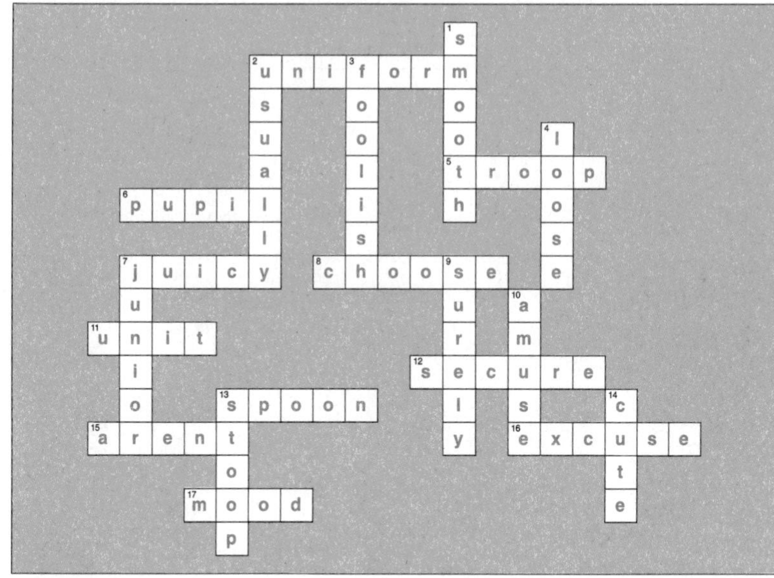


**Across**

**2.** an outfit
**5.** to move together in a large group
**6.** a student
**7.** watery
**8.** to decide or select
**11.** one thing
**12.** to fasten firmly
**13.** not a fork or a knife
**15.** are not (contraction)
**16.** a reason given
**17.** a state of mind

**Down**

**1.** to make flat
**2.** ordinarily
**3.** without sense
**4.** not tight
**7.** younger
**9.** certainly
**10.** to entertain
**13.** to bend down
**14.** pretty



## CONTROLLED DICTATION (Optional)

These dictation sentences provide maintenance for spelling words previously taught and practice for words currently being studied. Dictation should be administered on Day 4. The teacher or another student may dictate the sentences. Be sure to dictate all marks of punctuation. Challenge Word sentences are preceded by an asterisk.

1. One **pupil** in the **junior** class gave a **foolish excuse.**
2. The **uniform** is **loose** but has a **smooth** texture.
3. **Cute** clowns **stoop** down to **amuse** lively children.
4. The **troop** worked safely as a **unit.**
5. I **choose** to eat **juicy** oranges with a **spoon.**
6. The workers **usually secure** the door.
7. **Surely** her friends **aren't** going to change her sad **mood.**

*8. **You've** built a most **unusual scooter.**
*9. **Wolves** are **purely** wild animals.

**G. Using Other Word Forms** Write the Other Word Form that fits each clue.

Base Words: cute(er) sure(er) smooth(er) juicy(er) loose(er)

1. more moist juicier
2. more adorable cuter
3. more even smoother
4. more baggy looser
5. more certain surer

**H. Challenge Words** Write the Challenge Word that completes each question.

| scooter | purely | unusual | wolves | you've |
|---|---|---|---|---|

1. Isn't that an unusual sight to see?
2. How did the wolves track the sheep?
3. Is the scooter similar to the skateboard?
4. Are you sure you've looked everywhere?
5. Was the idea purely yours?

**I. Spelling and Writing** Use each phrase in a sentence. You may want to use the words in a different order or use Other Word Forms. Proofread for spelling using one of the Proofreading Tips from the Yellow Pages.

1. cute and clever trick
2. amuse the children
3. will surely excuse them
4. are usually read
5. of uniform length
6. a unit of measure
7. pupil of his eye
8. will choose a partner
9. sat on the stoop
10. scout troop
11. a foolish remark
12. is loose in the yard
13. spoon the pudding
14. a smooth manner
15. the mood of the crowd
16. a junior partner
17. such a juicy tale
18. aren't safe and secure



## USING OTHER WORD FORMS

Vocabulary is expanded through the use of other forms of basic spelling words. Emphasis is on the relationship of syntax to suffix choices. The following generalizations apply to the Other Word Forms used in Exercise G.

### Spelling Rule

Adding suffixes to words ending in **y**

When adding a suffix to words ending with consonant-**y**, change the **y** to **i**, unless the suffix begins with **i**.
(**juicy, juicier**)

Adding suffixes to words ending in silent **e**

When adding a suffix that begins with a vowel to words that end with silent **e**, drop the final **e**.
(**cute, cuter**)

## POSTTEST AND PROOFREADING

Follow the same testing procedures used in the Pretest, although you may wish to correct the tests yourself. Have students write any misspelled words on the Words to Learn Sheet and record spelling success on the Progress Chart.

## THE SPELLING-WRITING LINK

**Purpose** This activity helps students transfer lesson words into their daily writing. Students write complete sentences using the listed phrases.

**Procedure** On the chalkboard write the phrase from line one: **cute and clever trick.** Have the students read the phrase and note how it could be used in a sentence. Have them think about things or people the phrase suggests. You can provide a sample sentence: **My brother performed a cute and clever trick.**

**Practice** Tell the students to write original sentences using the phrases. Remind them they can use Other Word Forms or change the phrases around if it will improve the sentences.

# LESSON 6 REVIEW

## OBJECTIVES

- to review the spelling of the 100 words studied in Lessons 1-5
- to promote the use of other forms of the 100 spelling words
- to apply high-utility generalizations for the addition of suffixes

| Summary of Skills | Exercises |
|---|---|
| Proofreading | A |
| Visual Discrimination | A |
| Context Usage | B, D |
| Vocabulary Development | C |

## REVIEW OF LESSONS 1-5

The goal of the review exercises is to expand each student's spelling power. The one hundred spelling words studied in the five preceding lessons are presented in challenging formats where the focus is shifted from the spelling words to the Other Word Forms.

## WORD REVIEW PROCEDURE

Students are encouraged to use this abbreviated version of the **S-H-A-R-P** procedure when reviewing the spelling words at the top of each review page.

**LOOK** at each word.
**SAY** the word to yourself.
**THINK** about the letters that spell the word.

# 6 REVIEW

### REVIEWING LESSONS 1-5

| | | | | |
|---|---|---|---|---|
| beam | dried | final | knives | ore |
| beaten | eastern | frozen | lonely | safely |
| compare | easy | grace | mood | spoon |
| cute | excuse | ideal | northern | tones |
| decide | fare | item | operate | unit |

**A. Word Search** Twenty-five Other Word Forms of the spelling words can be found in the word puzzle. The words appear across, down, and diagonally. Circle and write each word. Use the **Spelling Dictionary**.

| o | p | e | r | a | t | e | s | c | u | t | e | s | t | s |
|---|---|---|---|---|---|---|---|---|---|---|---|---|---|---|
| b | f | x | f | i | n | a | l | i | s | t | l | m | o | f |
| e | a | c | o | r | i | t | s | t | m | p | o | o | n | e |
| a | r | b | o | e | a | s | i | e | r | q | n | o | i | x |
| t | e | d | e | m | a | e | l | m | h | i | e | d | n | c |
| n | s | e | t | o | p | d | r | i | e | s | t | y | g | u |
| n | g | c | i | f | x | a | o | z | d | g | a | e | f | s |
| g | h | i | e | k | e | s | r | e | e | e | k | o | r | i |
| u | g | d | r | c | a | f | f | e | i | j | n | a | e | n |
| i | d | e | a | l | s | o | a | n | s | d | i | l | e | g |
| v | t | d | a | o | t | p | u | a | i | r | f | l | z | t |
| u | n | i | t | s | m | c | b | e | a | m | e | d | e | o |
| s | l | f | i | o | r | e | s | a | f | e | s | t | i | w |
| g | r | a | c | e | f | u | l | s | p | o | o | n | s | s |
| n | o | r | t | h | w | a | r | d | a | n | a | g | l | s |

**Across**

1. operates
2. cutest
3. finalist
4. easier
5. driest
6. ideals
7. units
8. beamed
9. ores
10. safest
11. graceful
12. spoons
13. northward

**Diagonally**

14. compares

**Down**

15. beat
16. fares
17. decided
18. east
19. itemize
20. lone
21. knife
22. moody
23. toning
24. freeze
25. excusing



## MEETING INDIVIDUAL NEEDS / ASSIGNMENT GUIDE

| 5-Day Plan | 3-Day Plan | Limited Spellers | Average Spellers | Advanced Spellers |
|---|---|---|---|---|
| 1 and 2 | 1 | • Modified Lesson Visual Warm-up Word Parts | • Regular Lesson Spelling Activities<br>• Home Activity | • Regular Lesson Spelling Activities<br>• Home Activity |
| 3 and 4 | 2 | • Modified Lesson Vowel Puzzle Word Match Finish the Sentence | • Regular Lesson Spelling Activities<br>• Proofreading Exercise(s) | • Regular Lesson Spelling Activities<br>• Proofreading Exercise(s)<br>• Challenge Word Review |
| 5 | 3 | • Test Modified Lesson Words<br>• Words to Learn Sheet | • Review Test or Standardized-format Test<br>• Words to Learn Sheet | • Review Test or Standardized-format Test<br>• Words to Learn Sheet |

| ■ | ☆ | ▲ | ♦ | ● |
|---|---|---|---|---|
| crazy | invite | cheat | heap | juicy |
| seal | escape | chosen | border | lively |
| whale | rare | tied | guide | forbid |
| jokes | junior | ordered | rise | smooth |
| greatest | foolish | pupil | meanwhile | meantime |

REVIEW

**B. Books and Authors** Write Other Word Forms or the spelling words to complete the book titles. The shape tells you in what column you can find the spelling word. Write each word or its Other Word Form only once. Capitalize each word.

1. Manual for ▲ ___Tying___ and Loosening Knots by B. A. Scout
2. Across Many ♦ ___Borders___ by Tex S. Rangers
3. The Magic of the ■ ___Great___ Houdini by Otis Appear
4. A Place for ☆ ___Juniors___ and Seniors by Hy School
5. The Mystery of the ■ ___Sealed___ Envelope by O. Penn Upp
6. And ♦ ___Meanwhile___, Time Passes By! by Howe I. Linger
7. The Noisiest and ● ___Liveliest___ Children by Anita Rest
8. A ▲ ___Cheater___ Is Never a Winner by A. Lou Zerr
9. Tammy Twig's Zaniest and ■ ___Craziest___ Adventures by R. U. Square
10. How ☆ ___Foolishly___ We Behave! by Letts B. Quiet
11. Law and ▲ ___Order___ by Jay Walker
12. Famous ■ ___Whalers___ and Other Sailing Vessels by Ima Shipp
13. How ● ___Smoothly___ We Ride! by Iva Neucarr
14. The ● ___Forbidden___ Planet by Astro Knotts
15. Only the Tangiest and ● ___Juiciest___ Lemons! by Wee R. Squirts
16. The Largest and ☆ ___Rarest___ Jewel in the Crown by Ruby Rich
17. How Wild Is the ■ ___Joker___? by Decca Cards
18. Six ▲ ___Pupils___ for the School by Getta T. Chur
19. Land of the ♦ ___Rising___ Sun by Orrie Ental
20. The Leaders Our Forefathers ▲ ___Chose___ by U. R. King
21. The Last ☆ ___Invited___ Dinner Guest by I. M. Hungry
22. In the ● ___Meantime___, There's Work to Do! by Wee R. Lazy
23. Great ♦ ___Heaping___ Piles by Hyer and Hyer
24. The Book of Daring ☆ ___Escapes___ by U. May Runn
25. Lighthouses: Great ♦ ___Guiding___ Lights by I. C. Better



REVIEW

## CREATIVE WRITING

**(An optional writing activity)**

**Recipe for Writing:** This imaginative writing activity uses spelling words and Other Word Forms studied in Lessons 1-5.

COMBINE:
1 crazy whale
1 lively seal
2 peaceful seashores
a whole heap of juicy grapes

SEASON with your own original ideas and COOK UP a story with a unique FLAVOR. Proofread before SERVING.

The RECIPE words appear in the following lessons.

| Lesson | Words |
|---|---|
| 1 | crazy, whale, grapes |
| 2 | seal, seashores, peaceful, heap |
| 3 | lively |
| 4 | whole |
| 5 | juicy |

## Optional Activity Masters

Those using the Hardcover Pupil Edition may wish to use the Optional Activity Masters in the Teacher's Resource Book for Exercise A.

Home Activity #6

12

Modified Lesson #6

53

Modified Lesson #6 *(continued)*

54

## Home Activity

A weekly homework assignment

## Modified Lesson

An alternative lesson for limited spellers

*(The Answer Key can be found in the Teacher's Resource Book.)*

LESSON

# 6

CONTINUED

## Challenge Word Review

The Challenge Words from the previous five lessons are listed below if you wish to review the Challenge Words with your more advanced students.

1. canary
2. rarely
3. related
4. relaxation
5. reputation
6. agreeable
7. easier
8. decrease
9. meaningful
10. peacefully
11. bridle
12. guidance
13. identify
14. advised
15. miser
16. polar
17. post office
18. rodent
19. unknown
20. wholesale
21. scooter
22. purely
23. unusual
24. wolves
25. you've

| ■ | ★ | ▲ | ◆ | ● |
|---|---|---|---|---|
| break | bare | scare | I'll | mistake |
| peace | we're | dealing | reached | we've |
| divide | hadn't | doesn't | I'd | I've |
| hose | votes | formed | forward | don't |
| amuse | usually | uniform | troop | aren't |

REVIEW

**C. Word Clues** Write the spelling word that goes with each clue. The shape tells you in what column you can find the spelling word. Then write an Other Word Form for each spelling word.

| Word Clues | Spelling Words | Other Word Forms |
|---|---|---|
| **1.** ahead ◆ | f o r w a r d | forwardness |
| **2.** unclothed ★ | b a r e | barely |
| **3.** a tube to carry liquid ■ | h o s e | hoses |
| **4.** a group's outfit ▲ | u n i f o r m | uniformly |
| **5.** to move in a large group ◆ | t r o o p | troops |
| **6.** a mathematical term ■ | d i v i d e | divides |
| **7.** to frighten ▲ | s c a r e | scared |
| **8.** election choices ★ | v o t e s | voter |
| **9.** an error ● | m i s t a k e | mistakes |
| **10.** to make someone laugh ■ | a m u s e | amused |
| **11.** ordinarily ★ | u s u a l l y | usual |
| **12.** giving out playing cards ▲ | d e a l i n g | deal |
| **13.** freedom from war ■ | p e a c e | peaceful |
| **14.** stretched out a hand ◆ | r e a c h e d | reach |
| **15.** made or shaped ▲ | f o r m e d | forming |
| **16.** to come apart by force ■ | b r e a k | broke |

**17.** From the list above, write the nine contractions and their meanings.

**a.** we're — we are
**b.** hadn't — had not
**c.** doesn't — does not
**d.** I'll — I will
**e.** I'd — I would
**f.** we've — we have
**g.** I've — I have
**h.** don't — do not
**i.** aren't — are not

**26** Review—Lesson 6

### Proofreading Exercise Lesson #6

Name ______________________ Date __________

**Proofreading the Spelling of Others**

Some sign makers made signs for the fruit store. They made some spelling errors. Circle the misspelled words. Write the correct words on the lines. (Some items contain two errors; others contain one error. Leave blank the lines that have no corrections.)

**Signs in a Fruit Store**

1. Crisp apples grown in our own nothern orcherd — 1a. ________ 1b. ________
2. Our jiucy oranges are the finast — 2a. ________ 2b. ________
3. Another pear just doesnt compair! — 3a. ________ 3b. ________
4. The best grapa chozen from the best vines — 4a. ________ 4b. ________
5. Try our delicious frozin berries — 5a. ________ 5b. ________
6. Choose rair fruit from easturn Asia — 6a. ________ 6b. ________
7. Fruit salad: the ideel way to end a meal — 7a. ________ 7b. ________
8. Only dryed figs give that finel touch — 8a. ________ 8b. ________
9. Fresh plums oddered daily from local farms — 9a. ________ 9b. ________
10. You buy the fruit were realy proud to sell! — 10a. ________ 10b. ________



145

## Proofreading Exercise

| ■ | ★ | ▲ | ◆ | ● |
|---|---|---|---|---|
| graze | secure | filing | scorn | seashore |
| brake | preach | lonesome | stoop | ninth |
| square | grapes | choose | reaches | orchard |
| scarce | bore | really | lining | loose |
| preparing | reason | finest | surely | whole |

**D. Sentence Completion** Write Other Word Forms or the spelling words to complete the sentences. The shape tells you in what column you can find the spelling word. Write each word or its Other Word Form only once. If you need help, use the **Spelling Dictionary**.

REVIEW

1. I ▲ ___*chose*___ not to eat the one ★ ___grape___ that looked soft.
2. The ■ ___brakes___ in a car should be tightened ★ ___securely___.
3. Our math teacher told us the many ★ ___reasons___ for teaching the area of triangles and ■ ___squares___.
4. Southern farmers are ◆ ___sure___ that oranges will be ■ ___scarce___ this summer because of the cold winter.
5. My dad ■ ___prepared *or* prepares___ a ● ___wholesome___ meal for us.
6. The cow looked ▲ ___lonesome *or* lonely___ as it ■ ___grazed___ in the pasture.
7. Some children were ★ ___bored___ when the teacher ★ ___preached___ about safety.
8. He ◆ ___stooped___ down to put the ▲ ___files___ into the metal cabinet.
9. Her painting of the apple ● ___orchards___ looked very ▲ ___real *or* realistic___.
10. The ● ___nine___ yards of material was of ▲ ___fine___ quality.
11. My little brother ◆ ___scorns___ the idea of making straight ◆ ___lines___ on his homework paper.
12. When I ◆ ___reached___ for the ● ___loosely___ tied rope, the knot came undone.
13. We visited many ● ___seashores___ on our vacation.



## REVIEW TEST

REVIEW

Twenty-five words, selected randomly from the five spelling lists, constitute the test and are listed with the appropriate phrases. Follow the same testing procedure used to administer the weekly Pretest and Posttest. Have students write any misspelled words on the Words to Learn Sheet. As an alternative testing option, you may wish to use the Standardized-format Test for this Review Lesson, found in the Teacher's Resource Book.

### Test Words and Phrases

1. grapes — a bunch of **grapes**
2. crazy — a **crazy** day
3. fare — paid a full **fare**
4. bare — running in **bare** feet
5. preparing — **preparing** a meal
6. beam — a **beam** of light
7. cheat — caught the **cheat**
8. dealing — **dealing** the cards
9. really — if it **really** matters
10. beaten — the **beaten** team
11. rise — saw the balloon **rise**
12. decide — will **decide** on a color
13. finest — the **finest** piece of work
14. knives — sharpened the **knives**
15. I'd — if **I'd** tried
16. hose — the garden **hose**
17. whole — ate it **whole**
18. lonesome — **lonesome** and homesick
19. border — around the **border**
20. formed — **formed** a straight line
21. excuse — made no **excuse**
22. usually — **usually** done on time
23. pupil — one for each **pupil**
24. foolish — seemed rather **foolish**
25. mood — in a bad **mood**

**Review Test: Lesson 6**

Name________________ Date________

**Directions:** Read each sentence. Select the word with the correct spelling to complete each sentence. Fill in the correct letter in the answer column.

1. The cook is _____ a meal. A. prepairing B. preparing C. perparing D. prepareing
2. They are running in _____ feet. A. baire B. bayer C. bair D. bare
3. Today is a _____ day. A. craizy B. crazy C. crasy D. crazey
4. We paid a full _____ . A. fare B. faire C. fayer D. faer
5. The dog ate a bunch of _____ . A. graipes B. graipe C. grappes D. grapes
6. We saw a _____ of light. A. beem B. beim C. beam D. beame
7. The teacher caught the _____ . A. cheet B. cheete C. cheat D. cheate
8. Who is _____ the cards? A. deling B. deiling C. deeling D. dealing
9. The _____ team left the field. A. beaten B. beeten C. beatin D. beten
10. I wonder if it _____ matters. A. realy B. reely C. really D. reelly
11. They will _____ on a color. A. deside B. decide C. decied D. desighed
12. The cook sharpened the _____ . A. nifes B. nives C. knifes D. knives
13. We saw the _____ piece of work. A. finnest B. finast C. finist D. finest
14. We saw the balloon _____ . A. ryze B. rize C. rise D. wrise
15. He wondered if _____ tried. A. Id B. id C. I'd D. Id'
16. Use the garden _____ . A. hose B. hoze C. hos D. hoos
17. The shark ate it _____ . A. whol B. whole C. hole D. whoal
18. We were _____ and homesick. A. lonsome B. lonesum C. loansome D. lonesome
19. We _____ a straight line. A. formd B. foarmed C. formed D. formde
20. A hem was sewn around the _____ . A. bordar B. bordder C. boarder D. border
21. I am in a bad _____ . A. mude B. mood C. muod D. moud
22. It seemed rather _____ . A. foolish B. folish C. foollish D. follish
23. Use one for each _____ . A. pupill B. pupile C. pupil D. piupil
24. It's _____ done on time. A. usualy B. usually C. useually D. uzually
25. The child made no _____ . A. excus B. excuze C. excouse D. excuse

Answer Column: 1.–25. A B C D

154



**Standardized-format Test**

# LESSON 7

## OBJECTIVES

- to spell 20 high-frequency **ai** and **ay** words with the /ā/ and /âr/
- to proofread these words in daily writing
- to become familiar with 38 other forms of the spelling words

| Summary of Skills | Exercises |
|---|---|
| Auditory Discrimination | A |
| Proofreading | A, C, I |
| Visual Discrimination | C |
| Word Analysis | D, G |
| Vocabulary Development | E, F |
| Dictionary Skills | F |
| Context Usage | H |
| Original Writing | I |

## PRETEST AND PROOFREADING

The Pretest identifies the words students are able to spell, as well as the words they need to learn. You may wish to use Other Word Forms when giving the Pretest. Five suggested Other Word Forms are underlined on this page.

To administer the Pretest:

**READ** each word aloud.
**SAY** the phrase containing the word.
**REPEAT** the word.

Have students correct the Pretest using the Corrected-test Procedure. They may record their scores on a personal Progress Chart (see the Teacher's Resource Book) and study misspelled words using the **S-H-A-R-P** procedure.

## OTHER WORD FORMS

This section presents related forms of the spelling words to strengthen spelling power and vocabulary knowledge.

### Enrichment Activity

Have students write opposite words or phrases for these Other Word Forms. Be sure they write the Other Word Form with its opposite next to it.

**gained, straighten, delay, remaining**

# 7

**A. Pretest and Proofreading**

**B. Spelling Words and Phrases**

| | |
|---|---|
| **1. aim*** | took aim |
| **2. bait** | the last worm for bait |
| **3. gain*** | to gain weight |
| **4. braid** | a ribbon on each braid |
| **5. brain*** | controlled by the brain |
| **6. strain** | to strain on the rope |
| **7. remain*** | will remain here |
| **8. faint*** | will faint in the heat |
| **9. waist** | around your waist |
| **10. sailor*** | the sailor in uniform |
| **11. daily*** | a daily delivery |
| **12. praise** | praise for good work |
| **13. straight** | drew a straight line |
| **14. fairly*** | was treated fairly |
| **15. sway*** | will sway in the wind |
| **16. spray** | a spray of water |
| **17. stray** | to stray from course |
| **18. payment*** | a monthly payment |
| **19. mayor** | the office of the mayor |
| **20. delayed** | delayed the plane |

*Other Word Forms*

| | |
|---|---|
| aimed, aimless | day |
| baited | praises, praising |
| gained, gainful | straighten, straightest, |
| braided, braiding | straightening |
| brains, brainy | fair, fairer, fairest |
| strained, strainer | swaying |
| remains, remained, | sprayed |
| remaining | strayed |
| fainted, faintly | pay, pays, paid, paying |
| waists | mayors |
| sailors | delay, delays, delaying |

**C. Visual Warm-up** Write each word in its correct shape.

a. braid
b. bait
c. fairly
d. mayor
e. payment
f. sway
g. straight
h. spray
i. remain
j. strain
k. brain
l. delayed
m. daily
n. praise
o. aim
p. waist
q. stray
r. faint
s. sailor
t. gain



*Modified Lesson words are asterisked.
The Modified Lesson is found in the Teacher's Resource Book.

## MEETING INDIVIDUAL NEEDS / ASSIGNMENT GUIDE

| 5-Day Plan | 3-Day Plan | Limited Spellers | Average Spellers | Advanced Spellers |
|---|---|---|---|---|
| 1 | 1 | • Pretest<br>• Progress Chart | • Pretest<br>• Progress Chart<br>• Home Activity | • Pretest<br>• Progress Chart<br>• Home Activity |
| 2 | 1 | • Modified Lesson Visual Warm-up Ending Sounds | • Regular Lesson Visual Warm-up | • Regular Lesson Visual Warm-up |
| 3 and 4 | 2 | • Modified Lesson Vowel Puzzle Word Match Finish the Sentence | Spelling Activities | Spelling Activities<br>• Challenge Exercise |
| 5 | 3 | • Posttest<br>• Words to Learn Sheet<br>• Progress Chart | • Posttest<br>• Words to Learn Sheet<br>• Progress Chart | • Posttest<br>• Words to Learn Sheet<br>• Progress Chart |

**D. Patterns** Complete the words below by adding the correct spelling for the *a* sound. Write the spelling words. Each word can be found in the spelling list.

| | Patterns | Spelling Words | | Patterns | Spelling Words |
|---|---|---|---|---|---|
| 1. | rem a i n | remain | 11. | spr a y | spray |
| 2. | d a i ly | daily | 12. | s a i lor | sailor |
| 3. | br a i n | brain | 13. | f a i nt | faint |
| 4. | del a y ed | delayed | 14. | g a i n | gain |
| 5. | m a y or | mayor | 15. | f a i rly | fairly |
| 6. | sw a y | sway | 16. | p a y ment | payment |
| 7. | pr a i se | praise | 17. | w a i st | waist |
| 8. | b a i t | bait | 18. | a i m | aim |
| 9. | str a i n | strain | 19. | str a i ght | straight |
| 10. | br a i d | braid | 20. | str a y | stray |

**E. BrAIn Game** Answer each question with an ai word from the spelling list. Write the words.

1. What ai do you use to think? brain
2. What ai has to do with fishing? bait
3. What ai leaves you behind? remain
4. What ai separates out the water? strain
5. What ai goes to sea? sailor
6. What ai occurs when you are ill? faint
7. What ai is part of your body? waist
8. What ai is found each day? daily
9. What ai is what the girl did to her hair? braid
10. What ai do you get when you have done well? praise
11. What ai does not curve? straight
12. What ai helps you reach your goal? aim
13. What ai increases your weight? gain
14. What ai treats you honestly? fairly



## OPTIONAL TEACHING PLAN

Write the three Word Group headings on the chalkboard. Ask the students to name the thirteen spelling words with the long **a** sound that are spelled with **ai**. Write the words on the chalkboard as the students say them. Proceed in the same manner for identifying the other Word Groups. Note that the long **a** sound is spelled with **ai** in words such as **aim** and with **ay** in words such as **sway**.

| Word Groups | | |
|---|---|---|
| /ā/ words | aim | bait |
| | gain | braid |
| | brain | strain |
| | remain | faint |
| | waist | sailor |
| | daily | praise |
| | straight | **faithful** |
| | **popula-tion** | **laser** |
| /âr/ words | fairly | **stairway** |
| | **welfare** | |
| /ā/: **ay** words | sway | spray |
| | stray | payment |
| | mayor | delayed |

*Challenge Words are boldfaced.*

**Optional Activity Masters**

Those using the Hardcover Pupil Edition may wish to use the Optional Activity Masters in the Teacher's Resource Book for Exercises C and D.

### Home Activity #7

Name______ Date______

Use the spelling words to complete the sentences. The number before each blank tells you in what column you can find the correct word. Use each word only once.

| 1 | 2 | 3 | 4 |
|---|---|---|---|
| remain | braid | daily | payment |
| strain | faint | bait | stray |
| aim | fairly | waist | mayor |
| straight | praise | sailor | spray |
| gain | brain | sway | delayed |

1. You can go but I will (1) ______ here.
2. I just used the last worm for (3) ______ .
3. The child drew a (1) ______ line on the paper.
4. It is dangerous for ships to (4) ______ from course.
5. The fisherman had to (1) ______ on the rope to bring in the huge swordfish.
6. Let's give them (2) ______ for good work.
7. We saluted the (3) ______ in uniform.
8. I don't think the witness was treated (2) ______ by the judge.
9. Welcome to the office of the (4) ______ .
10. Buckle the belt around your (3) ______ .
11. I think I will (2) ______ in the heat.
12. The sail will (3) ______ in the wind.
13. The elephant squirted a (4) ______ of water at us.
14. The bowler took (1) ______ and scored a strike.
15. The girl had a ribbon on each (2) ______ .
16. The winter storm (4) ______ the plane.
17. All eye movements are controlled by the (2) ______ .
18. The thin man needed to (1) ______ weight.
19. She makes a monthly (4) ______ on her car.
20. The baker makes a (3) ______ delivery to our store.



13

### Modified Lesson #7

Name______ Date______

**Spelling Words** aim gain brain remain faint sailor daily fairly sway payment

I. **Visual Warm-up.** Write each spelling word in its correct shape.

II. **Vowel Hunt.** Fill in the missing vowels and write the spelling words.

a. d _ _ l _ ______ f. p _ _ m _ nt ______
b. sw _ _ ______ g. g _ _ n ______
c. _ _ m ______ h. br _ _ n ______
d. r _ m _ _ n ______ i. s _ _ l _ r ______
e. f _ _ rl _ ______ j. f _ _ nt ______

III. **Word Maze.** Fill in the missing letters to find the spelling words. Write the words in the blanks beside the numbers.

Across: 4. ___ 5. ___ 7. ___ 8. ___ 9. ___

Down: 1. ___ 2. ___ 3. ___ 6. ___ 7. ___



55

### Modified Lesson #7 *(continued)*

Name______ Date______

**Spelling Words** aim gain brain remain faint sailor daily fairly sway payment

IV. **Word Parts.** Write the spelling words that have the word parts below. A word may be used more than once.

a. ain words: ______, ______, ______, ______
b. or word: ______
c. ly words: ______, ______
d. air word: ______
e. ment word: ______
f. sw word: ______
g. br word: ______
h. word beginning with ai: ______

V. **Sentence Sense.** Write each spelling word in the correct sentence.

**Words** aim brain faint daily sway

a. The senses are controlled by the ______ .
b. Sick people will ______ in the heat.
c. The hunter took ______ at the target.
d. The tree will ______ in the wind.
e. The market needs a ______ delivery of bread.

**Words** gain remain sailor fairly payment

f. Each child was treated ______ .
g. The dog will ______ here overnight.
h. Does anyone need to ______ weight?
i. I must make a monthly ______ for rent.
j. The ______ in uniform fixed the sail.

56



**Home Activity**

A weekly homework assignment

**Modified Lesson**

An alternative lesson for limited spellers

*(The Answer Key can be found in the Teacher's Resource Book.)*

LESSON 7 CONTINUED

### Challenge Exercise #7

Name__________ Date__________

**Word Watch.** Seven hundred years ago, the French word *faint* meant "to avoid duty by false pretenses." A popular way to avoid duty was for one to pretend to lose consciousness. Persons unable to cope with life might choose to avoid a problem by pretending to pass out, usually at a very convenient moment. However, it was considered cowardly for a man to do this. In medieval days, men were expected to face their problems head-on. Today the word *faint* no longer includes the idea of false pretenses. Generally, a faint idea is a feeble one, and a person who faints usually loses consciousness because of a circulation problem.

**Word Analogies.** Decide on the relationship that exists between the first pair of words. Using the Other Word Forms on page 28, find a word that completes the second pair of words and establishes the same relationship.

1. *pilots* is to *planes* as __________ is to *ships*
2. *woven* is to *cloth* as __________ is to *hair*
3. *wrists* is to *bracelets* as __________ is to *belts*
4. *collecting* is to *stamps* as __________ is to *bills*
5. *stupid* is to *dumb* as __________ is to *smart*

**Challenge Words Student Activity**

Use the challenge words below to complete the statements about people.

**laser stairway welfare population faithful**

1. You are responsible for the __________ of your pet.
2. A business owner would look for __________ employees.
3. The carpenter should rebuild a shaky __________.
4. A census taker would check the town's __________.
5. A doctor might treat a patient with a __________ beam.

**Working With Words: Student Writing Activity**

Use as many Other Word Forms as you can from page 28 to write five sentences that review a movie. (Example: The plot was *aimless* and *remained* so until the end of the movie.)

120



## Challenge Exercise

Additional activities for advanced spellers

**Spelling Words**

| | | | | |
|---|---|---|---|---|
| aim | bait | gain | braid | brain |
| strain | remain | faint | waist | sailor |
| daily | praise | straight | fairly | sway |
| spray | stray | payment | mayor | delayed |

**F. Words and Meanings** Write a spelling word for each meaning. Check your answers in the **Spelling Dictionary**.

1. done every day daily
2. the body part above the hips waist
3. words that tell the worth of something praise
4. strands of hair woven together braid
5. the head of a city's government mayor
6. to increase in weight gain
7. a member of a ship's crew sailor
8. to move back and forth sway
9. not bent or curved straight
10. to pull hard strain
11. a moving group of water droplets spray
12. to stay in a place remain
13. to wander from the right path stray
14. an amount paid payment
15. honestly and justly fairly
16. to lose consciousness for a short time faint
17. anything used to attract animals to be caught bait
18. put off until later delayed
19. the part of the nervous system in the skull brain
20. a purpose or goal aim



## CONTROLLED DICTATION (Optional)

These dictation sentences provide maintenance for spelling words previously taught and practice for words currently being studied. Dictation should be administered on Day 4. The teacher or another student may dictate the sentences. Be sure to dictate all marks of punctuation. Challenge Word sentences are preceded by an asterisk.

1. Did the lonely **sailor stray** from the ship?
2. I **aim** to **praise** you **daily**.
3. **Spray** a little water on the **bait**.
4. Each **braid** will **sway** when she runs.
5. The **mayor delayed** the **payment**.
6. The ninth line must **remain fairly straight**.
7. You will **gain** inches around the **waist**.
8. Any **strain** on the **brain** may cause me to **faint**.

*9. The whole school **population** has your **welfare** at heart.
*10. Our **laser** printer has been **faithful**.
*11. Be careful on the **stairway**.

**G. Using Other Word Forms** Write the Other Word Form that completes each series.

Base Words: remain(ing) pay(ing) straighten(ing) braid(ing) praise(ing)

1. braids, braided, braiding
2. remains, remained, remaining
3. praises, praised, praising
4. straightens, straightened, straightening
5. pays, paid, paying

**H. Challenge Words** Write the Challenge Word that completes each sentence.

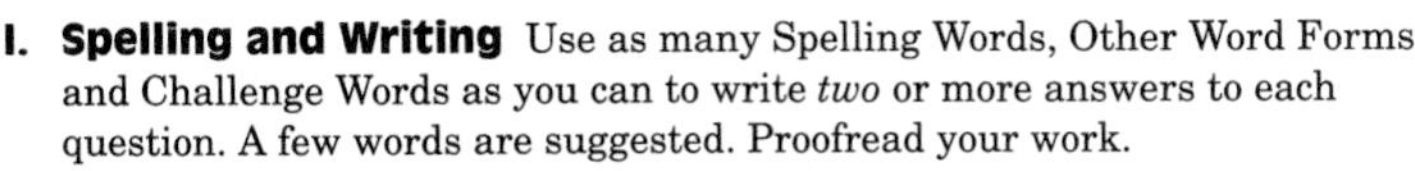

| stairway | faithful | population | laser | welfare |
|---|---|---|---|---|

1. A laser beam may be used to melt hard materials.
2. The male population of the city has increased.
3. A collie can be a faithful pet.
4. I'm concerned about your welfare .
5. A circular stairway connects both floors.

**I. Spelling and Writing** Use as many Spelling Words, Other Word Forms, and Challenge Words as you can to write *two* or more answers to each question. A few words are suggested. Proofread your work.

1. What would you do to reach your goal of becoming a good basketball player?

   daily – aim – delayed – remain – stray

   Example: *I would not stray from my daily practice schedule.*

2. What could you do to help an honest person become an elected official in your city or town?

   mayor – welfare – praise – fairly – faithful – population

3. What would you do if you saw a 50-pound fish about to grab your fishing line?

   bait – waist – sailor – spray – straight



## USING OTHER WORD FORMS

Vocabulary is expanded through the use of other forms of basic spelling words. Emphasis is on the relationship of syntax to suffix choices. The following generalizations apply to the Other Word Forms used in Exercise G.

### Spelling Rule

Adding suffixes to words ending in silent **e**

When adding a suffix that begins with a vowel to words that end with silent **e**, drop the final **e**.
**(praise, praising)**

Adding suffixes to words ending in **y**

When adding a suffix to words ending with vowel-**y**, do not change the **y** to **i**.
**(pay, paying)**

## POSTTEST AND PROOFREADING

Follow the same testing procedures used in the Pretest, although you may wish to correct the tests yourself. Have students write any misspelled words on the Words to Learn Sheet and record spelling success on the Progress Chart.

## THE SPELLING-WRITING LINK

**Purpose** This activity helps students retain the correct spelling of words and transfer the words to their daily writing. Students use lesson words to answer questions promoting higher-order thinking skills.

**Procedure** Read the first question and write the suggested words on the chalkboard: **daily, aim, delayed, remain, stray.** Have students list some Other Word Forms of the lesson words on the chalkboard. Write the example answer on the chalkboard, noting the lesson words: **stray, daily.** Brainstorm with the class other possible answers to question 1. Remind students to look at all the lesson words for ideas. Write the answers on the chalkboard, noting any lesson words.

**Practice** Tell students to finish the activity by writing two or more answers to each question. Remind them to proofread their work.

# LESSON 8

## OBJECTIVES

- to spell 20 high-frequency words, including words with the /ē/, /yōō/, and /ī/
- to proofread these words in daily writing
- to become familiar with 34 other forms of the spelling words

| Summary of Skills | Exercises |
|---|---|
| Auditory Discrimination | A, E |
| Proofreading | A, C, I |
| Visual Discrimination | C |
| Vocabulary Development | D, G, H |
| Dictionary Skills | D, F |
| Original Writing | I |

## PRETEST AND PROOFREADING

The Pretest identifies the words students are able to spell, as well as the words they need to learn. You may wish to use Other Word Forms when giving the Pretest. Five suggested Other Word Forms are underlined on this page.

To administer the Pretest:

**READ** each word aloud.
**SAY** the phrase containing the word.
**REPEAT** the word.

Have students correct the Pretest using the Corrected-test Procedure. They may record their scores on a personal Progress Chart (see the Teacher's Resource Book) and study misspelled words using the **S-H-A-R-P** procedure.

## OTHER WORD FORMS

This section presents related forms of the spelling words to strengthen spelling power and vocabulary knowledge.

### Enrichment Activity

Have students write sentences that include these Other Word Forms.

1. **viewed – flights**
2. **frozen – pieces**
3. **blood – sleeves**
4. **excited – freely**

**A. Pretest and Proofreading**

**B. Spelling Words and Phrases**

| | |
|---|---|
| **1. deed*** | good deed |
| **2. needle** | knitting needle |
| **3. creek*** | fish in the creek |
| **4. sleeve** | patch on my sleeve |
| **5. freeze*** | began to freeze |
| **6. freedom*** | enjoyed freedom |
| **7. bleeding*** | stopped the bleeding |
| **8. Halloween** | Halloween party |
| **9. piece** | a piece of paper |
| **10. chief*** | reported to the chief |
| **11. view** | view from the top |
| **12. ironing*** | a stack of ironing |
| **13. rifle** | held the rifle |
| **14. climate** | cool, dry climate |
| **15. excite** | will excite the crowd |
| **16. exciting** | an exciting vacation |
| **17. replied*** | replied without delay |
| **18. flight*** | took the next flight |
| **19. fright*** | recovered from our fright |
| **20. all right** | all right and safe |

***Other Word Forms***

| | |
|---|---|
| deeded | viewed, viewer |
| needles, needled | iron, ironed |
| creeks | rifles, rifled |
| sleeves | climates |
| froze, frozen, freezer, freezes, freezing | excited |
| free, freely | reply, replies, replying |
| bleed, bled, blood | flights |
| pieces, pieced | frighten, frightened, frightening |
| chiefs, chiefly | |

**C. Visual Warm-up** Write each word in its correct shape.

a. chief
b. bleeding
c. Halloween
d. needle
e. sleeve
f. view
g. excite
h. climate
i. all right
j. fright
k. freedom
l. piece
m. deed
n. creek
o. freeze
p. exciting
q. replied
r. ironing
s. rifle
t. flight



*Modified Lesson words are asterisked.
The Modified Lesson is found in the Teacher's Resource Book.

## MEETING INDIVIDUAL NEEDS / ASSIGNMENT GUIDE

| 5-Day Plan | 3-Day Plan | Limited Spellers | Average Spellers | Advanced Spellers |
|---|---|---|---|---|
| 1 | 1 | • Pretest<br>• Progress Chart | • Pretest<br>• Progress Chart<br>• Home Activity | • Pretest<br>• Progress Chart<br>• Home Activity |
| 2 | | • Modified Lesson Visual Warm-up Ending Sounds | • Regular Lesson Visual Warm-up | • Regular Lesson Visual Warm-up |
| 3 and 4 | 2 | • Modified Lesson Vowel Puzzle Word Match Finish the Sentence | Spelling Activities | Spelling Activities<br>• Challenge Exercise |
| 5 | 3 | • Posttest<br>• Words to Learn Sheet<br>• Progress Chart | • Posttest<br>• Words to Learn Sheet<br>• Progress Chart | • Posttest<br>• Words to Learn Sheet<br>• Progress Chart |

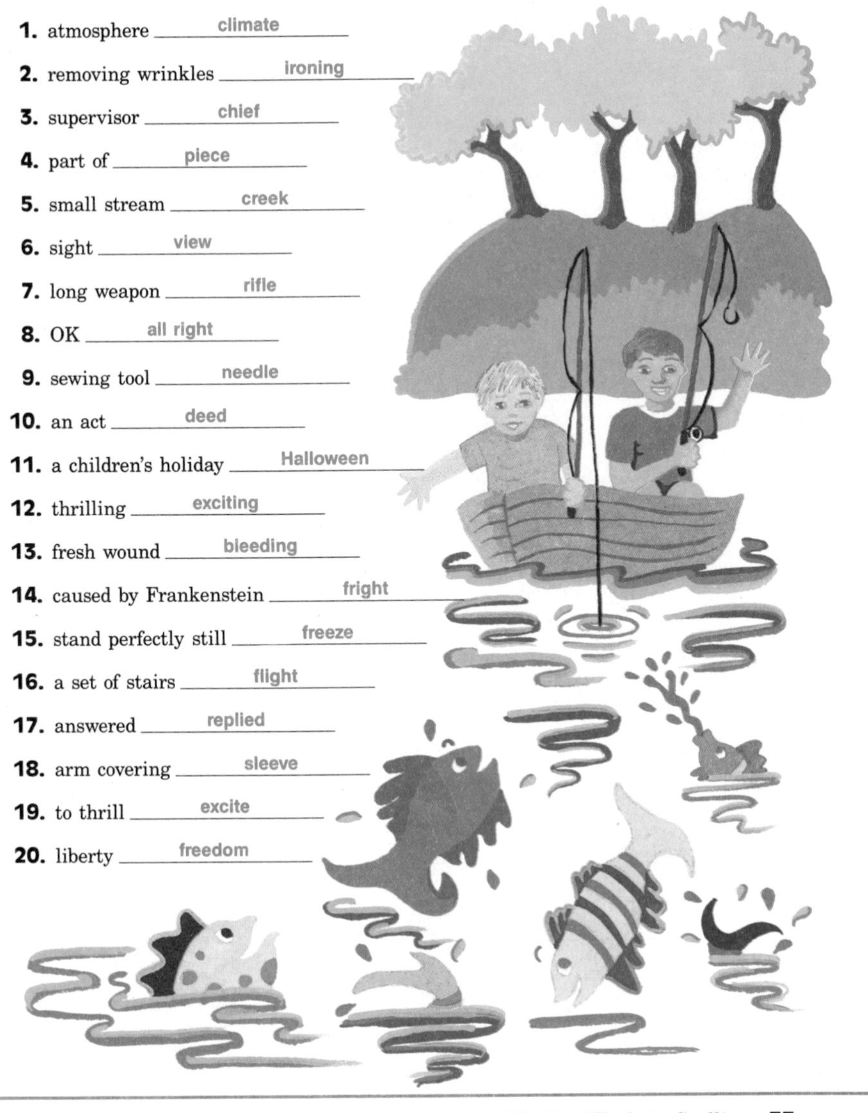

**D. Word Match-ups** Write a word from the spelling list that best fits each phrase or word below. Check your answers in the **Spelling Dictionary**.

1. atmosphere ___climate___
2. removing wrinkles ___ironing___
3. supervisor ___chief___
4. part of ___piece___
5. small stream ___creek___
6. sight ___view___
7. long weapon ___rifle___
8. OK ___all right___
9. sewing tool ___needle___
10. an act ___deed___
11. a children's holiday ___Halloween___
12. thrilling ___exciting___
13. fresh wound ___bleeding___
14. caused by Frankenstein ___fright___
15. stand perfectly still ___freeze___
16. a set of stairs ___flight___
17. answered ___replied___
18. arm covering ___sleeve___
19. to thrill ___excite___
20. liberty ___freedom___

Working Words in Spelling **33**

## OPTIONAL TEACHING PLAN

Write the four Word Group headings on the chalkboard. Ask the students to name the eight spelling words with the long **e** sound that are spelled with **ee**. Write the words on the chalkboard as the students say them. Proceed in the same manner for identifying the other Word Groups. Note the long **e** sound of **ie** in words such as **piece** and the /yo͞o/ sound of **ie** in **view**.

| Word Groups | | |
|---|---|---|
| /ē/: **ee** and **ea** words | deed<br>creek<br>freeze<br>bleeding<br>**breezes**<br>**gleefully** | needle<br>sleeve<br>freedom<br>Hal-loween<br>**bleachers** |
| /ē/: **ie** words | piece | chief |
| /yo͞o/: **ie** word | view | |
| /ī/: **i** words | ironing<br>climate<br>exciting<br>flight<br>all right<br>**violin** | rifle<br>excite<br>replied<br>fright<br>**limestone** |

*Challenge Words are boldfaced.*

### Optional Activity Masters

Those using the Hardcover Pupil Edition may wish to use the Optional Activity Masters in the Teacher's Resource Book for Exercise C.

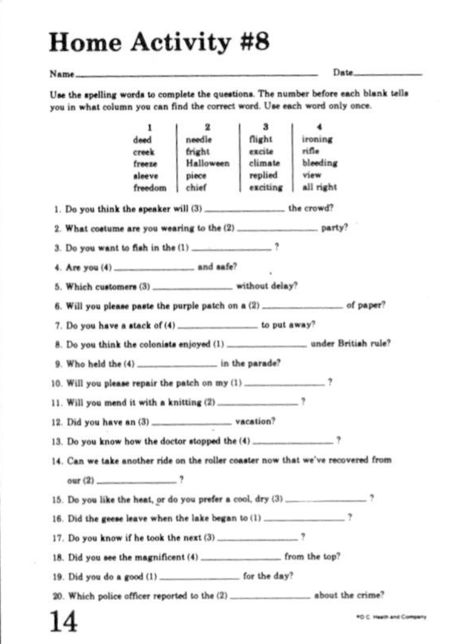

**Home Activity #8**

Name______________________ Date__________

Use the spelling words to complete the questions. The number before each blank tells you in what column you can find the correct word. Use each word only once.

| 1 | 2 | 3 | 4 |
|---|---|---|---|
| deed | needle | flight | ironing |
| creek | fright | excite | rifle |
| freeze | Halloween | climate | bleeding |
| sleeve | piece | replied | view |
| freedom | chief | exciting | all right |

1. Do you think the speaker will (3) __________ the crowd?
2. What costume are you wearing to the (2) __________ party?
3. Do you want to fish in the (1) __________ ?
4. Are you (4) __________ and safe?
5. Which customers (3) __________ without delay?
6. Will you please paste the purple patch on a (2) __________ of paper?
7. Do you have a stack of (4) __________ to put away?
8. Do you think the colonists enjoyed (1) __________ under British rule?
9. Who held the (4) __________ in the parade?
10. Will you please repair the patch on my (1) __________ ?
11. Will you mend it with a knitting (2) __________ ?
12. Did you have an (3) __________ vacation?
13. Do you know how the doctor stopped the (4) __________ ?
14. Can we take another ride on the roller coaster now that we've recovered from our (2) __________ ?
15. Do you like the heat, or do you prefer a cool, dry (3) __________ ?
16. Did the geese leave when the lake began to (1) __________ ?
17. Do you know if he took the next (3) __________ ?
18. Did you see the magnificent (4) __________ from the top?
19. Did you do a good (1) __________ for the day?
20. Which police officer reported to the (2) __________ about the crime?

14 ©D.C. Heath and Company

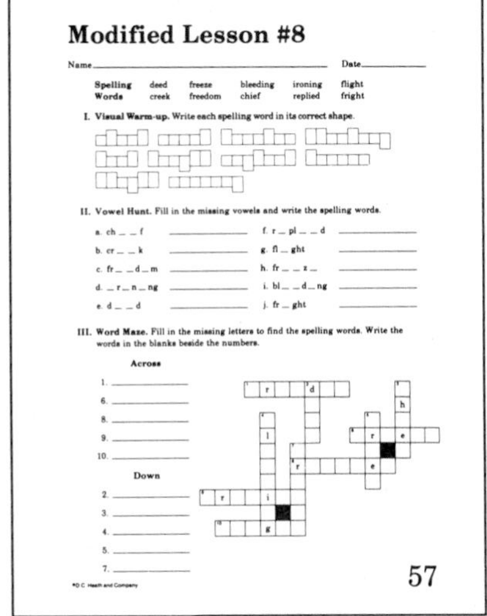

**Modified Lesson #8**

Name______________________ Date__________

**Spelling Words** deed, creek, freeze, freedom, bleeding, chief, ironing, replied, flight, fright

I. **Visual Warm-up.** Write each spelling word in its correct shape.

II. **Vowel Hunt.** Fill in the missing vowels and write the spelling words.

a. ch _ _ f __________
b. cr _ _ k __________
c. fr _ _ d _ m __________
d. _ r _ n _ ng __________
e. d _ _ d __________
f. r _ pl _ _ d __________
g. fl _ ght __________
h. fr _ _ z _ __________
i. bl _ _ d _ ng __________
j. fr _ ght __________

III. **Word Maze.** Fill in the missing letters to find the spelling words. Write the words in the blanks beside the numbers.

Across
1. __________
6. __________
8. __________
9. __________
10. __________

Down
2. __________
3. __________
4. __________
5. __________
7. __________

©D.C. Heath and Company 57

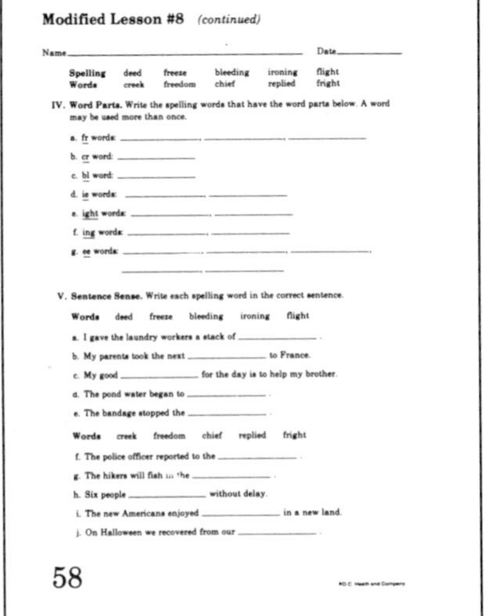

**Modified Lesson #8** *(continued)*

Name______________________ Date__________

**Spelling Words** deed, creek, freeze, freedom, bleeding, chief, ironing, replied, flight, fright

IV. **Word Parts.** Write the spelling words that have the word parts below. A word may be used more than once.

a. fr words: __________, __________, __________
b. cr word: __________
c. bl word: __________
d. ie words: __________, __________
e. ight words: __________, __________
f. ing words: __________, __________
g. ee words: __________, __________, __________, __________, __________

V. **Sentence Sense.** Write each spelling word in the correct sentence.

**Words** deed freeze bleeding ironing flight

a. I gave the laundry workers a stack of __________ .
b. My parents took the next __________ to France.
c. My good __________ for the day is to help my brother.
d. The pond water began to __________ .
e. The bandage stopped the __________ .

**Words** creek freedom chief replied fright

f. The police officer reported to the __________ .
g. The hikers will fish in the __________ .
h. Six people __________ without delay.
i. The new Americans enjoyed __________ in a new land.
j. On Halloween we recovered from our __________ .

58 ©D.C. Heath and Company

**Home Activity**
A weekly homework assignment

**Modified Lesson**
An alternative lesson for limited spellers

*(The Answer Key can be found in the Teacher's Resource Book.)*

# LESSON 8 CONTINUED

### Challenge Exercise #8

Name__________ Date__________

**Word Watch.** The word *climate* derives from the Greek word *klimatis*, which means "an inclination or slope, such as a slope of ground." The ancient Greeks believed that ships traveling beyond the horizon went down a slope. They called this slope *klimatis* and believed it affected the temperature and weather. Greek geographers developed several klimatis zones to explain what they thought were seven different climates of the world. The Romans adopted the word, changed it to *climatis*, and gave us the beginning of our spelling of the word *climate*.

**Word Analogies.** Decide on the relationship that exists between the first pair of words. Using the Other Word Forms on page 32, find a word that completes the second pair of words and establishes the same relationship.

1. *tripped* is to *stumbled* as __________ is to *scared*
2. *bows* is to *arrows* as __________ is to *bullets*
3. *admirals* is to *sailors* as __________ is to *braves*
4. *pulleys* is to *ropes* as __________ is to *threads*
5. *warming* is to *hot* as __________ is to *cold*

**Challenge Words Student Activity**

Use the challenge words below to locate each item.

**gleefully breezes violin bleachers limestone**

1. found in rock formations: __________
2. found in an orchestra: __________
3. found at a football field: __________
4. found at a parade: people __________ cheering.
5. found in the air: __________

**Working With Words: Student Writing Activity**

Use as many Other Word Forms as you can from page 32 to write instructions for a baby-sitter on how to deal with a crying child. (Example: Read fun stories that are not *frightening*.)



121

## Challenge Exercise

Additional activities for advanced spellers

### Spelling Words

| | | | | |
|---|---|---|---|---|
| deed | needle | creek | sleeve | freeze |
| freedom | bleeding | Halloween | piece | chief |
| view | ironing | rifle | climate | excite |
| exciting | replied | flight | fright | all right |

**E. Rhyming Words** Write the words from the spelling list that rhyme with the words below.

| | | | |
|---|---|---|---|
| **1.** do | view | **10.** tweedle | needle |
| **2.** beside | replied | **11.** believe | sleeve |
| **3.** delighting | exciting | **12.** beak | creek |
| **4.** bead | deed | **13.** trifle | rifle |
| **5.** admiring | ironing | **14.** feeding | bleeding |
| **6.** mean | Halloween | **15.** Fahrenheit | excite |
| **7.** seize | freeze | **16.** site | flight |
| **8.** niece | piece | **17.** might | fright |
| **9.** leaf | chief | **18.** good night | all right |

**19.** Write the two spelling words that do not have a rhyming word.

**a.** freedom **b.** climate

**F. Finding Words** The words in the spelling list appear in the beginning (A-H), middle (I-Q), or end (R-Z) of the **Spelling Dictionary**. Write each word.

**Beginning A-H**

1. deed
2. creek
3. freeze
4. freedom
5. bleeding
6. Halloween
7. chief
8. climate
9. excite
10. exciting
11. flight
12. fright
13. all right

**Middle I-Q**

14. needle
15. piece
16. ironing

**End R-Z**

17. sleeve
18. view
19. rifle
20. replied

**34** Lesson 8

## CONTROLLED DICTATION (Optional)

These dictation sentences provide maintenance for spelling words previously taught and practice for words currently being studied. Dictation should be administered on Day 4. The teacher or another student may dictate the sentences. Be sure to dictate all marks of punctuation. Challenge Word sentences are preceded by an asterisk.

1. It's **all right** to **excite** children on **Halloween**.
2. Before **ironing** the coat, fix the lining of the **sleeve** with a **needle** and thre
3. The **chief replied** that he had secured a new **rifle**.
4. Our **fright** grew when we saw that they were **bleeding**.
5. They have a **deed** to a **piece** of land with an orchard **view**.
6. Their **flight** to **freedom** was **exciting**.
7. The **creek** will not **freeze** in this **climate**.

*8. The fans in the **bleachers** welcomed the cooling **breezes**.
*9. She was playing the **violin gleefully**.
*10. The rock is made of **limestone**.

**G. Using Other Word Forms** Write the Other Word Form that fits each clue.

Base Words: reply(es) chief(s) needle(s) sleeve(s) piece(s)

1. more than one arm of a shirt sleeves
2. more than one boss chiefs
3. more than one part pieces
4. more than one sewing instrument needles
5. more than one answer replies

**H. Challenge Words** Write the Challenge Word that completes each phrase.

| breezes | gleefully | limestone | bleachers | violin |
|---|---|---|---|---|

1. either a guitar or a violin
2. either winds or breezes
3. either happily or gleefully
4. either seats or bleachers
5. either granite or limestone

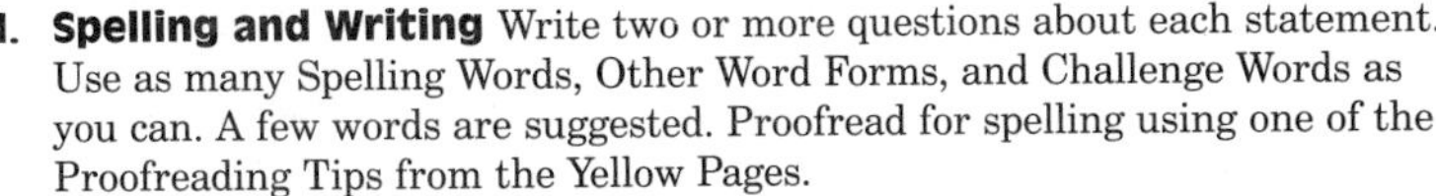

**I. Spelling and Writing** Write two or more questions about each statement. Use as many Spelling Words, Other Word Forms, and Challenge Words as you can. A few words are suggested. Proofread for spelling using one of the Proofreading Tips from the Yellow Pages.

1. Everyone was making unusual costumes.
   sleeve Halloween ironing frightful chief bleeding needle

   Example: Did they have time to iron the sleeves?
2. A short trip on a raft can be a good way to see wildlife.
   creek freedom viewing replied climate all right breezes
3. Many people go on a safari with a camera instead of a gun.
   deed freeze pieces rifle flight exciting



## USING OTHER WORD FORMS

Vocabulary is expanded through the use of other forms of basic spelling words. Emphasis is on the relationship of syntax to suffix choices. The following generalizations apply to the Other Word Forms used in Exercise G.

### Spelling Rule

Forming plurals

Add **s** to most nouns to form plurals. **(sleeve, sleeves)**

To form the plurals of nouns ending with consonant **-y**, change the **y** to **i** and add **es**. **(reply, replies)**

## POSTTEST AND PROOFREADING

Follow the same testing procedures used in the Pretest, although you may wish to correct the tests yourself. Have students write any misspelled words on the Words to Learn Sheet and record spelling success on the Progress Chart.

## THE SPELLING-WRITING LINK

**Purpose** This activity helps students to retain the correct spelling of words and transfer the words to their daily writing. Students use lesson words to create questions, which promotes inquiry and research skills.

**Procedure** Read the first statement and write the suggested words on the chalkboard: **sleeve, Halloween, ironing, frightful, chief, bleeding, needle.** Brainstorm with the class possible questions about statement 1. Remind students to look at all the lesson words for ideas, not just the suggested words. Write the questions on the chalkboard, noting any lesson words.

**Practice** Tell students to finish the activity by writing two or more questions about each statement. Remind them to proofread their work for spelling.

# LESSON 9

## OBJECTIVES

- to spell 20 high-frequency words, including vowel-**r** words and words with the /ō/, /ŏ/, and /ŭ/
- to proofread these words in daily writing
- to become familiar with 32 other forms of the spelling words

| Summary of Skills | Exercises |
|---|---|
| Auditory Discrimination | A |
| Proofreading | A, C, E, I |
| Visual Discrimination | C, E |
| Dictionary Skills | D, F |
| Vocabulary Development | F, H |
| Context Usage | G |
| Original Writing | I |

## PRETEST AND PROOFREADING

The Pretest identifies the words students are able to spell, as well as the words they need to learn. You may wish to use Other Word Forms when giving the Pretest. Five suggested Other Word Forms are underlined on this page.

To administer the Pretest:

**READ** each word aloud.
**SAY** the phrase containing the word.
**REPEAT** the word.

Have students correct the Pretest using the Corrected-test Procedure. They may record their scores on a personal Progress Chart (see the Teacher's Resource Book) and study misspelled words using the **S-H-A-R-P** procedure.

## OTHER WORD FORMS

This section presents related forms of the spelling words to strengthen spelling power and vocabulary knowledge.

### Enrichment Activity

Have students write synonyms or related phrases for these Other Word Forms. Be sure they write the Other Word Form with its synonym next to it.

**moments, bonding, stuffed, protester**

### A. Pretest and Proofreading

### B. Spelling Words and Phrases

| | | |
|---|---|---|
| **1.** | **burst** | to burst through the door |
| **2.** | **burglar** | startled the burglar |
| **3.** | **further** | for further information |
| **4.** | **surprises** | enjoys surprises |
| **5.** | **overturn** | to overturn the boat |
| **6.** | **overcome*** | overcome with joy |
| **7.** | **forever*** | forever and a day |
| **8.** | **motor** | started the motor |
| **9.** | **moment*** | at the last moment |
| **10.** | **program*** | a different program |
| **11.** | **protest*** | to protest the decision |
| **12.** | **odd*** | odd or even |
| **13.** | **golf*** | a game of golf |
| **14.** | **bond*** | their bond of friendship |
| **15.** | **moss** | covered with moss |
| **16.** | **toss*** | began to toss and turn |
| **17.** | **lodge** | stayed at the lodge |
| **18.** | **topic** | chose a topic |
| **19.** | **crops*** | harvested their crops |
| **20.** | **stuff** | will stuff with newspaper |

*Other Word Forms*

| | |
|---|---|
| bursting | oddly, oddest |
| burglary | golfer, golfing |
| furthered, furthermore | bonding, bondage |
| surprised, surprising | mossy |
| overturned, overturning | tossed |
| overcame, overcoming | lodged, lodging, |
| motorist, motoring | lodger |
| moments | topics |
| programmed, programmer, programming | cropped |
| protested, protester | stuffed |

### C. Visual Warm-up
Write each word in its correct shape.

a. moment
b. surprises
c. stuff
d. burglar
e. burst
f. bond
g. golf
h. topic
i. lodge
j. crops
k. further
l. program
m. forever
n. overcome
o. overturn
p. protest
q. motor
r. moss
s. odd
t. toss



*Modified Lesson words are asterisked.
The Modified Lesson is found in the Teacher's Resource Book.

## MEETING INDIVIDUAL NEEDS / ASSIGNMENT GUIDE

| 5-Day Plan | 3-Day Plan | Limited Spellers | Average Spellers | Advanced Spellers |
|---|---|---|---|---|
| 1 | 1 | • Pretest<br>• Progress Chart | • Pretest<br>• Progress Chart<br>• Home Activity | • Pretest<br>• Progress Chart<br>• Home Activity |
| 2 | | • Modified Lesson Visual Warm-up Ending Sounds | • Regular Lesson Visual Warm-up | • Regular Lesson Visual Warm-up |
| 3 and 4 | 2 | • Modified Lesson Vowel Puzzle Word Match Finish the Sentence | Spelling Activities | Spelling Activities<br>• Challenge Exercise |
| 5 | 3 | • Posttest<br>• Words to Learn Sheet<br>• Progress Chart | • Posttest<br>• Words to Learn Sheet<br>• Progress Chart | • Posttest<br>• Words to Learn Sheet<br>• Progress Chart |

**D. All in a Row** Write the twenty spelling words in alphabetical order. Then join the boxed letters and write four hidden words.

1. b o [n] d
2. b [u] r g l a r
3. b u [r] s t
4. c r o p [s]
5. f o r [e] v e r
6. Hidden Word: nurse
7. f u [r] t h e r
8. g [o] l f
9. l [o] d g e
10. [m] o m e n t
11. m o s [s]
12. Hidden Word: rooms
13. [m] o t o r
14. [o] d d
15. o [v] e r c o m e
16. o v [e] r t u r n
17. p [r] o g r a m
18. Hidden Word: mover
19. p r o t e [s] t
20. s [t] u f f
21. s u r p r i s [e] s
22. t o [p] i c
23. t o s [s]
24. Hidden Word: steps

**E. Word Search** The spelling words can be found in the word puzzle. The words appear across and down. Circle and write the words.

Across
1. forever
2. overturn
3. motor
4. crops
5. topic
6. bond
7. moment
8. program
9. moss
10. further
11. lodge
12. protest
13. toss

Down
14. stuff
15. burglar
16. burst
17. golf
18. odd
19. overcome
20. surprises

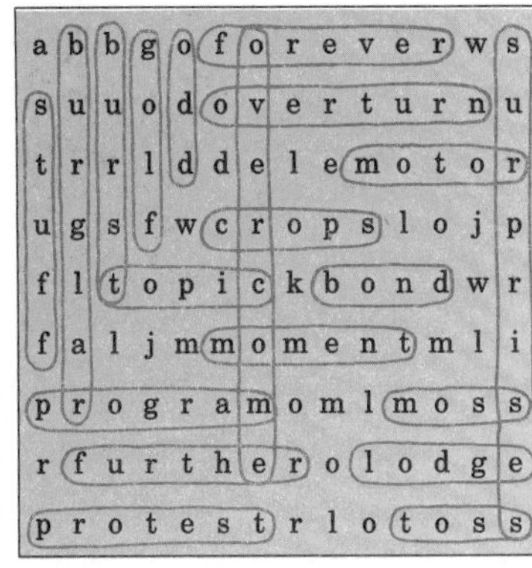


37

## OPTIONAL TEACHING PLAN

Write the five Word Group headings on the chalkboard. Ask the students to name the five **ur** spelling words. Write the words on the chalkboard as the students say them. Proceed in the same manner for identifying the other Word Groups. Note that the **er** in **forever** and the **ar** in **burglar** both have the /ə/ (schwa) sound, indicating that the vowel sound is ambiguous.

| Word Groups | | |
|---|---|---|
| **ur** words | burst<br>further<br>overturn | burglar<br>surprises |
| **er** words | overcome | forever |
| /ō/ words | motor<br>program<br>**solar** | moment<br>protest<br>**oppose** |
| /ŏ/ words | odd<br>bond<br>toss<br>topic<br>**operators** | golf<br>moss<br>lodge<br>crops |
| /ŭ/ words | stuff<br>**sections** | **wonder-fully** |

*Challenge Words are boldfaced.*

### Optional Activity Masters

Those using the Hardcover Pupil Edition may wish to use the Optional Activity Masters in the Teacher's Resource Book for Exercises C, D, and E.

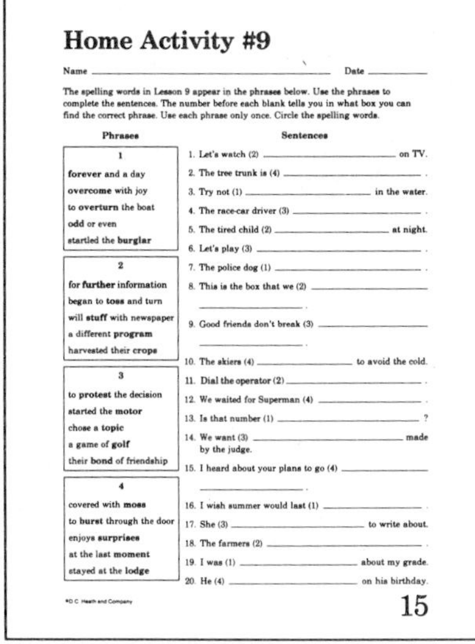

**Home Activity #9**

Name ________ Date ________

The spelling words in Lesson 9 appear in the phrases below. Use the phrases to complete the sentences. The number before each blank tells you in what box you can find the correct phrase. Use each phrase only once. Circle the spelling words.

Phrases

1: forever and a day; overcome with joy; to overturn the boat; odd or even; startled the burglar

2: for further information; began to toss and turn; will stuff with newspaper; a different program; harvested their crops

3: to protest the decision; started the motor; chose a topic; a game of golf; their bond of friendship

4: covered with moss; to burst through the door; enjoys surprises; at the last moment; stayed at the lodge

Sentences

1. Let's watch (2) ________ on TV.
2. The tree trunk is (4) ________.
3. Try not (1) ________ in the water.
4. The race-car driver (3) ________.
5. The tired child (2) ________ at night.
6. Let's play (3) ________.
7. The police dog (1) ________.
8. This is the box that we (2) ________.
9. Good friends don't break (3) ________.
10. The skiers (4) ________ to avoid the cold.
11. Dial the operator (2) ________.
12. We waited for Superman (4) ________.
13. Is that number (1) ________?
14. We want (3) ________ made by the judge.
15. I heard about your plans to go (4) ________.
16. I wish summer would last (1) ________.
17. She (3) ________ to write about.
18. The farmers (2) ________.
19. I was (1) ________ about my grade.
20. He (4) ________ on his birthday.

15

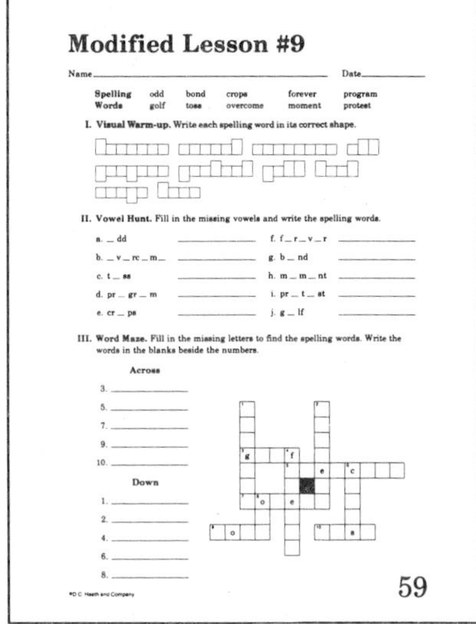

**Modified Lesson #9**

Name ________ Date ________

Spelling Words: odd, golf, bond, toss, crops, overcome, forever, moment, program, protest

I. Visual Warm-up. Write each spelling word in its correct shape.

II. Vowel Hunt. Fill in the missing vowels and write the spelling words.

a. _dd
b. _v_rc_m_
c. t_ss
d. pr_gr_m
e. cr_ps
f. f_r_v_r
g. b_nd
h. m_m_nt
i. pr_t_st
j. g_lf

III. Word Maze. Fill in the missing letters to find the spelling words. Write the words in the blanks beside the numbers.

Across: 3. 5. 7. 9. 10.

Down: 1. 2. 4. 6. 8.

59

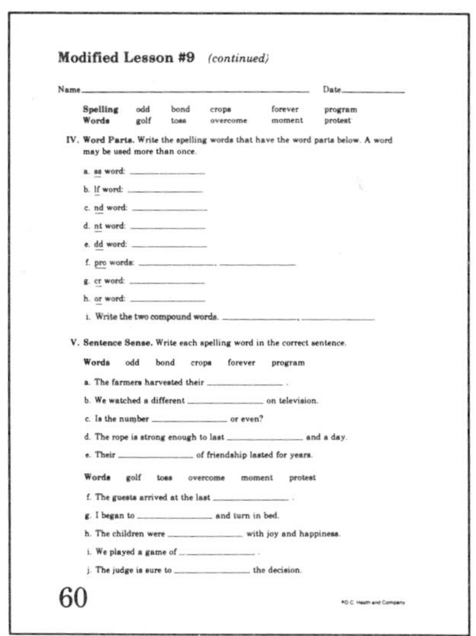

**Modified Lesson #9** *(continued)*

Name ________ Date ________

Spelling Words: odd, golf, bond, toss, crops, overcome, forever, moment, program, protest

IV. Word Parts. Write the spelling words that have the word parts below. A word may be used more than once.

a. ss word: ________
b. lf word: ________
c. nd word: ________
d. nt word: ________
e. dd word: ________
f. pro words: ________
g. cr word: ________
h. or word: ________
i. Write the two compound words. ________

V. Sentence Sense. Write each spelling word in the correct sentence.

Words: odd, bond, crops, forever, program

a. The farmers harvested their ________.
b. We watched a different ________ on television.
c. Is the number ________ or even?
d. The rope is strong enough to last ________ and a day.
e. Their ________ of friendship lasted for years.

Words: golf, toss, overcome, moment, protest

f. The guests arrived at the last ________.
g. I began to ________ and turn in bed.
h. The children were ________ with joy and happiness.
i. We played a game of ________.
j. The judge is sure to ________ the decision.

60

### Home Activity

A weekly homework assignment

### Modified Lesson

An alternative lesson for limited spellers

*(The Answer Key can be found in the Teacher's Resource Book.)*

LESSON

9

CONTINUED

## Challenge Exercise #9

Name________________ Date________

**Word Watch.** The sport of golf has been around for at least a thousand years. The origin of the word *golf* is uncertain. Some say the word derives from the Dutch word *kolf*, the name for a wooden club used in early hockeylike games. The word traveled across the North Sea to Scotland, where it became the name for the Scottish game that consisted of hitting small balls with clubs into a series of holes in the ground. In 1457 the Scottish government passed a law forbidding the game because government officials worried that practice in archery was being neglected. For the Scots, accuracy in archery, not golf, was essential to winning wars. However, golf prevailed, no matter how much the government tried to eliminate it.

**Word Analogies.** Decide on the relationship that exists between the first pair of words. Using the Other Word Forms on page 36, find a word that completes the second pair of words and establishes the same relationship.

1. *hiker* is to *trail* as ________ is to *highway*
2. *hair* is to *combed* as *salad* is to ________
3. *taught* is to *instructed* as ________ is to *astonished*
4. *bat* is to *shortstop* as *club* is to ________
5. *quickly* is to *rapidly* as ________ is to *strangely*

**Challenge Words Student Activity**

Use the challenge words below to complete the statements.

**oppose** **operators** **solar** **wonderfully** **sections**

1. The telephone company needs to hire new ________.
2. I like to divide an orange into ________.
3. If you don't like their plan, then you ________ it.
4. If something is nicely made, you can say it is ________ done.
5. Electricity from the sun's energy is called ________ power.

**Working With Words: Student Writing Activity**

Use as many Other Word Forms as you can from page 36 to write four road signs you might see while driving on the highway. (Example: Bear Right for Food and *Lodging*)

122



## Challenge Exercise

Additional activities for advanced spellers

### Spelling Words

| | | | | |
|---|---|---|---|---|
| burst | burglar | further | surprises | overturn |
| overcome | forever | motor | moment | program |
| protest | odd | golf | bond | moss |
| toss | lodge | topic | crops | stuff |

**F. Words and Meanings** Write a spelling word for each meaning. Check your answers in the **Spelling Dictionary**. You may wish to look up the meanings of *burst* and *toss*.

1. a length of time that never ends forever
2. something that ties or unites bond
3. a very brief space of time moment
4. made helpless overcome
5. at a greater amount further
6. a subject topic
7. to show objection to protest
8. to do suddenly or by force burst
9. not even odd
10. a person who steals burglar
11. an engine motor
12. to turn upside down overturn
13. things not expected surprises
14. green plants that form on trees moss
15. an outdoor game played with clubs and a ball golf
16. plants grown for food crops
17. a plan of what will be done program
18. a countrylike house lodge
19. to pack too fully stuff
20. to move about with force toss



## CONTROLLED DICTATION (Optional)

These dictation sentences provide maintenance for spelling words previously taught and practice for words currently being studied. Dictation should be administered on Day 4. The teacher or another student may dictate the sentences. Be sure to dictate all marks of punctuation. Challenge Word sentences are preceded by an asterisk.

1. Many **odd surprises** delayed us as we gathered the **crops**.
2. They formed a **bond** to be friends **forever**.
3. The **burglar** was **overcome** at the **golf** club.
4. The beams of the **lodge** were covered with **moss**.
5. He may **protest** our pick of a **topic** for the radio **program**.
6. At that **moment**, the **motor** did **overturn** and **burst**.
7. **Toss** fresh grapes into the dressing before you **stuff** the chicken **further**.

*8. The **solar** rays helped the flowers bloom **wonderfully**.
*9. Do the **operators** work alone or in **sections**?
*10. Do you **oppose** the idea?

**G. Using Other Word Forms** Write the Other Word Form that completes each sentence.

Base Words: motor(ist) burglar(y) lodge(er) program(er) golf(er)

1. A person who plays golf is a golfer.
2. A person who stays at an inn is a lodger.
3. A person who steals commits burglary.
4. A person who drives a car is a motorist.
5. A person who writes programs for a computer is a programmer.

**H. Challenge Words** Write the Challenge Word that completes each phrase.

| solar | operators | sections | oppose | wonderfully |
|---|---|---|---|---|

1. either marvelously or wonderfully
2. either lunar or solar
3. either segments or sections
4. either drivers or operators
5. either to disagree or to oppose

**I. Spelling and Writing** Write each set of words in a sentence. You may use Other Word Forms. Proofread your work.

1. crops – odd – topic
2. motor – overturn – burst
3. surprises – further – moment
4. golf – program – forever
5. protest – bond – overcome
6. lodge – stuff – moss
7. burglar – toss – overturned
8. sections – oppose – protester
9. solar – operators – wonderfully

## USING OTHER WORD FORMS

Vocabulary is expanded through the use of other forms of basic spelling words. Emphasis is on the relationship of syntax to suffix choices. The following generalization applies to the Other Word Forms used in Exercise G.

### Spelling Rule

Adding suffixes to words ending in silent **e**

> When adding a suffix that begins with a vowel to words that end with silent **e**, drop the final **e**.
> **(lodge, lodger)**

## POSTTEST AND PROOFREADING

Follow the same testing procedures used in the Pretest, although you may wish to correct the tests yourself. Have students write any misspelled words on the Words to Learn Sheet and record spelling success on the Progress Chart.

## THE SPELLING-WRITING LINK

**Purpose** This activity helps students effectively transfer lesson words into their daily writing. Students (a) determine a relationship among three given words and (b) write a complete sentence.

**Procedure** On the chalkboard, write the three words from line 1 (**crops, odd, topic**) and the Other Word Forms (**cropped, oddly, oddest, topics**). Have students read the words and think of ways the three words might be related. Have them think of things or people the words suggest. Ask students to create sentences using some of their ideas. You can provide an example sentence: **We thought a discussion about crops was an odd topic for the drama club.**

**Practice** Tell students to write original sentences using the word sets and to proofread their work. You may want them to circle the lesson words.

LESSON

# 10

## OBJECTIVES

- to spell 20 high-frequency words with the /ō/ and /ou/
- to proofread these words in daily writing
- to become familiar with 30 other forms of the spelling words

| Summary of Skills | Exercises |
|---|---|
| Auditory Discrimination | A |
| Proofreading | A, C, I |
| Visual Discrimination | C |
| Dictionary Skills | D |
| Word Analysis | E |
| Vocabulary Development | F, H |
| Context Usage | G |
| Original Writing | I |

## PRETEST AND PROOFREADING

The Pretest identifies the words students are able to spell, as well as the words they need to learn. You may wish to use Other Word Forms when giving the Pretest. Five suggested Other Word Forms are underlined on this page.

To administer the Pretest:

**READ** each word aloud.
**SAY** the phrase containing the word.
**REPEAT** the word.

Have students correct the Pretest using the Corrected-test Procedure. They may record their scores on a personal Progress Chart (see the Teacher's Resource Book) and study misspelled words using the **S-H-A-R-P** procedure.

## OTHER WORD FORMS

This section presents related forms of the spelling words to strengthen spelling power and vocabulary knowledge.

### Enrichment Activity

Have students write Other Word Forms under the appropriate vowel sound.

**long o** **/ou/ sound** **/our/ sound**

**A. Pretest and Proofreading**

**B. Spelling Words and Phrases**

| | |
|---|---|
| **1. soak** | to soak for ten minutes |
| **2. loan*** | a loan from the bank |
| **3. loafing** | no time for loafing |
| **4. unload** | to unload the truck |
| **5. foul** | to hit another foul |
| **6. trout** | stocked with trout |
| **7. crouch** | to crouch low for the ball |
| **8. blouse*** | tucked in the blouse |
| **9. county*** | into the next county |
| **10. mountain*** | a mountain trail |
| **11. pronounce** | hard to pronounce |
| **12. howl*** | a howl of pain |
| **13. scowl** | an angry scowl |
| **14. growl** | a frightening growl |
| **15. coward*** | scared the coward |
| **16. crowded*** | across the crowded room |
| **17. powder*** | crushed into powder |
| **18. however*** | however they tried |
| **19. downstairs*** | dashed downstairs |
| **20. sour** | sour milk |

*Other Word Forms*

| | |
|---|---|
| soaked | mountainous |
| loaned | pronounces, pronounced, pronouncing |
| loaf, loafs, loafed, loafer | howled, howling |
| unloaded, unloading | scowls, scowled |
| fouled, fouling | growled |
| trouts | cowards |
| crouches, crouched | crowd |
| blouses | powdered, powdering |
| counties | soured, sourest |

**C. Visual Warm-up** Write each word in its correct shape.

a. loan
b. pronounce
c. sour
d. however
e. powder
f. coward
g. trout
h. foul
i. crouch
j. growl
k. loafing
l. unload
m. soak
n. downstairs
o. scowl
p. crowded
q. mountain
r. county
s. blouse
t. howl



*Modified Lesson words are asterisked.
The Modified Lesson is found in the Teacher's Resource Book.

## MEETING INDIVIDUAL NEEDS / ASSIGNMENT GUIDE

| 5-Day Plan | 3-Day Plan | Limited Spellers | Average Spellers | Advanced Spellers |
|---|---|---|---|---|
| 1 | 1 | • Pretest<br>• Progress Chart | • Pretest<br>• Progress Chart<br>• Home Activity | • Pretest<br>• Progress Chart<br>• Home Activity |
| 2 | | • Modified Lesson Visual Warm-up Ending Sounds | • Regular Lesson Visual Warm-up | • Regular Lesson Visual Warm-up |
| 3 and 4 | 2 | • Modified Lesson Vowel Puzzle Word Match Finish the Sentence | Spelling Activities | Spelling Activities<br>• Challenge Exercise |
| 5 | 3 | • Posttest<br>• Words to Learn Sheet<br>• Progress Chart | • Posttest<br>• Words to Learn Sheet<br>• Progress Chart | • Posttest<br>• Words to Learn Sheet<br>• Progress Chart |

**D. Finding Words** The words in the spelling list appear in the beginning (A-H), middle (I-Q), or end (R-Z) of the **Spelling Dictionary**. Write each word.

| Beginning A-H | Middle I-Q | End R-Z |
|---|---|---|
| 1. foul | 11. loan | 16. soak |
| 2. crouch | 12. loafing | 17. unload |
| 3. blouse | 13. mountain | 18. trout |
| 4. county | 14. pronounce | 19. scowl |
| 5. howl | 15. powder | 20. sour |
| 6. growl | | |
| 7. coward | | |
| 8. crowded | | |
| 9. however | | |
| 10. downstairs | | |

**E. Oh, the Pain!** Find the missing letters and soothe the hurt. Write the words.

1. h o w ever — however
2. m o u ntain — mountain
3. gr o w l — growl
4. f o u l — foul
5. p o w der — powder
6. c o u nty — county
7. c o w ard — coward
8. s o a k — soak
9. tr o u t — trout
10. sc o w l — scowl
11. l o a fing — loafing
12. bl o u se — blouse
13. cr o u ch — crouch
14. unl o a d — unload
15. h o w l — howl
16. d o w nstairs — downstairs
17. l o a n — loan
18. cr o w ded — crowded
19. pron o u nce — pronounce
20. s o u r — sour

## OPTIONAL TEACHING PLAN

Write the three Word Group headings on the chalkboard. Ask the students to name the four spelling words with the long **o** sound. Help them identify the other Word Groups. Note that the /ou/ sound is spelled with **ou** in words such as **foul** and with **ow** in words such as **howl**.

| Word Groups | | |
|---|---|---|
| /ō/: **oa** words | soak<br>loafing<br>**moat** | loan<br>unload |
| /ou/: **ou** words | foul<br>crouch<br>county<br>pronounce<br>sour | trout<br>blouse<br>mountain<br>**pounced**<br>**proudly** |
| /ou/: **ow** words | howl<br>growl<br>crowded<br>however<br>**vowel**<br>**prowling** | scowl<br>coward<br>powder<br>down-stairs |

*Challenge Words are boldfaced.*

**Optional Activity Masters**

Those using the Hardcover Pupil Edition may wish to use the Optional Activity Masters in the Teacher's Resource Book for Exercises C, E, and F.

### Home Activity #10

Name________________ Date________

Use the spelling words to complete each pair of sentences. The spelling words appear scrambled below the blanks. The number before each blank tells you in what column you can find the correct word. Use each word only once.

| 1 | 2 | 3 | 4 |
|---|---|---|---|
| crouch | crowded | trout | pronounce |
| scowl | growl | howl | soak |
| foul | however | blouse | mountain |
| powder | downstairs | county | loan |
| coward | sour | loafing | unload |

1. The child had an angry look on his face when he drank the (2) ________ (srou) milk. He gave his father an angry (1) ________ (oscwl).
2. The big man jumped when the little dog gave a frightening (2) ________ (ogrwl). The dog's barking scared the (1) ________ (cawrdo).
3. The children found the word *spaghetti* hard to (4) ________ (ouprnneco). They couldn't say it; (2) ________ (wvrheoe) they tried.
4. First, the pill must be crushed into (1) ________ (prdoew). Then you must set it to (4) ________ (koas) for ten minutes in a glass of water.
5. The girl was in a hurry when she dashed (2) ________ (datraoiwns). At the bottom, she ran across the (2) ________ (dewdocr) room.
6. The bear hurt its paw while fishing in a stream stocked with (3) ________ (ttrou). The bear let out a (3) ________ (wloh) of pain.
7. There is no time for (3) ________ (nglfaoi). We need to (4) ________ (doanlu) the truck now.
8. The woman tucked in the (3) ________ (obleus) she was wearing. She wanted to look neat when she applied for a (4) ________ (naol) from the bank.
9. The batter tried not to hit another (1) ________ (louf). When he hit to second base, the fielder had to (1) ________ (chuocr) low for the ball.
10. The campers became lost on a (4) ________ (mntauoni) trail. They had hiked into the next (3) ________ (yntuoc) by the time they were found.

16 ©D.C. Heath and Company

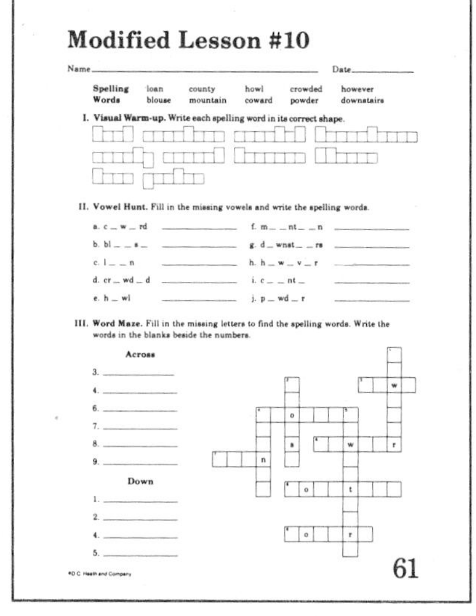

### Modified Lesson #10

Name________________ Date________

| Spelling Words | loan | county | howl | crowded | however |
|---|---|---|---|---|---|
| | blouse | mountain | coward | powder | downstairs |

I. **Visual Warm-up.** Write each spelling word in its correct shape.

II. **Vowel Hunt.** Fill in the missing vowels and write the spelling words.

a. c _ w _ rd ________ f. m _ _ nt _ _ n ________
b. bl _ _ s _ ________ g. d _ wnst _ _ rs ________
c. l _ _ n ________ h. h _ w _ v _ r ________
d. cr _ wd _ d ________ i. c _ _ nt _ ________
e. h _ wl ________ j. p _ wd _ r ________

III. **Word Maze.** Fill in the missing letters to find the spelling words. Write the words in the blanks beside the numbers.

Across
3. ________
4. ________
6. ________
7. ________
8. ________
9. ________

Down
1. ________
2. ________
4. ________
5. ________

©D.C. Heath and Company 61

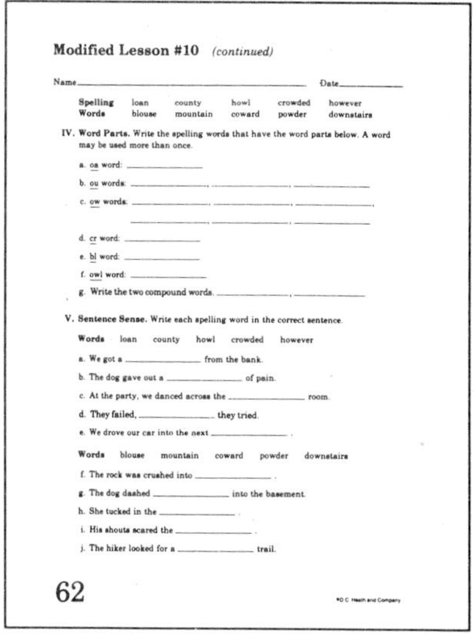

### Modified Lesson #10 *(continued)*

Name________________ Date________

| Spelling Words | loan | county | howl | crowded | however |
|---|---|---|---|---|---|
| | blouse | mountain | coward | powder | downstairs |

IV. **Word Parts.** Write the spelling words that have the word parts below. A word may be used more than once.

a. oa word: ________
b. ou words: ________, ________, ________
c. ow words: ________, ________, ________, ________, ________, ________
d. cr word: ________
e. bl word: ________
f. owl word: ________
g. Write the two compound words. ________, ________

V. **Sentence Sense.** Write each spelling word in the correct sentence.

**Words** loan county howl crowded however

a. We got a ________ from the bank.
b. The dog gave out a ________ of pain.
c. At the party, we danced across the ________ room.
d. They failed, ________ they tried.
e. We drove our car into the next ________.

**Words** blouse mountain coward powder downstairs

f. The rock was crushed into ________.
g. The dog dashed ________ into the basement.
h. She tucked in the ________.
i. His shouts scared the ________.
j. The hiker looked for a ________ trail.

62 ©D.C. Heath and Company

**Home Activity**
A weekly homework assignment

**Modified Lesson**
An alternative lesson for limited spellers

*(The Answer Key can be found in the Teacher's Resource Book.)*

LESSON

# 10

CONTINUED

### Challenge Exercise #10

Name________________ Date________

**Word Watch.** The word *coward* comes from the name of a rabbit. It seems that the rabbit in the old French fables of *Reynard the Fox* was called Coart, a name derived from the word *coue*, meaning "tail." Coart was a cowardly rabbit who was known to "turn tail," or to run away from a good fight. In France the word eventually became *couard*, only to be changed to *coward* when it traveled to England.

**Word Analogies.** Decide on the relationship that exists between the first pair of words. Using the Other Word Forms on page 40, find a word that completes the second pair of words and establishes the same relationship.

1. *trousers* is to *shirts* as *skirts* is to ________
2. *cackling* is to *hens* as ________ is to *wolves*
3. *birds* is to *swallows* as *fishes* is to ________
4. *one* is to *many* as *person* is to ________
5. *losers* is to *winners* as ________ is to *heroes*

**Challenge Words Student Activity**

Use the challenge words below to complete the statements.

**pounced moat proudly prowling vowel**

1. A deep ________ surrounded the castle.
2. The cat ________ on the scurrying mouse.
3. A wolf was ________ through the forest.
4. My brother announced ________ that he had won the race.
5. The word *related* has three different ________ sounds.

**Working With Words: Student Writing Activity**

Use as many Other Word Forms as you can from page 40 to write advertisements that might appear in the window of a sporting goods store. (Example: Protect your feet in *mountainous* country: use *powdered* foot pads.)



123

## Challenge Exercise

Additional activities for advanced spellers

**Spelling Words**

| | | | |
|---|---|---|---|
| soak | loan | loafing | unload |
| foul | trout | crouch | blouse |
| county | mountain | pronounce | howl |
| scowl | growl | coward | crowded |
| powder | however | downstairs | sour |

**F. Name the Book** Solve the puzzles. Write each spelling word. Then join the boxed letters and write the two-word title of a classic children's book.

1. a brook fish — [t] r o u t
2. snarl — g [r] o w l
3. dustlike material — p o w d [e] r
4. remove a cargo — u n l o [a] d
5. not upstairs — d o w n [s] t a i r s
6. not a fair ball — f o [u] l
7. speak sounds — p [r] o n o u n c e
8. a woman's shirt — b l o u s [e]
9. idling — l o a f [i] n g
10. place in water — [s] o a k
11. money borrowed — [l] o a n
12. a steep hill — m o u n t [a] i n
13. not a state — c o u [n] t y
14. not a hero — c o w a r [d]
15. What is the name of the book?

Treasure Island

## CONTROLLED DICTATION (Optional)

These dictation sentences provide maintenance for spelling words previously taught and practice for words currently being studied. Dictation should be administered on Day 4. The teacher or another student may dictate the sentences. Be sure to dictate all marks of punctuation. Challenge Word sentences are preceded by an asterisk.

1. **Downstairs** in a **crowded** room at the lodge, I found the workers **loafing**.
2. The milk we drank at the **county** fair was **sour**.
3. When **powder** spills or the ball rolls **foul**, the clowns **howl**.
4. **However**, you must **unload** the **trout**.
5. The **coward** did **crouch** down when he heard the **mountain** lion **growl**.
6. Don't **scowl** when I **pronounce** the words.
7. If I **loan** you the silk **blouse**, do not **soak** it in water.

*8. Near the **moat** a **prowling** cat **pounced** upon its dinner.

*9. The tiny child **proudly** pronounced each **vowel** clearly.

**G. Using Other Word Forms** Write the Other Word Form that completes each sentence.

Base Words: growl(ed) crouch(ed) coward(s) soak(ed) howl(ing)

1. The black cat crouched behind the tree.
2. In the distance, a hungry wolf was howling at the moon.
3. The beating rain soaked our clothes.
4. The angry dog growled as we passed by.
5. Do you understand why we felt like cowards on that spooky night?

**H. Challenge Words** Write the Challenge Word that completes each analogy.

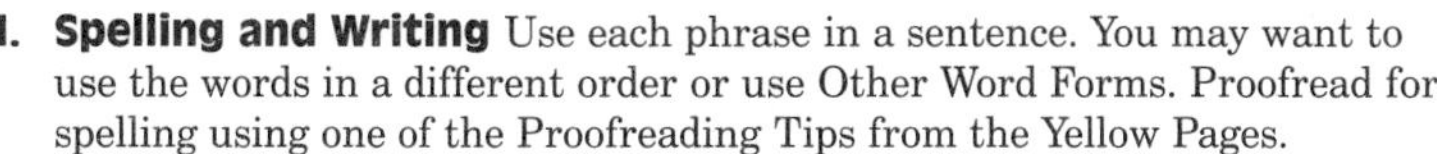

| vowel | pounced | proudly | prowling | moat |
|---|---|---|---|---|

1. **house** is to **fence** as **castle** is to moat
2. **sadly** is to **happily** as **meekly** is to proudly
3. **b** is to **a** as **consonant** is to vowel
4. **escaped** is to **fled** as **leaped** is to pounced
5. **horse** is to **galloping** as **tiger** is to prowling

**I. Spelling and Writing** Use each phrase in a sentence. You may want to use the words in a different order or use Other Word Forms. Proofread for spelling using one of the Proofreading Tips from the Yellow Pages.

1. soak the beans
2. loan him money
3. is loafing around
4. unload the weapon
5. foul weather
6. caught several trout
7. crouch down
8. a silk blouse
9. the county jail
10. the mountain lion
11. pronounce the words
12. the dog's howl
13. scowl and growl at us
14. a sour look
15. is not a coward
16. crowded the downstairs room
17. bath powder
18. however you travel



## THE SPELLING-WRITING LINK

**Purpose** This activity helps students transfer lesson words into their daily writing. Students write complete sentences using the listed phrases.

**Procedure** On the chalkboard write the phrase from line one: **will soak the beans.** Have the students read the phrase and note how it could be used in a sentence. Have them think about things or people the phrase suggests. You can provide a sample sentence: **My father will soak the beans overnight.**

**Practice** Tell the students to write original sentences using the phrases. Remind them they can use Other Word Forms or change the phrases around if it will improve the sentences.

## USING OTHER WORD FORMS

Vocabulary is expanded through the use of other forms of basic spelling words. Emphasis is on the relationship of syntax to suffix choices. The following generalization applies to the Other Word Forms used in Exercise G.

### Spelling Rule

Forming plurals

Add **s** to most nouns to form plurals.
(**coward, cowards**)

## POSTTEST AND PROOFREADING

Follow the same testing procedures used in the Pretest, although you may wish to correct the tests yourself. Have students write any misspelled words on the Words to Learn Sheet and record spelling success on the Progress Chart.

# LESSON 11

## OBJECTIVES

- to spell 20 high-frequency words with the /ĕ/ and /ûr/
- to proofread these words in daily writing
- to become familiar with 33 other forms of the spelling words

| Summary of Skills | Exercises |
|---|---|
| Auditory Discrimination | A |
| Proofreading | A, C, H |
| Visual Discrimination | C |
| Vocabulary Development | D, E, G |
| Context Usage | F |
| Original Writing | H |

## PRETEST AND PROOFREADING

The Pretest identifies the words students are able to spell, as well as the words they need to learn. You may wish to use Other Word Forms when giving the Pretest. Five suggested Other Word Forms are underlined on this page.

To administer the Pretest:

**READ** each word aloud.
**SAY** the phrase containing the word.
**REPEAT** the word.

Have students correct the Pretest using the Corrected-test Procedure. They may record their scores on a personal Progress Chart (see the Teacher's Resource Book) and study misspelled words using the **S-H-A-R-P** procedure.

## OTHER WORD FORMS

This section presents related forms of the spelling words to strengthen spelling power and vocabulary knowledge.

### Enrichment Activity

Have students write Other Word Forms under the appropriate ending.

-ing -ed -s -al -able -ity

# 11

**A. Pretest and Proofreading**

**B. Spelling Words and Phrases**

1. **sentence** — the verb in the sentence
2. **depend*** — to depend on others
3. **invent*** — to invent the wheel
4. **intend*** — intend to travel
5. **intent** — to know their intent
6. **empty** — the empty house
7. **helmet** — a motorcycle helmet
8. **herd*** — a herd of elephants
9. **person*** — a friendly person
10. **clerk** — the store clerk
11. **perhaps*** — will do it later perhaps
12. **merchant** — supplied by a merchant
13. **perfume** — the smell of perfume
14. **weren't** — if you weren't certain
15. **American** — the American flag
16. **desert*** — a trip across the desert
17. **member*** — greeted the new member
18. **temper*** — in control of my temper
19. **general** — the general idea
20. **entered*** — entered the room

*Other Word Forms*

sentenced, sentencing
depended, dependable, dependent
invented, inventor
intended, intention, intentional
emptied, emptying
helmets
herded, herding
personal, personally, personality, personable
clerking, clerical
merchandise
perfumed
America
deserted, deserting, deserter
membership
tempered
generally, generality
enter, entering

**C. Visual Warm-up** Write each word in its correct shape.

a. intend
b. intent
c. general
d. desert
e. American
f. herd
g. clerk
h. person
i. entered
j. empty
k. perfume
l. weren't
m. sentence
n. depend
o. invent
p. merchant
q. perhaps
r. temper
s. helmet
t. member



*Modified Lesson words are asterisked.
The Modified Lesson is found in the Teacher's Resource Book.

## MEETING INDIVIDUAL NEEDS / ASSIGNMENT GUIDE

| 5-Day Plan | 3-Day Plan | Limited Spellers | Average Spellers | Advanced Spellers |
|---|---|---|---|---|
| 1 | 1 | • Pretest<br>• Progress Chart | • Pretest<br>• Progress Chart<br>• Home Activity | • Pretest<br>• Progress Chart<br>• Home Activity |
| 2 | | • Modified Lesson Visual Warm-up Ending Sounds | • Regular Lesson Visual Warm-up | • Regular Lesson Visual Warm-up |
| 3 and 4 | 2 | • Modified Lesson Vowel Puzzle Word Match Finish the Sentence | Spelling Activities | Spelling Activities<br>• Challenge Exercise |
| 5 | 3 | • Posttest<br>• Words to Learn Sheet<br>• Progress Chart | • Posttest<br>• Words to Learn Sheet<br>• Progress Chart | • Posttest<br>• Words to Learn Sheet<br>• Progress Chart |

**D. Crossword Puzzle** Solve the puzzle by using all the words from the spelling list. Write each word. Check your answers in the **Spelling Dictionary**.

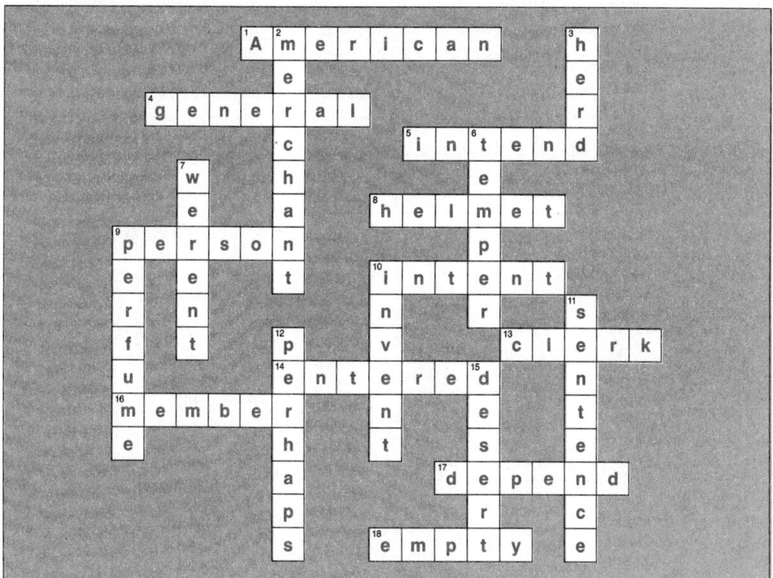

**Across**

1. a citizen of the U.S.
4. an army officer
5. to plan or to mean
8. a protective hat
9. a human being
10. purpose
13. a salesperson
14. came in
16. one of a group
17. to rely
18. not full

**Down**

2. one who sells
3. a group of cows
6. one's mood
7. were not (contraction)
9. a sweet-smelling liquid
10. to create something new
11. has a subject and predicate
12. maybe
15. a dry region



## OPTIONAL TEACHING PLAN

Write the three Word Group headings on the chalkboard. Ask the students to name the seven spelling words with the short **e** sound that don't have **er** in them. (One word, **American**, has the short **e** sound even though **r** follows **e**.) Continue identifying the other Word Groups. Note that five words have the short **e** sound followed by the **er** letter combination. The **er** has the /ə/ sound in each of these words.

| Word Groups | | |
|---|---|---|
| /ĕ/ words | sentence<br>invent<br>intent<br>helmet<br>American<br>depend | intend<br>empty<br>**rescue**<br>**revenge**<br>**restless** |
| /ûr/ words | herd<br>clerk<br>merchant<br>weren't | person<br>perhaps<br>perfume<br>**verses** |
| /ĕ/ and /ər/ words | desert<br>temper<br>entered | member<br>general<br>**reference** |

*Challenge Words are boldfaced.*

## Optional Activity Masters

Those using the Hardcover Pupil Edition may wish to use the Optional Activity Masters in the Teacher's Resource Book for Exercises C and D.

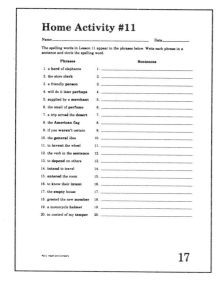

Home Activity #11 — 17

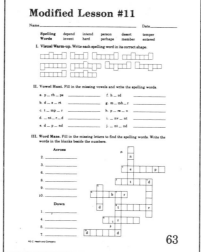

Modified Lesson #11 — 63

Modified Lesson #11 (continued) — 64

## Home Activity

A weekly homework assignment

## Modified Lesson

An alternative lesson for limited spellers

*(The Answer Key can be found in the Teacher's Resource Book.)*

LESSON

# 11

CONTINUED

## Challenge Exercise #11

Name____________________ Date__________

**Word Watch.** Oddly enough, the words *perfume* and *fumigate* share the same origin. At one time, the word *perfume*, meaning "to fill the air with smoke," was a synonym for *fumigate*. During the time of the Pilgrims, one perfumed the house, filling the inside air with smoke to fumigate and kill unwanted insects. In time, the meaning of the word *perfume* softened to mean "the release of pleasant odors into the air." The word *fumigate* remained to represent the idea of extermination by filling the air with a smoky substance.

**Word Analogies.** Decide on the relationship that exists between the first pair of words. Using the Other Word Forms on page 44, find a word that completes the second pair of words and establishes the same relationship.

1. *shoes* is to *boots* as *hats* is to __________
2. *leave* is to *come* as *exit* is to __________
3. *Columbus* is to *explorer* as *Edison* is to __________
4. *exiled* is to *king* as __________ is to *criminal*
5. *swarming* is to *queen bee* as __________ is to *shepherd*

**Challenge Words Student Activity**

Use the challenge words below to complete the titles for the following horror stories.

**revenge** **rescue** **verses** **reference** **restless**

1. Horror Tales for a __________ Night
2. Poems and __________ for Fun and Fright
3. Wanted: Monster Hunter—No __________ Required.
4. The Daring __________ From the Forbidden Planet
5. __________ of the Cosmic Creature

**Working With Words: Student Writing Activity**

Use as many Other Word Forms as you can from page 44 to write a speech that will persuade your classmates to vote for your friend who is running for class president.

124



## Challenge Exercise

Additional activities for advanced spellers

**Spelling Words**

| | | | | |
|---|---|---|---|---|
| sentence | depend | invent | intend | intent |
| empty | helmet | herd | clerk | person |
| perhaps | merchant | perfume | weren't | American |
| desert | member | temper | general | entered |

**E. Compare and Contrast** Write a spelling word for each phrase below.

1. not a phrase, but a sentence
2. not an outsider, but a member
3. not entered, but exited
4. not specific, but general
5. not a desert, but a swamp
6. not a helmet, but a hat
7. not copy, but invent
8. not full, but empty
9. not a buyer, but a clerk *or* merchant
10. not a flock, but a herd
11. not American, but English
12. not were, but weren't
13. not a manager, but a clerk *or* merchant
14. not an animal, but a person
15. not perhaps, but definitely
16. not an intent, but a purpose
17. not a skunk smell, but perfume
18. not intend, but do not plan to
19. not to distrust, but to depend on
20. not calm and peaceful, but with a temper



## CONTROLLED DICTATION (Optional)

These dictation sentences provide maintenance for spelling words previously taught and practice for words currently being studied. Dictation should be administered on Day 4. The teacher or another student may dictate the sentences. Be sure to dictate all marks of punctuation. Challenge Word sentences are preceded by an asterisk.

1. Did the **American merchant** buy the **herd** of cattle?
2. **Perhaps** the **clerk** will fill the **empty perfume** jars.
3. Only a foolish **person** would **intend** to cross the hot **desert**.
4. The troops **weren't** delayed by the **general** or any other **member** of the ar
5. When I **entered** the room, my **intent** was to hold my **temper**.
6. I'll **invent** a **helmet** that fits better.
7. May I **depend** on you to write the **sentence**?

*8. The soldiers were **restless** and wanted to begin the **rescue** mission.
*9. They sought **revenge** for the attack on the village.
*10. She made a **reference** to these **verses** in her report.

**F. Using Other Word Forms** Write the Other Word Form that completes each sentence.

Base Words: personal(ly) general(ly) invent(or) enter(ing) intention(al)

1. My neighbor, the inventor, created a new type of bicycle.
2. Greg personally chose the present for his mother.
3. Upon entering the room, the students were asked to be quiet.
4. Bob forgot to set his alarm clock. His oversleeping was not intentional.
5. Although not always true, students generally like the school lunches.

**G. Challenge Words** Write the Challenge Word that fits each group of words.

| reference | rescue | restless | revenge | verses |
|---|---|---|---|---|

1. nervous, unsettled, restless
2. poems, stanzas, verses
3. get back at, get even, revenge
4. example, quotation, reference
5. save, set free, rescue

**H. Spelling and Writing** Write two or more answers to each question. Use as many Spelling Words, Other Word Forms, and Challenge Words as you can. A few words are suggested. Proofread for spelling using one of the Proofreading Tips from the Yellow Pages.

1. Who will discover the broken glass?
   perfume members American person general revenge
2. How did the scientist invent the new safety helmet?
   intent inventing helmet depend emptied rescue
3. Where do they sell the new computer game?
   merchant clerk perhaps intended weren't reference



## USING OTHER WORD FORMS

Vocabulary is expanded through the use of other forms of basic spelling words. Emphasis is on the relationship of syntax to suffix choices.

## POSTTEST AND PROOFREADING

Follow the same testing procedures used in the Pretest, although you may wish to correct the tests yourself. Have students write any misspelled words on the Words to Learn Sheet and record spelling success on the Progress Chart.

## THE SPELLING-WRITING LINK

**Purpose** This activity helps students retain the correct spelling of words and transfer the words to their daily writing. Students use lesson words to answer questions.

**Procedure** Read the first question and write the suggested words on the chalkboard: **perfume, members, American, person, general, revenge.** Have students list some Other Word Forms of the lesson words. Brainstorm with the class possible answers to question 1. Remind students to look at all the lesson words for ideas. Write the answers on the chalkboard, noting any lesson words.

**Practice** Tell students to finish the activity by writing two or more answers to each question. Remind them to proofread their work for spelling.

# LESSON 12 REVIEW

## OBJECTIVES

- to review the spelling of the 100 words studied in Lessons 7-11
- to promote the use of other forms of the 100 spelling words
- to apply high-utility generalizations for the addition of suffixes

| Summary of Skills | Exercises |
|---|---|
| Visual Discrimination | A, B |
| Proofreading | A, B |
| Word Analysis | C |
| Context Usage | D |

## REVIEW OF LESSONS 7-11

The goal of the review exercises is to expand each student's spelling power. The one hundred spelling words studied in the five preceding lessons are presented in challenging formats where the focus is shifted from the spelling words to the Other Word Forms.

## WORD REVIEW PROCEDURE

Students are encouraged to use this abbreviated version of the **S-H-A-R-P** procedure when reviewing the spelling words at the top of each review page.

**LOOK** at each word.
**SAY** the word to yourself.
**THINK** about the letters that spell the word.

# 12 REVIEW

### REVIEWING LESSONS 7-11

| | | | | |
|---|---|---|---|---|
| bait | depend | helmet | moment | replied |
| bond | desert | however | mountain | scowl |
| chief | freedom | invent | odd | strain |
| county | freeze | member | powder | topic |
| delayed | fright | merchant | pronounce | trout |

**A. Break the Code** Use the code to write spelling words or Other Word Forms. Write each word.

| a | b | c | d | e | f | g | h | i | j | k | l | m | n | o | p | q | r | s | t | u | v | w | x | y | z |
|---|---|---|---|---|---|---|---|---|---|---|---|---|---|---|---|---|---|---|---|---|---|---|---|---|---|
| ↓ | ↓ | ↓ | ↓ | ↓ | ↓ | ↓ | ↓ | ↓ | ↓ | ↓ | ↓ | ↓ | ↓ | ↓ | ↓ | ↓ | ↓ | ↓ | ↓ | ↓ | ↓ | ↓ | ↓ | ↓ | ↓ |
| g | d | j | r | u | e | y | w | k | a | c | p | s | h | b | n | l | m | f | o | t | x | z | v | q | i |

1. tbbqg — oddly
2. sdtwfp — frozen
3. otpbm — bonds
4. utlzkm — topics
5. knzfsm — chiefs
6. dflqzfm — replies
7. rtrfpum — moments
8. sdffqg — freely
9. ojzuzpa — baiting
10. bfmfdum — deserts
11. nfqrfum — helmets
12. udteu — trout
13. nthfxfd — however
14. bflfpbzpa — depending
15. zpxfputd — inventor
16. sdzanufpfb — frightened
17. ktepuzfm — counties
18. mudjzpfd — strainer
19. bfqjgzpa — delaying
20. lthbfdfb — powdered
21. mkthqzpa — scowling
22. ldtpepkzjuztp — pronunciation
23. rfrofdmnzl — membership
24. rtepujzptem — mountainous
25. rfdknjpum — merchants



## MEETING INDIVIDUAL NEEDS / ASSIGNMENT GUIDE

| 5-Day Plan | 3-Day Plan | Limited Spellers | Average Spellers | Advanced Spellers |
|---|---|---|---|---|
| 1 and 2 | 1 | • Modified Lesson Visual Warm-up Word Parts | • Regular Lesson Spelling Activities • Home Activity | • Regular Lesson Spelling Activities • Home Activity |
| 3 and 4 | 2 | • Modified Lesson Vowel Puzzle Word Match Finish the Sentence | • Regular Lesson Spelling Activities • Proofreading Exercise(s) | • Regular Lesson Spelling Activities • Proofreading Exercise(s) • Challenge Word Review |
| 5 | 3 | • Test Modified Lesson Words • Words to Learn Sheet | Review Test or Standardized-format Test Words to Learn Sheet | • Review Test or Standardized-format Test • Words to Learn Sheet |

| American | downstairs | ironing | perfume | spray |
|---|---|---|---|---|
| blouse | empty | loafing | perhaps | straight |
| burglar | excite | needle | protest | surprises |
| coward | forever | overcome | sailor | temper |
| deed | golf | payment | sentence | weren't |

**B. Word Search** Twenty-one Other Word Forms and four spelling words can be found in the word puzzle. The words appear across and down. Circle and write the words. Capitalize the other form of *American*. Use the **Spelling Dictionary**.

**Across**

1. overcame
2. golfer
3. perhaps
4. tempers
5. loafer
6. payments
7. deeds
8. burglars
9. exciting
10. sentencing
11. blouses
12. straighten
13. forever

| | | | | | | | | | | | | | | |
|---|---|---|---|---|---|---|---|---|---|---|---|---|---|---|
| i | o | v | e | r | c | a | m | e | d | e | w | s | d | a |
| r | o | e | s | g | o | l | f | e | r | n | e | u | o | m |
| o | t | i | p | e | r | h | a | p | s | t | r | r | w | e |
| n | x | t | e | m | p | e | r | s | p | p | e | p | n | r |
| s | y | z | r | w | s | l | n | s | r | s | n | r | s | i |
| l | o | a | f | e | r | t | t | a | a | n | t | i | t | c |
| f | o | m | u | o | s | h | o | i | y | e | c | s | a | a |
| p | a | y | m | e | n | t | s | l | i | e | o | e | i | l |
| r | d | d | e | e | d | s | w | o | n | d | w | d | r | m |
| o | n | d | s | l | e | b | u | r | g | l | a | r | s | e |
| t | c | m | o | r | i | u | a | s | f | e | r | m | i | m |
| e | x | c | i | t | i | n | g | o | r | s | d | r | u | p |
| s | e | n | t | e | n | c | i | n | g | g | l | o | u | t |
| t | o | b | l | o | u | s | e | s | t | o | y | e | r | i |
| e | n | r | e | s | t | r | a | i | g | h | t | e | n | e |
| d | f | o | r | e | v | e | r | p | r | o | t | h | s | s |

REVIEW

**Down**

14. irons
15. protested
16. perfumes
17. sailors
18. spraying
19. needles
20. weren't
21. cowardly
22. surprised
23. downstairs
24. America
25. empties



## CREATIVE WRITING

**(An optional writing activity)**

**Recipe for Writing:** This imaginative writing activity uses spelling words and Other Word Forms studied in Lessons 7-11.

COMBINE:
1 mossy, mountain lodge
1 frightened clerk
1 surprised burglar
9 cowards crouched downstairs
1 excited general in a helmet
4 swaying sailors

SEASON with your own original ideas and COOK UP a story with a unique FLAVOR. Proofread before SERVING.

The RECIPE words appear in the following lessons.

| Lesson | Words |
|---|---|
| 7 | sailors, swaying |
| 8 | excited, frightened |
| 9 | surprised, burglar, lodge, mossy |
| 10 | cowards, mountain, crouched, downstairs |
| 11 | clerk, general, helmet |

REVIEW

## Optional Activity Masters

Those using the Hardcover Pupil Edition may wish to use the Optional Activity Masters in the Teacher's Resource Book for Exercises A and B.

**Home Activity #12**

Name ______ Date ______

Review the words in Lessons 7-11.

| Lesson 7 | Lesson 8 | Lesson 9 |
|---|---|---|
| aim | deed | burst |
| bait | needle | burglar |
| gain | creek | further |
| braid | sleeve | surprises |
| brain | freeze | overturn |
| strain | freedom | overcome |
| remain | bleeding | forever |
| faint | Halloween | motor |
| waist | piece | moment |
| sailor | chief | program |
| daily | view | protest |
| praise | ironing | odd |
| straight | rifle | golf |
| fairly | climate | bond |
| away | excite | moss |
| spray | exciting | toss |
| stray | replied | lodge |
| payment | flight | topic |
| mayor | fright | crops |
| delayed | all right | stuff |

| Lesson 10 | Lesson 11 |
|---|---|
| soak | sentence |
| loan | depend |
| loafing | invent |
| unload | intend |
| foul | intent |
| trout | empty |
| crouch | helmet |
| blouse | herd |
| county | person |
| mountain | clerk |
| pronounce | perhaps |
| howl | merchant |
| scowl | perfume |
| growl | weren't |
| coward | American |
| crowded | desert |
| powder | member |
| however | temper |
| downstairs | general |
| sour | entered |

18 ©D.C. Heath and Company

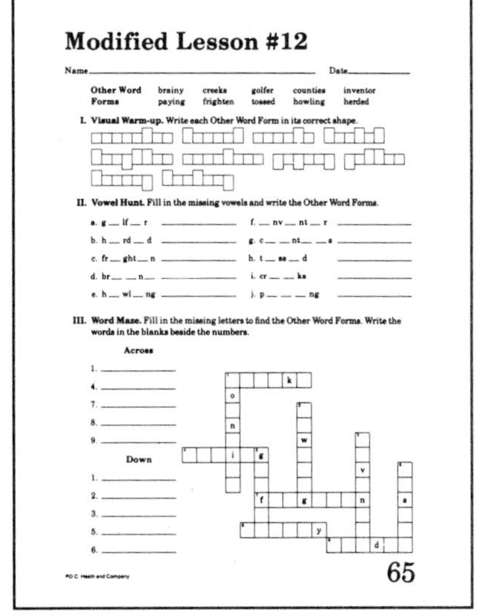

**Modified Lesson #12**

Name ______ Date ______

| Other Word Forms | brainy | creeks | golfer | counties | inventor |
|---|---|---|---|---|---|
| | paying | frighten | tossed | howling | herded |

I. **Visual Warm-up.** Write each Other Word Form in its correct shape.

II. **Vowel Hunt.** Fill in the missing vowels and write the Other Word Forms.

a. g __ lf __ r ______ f. __ nv __ nt __ r ______
b. h __ rd __ d ______ g. c __ __ nt __ __ s ______
c. fr __ ght __ n ______ h. t __ ss __ d ______
d. br __ __ n __ ______ i. cr __ __ ks ______
e. h __ wl __ ng ______ j. p __ __ __ ng ______

III. **Word Maze.** Fill in the missing letters to find the Other Word Forms. Write the words in the blanks beside the numbers.

Across: 1. ______ 4. ______ 7. ______ 8. ______ 9. ______

Down: 1. ______ 2. ______ 3. ______ 5. ______ 6. ______

©D.C. Heath and Company 65

**Modified Lesson #12** *(continued)*

Name ______ Date ______

| Other Word Forms | brainy | creeks | golfer | counties | inventor |
|---|---|---|---|---|---|
| | paying | frighten | tossed | howling | herded |

IV. **Word Parts.** Write the Other Word Forms that have the word parts below. A word may be used more than once.

a. fr word: ______
b. br word: ______
c. cr word: ______
d. ing words: ______, ______
e. er words: ______, ______
f. or word: ______
g. ed words: ______, ______
h. word ending in y: ______
i. ight word: ______
j. words ending in s: ______, ______
k. lf word: ______

V. **Sentence Sense.** Write each Other Word Form in the correct sentence.

Words brainy creeks golfer counties inventor

a. The water rose high in several ______ during the storm.
b. Thomas Edison was a famous ______.
c. Our state is divided into ______.
d. Smart people are ______.
e. The ______ searched for the lost ball.

Words paying frighten tossed howling herded

f. The farmer ______ the cows into the barn.
g. Who is ______ the bill?
h. A ______ wind awakened me.
i. I ______ and turned in bed all night.
j. Scary stories will ______ the campers.

66 ©D.C. Heath and Company

**Home Activity**

A weekly homework assignment

**Modified Lesson**

An alternative lesson for limited spellers

*(The Answer Key can be found in the Teacher's Resource Book.)*

**LESSON**

# 12

**CONTINUED**

## Challenge Word Review

The Challenge Words from the previous five lessons are listed below if you wish to review the Challenge Words with your more advanced students.

1. stairway
2. faithful
3. population
4. laser
5. welfare
6. breezes
7. gleefully
8. limestone
9. bleachers
10. violin
11. solar
12. operators
13. sections
14. oppose
15. wonderfully
16. vowel
17. pounced
18. proudly
19. prowling
20. moat
21. reference
22. rescue
23. restless
24. revenge
25. verses

| faint | praise | remain | aim | gain |
|---|---|---|---|---|
| sleeve | piece | flight | rifle | mayor |
| further | overturn | motor | program | moss |
| foul | loan | unload | all right | crouch |
| Halloween | intent | intend | general | entered |

**REVIEW**

**C. Word Building** Add word parts to each spelling word or its base word to make Other Word Forms. Write the words.

| | ***s* or *es*** | ***ed*** | ***ing*** |
|---|---|---|---|
| **1.** faint | *faints* | *fainted* | *fainting* |
| **2.** sleeve | sleeves | | |
| **3.** further | furthers | furthered | furthering |
| **4.** foul | fouls | fouled | fouling |
| **5.** praise | praises | praised | praising |
| **6.** piece | pieces | pieced | piecing |
| **7.** overturn | overturns | overturned | overturning |
| **8.** loan | loans | loaned | loaning |
| **9.** intent | intents | | |
| **10.** remain | remains | remained | remaining |
| **11.** flight | flights | | |
| **12.** motor | motors | motored | motoring |
| **13.** unload | unloads | unloaded | unloading |
| **14.** intend | intends | intended | intending |
| **15.** aim | aims | aimed | aiming |
| **16.** rifle | rifles | | |
| **17.** program | programs | programmed | programming |
| **18.** general | generals | | |
| **19.** gain | gains | gained | gaining |
| **20.** mayor | mayors | | |
| **21.** moss | mosses | | |
| **22.** crouch | crouches | crouched | crouching |
| **23.** entered | enters | | entering |

**24.** Write the two remaining spelling words that have no Other Word Forms.

**a.** Halloween **b.** all right

**50** Review—Lesson 12

### Proofreading Exercise Lesson #12

Name ______________________ Date __________

**Proofreading the Spelling of Others**

A movie critic wrote a review of a new movie. She made some spelling errors. Circle the misspelled words. Write the correct words on the lines.

**Movie Review**

Haloween Horror is not a great movie. It does, howevor, contain one or two eksiting momments and serprises. For this reason, purhaps, the movie may be worthy of some small praize. But not much. The plot is much too emptey and deepends heavily on frite. The story centrs on an Amarican genarel who is lost in the dessert. A hurd of strey camels berst on the screen and provide two hours of horror for the hero. What good action ther is is delayd until it's too late to save the movie. Frankly, I found it a strane to remaine in my seat until the end of the programe.

1. ________ 6. ________ 11. ________ 16. ________
2. ________ 7. ________ 12. ________ 17. ________
3. ________ 8. ________ 13. ________ 18. ________
4. ________ 9. ________ 14. ________ 19. ________
5. ________ 10. ________ 15. ________ 20. ________

146



**Proofreading Exercise**

| ■ | ★ | ▲ | ◆ | ● |
|---|---|---|---|---|
| braid | brain | sway | fairly | stray |
| waist | climate | exciting | view | bleeding |
| burst | lodge | crops | stuff | toss |
| growl | howl | soak | sour | crowded |
| clerk | herd | person | daily | creek |

**D. Not So Tall Tales** Write Other Word Forms or the spelling words to complete the sentences. The shape tells you in what column you can find the spelling word. Write each word or its Other Word Form only once. If you need help, use the **Spelling Dictionary**.

The Howling Clerks

At a supermarket in a cold ★ **(1.)** ___climate___, two grocery ■ **(2.)** ___clerks___ often ★ **(3.)** ___howled___ loudly when the ● **(4.)** ___crowd___ entered. Each day was exciting for these two ▲ **(5.)** ___persons___. Somehow it seemed that their ★ **(6.)** ___brains___ were ■ **(7.)** ___bursting___ with mischief. How their ● **(8.)** ___blood___ boiled! Some days they were seen ▲ **(9.)** ___swaying___ back and forth and ■ **(10.)** ___growling___ at the ★ **(11.)** ___herds___ of people who shopped. Most shoppers lived in ski ★ **(12.)** ___lodges___ near the ● **(13.)** ___creek___ that ran by the store. They put up with the madness ◆ **(14.)** ___daily___ because the clerks' work was always well done. With aprons around their ■ **(15.)** ___waists___, the clerks ● **(16.)** ___tossed___ the salad for the deli, ▲ **(17.)** ___soaked___ the dirt from the ▲ **(18.)** ___crop___ of lettuce, ◆ **(19.)** ___stuffed___ the turkeys for cooking, ■ **(20.)** ___braided___ the bread dough into designs, and sliced the ◆ **(21.)** ___sour___ pickles into fancy shapes. They were always ▲ **(22.)** ___excited___ about their work and seldom ● **(23.)** ___strayed___ from the work area. The manager ◆ **(24.)** ___viewed___ them ◆ **(25.)** ___fairly___, but he kept them out of sight as much as possible.

REVIEW



## REVIEW TEST

REVIEW

Twenty-five words, selected randomly from the five spelling lists, constitute the test and are listed with the appropriate phrases. Follow the same testing procedure used to administer the weekly Pretest and Posttest. Have students write any misspelled words on the Words to Learn Sheet. As an alternative testing option, you may wish to use the Standardized-format Test for this Review Lesson, found in the Teacher's Resource Book.

### Test Words and Phrases

| | |
|---|---|
| 1. braid | a ribbon on each **braid** |
| 2. faint | will **faint** in the heat |
| 3. praise | **praise** for good work |
| 4. spray | a **spray** of water |
| 5. delayed | **delayed** the plane |
| 6. deed | good **deed** |
| 7. freeze | began to **freeze** |
| 8. piece | a **piece** of paper |
| 9. rifle | held the **rifle** |
| 10. replied | **replied** without delay |
| 11. surprises | enjoys **surprises** |
| 12. motor | started the **motor** |
| 13. odd | **odd** or even |
| 14. toss | began to **toss** and turn |
| 15. stuff | will **stuff** with newspaper |
| 16. soak | to **soak** for ten minutes |
| 17. foul | to hit another **foul** |
| 18. county | into the next **county** |
| 19. scowl | an angry **scowl** |
| 20. powder | crushed into **powder** |
| 21. intend | **intend** to travel |
| 22. herd | a **herd** of elephants |
| 23. merchant | supplied by a **merchant** |
| 24. desert | a trip across the **desert** |
| 25. entered | **entered** the room |

**Review Test: Lesson 12**

Name________________ Date__________

**Directions:** Read each sentence. Select the word with the correct spelling to complete each sentence. Fill in the correct letter in the answer column.

1. Put a ribbon on each ____. A. brade C. braid B. braed D. braide
2. They will ____ in the heat. A. fante C. fant B. faynt D. faint
3. I get ____ for good work. A. praize C. praise B. prase D. praze
4. I felt a ____ of water. A. spray C. sparay B. sprai D. sprae
5. The storm ____ the plane. A. delayd C. delaied B. delayed D. delade
6. The child did a good ____. A. dede C. deade B. dead D. deed
7. The water began to ____. A. freze C. freaze B. freeze D. freez
8. I need a ____ of paper. A. peice C. pease B. piece D. pece
9. One person held the ____. A. riffle C. rifel B. rifle D. riffel
10. She ____ without delay. A. replied C. replide B. replyed D. replid
11. My brother enjoys ____. A. serprizes C. surprizes B. serprises D. surprises
12. The driver started the ____. A. moter C. mottor B. motor D. moater
13. Is the number ____ or even? A. od C. odde B. aud D. odd
14. I began to ____ and turn. A. toss C. tause B. taus D. tos
15. This is what I will ____ with newspaper. A. stufe C. stuf B. stuffe D. stuff
16. It needs to ____ for ten minutes. A. sok C. soke B. soak D. soake
17. You don't need to hit another ____. A. faul C. foul B. fowle D. foule
18. We drove into the next ____. A. countey C. conty B. cownty D. county
19. The man had an angry ____. A. scoul C. scowl B. skoul D. skowl
20. The rock was crushed into ____. A. powder C. powdar B. pouder D. poudar
21. We ____ to travel. A. intened C. intind B. intend D. intand
22. We saw a ____ of elephants. A. heard C. hurd B. hird D. herd
23. The food was supplied by a ____. A. merchent C. merchant B. mirchant D. murchant
24. We took a trip across the ____. A. dezert C. desert B. dessert D. dezzert
25. Who ____ the room? A. entered C. entirred B. intered D. enterred

Answer Column

1. A B C D
2. A B C D
3. A B C D
4. A B C D
5. A B C D
6. A B C D
7. A B C D
8. A B C D
9. A B C D
10. A B C D
11. A B C D
12. A B C D
13. A B C D
14. A B C D
15. A B C D
16. A B C D
17. A B C D
18. A B C D
19. A B C D
20. A B C D
21. A B C D
22. A B C D
23. A B C D
24. A B C D
25. A B C D



155

**Standardized-format Test**

# LESSON 13

## OBJECTIVES

- to spell 20 high-frequency words with the /ĭ/
- to proofread these words in daily writing
- to become familiar with 42 other forms of the spelling words

| Summary of Skills | Exercises |
|---|---|
| Auditory Discrimination | A |
| Proofreading | A, C, H |
| Visual Discrimination | C |
| Vocabulary Development | D, G |
| Dictionary Skills | E |
| Word Analysis | F |
| Original Writing | H |

## PRETEST AND PROOFREADING

The Pretest identifies the words students are able to spell, as well as the words they need to learn. You may wish to use Other Word Forms when giving the Pretest. Five suggested Other Word Forms are underlined on this page.

To administer the Pretest:

**READ** each word aloud.
**SAY** the phrase containing the word.
**REPEAT** the word.

Have students correct the Pretest using the Corrected-test Procedure. They may record their scores on a personal Progress Chart (see the Teacher's Resource Book) and study misspelled words using the **S-H-A-R-P** procedure.

## OTHER WORD FORMS

This section presents related forms of the spelling words to strengthen spelling power and vocabulary knowledge.

### Enrichment Activity

Have students write variations of the same sentence using each of the Other Word Forms for a spelling word.

The boy will **skim** the rock across the water.

**skimmed, skimming, skimmer**



# 13

**A. Pretest and Proofreading**

**B. Spelling Words and Phrases**

| | |
|---|---|
| **1. risk*** | to take a risk |
| **2. limb*** | a sawed-off tree limb |
| **3. limp** | walked with a limp |
| **4. skim** | to skim these pages |
| **5. split*** | did a split |
| **6. strip*** | a short strip of tape |
| **7. slipped** | slipped and fell |
| **8. swimming** | swimming to the raft |
| **9. beginning** | beginning to rain |
| **10. skinned** | skinned your elbow |
| **11. wicked*** | the wicked witch |
| **12. quickly*** | moved away quickly |
| **13. wrist** | twisted my wrist |
| **14. ditch** | to dig a ditch |
| **15. kitchen*** | opened the kitchen window |
| **16. pitcher** | the baseball pitcher |
| **17. fifth*** | a fifth of the class |
| **18. fifteenth** | the fifteenth of the month |
| **19. printing*** | writing rather than printing |
| **20. prince*** | turned into a prince |

*Other Word Forms*

risky, risked
limbs, limber
limps, limped
skimmed, skimming, skimmer
splitting
stripped, stripping
slip, slips, slipping, slipper
swim, swam, swum, swimmer
begin, begins, began, begun
skin, skinning
wickedly
quick, quicker, quickest
wrists
ditches, ditched
kitchens
pitchers
five
fifteen
print, printed, printer
princes, princely

**C. Visual Warm-up** Write each word in its correct shape.

a. kitchen
b. quickly
c. wrist
d. limb
e. split
f. strip
g. skinned
h. printing
i. fifth
j. wicked
k. ditch
l. risk
m. limp
n. swimming
o. skim
p. beginning
q. slipped
r. pitcher
s. prince
t. fifteenth



*Modified Lesson words are asterisked.
The Modified Lesson is found in the Teacher's Resource Book.

## MEETING INDIVIDUAL NEEDS / ASSIGNMENT GUIDE

| 5-Day Plan | 3-Day Plan | Limited Spellers | Average Spellers | Advanced Spellers |
|---|---|---|---|---|
| 1 | 1 | • Pretest<br>• Progress Chart | • Pretest<br>• Progress Chart<br>• Home Activity | • Pretest<br>• Progress Chart<br>• Home Activity |
| 2 | | • Modified Lesson Visual Warm-up Ending Sounds | • Regular Lesson Visual Warm-up | • Regular Lesson Visual Warm-up |
| 3 and 4 | 2 | • Modified Lesson Vowel Puzzle Word Match Finish the Sentence | Spelling Activities | Spelling Activities<br>• Challenge Exercise |
| 5 | 3 | • Posttest<br>• Words to Learn Sheet<br>• Progress Chart | • Posttest<br>• Words to Learn Sheet<br>• Progress Chart | • Posttest<br>• Words to Learn Sheet<br>• Progress Chart |

### D. Word Changes

Add *ed* to each of the following words. Write the new word and circle it if you had to double the final consonant.

**1.** risk risked
**2.** skim (skimmed)
**3.** ditch ditched
**4.** slip (slipped)
**5.** skin (skinned)
**6.** limp limped
**7.** strip (stripped)

Write the plural forms of the words.

**8.** limb limbs
**9.** wrist wrists
**10.** prince princes
**11.** ditch ditches
**12.** pitcher pitchers
**13.** kitchen kitchens
**14.** Do the plurals that end in *es* gain a syllable? yes

Circle the words below that have double consonants. Then write the base word for each word. Use the **Spelling Dictionary**.

**15.** (slipped) slip
**16.** wickedly wicked
**17.** (skinned) skin
**18.** fifteenth fifteen
**19.** (beginning) begin
**20.** quickly quick
**21.** fifth five
**22.** (splitting) split
**23.** printing print
**24.** (swimming) swim

## OPTIONAL TEACHING PLAN

Write the four Word Group headings on the chalkboard. Ask the students to name the nine spelling words with the short **i** sound. Write the words on the chalkboard as the students say them. Proceed in the same manner for identifying the other Word Groups. Note that five words have the sound **ar** spells in **chart**. The word **reward**, however, has the sound **or** spells in **sort**.

| Word Groups | | |
|---|---|---|
| /i/ words | risk | strip |
| | limp | swimming |
| | split | wicked |
| | slipped | wrist |
| | beginning | kitchen |
| | skinned | fifth |
| | quickly | printing |
| | ditch | **ridges** |
| | pitcher | **lizard** |
| | fifteenth | **whistle** |
| | prince | **vision** |
| | limb | **innumerable** |
| | skim | |

*Challenge Words are boldfaced.*

### Optional Activity Masters

Those using the Hardcover Pupil Edition may wish to use the Optional Activity Masters in the Teacher's Resource Book for Exercise C.

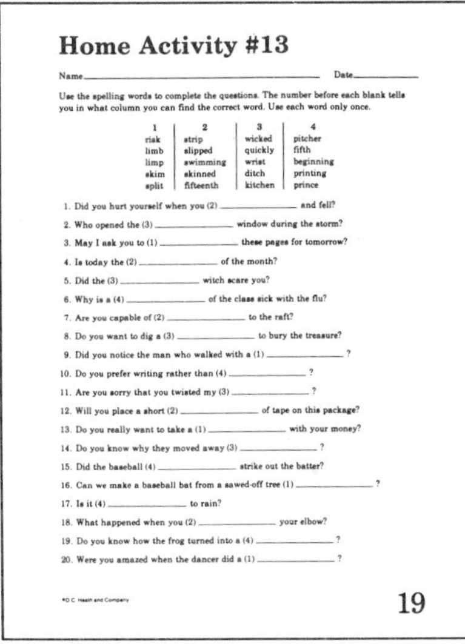

**Home Activity #13**

Name________ Date________

Use the spelling words to complete the questions. The number before each blank tells you in what column you can find the correct word. Use each word only once.

| 1 | 2 | 3 | 4 |
|---|---|---|---|
| risk | strip | wicked | pitcher |
| limb | slipped | quickly | fifth |
| limp | swimming | wrist | beginning |
| skim | skinned | ditch | printing |
| split | fifteenth | kitchen | prince |

1. Did you hurt yourself when you (2) ________ and fell?
2. Who opened the (3) ________ window during the storm?
3. May I ask you to (1) ________ these pages for tomorrow?
4. Is today the (2) ________ of the month?
5. Did the (3) ________ witch scare you?
6. Why is a (4) ________ of the class sick with the flu?
7. Are you capable of (2) ________ to the raft?
8. Do you want to dig a (3) ________ to bury the treasure?
9. Did you notice the man who walked with a (1) ________ ?
10. Do you prefer writing rather than (4) ________ ?
11. Are you sorry that you twisted my (3) ________ ?
12. Will you place a short (2) ________ of tape on this package?
13. Do you really want to take a (1) ________ with your money?
14. Do you know why they moved away (3) ________ ?
15. Did the baseball (4) ________ strike out the batter?
16. Can we make a baseball bat from a sawed-off tree (1) ________ ?
17. Is it (4) ________ to rain?
18. What happened when you (2) ________ your elbow?
19. Do you know how the frog turned into a (4) ________ ?
20. Were you amazed when the dancer did a (1) ________ ?



19

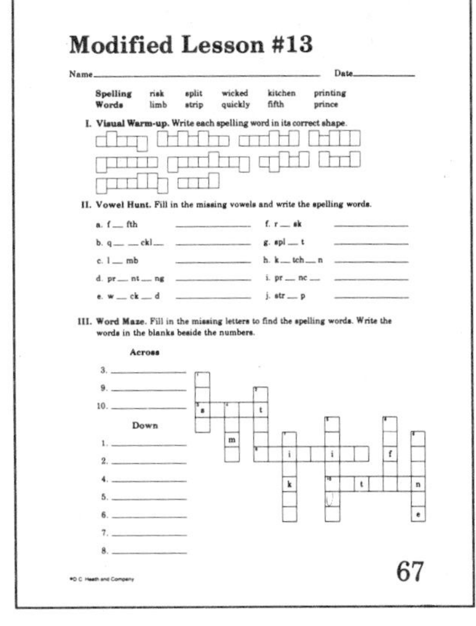

**Modified Lesson #13**

Name________ Date________

**Spelling Words** risk limb split strip wicked quickly kitchen fifth printing prince

**I. Visual Warm-up.** Write each spelling word in its correct shape.

**II. Vowel Hunt.** Fill in the missing vowels and write the spelling words.

a. f__fth ________
b. q__ __ckl__ ________
c. l__mb ________
d. pr__nt__ng ________
e. w__ck__d ________
f. r__sk ________
g. spl__t ________
h. k__tch__n ________
i. pr__nc__ ________
j. str__p ________

**III. Word Maze.** Fill in the missing letters to find the spelling words. Write the words in the blanks beside the numbers.

**Across**
3. ________
9. ________
10. ________

**Down**
1. ________
2. ________
4. ________
5. ________
6. ________
7. ________
8. ________



67

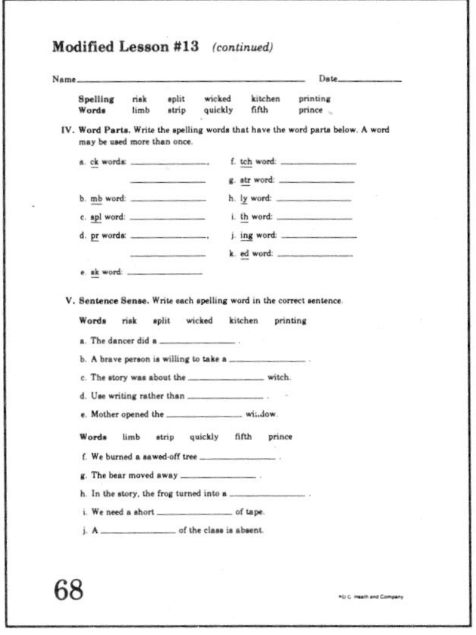

**Modified Lesson #13** *(continued)*

Name________ Date________

**Spelling Words** risk limb split strip wicked quickly kitchen fifth printing prince

**IV. Word Parts.** Write the spelling words that have the word parts below. A word may be used more than once.

a. ck words: ________, ________
b. mb word: ________
c. spl word: ________
d. pr words: ________, ________
e. sk word: ________
f. tch word: ________
g. str word: ________
h. ly word: ________
i. th word: ________
j. ing word: ________
k. ed word: ________

**V. Sentence Sense.** Write each spelling word in the correct sentence.

**Words** risk split wicked kitchen printing

a. The dancer did a ________ .
b. A brave person is willing to take a ________ .
c. The story was about the ________ witch.
d. Use writing rather than ________ .
e. Mother opened the ________ window.

**Words** limb strip quickly fifth prince

f. We burned a sawed-off tree ________ .
g. The bear moved away ________ .
h. In the story, the frog turned into a ________ .
i. We need a short ________ of tape.
j. A ________ of the class is absent.

68



### Home Activity

A weekly homework assignment

### Modified Lesson

An alternative lesson for limited spellers

*(The Answer Key can be found in the Teacher's Resource Book.)*

# LESSON 13 CONTINUED

### Challenge Exercise #13

Name________________________ Date__________

**Word Watch.** The word *kitchen* traces back to the Latin word *coquere*, meaning "to cook." The Romans called the room where food was prepared the *coquina*, meaning "the cooking place." The word was adopted by the English as *cycene*, eventually being changed to *kitchene*. The spelling of *kitchen* has remained unchanged for only 300 years; however, the meaning of the word has remained unchanged for over 2,000 years.

**Word Analogies.** Decide on the relationship that exists between the first pair of words. Using the Other Word Forms on page 52, find a word that completes the second pair of words and establishes the same relationship.

1. *runner* is to *track* as ____________ is to *pool*
2. *mother* is to *sons* as *queen* is to ____________
3. *ankles* is to *legs* as ____________ is to *arms*
4. *tortoise* is to *slower* as *hare* is to ____________
5. *sleeping* is to *bedrooms* as *cooking* is to ____________

**Challenge Words Student Activity**
Use the challenge words below to complete the science fiction story.

**lizards vision innumerable ridges whistle**

I was nearly blinded by the blow, but soon my ____________ cleared. I saw ____________ creatures crawling across the rocky ____________ before me. Suddenly one stood on its hind legs and gave a warning ____________. At once, the whole troop of ____________ raced toward me.

**Working With Words: Student Writing Activity**
Use as many Other Word Forms as you can from page 52 to write an invitation to your birthday party. Include information using these question words as a guide: *who, what, when, where,* and *why.*

 125

## Challenge Exercise
Additional activities for advanced spellers

**Spelling Words**

| | | | | |
|---|---|---|---|---|
| risk | limb | limp | skim | split |
| strip | slipped | swimming | skinned | beginning |
| wicked | quickly | wrist | ditch | kitchen |
| pitcher | fifth | fifteenth | printing | prince |

**E. Scrambled Words**

Unscramble each word to find a word from the spelling list. Write the word.

1. ngiimmsw **swimming**
2. tispl **split**
3. pistr **strip**
4. pidslpe **slipped**
5. nggeiinbn **beginning**
6. retchpi **pitcher**
7. tchid **ditch**
8. niskend **skinned**
9. misk **skim**
10. inktche **kitchen**

Unscramble the scrambled word to find the spelling word that completes the sentence. Write the word.

11. The injured man walked with a **limp** (mpli).
12. Chris is in **fifth** (thiff) grade.
13. **Wicked** (deckwi) actions should be avoided.
14. The **prince** (inprec) is heir to the throne.
15. The watch is on your **wrist** (stiwr).
16. Move **quickly** (lckyqui) to avoid injury.
17. Daredevils **risk** (skir) their lives.
18. Marta celebrated her **fifteenth** (theneffit) birthday.
19. The tree **limb** (mbli) cracked during the storm.
20. Gutenberg invented the **printing** (ntprngii) press.

54 Lesson 13

## CONTROLLED DICTATION (Optional)

These dictation sentences provide maintenance for spelling words previously taught and practice for words currently being studied. Dictation should be administered on Day 4. The teacher or another student may dictate the sentences. Be sure to dictate all marks of punctuation. Challenge Word sentences are preceded by an asterisk.

1. The **fifth pitcher** of the season was **quickly** chosen.
2. Our finest book is in its **fifteenth printing**.
3. The **prince** is **swimming** in the lake at his own **risk**.
4. My **wrist** is **beginning** to feel all right, but I still walk with a **limp**.
5. Perhaps I **skinned** my fingers when I **split** the **strip** of wood.
6. In the story, the **wicked** man **slipped** from the **limb** and fell into the **ditch**.
7. After you **skim** the pages, place the book on the **kitchen** table.

*8. She had a strange **vision** of **innumerable lizards**.
*9. The **ridges** on the **whistle** change the sound.

**F. Using Other Word Forms** Write the Other Word Form of each base word that rhymes with each word pair.

Base Words: print(ed) skim(ed) split(ing) swim(um) ditch(es)

1. sprinted, minted, printed
2. stitches, witches, ditches
3. dimmed, slimmed, skimmed
4. spitting, fitting, splitting
5. hum, glum, swum

**G. Challenge Words** Write the Challenge Word that replaces each underlined word or phrase.

| innumerable | ridges | lizards | vision | whistle |
|---|---|---|---|---|

1. We climbed both mountain ledges. ridges
2. Those animals are reptiles. lizards
3. My range of sight was limited by fog. vision
4. You have countless opportunities. innumerable
5. Put your lips together and make a sound. whistle

**H. Spelling and Writing** Write two or more questions about each statement. Use as many Spelling Words, Other Word Forms, and Challenge Words as you can. A few words are suggested. Proofread for spelling using one of the Proofreading Tips from the Yellow Pages.

1. It is a good idea to examine a location before you play there.
   risky limb ditches fifth split strip quickly vision

   Example: Does the strip of land have any ditches or other risky areas?

2. An afternoon at the pool should be free of accidents.
   limp slipped swimming wrist
   skimming skinned fifteenth whistle

3. A fanciful tale often starts with "once upon a time."
   printing beginning wicked kitchen pitchers prince lizards



## USING OTHER WORD FORMS

Vocabulary is expanded through the use of other forms of basic spelling words. Emphasis is on the relationship of syntax to suffix choices. The following generalizations apply to the Other Word Forms used in Exercise F.

### Spelling Rule

Forming plurals

To form plurals of nouns ending with **s**, **ss**, **sh**, **ch**, or **x**, add **es**. (**ditch**, **ditches**)

Doubling the final consonant when adding suffixes

When adding a suffix that begins with a vowel to one-syllable words that end with one vowel and one consonant, double the final consonant. (**skim**, **skimmed**)

## POSTTEST AND PROOFREADING

Follow the same testing procedures used in the Pretest, although you may wish to correct the tests yourself. Have students write any misspelled words on the Words to Learn Sheet and record spelling success on the Progress Chart.

## THE SPELLING-WRITING LINK

**Purpose** This activity helps students to retain the correct spelling of words and transfer the words to their daily writing. Students use lesson words to create questions, which promotes inquiry and research skills.

**Procedure** Read the first statement and write the suggested words on the chalkboard: **risky, limb, ditches, fifth, split, strip, quickly, vision.** Brainstorm with the class possible questions about statement 1. Remind students to look at all the lesson words for ideas, not just the suggested words. Write the questions on the chalkboard, noting any lesson words.

**Practice** Tell students to finish the activity by writing two or more questions about each statement. Remind them to proofread their work for spelling.

# LESSON 14

## OBJECTIVES

- to spell 20 high-frequency words, including vowel-**r** words and words with the /ŏ/, /o͞o/, and /ŭ/
- to proofread these words in daily writing
- to become familiar with 37 other forms of the spelling words

| Summary of Skills | Exercises |
|---|---|
| Auditory Discrimination | A |
| Proofreading | A, C, D, J |
| Visual Discrimination | C, D |
| Vocabulary Development | E, G |
| Word Analysis | F |
| Dictionary Skills | G |
| Context Usage | H, I |
| Original Writing | J |

## PRETEST AND PROOFREADING

The Pretest identifies the words students are able to spell, as well as the words they need to learn. You may wish to use Other Word Forms when giving the Pretest. Five suggested Other Word Forms are underlined on this page.

To administer the Pretest:

**READ** each word aloud.
**SAY** the phrase containing the word.
**REPEAT** the word.

Have students correct the Pretest using the Corrected-test Procedure. They may record their scores on a personal Progress Chart (see the Teacher's Resource Book) and study misspelled words using the **S-H-A-R-P** procedure.

## OTHER WORD FORMS

This section presents related forms of the spelling words to strengthen spelling power and vocabulary knowledge.

### Enrichment Activity

Have students write opposite words or phrases next to these Other Word Forms.

**towards, offering, dropping, copier**

# 14

**A. Pretest and Proofreading**

**B. Spelling Words and Phrases**

| | |
|---|---|
| **1. model** | building a model plane |
| **2. bodies** | large bodies of water |
| **3. copies** | made two copies |
| **4. problem** | solved the problem |
| **5. offer*** | an offer to help |
| **6. copper*** | gold and copper |
| **7. dropped** | dropped the dish |
| **8. shopping*** | the plastic shopping bag |
| **9. dollar*** | cost one dollar |
| **10. collar** | turned-up collar |
| **11. bottom*** | the top and the bottom |
| **12. blossom** | a blossom on the tree |
| **13. cloth*** | a cotton cloth |
| **14. toward*** | walked toward the shore |
| **15. quart*** | a quart of milk |
| **16. quarter** | a quarter and a dime |
| **17. court*** | went to court |
| **18. course** | changed their course |
| **19. balloon** | blew up the balloon |
| **20. shovel*** | a shovel and a rake |

***Other Word Forms***

| | |
|---|---|
| models, modeled | collared |
| body | bottomless |
| copy, copied, copying, copier | blossoms, blossomed |
| problems | cloths, clothing, clothes |
| offers, offered, offering | towards |
| coppery | quarts |
| drop, drops, dropping, dropper | quartered, quartering |
| shop, shopped, shops, shopper | courted |
| dollars | courses, coursed |
| | balloons |
| | shoveled |

**C. Visual Warm-up** Write each word in its correct shape.

a. collar
b. balloon
c. dollar
d. bottom
e. model
f. shovel
g. problem
h. toward
i. quart
j. bodies
k. shopping
l. offer
m. copies
n. course
o. quarter
p. court
q. dropped
r. cloth
s. blossom
t. copper



*Modified Lesson words are asterisked.
The Modified Lesson is found in the Teacher's Resource Book.

## MEETING INDIVIDUAL NEEDS / ASSIGNMENT GUIDE

| 5-Day Plan | 3-Day Plan | Limited Spellers | Average Spellers | Advanced Spellers |
|---|---|---|---|---|
| 1 | 1 | • Pretest<br>• Progress Chart | • Pretest<br>• Progress Chart<br>• Home Activity | • Pretest<br>• Progress Chart<br>• Home Activity |
| 2 | | • Modified Lesson Visual Warm-up Ending Sounds | • Regular Lesson Visual Warm-up | • Regular Lesson Visual Warm-up |
| 3 and 4 | 2 | • Modified Lesson Vowel Puzzle Word Match Finish the Sentence | Spelling Activities | Spelling Activities<br>• Challenge Exercise |
| 5 | 3 | • Posttest<br>• Words to Learn Sheet<br>• Progress Chart | • Posttest<br>• Words to Learn Sheet<br>• Progress Chart | • Posttest<br>• Words to Learn Sheet<br>• Progress Chart |

**D. Break the Code** Use the code to write the spelling words.

| a | b | c | d | e | f | g | h | i | j | k | l | m | n | o | p | q | r | s | t | u | v | w | x | y | z |
|---|---|---|---|---|---|---|---|---|---|---|---|---|---|---|---|---|---|---|---|---|---|---|---|---|---|
| ↕ | ↕ | ↕ | ↕ | ↕ | ↕ | ↕ | ↕ | ↕ | ↕ | ↕ | ↕ | ↕ | ↕ | ↕ | ↕ | ↕ | ↕ | ↕ | ↕ | ↕ | ↕ | ↕ | ↕ | ↕ | ↕ |
| c | d | a | b | g | h | e | f | k | l | i | j | o | p | m | n | s | t | q | r | w | x | u | v | z | y |

1. rmuctb toward
2. swctr quart
3. swctrgt quarter
4. dcjjmmp balloon
5. amwtqg course
6. amwtr court
7. amnngt copper
8. mhhgt offer
9. djmqqmo blossom
10. ntmdjgo problem
11. dmrrmo bottom
12. amjjct collar
13. bmjjct dollar
14. ombgj model
15. qfmxgj shovel
16. amnkgq copies
17. btmnngb dropped
18. qfmnnkpe shopping
19. ajmrf cloth
20. dmbkgq bodies

**E. Generally Speaking** Write a spelling word for the group it best fits.

1. pint, quart, gallon
2. fabric, material, cloth
3. hoe, rake, shovel
4. closer, nearer, toward
5. nickel, dime, quarter
6. crime, trial, court
7. copy, pattern, model
8. trouble, difficulty, problem

**F. Be a Word Doctor** Write the one operation you must perform before adding the suffix to each word. Write the new word.

| | Operations | | | New Words |
|---|---|---|---|---|
| Example: swim | *double the m* | + ing | = | *swimming* |
| 1. body | change y to *i* | + es | = | bodies |
| 2. copy | change y to *i* | + es | = | copies |
| 3. shop | double the *p* | + ing | = | shopping |
| 4. drop | double the *p* | + ed | = | dropped |



## OPTIONAL TEACHING PLAN

Write the five Word Group headings on the chalkboard. Ask the students to name the thirteen spelling words with the short **o** sound. Continue identifying the other Word Groups. Note the two-syllable words with double consonants and the short **o** sound: **offer, copper, dropped, shopping, dollar, collar, bottom, blossom.**

| Word Groups | | |
|---|---|---|
| /ŏ/ words | model | bodies |
| | copies | problem |
| | offer | copper |
| | dropped | shopping |
| | dollar | collar |
| | bottom | blossom |
| | cloth | **forgotten** |
| | **operated** | **property** |
| | **softened** | |
| **ar** words | toward | quart |
| | quarter | |
| **our** words | court | course |
| /o͞o/ word | balloon | |
| /ŭ/ words | shovel | **youngster** |

*Challenge Words are boldfaced.*

### Optional Activity Masters

Those using the Hardcover Pupil Edition may wish to use the Optional Activity Masters in the Teacher's Resource Book for Exercise C.

### Home Activity #14

Name________________ Date________

The spelling words in Lesson 14 appear in the phrases below. Use the phrases to complete the sentences. The number before each blank tells you in what box you can find the correct phrase. Use each phrase only once. Circle the spelling words.

**Phrases**

1: cost one **dollar**; walked **toward** the shore; a **quarter** and a dime; made two **copies**; went to **court**

2: a cotton **cloth**; large **bodies** of water; changed their **course**; a **shovel** and a rake; building a **model** plane

3: solved the **problem**; **dropped** the dish; the plastic **shopping** bag; a **quart** of milk; the top and the **bottom**

4: turned-up **collar**; blew up the **balloon**; a **blossom** on the tree; an **offer** to help; gold and **copper**

**Sentences**

1. I used (2) ________ in the garden.
2. Show me (3) ________ of the box.
3. Can you loan me (1) ________?
4. The groceries are in (3) ________.
5. The lawyers (1) ________ to argue the case.
6. The Great Lakes are (2) ________.
7. He wore a (4) ________ to shield the wind.
8. The child (3) ________ and broke it.
9. This dress is made from (2) ________.
10. We (1) ________ to find seashells.
11. Please pick (4) ________.
12. The student (3) ________ given by the math teacher.
13. The clerk (1) ________ of the letter.
14. He (4) ________ and let it go.
15. The purchase (1) ________.
16. This coin is made of (4) ________.
17. She is (2) ________ out of wood.
18. He gave me (4) ________ with my work.
19. We bought (3) ________ and some eggs.
20. The sailors (2) ________ from east to west.

20 ©D.C. Heath and Company

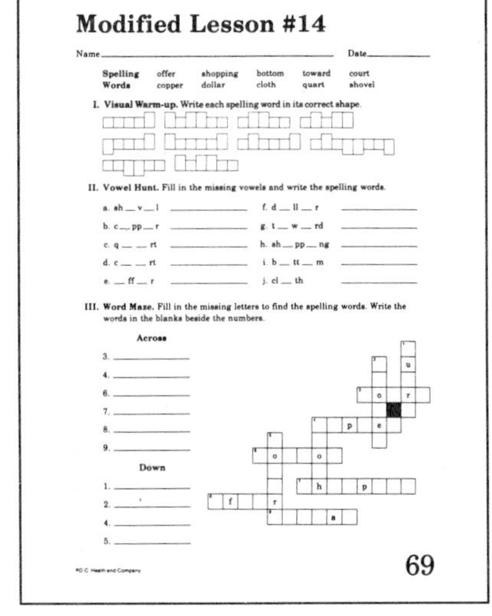

### Modified Lesson #14

Name________________ Date________

**Spelling Words** offer, copper, shopping, dollar, bottom, cloth, toward, quart, court, shovel

**I. Visual Warm-up.** Write each spelling word in its correct shape.

**II. Vowel Hunt.** Fill in the missing vowels and write the spelling words.

a. sh _ v _ l ________
b. c _ pp _ r ________
c. q _ _ rt ________
d. c _ _ rt ________
e. _ ff _ r ________
f. d _ ll _ r ________
g. t _ w _ rd ________
h. sh _ pp _ ng ________
i. b _ tt _ m ________
j. cl _ th ________

**III. Word Maze.** Fill in the missing letters to find the spelling words. Write the words in the blanks beside the numbers.

Across: 3. ____ 4. ____ 6. ____ 7. ____ 8. ____ 9. ____

Down: 1. ____ 2. ____ 4. ____ 5. ____

©D.C. Heath and Company 69

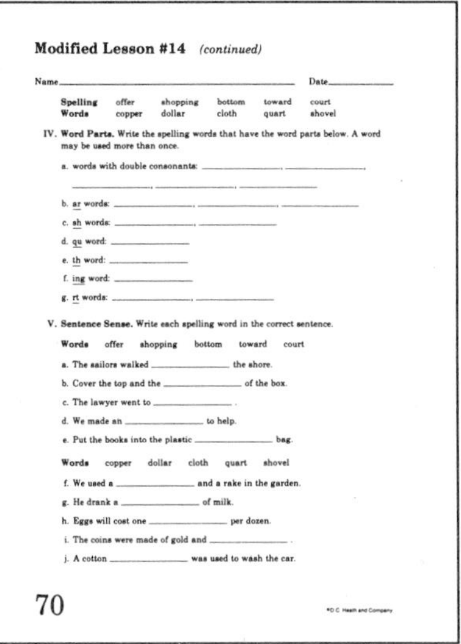

### Modified Lesson #14 *(continued)*

Name________________ Date________

**Spelling Words** offer, copper, shopping, dollar, bottom, cloth, toward, quart, court, shovel

**IV. Word Parts.** Write the spelling words that have the word parts below. A word may be used more than once.

a. words with double consonants: ____, ____, ____, ____, ____
b. ar words: ____, ____, ____
c. sh words: ____, ____
d. qu word: ____
e. th word: ____
f. ing word: ____
g. rt words: ____, ____

**V. Sentence Sense.** Write each spelling word in the correct sentence.

**Words** offer shopping bottom toward court

a. The sailors walked ________ the shore.
b. Cover the top and the ________ of the box.
c. The lawyer went to ________.
d. We made an ________ to help.
e. Put the books into the plastic ________ bag.

**Words** copper dollar cloth quart shovel

f. We used a ________ and a rake in the garden.
g. He drank a ________ of milk.
h. Eggs will cost one ________ per dozen.
i. The coins were made of gold and ________.
j. A cotton ________ was used to wash the car.

70 ©D.C. Heath and Company

## Home Activity

A weekly homework assignment

## Modified Lesson

An alternative lesson for limited spellers

*(The Answer Key can be found in the Teacher's Resource Book.)*

LESSON
# 14
CONTINUED

### Challenge Exercise #14

Name__________ Date__________

**Word Watch.** The word *dollar* had its beginning four hundred years ago in Bohemia, where money was minted from silver produced in the regional mines. The mint was located in Joachimsthal, meaning "Joachim's Valley." The German word *thal* means "valley." The Bohemians called their silver coin *Joachimsthaler* and later shortened the name to *thaler*. Our English word *dollar* came from this shortened form.

**Word Analogies.** Decide on the relationship that exists between the first pair of words. Using the Other Word Forms on page 56, find a word that completes the second pair of words and establishes the same relationship.

1. *gasoline* is to *gallons* as *oil* is to ________
2. *raises* is to *lowers* as *lifts* is to ________
3. *raked* is to *leaves* as ________ is to *snow*
4. *shell* is to *nut* as ________ is to *person*
5. *peak* is to *mountain* as *head* is to ________

**Challenge Words Student Activity**
Use the challenge words below to complete the paragraph.

**forgotten property youngster operated softened**

For two days, a small boy ________ a lemonade stand outside our office building. The ________ smiled happily as he served his customers. For some, the boy's grin ________ the problems of the day. Then the building owner told him to leave the ________. The workers, who had not ________ their own childhoods, protested.

**Working With Words: Student Writing Activity**
Use as many Other Word Forms as you can from page 56 to write the five messages that you might find inside fortune cookies. (Example: You will become a good *shopper* when you become a careful spender.)

126



## Challenge Exercise
Additional activities for advanced spellers

**Spelling Words**

| | | | | |
|---|---|---|---|---|
| model | bodies | copies | problem | offer |
| copper | dropped | shopping | dollar | collar |
| bottom | blossom | cloth | toward | quart |
| quarter | court | course | balloon | shovel |

**G. Words and Meanings** Write a spelling word for each meaning. Check your answers in the **Spelling Dictionary**. You may wish to look up the meanings of *course, offer,* and *toward.*

1. a math question to be solved problem
2. in the direction of toward
3. let fall dropped
4. material made by weaving fibers together cloth
5. a band of clothing around the neck collar
6. one fourth of a gallon quart
7. a small-scale copy model
8. a rubber bag to be filled with air balloon
9. a tool for lifting snow shovel
10. masses of matter bodies
11. the direction taken course
12. buying things in a store shopping
13. the lowest part bottom
14. things made just like others copies
15. a reddish-brown element copper
16. a place where legal cases are decided court
17. 100 cents dollar
18. a suggestion or plan offer
19. 25 cents quarter
20. a flower blossom



## CONTROLLED DICTATION (Optional)

These dictation sentences provide maintenance for spelling words previously taught and practice for words currently being studied. Dictation should be administered on Day 4. The teacher or another student may dictate the sentences. Be sure to dictate all marks of punctuation. Challenge Word sentences are preceded by an asterisk.

1. They will **offer** to set aside a **quarter** for each **dollar** earned.
2. The **blossom dropped** to the **bottom** of the empty box.
3. The **problem** with the **copper** pitcher is that it holds only one **quart**.
4. Of **course**, your **bodies** will be sore after you **shovel** snow.
5. Carrying a red **balloon**, the child walked **toward** the open **court**.
6. **Model** planes are **copies** of larger planes.
7. We are **shopping** for a **collar** made of the finest silk **cloth**.

*8. The bus driver said that the **youngster** had **forgotten** her lunch.
*9. The gate for this **property** is **operated** by a guard.
*10. This new soap **softened** the rough cloth.

**H. Using Other Word Forms** Write the Other Word Form that completes each sentence.

Base Words: course(s) drop(ing) model(s) shovel(ed) shop(er)

1. A person who models wears the new fashions.
2. A person who lets something fall is dropping it.
3. A person who buys in a store is a shopper.
4. A person who plays golf plays on golf courses.
5. A person who moved a pile of dirt shoveled it.

**I. Challenge Words** Write the Challenge Word that completes each question.

| forgotten | operated | property | softened | youngster |
|---|---|---|---|---|

1. How much property do they own?
2. Has the butter softened?
3. Who operated the computer?
4. Where does the youngster attend school?
5. Have you forgotten to do your homework?

**J. Spelling and Writing** Write each set of words in a sentence. You may use Other Word Forms. Proofread your work.

1. quarter – copper – dollar
2. balloon – dropped – course
3. shopping – collar – cloth
4. bottom – shovel – court
5. bodies – copies – model
6. offer – toward – problem
7. quart – blossom – drops
8. operated – softened – problems
9. youngster – forgotten – property

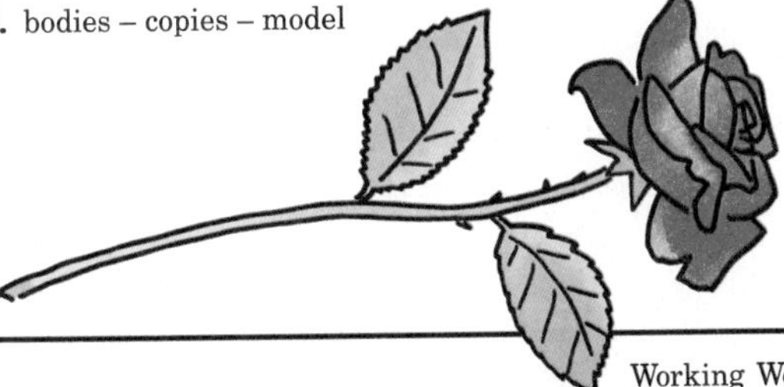



## USING OTHER WORD FORMS

Vocabulary is expanded through the use of other forms of basic spelling words. Emphasis is on the relationship of syntax to suffix choices. The following generalizations apply to the Other Word Forms used in Exercise H.

### Spelling Rule

Forming plurals

Add **s** to most nouns to form plurals.
**(model, models)**

Doubling the final consonant when adding suffixes

When adding a suffix that begins with a vowel to one-syllable words that end with one vowel and one consonant, double the final consonant.
**(drop, dropping)**

## POSTTEST AND PROOFREADING

Follow the same testing procedures used in the Pretest, although you may wish to correct the tests yourself. Have students write any misspelled words on the Words to Learn Sheet and record spelling success on the Progress Chart.

## THE SPELLING-WRITING LINK

**Purpose** This activity helps students effectively transfer lesson words into their daily writing. Students (a) determine a relationship among three given words and (b) write a complete sentence.

**Procedure** On the chalkboard, write the three words from line 1 (**quarter, copper, dollar**) and the Other Word Forms (**quartered, quartering, coppery, dollars**). Have students read the words and think of ways the three words might be related. Have them think of things or people the words suggest. Ask students to create sentences using some of their ideas. You can provide an example sentence: **A paper dollar and silvery quarter are worth more than a copper penny.**

**Practice** Tell students to write original sentences using the word sets and to proofread their work. You may want them to circle the lesson words.

# LESSON 15

## OBJECTIVES

- to spell 20 high-frequency words with the /ŭ/, /ŏ/, /o͝o/, and /ou/
- to proofread these words in daily writing
- to become familiar with 37 other forms of the spelling words

| Summary of Skills | Exercises |
|---|---|
| Auditory Discrimination | A |
| Proofreading | A, C, H |
| Visual Discrimination | C |
| Vocabulary Development | D, G |
| Dictionary Skills | E |
| Word Analysis | F |
| Original Writing | H |

## PRETEST AND PROOFREADING

The Pretest identifies the words students are able to spell, as well as the words they need to learn. You may wish to use Other Word Forms when giving the Pretest. Five suggested Other Word Forms are underlined on this page.

To administer the Pretest:

**READ** each word aloud.
**SAY** the phrase containing the word.
**REPEAT** the word.

Have students correct the Pretest using the Corrected-test Procedure. They may record their scores on a personal Progress Chart (see the Teacher's Resource Book) and study misspelled words using the **S-H-A-R-P** procedure.

## OTHER WORD FORMS

This section presents related forms of the spelling words to strengthen spelling power and vocabulary knowledge.

### Enrichment Activity

Have students write sentences that include these Other Word Forms.

1. **doubling – production**
2. **roughest – outlines**
3. **troubled – touched**
4. **flooded – southerly**

# 15

**A. Pretest and Proofreading**

**B. Spelling Words and Phrases**

| | |
|---|---|
| **1. touch** | too hot to touch |
| **2. cousin** | wrote to my cousin |
| **3. southern** | the southern route |
| **4. double** | rode double on the sled |
| **5. trouble*** | asking for trouble |
| **6. rough** | a rough surface |
| **7. enough*** | not enough for three |
| **8. dozen*** | a dozen yellow roses |
| **9. govern** | will govern the nation |
| **10. flood** | flood in the cellar |
| **11. blood*** | several drops of blood |
| **12. product*** | the best-selling product |
| **13. brook** | trout in the brook |
| **14. shook** | shook them fiercely |
| **15. goodness*** | my goodness |
| **16. couldn't*** | couldn't swim |
| **17. wouldn't*** | if they wouldn't wait |
| **18. outline*** | traced an outline |
| **19. household*** | for household use only |
| **20. fountain** | brightly lighted fountain |

*Other Word Forms*

| | |
|---|---|
| touches, touched | bloody, bleed, bled, bleeding |
| cousins, | products, production |
| south, southerly, | brooks |
| doubled, doubles, doubling, doubly | shake, shakes, shaking, shaky |
| troubles, troubling, troubled | good |
| rougher, roughest, roughly | outlines, outlined, outlining |
| dozens | households |
| governing, government | fountains |
| floods, flooded | |

**C. Visual Warm-up** Write each word in its correct shape.

a. blood
b. flood
c. southern
d. trouble
e. enough
f. shook
g. touch
h. outline
i. household
j. couldn't
k. product
l. double
m. rough
n. brook
o. goodness
p. dozen
q. cousin
r. fountain
s. wouldn't
t. govern

60 Lesson 15

*Modified Lesson words are asterisked.
The Modified Lesson is found in the Teacher's Resource Book.

## MEETING INDIVIDUAL NEEDS / ASSIGNMENT GUIDE

| 5-Day Plan | 3-Day Plan | Limited Spellers | Average Spellers | Advanced Spellers |
|---|---|---|---|---|
| 1 | 1 | • Pretest<br>• Progress Chart | • Pretest<br>• Progress Chart<br>• Home Activity | • Pretest<br>• Progress Chart<br>• Home Activity |
| 2 | | • Modified Lesson Visual Warm-up Ending Sounds | • Regular Lesson Visual Warm-up | • Regular Lesson Visual Warm-up |
| 3 and 4 | 2 | • Modified Lesson Vowel Puzzle Word Match Finish the Sentence | Spelling Activities | Spelling Activities<br>• Challenge Exercise |
| 5 | 3 | • Posttest<br>• Words to Learn Sheet<br>• Progress Chart | • Posttest<br>• Words to Learn Sheet<br>• Progress Chart | • Posttest<br>• Words to Learn Sheet<br>• Progress Chart |

## D. Look Out!

Answer each question with an ou word from the spelling list. Write the word.

1. What ou is twice as much? **double**
2. What ou shows the edge? **outline**
3. What ou was not able to? **couldn't**
4. What ou didn't want to? **wouldn't**
5. What ou sprays toward the sky? **fountain**
6. What ou causes problems? **trouble**
7. What ou is a relative? **cousin**
8. What ou is done by feeling? **touch**
9. What ou is opposite of northern? **southern**
10. What ou is found where you live? **household**
11. What ou is as much as needed? **enough**
12. What ou is not smooth? **rough**

Answer each question with an oo word from the spelling list. Write the word.

13. What oo did you do when you were frightened? **shook**
14. What oo is red in color? **blood**
15. What oo is like a stream? **brook**
16. What oo can bring great damage? **flood**
17. What oo shows kindness? **goodness**
18. Write the three remaining spelling words or their Other Word Forms (p. 60) in sentences.

**Sample responses:**

**The President holds the highest *government* office.**

**We shared a *dozen* donuts.**

**Some people buy only brand-name *products*.**



## OPTIONAL TEACHING PLAN

Write the seven Word Group headings on the chalkboard. Ask the students to name the seven spelling words with the short **u** sound that are spelled **ou**. Continue identifying the other Word Groups. Note the three different sounds of **ou** (short **u**, /o͞o/, and /ou/).

| Word Groups | | |
|---|---|---|
| /ŭ/: **ou** words | touch<br>southern<br>trouble<br>enough | cousin<br>double<br>rough |
| /ŭ/: **o** words | dozen<br>**uncomfortable** | govern |
| /ŭ/ words | flood<br>**mumble** | blood<br>**luckily** |
| /ŏ/ word | product | |
| /o͝o/: **oo** words | brook<br>goodness | shook |
| /o͝o/: **ou** words | couldn't | wouldn't |
| /ou/ words | outline<br>fountain<br>**compound** | household<br>**powerfully** |

*Challenge Words are boldfaced.*

### Optional Activity Masters

Those using the Hardcover Pupil Edition may wish to use the Optional Activity Masters in the Teacher's Resource Book for Exercise C.

**Home Activity #15**

Name_______________ Date_______

Use the spelling words to complete the sentences. The number before each blank tells you in what column you can find the correct word. Use each word only once.

| 1 | 2 | 3 | 4 |
|---|---|---|---|
| brook | wouldn't | rough | household |
| goodness | cousin | enough | fountain |
| shook | trouble | flood | product |
| blood | southern | govern | couldn't |
| touch | double | outline | dozen |

1. He stayed on shore because he (4) __________ swim.
2. The president will (3) __________ the nation.
3. My (1) __________, how you've grown!
4. Let's take the (2) __________ route instead.
5. The bear seemed angry at her cubs and (1) __________ them fiercely.
6. This rocky road has a (3) __________ surface.
7. The florist sold a (4) __________ yellow roses.
8. Don't sit too close or you may be asking for (2) __________!
9. Let's watch the trout in the (1) __________.
10. This cleaner is for (4) __________ use only.
11. The twins rode (2) __________ on the sled.
12. Bring the buckets because there is a (3) __________ in the cellar!
13. Look at the sprays of water in the brightly lighted (4) __________.
14. It's not our fault if they (2) __________ wait.
15. There is not (3) __________ for three.
16. He lost several drops of (1) __________ before he bandaged his finger.
17. The student traced an (3) __________ on the paper.
18. This item is the best-selling (4) __________ in the store.
19. The grill is too hot to (1) __________.
20. I wrote to my (2) __________ about the family reunion.

©D.C. Heath and Company 21

**Modified Lesson #15**

Name_______________ Date_______

**Spelling Words** trouble enough dozen blood product goodness couldn't wouldn't outline household

I. **Visual Warm-up.** Write each spelling word in its correct shape.

II. **Vowel Hunt.** Fill in the missing vowels and write the spelling words.

a. g _ _ dn _ ss __________ f. tr _ _ bl _ __________
b. _ n _ _ gh __________ g. bl _ _ d __________
c. h _ _ s _ h _ ld __________ h. pr _ d _ ct __________
d. _ _ tl _ n _ __________ i. d _ z _ n __________
e. w _ _ ldn't __________ j. c _ _ ldn't __________

III. **Word Maze.** Fill in the missing letters to find the spelling words. Write the words in the blanks beside the numbers.

Across: 2. ___ 3. ___ 5. ___ 7. ___ 8. ___ 9. ___ 10. ___

Down: 1. ___ 4. ___ 6. ___

©D.C. Heath and Company 71

**Modified Lesson #15** *(continued)*

Name_______________ Date_______

**Spelling Words** trouble enough dozen blood product goodness couldn't wouldn't outline household

IV. **Word Parts.** Write the spelling words that have the word parts below. A word may be used more than once.

a. tr word: __________
b. pr word: __________
c. bl word: __________
d. ness word: __________
e. ough word: __________
f. en words: __________, __________
g. ld words: __________, __________, __________
h. ct word: __________
i. Write the two compound words. __________, __________
j. Write the two contractions. __________, __________

V. **Sentence Sense.** Write each spelling word in the correct sentence.

**Words** trouble dozen product couldn't outline

a. The loud children were asking for __________.
b. That soap is the best-selling __________.
c. The student traced an __________ of a map.
d. She received a __________ yellow roses.
e. I jumped into the water but I __________ swim.

**Words** enough blood goodness wouldn't household

f. The wax is for __________ use only.
g. I have some dessert but not __________ for three.
h. The teacher praised me for my __________.
i. If they __________ wait, we would be upset.
j. The doctor took several drops of __________.

72 ©D.C. Heath and Company

### Home Activity

A weekly homework assignment

### Modified Lesson

An alternative lesson for limited spellers

*(The Answer Key can be found in the Teacher's Resource Book.)*

# LESSON 15 CONTINUED

### Challenge Exercise #15

Name____________________ Date__________

**Word Watch.** The Latin word for *twelve* is *duodecim*, meaning "two plus ten." The word was borrowed by the early French and changed to *douzaine*. When the word entered the English language, additional changes occurred. Over the years, the spellings included *dozyne, duzan, dousayne,* and *doozen*. During the 16th century, the spelling *dozen* came into general use. Today the word *dozen* still means "a group of twelve." Of special interest is the fact that the Latin word *duodecim* is still used by mathematicians. The duodecimal system is a number system based on a dozen digits.

**Word Analogies.** Decide on the relationship that exists between the first pair of words. Using the Other Word Forms on page 60, find a word that completes the second pair of words and establishes the same relationship.

1. *wind* is to *tornadoes* as *water* is to __________
2. *motionless* is to *steady* as *trembling* is to __________
3. *cloudy* is to *gray* as __________ is to *red*
4. *better* is to *worse* as __________ is to *bad*
5. *three* is to *tripled* as *two* is to __________

**Challenge Words Student Activity**

Use the challenge words below to complete the statements about people.

**compound** **luckily** **mumble** **uncomfortable** **powerfully**

1. That champion weight lifter needs to be __________ built.
2. A scientist can combine elements to make a __________ .
3. A shy person might __________ when giving a speech.
4. The lost hiker __________ was found before night.
5. A camper without a sleeping bag could be __________ .

**Working With Words: Student Writing Activity**

Use as many Other Word Forms as you can from page 60 to write short, silly rhymes to include in a children's nursery rhyme book. (Example: *Troubled* trolls pay double tolls.



127

## Challenge Exercise

Additional activities for advanced spellers

**Spelling Words**

| | | | | |
|---|---|---|---|---|
| touch | cousin | southern | double | trouble |
| rough | enough | dozen | govern | blood |
| flood | product | brook | shook | goodness |
| couldn't | wouldn't | outline | household | fountain |

**E. Guide Words** These word pairs are guide words that might appear in a dictionary. Write the words from the spelling list that would appear on the same page as each pair of guide words.

**balloon – bottom**
1. blood

**bought – canyon**
2. brook

**copy – daughter**
3. cousin
4. couldn't

**day – dropped**
5. double
6. dozen

**dry – escape**
7. enough

**fifteen – freedom**
8. flood
9. fountain

**freeze – graze**
10. goodness
11. govern

**help – ironing**
12. household

**often – pasture**
13. outline

**president – quart**
14. product

**reply – scarf**
15. rough

**schoolmate – skinned**
16. shook

**skirt – strain**
17. southern

**taught – ugly**
18. touch
19. trouble

**western – wrist**
20. wouldn't



## CONTROLLED DICTATION (Optional)

These dictation sentences provide maintenance for spelling words previously taught and practice for words currently being studied. Dictation should be administered on Day 4. The teacher or another student may dictate the sentences. Be sure to dictate all marks of punctuation. Challenge Word sentences are preceded by an asterisk.

1. I **wouldn't** choose that **household product**.
2. Why **couldn't** they **govern** the **southern** county?
3. The **brook** rose high **enough** to **flood** the field.
4. A **dozen** new problems would **double** my **trouble**.
5. My hand **shook** as I drew an **outline** of the water **fountain**.
6. Though he seems **rough**, there is a **touch** of **goodness** within him.
7. Do my **cousin** and I really have the same type of **blood**?

*8. **Luckily** for us, it was a **powerfully** strong **compound**.
*9. Did you hear him **mumble** that he was **uncomfortable**?

**F. Using Other Word Forms** Write the Other Word Form that completes each series.

Base Words: shake(ing) touch(es) bleed(ed) outline(ing) govern(ing)

1. bleeds, bled, bleeding
2. shakes, shook, shaking
3. touches, touched, touching
4. governs, governed, governing
5. outlines, outlined, outlining

**G. Challenge Words** Write the Challenge Word that completes each phrase.

| powerfully | uncomfortable | compound | mumble | luckily |
|---|---|---|---|---|

1. not unfortunately, but luckily
2. not weakly, but powerfully
3. not a shout, but a mumble
4. not comfortable, but uncomfortable
5. not an element, but a compound

**H. Spelling and Writing** Use as many Spelling Words, Other Word Forms, and Challenge Words as you can to write *two* or more answers to each question. A few words are suggested. Proofread your work.

1. What might you say about your neighborhood after a week of heavy rain?
   flood – enough – brook – double – trouble – powerfully
2. What might you say during a phone call to a relative living in Florida?
   touch – couldn't – cousin – southern – household – mumble
3. What could you say to someone who has just scraped his or her knee?
   rough – shook – blood – goodness – uncomfortable – luckily



## USING OTHER WORD FORMS

Vocabulary is expanded through the use of other forms of basic spelling words. Emphasis is on the relationship of syntax to suffix choices. The following generalization applies to the Other Word Forms used in Exercise F.

### Spelling Rule

Adding suffixes to words ending in silent **e**

When adding a suffix that begins with a vowel to words that end with silent **e**, drop the final **e**.
**(shake, shaking)**

## POSTTEST AND PROOFREADING

Follow the same testing procedures used in the Pretest, although you may wish to correct the tests yourself. Have students write any misspelled words on the Words to Learn Sheet and record spelling success on the Progress Chart.

## THE SPELLING-WRITING LINK

**Purpose** This activity helps students retain the correct spelling of words and transfer the words to their daily writing. Students use lesson words to answer questions promoting higher-order thinking skills.

**Procedure** Read the first question and write the suggested words on the chalkboard: **flood, enough, brook, double, trouble, powerfully.** Have students list some Other Word Forms of the lesson words. Brainstorm with the class possible answers to question 1. Remind students to look at all the lesson words for ideas. Write the answers on the chalkboard, noting any lesson words.

**Practice** Tell students to finish the activity by writing two or more answers to each question. Remind them to proofread their work.

# LESSON 16

## OBJECTIVES

- to spell 20 high-frequency words with the /ă/
- to proofread these words in daily writing
- to become familiar with 37 other forms of the spelling words

| Summary of Skills | Exercises |
|---|---|
| Auditory Discrimination | A |
| Proofreading | A, C, I |
| Visual Discrimination | C |
| Word Analysis | D, F |
| Dictionary Skills | E |
| Context Usage | G |
| Vocabulary Development | H |
| Original Writing | I |

## PRETEST AND PROOFREADING

The Pretest identifies the words students are able to spell, as well as the words they need to learn. You may wish to use Other Word Forms when giving the Pretest. Five suggested Other Word Forms are underlined on this page.

To administer the Pretest:

**READ** each word aloud.
**SAY** the phrase containing the word.
**REPEAT** the word.

Have students correct the Pretest using the Corrected-test Procedure. They may record their scores on a personal Progress Chart (see the Teacher's Resource Book) and study misspelled words using the **S-H-A-R-P** procedure.

## OTHER WORD FORMS

This section presents related forms of the spelling words to strengthen spelling power and vocabulary knowledge.

### Enrichment Activity

Have students write synonyms or related phrases for these Other Word Forms. Be sure they write the Other Word Form with its synonym next to it.

**jackets, hatched, thankfully, action**

# 16

**A. Pretest and Proofreading**

**B. Spelling Words and Phrases**

| | |
|---|---|
| **1. acts*** | two acts in the play |
| **2. angle** | a wide angle |
| **3. ankle** | a broken ankle |
| **4. rank*** | the rank of lieutenant |
| **5. thankful*** | thankful to be here |
| **6. fact*** | as a matter of fact |
| **7. grasp** | a tight grasp |
| **8. brass*** | made of brass |
| **9. canyon*** | a deep, narrow canyon |
| **10. sample*** | a sample of their work |
| **11. stack** | tall stack of books |
| **12. shack** | build their own shack |
| **13. jacket** | a wool jacket |
| **14. racket** | wooden tennis racket |
| **15. hatch** | a hatch of chicks |
| **16. patch*** | patch of blue sky |
| **17. catcher** | catcher and batter |
| **18. matches*** | book of matches |
| **19. branches** | several tree branches |
| **20. hasn't*** | hasn't arrived yet |

*Other Word Forms*

| | |
|---|---|
| act, acted, action | shacks |
| angles | jackets |
| ankles | rackets |
| ranks, ranked | hatches, hatched |
| thankfully | patches, patched, patching |
| facts, factual, factually | catch, catches, catching |
| grasps | caught, catchers |
| brasses, brassy | match, matched, matching |
| canyons | branch, branched |
| samples | |
| stacks, stacked, stacking | |

**C. Visual Warm-up** Write each word in its correct shape.

a. fact
b. sample
c. thankful
d. angle
e. hasn't
f. matches
g. shack
h. brass
i. ankle
j. acts
k. rank
l. canyon
m. patch
n. catcher
o. branches
p. grasp
q. stack
r. jacket
s. hatch
t. racket



*Modified Lesson words are asterisked.
The Modified Lesson is found in the Teacher's Resource Book.

## MEETING INDIVIDUAL NEEDS / ASSIGNMENT GUIDE

| 5-Day Plan | 3-Day Plan | Limited Spellers | Average Spellers | Advanced Spellers |
|---|---|---|---|---|
| 1 | 1 | • Pretest<br>• Progress Chart | • Pretest<br>• Progress Chart<br>• Home Activity | • Pretest<br>• Progress Chart<br>• Home Activity |
| 2 | | • Modified Lesson Visual Warm-up Ending Sounds | • Regular Lesson Visual Warm-up | • Regular Lesson Visual Warm-up |
| 3 and 4 | 2 | • Modified Lesson Vowel Puzzle Word Match Finish the Sentence | Spelling Activities | Spelling Activities<br>• Challenge Exercise |
| 5 | 3 | • Posttest<br>• Words to Learn Sheet<br>• Progress Chart | • Posttest<br>• Words to Learn Sheet<br>• Progress Chart | • Posttest<br>• Words to Learn Sheet<br>• Progress Chart |

### D. Whose Serve?

Write the fifteen singular nouns found on the spelling list. Then write their plural forms.

| | Singular | Plural |
|---|---|---|
| 1. | *angle* | angles |
| 2. | ankle | ankles |
| 3. | rank | ranks |
| 4. | fact | facts |
| 5. | grasp | grasps |
| 6. | brass | brasses |
| 7. | canyon | canyons |
| 8. | sample | samples |
| 9. | shack | shacks |
| 10. | stack | stacks |
| 11. | jacket | jackets |
| 12. | racket | rackets |
| 13. | hatch | hatches |
| 14. | patch | patches |
| 15. | catcher | catchers |

**16.** Write the three plural nouns found on the spelling list. Then write their singular forms.

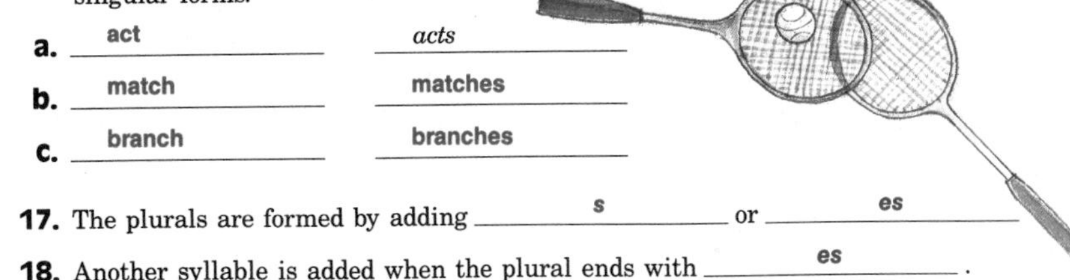

a. act — *acts*

b. match — matches

c. branch — branches

**17.** The plurals are formed by adding s or es

**18.** Another syllable is added when the plural ends with es .



## OPTIONAL TEACHING PLAN

Write the Word Group heading on the chalkboard. Ask the students to name the twenty spelling words with the short **a** sound. Write the words on the chalkboard as the students say them. Note the silent consonant **t** in **hatch**, **patch**, **catcher**, and **matches**. Point out the consonant digraph **ck** in **stack**, **shack**, **jacket**, and **racket**.

| Word Group | | |
|---|---|---|
| /ă/ words | acts | racket |
| | angle | hatch |
| | ankle | patch |
| | rank | catcher |
| | thankful | matches |
| | fact | branches |
| | grasp | hasn't |
| | brass | **aspect** |
| | canyon | **attaching** |
| | sample | **attacking** |
| | stack | **calendar** |
| | shack | **antenna** |
| | jacket | |

*Challenge Words are boldfaced.*

## Optional Activity Masters

Those using the Hardcover Pupil Edition may wish to use the Optional Activity Masters in the Teacher's Resource Book for Exercises C and E.

**Home Activity #16**

Name________________ Date________

The spelling words in Lesson 16 appear in the phrases below. Write each phrase in a sentence and circle the spelling word.

| Phrases | Sentences |
|---|---|
| 1. a tight **grasp** | 1. ________ |
| 2. as a matter of **fact** | 2. ________ |
| 3. made of **brass** | 3. ________ |
| 4. two **acts** in the play | 4. ________ |
| 5. a broken **ankle** | 5. ________ |
| 6. the **rank** of lieutenant | 6. ________ |
| 7. **thankful** to be here | 7. ________ |
| 8. a wide **angle** | 8. ________ |
| 9. a deep, narrow **canyon** | 9. ________ |
| 10. a **sample** of their work | 10. ________ |
| 11. tall **stack** of books | 11. ________ |
| 12. wooden tennis **racket** | 12. ________ |
| 13. build their own **shack** | 13. ________ |
| 14. a wool **jacket** | 14. ________ |
| 15. a **hatch** of chicks | 15. ________ |
| 16. **catcher** and batter | 16. ________ |
| 17. **patch** of blue sky | 17. ________ |
| 18. book of **matches** | 18. ________ |
| 19. several tree **branches** | 19. ________ |
| 20. **hasn't** arrived yet | 20. ________ |

22 ©D.C. Heath and Company

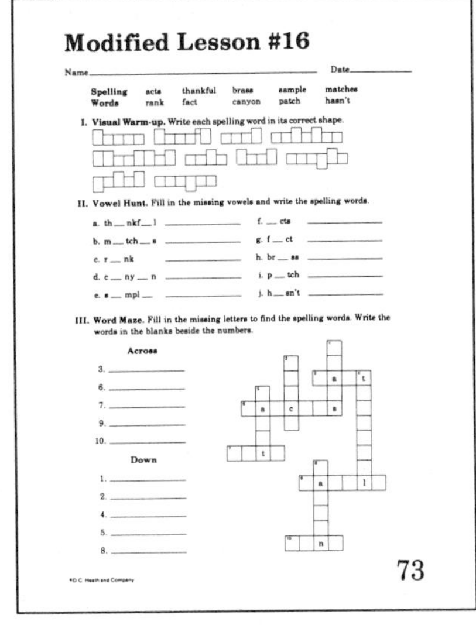

**Modified Lesson #16**

Name________________ Date________

**Spelling Words** acts, rank, thankful, fact, brass, canyon, sample, patch, matches, hasn't

**I. Visual Warm-up.** Write each spelling word in its correct shape.

**II. Vowel Hunt.** Fill in the missing vowels and write the spelling words.

a. th__nkf__l ________ f. __cts ________
b. m__tch__s ________ g. f__ct ________
c. r__nk ________ h. br__ss ________
d. c__ny__n ________ i. p__tch ________
e. s__mpl__ ________ j. h__sn't ________

**III. Word Maze.** Fill in the missing letters to find the spelling words. Write the words in the blanks beside the numbers.

Across: 3. ____ 6. ____ 7. ____ 9. ____ 10. ____

Down: 1. ____ 2. ____ 4. ____ 5. ____ 8. ____

©D.C. Heath and Company 73

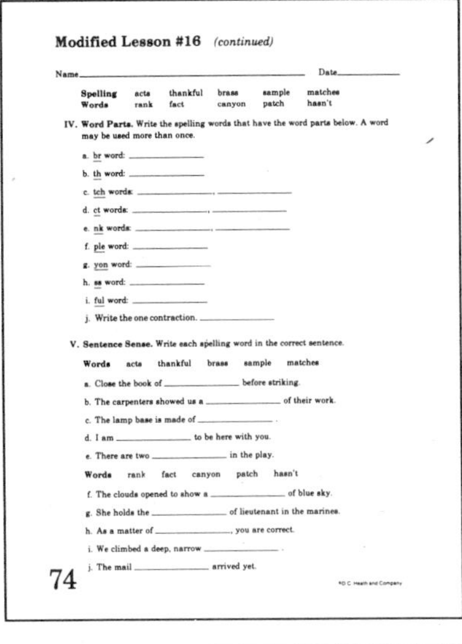

**Modified Lesson #16** *(continued)*

Name________________ Date________

**Spelling Words** acts, rank, thankful, fact, brass, canyon, sample, patch, matches, hasn't

**IV. Word Parts.** Write the spelling words that have the word parts below. A word may be used more than once.

a. br word: ________
b. th word: ________
c. tch words: ________, ________
d. ct words: ________, ________
e. nk words: ________, ________
f. ple word: ________
g. yon word: ________
h. ss word: ________
i. ful word: ________
j. Write the one contraction. ________

**V. Sentence Sense.** Write each spelling word in the correct sentence.

**Words** acts thankful brass sample matches

a. Close the book of ________ before striking.
b. The carpenters showed us a ________ of their work.
c. The lamp base is made of ________ .
d. I am ________ to be here with you.
e. There are two ________ in the play.

**Words** rank fact canyon patch hasn't

f. The clouds opened to show a ________ of blue sky.
g. She holds the ________ of lieutenant in the marines.
h. As a matter of ________, you are correct.
i. We climbed a deep, narrow ________ .
j. The mail ________ arrived yet.

74 ©D.C. Heath and Company

## Home Activity

A weekly homework assignment

## Modified Lesson

An alternative lesson for limited spellers

*(The Answer Key can be found in the Teacher's Resource Book.)*

# LESSON 16 CONTINUED

## Challenge Exercise #16

Name_______________________ Date__________

**Word Watch.** Long ago, English foot soldiers going into battle wore a coat of mail called a *jack*. The name of the garment was the English form of the French word *jaque*. This armored coat was constructed of overlapping metal plates and was a heavy garment that weighed down the soldier. Some battlers preferred a lighter version of the jack, called a *jacket*, meaning "little jack." Today the jacket is still used as a protective garment, but only to protect wearers from the cold and precipitation.

**Word Analogies.** Decide on the relationship that exists between the first pair of words. Using the Other Word Forms on page 64, find a word that completes the second pair of words and establishes the same relationship.

1. *buds* is to *blossomed* as *eggs* is to ____________
2. *arcs* is to *circles* as ____________ is to *squares*
3. *piled* is to *sand* as ____________ is to *hay*
4. *arm* is to *person* as ____________ is to *tree*
5. *goalies* is to *hockey* as ____________ is to *baseball*

**Challenge Words Student Activity**

Use the challenge words below to complete the statements about people.

**antenna calendar aspect attacking attaching**

1. A lawyer might study each ____________ of a case.
2. A radio operator might need a new ____________ .
3. A busy person might check the ____________ often.
4. A firefighter might be ____________ a hose to a hydrant.
5. The Vikings might have considered ____________ an enemy outpost.

**Working With Words: Student Writing Activity**

Use as many Other Word Forms as you can from page 64 to write a plan to your principal for extending the recess period. Use the format of a friendly letter.

128



## Challenge Exercise

Additional activities for advanced spellers

### Spelling Words

| | | | | |
|---|---|---|---|---|
| acts | angle | ankle | rank | thankful |
| fact | grasp | brass | canyon | sample |
| shack | stack | jacket | racket | hatch |
| patch | catcher | matches | branches | hasn't |

**E. All in a Row** Write the twenty spelling words in alphabetical order. Then join the boxed letters and write four hidden words.

1. a [c] t s
2. a n g [l] e
3. a n k l [e]
4. b r [a] n c h e s
5. b [r] a s s
6. Hidden Word: clear
7. [c] a n y o n
8. c a t c [h] e r
9. f [a] c t
10. g [r] a s p
11. h a s n ' [t]
12. Hidden Word: chart
13. h [a] t c h
14. j a c k e [t]
15. m a [t] c h e s
16. p [a] t [c] h
17. r a c [k] e t
18. Hidden Word: attack
19. [r] a n k
20. s a m p l [e]
21. s h [a] c k
22. s t a [c] k
23. [t] h a n k f u l
24. Hidden Word: react

**F. Word Building** Add a word part to each word to build words from the spelling list. Write the words.

s et es er ful n't

1. jack jacket
2. act acts
3. match matches
4. rack racket
5. has hasn't
6. catch catcher
7. branch branches
8. thank thankful



## CONTROLLED DICTATION (Optional)

These dictation sentences provide maintenance for spelling words previously taught and practice for words currently being studied. Dictation should be administered on Day 4. The teacher or another student may dictate the sentences. Be sure to dictate all marks of punctuation. Challenge Word sentences are preceded by an asterisk.

1. The **catcher** wore a **patch** on his **jacket**.
2. We placed a **stack** of **branches** behind the **shack**.
3. The clerk stored the **matches** in a **brass** box.
4. The **angle** of the **racket** handle **hasn't** been changed.
5. One of the final **acts** will be to **grasp** each **ankle** without bending the knee
6. How do you **rank** the **sample** chicks from the latest **hatch**?
7. We were **thankful** that my cousin knew that **fact** about the **canyon**.

*8. They are **attaching** another **antenna** to the roof.
*9. The **calendar** shows one **aspect** of time.
*10. The bee is **attacking** the dog.

**G. Using Other Word Forms** Write the Other Word Form that completes each sentence.

Base Words: branch(ed) match(ed) patch(ed) fact(al) catch(ught)

1. A non-fiction report is like a true story. Both are factual.
2. Like a river, the road branched in many directions.
3. A torn jacket is like a hole in the ceiling. Both need to be patched.
4. A cold is like a fish. Both are caught.
5. Bookends are like a pair of socks. Both are matched.

**H. Challenge Words** Write the Challenge Word that replaces each underlined word.

| aspect | attaching | attacking | calendar | antenna |
|---|---|---|---|---|

1. The child is connecting the tail to the donkey. attaching
2. Check each day on the timetable. calendar
3. The raiders are storming the village. attacking
4. The television aerial is located on the roof. antenna
5. You missed one important part of the problem. aspect

**I. Spelling and Writing** Use as many Spelling Words, Other Word Forms, and Challenge Words as you can to write *two* or more answers to each question. A few words are suggested. Proofread your work.

1. What would you do if a classmate asked you to help with a math project?

   thankful – sample – fact – angle – calendar – aspect

2. How would you describe to a friend what happened the first time you went hiking or skiing?

   ankle – canyon – attacking – jacket – patch – branches

3. What would you do if you lost your pet lizard in the kitchen just as company arrived?

   stack – racket – catcher – grasp – attaching



## USING OTHER WORD FORMS

Vocabulary is expanded through the use of other forms of basic spelling words. Emphasis is on the relationship of syntax to suffix choices.

## POSTTEST AND PROOFREADING

Follow the same testing procedures used in the Pretest, although you may wish to correct the tests yourself. Have students write any misspelled words on the Words to Learn Sheet and record spelling success on the Progress Chart.

## THE SPELLING-WRITING LINK

**Purpose** This activity helps students retain the correct spelling of words and transfer the words to their daily writing. Students use lesson words to answer questions promoting higher-order thinking skills.

**Procedure** Read the first question and write the suggested words on the chalkboard: **thankful, sample, fact, angle, calendar, aspect.** Have students list some Other Word Forms of the lesson words. Brainstorm with the class possible answers to question 1. Remind students to look at all the lesson words for ideas. Write the answers on the chalkboard, noting any lesson words.

**Practice** Tell students to finish the activity by writing two or more answers to each question. Remind them to proofread their work.

## OBJECTIVES

- to spell 20 high-frequency words, including **au** words with the /ô/ and /ă/, and **o** words with the /ô/, /ə/, and /ŏ/
- to proofread these words in daily writing
- to become familiar with 39 other forms of the spelling words

| Summary of Skills | Exercises |
|---|---|
| Auditory Discrimination | A |
| Proofreading | A, C, E, I |
| Visual Discrimination | C, E |
| Word Analysis | D |
| Vocabulary Development | F, H |
| Context Usage | G |
| Original Writing | I |

## PRETEST AND PROOFREADING

The Pretest identifies the words students are able to spell, as well as the words they need to learn. You may wish to use Other Word Forms when giving the Pretest. Five suggested Other Word Forms are underlined on this page.

To administer the Pretest:

**READ** each word aloud.
**SAY** the phrase containing the word.
**REPEAT** the word.

Have students correct the Pretest using the Corrected-test Procedure. They may record their scores on a personal Progress Chart (see the Teacher's Resource Book) and study misspelled words using the **S-H-A-R-P** procedure.

## OTHER WORD FORMS

This section presents related forms of the spelling words to strengthen spelling power and vocabulary knowledge.

### Enrichment Activity

Have students write Other Word Forms under the appropriate ending.

-ing -ed -s -er

# 17

**A. Pretest and Proofreading**

**B. Spelling Words and Phrases**

| | |
|---|---|
| **1. August** * | an August thunderstorm |
| **2. audience** | a noisy audience |
| **3. autumn** | colorful autumn leaves |
| **4. automobile** | inspected the automobile |
| **5. caused** * | has caused an accident |
| **6. caught** * | caught a cold |
| **7. taught** * | taught social studies |
| **8. daughter** | the oldest daughter |
| **9. naughty** | a naughty thing to do |
| **10. astronaut** | first astronaut on the moon |
| **11. aunt** * | my aunt and uncle |
| **12. often** * | as often as possible |
| **13. honest** * | an honest person |
| **14. holiday** | summer holiday |
| **15. knock** * | a knock on the door |
| **16. control** | lost control of the surfboard |
| **17. consent** | asked for consent |
| **18. content** * | was content to wait |
| **19. conduct** | will conduct the orchestra |
| **20. contract** * | signed the contract |

*Other Word Forms*

| | |
|---|---|
| Aug. | aunts |
| <u>audiences</u> | honestly, honesty |
| autumns, autumnal | holidays |
| automobiles | knocks, knocked, knocking |
| cause, causes, causing | controls, controlled |
| catch, <u>catcher</u>, catches, catching | consents, consented, consenting |
| teach, teaches, teaching, teacher | contents, contented |
| daughters | conducts, conducting, <u>conductor</u> |
| naughtier, <u>naughtiest</u> | contracts |
| <u>astronauts</u> | |

**C. Visual Warm-up** Write each word in its correct shape.

a. control
b. content
c. conduct
d. caused
e. taught
f. aunt
g. naughty
h. knock
i. August
j. astronaut
k. autumn
l. caught
m. contract
n. daughter
o. honest
p. often
q. holiday
r. automobile
s. audience
t. consent



*Modified Lesson words are asterisked.
The Modified Lesson is found in the Teacher's Resource Book.

## MEETING INDIVIDUAL NEEDS / ASSIGNMENT GUIDE

| 5-Day Plan | 3-Day Plan | Limited Spellers | Average Spellers | Advanced Spellers |
|---|---|---|---|---|
| 1 | 1 | • Pretest<br>• Progress Chart | • Pretest<br>• Progress Chart<br>• Home Activity | • Pretest<br>• Progress Chart<br>• Home Activity |
| 2 | | • Modified Lesson Visual Warm-up Ending Sounds | • Regular Lesson Visual Warm-up | • Regular Lesson Visual Warm-up |
| 3 and 4 | 2 | • Modified Lesson Vowel Puzzle Word Match Finish the Sentence | Spelling Activities | Spelling Activities<br>• Challenge Exercise |
| 5 | 3 | • Posttest<br>• Words to Learn Sheet<br>• Progress Chart | • Posttest<br>• Words to Learn Sheet<br>• Progress Chart | • Posttest<br>• Words to Learn Sheet<br>• Progress Chart |

**D. Sort Your Words** Divide the spelling words into two alphabetical lists under the correct headings. Write the words. Two words go in both lists.

| Vowel Sound Spelled with *o* | Vowel Sound Spelled with *au* |
|---|---|
| 1. astronaut | 12. astronaut |
| 2. automobile | 13. audience |
| 3. conduct | 14. August |
| 4. consent | 15. aunt |
| 5. content | 16. automobile |
| 6. contract | 17. autumn |
| 7. control | 18. caught |
| 8. holiday | 19. caused |
| 9. honest | 20. daughter |
| 10. knock | 21. naughty |
| 11. often | 22. taught |

**E. Knock Down** As you knock down each bottle, unscramble the letters and write the spelling word. Then write an Other Word Form (p. 68) beside all but one word.

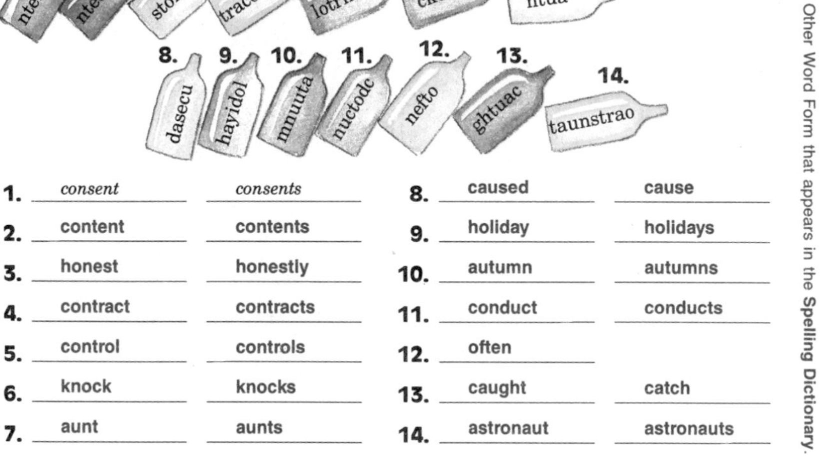


| | | | | | |
|---|---|---|---|---|---|
| 1. | *consent* | *consents* | 8. | caused | cause |
| 2. | content | contents | 9. | holiday | holidays |
| 3. | honest | honestly | 10. | autumn | autumns |
| 4. | contract | contracts | 11. | conduct | conducts |
| 5. | control | controls | 12. | often | |
| 6. | knock | knocks | 13. | caught | catch |
| 7. | aunt | aunts | 14. | astronaut | astronauts |

Accept any Other Word Form that appears in the **Spelling Dictionary**.



## OPTIONAL TEACHING PLAN

Write the five Word Group headings on the chalkboard. Ask the students to name the ten spelling words with the /ô/ sound that are spelled with **au**. Continue identifying the other Word Groups. Note the /ô/ sound of **au** in words such as **August** and the short **a** sound of **au** in **aunt**. Point out the silent consonant **k** in **knock**.

| Word Groups | | |
|---|---|---|
| /ô/: **au** words | August<br>audience<br>autumn<br>automobile<br>caused<br>caught | taught<br>daughter<br>naughty<br>astronaut<br>**automatic**<br>**sausage** |
| /ă/: **au** word | aunt | |
| /ô/ words | often<br>honest<br>holiday<br>knock | **lobster**<br>**offered**<br>**volume** |
| /ə/: **o** words | control | consent |
| /ŏ/ or /ə/ words | content<br>contract | conduct |

*Challenge Words are boldfaced.*

### Optional Activity Masters

Those using the Hardcover Pupil Edition may wish to use the Optional Activity Masters in the Teacher's Resource Book for Exercise C.

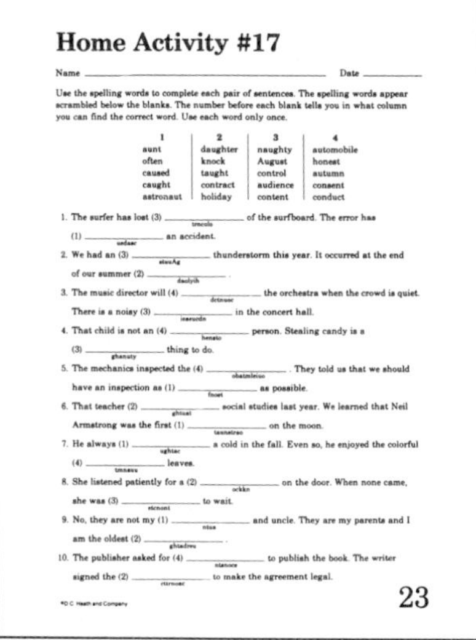

### Home Activity #17

Name ____________ Date ______

Use the spelling words to complete each pair of sentences. The spelling words appear scrambled below the blanks. The number before each blank tells you in what column you can find the correct word. Use each word only once.

| 1 | 2 | 3 | 4 |
|---|---|---|---|
| aunt | daughter | naughty | automobile |
| often | knock | August | honest |
| caused | taught | control | autumn |
| caught | contract | audience | consent |
| astronaut | holiday | content | conduct |

1. The surfer has lost (3) ________ of the surfboard. The error has (1) ________ an accident.
2. We had an (3) ________ thunderstorm this year. It occurred at the end of our summer (2) ________.
3. The music director will (4) ________ the orchestra when the crowd is quiet. There is a noisy (3) ________ in the concert hall.
4. That child is not an (4) ________ person. Stealing candy is a (3) ________ thing to do.
5. The mechanics inspected the (4) ________. They told us that we should have an inspection as (1) ________ as possible.
6. That teacher (2) ________ social studies last year. We learned that Neil Armstrong was the first (1) ________ on the moon.
7. He always (1) ________ a cold in the fall. Even so, he enjoyed the colorful (4) ________ leaves.
8. She listened patiently for a (2) ________ on the door. When none came, she was (3) ________ to wait.
9. No, they are not my (1) ________ and uncle. They are my parents and I am the oldest (2) ________.
10. The publisher asked for (4) ________ to publish the book. The writer signed the (2) ________ to make the agreement legal.

©D.C. Heath and Company 23

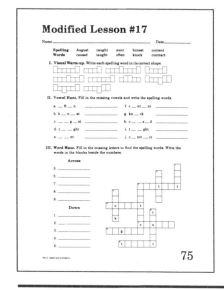

### Modified Lesson #17

Name ____________ Date ______

**Spelling Words** August caught aunt honest content caused taught often knock contract

**I. Visual Warm-up.** Write each spelling word in its correct shape.

**II. Vowel Hunt.** Fill in the missing vowels and write the spelling words.

a. __ ft __ n ________ f. c __ nt __ nt ________
b. h __ n __ st ________ g. kn __ ck ________
c. __ __ g __ st ________ h. c __ __ s __ d ________
d. c __ __ ght ________ i. t __ __ ght ________
e. __ __ nt ________ j. c __ ntr __ ct ________

**III. Word Maze.** Fill in the missing letters to find the spelling words. Write the words in the blanks beside the numbers.

Across: 3. ____ 5. ____ 7. ____ 8. ____ 9. ____
Down: 1. ____ 2. ____ 3. ____ 4. ____ 6. ____

©D.C. Heath and Company 75

### Modified Lesson #17 *(continued)*

Name ____________ Date ______

**Spelling Words** August caught aunt honest content caused taught often knock contract

**IV. Word Parts.** Write the spelling words that have the word parts below. A word may be used more than once.

a. au words: ________
b. con words: ________
c. kn word: ________
d. tent word: ________
e. ct word: ________
f. est word: ________
g. ght words: ________
h. ed word: ________
i. of word: ________
j. ck word: ________

**V. Sentence Sense.** Write each spelling word in the correct sentence.

**Words** August caught aunt honest content

a. Never swim during an ________ thunderstorm.
b. Abraham Lincoln was an ________ person.
c. My ________ and uncle visited us last week.
d. Last winter I ________ a cold.
e. Each child was ________ to wait for a turn.

**Words** caused taught often knock contract

f. My sister once ________ social studies.
g. Their carelessness has ________ an accident.
h. We exercise as ________ as possible.
i. The baseball player signed the ________.
j. I heard a ________ on the door.

76 ©D.C. Heath and Company

**Home Activity**
A weekly homework assignment

**Modified Lesson**
An alternative lesson for limited spellers

*(The Answer Key can be found in the Teacher's Resource Book.)*

## LESSON 17 CONTINUED

### Challenge Exercise #17

Name ____________________ Date __________

**Word Watch.** Originally the word *naughty* meant "good for nothing." In 1621, the Pilgrims spoke of the naughty canoes of the Indians because the crafts overturned easily. Years later, the word *naughty* came to mean "evil." Those thought to be witches and wizards were considered naughty people. Only recently has the word *naughty* softened in meaning to describe the playful actions of an impish child.

**Word Analogies.** Decide on the relationship that exists between the first pair of words. Using the Other Word Forms on page 68, find a word that completes the second pair of words and establishes the same relationship.

1. *nephews* is to *uncles* as *nieces* is to ______
2. *director* is to *cast* as ______ is to *orchestra*
3. *artist* is to *painter* as ______ is to *instructor*
4. *disagreeing* is to *agreeing* as *refusing* is to ______
5. *water* is to *steamboats* as *gasoline* is to ______

**Challenge Words Student Activity**

Use the challenge words below to complete the paragraph.

**automatic** **volume** **lobster** **offered** **sausage**

I shopped early because the ______ of shoppers rises near noon. As I left the market, the ______ door stuck. My grocery bag ripped and the frozen ______ rolled across the floor. Then my live ______ crawled under a counter! Laughing shoppers ______ to help me catch it.

**Working With Words: Student Writing Activity**

Use as many Other Word Forms as you can from page 68 to write a paragraph to be placed in the school handbook. Write about the many ways your school is important to you and your schoolmates.



129

### Challenge Exercise

Additional activities for advanced spellers

**Spelling Words**

| | | | |
|---|---|---|---|
| August | audience | autumn | automobile |
| caused | caught | taught | daughter |
| naughty | astronaut | aunt | often |
| honest | holiday | knock | control |
| consent | content | conduct | contract |

**F. Generally Speaking** Write each spelling word for the group it best fits.

1. vehicle, car, **automobile**
2. seized, trapped, **caught**
3. tap, rap, **knock**
4. youngster, girl, **daughter**
5. rest, vacation, **holiday**
6. pleased, happy, **content**
7. agreement, document, **contract**
8. lead, organize, **conduct**
9. brought about, made happen, **caused**
10. power, command, **control**
11. June, July, **August**
12. instructed, informed, **taught**
13. OK, agree, **consent**
14. cousin, uncle, **aunt**
15. crew member, pilot, **astronaut**
16. spring, summer, **autumn**
17. frequently, usually, **often**
18. truthful, fair, **honest**
19. bad, mean, **naughty**
20. listeners, viewers, **audience**



### CONTROLLED DICTATION (Optional)

These dictation sentences provide maintenance for spelling words previously taught and practice for words currently being studied. Dictation should be administered on Day 4. The teacher or another student may dictate the sentences. Be sure to dictate all marks of punctuation. Challenge Word sentences are preceded by an asterisk.

1. **Honest** workers have never **caused** a problem.
2. Last **autumn** I gave him my **consent** to **conduct** the course.
3. Before the space mission in **August**, the **astronaut** spent the **holiday** at hom
4. **Often** my **aunt** is **content** to drive her **automobile**.
5. My **daughter caught** the **naughty** puppy as it ran through the **audience**.
6. Weren't you **taught** to **knock** before entering a room?
7. They may protest but, by **contract**, you **control** oil prices.

*8. It's loud because the **automatic volume** control is stuck.
*9. The cook **offered** us **lobster** and **sausage**.

**G. Using Other Word Forms** Write the Other Word Form that completes each sentence.

Base Words: catch(er) conduct(or) astronaut(s) audience(s) naughty(est)

1. People who work in outer space are called astronauts.
2. A person who plays behind home plate is a catcher.
3. Different groups of people who attend shows are called audiences.
4. The child who misbehaves the most is the naughtiest.
5. A person who leads a band is called a conductor.

**H. Challenge Words** Write the Challenge Word that completes each analogy.

| automatic | sausage | lobster | offered | volume |
|---|---|---|---|---|

1. **vegetable** is to **carrot** as **meat** is to sausage
2. **heat** is to **temperature** as **noise** is to volume
3. **accept** is to **accepted** as **offer** is to offered
4. **fresh water** is to **crayfish** as **salt water** is to lobster
5. **handmade** is to **machine-made** as **manual** is to automatic

**I. Spelling and Writing** Write each set of words in a sentence. You may use Other Word Forms. Proofread your work.

1. astronaut – control – August
2. audience – conduct – often
3. contract – aunt – automobile
4. honest – caused – knock
5. content – taught – daughter
6. consent – catcher – holiday
7. autumn – naughty – caught
8. automatic – volume – audiences
9. sausage – lobster – offered

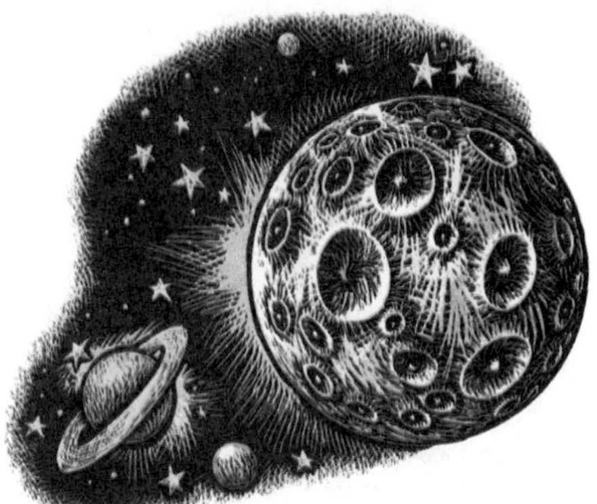

Working Words in Spelling

## USING OTHER WORD FORMS

Vocabulary is expanded through the use of other forms of basic spelling words. Emphasis is on the relationship of syntax to suffix choices. The following generalizations apply to the Other Word Forms used in Exercise G.

### Spelling Rule

Forming plurals

Add **s** to most nouns to form plurals. **(astronaut, astronauts)**

Adding suffixes to words ending in **y**

When adding a suffix to words ending in consonant-**y**, change the **y** to **i**, unless the suffix begins with **i**. **(naughty, naughtiest)**

## POSTTEST AND PROOFREADING

Follow the same testing procedures used in the Pretest, although you may wish to correct the tests yourself. Have students write any misspelled words on the Words to Learn Sheet and record spelling success on the Progress Chart.

## THE SPELLING-WRITING LINK

**Purpose** This activity helps students effectively transfer lesson words into their daily writing. Students (a) determine a relationship among three given words and (b) write a complete sentence.

**Procedure** On the chalkboard, write the three words from line 1 (**astronaut, control, August**) and the Other Word Forms (**astronauts, controls, controlled**). Have students read the words and think of ways the three words might be related. Have them think of things or people the words suggest. Ask students to create sentences using some of their ideas. You can provide an example sentence: **By August, the astronaut could control the spacecraft.**

**Practice** Tell students to write original sentences using the word sets and to proofread their work. You may want them to circle the lesson words.

LESSON
# 18
REVIEW

## OBJECTIVES

- to review the spelling of the 100 words studied in Lessons 13-17
- to promote the use of other forms of the 100 spelling words
- to apply high-utility generalizations for the addition of suffixes

| Summary of Skills | Exercises |
|---|---|
| Vocabulary Development | A |
| Word Analysis | B |
| Context Usage | C |
| Dictionary Skills | D |

## REVIEW OF LESSONS 13-17

The goal of the review exercises is to expand each student's spelling power. The one hundred spelling words studied in the five preceding lessons are presented in challenging formats where the focus is shifted from the spelling words to the Other Word Forms.

## WORD REVIEW PROCEDURE

Students are encouraged to use this abbreviated version of the **S-H-A-R-P** procedure when reviewing the spelling words at the top of each review page.

**LOOK** at each word.
**SAY** the word to yourself.
**THINK** about the letters that spell the word.

18

REVIEW

### REVIEWING LESSONS 13-17

| ■ | ★ | ▲ | ◆ | ● |
|---|---|---|---|---|
| swimming | beginning | quickly | split | skinned |
| shopping | dropped | shovel | blossom | quarter |
| outline | trouble | southern | couldn't | wouldn't |
| branches | brass | grasp | matches | hasn't |
| automobile | knock | astronaut | holiday | August |

**A. Word Clues** Write the spelling word that goes with each clue. The shape tells you in what column you can find the spelling word. Then write an Other Word Form for each spelling word.

| Word Clues | Spelling Words | Other Word Forms |
|---|---|---|
| 1. a firm hold ▲ | grasp | grasps |
| 2. injured by scrapping ● | skinned | skin |
| 3. a pounding noise ★ | knock | knocks |
| 4. a flower ◆ | blossom | blossoms |
| 5. to trace an object ■ | outline | outlines |
| 6. the eighth month ● | August | Aug. |
| 7. rapidly ▲ | quickly | quick |
| 8. let fall ★ | dropped | drop |
| 9. a car ■ | automobile | automobiles |
| 10. used to light an oven ◆ | matches | match |
| 11. buying things ■ | shopping | shop |
| 12. from the south ▲ | southern | south |
| 13. starting ★ | beginning | begin |
| 14. a tool for digging a hole ▲ | shovel | shoveled |
| 15. twenty-five cents ● | quarter | quartered |
| 16. to break apart ◆ | split | splitting |
| 17. difficulty ★ | trouble | troubles |
| 18. a spacecraft's crew member ▲ | astronaut | astronauts |
| 19. limbs of a tree ■ | branches | branch |
| 20. a copper and zinc alloy ★ | brass | brasses |
| 21. a day of celebration ◆ | holiday | holidays |
| 22. moving through the water ■ | swimming | swim |

23. From the list above, write the three contractions and their meanings.

a. couldn't — could not
b. hasn't — has not
c. wouldn't — would not

Accept any Other Word Form that appears in the Spelling Dictionary.

72 Review—Lesson 18

## MEETING INDIVIDUAL NEEDS / ASSIGNMENT GUIDE

| 5-Day Plan | 3-Day Plan | Limited Spellers | Average Spellers | Advanced Spellers |
|---|---|---|---|---|
| 1 and 2 | 1 | • Modified Lesson Visual Warm-up Word Parts | • Regular Lesson Spelling Activities<br>• Home Activity | • Regular Lesson Spelling Activities<br>• Home Activity |
| 3 and 4 | 2 | • Modified Lesson Vowel Puzzle Word Match Finish the Sentence | • Regular Lesson Spelling Activities<br>• Proofreading Exercise(s) | • Regular Lesson Spelling Activities<br>• Proofreading Exercise(s)<br>• Challenge Word Review |
| 5 | 3 | • Test Modified Lesson Words<br>• Words to Learn Sheet | • Review Test or Standardized-format Test<br>• Words to Learn Sheet | • Review Test or Standardized-format Test<br>• Words to Learn Sheet |

| wicked | printing | prince | pitcher | kitchen |
|---|---|---|---|---|
| problem | quart | dollar | bottom | copper |
| product | govern | dozen | cousin | household |
| thankful | fact | catcher | acts | jacket |
| control | conduct | honest | contract | content |

**B. Word Building** Add word parts to each spelling word or its base word to make Other Word Forms. Write the words.

| Spelling Words | *s* or *es* | *ed* | *ing* |
|---|---|---|---|
| Example: **play** | *plays* | *played* | *playing* |
| **1.** problem | problems | | |
| **2.** product | products | | |
| **3.** printing | prints | printed | |
| **4.** control | controls | controlled | controlling |
| **5.** fact | facts | | |
| **6.** govern | governs | governed | governing |
| **7.** quart | quarts | | |
| **8.** dozen | dozens | | |
| **9.** cousin | cousins | | |
| **10.** content | contents | contented | |
| **11.** contract | contracts | contracted | contracting |
| **12.** jacket | jackets | | |
| **13.** kitchen | kitchens | | |
| **14.** household | households | | |
| **15.** acts | | acted | acting |
| **16.** dollar | dollars | | |
| **17.** catcher | catches | | catching |
| **18.** bottom | bottoms | | |
| **19.** pitcher | pitches | pitched | pitching |
| **20.** conduct | conducts | conducted | conducting |

Add *ly* or *y* to each spelling word to write Other Word Forms.

**21.** wicked wickedly
**22.** thankful thankfully
**23.** prince princely
**24.** honest honestly
**25.** copper coppery

REVIEW



REVIEW

## CREATIVE WRITING

**(An optional writing activity)**

**Recipe for Writing:** This imaginative writing activity uses spelling words and Other Word Forms studied in Lessons 13-17.

COMBINE:
1 dozen copper and brass quart pitchers
1 flooded kitchen
1 wicked prince
1 troubled aunt
fifteen balloons

SEASON with your own original ideas and COOK UP a story with a unique FLAVOR. Proofread before SERVING.

The RECIPE words appear in the following lessons.

| Lesson | Words |
|---|---|
| 13 | wicked, prince, fifteen, pitchers, kitchen |
| 14 | copper, quart, balloons |
| 15 | flooded, dozen, troubled |
| 16 | brass |
| 17 | aunt |

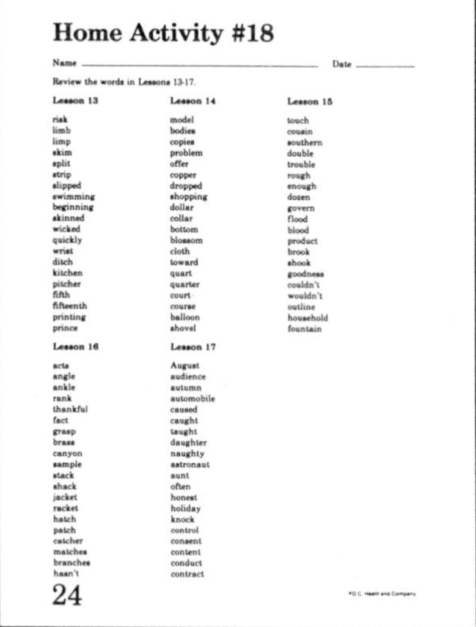

# Home Activity #18

Name ____________ Date ______

Review the words in Lessons 13-17.

| Lesson 13 | Lesson 14 | Lesson 15 |
|---|---|---|
| risk | model | touch |
| limb | bodies | cousin |
| limp | copies | southern |
| skim | problem | double |
| split | offer | trouble |
| strip | copper | rough |
| slipped | dropped | enough |
| swimming | shopping | dozen |
| beginning | dollar | govern |
| skinned | collar | flood |
| wicked | bottom | blood |
| quickly | blossom | product |
| wrist | cloth | brook |
| ditch | toward | shook |
| kitchen | quart | goodness |
| pitcher | quarter | couldn't |
| fifth | court | wouldn't |
| fifteenth | course | outline |
| printing | balloon | household |
| prince | shovel | fountain |

| Lesson 16 | Lesson 17 |
|---|---|
| acts | August |
| angle | audience |
| ankle | autumn |
| rank | automobile |
| thankful | caused |
| fact | caught |
| grasp | taught |
| brass | daughter |
| canyon | naughty |
| sample | astronaut |
| stack | aunt |
| shack | often |
| jacket | honest |
| racket | holiday |
| hatch | knock |
| patch | control |
| catcher | consent |
| matches | content |
| branches | conduct |
| hasn't | contract |

24



# Modified Lesson #18

Name ____________ Date ______

| Other Word Forms | risky | quarts | troubles | thankfully | honesty |
|---|---|---|---|---|---|
| | printer | offered | outlined | catching | knocking |

I. **Visual Warm-up.** Write each Other Word Form in its correct shape.

II. **Vowel Hunt.** Fill in the missing vowels and write the Other Word Forms.

a. q __ __ rts ______
b. __ __ tl __ n __ d ______
c. kn __ ck __ ng ______
d. h __ n __ st __ ______
e. th __ nkf __ ll __ ______
f. r __ sk __ ______
g. __ ff __ r __ d ______
h. pr __ nt __ r ______
i. tr __ __ bl __ s ______
j. c __ tch __ ng ______

III. **Word Maze.** Fill in the missing letters to find the Other Word Forms. Write the words in the blanks beside the numbers.

Across
1. ______
5. ______
7. ______
10. ______

Down
2. ______
3. ______
4. ______
6. ______
8. ______
9. ______



77

## Modified Lesson #18 *(continued)*

Name ____________ Date ______

| Other Word Forms | risky | quarts | troubles | thankfully | honesty |
|---|---|---|---|---|---|
| | printer | offered | outlined | catching | knocking |

IV. **Word Parts.** Write the Other Word Forms that have the word parts below. A word may be used more than once.

a. word ending in fully: ______
b. words ending in s: ______, ______, ______
c. ing words: ______, ______
d. ed words: ______, ______
e. er words: ______, ______
f. kn word: ______
g. qu word: ______
h. words ending in y: ______, ______, ______
i. ck word: ______
j. th word: ______

V. **Sentence Sense.** Write each Other Word Form in the correct sentence.

**Words** risky quarts troubles thankfully honesty

a. Some say that ______ is the best policy.
b. Swinging on a trapeze can be very ______
c. There are four ______ in one gallon.
d. The winner accepted the prize ______
e. May all your ______ be problems you can handle.

**Words** printer offered outlined catching knocking

f. She was ______ a new job.
g. We are ______ many fish with the new bait.
h. The ______ was covered with black ink.
i. Who's ______ on the door?
j. I ______ the science chapter.

78



## Home Activity

A weekly homework assignment

## Modified Lesson

An alternative lesson for limited spellers

*(The Answer Key can be found in the Teacher's Resource Book.)*

# LESSON 18 CONTINUED

## Challenge Word Review

The Challenge Words from the previous five lessons are listed below if you wish to review the Challenge Words with your more advanced students.

1. innumerable
2. ridges
3. lizards
4. vision
5. whistle
6. forgotten
7. operated
8. property
9. softened
10. youngster
11. powerfully
12. uncomfortable
13. compound
14. mumble
15. luckily
16. aspect
17. attaching
18. attacking
19. calendar
20. antenna
21. automatic
22. sausage
23. lobster
24. offered
25. volume

| ■ | ★ | ▲ | ◆ | ○ |
|---|---|---|---|---|
| risk | ditch | slipped | strip | wrist |
| court | collar | offer | course | toward |
| shook | rough | flood | brook | fountain |
| rank | shack | ankle | racket | canyon |
| consent | aunt | audience | naughty | caused |

REVIEW

**C. Raising Questions** Complete each question by writing Other Word Forms or the spelling words. The shape tells you in what column you can find the spelling word. Use each word or its Other Word Form only once. If you need help, use the **Spelling Dictionary**.

1. Were the players holding tennis ◆ **rackets** when they ▲ **slipped** and fell on the ice?
2. Did your uncles and ★ **aunts** walk ○ **toward** the shore?
3. Why are you ■ **risking** broken ▲ **ankles** and ○ **wrists**?
4. Is the water ▲ **flooding** the ★ **ditch *or* ditches**?
5. Were the ★ **shacks** ★ **roughly** built?
6. Why do the ◆ **naughty** children ○ **cause** so many problems?
7. Has the tailor ◆ **stripped** the ★ **collars** from the coats?
8. Have most ▲ **audiences** ■ **ranked** the play a success?
9. Are the ■ **courts** ▲ **offering** more help to people?
10. Can nature's ○ **fountains** be found in most ○ **canyons**?
11. How many golf ◆ **courses** include small ◆ **brooks** and streams near the greens?
12. Did you ■ **shake** his hand until he ■ **consented** to join the club?



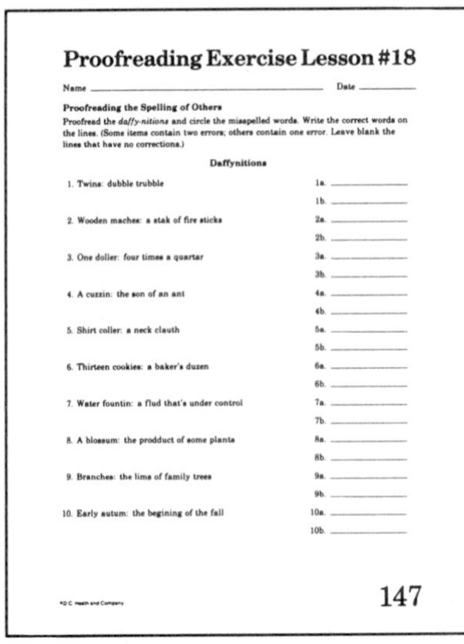

## Proofreading Exercise Lesson #18

Name ______________ Date ________

**Proofreading the Spelling of Others**

Proofread the *daffy-nitions* and circle the misspelled words. Write the correct words on the lines. (Some items contain two errors; others contain one error. Leave blank the lines that have no corrections.)

**Daffynitions**

1. Twins: dubble trubble — 1a. ______ 1b. ______
2. Wooden maches: a stak of fire sticks — 2a. ______ 2b. ______
3. One doller: four times a quartar — 3a. ______ 3b. ______
4. A cuzzin: the son of an ant — 4a. ______ 4b. ______
5. Shirt coller: a neck clauth — 5a. ______ 5b. ______
6. Thirteen cookies: a baker's duzen — 6a. ______ 6b. ______
7. Water fountin: a flud that's under control — 7a. ______ 7b. ______
8. A blossum: the prodduct of some plants — 8a. ______ 8b. ______
9. Branches: the lims of family trees — 9a. ______ 9b. ______
10. Early autum: the begining of the fall — 10a. ______ 10b. ______

©D.C. Heath and Company

147

**Proofreading Exercise**

## Half-year Proofreading Review

Name ______________ Date ________

**Directions:** Circle the misspelled word in each group. Write each word correctly on the line.

| | | | | | |
|---|---|---|---|---|---|
| 1. | naughty | loan | modle | waist | 1. ______ |
| 2. | filing | greatest | stoop | surprizes | 2. ______ |
| 3. | audience | waist | coward | preech | 3. ______ |
| 4. | sailer | reason | shack | remain | 4. ______ |
| 5. | scowl | fact | hadn't | dubble | 5. ______ |
| 6. | offer | nineth | intend | knives | 6. ______ |
| 7. | really | excite | juisy | shovel | 7. ______ |
| 8. | burgler | square | control | collar | 8. ______ |
| 9. | jacket | beginning | peice | ideal | 9. ______ |
| 10. | whole | dryed | lodge | wished | 10. ______ |
| 11. | merchant | baite | American | doesn't | 11. ______ |
| 12. | troubel | motor | cloth | blouse | 12. ______ |
| 13. | straight | choose | orchard | conduct | 13. ______ |
| 14. | kwarter | rare | smooth | chosen | 14. ______ |
| 15. | beeten | quickly | matches | entered | 15. ______ |
| 16. | forever | ordered | replied | baloon | 16. ______ |
| 17. | seashore | corntract | invent | golf | 17. ______ |
| 18. | court | forbid | mayer | hasn't | 18. ______ |
| 19. | usually | sour | enough | Haloween | 19. ______ |
| 20. | sleave | scarce | view | knock | 20. ______ |
| 21. | dozin | temper | moss | scorn | 21. ______ |
| 22. | bore | forward | strip | purhaps | 22. ______ |
| 23. | skinned | shurely | braid | fountain | 23. ______ |
| 24. | trout | divide | catcher | amuze | 24. ______ |
| 25. | escape | berst | eastern | powder | 25. ______ |
| 26. | could'nt | decide | wrist | needle | 26. ______ |
| 27. | rough | mistake | taught | ankel | 27. ______ |
| 28. | opperate | pitcher | break | spray | 28. ______ |
| 29. | rifle | outline | montain | easy | 29. ______ |
| 30. | daughter | angle | clurk | fifteenth | 30. ______ |

148

©D.C. Heath and Company

**Half-year Proofreading Review**

| angle | caught | enough | limb | sample |
|---|---|---|---|---|
| autumn | cloth | fifteenth | limp | skim |
| balloon | copies | fifth | model | stack |
| blood | daughter | goodness | often | taught |
| bodies | double | hatch | patch | touch |

**D. Alphabetical Order** Find the spelling word that comes alphabetically right *before* each word below. Write the spelling word and an Other Word Form for all but two spelling words.

| | Before | Spelling Words | Other Word Forms |
|---|---|---|---|
| **1.** | headquarters | *h a t c h* | hatches |
| **2.** | cause | c a u g h t | catch |
| **3.** | downstairs | d o u b l e | doubled |
| **4.** | day | d a u g h t e r | daughters |
| **5.** | enter | e n o u g h | |
| **6.** | limp | l i m b | limbs |
| **7.** | fifth | f i f t e e n t h | fifteen |
| **8.** | pay | p a t c h | patches |
| **9.** | teach | t a u g h t | teach |
| **10.** | moment | m o d e l | models |
| **11.** | body | b o d i e s | body |
| **12.** | stalk | s t a c k | stacks |
| **13.** | awaken | a u t u m n | autumns |
| **14.** | sleeve | s k i m | skimmed |
| **15.** | cozy | c o p i e s | copy |
| **16.** | coast | c l o t h | cloths |
| **17.** | flashlight | f i f t h | five |
| **18.** | tough | t o u c h | touches |
| **19.** | sausage | s a m p l e | samples |
| **20.** | olive | o f t e n | |
| **21.** | government | g o o d n e s s | good |
| **22.** | banner | b a l l o o n | balloons |
| **23.** | liquid | l i m p | limps |
| **24.** | boast | b l o o d | bloody |
| **25.** | arch | a n g l e | angles |

REVIEW

Accept any Other Word Form that appears in the **Spelling Dictionary.**



## Review Test: Lesson 18

Name ______________________ Date ____________

**Directions:** Read each sentence. Select the word with the correct spelling to complete each sentence. Fill in the correct letter in the answer column.

1. We found a sawed-off tree ______ . A. limm C. limb B. lim D. lem
2. Dad needs a short ______ of tape. A. stripe C. stirip B. stripp D. strip
3. It was ______ to rain. A. begining C. beggining B. beginning D. biginning
4. We need to dig a ______ . A. ditch C. ditche B. dich D. ditsh
5. Today is the ______ of the month. A. fiftenth C. fiveteenth B. fiveteenth D. fifteenth
6. Oceans are large ______ of water. A. boddies C. bodys B. bodies D. boddys
7. The metals are gold and ______ . A. coper C. copper B. coppor D. copor
8. Fix your turned-up ______ . A. callar C. coller B. caller D. collar
9. We walked ______ the shore. A. tored C. toward B. toared D. towerd
10. The pilots changed their ______ . A. course C. coure B. corse D. coarse
11. No one wrote to my ______ . A. couzin C. cusin B. cuzzin D. cousin
12. The table has a ______ surface. A. ruff C. rough B. rouff D. rufe
13. I noticed several drops of ______ . A. blod C. blud B. blood D. bloud
14. We ______ them fiercely. A. shouk C. shoke B. shook D. shoock
15. The artist traced an ______ . A. outlign C. outlien B. outlin D. outline
16. The lines form a wide ______ . A. angal C. angul B. angle D. angel
17. She replied as a matter of ______ . A. fakt C. fact B. fack D. facked
18. I saw a ______ of their work. A. sample C. sampple B. sampel D. sampul
19. She used a wooden tennis ______ . A. raket C. rackette B. racket D. rackit
20. Close the book of ______ . A. maches C. macthes B. machtes D. matches
21. Actors don't like a noisy ______ . A. oddience C. audience B. audiants D. audiance
22. I wonder how I ______ a cold. A. caught C. cought B. caght D. caut
23. My ______ and uncle arrived early. A. ant C. aunt B. arent D. arnt
24. There was a ______ on the door. A. nok C. knok B. nock D. knock
25. Who will ______ the orchestra? A. cornduct C. conduct B. condduct D. conduck

Answer Column: 1.–25. A B C D

156 ©D.C. Heath and Company

### Standardized-format Test

## Half-year Test

Name ______________________ Date ____________

**Directions:** Look at each group of words. Find the one word that is spelled correctly. Fill in the correct space in the answer column.

| | A | B | C | D |
|---|---|---|---|---|
| 1. | greatest | gratest | graitest | gratest |
| 2. | perparing | prepairing | preparring | preparing |
| 3. | reched | reached | reiched | reashed |
| 4. | beatten | beaten | beeten | beatin |
| 5. | linning | lineing | lining | lyning |
| 6. | knives | knifes | nives | nifes |
| 7. | doen't | dont | do'nt | don't |
| 8. | nothurn | northen | nothern | northern |
| 9. | aren't | are'nt | arent | arn't |
| 10. | junier | juniar | junior | juinor |
| 11. | daly | daily | dailey | daley |
| 12. | strayt | straeght | straight | straght |
| 13. | needle | neidle | neadle | kneadle |
| 14. | allright | alrite | all rite | all right |
| 15. | surprises | surprizes | serprises | serprizes |
| 16. | lawdge | lodge | lorge | lordge |
| 17. | pronounse | prononce | pronownse | pronounce |
| 18. | blouss | blause | blouse | blous |
| 19. | sentence | sentance | santence | sentince |
| 20. | perfume | purfume | perfum | perfiume |
| 21. | picher | pitcher | pitsher | pichure |
| 22. | wriste | riste | rist | wrist |
| 23. | corse | cours | course | coorse |
| 24. | ofer | offer | orfer | aufer |
| 25. | cousin | couzin | cuzzin | cousine |
| 26. | guvern | govin | goven | govern |
| 27. | maches | matshes | matches | matchs |
| 28. | canyin | cannion | canyon | canyen |
| 29. | daughter | dawter | daghter | doughter |
| 30. | corntract | contract | contrakt | contracte |

Answer Column: 1.–30. A B C D

©D.C. Heath and Company 157

### Half-year Standardized-format Test

## REVIEW TEST

Twenty-five words, selected randomly from the five spelling lists, constitute the test and are listed with the appropriate phrases. Follow the same testing procedure used to administer the weekly Pretest and Posttest. Have students write any misspelled words on the Words to Learn Sheet. As an alternative testing option, you may wish to use the Standardized-format Test for this Review Lesson, found in the Teacher's Resource Book.

REVIEW

### Test Words and Phrases

1. limb — a sawed-off tree **limb**
2. strip — a short **strip** of tape
3. beginning — **beginning** to rain
4. ditch — to dig a **ditch**
5. fifteenth — the **fifteenth** of the month
6. bodies — large **bodies** of water
7. copper — gold and **copper**
8. collar — turned-up **collar**
9. toward — walked **toward** the shore
10. course — changed their **course**
11. cousin — wrote to my **cousin**
12. rough — a **rough** surface
13. blood — several drops of **blood**
14. shook — **shook** them fiercely
15. outline — traced an **outline**
16. angle — a wide **angle**
17. fact — as a matter of **fact**
18. sample — a **sample** of their work
19. racket — wooden tennis **racket**
20. matches — book of **matches**
21. audience — a noisy **audience**
22. caught — **caught** a cold
23. aunt — my **aunt** and uncle
24. knock — a **knock** on the door
25. conduct — will **conduct** the orchestra

LESSON

# 19

## OBJECTIVES

- to spell 20 high-frequency words with the /ā/ and /ûr/
- to proofread these words in daily writing
- to become familiar with 35 other forms of the spelling words

| Summary of Skills | Exercises |
|---|---|
| Auditory Discrimination | A |
| Proofreading | A, C, H |
| Visual Discrimination | C |
| Word Analysis | D |
| Dictionary Skills | E |
| Context Usage | F, G |
| Original Writing | H |

## PRETEST AND PROOFREADING

The Pretest identifies the words students are able to spell, as well as the words they need to learn. You may wish to use Other Word Forms when giving the Pretest. Five suggested Other Word Forms are underlined on this page.

To administer the Pretest:

**READ** each word aloud.
**SAY** the phrase containing the word.
**REPEAT** the word.

Have students correct the Pretest using the Corrected-test Procedure. They may record their scores on a personal Progress Chart (see the Teacher's Resource Book) and study misspelled words using the **S-H-A-R-P** procedure.

## OTHER WORD FORMS

This section presents related forms of the spelling words to strengthen spelling power and vocabulary knowledge.

### Enrichment Activity

Have students write Other Word Forms under the appropriate heading.

long **a** (**a-e** pattern)   long **a** (**a**)
long **a** (**ay**)   /**ûr**/



# 19

**A. Pretest and Proofreading**

**B. Spelling Words and Phrases**

| | |
|---|---|
| **1. parade** | followed the parade |
| **2. safety** | wore safety glasses |
| **3. basement*** | went into the basement |
| **4. grapefruit** | an apple and a grapefruit |
| **5. savings*** | savings in the bank |
| **6. changing*** | changing the flat tire |
| **7. ashamed** | ashamed to tell |
| **8. apron** | a red-checked apron |
| **9. April*** | April showers |
| **10. navy*** | navy blue sweater |
| **11. famous** | famous last words |
| **12. favor** | did us a favor |
| **13. ladies** | ladies and gentlemen |
| **14. nature*** | the world of nature |
| **15. nation*** | traveled across the nation |
| **16. station** | turned to another station |
| **17. plantation** | southern plantation |
| **18. information*** | dialed for information |
| **19. betray*** | to betray a friend |
| **20. worse*** | worse than before |

*Other Word Forms*

| | |
|---|---|
| paraded, parading, parades | fame |
| safe, safest, safely | favored, favorite |
| basements | lady |
| grapefruits | natures, natural |
| save, saving | national |
| change, changed, changes | stations, stationed |
| shame, ashamedly | plantations |
| aprons | inform, informed informing, informer |
| Apr. | betrayed, betrayal |
| navies | worst |

**C. Visual Warm-up** Write each word in its correct shape.

a. nature
b. nation
c. safety
d. basement
e. grapefruit
f. April
g. station
h. ladies
i. favor
j. plantation
k. apron
l. changing
m. ashamed
n. savings
o. parade
p. navy
q. betray
r. information
s. famous
t. worse

*Modified Lesson words are asterisked.
The Modified Lesson is found in the Teacher's Resource Book.



## MEETING INDIVIDUAL NEEDS / ASSIGNMENT GUIDE

| 5-Day Plan | 3-Day Plan | Limited Spellers | Average Spellers | Advanced Spellers |
|---|---|---|---|---|
| 1 | 1 | • Pretest<br>• Progress Chart | • Pretest<br>• Progress Chart<br>• Home Activity | • Pretest<br>• Progress Chart<br>• Home Activity |
| 2 | | • Modified Lesson Visual Warm-up Ending Sounds | • Regular Lesson Visual Warm-up | • Regular Lesson Visual Warm-up |
| 3 and 4 | 2 | • Modified Lesson Vowel Puzzle Word Match Finish the Sentence | Spelling Activities | Spelling Activities<br>• Challenge Exercise |
| 5 | 3 | • Posttest<br>• Words to Learn Sheet<br>• Progress Chart | • Posttest<br>• Words to Learn Sheet<br>• Progress Chart | • Posttest<br>• Words to Learn Sheet<br>• Progress Chart |

**D. Add and Subtract** Complete each puzzle to find a spelling word. Write the word.

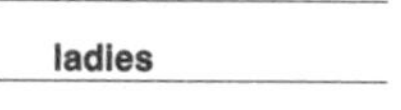

1. plant + station − st = a large farm — plantation
2. lad + tries − tr = women — ladies
3. favorite − ite = an act of kindness — favor
4. as + ham + bed − b = feeling guilt — ashamed
5. c + hang + ring − r = making different — changing
6. in + form + station − st = facts and figures — information
7. be + stray − s = double-cross — betray
8. sad + feet + by − bed = freedom from danger — safety
9. gray − y + pen − n + fruit = a citrus fruit — grapefruit
10. slave + kings − elks = money in the bank — savings
11. no + station − ost = a country — nation
12. tape + rile − tee = a month — April
13. way + horse − hay = less good — worse
14. fame + to + us − et = well-known — famous
15. part + ade − t = a grand march — parade
16. state + lion − el = a train stop — station
17. signature − sig = outdoor world — nature
18. cap + round − cud = a cook's protective garment — apron
19. nap + wavy − paw = a branch of the armed forces — navy
20. base + statement − state = cellar — basement

## OPTIONAL TEACHING PLAN

Write the four Word Group headings on the chalkboard. Ask the students to name the seven spelling words with the long **a** sound that follow the **a-e** pattern. Write the words on the chalkboard as the students say them. Continue identifying the other Word Groups. Note that the long **a** sound is spelled with the **a-e** pattern in some words, with **a** in some words, and with **ay** in **betray**.

| Word Groups | | |
|---|---|---|
| /ā/: **a-e** pattern | parade<br>safety<br>basement<br>grapefruit | changing<br>ashamed<br>savings<br>**nickname** |
| /ā/: **a** words | apron<br>April<br>navy<br>famous<br>favor<br>ladies<br>nature | nation<br>station<br>plantation<br>information<br>**bathing**<br>**crater**<br>**decoration** |
| /ā/: **ay** and **ey** words | betray | **prey** |
| /ûr/ word | worse | |

*Challenge Words are boldfaced.*

### Optional Activity Masters

Those using the Hardcover Pupil Edition may wish to use the Optional Activity Master in the Teacher's Resource Book for Exercise C.

**Home Activity #19** (25)

**Modified Lesson #19** (79)

**Modified Lesson #19** *(continued)* (80)

### Home Activity

A weekly homework assignment

### Modified Lesson

An alternative lesson for limited spellers

*(The Answer Key can be found in the Teacher's Resource Book.)*

# LESSON 19 CONTINUED

### Challenge Exercise #19

Name________________ Date________

**Word Watch.** The word *apron* is the result of a language error. Like the word *napkin*, *apron* had its beginning in the French word *nape*, meaning "tablecloth." The French word *naperon*, meaning "a cook's protective cloth," was adopted by the English, who called the covering "a napron." By some error, the *n* was joined with the *a*, and the object became "an apron." Since its unusual birth, the protective garment for those who work around food has continued to be known as "an apron."

**Word Analogies.** Decide on the relationship that exists between the first pair of words. Using the Other Word Forms on page 76, find a word that completes the second pair of words and establishes the same relationship.

1. *cellars* is to *attics* as ________ is to *lofts*
2. *hazardous* is to *secure* as *dangerous* is to ________
3. *mayor* is to *local* as *president* is to ________
4. *airports* is to *jets* as ________ is to *trains*
5. *running* is to *marathons* as *marching* is to ________

**Challenge Words Student Activity**
Write the correct challenge word from below to complete each sentence.

**crater decoration bathing nickname prey**

1. My brother's ________ is "The Pest."
2. Steam rose from the volcano's huge ________ .
3. I love ________ in icy mountain streams.
4. The baby rabbit would be easy ________ for the fox.
5. The only ________ on the table was a big red candle.

**Working With Words: Student Writing Activity**
Use as many Other Word Forms as you can from page 76 to write a tall tale about an unusual being or creature. Remember to exaggerate your ideas. (Sample idea: Gusher George stuck his index finger deep into the soil, and a *natural* spring of water shot four miles into the sky.)

130



## Challenge Exercise
Additional activities for advanced spellers

### Spelling Words

| | | | |
|---|---|---|---|
| parade | safety | basement | grapefruit |
| savings | changing | ashamed | apron |
| April | navy | famous | favor |
| ladies | nature | nation | station |
| plantation | information | betray | worse |

**E. Guide Words** These word pairs are guide words that might appear in a dictionary. Write the words from the spelling list that would appear on the same page as each pair of guide words.

**appoint - bait**
1. ashamed
2. apron
3. April

**balloon - bottom**
4. basement
5. betray

**captain - chosen**
6. changing

**everywhere - festive**
7. famous
8. favor

**freeze - graze**
9. grapefuit

**help - ironing**
10. information

**known - machine**
11. ladies

**mud - offer**
12. navy
13. nature
14. nation

**often - pasture**
15. parade

**patch - preparing**
16. plantation

**replay - scarf**
17. safety
18. savings

**skirt - strain**
19. station

**western - wrist**
20. worse



## CONTROLLED DICTATION (Optional)

These dictation sentences provide maintenance for spelling words previously taught and practice for words currently being studied. Dictation should be administered on Day 4. The teacher or another student may dictate the sentences. Be sure to dictate all marks of punctuation. Challenge Word sentences are preceded by an asterisk.

1. I **favor** storing the **grapefruit** in the **basement**.
2. The **ladies** gave out **information** on automobile **safety**.
3. A **famous parade** is held in **April**.
4. They were **ashamed** to spend the **savings** from the **plantation**.
5. In our **nation**, we could be **changing nature** for the **worse**.
6. Would a sailor **betray** a **navy** buddy?
7. The clerk at the bus **station** wore an **apron**.

*8. The lion did not find any **prey** near the **crater**.
*9. She added a pink **decoration** to her **bathing** suit.
*10. Do you have a **nickname**?

**F. Using Other Word Forms** Write the Other Word Form that completes each sentence.

Base Words: inform(ed) station(s) nation(al) change(ed) favor(ite)

1. An important ___national___ event is the election of the President.
2. The media keeps us ___informed___ of this event.
3. It is my ___favorite___ topic on the nightly news.
4. Many television ___stations___ run programs about the candidates.
5. Television has really ___changed___ election coverage.

**G. Challenge Words** Write the Challenge Word that completes each sentence.

| bathing | crater | decoration | nickname | prey |
|---|---|---|---|---|

1. Father is ___bathing___ the baby.
2. Each child was called by a special ___nickname___ .
3. The hawk is a bird of ___prey___ .
4. The telescope reveals each ___crater___ of the moon.
5. Each child made a colorful ___decoration___ for the surprise party.

**H. Spelling and Writing** Write each set of words in a sentence. You may use Other Word Forms. Proofread for spelling using one of the Proofreading Tips from the Yellow Pages.

1. parade, famous, April
2. worse, ashamed, plantation
3. betray, nation, navy
4. information, ladies, safety
5. basement, station, changing
6. saving, nature, grapefruit
7. apron, favor, safety
8. nickname, crater, decoration
9. prey, bathing, safety



## USING OTHER WORD FORMS

Vocabulary is expanded through the use of other forms of basic spelling words. Emphasis is on the relationship of syntax to suffix choices. The following generalizations apply to the Other Word Forms used in Exercise F.

### Spelling Rule

Forming plurals

Add **s** to most nouns to form plurals.
(**station, stations**)

Adding suffixes to words ending in silent **e**

When adding a suffix that begins with a vowel to words that end with silent **e**, drop the final **e**.
(**change, changed**)

## POSTTEST AND PROOFREADING

Follow the same testing procedures used in the Pretest, although you may wish to correct the tests yourself. Have students write any misspelled words on the Words to Learn Sheet and record spelling success on the Progress Chart.

## THE SPELLING-WRITING LINK

**Purpose** This activity helps students effectively transfer lesson words into their daily writing. Students (a) determine a relationship among three given words and (b) write a complete sentence.

**Procedure** On the chalkboard, write the three words from line 1: **parade, famous, April,** and the Other Word Forms: **parading, fame, Apr.** Have students read the words and think of ways the three words might be related. Have them think of things or people the words suggest. Ask students to create sentences using some of their ideas. You can provide a sample sentence: **Each April our town has a parade for famous local people.**

**Practice** Tell students to write original sentences using the word sets and to proofread their work. You may want them to circle the lesson words.

## LESSON 20

### OBJECTIVES

- to spell 20 high-frequency words with the /ŭ/, /o͝o/, /ûr/, and /ō/
- to proofread these words in daily writing
- to become familiar with 40 other forms of the spelling words

| Summary of Skills | Exercises |
|---|---|
| Auditory Discrimination | A, E, F |
| Proofreading | A, C, J |
| Visual Discrimination | C |
| Word Analysis | D, G, H |
| Vocabulary Development | E, F, I |
| Original Writing | J |

### PRETEST AND PROOFREADING

The Pretest identifies the words students are able to spell, as well as the words they need to learn. You may wish to use Other Word Forms when giving the Pretest. Five suggested Other Word Forms are underlined on this page.

To administer the Pretest:

**READ** each word aloud.
**SAY** the phrase containing the word.
**REPEAT** the word.

Have students correct the Pretest using the Corrected-test Procedure. They may record their scores on a personal Progress Chart (see the Teacher's Resource Book) and study misspelled words using the **S-H-A-R-P** procedure.

### OTHER WORD FORMS

This section presents related forms of the spelling words to strengthen spelling power and vocabulary knowledge.

### Enrichment Activity

Have students write variations of the same sentence using each of the Other Word Forms for a spelling word.

She **studies** long hours for tests.
**study**, **studied**, **studying**

**A. Pretest and Proofreading**

**B. Spelling Words and Phrases**

| | |
|---|---|
| **1. gulf*** | sailed across the gulf |
| **2. judge** | to judge the contest |
| **3. crush** | will crush the ice |
| **4. thumb** | a broken thumb |
| **5. stump*** | the stump of the tree |
| **6. studies** | studies for the test |
| **7. struck*** | struck by lightning |
| **8. uncle*** | my aunt and uncle |
| **9. bundle** | a bundle of dirty laundry |
| **10. jungle** | tigers in the jungle |
| **11. puzzle** | a piece of the puzzle |
| **12. upper*** | into the upper bunk |
| **13. sunny*** | across the sunny meadow |
| **14. muddy*** | with muddy shoes |
| **15. stubborn** | a stubborn mule |
| **16. button*** | lost the top button |
| **17. cutting*** | cutting the lawn |
| **18. putting*** | putting on the boots |
| **19. current** | swam against the current |
| **20. swallow** | will swallow the juice |

*Other Word Forms*

| | |
|---|---|
| gulfs | puzzled, puzzling |
| judges, judged, judging | up |
| crushes, crushed, crushing | sun, sunnier, sunniest |
| thumbs | mud, muddier, muddiest |
| stumps, stumped | stubbornly, stubbornest |
| study, studied, studying | buttons, buttoned |
| strike | cut, cuts, cutter |
| uncles | put, puts |
| bundles, bundled, bundling | currents, currently |
| jungles | swallowed |

**C. Visual Warm-up** Write each word in its correct shape.

**a.** struck
**b.** gulf
**c.** button
**d.** bundle
**e.** puzzle
**f.** swallow
**g.** putting
**h.** judge
**i.** sunny
**j.** stump
**k.** jungle
**l.** current
**m.** crush
**n.** stubborn
**o.** uncle
**p.** muddy
**q.** studies
**r.** cutting
**s.** thumb
**t.** upper



*Modified Lesson words are asterisked.
The Modified Lesson is found in the Teacher's Resource Book.

### MEETING INDIVIDUAL NEEDS / ASSIGNMENT GUIDE

| 5-Day Plan | 3-Day Plan | Limited Spellers | Average Spellers | Advanced Spellers |
|---|---|---|---|---|
| 1 | 1 | • Pretest<br>• Progress Chart | • Pretest<br>• Progress Chart<br>• Home Activity | • Pretest<br>• Progress Chart<br>• Home Activity |
| 2 | | • Modified Lesson Visual Warm-up Ending Sounds | • Regular Lesson Visual Warm-up | • Regular Lesson Visual Warm-up |
| 3 and 4 | 2 | • Modified Lesson Vowel Puzzle Word Match Finish the Sentence | Spelling Activities | Spelling Activities<br>• Challenge Exercise |
| 5 | 3 | • Posttest<br>• Words to Learn Sheet<br>• Progress Chart | • Posttest<br>• Words to Learn Sheet<br>• Progress Chart | • Posttest<br>• Words to Learn Sheet<br>• Progress Chart |

**D. Find the Right List** In alphabetical order, write the spelling words where they belong.

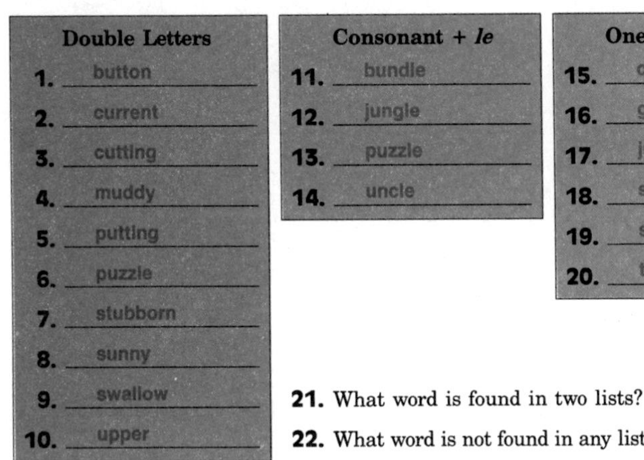

| Double Letters | Consonant + *le* | One-syllable Words |
|---|---|---|
| 1. button | 11. bundle | 15. crush |
| 2. current | 12. jungle | 16. gulf |
| 3. cutting | 13. puzzle | 17. judge |
| 4. muddy | 14. uncle | 18. struck |
| 5. putting | | 19. stump |
| 6. puzzle | | 20. thumb |
| 7. stubborn | | |
| 8. sunny | | |
| 9. swallow | | |
| 10. upper | | |

21. What word is found in two lists? puzzle

22. What word is not found in any list? studies

**E. Hink Pink** The solution to each Hink Pink requires two rhyming words, each with one syllable. Solve each Hink Pink. Write the words. One word of each Hink Pink will be a spelling word.

Example: a foot covering made of stone

*rock*

*sock*

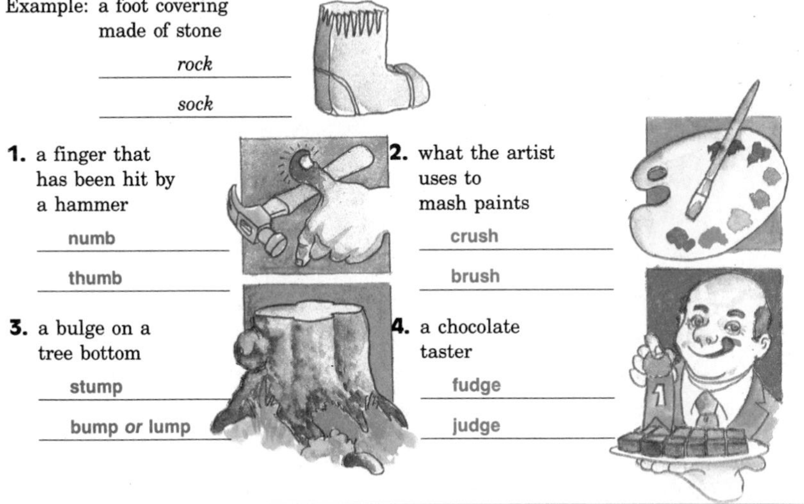

1. a finger that has been hit by a hammer
   numb
   thumb

2. what the artist uses to mash paints
   crush
   brush

3. a bulge on a tree bottom
   stump
   bump *or* lump

4. a chocolate taster
   fudge
   judge



## OPTIONAL TEACHING PLAN

Write the four Word Group headings on the chalkboard. Ask the students to name the seventeen spelling words with the short **u** sound. Write the words on the chalkboard as the students say them. Continue identifying the other Word Groups. Note the consonant-**le** combination in words such as **uncle**, and the double consonants in words such as **puzzle**.

| Word Groups | | |
|---|---|---|
| /ŭ/ words | gulf | upper |
| | judge | sunny |
| | crush | muddy |
| | thumb | stubborn |
| | stump | button |
| | studies | cutting |
| | struck | **construct** |
| | uncle | **underneath** |
| | bundle | **dumb** |
| | jungle | **instructions** |
| | puzzle | **couple** |
| /o͝o/: **u** word | putting | |
| /ûr/ word | current | |
| /ō/: **ow** word | swallow | |

*Challenge Words are boldfaced.*

### Optional Activity Masters

Those using the Hardcover Pupil Edition may wish to use the Optional Activity Master in the Teacher's Resource Book for Exercise C.

**Home Activity #20**

Name________ Date________

Use the spelling words to complete the questions. The number before each blank tells you in what column you can find the correct word. Use each word only once.

| 1 | 2 | 3 | 4 |
|---|---|---|---|
| upper | stubborn | stump | judge |
| gulf | puzzle | jungle | studies |
| cutting | thumb | sunny | putting |
| muddy | uncle | crush | current |
| button | bundle | struck | swallow |

1. Do you have a (2) ________ of dirty laundry?
2. When was the tree (3) ________ by lightning?
3. Did you stomp into the house with (1) ________ shoes?
4. Shall we count the rings on the (3) ________ of the tree?
5. Will you stop being a (2) ________ mule?
6. Who (4) ________ for the test and who plays outside instead?
7. Who is (1) ________ the lawn?
8. Do tigers in the (3) ________ fascinate you?
9. Did you see the eel as it swam against the (4) ________ ?
10. Have you lost the top (1) ________ of your shirt?
11. Can you solve a piece of the (2) ________ ?
12. Would you like to (4) ________ the contest?
13. Who sailed across the (1) ________ during the storm?
14. Have you met my aunt and (2) ________ ?
15. Who will (4) ________ the juice?
16. Who will (3) ________ the ice for the water?
17. Who jumped into the (1) ________ bunk?
18. How did you get a broken (2) ________ ?
19. Why are you (4) ________ on boots to go swimming?
20. Do you see the colt galloping across the (3) ________ meadow?

26 ©D.C. Heath and Company

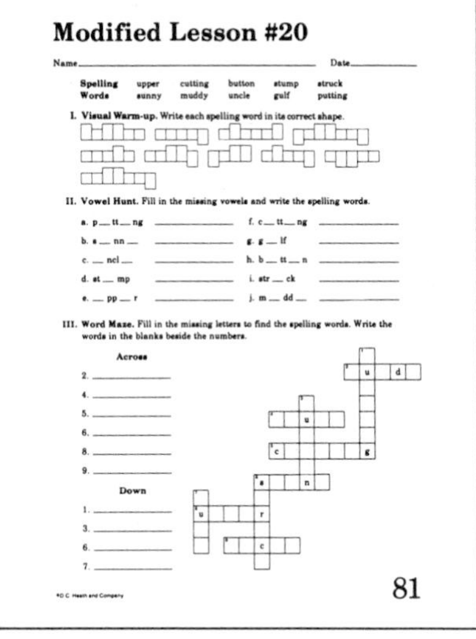

**Modified Lesson #20**

Name________ Date________

| Spelling Words | upper | cutting | button | stump | struck |
|---|---|---|---|---|---|
| | sunny | muddy | uncle | gulf | putting |

I. **Visual Warm-up.** Write each spelling word in its correct shape.

II. **Vowel Hunt.** Fill in the missing vowels and write the spelling words.

a. p__tt__ng ________ f. c__tt__ng ________
b. s__nn__ ________ g. g__lf ________
c. __ncl__ ________ h. b__tt__n ________
d. st__mp ________ i. str__ck ________
e. __pp__r ________ j. m__dd__ ________

III. **Word Maze.** Fill in the missing letters to find the spelling words. Write the words in the blanks beside the numbers.

Across: 2. ____ 4. ____ 5. ____ 6. ____ 8. ____ 9. ____

Down: 1. ____ 3. ____ 6. ____ 7. ____

©D.C. Heath and Company 81

**Modified Lesson #20** *(continued)*

Name________ Date________

| Spelling Words | upper | cutting | button | stump | struck |
|---|---|---|---|---|---|
| | sunny | muddy | uncle | gulf | putting |

IV. **Word Parts.** Write the spelling words that have the word parts below. A word may be used more than once.

a. ing words: ________, ________
b. words with double consonants: ________, ________, ________, ________, ________, ________
c. un words: ________, ________
d. words ending in y: ________, ________
e. mp word: ________
f. ck word: ________
g. lf word: ________
h. str word: ________
i. er word: ________

V. **Sentence Sense.** Write each spelling word in the correct sentence.

**Words** upper cutting button stump muddy

a. My mother was ________ the lawn when the storm came.
b. The ________ of the tree was rotten.
c. With ________ shoes, the child walked across the carpet.
d. I crawled into the ________ bunk to sleep.
e. He lost the top ________ from his shirt.

**Words** sunny struck uncle gulf putting

f. The cows roamed across the ________ meadow.
g. I visited with my aunt and ________ .
h. They sailed across the ________ .
i. The house was ________ by lightning.
j. Why are you ________ on boots?

82 ©D.C. Heath and Company

### Home Activity

A weekly homework assignment

### Modified Lesson

An alternative lesson for limited spellers

*(The Answer Key can be found in the Teacher's Resource Book.)*

# LESSON 20 CONTINUED

### Challenge Exercise #20

Name______________________ Date__________

**Word Watch.** Long ago the French referred to the tiny object used to fasten their clothes as a *bouton*, their word for *bud* as well as for anything of small value. It seems that the small round disk reminded them of the small round bud of a flower or leaf, ready to open. The English were quick to borrow the word, first changing it to *boton* and later to *button*. Today the button not only fastens our clothes but decorates them as well. Oddly, through the years the button has remained an item of some small value.

**Word Analogies.** Decide on the relationship that exists between the first pair of words. Using the Other Word Forms on page 80, find a word that completes the second pair of words and establishes the same relationship.

1. *boxes* is to *crayons* as ______________ is to *groceries*
2. *coves* is to *lakes* as ______________ is to *oceans*
3. *coldness* is to *polar regions* as *warmth* is to ______________
4. *home run* is to *baseball* as ______________ is to *bowling*
5. *shovel* is to *digger* as *scissors* is to ______________

**Challenge Words Student Activity**
Use the challenge words below to complete the paragraph.

**instructions  construct  dumb  couple  underneath**

I love to ______________ model airplanes. The ______________ are easy to follow. Today, though, I had trouble finding a ______________ of parts. While I was calling the hobby shop to ask for a new model, I found them ______________ my chair. I felt pretty ______________!

**Working With Words: Student Writing Activity**
Use as many Other Word Forms as you can from page 80 to write a paragraph describing a trip, real or imaginary, to an unusual place.



131

## Challenge Exercise
Additional activities for advanced spellers

**Spelling Words**

| | | | | |
|---|---|---|---|---|
| gulf | judge | crush | thumb | stump |
| studies | struck | uncle | bundle | jungle |
| puzzle | upper | sunny | muddy | stubborn |
| button | cutting | putting | current | swallow |

**F. Hinky Pinky** The solution to each Hinky Pinky requires two rhyming words, each with two syllables. Write the words. One word of each Hinky Pinky will be a spelling word.

Example: a band member who plays only in June, July, and August — *summer* — *drummer*

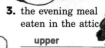

1. a happy rabbit — sunny — bunny
2. the navel of a lamb — mutton — button
3. the evening meal eaten in the attic — upper — supper

4. an empty bird — hollow — swallow
5. a friend who fell on wet ground — muddy — buddy

**G. Circles and Squares** Join circle syllables with square syllables to form fourteen words from the spelling list. Write the words.

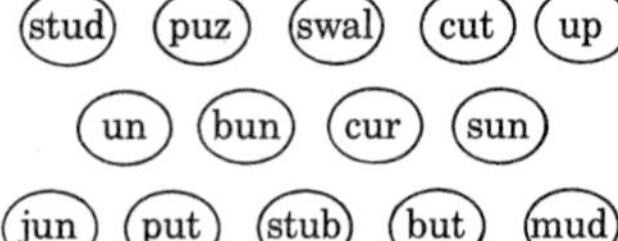


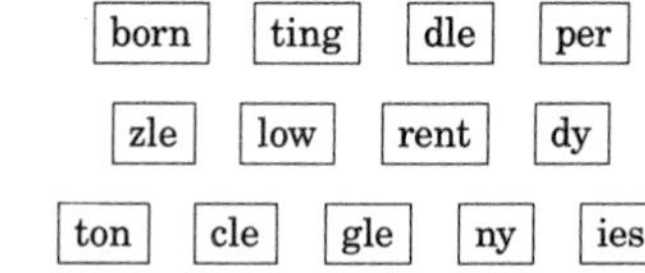


1. studies
2. puzzle
3. swallow
4. cutting
5. upper
6. uncle
7. bundle
8. current
9. sunny
10. jungle
11. putting
12. stubborn
13. button
14. muddy



## CONTROLLED DICTATION (Optional)

These dictation sentences provide maintenance for spelling words previously taught and practice for words currently being studied. Dictation should be administered on Day 4. The teacher or another student may dictate the sentences. Be sure to dictate all marks of punctuation. Challenge Word sentences are preceded by an asterisk.

1. From the **muddy gulf** we moved forward toward the **jungle**.
2. My **uncle** can be a **stubborn judge**.
3. Did you **crush** the **upper** part of your **thumb** when you **struck** it?
4. A **swallow** of cold water feels good on a hot, **sunny** day.
5. My **current studies** can be a **puzzle** to me.
6. I saw her **putting** the **bundle** of branches near the tree **stump**.
7. Why is he **cutting** the **button** from the sleeve?

*8. With **instructions** I'll be able to **construct** the stairs.
*9. I felt **dumb** when I forgot his name.
*10. A **couple** of cats are sleeping **underneath** the steps.

**H. Using Other Word Forms** Add an ending to each word to write an Other Word Form.

Base Words: sunny(est) judge(ing) muddy(est) study(ing) bundle(ing)

1. judge + ing = judging
2. study + ing = studying
3. bundle + ing = bundling
4. sunny + est = sunniest
5. muddy + est = muddiest

**I. Challenge Words** Write the Challenge Word that fits each group of words.

| construct | couple | underneath | dumb | instructions |
|---|---|---|---|---|

1. bottom, surface, below, underneath
2. carpenter, wood, build, construct
3. words, directions, how to, instructions
4. silent, without speech, can't talk, dumb
5. two, pair, people, couple

**J. Spelling and Writing** Use as many Spelling Words, Other Word Forms, and Challenge Words as you can to write *two* or more answers to each question. A few words are suggested. Proofread your work.

1. If you were a researcher, what topics might you examine?

   gulf – studies – muddy – sunny – jungle – construct

2. How would you describe what happened at your school or clubhouse during a bad storm?

   struck – upper – crush – stump – underneath

3. What could you say about a relative who always thinks that he or she is right?

   puzzle – judge – stubborn – instructions – putting



## USING OTHER WORD FORMS

Vocabulary is expanded through the use of other forms of basic spelling words. Emphasis is on the relationship of syntax to suffix choices. The following generalizations apply to the Other Word Forms used in Exercise H.

### Spelling Rule

Adding suffixes to words ending in silent **e**

When adding a suffix that begins with a vowel to words that end with silent **e**, drop the final **e**.
**(judge, judging)**

Adding suffixes to words ending in **y**

When adding a suffix to words ending with consonant-**y**, change the **y** to **i**, unless the suffix begins with **i**.
**(study, studying; sunny, sunniest)**

## POSTTEST AND PROOFREADING

Follow the same testing procedures used in the Pretest, although you may wish to correct the tests yourself. Have students write any misspelled words on the Words to Learn Sheet and record spelling success on the Progress Chart.

## THE SPELLING-WRITING LINK

**Purpose** This activity helps students retain the correct spelling of words and transfer the words to their daily writing. Students use lesson words to answer questions promoting higher-order thinking skills.

**Procedure** Read the first question and write the suggested words on the chalkboard: **gulf, studies, muddy, sunny, jungle, construct.** Have students list some Other Word Forms of the lesson words. Brainstorm with the class possible answers to question 1. Remind students to look at all the lesson words for ideas. Write the answers on the chalkboard, noting any lesson words.

**Practice** Tell students to finish the activity by writing two or more answers to each question. Remind them to proofread their work.

## LESSON 21

### OBJECTIVES

- to spell 20 high-frequency words with the /ă/, /ăr/, and other vowel sounds
- to proofread these words in daily writing
- to become familiar with 34 other forms of the spelling words

| Summary of Skills | Exercises |
|---|---|
| Auditory Discrimination | A |
| Proofreading | A, C, F, I |
| Visual Discrimination | C, F |
| Vocabulary Development | D, E, G |
| Context Usage | H |
| Original Writing | I |

### PRETEST AND PROOFREADING

The Pretest identifies the words students are able to spell, as well as the words they need to learn. You may wish to use Other Word Forms when giving the Pretest. Five suggested Other Word Forms are underlined on this page.

To administer the Pretest:

**READ** each word aloud.
**SAY** the phrase containing the word.
**REPEAT** the word.

Have students correct the Pretest using the Corrected-test Procedure. They may record their scores on a personal Progress Chart (see the Teacher's Resource Book) and study misspelled words using the **S-H-A-R-P** procedure.

### OTHER WORD FORMS

This section presents related forms of the spelling words to strengthen spelling power and vocabulary knowledge.

### Enrichment Activity

Have students write opposite words or phrases for these Other Word Forms. Be sure they write the Other Word Form with its opposite next to it.

**carrying, valleys, attaches, bitterly**

# 21

**A. Pretest and Proofreading**

**B. Spelling Words and Phrases**

| | |
|---|---|
| **1. attack** | after the attack |
| **2. attached** | attached to the house |
| **3. cabbage** | a small head of cabbage |
| **4. planning** | planning a party |
| **5. passenger** | an extra passenger |
| **6. ragged** | cut by the ragged edge |
| **7. gallon*** | gallon of cold cider |
| **8. valley*** | echoed across the valley |
| **9. arrow*** | lost another arrow |
| **10. carries*** | carries a heavier load |
| **11. carried*** | was carried home |
| **12. married*** | were married today |
| **13. sparrow*** | a nesting sparrow |
| **14. barrel*** | a barrel of pickles |
| **15. allow*** | will allow us to go |
| **16. bitter*** | a bitter taste |
| **17. mirror** | a crack in the mirror |
| **18. potato** | one baked potato |
| **19. tomato** | lettuce and tomato |
| **20. envied** | envied their courage |

*Other Word Forms*

| | |
|---|---|
| attacks, attacked, attacker | marry, marries, marrying |
| attach, attaches | sparrows |
| cabbages | barrels |
| plan, plans, planned, planner | allows, allowed, allowing, allowance |
| passengers | bitterly |
| rag, rags | mirrors |
| gallons | potatoes |
| valleys | tomatoes |
| arrows | envy, envious |
| carry, carrying, carrier | |

**C. Visual Warm-up** Write each word in its correct shape.

a. carried
b. married
c. bitter
d. sparrow
e. potato
f. allow
g. attached
h. attack
i. tomato
j. cabbage
k. envied
l. planning
m. passenger
n. carries
o. ragged
p. arrow
q. barrel
r. gallon
s. valley
t. mirror

*Modified Lesson words are asterisked.
The Modified Lesson is found in the Teacher's Resource Book.



### MEETING INDIVIDUAL NEEDS / ASSIGNMENT GUIDE

| 5-Day Plan | 3-Day Plan | Limited Spellers | Average Spellers | Advanced Spellers |
|---|---|---|---|---|
| 1 | 1 | • Pretest<br>• Progress Chart | • Pretest<br>• Progress Chart<br>• Home Activity | • Pretest<br>• Progress Chart<br>• Home Activity |
| 2 | | • Modified Lesson Visual Warm-up Ending Sounds | • Regular Lesson Visual Warm-up | • Regular Lesson Visual Warm-up |
| 3 and 4 | 2 | • Modified Lesson Vowel Puzzle Word Match Finish the Sentence | Spelling Activities | Spelling Activities<br>• Challenge Exercise |
| 5 | 3 | • Posttest<br>• Words to Learn Sheet<br>• Progress Chart | • Posttest<br>• Words to Learn Sheet<br>• Progress Chart | • Posttest<br>• Words to Learn Sheet<br>• Progress Chart |

**D. Categories** Below are several categories with one word under each. Choose a spelling word for each category and write the word.

1. Things Growing Underground
   beet, potato
2. People Who Ride
   engineer, passenger
3. Vegetables in Heads
   lettuce, cabbage
4. Birds
   robin, sparrow
5. Red Things to Eat
   apple, tomato
6. Tastes
   sour, bitter
7. Measures
   pint, gallon
8. Containers
   bottle, barrel
9. Pointed Things
   dart, arrow
10. Types of Land
    hill, valley
11. Breakable Things
    dish, mirror

**E. Sequences and Consequences** Show what might happen next by using these nine spelling words. Write the words.

allow attached attack carried carries envied married planning ragged

1. dated ➡ engaged ➡ married
2. new ➡ worn ➡ ragged
3. stooped ➡ lifted ➡ carried
4. threaded ➡ sewed ➡ attached
5. refused ➡ wanted ➡ envied
6. prepare ➡ attack ➡ win
7. carries ➡ drops ➡ cleans up
8. planning ➡ doing ➡ finishing
9. allow ➡ disapprove ➡ prevent

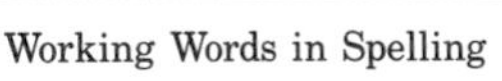



## OPTIONAL TEACHING PLAN

Write the seven Word Group headings on the chalkboard. Ask the students to name the eight spelling words with the short **a** sound. Continue identifying the other Word Groups. Note that the short **a** and /ăr/ words have double consonants. Compare the **ow** ending sounds of **sparrow** and **allow**.

| Word Groups | | |
|---|---|---|
| /ă/ words | attack | gallon |
| | attached | valley |
| | cabbage | **atlas** |
| | planning | **fashionable** |
| | passenger | **dandelion** |
| | ragged | **nationally** |
| /ăr/ words | arrow | married |
| | carries | sparrow |
| | carried | barrel |
| /ĭ/ word | bitter | |
| **ir** word | mirror | |
| /ā/ and /ō/ words | potato | tomato |
| /ou/: **ow** word | | allow |
| /ĕ/ and /ē/ word | | envied |

*Challenge Words are boldfaced.*

### Optional Activity Masters

Those using the Hardcover Pupil Edition may wish to use the Optional Activity Masters in the Teacher's Resource Book for Exercises C and F.

**Home Activity #21**

Name________ Date______

The spelling words in Lesson 21 appear in the phrases below. Write each phrase in a sentence and circle the spelling word.

| Phrases | Sentences |
|---|---|
| 1. was **carried** home | 1. |
| 2. lost another **arrow** | 2. |
| 3. **carries** a heavier load | 3. |
| 4. were **married** today | 4. |
| 5. a crack in the **mirror** | 5. |
| 6. a nesting **sparrow** | 6. |
| 7. will **allow** us to go | 7. |
| 8. after the **attack** | 8. |
| 9. a small head of **cabbage** | 9. |
| 10. **planning** a party | 10. |
| 11. an extra **passenger** | 11. |
| 12. cut by the **ragged** edge | 12. |
| 13. a **barrel** of pickles | 13. |
| 14. **gallon** of cold cider | 14. |
| 15. echoed across the **valley** | 15. |
| 16. a **bitter** taste | 16. |
| 17. **attached** to the house | 17. |
| 18. one baked **potato** | 18. |
| 19. lettuce and **tomato** | 19. |
| 20. **envied** their courage | 20. |

 27

**Modified Lesson #21**

Name________ Date______

**Spelling Words** carried carries sparrow barrel valley arrow married allow gallon bitter

**I. Visual Warm-up.** Write each spelling word in its correct shape.

**II. Vowel Hunt.** Fill in the missing vowels and write the spelling words.

a. v__ll__ __
b. m__rr__ __d
c. b__rr__l
d. __ll__w
e. c__rr__ __d
f. g__ll__n
g. b__tt__r
h. sp__rr__w
i. c__rr__ __s
j. __rr__w

**III. Word Maze.** Fill in the missing letters to find the spelling words. Write the words in the blanks beside the numbers.

Across: 1. 4. 6. 7. 9.
Down: 1. 2. 3. 5. 8.

 83

**Modified Lesson #21** *(continued)*

Name________ Date______

**Spelling Words** carried carries sparrow barrel valley arrow married allow gallon bitter

**IV. Word Parts.** Write the spelling words that have the word parts below. A word may be used more than once.

a. rr words:
b. ll words:
c. tt word:
d. ied words:
e. ies word:
f. ow words:
g. sp word:

**V. Sentence Sense.** Write each spelling word in the correct sentence.

**Words** carried married sparrow barrel valley

a. The gray bird is a nesting ______.
b. The sound echoed across the ______.
c. The bride and groom were ______ today.
d. The injured dog was ______ home.
e. The storekeeper sold a ______ of pickles.

**Words** arrow carries allow gallon bitter

f. Lemon has a ______ taste.
g. The archer lost another ______.
h. The teacher will ______ us to go on the field trip.
i. Who drank the ______ of cold cider?
j. This cart ______ a heavier load.

84 

### Home Activity

A weekly homework assignment

### Modified Lesson

An alternative lesson for limited spellers

*(The Answer Key can be found in the Teacher's Resource Book.)*

# LESSON 21 CONTINUED

Challenge Exercise #21

Name__________ Date__________

**Word Watch.** The word *cabbage* was born of the old French word *boche*, meaning "a bulge or swelling." The word was expanded to *caboche* to mean "a swollen head." When the English adopted the word, they changed it to *cabidge*, which later became our word *cabbage*. In a sense, the cabbage plant, with its tight overlapping leaves, resembles a swollen head. Even today, when we speak of cabbage, we refer to the plant as a head of cabbage.

**Word Analogies.** Decide on the relationship that exists between the first pair of words. Using the Other Word Forms on page 84, find a word that completes the second pair of words and establishes the same relationship.

1. *sharks* is to *fins* as ________ is to *wings*
2. *ears* is to *corn* as *heads* is to ________
3. *hikers* is to *trail* as ________ is to *vehicle*
4. *prevented* is to *halted* as *permitted* is to ________
5. *highs* is to *lows* as *peaks* is to ________

**Challenge Words Student Activity**

Use the challenge words below to complete each series.

**fashionable atlas nationally shatter dandelion**

1. country-wide, federally, ________
2. aster, daisy, ________
3. modern, stylish, ________
4. globe, maps, ________
5. break, crumble, ________

**Working With Words: Student Writing Activity**

Use as many Other Word Forms as you can from page 84 to write five math problems. (Example: If our quarts equal one gallon, how many quarts of water are needed to fill six one-gallon *barrels*?)

132



## Challenge Exercise

Additional activities for advanced spellers

**Spelling Words**

| | | | | |
|---|---|---|---|---|
| attack | attached | cabbage | planning | passenger |
| ragged | gallon | valley | arrow | carries |
| carried | married | sparrow | barrel | allow |
| bitter | mirror | potato | tomato | envied |

**F. Word Search** The spelling words and some Other Word Forms (p. 84) can be found in the word puzzle. The words appear across and down. Circle and write the words.

**Spelling Words**

**Across**

1. carries
2. passenger
3. arrow
4. barrel
5. bitter
6. valley
7. married
8. tomato
9. attached
10. cabbage

**Down**

11. carried
12. allow
13. potato
14. gallon
15. sparrow
16. attack
17. envied
18. mirror
19. ragged
20. planning

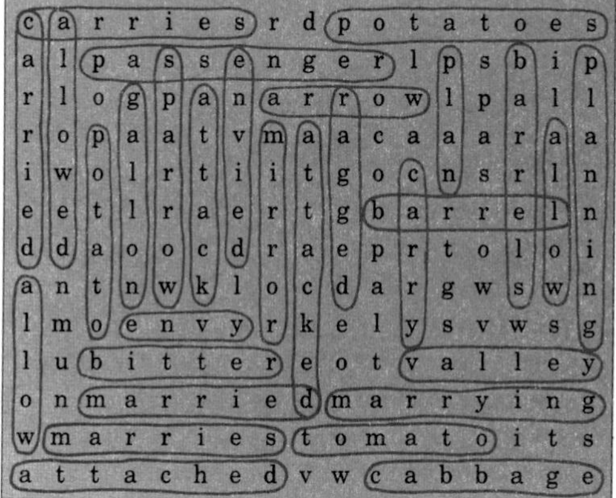


**Other Word Forms**

**Across**

21. potatoes
22. envy
23. marrying
24. marries

**Down**

25. allowed
26. attacked
27. carry
28. plan
29. barrels
30. allows



## CONTROLLED DICTATION (Optional)

These dictation sentences provide maintenance for spelling words previously taught and practice for words currently being studied. Dictation should be administered on Day 4. The teacher or another student may dictate the sentences. Be sure to dictate all marks of punctuation. Challenge Word sentences are preceded by an asterisk.

1. I **carried** home a head of **cabbage**, one **gallon** of milk, and a very **bitter** grapefruit.
2. The cat is **planning** to **attack** the **sparrow**.
3. The man in **ragged** pants lives in the **valley** and usually **carries** a bow and **arrow**.
4. **Allow** me to slice a **potato** and a **tomato** for you.
5. A copper **mirror** was **attached** to the top of the **barrel**.
6. Every **passenger envied** my aunt and her **married** daughter.

*7. This **atlas** of cities is sold **nationally**.

*8. The picture showed a **fashionable** woman picking a **dandelion**.

*9. Luckily the vase did not **shatter**.

**G. Using Other Word Forms** Write the Other Word Form that fits each clue.

Base Words: attack(ed) plan(ed) marry(ing) allow(ed) potato(es)

1. plotted or thought out planned
2. can be mashed, boiled, or baked potatoes
3. permitted or let do something allowed
4. started a fight attacked
5. becoming husband or wife marrying

**H. Challenge Words** Write the Challenge Word that completes each sentence.

| atlas | fashionable | dandelion | shatter | nationally |
|---|---|---|---|---|

1. Once the business was run locally; now it's run nationally.
2. Once it was out of style; now it's fashionable.
3. Once it was the book of maps; now it's the atlas.
4. Once it was a weed; now it's a dandelion.
5. Once it could break; now it could shatter.

**I. Spelling and Writing** Write each set of words in a sentence. You may use Other Word Forms. Proofread your work.

1. married – planning – allow
2. envied – passenger – carries
3. ragged – arrow – carried
4. valley – sparrow – cabbage
5. potato – tomato – attack
6. gallon – bitter – barrel
7. mirror – attached – shatter
8. atlas – nationally – planned
9. fashionable – dandelion – carry



## USING OTHER WORD FORMS

Vocabulary is expanded through the use of other forms of basic spelling words. Emphasis is on the relationship of syntax to suffix choices. The following generalizations apply to the Other Word Forms used in Exercise G.

### Spelling Rule

Doubling the final consonant when adding suffixes

When adding a suffix that begins with a vowel to one-syllable words that end with one vowel and one consonant, double the final consonant.
**(plan, planned)**

Adding suffixes to words ending in y

When adding a suffix to words ending with consonant-**y**, change the **y** to **i**, unless the suffix begins with **i**.
**(marry, marrying)**

## POSTTEST AND PROOFREADING

Follow the same testing procedures used in the Pretest, although you may wish to correct the tests yourself. Have students write any misspelled words on the Words to Learn Sheet and record spelling success on the Progress Chart.

## THE SPELLING-WRITING LINK

**Purpose** This activity helps students effectively transfer lesson words into their daily writing. Students (a) determine a relationship among three given words and (b) write a complete sentence.

**Procedure** On the chalkboard, write the three words from line 1 (**married, planning, allow**) and the Other Word Forms (**marry, marries, marrying, plan, plans, planned, planner, allows, allowed, allowing, allowance**). Have students read the words and think of ways the three words might be related. Have them think of things or people the words suggest. Ask students to create sentences using some of their ideas. You can provide an example sentence: **After they marry, they are planning to allow two weeks for a trip.**

**Practice** Tell students to write original sentences using the word sets and to proofread their work. You may want them to circle the lesson words.

LESSON 22

## OBJECTIVES

- to spell 20 high-frequency words with the /ĭ/ and /ŭ/
- to proofread these words in daily writing
- to become familiar with 39 other forms of the spelling words

| Summary of Skills | Exercises |
|---|---|
| Auditory Discrimination | A |
| Proofreading | A, C, I |
| Visual Discrimination | C |
| Vocabulary Development | D, G, H |
| Word Analysis | E, F |
| Original Writing | I |

## PRETEST AND PROOFREADING

The Pretest identifies the words students are able to spell, as well as the words they need to learn. You may wish to use Other Word Forms when giving the Pretest. Five suggested Other Word Forms are underlined on this page.

To administer the Pretest:

**READ** each word aloud.
**SAY** the phrase containing the word.
**REPEAT** the word.

Have students correct the Pretest using the Corrected-test Procedure. They may record their scores on a personal Progress Chart (see the Teacher's Resource Book) and study misspelled words using the **S-H-A-R-P** procedure.

## OTHER WORD FORMS

This section presents related forms of the spelling words to strengthen spelling power and vocabulary knowledge.

### Enrichment Activity

Have students write sentences that include these Other Word Forms.

1. **buildings – compasses**
2. **villages – signals**
3. **thriller – differently**
4. **finishing – unwillingly**

# 22

**A. Pretest and Proofreading**

**B. Spelling Words and Phrases**

| | |
|---|---|
| **1. cliff** | the edge of the cliff |
| **2. thrill*** | the thrill of winning |
| **3. unwilling** | unwilling to give up |
| **4. silly*** | a silly reason |
| **5. ribbon*** | tied a yellow ribbon |
| **6. village** | the village post office |
| **7. million** | into a million pieces |
| **8. different** | different from the others |
| **9. finger*** | a paper cut on my finger |
| **10. listen*** | will stop, look, and listen |
| **11. chimney** | cleaned the chimney |
| **12. pilgrims** | traveled with the pilgrims |
| **13. signal** | watching for the signal |
| **14. finish*** | a close finish |
| **15. midnight*** | stayed up until midnight |
| **16. bridge** | felt the bridge shaking |
| **17. minute*** | had one more minute |
| **18. cities*** | several eastern cities |
| **19. building*** | the building site |
| **20. compass** | lost without a compass |

*Other Word Forms*

| | |
|---|---|
| cliffs | pilgrim, pilgrimage |
| thrills, thrilled, thriller | signals, signaled, signaling |
| will, unwillingly | finishes, finished, finishing |
| sillier, silliest | midnights, night |
| ribbons | bridges, bridged, bridging |
| villages, villager | minutes |
| millionaire | city |
| differ, differently | buildings, builds, built, builder |
| fingered, fingering | compasses |
| listened, listener | |
| chimneys | |

**C. Visual Warm-up** Write each word in its correct shape.

**a.** midnight
**b.** ribbon
**c.** bridge
**d.** village
**e.** thrill
**f.** million
**g.** unwilling
**h.** signal
**i.** finger
**j.** building
**k.** listen
**l.** cliff
**m.** chimney
**n.** minute
**o.** pilgrims
**p.** compass
**q.** different
**r.** cities
**s.** silly
**t.** finish



*Modified Lesson words are asterisked.
The Modified Lesson is found in the Teacher's Resource Book.

## MEETING INDIVIDUAL NEEDS / ASSIGNMENT GUIDE

| 5-Day Plan | 3-Day Plan | Limited Spellers | Average Spellers | Advanced Spellers |
|---|---|---|---|---|
| 1 | 1 | • Pretest<br>• Progress Chart | • Pretest<br>• Progress Chart<br>• Home Activity | • Pretest<br>• Progress Chart<br>• Home Activity |
| 2 | | • Modified Lesson Visual Warm-up Ending Sounds | • Regular Lesson Visual Warm-up | • Regular Lesson Visual Warm-up |
| 3 and 4 | 2 | • Modified Lesson Vowel Puzzle Word Match Finish the Sentence | Spelling Activities | Spelling Activities<br>• Challenge Exercise |
| 5 | 3 | • Posttest<br>• Words to Learn Sheet<br>• Progress Chart | • Posttest<br>• Words to Learn Sheet<br>• Progress Chart | • Posttest<br>• Words to Learn Sheet<br>• Progress Chart |

**D. Compare and Contrast** Write a spelling word for each phrase below.

1. not a chimney, but a smokestack
2. not a tunnel, but a bridge
3. not an hour, but a minute
4. not a map, but a compass
5. not the same, but different
6. not villages, but cities
7. not a million, but a thousand
8. not a canyon, but a cliff
9. not destroying, but building
10. not a warning, but a signal
11. not a city, but a village
12. not midnight, but noon
13. not willing, but unwilling
14. not silly, but serious
15. not a bore, but a thrill
16. not settlers, but pilgrims
17. not listen, but speak
18. not a finger, but a toe
19. not string, but ribbon
20. not start, but finish

**E. Mix and Match** Match the first syllables in Column 1 with the last syllables in Column 2. Write the words.

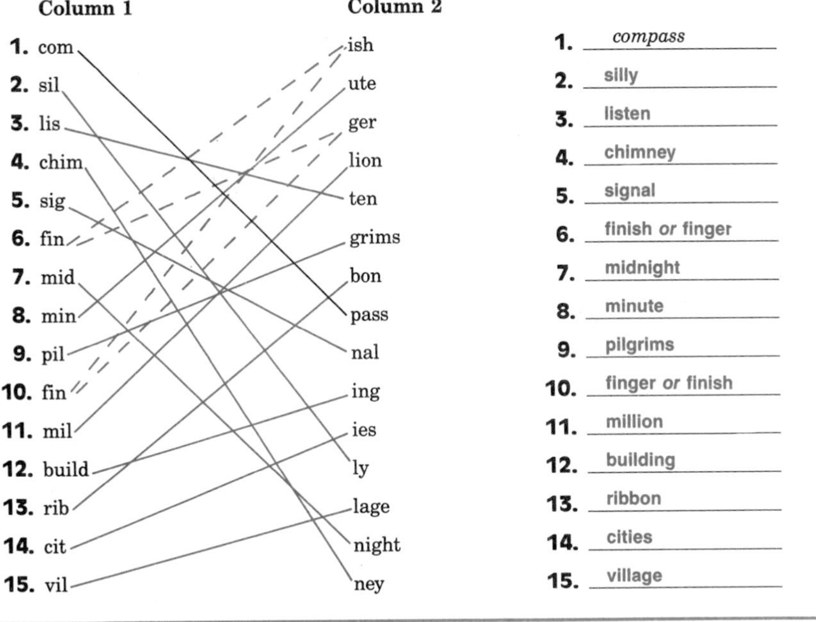

| Column 1 | Column 2 |
|---|---|
| 1. com | ish |
| 2. sil | ute |
| 3. lis | ger |
| 4. chim | lion |
| 5. sig | ten |
| 6. fin | grims |
| 7. mid | bon |
| 8. min | pass |
| 9. pil | nal |
| 10. fin | ing |
| 11. mil | ies |
| 12. build | ly |
| 13. rib | lage |
| 14. cit | night |
| 15. vil | ney |

1. *compass*
2. silly
3. listen
4. chimney
5. signal
6. finish *or* finger
7. midnight
8. minute
9. pilgrims
10. finger *or* finish
11. million
12. building
13. ribbon
14. cities
15. village



## OPTIONAL TEACHING PLAN

Write the two Word Group headings on the chalkboard. Ask the students to name the nineteen spelling words with the short **i** sound. Write the words on the chalkboard as the students say them. Proceed in the same manner for identifying the other Word Group. Note that the **dge** ending in **bridge** and the silent consonants **gh** in **midnight**. Point out the short **u** sound of **o** in **compass**.

| Word Groups | | |
|---|---|---|
| /ĭ/ words | cliff | signal |
| | thrill | finish |
| | unwilling | midnight |
| | silly | bridge |
| | ribbon | minute |
| | village | cities |
| | million | building |
| | different | **comic** |
| | finger | **digits** |
| | listen | **windshield** |
| | chimney | **military** |
| | pilgrims | **miserable** |
| /ŭ/: o word | compass | |

*Challenge Words are boldfaced.*

### Optional Activity Masters

Those using the Hardcover Pupil Edition may wish to use the Optional Activity Masters in the Teacher's Resource Book for Exercises C and E.

Home Activity #22

Name ________ Date ________

Use the spelling words to complete each pair of sentences. The spelling words appear scrambled below the blanks. The number before each blank tells you in what column you can find the correct word. Use each word only once.

| 1 | 2 | 3 | 4 |
|---|---|---|---|
| cliff | village | chimney | listen |
| thrill | million | pilgrims | minute |
| unwilling | different | signal | cities |
| silly | finger | finish | building |
| ribbon | bridge | midnight | compass |

28

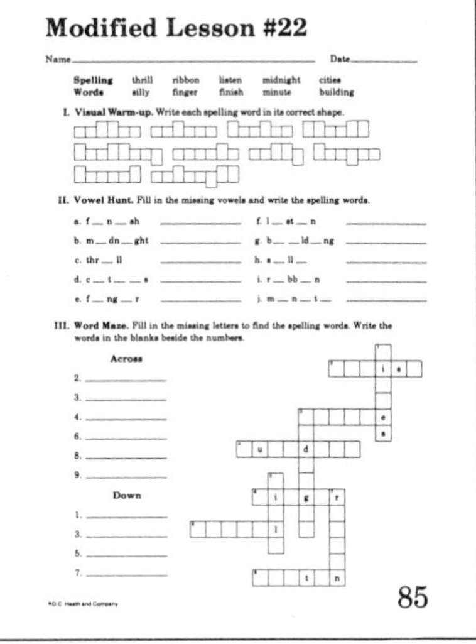
Modified Lesson #22

Name ________ Date ________

Spelling Words: thrill, ribbon, listen, midnight, cities, silly, finger, finish, minute, building

I. Visual Warm-up. Write each spelling word in its correct shape.

II. Vowel Hunt. Fill in the missing vowels and write the spelling words.

III. Word Maze. Fill in the missing letters to find the spelling words. Write the words in the blanks beside the numbers.

Across

Down

85

Modified Lesson #22 *(continued)*

Name ________ Date ________

IV. Word Parts. Write the spelling words that have the word parts below. A word may be used more than once.

V. Sentence Sense. Write each spelling word in the correct sentence.

86

### Home Activity

A weekly homework assignment

### Modified Lesson

An alternative lesson for limited spellers

*(The Answer Key can be found in the Teacher's Resource Book.)*

**LESSON**

# 22

**CONTINUED**

## Challenge Exercise #22

Name________________ Date________

**Word Watch.** Our word *chimney* can be traced far back to the Greek word *kaminos*, meaning "furnace." When the Romans borrowed the word, they changed it to *caminata*, and it became the name for a fireplace. The French changed the word to *cheminee* when it entered their language. The English put the finishing touches on the word when they changed the word to *chimney*, no longer a word for a fireplace but for a smokestack.

**Word Analogies.** Decide on the relationship that exists between the first pair of words. Using the Other Word Forms on page 88, find a word that completes the second pair of words and establishes the same relationship.

1. *flat* is to *plains* as *steep* is to ________
2. *watches* is to *time* as ________ is to *direction*
3. *eye* is to *viewer* as *ear* is to ________
4. *laughter* is to *comedy* as *fright* is to ________
5. *starts* is to *begins* as ________ is to *concludes*

**Challenge Words Student Activity**

Use the challenge words below to complete the sentences.

**comic** **digits** **military** **miserable** **windshield**

1. I was ________ when I was sick.
2. The number of people at each event could be counted in single ________ .
3. The clown's face was painted with a truly ________ grin.
4. The ________ vehicle was full of soldiers.
5. Dad asked me to clean our car's ________ .

**Working With Words: Student Writing Activity**

Use as many Other Word Forms as you can from page 88 to write six real-estate ads. The ads can be real or imaginary. (Example: For sale. Dirt road used by Paul Revere. Open at *night* and early morning. *Compasses* required to find direction back to city.)





**Challenge Exercise**
Additional activities for advanced spellers

**Spelling Words**

| | | | | |
|---|---|---|---|---|
| cliff | thrill | unwilling | silly | ribbon |
| village | million | different | finger | listen |
| chimney | pilgrims | signal | finish | midnight |
| bridge | minute | cities | building | compass |

**F. Bases, Prefixes, and Suffixes** The spelling list contains fourteen base words and six words with prefixes, suffixes, or both. Write each spelling word.

| | Words with Prefixes, Suffixes, or Both | Base Words |
|---|---|---|
| 1. | millionaire | million |
| 2. | listener | listen |
| 3. | finishes | finish |
| 4. | villager | village |
| 5. | signaled | signal |
| 6. | ribbons | ribbon |
| 7. | bridging | bridge |
| 8. | fingered | finger |
| 9. | minutes | minute |
| 10. | silliest | silly |
| 11. | thriller | thrill |
| 12. | compasses | compass |
| 13. | cliffs | cliff |
| 14. | chimneys | chimney |
| 15. | different | differ |
| 16. | cities | city |
| 17. | midnight | night |
| 18. | pilgrims | pilgrim |
| 19. | unwilling | will |
| 20. | building | build |



## CONTROLLED DICTATION (Optional)

These dictation sentences provide maintenance for spelling words previously taught and practice for words currently being studied. Dictation should be administered on Day 4. The teacher or another student may dictate the sentences. Be sure to dictate all marks of punctuation. Challenge Word sentences are preceded by an asterisk.

1. They are **unwilling** to **finish** putting the **chimney** on my **building**.
2. The **pilgrims** have no **compass**, so they must **listen** for a **signal**.
3. It is a **thrill** to look down on the **village** at **midnight**.
4. Did you climb the **cliff** near the eastern **bridge**?
5. A **million** persons drive **different** automobiles in **cities** every **minute** of the day.
6. I felt **silly** with the **ribbon** attached to my **finger**.

*7. Not every **military** truck has a **windshield**.
*8. The **comic** was **miserable** when he forgot his lines.
*9. How many **digits** are there in your code?

**G. Using Other Word Forms** Write the Other Word Form that replaces each underlined word or phrase.

Base Words: listen(ed) chimney(s) silly(est) million(aire) different(ly)

1. The man with a million dollars had a unique idea. millionaire
2. He became rich by designing smokestacks. chimneys
3. He paid attention to our requests. listened
4. We needed chimneys built in a different way. differently
5. Isn't that the most ridiculous way to become rich? silliest

**H. Challenge Words** Write the Challenge Word that completes each analogy.

| comic | digits | windshield | military | miserable |
|---|---|---|---|---|

1. **sad** is to **tragic** as **funny** is to comic
2. **wood** is to **door** as **glass** is to windshield
3. **happy** is to **joyous** as **unhappy** is to miserable
4. **letters** is to **vowels** as **numbers** is to digits
5. **doctor** is to **medical** as **soldier** is to military

**I. Spelling and Writing** Use each phrase in a sentence. You may want to use the words in a different order or use Other Word Forms. Proofread for spelling using one of the Proofreading Tips from the Yellow Pages.

1. stood near the cliff
2. thrill the audience
3. an unwilling patient
4. silly mistakes
5. decorate with ribbon
6. every village and town
7. a million people
8. alike or different
9. pointed a finger
10. compass needle
11. building a chimney
12. land of the pilgrims
13. listen for the signal
14. finish her homework
15. the midnight ride
16. bridge the gap
17. minute grain of sand
18. the capital cities



## USING OTHER WORD FORMS

Vocabulary is expanded through the use of other forms of basic spelling words. Emphasis is on the relationship of syntax to suffix choices. The following generalizations apply to the Other Word Forms used in Exercise G.

### Spelling Rule

Forming plurals

To form the plurals of nouns ending with vowel-**y**, add **s**. (**chimney**, **chimneys**)

Adding suffixes to words ending in **y**

When adding a suffix to words ending with consonant-**y**, change the **y** to **i**, unless the suffix begins with **i**. (**silly**, **silliest**)

## POSTTEST AND PROOFREADING

Follow the same testing procedures used in the Pretest, although you may wish to correct the tests yourself. Have students write any misspelled words on the Words to Learn Sheet and record spelling success on the Progress Chart.

## THE SPELLING-WRITING LINK

**Purpose** This activity helps students transfer lesson words into their daily writing. Students write complete sentences using the listed phrases.

**Procedure** On the chalkboard write the phrase from line one: **stood near the cliff.** Have the students read the phrase and note how it could be used in a sentence. Have them think about things or people the phrase suggests. You can provide a sample sentence: **The hiker stood near the edge of the cliff.**

**Practice** Tell the students to write original sentences using the phrases. Remind them they can use Other Word Forms or change the phrases around if it will improve the sentences.

# LESSON 23

## OBJECTIVES

- to spell 20 high-frequency words with the /ō/, /ŭ/, /oi/, and /ôr/
- to proofread these words in daily writing
- to become familiar with 33 other forms of the spelling words

| Summary of Skills | Exercises |
|---|---|
| Auditory Discrimination | A |
| Proofreading | A, C, F, I |
| Visual Discrimination | C, F |
| Word Analysis | D |
| Vocabulary Development | E, H |
| Context Usage | F, G |
| Original Writing | I |

## PRETEST AND PROOFREADING

The Pretest identifies the words students are able to spell, as well as the words they need to learn. You may wish to use Other Word Forms when giving the Pretest. Five suggested Other Word Forms are underlined on this page.

To administer the Pretest:

**READ** each word aloud.
**SAY** the phrase containing the word.
**REPEAT** the word.

Have students correct the Pretest using the Corrected-test Procedure. They may record their scores on a personal Progress Chart (see the Teacher's Resource Book) and study misspelled words using the **S-H-A-R-P** procedure.

## OTHER WORD FORMS

This section presents related forms of the spelling words to strengthen spelling power and vocabulary knowledge.

### Enrichment Activity

Have students write synonyms or related phrases for these Other Word Forms. Be sure they write the Other Word Form with its synonym next to it.

**wonderful, appointed, owing, grew**

**A. Pretest and Proofreading**

**B. Spelling Words and Phrases**

| | |
|---|---|
| **1. colt** | frisky colt |
| **2. owe*** | whatever we owe |
| **3. knowing*** | knowing the answer |
| **4. known** | if only they had known |
| **5. growth** | spoke of their growth |
| **6. throat** | a sore throat |
| **7. cocoa** | a cup of hot cocoa |
| **8. someone*** | asked someone else |
| **9. somehow*** | will do it somehow |
| **10. somewhat*** | was somewhat different |
| **11. somewhere*** | somewhere in the cellar |
| **12. comfort** | comfort of the campfire |
| **13. company*** | company for dinner |
| **14. colored*** | colored tablecloth |
| **15. monthly*** | arrived monthly |
| **16. wonder*** | made us wonder |
| **17. choice** | had no choice |
| **18. voices** | voices in the darkness |
| **19. appointment** | forgot the appointment |
| **20. organ** | played the organ |

*Other Word Forms*

| | |
|---|---|
| colts | color, colorful |
| owes, owed, owing | month |
| know, knew, knows, knowledge | wondered, wondering, wonderful, wonderfully |
| grows, grew, growing, grower | choices, choicest |
| throats | voice, voiced, voicing |
| comforted, comforting, comfortable, | appoints, appointed |
| companies, companion | organs |

**C. Visual Warm-up** Write each word in its correct shape.

a. appointment
b. voices
c. comfort
d. organ
e. wonder
f. colt
g. owe
h. someone
i. colored
j. choice
k. somewhat
l. knowing
m. company
n. throat
o. somewhere
p. known
q. cocoa
r. monthly
s. somehow
t. growth



*Modified Lesson words are asterisked.
The Modified Lesson is found in the Teacher's Resource Book.

## MEETING INDIVIDUAL NEEDS / ASSIGNMENT GUIDE

| 5-Day Plan | 3-Day Plan | Limited Spellers | Average Spellers | Advanced Spellers |
|---|---|---|---|---|
| 1 | 1 | • Pretest<br>• Progress Chart | • Pretest<br>• Progress Chart<br>• Home Activity | • Pretest<br>• Progress Chart<br>• Home Activity |
| 2 | 1 | • Modified Lesson Visual Warm-up Ending Sounds | • Regular Lesson Visual Warm-up | • Regular Lesson Visual Warm-up |
| 3 and 4 | 2 | • Modified Lesson Vowel Puzzle Word Match Finish the Sentence | Spelling Activities | Spelling Activities<br>• Challenge Exercise |
| 5 | 3 | • Posttest<br>• Words to Learn Sheet<br>• Progress Chart | • Posttest<br>• Words to Learn Sheet<br>• Progress Chart | • Posttest<br>• Words to Learn Sheet<br>• Progress Chart |

**D. Compare the *O* Sounds** There is an *o* sound in each of the spelling words. In alphabetical order, write the spelling words where they belong.

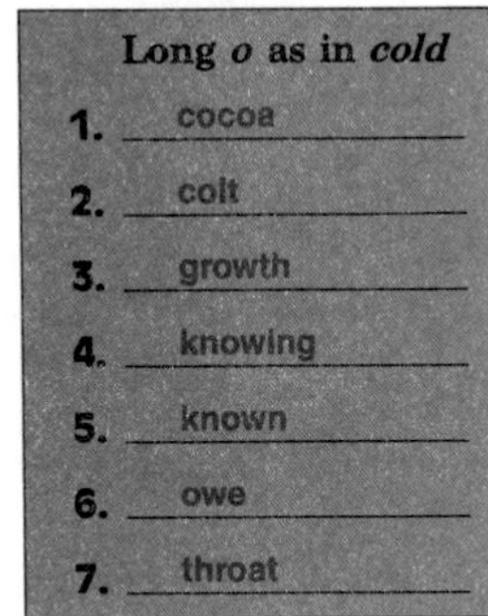
Long *o* as in *cold*

1. cocoa
2. colt
3. growth
4. knowing
5. known
6. owe
7. throat

**First Syllable Having *o* with the Sound of *u* as in *cup***

11. colored
12. comfort
13. company
14. monthly
15. somehow
16. someone
17. somewhat
18. somewhere
19. wonder

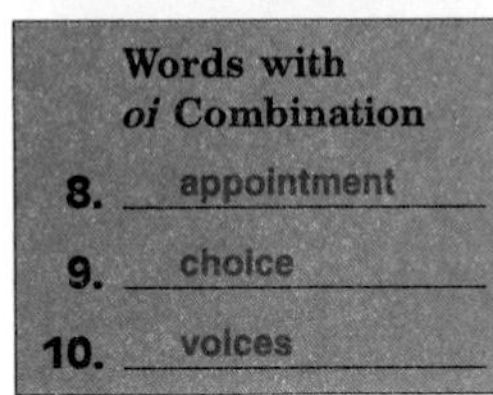
Words with *oi* Combination

8. appointment
9. choice
10. voices

**First Syllable Having *or* Controlled by *r***

20. organ

**E. Word Match-ups** Write a word from the spelling list that best fits each phrase or word below. Check your answers in the **Spelling Dictionary**.

1. young male horse colt
2. an unknown place somewhere
3. inside your neck throat
4. musical instrument organ
5. hot drink cocoa
6. an increase growth
7. something chosen choice
8. scheduled meeting appointment
9. periodically monthly
10. needed for a chorus voices
11. some person someone
12. learned known
13. debtor's problem owe
14. relieve from fear comfort
15. slightly somewhat
16. miracle wonder
17. understanding knowing
18. not black-and-white colored
19. house guests company
20. one way or another somehow



## OPTIONAL TEACHING PLAN

Write the four Word Group headings on the chalkboard. Ask the students to name the seven spelling words with the long **o** sound. Write the words as the students say them. Continue identifying the other Word Groups. Note that the long **o** sound is spelled **o** in **colt**, **ow** in **owe**, and **oa** in **cocoa**. Point out the short **u** sound of **o** in words such as **someone**.

| Word Groups | | |
|---|---|---|
| /ō/ words | colt<br>owe<br>knowing<br>known<br>growth | throat<br>cocoa<br>**ownership**<br>**poetry** |
| /ŭ/ words | someone<br>somehow<br>somewhat<br>somewhere<br>comfort<br>company | colored<br>monthly<br>wonder<br>**adjusting**<br>**insult** |
| /oi/ words | choice<br>voices | appointment<br>**royalty** |
| /ôr/ word | organ | |

*Challenge Words are boldfaced.*

### Optional Activity Masters

Those using the Hardcover Pupil Edition may wish to use the Optional Activity Masters in the Teacher's Resource Book for Exercises C and F.

Home Activity #23 — 29

Name _____ Date _____

Use the spelling words to complete the sentences. The number before each blank tells you in what column you can find the correct word. Use each word only once.

| 1 | 2 | 3 | 4 |
|---|---|---|---|
| appointment | somewhat | known | someone |
| colt | owe | wonder | somewhere |
| choice | company | throat | somehow |
| knowing | growth | somehow | colored |
| voices | monthly | cocoa | organ |

1. Though I have little time to complete the task, I will do it (3) _____.
2. The football player had no (1) _____ but to kick the ball.
3. We will be having (2) _____ for dinner.
4. Let's set the table with the (4) _____ tablecloth.
5. Please join me for a cup of hot (3) _____.
6. There is nothing like the (4) _____ of the campfire.
7. Robin heard (1) _____ in the darkness.
8. That magazine usually arrived (2) _____.
9. Don't raise your hand without (1) _____ the answer.
10. We'll pay whatever we (2) _____.
11. The director played the (4) _____ while the chorus sang.
12. I have a terrible cough and a sore (3) _____.
13. Each song was (2) _____ different from the next.
14. You will find a ladder (4) _____ in the cellar.
15. He forgot the (1) _____ to see the doctor.
16. Your failure to reply made us (3) _____ about your intentions.
17. When the girl's father didn't know the answer to her question, she asked (4) _____ else.
18. It will be hard to tame the frisky (1) _____.
19. If only they had (3) _____ about the accident, they would have helped.
20. The president spoke of their (2) _____ with the company.

©D.C. Heath and Company

Modified Lesson #23 — 87

Name _____ Date _____

| Spelling Words | knowing | owe | somehow | someone | company |
|---|---|---|---|---|---|
| | somewhat | wonder | monthly | somewhere | colored |

I. **Visual Warm-up.** Write each spelling word in its correct shape.

II. **Vowel Hunt.** Fill in the missing vowels and write the spelling words.

a. c __ mp __ n __
b. s __ m __ wh __ t
c. kn __ w __ ng
d. __ w __
e. w __ nd __ r

f. c __ l __ r __ d
g. s __ m __ __ n __
h. s __ m __ wh __ r __
i. m __ nthl __
j. s __ m __ h __ w

III. **Word Maze.** Fill in the missing letters to find the spelling words. Write the words in the blanks beside the numbers.

Across
4. _____
5. _____

©D.C. Heath and Company

Modified Lesson #23 *(continued)* — 88

Name _____ Date _____

| Spelling Words | knowing | owe | somehow | someone | company |
|---|---|---|---|---|---|
| | somewhat | wonder | monthly | somewhere | colored |

IV. **Word Parts.** Write the spelling words that have the word parts below. A word may be used more than once.

a. kn word: _____
b. wh words: _____
c. er words: _____
d. ed word: _____
e. ly word: _____
f. ow words: _____

g. ing word: _____
h. words ending in y _____
i. Write the four compound words:
_____
_____
_____
_____

V. **Sentence Sense.** Write each spelling word in the correct sentence.

Words: knowing somehow someone colored

a. A _____ tablecloth covered the table.
b. The teacher asked _____ else to erase the chalkboard.
c. The work is hard but she will do it _____.
d. We must pay whatever we _____.
e. _____ the answer, I raised my hand.

Words: somewhat wonder monthly somewhere company

f. The cat was hiding _____ in the cellar.
g. The couch we bought was _____ different.
h. Our family expects _____ for dinner.
i. The dog's strange actions made us _____.
j. The rent bill arrived _____.

©D.C. Heath and Company

### Home Activity

A weekly homework assignment

### Modified Lesson

An alternative lesson for limited spellers

*(The Answer Key can be found in the Teacher's Resource Book.)*

# LESSON 23 CONTINUED

## Challenge Exercise #23

Name______________________ Date__________

**Word Watch.** The word *company* has its origin in two Latin words: *cum*, meaning "with," and *panis*, meaning "bread." The *companis* were the people who came to your home to "eat bread with you." In early times, people spoke of breaking bread. Breaking bread was a sign of hospitality and neighborliness. Today, the company you entertain in your home often breaks bread with you as well as eats your food while you share your hospitality with them.

**Word Analogies.** Decide on the relationship that exists between the first pair of words. Using the Other Word Forms on page 92, find a word that completes the second pair of words and establishes the same relationship.

1. *Tuesday* is to *day* as *April* is to ____________
2. *valves* is to *trumpets* as *keys* is to ____________
3. *beautiful* is to *homely* as ____________ is to *awful*
4. *seals* is to *pups* as *horses* is to ____________
5. *knows* is to *nose* as ____________ is to *new*

**Challenge Words Student Activity**

Use the challenge words below to complete each *whodunit*.

**insult poetry adjusting ownership royalty**

1. Who was ____________ the car brakes?
2. Who shouted the ____________ to the chef?
3. Who claimed ____________ of the property?
4. Who was revealed to be ____________, with a claim to the throne?
5. Who tore the page from the ____________ book?

**Working With Words: Student Writing Activity**

Use as many Other Word Forms as you can from page 92 to write a menu for a restaurant. (Example: STRAWBERRY SURPRISE—the *choicest* strawberries resting on a *comfortable* bed of vanilla ice cream)

134



### Challenge Exercise

Additional activities for advanced spellers

**Spelling Words**

| | | | |
|---|---|---|---|
| growth | throat | cocoa | someone |
| colt | owe | knowing | known |
| somehow | somewhat | comfort | somewhere |
| company | colored | monthly | wonder |
| choice | voices | appointment | organ |

**F. Find the Missing Treasure**

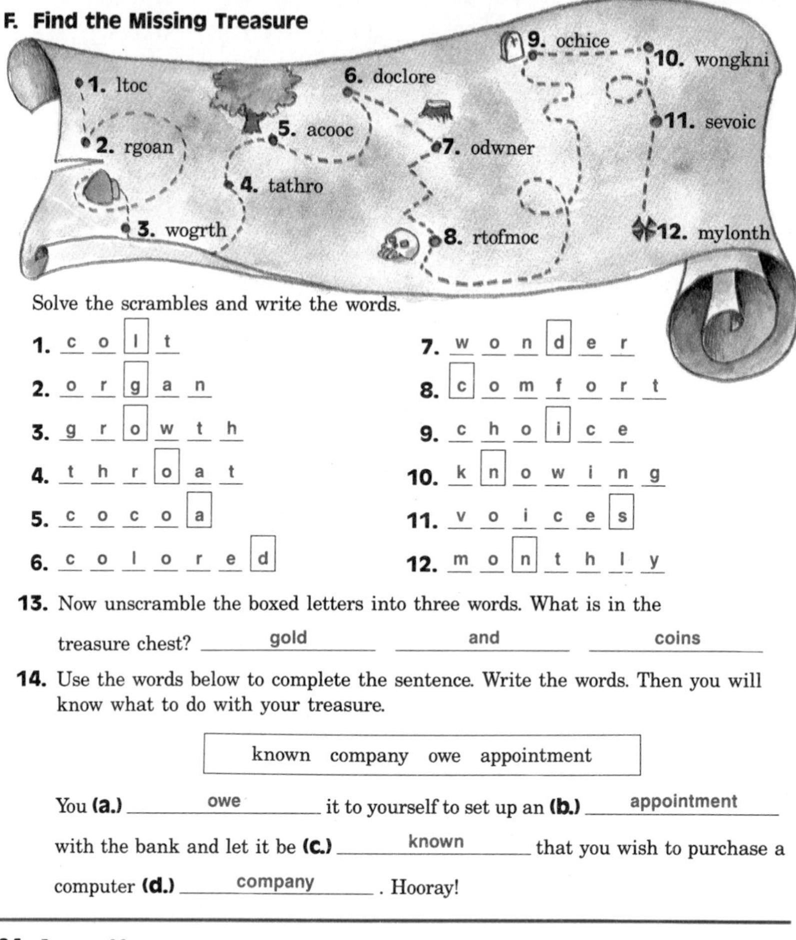


Solve the scrambles and write the words.

1. c o l t
2. o r g a n
3. g r o w t h
4. t h r o a t
5. c o c o a
6. c o l o r e d
7. w o n d e r
8. c o m f o r t
9. c h o i c e
10. k n o w i n g
11. v o i c e s
12. m o n t h l y

13. Now unscramble the boxed letters into three words. What is in the treasure chest? ___gold___ ___and___ ___coins___

14. Use the words below to complete the sentence. Write the words. Then you will know what to do with your treasure.

known company owe appointment

You **(a.)** ___owe___ it to yourself to set up an **(b.)** ___appointment___ with the bank and let it be **(c.)** ___known___ that you wish to purchase a computer **(d.)** ___company___. Hooray!



## CONTROLLED DICTATION (Optional)

These dictation sentences provide maintenance for spelling words previously taught and practice for words currently being studied. Dictation should be administered on Day 4. The teacher or another student may dictate the sentences. Be sure to dictate all marks of punctuation. Challenge Word sentences are preceded by an asterisk.

1. I **wonder** why the general wants a **monthly appointment**.
2. **Somehow** warm **cocoa** helps my **throat**.
3. There was **comfort knowing** the **colt** was **somewhere** near.
4. Had you **known** about the rapid **growth** of the printing **company**?
5. The **voices** were **somewhat** loud, but I could still hear the **organ**.
6. We **owe** each passenger a **choice** of seats.
7. Hasn't **someone colored** the eggs yet?

*8. Long ago **poetry** was written to **insult** or make fun of **royalty**.

*9. The men were **adjusting ownership** papers for the car.

**G. Using Other Word Forms** Write the Other Word Form that completes each sentence.

Base Words: color(ful) know(ledge) voice(ing) company(es) comfort(able)

1. Businesses are sometimes called companies.
2. A picture with many bright colors is colorful.
3. The knowing of information is called knowledge.
4. Having comfort means that you are comfortable.
5. When you tell your ideas, you are voicing your opinion.

**H. Challenge Words** Write the Challenge Word that completes each phrase.

| adjusting | insult | ownership | poetry | royalty |
|---|---|---|---|---|

1. prose or poetry
2. compliment or insult
3. peasants or royalty
4. possession or ownership
5. repairing or adjusting

**I. Spelling and Writing** Write two or more questions about each statement. Use as many Spelling Words, Other Word Forms, and Challenge Words as you can. A few words are suggested. Proofread for spelling using one of the Proofreading Tips from the Yellow Pages.

1. Receiving a new heart or kidney is a miracle of modern science.
   someone somewhere comfort organ
   owes knowing appointment

   Example: Is it a comfort to know that someone's life may be saved by a new organ?

2. Many hotels serve special meals to guests.
   known somewhat company colored choicest cocoa royalty

3. It is necessary for a horse to get used to human touch.
   colt throat somehow wonderful voices monthly growth



## USING OTHER WORD FORMS

Vocabulary is expanded through the use of other forms of basic spelling words. Emphasis is on the relationship of syntax to suffix choices. The following generalizations apply to the Other Word Forms used in Exercise G.

### Spelling Rule

Forming plurals

To form the plurals of nouns ending with consonant-**y**, change the **y** to **i** and add **es**. (**company, companies**)

Adding suffixes to words ending in silent **e**

When adding a suffix that begins with a vowel to words that end with silent **e**, drop the final **e**. (**voice, voicing**)

## POSTTEST AND PROOFREADING

Follow the same testing procedures used in the Pretest, although you may wish to correct the tests yourself. Have students write any misspelled words on the Words to Learn Sheet and record spelling success on the Progress Chart.

## THE SPELLING-WRITING LINK

**Purpose** This activity helps students to retain the correct spelling of words and transfer the words to their daily writing. Students use lesson words to create questions, which promotes inquiry and research skills.

**Procedure** Read the first statement and write the suggested words on the chalkboard: **someone, somewhere, comfort, organ, owes, knowing, appointment.** Brainstorm with the class possible questions about statement 1. Remind students to look at all the lesson words for ideas, not just the suggested words. Write the questions on the chalkboard, noting any lesson words.

**Practice** Tell students to finish the activity by writing two or more questions about each statement. Remind them to proofread their work for spelling.

LESSON

# 24

REVIEW

**OBJECTIVES**

- to review the spelling of the 100 words studied in Lessons 19-23
- to promote the use of other forms of the 100 spelling words
- to apply high-utility generalizations for the addition of suffixes

| Summary of Skills | Exercises |
|---|---|
| Context Usage | A, C |
| Word Analysis | B, D |

## REVIEW OF LESSONS 19-23

The goal of the review exercises is to expand each student's spelling power. The one hundred spelling words studied in the five preceding lessons are presented in challenging formats where the focus is shifted from the spelling words to the Other Word Forms.

## WORD REVIEW PROCEDURE

Students are encouraged to use this abbreviated version of the **S-H-A-R-P** procedure when reviewing the spelling words at the top of each review page.

**LOOK** at each word.
**SAY** the word to yourself.
**THINK** about the letters that spell the word.

24

**REVIEWING LESSONS 19-23**

| April | navy | nation | information | worse |
|---|---|---|---|---|
| muddy | judge | current | stubborn | struck |
| attack | carried | allow | planning | attached |
| village | bridge | signal | cities | minute |
| knowing | company | cocoa | someone | somewhere |

**A. Quotable Quotes** Write Other Word Forms to replace the spelling words printed under each blank. Four words have no Other Word Forms. If you need help, use the **Spelling Dictionary**.

1. "The judges (judge) stubbornly (stubborn) refused to change their minds," the senator added.
2. "The city (cities) bridges (bridge) will carry (carried) more traffic than we had planned," someone (someone) replied.
3. The president said, "Several nations (nation) have allowed (allow) both companies (company) to purchase cocoa (cocoa) beans."
4. 'The naval (naval) base is located somewhere (somewhere) in California," Jay answered.
5. The general stated, "In minutes (minute), the planes attacked (attack) the villages (village) beyond Pearl Harbor."
6. "In April (April), we had planned (planning) to attach (attached) new switches to all the traffic signals (signal)," the safety officer remarked.
7. The coach added, "I was informed (information) that the muddiest (muddy) fields present the worst (worse) problems to the players."
8. "We now know (knowing) that strong wind currents (current) will cause the storm to strike (struck) in the early morning hours," the newscaster reported.

R E V I E W



## MEETING INDIVIDUAL NEEDS / ASSIGNMENT GUIDE

| 5-Day Plan | 3-Day Plan | Limited Spellers | Average Spellers | Advanced Spellers |
|---|---|---|---|---|
| 1 and 2 | 1 | • Modified Lesson Visual Warm-up Word Parts | • Regular Lesson Spelling Activities • Home Activity | • Regular Lesson Spelling Activities • Home Activity |
| 3 and 4 | 2 | • Modified Lesson Vowel Puzzle Word Match Finish the Sentence | Regular Lesson Spelling Activities • Proofreading Exercise(s) | • Regular Lesson Spelling Activities • Proofreading Exercise(s) • Challenge Word Review |
| 5 | 3 | • Test Modified Lesson Words • Words to Learn Sheet | • Review Test or Standardized-format Test • Words to Learn Sheet | • Review Test or Standardized-format Test • Words to Learn Sheet |

| | | | | |
|---|---|---|---|---|
| changing | favor | station | swallow | betray |
| sunny | puzzle | button | bundle | choice |
| married | mirror | savings | carries | thrill |
| listen | finish | wonder | comfort | appointment |
| throat | ribbon | cliff | potato | tomato |

**B. Word Building** Add word parts to each spelling word or its base word to make Other Word Forms. Write the words.

| Spelling Words | *s* or *es* | *ed* | *ing* |
|---|---|---|---|
| Example: **act** | *acts* | *acted* | *acting* |
| **1.** changing | changes | changed | |
| **2.** married | marries | | marrying |
| **3.** listen | listens | listened | listening |
| **4.** throat | throats | | |
| **5.** favor | favors | favored | favoring |
| **6.** puzzle | puzzles | puzzled | puzzling |
| **7.** mirror | mirrors | mirrored | mirroring |
| **8.** finish | finishes | finished | finishing |
| **9.** station | stations | stationed | stationing |
| **10.** button | buttons | buttoned | buttoning |
| **11.** savings | saves | saved | saving |
| **12.** tomato | tomatoes | | |
| **13.** cliff | cliffs | | |
| **14.** swallow | swallows | swallowed | swallowing |
| **15.** bundle | bundles | bundled | bundling |
| **16.** carries | | carried | carrying |
| **17.** comfort | comforts | comforted | comforting |
| **18.** potato | potatoes | | |
| **19.** betray | betrays | betrayed | betraying |
| **20.** thrill | thrills | thrilled | thrilling |
| **21.** choice | choices | | |
| **22.** wonder | wonders | wondered | wondering |
| **23.** appointment | appoints | appointed | appointing |
| **24.** ribbon | ribbons | | |
| **25.** sunny | suns | sunned | sunning |

REVIEW



REVIEW

## CREATIVE WRITING

**(An optional writing activity)**

**Recipe for Writing:** This imaginative writing activity uses spelling words and Other Word Forms studied in Lessons 19-23.

COMBINE:

1 grapefruit plantation in a sunny jungle valley
5 puzzling mirror signals from the cliff
9 ladies with colored bundles
1 compass

SEASON with your own original ideas and COOK UP a story with a unique FLAVOR. Proofread before SERVING.

The RECIPE words appear in the following lessons.

| Lesson | Words |
|---|---|
| 19 | grapefruit, plantation, ladies |
| 20 | sunny, jungle, puzzling, bundles |
| 21 | valley, mirror |
| 22 | signals, cliff, compass |
| 23 | colored |

**Home Activity #24**

30

**Modified Lesson #24**

89

**Modified Lesson #24** *(continued)*

90

## Home Activity

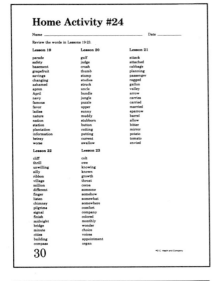

A weekly homework assignment

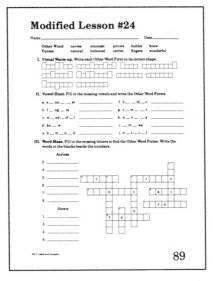

## Modified Lesson

An alternative lesson for limited spellers

*(The Answer Key can be found in the Teacher's Resource Book.)*

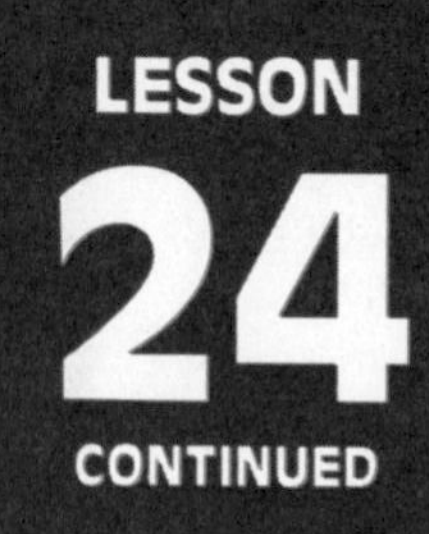

LESSON 24 CONTINUED

## Challenge Word Review

The Challenge Words from the previous five lessons are listed below if you wish to review the Challenge Words with your more advanced students.

1. bathing
2. crater
3. decoration
4. nickname
5. prey
6. construct
7. couple
8. underneath
9. dumb
10. instructions
11. atlas
12. fashionable
13. dandelion
14. shatter
15. nationally
16. comic
17. digits
18. windshield
19. military
20. miserable
21. adjusting
22. insult
23. ownership
24. poetry
25. royalty

| ■ | ★ | ▲ | ◆ | ● |
|---|---|---|---|---|
| safety | grapefruit | cutting | thumb | crush |
| ragged | barrel | silly | building | voices |
| chimney | owe | growth | monthly | colt |
| gallon | pilgrims | cabbage | sparrow | arrow |
| parade | ladies | plantation | putting | studies |

REVIEW

**C. Classified Ads** Complete each ad by writing Other Word Forms or the spelling words. The shape tells you in what column you can find the spelling word. Use each word or its Other Word Form only once. If you need help, use the **Spelling Dictionary**.

1. Gardener ad: We hire green ◆ thumbs only.
2. Roof cleaner ad: All ■ chimneys swept clean.
3. The *Mayflower* captain ad: Only ★ pilgrims need apply.
4. Robin Hood ad: We rent bows and ● arrows.
5. Comedian ad: A lot of ▲ silliness accepted.
6. Coleslaw maker ad: Firm ▲ cabbages required.
7. Fancy ★ grapefruit grower ad: We sell juice by the ■ gallons.
8. Bird seller ad: Buy ◆ sparrows cheap.
9. Choir director ad: Add your ● voice to ours.
10. Traffic guard ad: We promise you a ■ safe crossing.
11. Self-defense instructor ad: We deal ● crushing blows.
12. Diet planner ad: Eat right and ▲ grow slender.
13. Southern realtor ad: Old ▲ plantations bought and sold.
14. Writer ad: Go from ■ rags to riches.
15. Carpenter ad: We ◆ build your dreams.
16. Calendar maker ad: The weeks grow into ◆ months.
17. Stable owner ad: We rent spring ● colts.
18. Tutor ad: You can ● study with a buddy.
19. Amusement-park owner ad: Have ★ barrels of fun.
20. Barber ad: We make short ▲ cuts.
21. Kennel owner ad: Let's ◆ put a dog in your life.
22. Nail filer ad: We serve ★ lady fingers.
23. Moneylender ad: You ★ owe it to yourself.
24. Marcher ad: No ■ parades too small.



### Proofreading Exercise Lesson #24

Name ____________ Date ________

**Proofreading the Spelling of Others**
Proofread Sally's letter and circle the misspelled words.
Write the correct words on the lines.

April 13, 1988

Pilgrim Choices
25 Bridge Street
East Village, MA 01761

Dear Sirs:

Two weeks ago I sent for an aprin made by your famus cumpany. Your ad said that the product had ribons and small buttins and was made for cumfort in the kitchen.

A bundel arrived in the mail today. It contained a raggid piece of navey blue cloth. I can't help but wunder what happened! I feel that sumhow somone sumwhere made a silley mistake. The choise you sent me was very diferent from what I ordered and I am unwiling to keep it.

I am returning the collored cloth. Please faver me with my choice soon.

Yours truly,
Sally Swallow

1. ______ 6. ______ 11. ______ 16. ______
2. ______ 7. ______ 12. ______ 17. ______
3. ______ 8. ______ 13. ______ 18. ______
4. ______ 9. ______ 14. ______ 19. ______
5. ______ 10. ______ 15. ______ 20. ______





## Proofreading Exercise

| famous | ashamed | nature | stump | different |
|---|---|---|---|---|
| upper | envied | million | known | finger |
| organ | basement | apron | uncle | jungle |
| gulf | colored | passenger | midnight | valley |
| bitter | compass | unwilling | somehow | somewhat |

**D. Word Operations** Use words from the spelling list to complete the exercises below. If you need help, use the **Spelling Dictionary**.

**Operation Plural** Write the *s* or *es* form of each word. Use the **Spelling Dictionary**.

**1.** gulf *gulfs*
**2.** organ organs
**3.** million millions
**4.** compass compasses
**5.** apron aprons
**6.** passenger passengers
**7.** stump stumps
**8.** uncle uncles
**9.** finger fingers
**10.** jungle jungles
**11.** valley valleys
**12.** basement basements

**Operation Adverb** Write an Other Word Form that ends in *ly* for each word. Use the **Spelling Dictionary** to check your word. The starred words are difficult.

**13.** bitter bitterly
**14.** different differently
**15.** famous famously
***16.** envied enviously
***17.** colored colorfully
***18.** nature naturally
***19.** known knowingly
**20.** unwilling unwillingly
**21.** ashamed ashamedly

**Operation Addition** Add the word parts to make spelling words. Write the words. You will have to add a letter to one word to make the spelling word.

**22.** some + what = somewhat
**23.** mid + night = midnight
**24.** up + er = upper
**25.** some + how = somehow

REVIEW



## Review Test: Lesson 24

Name__________ Date__________

**Directions:** Read each sentence. Select the word with the correct spelling to complete each sentence. Fill in the correct letter in the answer column.

1. The children followed the _____. A. parad B. parade C. paraid D. perade
2. I have some _____ in the bank. A. saivings B. savigns C. saverngs D. savings
3. _____ showers bring May flowers. A. April B. Aprel C. Aprill D. Arpil
4. The _____ and gentlemen left. A. ladys B. ladies C. laides D. laidys
5. Tara was a southern _____. A. plantion B. plantachion C. plantasion D. plantation
6. We sailed across the _____. A. golf B. golfe C. gulf D. gulfe
7. The _____ of the tree rotted. A. stoump B. stump C. stomp D. stumpe
8. I have a _____ of dirty laundry. A. bundle B. bundel C. bundil D. bundal
9. I ran across the _____ meadow. A. sunney B. sunnie C. suny D. sunny
10. They are _____ the lawn. A. catting B. cuting C. cutting D. cuttin
11. The army rested after the _____. A. atack B. attack C. attak D. attacke
12. The bus has an extra _____. A. pasenger B. passenjer C. passinger D. passenger
13. Robin lost another _____. A. arro B. arow C. arrow D. arrou
14. There is a crack in the _____. A. mirror B. miror C. mirrer D. mirrar
15. That bird is a nesting _____. A. sparow B. sparrou C. sparrow D. sparough
16. We walked to the edge of the _____. A. clif B. clef C. cliffe D. cliff
17. He tied a yellow _____. A. ribon B. ribbon C. ribben D. ribban
18. I have a paper cut on my _____. A. finger B. fingre C. fingger D. fingar
19. I am watching for the _____. A. signol B. signel C. signal D. signell
20. We need one more _____ to work. A. minut B. minnit C. minnut D. minute
21. The horse is a frisky _____. A. kolt B. coolt C. colt D. koolt
22. The children spoke of their _____. A. groth B. groath C. grouth D. growth
23. We will do it _____. A. somhow B. somehow C. sumhow D. sumehow
24. Our family had _____ for dinner. A. companny B. cumpany C. company D. companey
25. We had no _____. A. choise B. choyce C. choice D. choce

Answer Column: 1.–25. A B C D

158



**Standardized-format Test**

## REVIEW TEST

Twenty-five words, selected randomly from the five spelling lists, constitute the test and are listed with the appropriate phrases. Follow the same testing procedure used to administer the weekly Pretest and Posttest. Have students write any misspelled words on the Words to Learn Sheet. As an alternative testing option, you may wish to use the Standardized-format Test for this Review Lesson, found in the Teacher's Resource Book.

REVIEW

## Test Words and Phrases

| | |
|---|---|
| 1. parade | followed the **parade** |
| 2. savings | **savings** in the bank |
| 3. April | **April** showers |
| 4. ladies | **ladies** and gentlemen |
| 5. plantation | southern **plantation** |
| 6. gulf | sailed across the **gulf** |
| 7. stump | the **stump** of the tree |
| 8. bundle | a **bundle** of dirty laundry |
| 9. sunny | across the **sunny** meadow |
| 10. cutting | **cutting** the lawn |
| 11. attack | after the **attack** |
| 12. passenger | an extra **passenger** |
| 13. arrow | lost another **arrow** |
| 14. sparrow | a nesting **sparrow** |
| 15. mirror | a crack in the **mirror** |
| 16. cliff | the edge of the **cliff** |
| 17. ribbon | tied a yellow **ribbon** |
| 18. finger | a paper cut on my **finger** |
| 19. signal | watching for the **signal** |
| 20. minute | had one more **minute** |
| 21. colt | frisky **colt** |
| 22. growth | spoke of their **growth** |
| 23. somehow | will do it **somehow** |
| 24. company | **company** for dinner |
| 25. choice | had no **choice** |

# LESSON 25

## OBJECTIVES

- to spell 20 high-frequency words including words with the /ŭ/, /ô/, and /ä/
- to proofread these words in daily writing
- to become familiar with 38 other forms of the spelling words

| Summary of Skills | Exercises |
|---|---|
| Auditory Discrimination | A |
| Proofreading | A, C, D, H |
| Visual Discrimination | C, D |
| Vocabulary Development | E |
| Word Analysis | F |
| Context Usage | G |
| Original Writing | H |

## PRETEST AND PROOFREADING

The Pretest identifies the words students are able to spell, as well as the words they need to learn. You may wish to use Other Word Forms when giving the Pretest. Five suggested Other Word Forms are underlined on this page.

To administer the Pretest:

**READ** each word aloud.
**SAY** the phrase containing the word.
**REPEAT** the word.

Have students correct the Pretest using the Corrected-test Procedure. They may record their scores on a personal Progress Chart (see the Teacher's Resource Book) and study misspelled words using the **S-H-A-R-P** procedure.

## OTHER WORD FORMS

This section presents related forms of the spelling words to strengthen spelling power and vocabulary knowledge.

### Enrichment Activity

Have students write Other Word Forms under the appropriate ending.

-ing -ed -s -ly -er -est

# 25

**A. Pretest and Proofreading**

**B. Spelling Words and Phrases**

| | |
|---|---|
| **1. ugly*** | ugly storm |
| **2. public** | open to the public |
| **3. husband** | husband and wife |
| **4. pumpkin** | turned into a pumpkin |
| **5. multiply** | learned to multiply |
| **6. thunder*** | afraid of thunder |
| **7. salty** | too salty to eat |
| **8. altered** | altered their plans |
| **9. false** | true or false |
| **10. smaller*** | smaller or larger |
| **11. stalk** | a stalk of corn |
| **12. awful** | thought it was awful |
| **13. crawl*** | had to crawl out |
| **14. drawn*** | drawn by the artist |
| **15. drawing*** | tore the drawing paper |
| **16. watered*** | watered the garden |
| **17. cough*** | a dose of cough medicine |
| **18. bought*** | bought my own lunch |
| **19. brought*** | brought our friend |
| **20. calm** | calm and peaceful |

*Other Word Forms*

| | |
|---|---|
| uglier, ugliest | small, smallest |
| publicity, publicly, publicize | stalked, stalking |
| husbands | awfully |
| pumpkins | crawls, crawled |
| multiplies, multiplying, multiplier | draw, drew |
| thundering | water, watering, watery |
| salt, salting | coughed, coughs, coughing |
| alter, alters | buy, buying |
| falsely | bring, bringing |
| | calmer, calmest, calmly |

**C. Visual Warm-up** Write each word in its correct shape.

a. awful
b. ugly
c. salty
d. cough
e. false
f. bought
g. smaller
h. brought
i. calm
j. watered
k. altered
l. public
m. drawn
n. husband
o. crawl
p. pumpkin
q. drawing
r. thunder
s. multiply
t. stalk



*Modified Lesson words are asterisked.
The Modified Lesson is found in the Teacher's Resource Book.

## MEETING INDIVIDUAL NEEDS / ASSIGNMENT GUIDE

| 5-Day Plan | 3-Day Plan | Limited Spellers | Average Spellers | Advanced Spellers |
|---|---|---|---|---|
| 1 | 1 | • Pretest • Progress Chart | • Pretest • Progress Chart • Home Activity | • Pretest • Progress Chart • Home Activity |
| 2 | 1 | • Modified Lesson Visual Warm-up Ending Sounds | • Regular Lesson Visual Warm-up | • Regular Lesson Visual Warm-up |
| 3 and 4 | 2 | • Modified Lesson Vowel Puzzle Word Match Finish the Sentence | Spelling Activities | Spelling Activities • Challenge Exercise |
| 5 | 3 | • Posttest • Words to Learn Sheet • Progress Chart | • Posttest • Words to Learn Sheet • Progress Chart | • Posttest • Words to Learn Sheet • Progress Chart |

**D. Scrambled Words** Unscramble the words in each of the columns. Then rearrange the boxed letters to write a word from the spelling list. If your answers are correct, you will have uncovered all the spelling words.

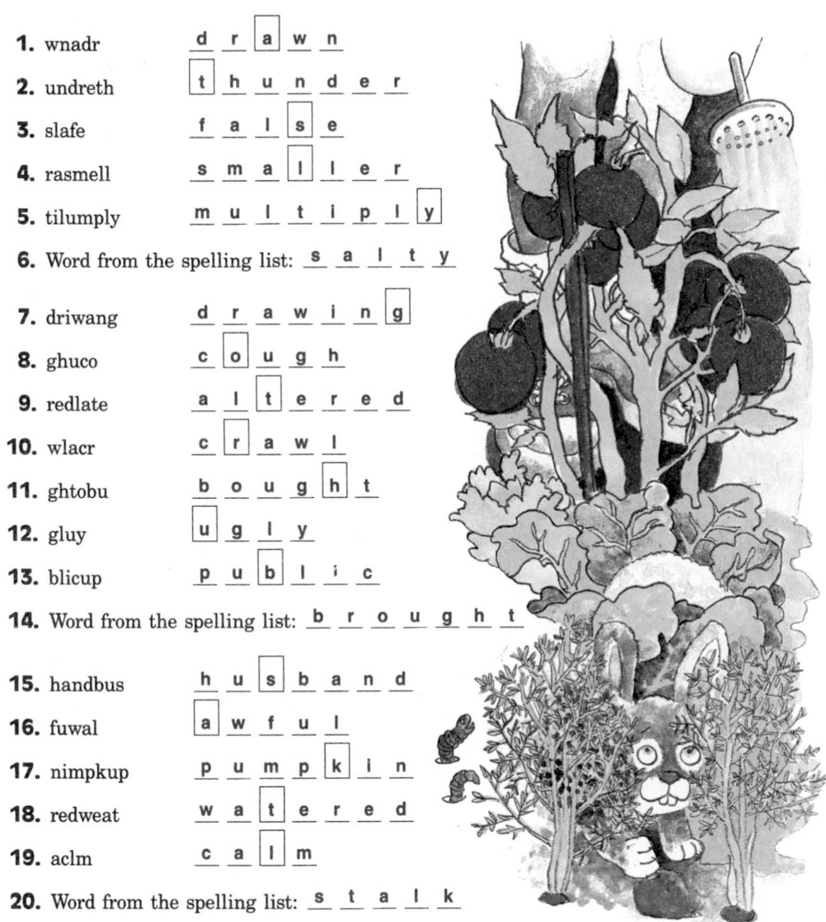

1. wnadr — d r [a] w n
2. undreth — [t] h u n d e r
3. slafe — f a l [s] e
4. rasmell — s m a [l] l e r
5. tilumply — m u l t i p l [y]
6. Word from the spelling list: s a l t y

7. driwang — d r a w i n [g]
8. ghuco — c [o] u g h
9. redlate — a l [t] e r e d
10. wlacr — c [r] a w l
11. ghtobu — b o u g [h] t
12. gluy — [u] g l y
13. blicup — p u [b] l i c
14. Word from the spelling list: b r o u g h t

15. handbus — h u [s] b a n d
16. fuwal — [a] w f u l
17. nimpkup — p u m p [k] i n
18. redweat — w a [t] e r e d
19. aclm — c a [l] m
20. Word from the spelling list: s t a l k



## OPTIONAL TEACHING PLAN

Write the six Word Group headings on the chalkboard. Ask the students to name the six spelling words with the short **u** sound. Write the words as the students say them. Continue identifying the other Word Groups. Note that the /ô/ sound is spelled with **al** in words such as **salty**, **a** in **watered**, **aw** in words such as **awful**, and **ou** in words such as **cough**.

| Word Groups | | |
|---|---|---|
| /ŭ/ words | ugly<br>public<br>husband | pumpkin<br>multiply<br>thunder |
| /ô/: **al** words | salty<br>altered<br>false | smaller<br>stalk |
| /ô/: **aw** and **au** words | awful<br>crawl<br>drawn<br>drawing | **cautious**<br>**vault**<br>**lawyer**<br>**awesome** |
| /ô/: **a** and **o** words | watered | **lofty** |
| /ô/: **ou** words | cough<br>bought | brought |
| /ä/: **al** word | calm | |

*Challenge Words are boldfaced.*

### Optional Activity Masters

Those using the Hardcover Pupil Edition may wish to use the Optional Activity Masters in the Teacher's Resource Book for Exercises C and D.

**Home Activity #25**

| 1 | 2 | 3 | 4 |
| ugly | thunder | stalk | crawl |
| public | salty | calm | drawing |
| husband | altered | watered | brought |
| pumpkin | false | awful | cough |
| multiply | smaller | drawn | bought |

1. Is this statement true or (2) _____? You will be turned into a (1) _____ if you stay out too late.
2. I took a dose of (4) _____ medicine. I thought it was (3) _____, but I swallowed it anyway.
3. The exhibition was open to the (1) _____. We (4) _____ our friend.
4. Is 2 times 3 (2) _____ or larger than 4 times 5? You should know if you have learned to (1) _____.
5. That German shepherd is afraid of (2) _____. He yelped in fear at the sounds of the (1) _____ storm.
6. This portrait was (3) _____ by the artist. It is slightly damaged because I tore the (4) _____ paper.
7. Chauncey (3) _____ the garden. He enjoyed the garden because it was (3) _____ and peaceful.
8. I (4) _____ my own lunch at the restaurant. I was disappointed, though, because my lunch was too (2) _____ to eat.
9. I found a beetle in a (3) _____ of corn. It had to (4) _____ out when I set the corn to soak.
10. They had planned on becoming (1) _____ and wife in June. However, they (2) _____ their plans and were married in July.

©D. C. Heath and Company       **31**

|---|---|---|---|
| ugly<br>public<br>husband<br>pumpkin<br>multiply | thunder<br>salty<br>altered<br>false<br>smaller | stalk<br>calm<br>watered<br>awful<br>drawn | crawl<br>drawing<br>brought<br>cough<br>bought |

31

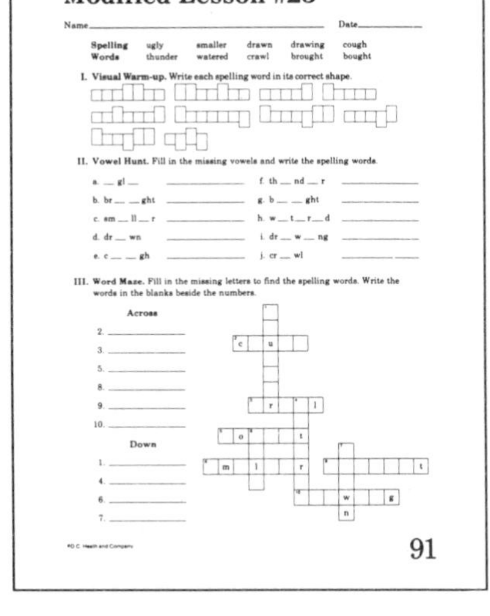

**Modified Lesson #25**

Spelling Words: ugly, thunder, smaller, watered, drawn, crawl, drawing, brought, cough, bought

I. Visual Warm-up. Write each spelling word in its correct shape.

II. Vowel Hunt. Fill in the missing vowels and write the spelling words.

a. __ gl __ _____
b. br __ __ ght _____
c. sm __ ll __ r _____
d. dr __ wn _____
e. c __ __ gh _____
f. th __ nd __ r _____
g. b __ __ ght _____
h. w __ t __ r __ d _____
i. dr __ w __ ng _____
j. cr __ wl _____

III. Word Maze. Fill in the missing letters to find the spelling words. Write the words in the blanks beside the numbers.

Across
2. _____
3. _____
5. _____
8. _____
9. _____
10. _____

Down
1. _____
4. _____
6. _____
7. _____

©D. C. Heath and Company

91

**Modified Lesson #25** *(continued)*

IV. Word Parts. Write the spelling words that have the word parts below. A word may be used more than once.

a. aw words: _____
b. ou words: _____
c. all word: _____
d. ly word: _____
e. word with gh having the sound of f: _____
f. er words: _____
g. ght words: _____
h. ed word: _____
i. dr words: _____
j. th word: _____

V. Sentence Sense.

92

### Home Activity

A weekly homework assignment

### Modified Lesson

An alternative lesson for limited spellers

*(The Answer Key can be found in the Teacher's Resource Book.)*

# LESSON 25 CONTINUED

### Challenge Exercise #25

Name__________________ Date__________

**Word Watch.** The word *calm* derives from the ancient Greek word meaning "burning heat." Greece is an intensely warm country where many people rest midday to avoid the hot sun. During this quiet hot period of the day, even the winds are still. To the early Greeks, this time was the *kauma*. When the French borrowed the word, it became *calme*. For them, it meant "the time of day when the flocks are at rest." Today, regardless of who or what is at rest, the word *calm* refers to "a peaceful time."

**Word Analogies.** Decide on the relationship that exists between the first pair of words. Using the Other Word Forms on page 100, find a word that completes the second pair of words and establishes the same relationship.

1. *sugar* is to *sweetening* as __________ is to *seasoning*
2. *purchase* is to *sale* as __________ is to *selling*
3. *females* is to *wives* as *males* is to __________
4. *secretly* is to *privately* as *openly* is to __________
5. *negative* is to *positive* as __________ is to *truly*

**Challenge Words Student Activity**
Use the challenge words below to complete the definition.

**awesome cautious lawyer vault lofty**

A good __________ is a person who has studied law for years, who proceeds in a __________ manner, and who has a __________ ideal of justice. A good lawyer feels an __________ responsibility for any client's rights. A few lawyers, however, think more about how they may __________ to fame through handling an important case.

**Working With Words: Student Writing Activity**
Use as many Other Word Forms as you can from page 100 to write five entries in the school's medical record book. You may describe illnesses or injuries. (Example: Kim *coughed* often during class and needed a *small* amount of water to ease the cough.)





## Challenge Exercise
Additional activities for advanced spellers

### Spelling Words

| | | | | |
|---|---|---|---|---|
| ugly | public | husband | pumpkin | multiply |
| thunder | salty | altered | false | smaller |
| stalk | awful | crawl | drawn | drawing |
| watered | cough | bought | brought | calm |

**E. Generally Speaking** Write each spelling word for the group it best fits.

1. small, smaller, smallest
2. poor, bad, awful
3. sketching, painting, drawing
4. male, spouse, husband
5. wrong, untrue, false
6. changed, fitted, altered
7. sniff, sneeze, cough
8. wet, sprayed, watered
9. spicy, seasoned, salty
10. unattractive, unpleasant, ugly
11. squash, cucumber, pumpkin
12. sketched, painted, drawn
13. windless, motionless, calm
14. storm, lightning, thunder
15. add, substract, multiply
16. creep, crawl, walk
17. purchased, shopped, bought
18. took, carried, brought
19. stem, trunk, stalk
20. citizens, people, public



## CONTROLLED DICTATION (Optional)

These dictation sentences provide maintenance for spelling words previously taught and practice for words currently being studied. Dictation should be administered on Day 4. The teacher or another student may dictate the sentences. Be sure to dictate all marks of punctuation. Challenge Word sentences are preceded by an asterisk.

1. An **awful** crash of **thunder** burst the afternoon **calm**.
2. I **watered** the **smaller stalk** so it would **multiply** faster.
3. Her **husband brought** an **ugly** mask to the Halloween party.
4. The **pumpkin** I **bought** had a **salty** taste.
5. When I **cough**, my **false** tooth moves forward somewhat.
6. Who **altered** the **drawing** of the **public** building?
7. The girl has **drawn** pictures of the kittens as they **crawl** and play.

*8. The **cautious lawyer** put the will in the **vault**.
*9. The height of those **lofty** mountains is **awesome**.

**F. Using Other Word Forms** Write the Other Word Form that completes each series.

Base Words: buy(ing) water(ing) stalk(ed) multiply(es) cough(ed)

1. multiplies, multiplied, multiplying
2. waters, watered, watering
3. coughs, coughed, coughing
4. buys, bought, buying
5. stalks, stalked, stalking

**G. Challenge Words** Write the Challenge Word that completes each question.

| cautious | vault | lawyer | lofty | awesome |
|---|---|---|---|---|

1. Was the money placed in a vault?
2. Is the Grand Canyon really an awesome sight?
3. Were the hikers cautious as they climbed the cliffs?
4. When did the lawyer enter the courtroom?
5. Does the condor nest at lofty heights?

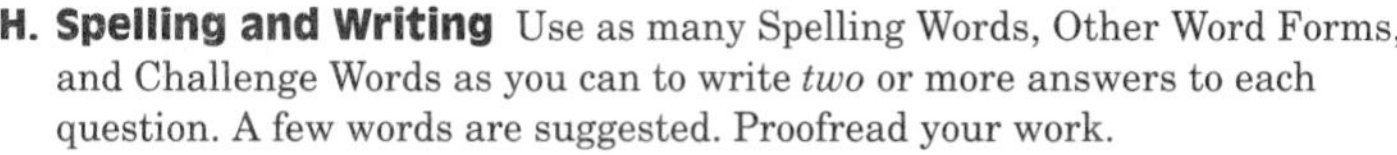

**H. Spelling and Writing** Use as many Spelling Words, Other Word Forms, and Challenge Words as you can to write *two* or more answers to each question. A few words are suggested. Proofread your work.

1. What advice would you give to someone who wants to plant a garden?

   stalk – watered – crawl – pumpkin – cautious – multiply

2. How would you try to convince people to help you clean up a littered, vacant lot?

   ugly – public – awful – drawing – brought

3. What would you do if a product you purchased didn't do what it was advertised to do?

   altered – bought – false – calm – lawyer – smaller



## USING OTHER WORD FORMS

Vocabulary is expanded through the use of other forms of basic spelling words. Emphasis is on the relationship of syntax to suffix choices. The following generalizations apply to the Other Word Forms used in Exercise F.

### Spelling Rule

Adding suffixes to words ending in **y**

When adding a suffix to words ending with consonant-**y**, change the **y** to **i**, unless the suffix begins with **i**.
(**multiply, multiplies**)

When adding a suffix to words ending with vowel-**y**, do not change the **y** to **i**.
(**buy, buying**)

## POSTTEST AND PROOFREADING

Follow the same testing procedures used in the Pretest, although you may wish to correct the tests yourself. Have students write any misspelled words on the Words to Learn Sheet and record spelling success on the Progress Chart.

## THE SPELLING-WRITING LINK

**Purpose** This activity helps students retain the correct spelling of words and transfer the words to their daily writing. Students use lesson words to answer questions promoting higher-order thinking skills.

**Procedure** Read the first question and write the suggested words on the chalkboard: **stalk, watered, crawl, pumpkin, cautious, multiply.** Have students list some Other Word Forms of the lesson words. Brainstorm with the class possible answers to question 1. Remind students to look at all the lesson words for ideas. Write the answers on the chalkboard, noting any lesson words.

**Practice** Tell students to finish the activity by writing two or more answers to each question. Remind them to proofread their work.

LESSON

# 26

## OBJECTIVES

- to spell 20 high-frequency words, including **eigh** and **ai** words with the /ā/, and words with the /ă/ and /ĕ/
- to proofread these words in daily writing
- to become familiar with 32 other forms of the spelling words

| Summary of Skills | Exercises |
|---|---|
| Auditory Discrimination | A |
| Proofreading | A, C, D, J |
| Visual Discrimination | C, D |
| Word Analysis | E, G |
| Vocabulary Development | F, H, I |
| Original Writing | J |

## PRETEST AND PROOFREADING

The Pretest identifies the words students are able to spell, as well as the words they need to learn. You may wish to use Other Word Forms when giving the Pretest. Five suggested Other Word Forms are underlined on this page.

To administer the Pretest:

**READ** each word aloud.
**SAY** the phrase containing the word.
**REPEAT** the word.

Have students correct the Pretest using the Corrected-test Procedure. They may record their scores on a personal Progress Chart (see the Teacher's Resource Book) and study misspelled words using the **S-H-A-R-P** procedure.

## OTHER WORD FORMS

This section presents related forms of the spelling words to strengthen spelling power and vocabulary knowledge.

### Enrichment Activity

Have students write Other Word Forms under the appropriate vowel sound.

**long a** **short a** **short e**

# 26

**A. Pretest and Proofreading**

**B. Spelling Words and Phrases**

| | |
|---|---|
| **1. eighteen*** | eighteen students |
| **2. eighty*** | eighty days |
| **3. weigh** | to weigh and measure |
| **4. neighborhood** | a friendly neighborhood |
| **5. plain*** | plain wrapper |
| **6. raise*** | had to raise it higher |
| **7. maintain** | to maintain order |
| **8. ashes*** | burned to ashes |
| **9. badge** | showed your badge |
| **10. flashlight*** | the dimming flashlight |
| **11. edge*** | at the edge of the wharf |
| **12. else** | nothing else to do |
| **13. kettle*** | heated the kettle |
| **14. settle*** | to settle in the town |
| **15. freckles** | covered with freckles |
| **16. quest** | their quest for gold |
| **17. question** | asked another question |
| **18. mention** | the mention of my name |
| **19. western*** | wore western clothes |
| **20. cherries** | a basket of cherries |

*Other Word Forms*

| | |
|---|---|
| eighteenth | flashlights |
| eightieth | edges, edging, edgy |
| weight, weighed | kettles |
| neighbor, neighboring, neighborly | settler, settled |
| plainly, plainer, plainest | freckled |
| raises, raised, raising | questing |
| maintained, maintenance | questions |
| ash | mentioned, mentioning |
| badges | west, westerly |
| | cherry |

**C. Visual Warm-up** Write each word in its correct shape.

a. mention
b. western
c. weigh
d. badge
e. flashlight
f. ashes
g. plain
h. quest
i. eighteen
j. else
k. freckles
l. neighborhood
m. settle
n. maintain
o. kettle
p. eighty
q. edge
r. cherries
s. raise
t. question



*Modified Lesson words are asterisked.
The Modified Lesson is found in the Teacher's Resource Book.

## MEETING INDIVIDUAL NEEDS / ASSIGNMENT GUIDE

| 5-Day Plan | 3-Day Plan | Limited Spellers | Average Spellers | Advanced Spellers |
|---|---|---|---|---|
| 1 | 1 | • Pretest<br>• Progress Chart | • Pretest<br>• Progress Chart<br>• Home Activity | • Pretest<br>• Progress Chart<br>• Home Activity |
| 2 | | • Modified Lesson<br>Visual Warm-up<br>Ending Sounds | • Regular Lesson<br>Visual Warm-up | • Regular Lesson<br>Visual Warm-up |
| 3 and 4 | 2 | • Modified Lesson<br>Vowel Puzzle<br>Word Match<br>Finish the Sentence | Spelling Activities | Spelling Activities<br>• Challenge Exercise |
| 5 | 3 | • Posttest<br>• Words to Learn Sheet<br>• Progress Chart | • Posttest<br>• Words to Learn Sheet<br>• Progress Chart | • Posttest<br>• Words to Learn Sheet<br>• Progress Chart |

**D. Word Search** Find each of the spelling words in the grid below. The words appear across and down. Circle and write the words.

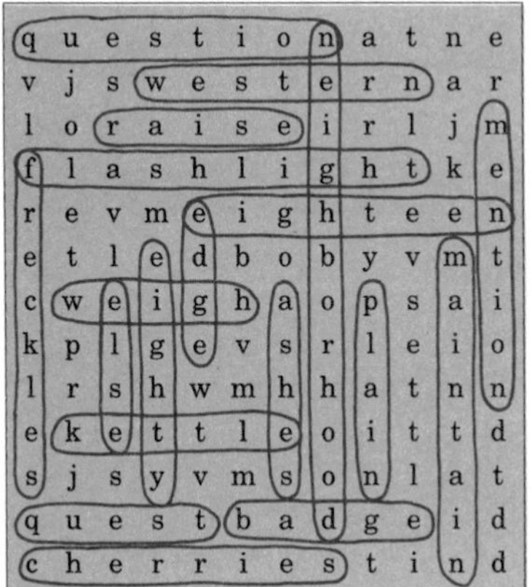

q u e s t i o n a t n e
v j s w e s t e r n a r
l o r a i s e i r l j m
f l a s h l i g h t k e
r e v m e i g h t e e n
e t l e d b o b y v m t
c w e i g h a o p s a i
k p l g e v s r l e i o
l r s h w m h h a t n n
e k e t t l e o i t t d
s j s y v m s o n l a t
q u e s t b a d g e i d
c h e r r i e s t i n d

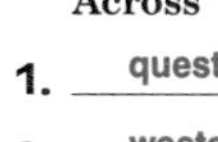

Across

1. question
2. western
3. raise
4. flashlight
5. eighteen
6. weigh
7. kettle
8. quest
9. badge
10. cherries

Down

11. freckles
12. else
13. eighty
14. edge
15. ashes
16. neighborhood
17. plain
18. settle
19. maintain
20. mention

**E. Build a Word** Write the four spelling words that use *eigh* to make the long *a* sound.

1. eighteen
2. eighty
3. weigh
4. neighborhood

## OPTIONAL TEACHING PLAN

Write the four Word Group headings on the chalkboard. Ask the students to name the four spelling words with the long **a** sound that are spelled with **eigh**. Write the words as the students say them. Continue identifying the other Word Groups. Note that the long **a** sound is spelled with **eigh** in some words and with **ai** in other words. Point out the **dge** ending in **badge** and **edge**.

| Word Groups | | |
|---|---|---|
| /ā/: **eigh** words | eighteen<br>eighty | neighborhood<br>weight |
| /ā/: **ai** words | plain<br>raise | maintain |
| /ă/ words | ashes<br>badge<br>flashlight | **under-standing** |
| /ĕ/ words | edge<br>else<br>kettle<br>settle<br>freckles<br>quest<br>cherries | question<br>mention<br>western<br>**projector**<br>**protection**<br>**reflected**<br>**refreshments** |

*Challenge Words are boldfaced.*

### Optional Activity Masters

Those using the Hardcover Pupil Edition may wish to use the Optional Activity Masters in the Teacher's Resource Book for Exercises C, D, and G.

**Home Activity #26**

Name______ Date______

Use the spelling words to complete the questions. The number before each blank tells you in what column you can find the correct word. Use each word only once.

| 1 | 2 | 3 | 4 |
|---|---|---|---|
| maintain | eighteen | edge | quest |
| weigh | raise | else | question |
| eighty | ashes | kettle | mention |
| neighborhood | flashlight | freckles | western |
| plain | badge | settle | cherries |

1. Would you mind if I asked another (4) ______ ?
2. Did you see the old school house as it burned to (2) ______ ?
3. Do you want to go around the world in (1) ______ days?
4. Did you count (2) ______ students?
5. Who heated the (3) ______ and served the soup?
6. Did the miners succeed in their (4) ______ for gold?
7. Is this a friendly (1) ______ ?
8. Are you prepared to (3) ______ in the town, or will you be moving soon?
9. Was everyone amazed when you showed your (2) ______ of honor?
10. Is this the season to pick a basket of (4) ______ ?
11. Are you so bored that you have nothing (3) ______ to do?
12. Do you know how to (1) ______ and measure the items?
13. Why do they laugh at the (4) ______ of my name?
14. Who carried the dimming (2) ______ into the dark forest?
15. Is she the person whose face is covered with (3) ______ ?
16. Did you see the girl who wore (4) ______ clothes?
17. Is it difficult to (1) ______ order in the classroom?
18. Can you see the canoe at the (3) ______ of the wharf?
19. What is wrapped in that (1) ______ wrapper?
20. Do you know why the flag was too low and why we had to (2) ______ it higher?

32



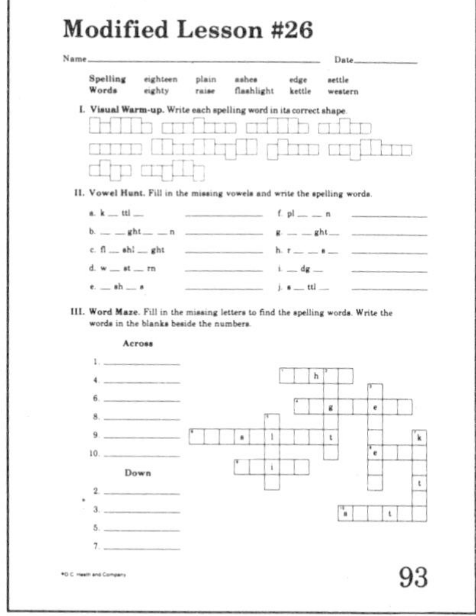

**Modified Lesson #26**

Name______ Date______

**Spelling Words** eighteen eighty plain raise ashes flashlight edge kettle settle western

**I. Visual Warm-up.** Write each spelling word in its correct shape.

**II. Vowel Hunt.** Fill in the missing vowels and write the spelling words.

a. k _ ttl _
b. _ _ ght _ _ n
c. fl _ shl _ ght
d. w _ st _ rn
e. _ sh _ s
f. pl _ _ n
g. _ _ ght _
h. r _ _ s _
i. _ dg _
j. s _ ttl _

**III. Word Maze.** Fill in the missing letters to find the spelling words. Write the words in the blanks beside the numbers.

Across

1. ______
4. ______
6. ______
8. ______
9. ______
10. ______

Down

2. ______
3. ______
5. ______
7. ______



93

**Modified Lesson #26** *(continued)*

Name______ Date______

**Spelling Words** eighteen eighty plain raise ashes flashlight edge kettle settle western

**IV. Word Parts.** Write the spelling words that have the word parts below. A word may be used more than once.

a. ai words: ______, ______
b. eigh words: ______, ______
c. tt words: ______, ______
d. ght words: ______, ______, ______
e. dge word: ______
f. sh words: ______, ______
g. rn word: ______
h. word ending in es: ______
i. Write the one compound word. ______

**V. Sentence Sense.** Write each spelling word in the correct sentence.

**Words** eighteen plain ashes edge settle

a. The gift came in a ______ wrapper.
b. The log burned to ______ .
c. There are ______ students in the class.
d. The boat was tied at the ______ of the wharf.
e. The pioneer wanted to ______ in the town.

**Words** eighty raise flashlight kettle western

f. The country singer wore ______ clothes.
g. Grandfather heated the ______ .
h. The dimming ______ caused a problem for the hikers.
i. We traveled around the world in ______ days.
j. We had to ______ it higher.

94



### Home Activity

A weekly homework assignment

### Modified Lesson

An alternative lesson for limited spellers

*(The Answer Key can be found in the Teacher's Resource Book.)*

LESSON

# 26

CONTINUED

### Challenge Exercise #26

Name ______________________ Date __________

**Word Watch.** Long ago in England, one's neighbor was the "farmer who lived on the next farm." The Old English word for "nearby farmer" was *neahgebur*. Formed of the two German words *nahe*, meaning "near," and *gebur*, meaning "farmer," the word traveled to England and was changed slightly in the process when *nahe* became *neah*. In early England, a person soon learned to rely on his or her *neahgebur* as we today have learned to rely on our own neighbors.

**Word Analogies.** Decide on the relationship that exists between the first pair of words. Using the Other Word Forms on page 104, find a word that completes the second pair of words and establishes the same relationship.

1. *third* is to *sixth* as *ninth* is to __________
2. *apple* is to *seed* as __________ is to *pit*
3. *inches* is to *height* as *pounds* is to __________
4. *replies* is to *answers* as *asks* is to __________
5. *centers* is to *middles* as __________ is to *rims*

**Challenge Words Student Activity**

Use the challenge words below to complete the statements about Greek gods.

**projector reflected protection understanding refreshments**

1. Greek gods often lacked __________ of people's needs.
2. Athena provided __________ to the people of Athens.
3. Zeus and Hera were served nectar and grapes as __________.
4. Narcissus saw his own face __________ and fell in love with his image.
5. We showed our slides of ancient Greek temples on the school __________.

**Working With Words: Student Writing Activity**

Use as many Other Word Forms as you can from page 104 to write catchy statements to put on six movie posters. Use any of the following types of movies: westerns, horror, science fiction. (Example: Horror so dark that a thousand *flashlights* cannot cut through the blackest night!)

136



## Challenge Exercise

Additional activities for advanced spellers

### Spelling Words

| | | | |
|---|---|---|---|
| eighteen | eighty | weigh | neighborhood |
| plain | raise | maintain | ashes |
| badge | flashlight | edge | else |
| kettle | settle | freckles | quest |
| question | mention | western | cherries |

**F. Generally Speaking** Write a spelling word for the group it best fits.

1. logs, fireplace, ashes
2. lantern, lamp, flashlight
3. grapes, apples, cherries
4. pot, pan, kettle
5. medal, pin, badge
6. ordinary, simple, plain
7. keep, continue, maintain

**G. Missing Vowel** The following words from the list are missing the same vowel. Write the words.

1. e ls e — else
2. s e ttl e — settle
3. qu e st — quest
4. fr e ckl e s — freckles
5. e dg e — edge
6. m e ntion — mention
7. w e st e rn — western
8. qu e stion — question
9. rais e — raise



## CONTROLLED DICTATION (Optional)

These dictation sentences provide maintenance for spelling words previously taught and practice for words currently being studied. Dictation should be administered on Day 4. The teacher or another student may dictate the sentences. Be sure to dictate all marks of punctuation. Challenge Word sentences are preceded by an asterisk.

1. **Eighty neighborhood** centers make up the **western** city.
2. In her **quest** to earn a **badge**, the troop member answers one **question** about camping.
3. Did anyone **else mention** the **freckles** on your face?
4. Place the **ashes** inside the **kettle** to **weigh** them.
5. They will **settle** near the **edge** of the village and **raise** potatoes.
6. He is putting the **cherries** on a **plain** white cake.
7. Each of the **eighteen** campers needed a **flashlight** to **maintain** order at night.

*8. Keep the **refreshments** under **protection** so no animals will eat them.

*9. My **understanding** about light being **reflected** from a **projector** is wrong.

**H. Using Other Word Forms** Write the Other Word Form that fits each clue.

Base Words: maintain(ed) neighbor(ly) edge(y) raise(ing) eighteen(th)

1. follows the seventeenth eighteenth
2. friendly with the people next door neighborly
3. kept in proper working condition maintained
4. lifting up raising
5. nervous or uptight edgy

**I. Challenge Words** Write the Challenge Word that fits each clue.

| understanding | projector | protection | reflected | refreshments |
|---|---|---|---|---|

1. This turns reels of film. projector
2. A seatbelt provides this. protection
3. You buy these snacks at the movies. refreshments
4. This image is given back by a mirror. reflected
5. This is knowledge. understanding

**J. Spelling and Writing** Use as many Spelling Words, Other Word Forms, and Challenge Words as you can to write *two* or more answers to each question. A few words are suggested. Proofread your work.

1. What could you do to start a safety-education program in your area?

   neighborhood – maintain – flashlight – badge – protection – understanding

2. What advice would you give to someone who wanted to capture a beautiful sunset on videotape?

   western – mention – quest – question – reflected – projector

3. What suggestions do you have for putting out a campfire?

   settle – edge – ashes – kettle – raise – else



## USING OTHER WORD FORMS

Vocabulary is expanded through the use of other forms of basic spelling words. Emphasis is on the relationship of syntax to suffix choices. The following generalization applies to the Other Word Forms used in Exercise H.

### Spelling Rule

Adding suffixes to words ending in silent **e**

> **When adding a suffix that begins with a vowel to words that end with silent e, drop the final e.**
> **(raise, raising)**

## POSTTEST AND PROOFREADING

Follow the same testing procedures used in the Pretest, although you may wish to correct the tests yourself. Have students write any misspelled words on the Words to Learn Sheet and record spelling success on the Progress Chart.

## THE SPELLING-WRITING LINK

**Purpose** This activity helps students retain the correct spelling of words and transfer the words to their daily writing. Students use lesson words to answer questions promoting higher-order thinking skills.

**Procedure** Read the first question and write the suggested words on the chalkboard: **neighborhood, maintain, flashlight, badge, protection, understanding.** Have students list some Other Word Forms of the lesson words. Brainstorm with the class possible answers to question 1. Remind students to look at all the lesson words for ideas. Write the answers on the chalkboard, noting any lesson words.

**Practice** Tell students to finish the activity by writing two or more answers to each question. Remind them to proofread their work.

# LESSON 27

## OBJECTIVES
- to spell 20 high-frequency words with the /ĕ/
- to proofread these words in daily writing
- to become familiar with 32 other forms of the spelling words

| Summary of Skills | Exercises |
|---|---|
| Auditory Discrimination | A |
| Proofreading | A, C, H |
| Visual Discrimination | C |
| Vocabulary Development | D, G |
| Dictionary Skills | E |
| Context Usage | F |
| Original Writing | H |

## PRETEST AND PROOFREADING
The Pretest identifies the words students are able to spell, as well as the words they need to learn. You may wish to use Other Word Forms when giving the Pretest. Five suggested Other Word Forms are underlined on this page.

To administer the Pretest:

**READ** each word aloud.
**SAY** the phrase containing the word.
**REPEAT** the word.

Have students correct the Pretest using the Corrected-test Procedure. They may record their scores on a personal Progress Chart (see the Teacher's Resource Book) and study misspelled words using the **S-H-A-R-P** procedure.

## OTHER WORD FORMS
This section presents related forms of the spelling words to strengthen spelling power and vocabulary knowledge.

### Enrichment Activity
Have students write variations of the same sentence using each of the Other Word Forms for a spelling word.

Good foods and exercise are important for your **health**.

**healthy**, **healthier**, **healthful**

# 27

**A. Pretest and Proofreading**

**B. Spelling Words and Phrases**

| | |
|---|---|
| **1. deaf** | thought I was deaf |
| **2. heavy*** | looks very heavy |
| **3. health*** | in good health |
| **4. treasure** | buried treasure |
| **5. meadow** | ran through the meadow |
| **6. feather*** | a bird's feather |
| **7. leather*** | dressed in leather |
| **8. sweater*** | has put on a sweater |
| **9. headquarters*** | visit to the headquarters |
| **10. except*** | except on Sunday |
| **11. erect** | will erect a building |
| **12. select** | will select another color |
| **13. direct** | had to direct traffic |
| **14. protect*** | to protect them from disease |
| **15. export*** | the export of wheat |
| **16. regular** | on a regular basis |
| **17. festival** | the annual festival |
| **18. remember*** | if you don't remember |
| **19. necktie** | struggled with my necktie |
| **20. president** | may meet a president |

***Other Word Forms***

deafen, deafness
heavier, heaviest
<u>healthy</u>, healthier, healthful
treasury
meadows
feathered, feathery
leathered, leathery
sweaters
excepted, <u>exception</u>
erected
selected, <u>selection</u>
directed, <u>direction</u>
protector, protection
exported
<u>regularly</u>, regulates, regulation
festive
remembrance
neckties
presidential, presidency

**C. Visual Warm-up** Write each word in its correct shape.

a. direct
b. treasure
c. feather
d. leather
e. health
f. select
g. deaf
h. except
i. festival
j. meadow
k. export
l. sweater
m. remember
n. headquarters
o. necktie
p. regular
q. erect
r. heavy
s. protect
t. president



*Modified Lesson words are asterisked.
The Modified Lesson is found in the Teacher's Resource Book.

## MEETING INDIVIDUAL NEEDS / ASSIGNMENT GUIDE

| 5-Day Plan | 3-Day Plan | Limited Spellers | Average Spellers | Advanced Spellers |
|---|---|---|---|---|
| 1 | 1 | • Pretest • Progress Chart | • Pretest • Progress Chart • Home Activity | • Pretest • Progress Chart • Home Activity |
| 2 | 1 | • Modified Lesson Visual Warm-up Ending Sounds | • Regular Lesson Visual Warm-up | • Regular Lesson Visual Warm-up |
| 3 and 4 | 2 | • Modified Lesson Vowel Puzzle Word Match Finish the Sentence | Spelling Activities | Spelling Activities • Challenge Exercise |
| 5 | 3 | • Posttest • Words to Learn Sheet • Progress Chart | • Posttest • Words to Learn Sheet • Progress Chart | • Posttest • Words to Learn Sheet • Progress Chart |

**D. Crossword Puzzle** Solve the puzzle by using all the words from the spelling list. Write each word. Check your answers in the **Spelling Dictionary**.

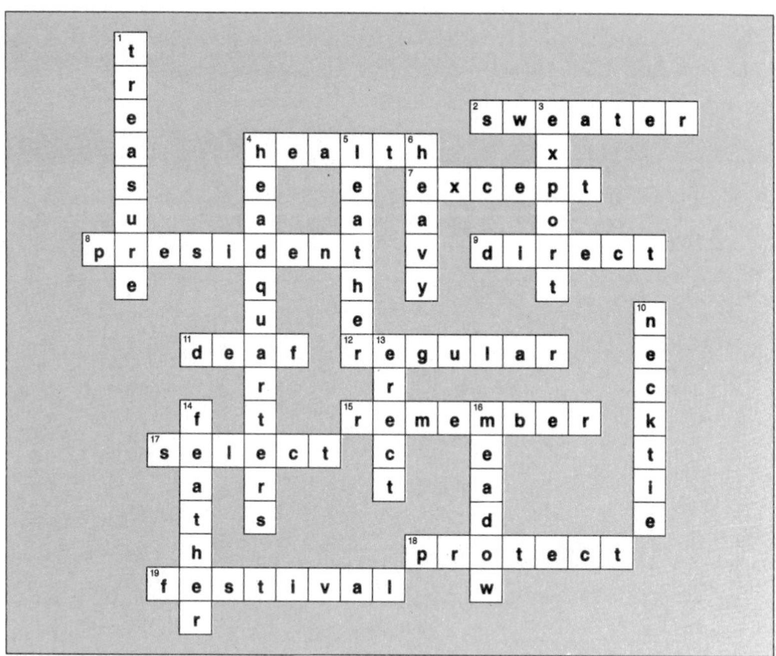

**Across**

2. an item of warm clothing
4. one's physical condition
7. not including
8. the leader of a nation
9. to conduct
11. unable to hear
12. usual
15. not to forget
17. to choose
18. to defend
19. a special celebration

**Down**

1. hidden wealth
3. to ship out of the country
4. the main office
5. tanned animal skin
6. not light in weight
10. clothing for decoration
13. up straight
14. bird clothing
16. a field



## OPTIONAL TEACHING PLAN

Write the two Word Group headings on the chalkboard. Ask the students to name the nine spelling words with the short **e** sound that are spelled with **ea**. Write the words as the students say them. Continue identifying the other Word Group. Note that the short **e** sound is spelled with **ea** in words such as **deaf** and with **e** in words such as **except**. Point out the five words that end with the **pt** or **ct** consonant blend.

| Word Groups | | |
|---|---|---|
| /ĕ/: **ea** words | deaf | feather |
| | heavy | leather |
| | health | sweater |
| | treasure | headquarters |
| | meadow | |
| /ĕ/: **e** words | except | remember |
| | erect | necktie |
| | select | president |
| | direct | **correctly** |
| | protect | **inspection** |
| | export | **lecture** |
| | regular | **mentally** |
| | festival | **tension** |

*Challenge Words are boldfaced.*

### Optional Activity Masters

Those using the Hardcover Pupil Edition may wish to use the Optional Activity Masters in the Teacher's Resource Book for Exercises C and D.

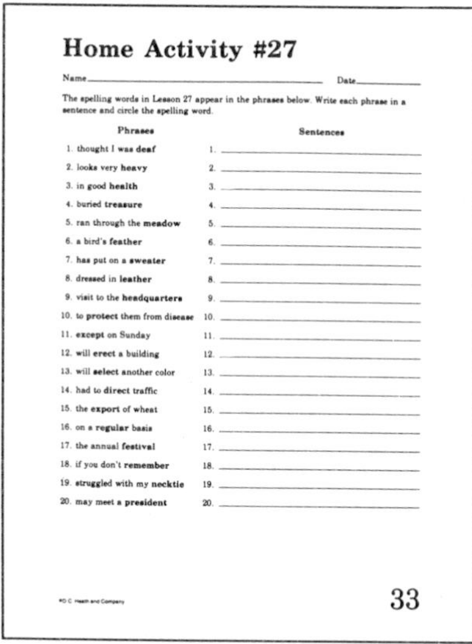

**Home Activity #27**

Name__________ Date______

The spelling words in Lesson 27 appear in the phrases below. Write each phrase in a sentence and circle the spelling word.

| Phrases | Sentences |
|---|---|
| 1. thought I was **deaf** | 1. ________ |
| 2. looks very **heavy** | 2. ________ |
| 3. in good **health** | 3. ________ |
| 4. buried **treasure** | 4. ________ |
| 5. ran through the **meadow** | 5. ________ |
| 6. a bird's **feather** | 6. ________ |
| 7. has put on a **sweater** | 7. ________ |
| 8. dressed in **leather** | 8. ________ |
| 9. visit to the **headquarters** | 9. ________ |
| 10. to **protect** them from disease | 10. ________ |
| 11. **except** on Sunday | 11. ________ |
| 12. will **erect** a building | 12. ________ |
| 13. will **select** another color | 13. ________ |
| 14. had to **direct** traffic | 14. ________ |
| 15. the **export** of wheat | 15. ________ |
| 16. on a **regular** basis | 16. ________ |
| 17. the annual **festival** | 17. ________ |
| 18. if you don't **remember** | 18. ________ |
| 19. struggled with my **necktie** | 19. ________ |
| 20. may meet a **president** | 20. ________ |



33

**Modified Lesson #27**

Name__________ Date______

**Spelling Words** heavy health feather sweater leather headquarters protect except export remember

**I. Visual Warm-up.** Write each spelling word in its correct shape.

**II. Vowel Hunt.** Fill in the missing vowels and write the spelling words.

a. pr _ t _ ct ______ f. sw _ _ t _ r ______
b. h _ _ v _ ______ g. l _ _ th _ r ______
c. _ xp _ rt ______ h. f _ _ th _ r ______
d. _ xc _ pt ______ i. r _ m _ mb _ r ______
e. h _ _ lth ______ j. h _ _ dq _ _ rt _ rs ______

**III. Word Maze.** Fill in the missing letters to find the spelling words. Write the words in the blanks beside the numbers.

**Across**
2. ______
4. ______
8. ______
9. ______
10. ______

**Down**
1. ______
3. ______
5. ______
6. ______
7. ______



95

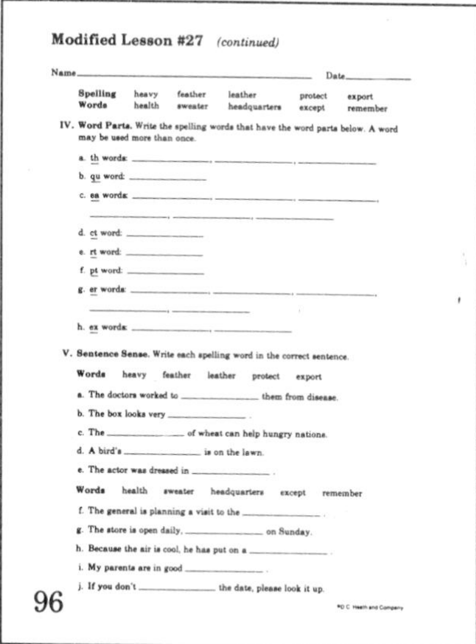

**Modified Lesson #27** *(continued)*

Name__________ Date______

**Spelling Words** heavy health feather sweater leather headquarters protect except export remember

**IV. Word Parts.** Write the spelling words that have the word parts below. A word may be used more than once.

a. th words: ______, ______, ______
b. qu word: ______
c. ea words: ______, ______, ______, ______, ______, ______
d. ct word: ______
e. rt word: ______
f. pt word: ______
g. er words: ______, ______, ______, ______, ______
h. ex words: ______, ______

**V. Sentence Sense.** Write each spelling word in the correct sentence.

**Words** heavy feather leather protect export

a. The doctors worked to ______ them from disease.
b. The box looks very ______ .
c. The ______ of wheat can help hungry nations.
d. A bird's ______ is on the lawn.
e. The actor was dressed in ______ .

**Words** health sweater headquarters except remember

f. The general is planning a visit to the ______ .
g. The store is open daily, ______ on Sunday.
h. Because the air is cool, he has put on a ______ .
i. My parents are in good ______ .
j. If you don't ______ the date, please look it up.

96



### Home Activity

A weekly homework assignment

### Modified Lesson

An alternative lesson for limited spellers

*(The Answer Key can be found in the Teacher's Resource Book.)*

LESSON

# 27

CONTINUED

### Challenge Exercise #27

Name__________________ Date________

**Word Watch.** The word *treasure* had its beginnings in early Greece and Rome. Originally, the Greek word *thesauros* and, later, the Latin word *thesaurus* referred to treasure. As the word traveled to England, it was altered, and *tresor* became the word for "hidden wealth." Of interest is the fact that the word *thesaurus* has returned to regular usage, unchanged from early times. Today a thesaurus, though no longer a treasure of coins and jewels, has come to be a "treasure of words."

**Word Analogies.** Decide on the relationship that exists between the first pair of words. Using the Other Word Forms on page 108, find a word that completes the second pair of words and establishes the same relationship.

1. *halibut* is to *scaly* as *robin* is to ________
2. *buffalo* is to *plains* as *cows* is to ________
3. *nominated* is to *appointed* as ________ is to *chosen*
4. *weakest* is to *strongest* as *lightest* is to ________
5. *pantry* is to *food* as ________ is to *money*

**Challenge Words Student Activity**

Use the challenge words below to complete the instructions.

**mentally lecture inspection tension correctly**

1. Give the room a careful ________.
2. Increase the ________ by tightening that rope.
3. Prepare a ten-minute ________ on any subject.
4. Be sure to spell the word ________.
5. Try to stay ________ alert at all times.

**Working With Words: Student Writing Activity**

Use as many Other Word Forms as you can from page 108 to write silly two-line verses about animals.
(Example: These parrots are such *feathery* birds,
But they only speak another's words.)



137

## Challenge Exercise

Additional activities for advanced spellers

**Spelling Words**

| | | | |
|---|---|---|---|
| meadow | feather | leather | sweater |
| deaf | heavy | health | treasure |
| headquarters | except | erect | select |
| direct | protect | export | regular |
| festival | remember | necktie | president |

**E. Guide Words** These word pairs are guide words that might appear in a dictionary. Write the words from the spelling list that would appear on the same page as each pair of guide words.

**day - dropped**
1. deaf
2. direct

**dry - escape**
3. erect

**everywhere - festive**
4. feather
5. except
6. export
7. festival

**great - helmet**
8. heavy
9. health
10. headquarters

**known - machine**
11. leather

**magazine - mountain**
12. meadow

**mud - offer**
13. necktie

**president - quart**
14. protect
15. president

**quarter - replied**
16. regular
17. remember

**schoolmate - skinned**
18. select

**stray - talent**
19. sweater

**taught - ugly**
20. treasure



## CONTROLLED DICTATION (Optional)

These dictation sentences provide maintenance for spelling words previously taught and practice for words currently being studied. Dictation should be administered on Day 4. The teacher or another student may dictate the sentences. Be sure to dictate all marks of punctuation. Challenge Word sentences are preceded by an asterisk.

1. **Select** only the brown **leather** belts for **export**.
2. The **president** wore a **sweater** and a **necktie**.
3. **Protect** yourself from becoming **deaf** by having **regular** and thorough **health** checks.
4. Does anyone **remember** who did **erect** the building?
5. We found nothing **except** a bird **feather** on the **meadow** path.
6. The planners of the **festival** must locate their **headquarters** near the parade grounds.
7. **Direct** the sailors to hide the **treasure** under a **heavy** rock.

*8. The car **inspection** must be done **correctly**.
*9. He was full of **tension** before giving his **lecture**.
*10. Working longer hours tires her **mentally**.

**F. Using Other Word Forms** Write the Other Word Form that completes each sentence.

Base Words: select(ion) direct(ed) health(y) except(ion) regular(ly)

1. Beth is a very ___healthy___ person.
2. Without ___exception___, she eats three balanced meals a day.
3. She enjoys a healthy ___selection___ of fruits and vegetables.
4. She visits a doctor ___regularly___ for check-ups.
5. He has ___directed___ her to follow an exercise program.

**G. Challenge Words** Write the Challenge Word that completes each phrase.

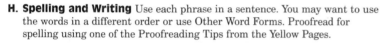

| correctly | inspection | lecture | mentally | tension |
|---|---|---|---|---|

1. physically and ___mentally___
2. talk and ___lecture___
3. stress and ___tension___
4. properly and ___correctly___
5. check-up and ___inspection___

**H. Spelling and Writing** Use each phrase in a sentence. You may want to use the words in a different order or use Other Word Forms. Proofread for spelling using one of the Proofreading Tips from the Yellow Pages.

1. some deaf people
2. heavy fog in the meadow
3. in good health
4. treasure your friendship
5. a striped necktie
6. a feather in my hat
7. leather gloves
8. woolen sweater
9. moving their headquarters
10. every day except today
11. must stand erect
12. can select one item
13. will fly direct
14. remember to protect your eyes
15. will export new cars
16. a regular customer
17. the music festival
18. elected president



## USING OTHER WORD FORMS

Vocabulary is expanded through the use of other forms of basic spelling words. Emphasis is on the relationship of syntax to suffix choices.

## POSTTEST AND PROOFREADING

Follow the same testing procedures used in the Pretest, although you may wish to correct the tests yourself. Have students write any misspelled words on the Words to Learn Sheet and record spelling success on the Progress Chart.

## THE SPELLING-WRITING LINK

**Purpose** This activity helps students transfer lesson words into their daily writing. Students write complete sentences using the listed phrases.

**Procedure** On the chalkboard write the phrase from line one: **some deaf people.** Have the students read the phrase and note how it could be used in a sentence. Have them think about things or people the phrase suggests. You can provide a sample sentence: **Some deaf people learn to sign.**

**Practice** Tell the students to write original sentences using the phrases. Remind them they can use Other Word Forms or change the phrases around if it will improve the sentences.

# LESSON 28

## OBJECTIVES

- to spell 20 high-frequency words with the /ă/, /ə/, /ä/, and /ĕ/
- to proofread these words in daily writing
- to become familiar with 35 other forms of the spelling words

| Summary of Skills | Exercises |
|---|---|
| Auditory Discrimination | A |
| Proofreading | A, C, D, I |
| Visual Discrimination | C, D |
| Vocabulary Development | E |
| Context Usage | F, G, H |
| Dictionary Skills | F |
| Original Writing | I |

## PRETEST AND PROOFREADING

The Pretest identifies the words students are able to spell, as well as the words they need to learn. You may wish to use Other Word Forms when giving the Pretest. Five suggested Other Word Forms are underlined on this page.

To administer the Pretest:

**READ** each word aloud.
**SAY** the phrase containing the word.
**REPEAT** the word.

Have students correct the Pretest using the Corrected-test Procedure. They may record their scores on a personal Progress Chart (see the Teacher's Resource Book) and study misspelled words using the **S-H-A-R-P** procedure.

## OTHER WORD FORMS

This section presents related forms of the spelling words to strengthen spelling power and vocabulary knowledge.

### Enrichment Activity

Have students write opposite words or phrases for the Other Word Forms. Be sure they write the Other Word Form with its opposite next to it.

**fanciest, answered, angrily, fastening**

# 28

**A. Pretest and Proofreading**

**B. Spelling Words and Phrases**

1. **anger*** filled with anger
2. **angry*** the angry mob
3. **answer*** did not answer
4. **average** figured the average
5. **fancy*** a fancy decoration
6. **calves** fed the calves
7. **canal** dug the canal
8. **tackle** a clean, low tackle
9. **castle** defended the castle
10. **fasten*** will fasten the seat belt
11. **platform*** stood on the platform
12. **magazine** our magazine subscription
13. **gasoline** a red can of gasoline
14. **valentine** mailed the last valentine
15. **savage*** the lion's savage roar
16. **language*** lost my language book
17. **garage** waited at the garage
18. **machine** an ancient flying machine
19. **palm*** in the palm of my hand
20. **engine*** started the engine

*Other Word Forms*

angered, angering, angrily, angrier, angriest
answers, answered
averages, averaged, averaging
fanciful, fancier, fanciest
calf
canals
tackles, tackled, tackling
castles
fastens, fastened, fastening, fastener
platforms
magazines
valentines
savages
languages
garages, garaged, garaging
machinery
palmed
engines, engineer

**C. Visual Warm-up** Write each word in its correct shape.

a. machine
b. fasten
c. magazine
d. answer
e. gasoline
f. average
g. valentine
h. calves
i. engine
j. castle
k. savage
l. platform
m. palm
n. garage
o. tackle
p. anger
q. language
r. angry
s. canal
t. fancy



*Modified Lesson words are asterisked.
The Modified Lesson is found in the Teacher's Resource Book.

## MEETING INDIVIDUAL NEEDS / ASSIGNMENT GUIDE

| 5-Day Plan | 3-Day Plan | Limited Spellers | Average Spellers | Advanced Spellers |
|---|---|---|---|---|
| 1 | 1 | • Pretest<br>• Progress Chart | • Pretest<br>• Progress Chart<br>• Home Activity | • Pretest<br>• Progress Chart<br>• Home Activity |
| 2 | | • Modified Lesson Visual Warm-up Ending Sounds | • Regular Lesson Visual Warm-up | • Regular Lesson Visual Warm-up |
| 3 and 4 | 2 | • Modified Lesson Vowel Puzzle Word Match Finish the Sentence | Spelling Activities | Spelling Activities<br>• Challenge Exercise |
| 5 | 3 | • Posttest<br>• Words to Learn Sheet<br>• Progress Chart | • Posttest<br>• Words to Learn Sheet<br>• Progress Chart | • Posttest<br>• Words to Learn Sheet<br>• Progress Chart |

**D. Hidden Words** The spelling words can be found in the word puzzle. The words appear across and down. Circle and write the words.

**Across**

1. engine
2. fasten
3. machine
4. fancy
5. gasoline
6. canal
7. garage
8. average
9. platform

| | | | | | | | | | | | | | |
|---|---|---|---|---|---|---|---|---|---|---|---|---|---|
| e | n | g | i | n | e | l | f | a | s | t | e | n | p |
| n | m | a | c | h | i | n | e | w | v | j | m | m | a |
| t | a | r | v | o | m | y | f | a | n | c | y | l | l |
| a | g | a | s | o | l | i | n | e | l | v | r | c | m |
| c | a | g | a | m | a | e | g | z | c | a | n | a | l |
| k | z | g | v | o | n | i | e | v | w | l | w | l | o |
| l | i | m | a | k | g | a | r | a | g | e | a | v | c |
| e | n | o | g | a | u | l | a | n | a | n | n | e | a |
| v | e | w | e | v | a | c | r | g | n | t | s | s | s |
| a | v | e | r | a | g | e | v | r | g | i | w | m | t |
| m | a | c | h | l | e | y | c | y | e | n | e | w | l |
| p | l | a | t | f | o | r | m | n | r | e | r | j | e |

**Down**

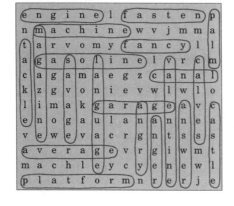

10. tackle
11. magazine
12. savage
13. language
14. angry
15. anger
16. valentine
17. answer
18. calves
19. palm
20. castle

**E. Generally Speaking** Write each spelling word for the group it best fits.

1. newspaper, journal, magazine
2. fuel, oil, gasoline
3. palace, chateau, castle
4. speech, expression, language
5. respond, reply, answer
6. attach, bind, fasten
7. card, heart-shaped, valentine
8. decorated, not plain, fancy
9. fuming, furious, angry
10. waterway, channel, canal
11. cows, bulls, calves
12. medium, usual, average
13. rage, fury, anger
14. seize, undertake, tackle
15. floor, stage, platform
16. motor, engine, machine
17. drive, park, garage
18. brutal, cruel, savage
19. oak, fern, palm



## OPTIONAL TEACHING PLAN

Write the four Word Group headings on the chalkboard. Ask the students to name the sixteen spelling words with the short **a** sound. Continue identifying the other Word Groups. Note that **a** has the short **a** sound in **anger**, the /ə/ (schwa) sound in **garage**, and the /ä/ sound in **palm**. Point out the different sounds of the ending **age** in **garage** and **average**.

| Word Groups | | |
|---|---|---|
| /ă/ words | anger<br>angry<br>answer<br>average<br>fancy<br>calves<br>canal<br>tackle<br>castle<br>fasten<br>platform | magazine<br>gasoline<br>valentine<br>savage<br>language<br>**commander**<br>**hand-icapped**<br>**data**<br>**mackerel**<br>**romantic** |
| /ə/: **a** words | garage | machine |
| /ĕ/ word | engine | |
| /ä/: **al** word | | palm |

*Challenge Words are boldfaced.*

### Optional Activity Masters

Those using the Hardcover Pupil Edition may wish to use the Optional Activity Masters in the Teacher's Resource Book for Exercises C and D.

**Home Activity #28**

Name_____ Date_____

Use the spelling words to complete the sentences. The number before each blank tells you in what column you can find the correct word. Use each word only once.

| 1 | 2 | 3 | 4 |
|---|---|---|---|
| engine | canal | machine | fancy |
| castle | savage | fasten | platform |
| magazine | palm | garage | answer |
| valentine | calves | language | average |
| gasoline | tackle | angry | anger |

1. I wasn't prepared for class because I had lost my (3) _____ book.
2. Our (1) _____ subscription for *Amazing Adventures* ran out.
3. I saw an ancient flying (3) _____ in the museum.
4. I mailed the last (1) _____ to a friend.
5. The clerk did not (4) _____ my question.
6. She took a red can of (1) _____ and filled the tank.
7. The farmers fed the (2) _____ and milked the cows.
8. The knights defended the _____.
9. The (3) _____ mob of tourists demanded better service.
10. She stood on the (4) _____ to give a speech.
11. I held my lunch in the (2) _____ of my hand.
12. He started the (1) _____ and drove away.
13. I will (3) _____ the seat belt for you.
14. He figured the (4) _____ score for the class.
15. I challenged the wrestler with a clean, low (2) _____.
16. I have a (4) _____ decoration hanging on my wall.
17. I heard the lion's (2) _____ roar.
18. The coach was filled with (4) _____ because a few players had missed practice.
19. I waited at the (3) _____ until the mechanics had finished repairing my car.
20. The workers dug the (2) _____ with shovels and hoes.

34

**Modified Lesson #28**

Name_____ Date_____

Spelling Words: engine palm language platform angry
savage fasten fancy answer anger

I. **Visual Warm-up.** Write each spelling word in its correct shape.

II. **Vowel Hunt.** Fill in the missing vowels and write the spelling words.
a. s __ v __ g __
b. p __ lm
c. f __ nc __
d. pl __ tf __ rm
e. __ ngr __
f. __ ng __ n __
g. f __ st __ n
h. l __ ng __ __ g __
i. __ nsw __ r
j. __ ng __ r

III. **Word Maze.** Fill in the missing letters to find the spelling words. Write the words in the blanks beside the numbers.
1. _____
4. _____
6. _____
7. _____

97

**Modified Lesson #28** *(continued)*

Name_____ Date_____

Spelling Words: engine palm language platform angry
savage fasten fancy answer anger

IV. **Word Parts.** Write the spelling words that have the word parts below. A word may be used more than once.
a. lm word: _____
b. age words: _____
c. words ending in y: _____
d. en words: _____
e. pl word: _____
f. word with silent w: _____
g. an words: _____
h. ine word: _____

V. **Sentence Sense.** Write each spelling word in the correct sentence.
Words: engine palm language platform angry
a. I lost my _____ book in the lunchroom.
b. The driver started the _____.
c. The _____ mob shouted at the marchers.
d. I held the coin in the _____ of my hand.
e. The speaker stood on the _____.
Words: savage fasten fancy answer anger
f. We hung a _____ decoration on the tree.
g. We heard the lion's _____ roar and became frightened.
h. The customer was filled with _____.
i. The passenger will _____ the seat belt.
j. I knocked on the door but she did not _____.

98

### Home Activity

A weekly homework assignment

### Modified Lesson

An alternative lesson for limited spellers

*(The Answer Key can be found in the Teacher's Resource Book.)*

LESSON

# 28

CONTINUED

### Challenge Exercise #28

Name__________ Date__________

**Word Watch.** The Crusaders returning from the Holy Land brought home to England several Arabic words, among them the word *makhazin*, meaning "a warehouse for storing weapons." In time, these military warehouses were built in England and were called *magazines*. The magazines eventually became storehouses for other kinds of goods as well. In 1731, an English publisher used the word *magazine* to mean "a storehouse of ideas" when he published the *Gentleman's Magazine*. He thus provided a new meaning for the word, a meaning that has not changed in over 250 years.

**Word Analogies.** Decide on the relationship that exists between the first pair of words. Using the Other Word Forms on page 112, find a word that completes the second pair of words and establishes the same relationship.

1. *manager* is to *office* as __________ is to *train*
2. *shamrocks* is to *green* as __________ is to *red*
3. *houses* is to *people* as __________ is to *automobiles*
4. *simple* is to *showy* as *plainer* is to __________
5. *baseball* is to *tagged* as *football* is to __________

**Challenge Words Student Activity**

Use the challenge words below to complete each definition.

**commander** **handicapped** **romantic** **data** **mackerel**

1. having a problem or disadvantage: __________
2. a collection of information: __________
3. a giver of orders: __________
4. a salt-water fish: __________
5. a lover of drama and adventure: __________

**Working With Words: Student Writing Activity**

Use as many Other Word Forms as you can from page 112 to write real or silly messages to put on valentine cards. (Example: I'm *fastening* my heart to yours. Will you "knot" be my valentine?)

138



## Challenge Exercise

Additional activities for advanced spellers

**Spelling Words**

| | | | | |
|---|---|---|---|---|
| anger | angry | answer | average | fancy |
| calves | canal | tackle | castle | fasten |
| platform | magazine | gasoline | valentine | savage |
| language | garage | machine | palm | engine |

**F. Many Meanings** Complete each pair of sentences with the same spelling word. Write the word and its meaning as it is used in the sentences. Use the **Spelling Dictionary**.

**1. a.** The weather here is too cold for growing a palm tree.
a tree with a tall trunk, leaves at the top, and no branches.

**b.** I have the prize in the palm of my hand.
the inside surface of the hand, between the fingers and the wrist

**2. a.** I think that 6 is the average of 2 and 10.
the number that is typical or representative of a group of numbers

**b.** We have had an average amount of snow this year.
usual

**3. a.** I will tackle that math problem later.
to undertake or try to deal with

**b.** The team's star player made that last tackle.
in football, stopping and throwing to the ground an opponent with the ball

**4. a.** I must have left my language book at home.
of languages

**b.** I wish I knew a language other than English.
speech and writing that a nation or a group uses to communicate



## CONTROLLED DICTATION (Optional)

These dictation sentences provide maintenance for spelling words previously taught and practice for words currently being studied. Dictation should be administered on Day 4. The teacher or another student may dictate the sentences. Be sure to dictate all marks of punctuation. Challenge Word sentences are preceded by an asterisk.

1. The **average machine** runs on **gasoline**.
2. My cousin will **tackle** the **language** problem and find the **answer**.
3. The **angry** crowd left the **castle** and ran toward the **canal**.
4. The **savage** growl of the dog caused trouble for the **calves**.
5. Use tape to **fasten** the **fancy valentine** to the **magazine** cover.
6. Was the **engine** repaired at the neighborhood **garage**?
7. In **anger** he pounded the **palm** of his hand on the **platform**.

*8. A **mackerel** is a saltwater fish.
*9. Our **romantic** picnic was **handicapped** by the rain.
*10. The wrong **data** was given to the **commander** of the ship.

**G. Using Other Word Forms** Write the Other Word Form that completes each sentence.

Base Words: fasten(er) average(ing) engine(er) language(s) angry(ly)

1. People speak different ___languages___ in foreign countries.
2. A clamp is one type of ___fastener___ .
3. When ___averaging___ 20, 24, and 28, the answer is 24.
4. People answer ___angrily___ when they are upset or annoyed.
5. A mechanical ___engineer___ might design engines.

**H. Challenge Words** Write the Challenge Word that completes each sentence.

| commander | handicapped | data | mackerel | romantic |
|---|---|---|---|---|

1. The love story was a ___romantic___ tale of the Civil War.
2. We caught cod, haddock, and ___mackerel___ .
3. Jennifer was not ___handicapped___ by her vision problem.
4. The ___commander___ of the spaceship was a brave leader.
5. All the ___data___ that we fed the computer was correct.

**I. Spelling and Writing** Write each set of words in a sentence. You may use Other Word Forms. Proofread your work.

1. machine – garage – gasoline
2. fasten – anger – calves
3. average – valentine – fancy
4. engine – canal – platform
5. palm – tackle – angry
6. magazine – language – answer
7. commander – mackerel – savage
8. castle – romantic – fanciful
9. handicapped – data – engines

## THE SPELLING-WRITING LINK

**Purpose** This activity helps students effectively transfer lesson words into their daily writing. Students (a) determine a relationship among three given words and (b) write a complete sentence.

**Procedure** On the chalkboard, write the three words from line 1 (**machine, garage, gasoline**) and the Other Word Forms (**machinery, garages, garaged, garaging**). Have students read the words and think of ways the three words might be related. Have them think of things or people the words suggest. Ask students to create sentences using some of their ideas. You can provide an example sentence: **The garage mechanic told us that the machine was simply out of gasoline.**

**Practice** Tell students to write original sentences using the word sets and to proofread their work. You may want them to circle the lesson words.

## USING OTHER WORD FORMS

Vocabulary is expanded through the use of other forms of basic spelling words. Emphasis is on the relationship of syntax to suffix choices. The following generalizations apply to the Other Word Forms used in Exercise G.

### Spelling Rule

Forming plurals

Add **s** to most nouns to form plurals.
(**language, languages**)

Adding suffixes to words ending in silent **e**

When adding a suffix that begins with a vowel to words that end with silent **e**, drop the final **e**.
(**average, averaging**)

Adding suffixes to words ending in **y**

When adding a suffix to words ending with consonant-**y**, change the **y** to **i**, unless the suffix begins with **i**.
(**angry, angrily**)

## POSTTEST AND PROOFREADING

Follow the same testing procedures used in the Pretest, although you may wish to correct the tests yourself. Have students write any misspelled words on the Words to Learn Sheet and record spelling success on the Progress Chart.

# LESSON 29

## OBJECTIVES

- to spell 20 high-frequency words with the /ĕ/, /ē/, /ĭ/, and /îr/
- to proofread these words in daily writing
- to become familiar with 35 other forms of the spelling words

| Summary of Skills | Exercises |
|---|---|
| Auditory Discrimination | A |
| Proofreading | A, C, H |
| Visual Discrimination | C |
| Vocabulary Development | D, E, F, G |
| Original Writing | H |

## PRETEST AND PROOFREADING

The Pretest identifies the words students are able to spell, as well as the words they need to learn. You may wish to use Other Word Forms when giving the Pretest. Five suggested Other Word Forms are underlined on this page.

To administer the Pretest:

**READ** each word aloud.
**SAY** the phrase containing the word.
**REPEAT** the word.

Have students correct the Pretest using the Corrected-test Procedure. They may record their scores on a personal Progress Chart (see the Teacher's Resource Book) and study misspelled words using the **S-H-A-R-P** procedure.

## OTHER WORD FORMS

This section presents related forms of the spelling words to strengthen spelling power and vocabulary knowledge.

### Enrichment Activity

Have students write sentences that include these Other Word Forms.

1. **lemony – jellies**
2. **fearing – messages**
3. **dresses – elbows**
4. **recesses – periodically**

**A. Pretest and Proofreading**

**B. Spelling Words and Phrases**

| | |
|---|---|
| **1. elbow** | sore elbow |
| **2. jelly*** | has spread the jelly |
| **3. begged** | begged us to come |
| **4. message*** | received the message |
| **5. dresser*** | into the dresser drawer |
| **6. unless** | unless you go |
| **7. attend** | will attend together |
| **8. cellar** | down the cellar stairs |
| **9. tennis** | learned to play tennis |
| **10. helpful*** | always very helpful |
| **11. shelter*** | shelter from the storm |
| **12. lemon** | orange, lemon, and lime |
| **13. record*** | played the new record |
| **14. people*** | elected by the people |
| **15. recess*** | waiting for recess |
| **16. secret** | kept the secret |
| **17. English*** | English, French, and Russian |
| **18. period** | a period or a comma |
| **19. nearby** | nearby field |
| **20. fearful*** | became fearful |

*Other Word Forms*

| | |
|---|---|
| elbows | recorded, recording, recorder |
| jellies, jellied | peoples |
| beg, begs, begging, beggar | recesses, recessed, recessing |
| messages, messenger | secretly, secretive |
| dress, dresses, dressing | England |
| attending, attendance | periodical, periodically |
| cellars | fearfully, fearing |
| helpfully, helpless | |
| sheltered, sheltering | |
| lemons, lemony | |

**C. Visual Warm-up** Write each word in its correct shape.

a. record
b. secret
c. elbow
d. unless
e. begged
f. English
g. message
h. period
i. attend
j. people
k. recess
l. jelly
m. nearby
n. helpful
o. fearful
p. shelter
q. lemon
r. dresser
s. tennis
t. cellar



*Modified Lesson words are asterisked.
The Modified Lesson is found in the Teacher's Resource Book.

## MEETING INDIVIDUAL NEEDS / ASSIGNMENT GUIDE

| 5-Day Plan | 3-Day Plan | Limited Spellers | Average Spellers | Advanced Spellers |
|---|---|---|---|---|
| 1 | 1 | • Pretest<br>• Progress Chart | • Pretest<br>• Progress Chart<br>• Home Activity | • Pretest<br>• Progress Chart<br>• Home Activity |
| 2 | | • Modified Lesson<br>Visual Warm-up<br>Ending Sounds | • Regular Lesson<br>Visual Warm-up | • Regular Lesson<br>Visual Warm-up |
| 3 and 4 | 2 | • Modified Lesson<br>Vowel Puzzle<br>Word Match<br>Finish the Sentence | Spelling Activities | Spelling Activities<br>• Challenge Exercise |
| 5 | 3 | • Posttest<br>• Words to Learn Sheet<br>• Progress Chart | • Posttest<br>• Words to Learn Sheet<br>• Progress Chart | • Posttest<br>• Words to Learn Sheet<br>• Progress Chart |

**D. Pandora's Box** Solve the puzzle by using spelling words and one Other Word Form (p. 116).* Write each word. Use the **Spelling Dictionary**. Then rearrange the four letters in the outlined squares, and you will know what was left in Pandora's Box.

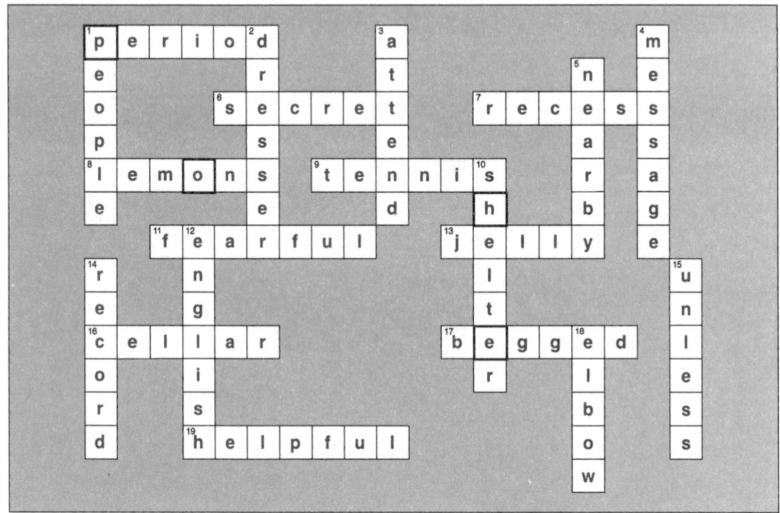

**Across**

1. the end of a sentence
6. hidden; concealed
7. a play period
8. citrus fruits*
9. a game played on a court
11. frightened
13. like jam
16. an underground room
17. pleaded
19. useful

**Down**

1. persons
2. furniture for clothing
3. to be present at
4. a note or letter
5. close; not faraway
10. a protective house
12. a language
14. an album
15. except if
18. a joint in the arm

20. What was left in Pandora's box? p o h e = hope



## OPTIONAL TEACHING PLAN

Write the five Word Group headings on the chalkboard. Ask the students to name the thirteen spelling words with the short **e** sound. Write the words on the chalkboard as the students say them. Continue identifying the other Word Groups. Note that the long **e** sound is spelled with **eo** in **people** and that **recess** has both a long **e** and a short **e** sound.

| Word Groups | | |
|---|---|---|
| /ĕ/ words | elbow<br>jelly<br>begged<br>message<br>dresser<br>unless<br>attend<br>cellar<br>tennis<br>helpful | shelter<br>lemon<br>record<br>**director**<br>**dreadful**<br>**elements**<br>**energy**<br>**gentle-men** |
| /ē/: **eo** word | people | |
| /ē/ words | recess | secret |
| /ĭ/ word | English | |
| /îr/: **er** and **ear** words | period<br>nearby | fearful |

*Challenge Words are boldfaced.*

### Optional Activity Masters

Those using the Hardcover Pupil Edition may wish to use the Optional Activity Masters in the Teacher's Resource Book for Exercises C and D.

**Home Activity #29**

Name ______ Date ______

The spelling words in Lesson 29 appear in the phrases below. Use the phrases to complete the sentences. The number before each blank tells you in what box you can find the correct phrase. Use each phrase only once. Circle the spelling words.

**Phrases**

1
elected by the **people**
sore **elbow**
a **period** or a comma
**English**, French, and Russian
kept the **secret**

2
waiting for **recess**
**nearby** field
into the **dresser** drawer
has spread the **jelly**
received the **message**

3
**begged** us to come
became **fearful**
**shelter** from the storm
down the **cellar** stairs
learned to play **tennis**

4
always very **helpful**
will **attend** together
orange, **lemon**, and lime
played the new **record**
**unless** you go

**Sentences**

1. The anxious child was (2) ______.
2. Follow me (3) ______.
3. Do I need (1) ______ after this phrase?
4. The three flavors are (4) ______.
5. I threw the socks (2) ______.
6. He (3) ______ of taking risks.
7. We (4) ______ on the stereo.
8. I fell and now have a (1) ______.
9. They (3) ______ to the party.
10. I (2) ______ that you called.
11. She speaks Spanish, (1) ______.
12. We need (3) ______.
13. The Halloween party is the one we (4) ______.
14. He (2) ______ on the bread.
15. Those tour guides are (4) ______.
16. The farmer plowed a (2) ______.
17. I (3) ______, not golf.
18. The president will be (1) ______.
19. I won't go (4) ______, too.
20. The spies (1) ______ to themselves.



35

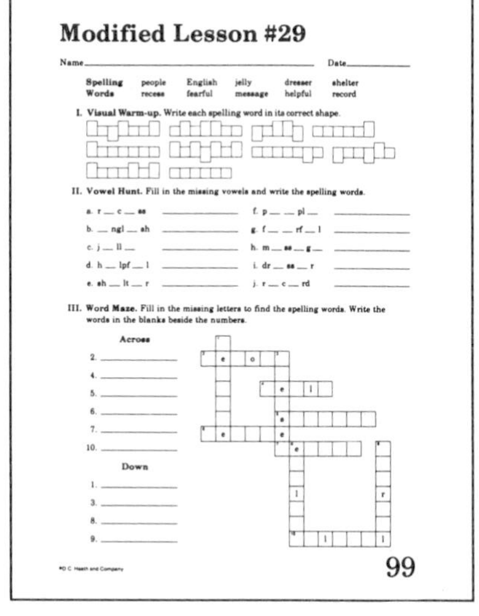

**Modified Lesson #29**

Name ______ Date ______

**Spelling Words** people recess English fearful jelly message dresser helpful shelter record

I. **Visual Warm-up.** Write each spelling word in its correct shape.

II. **Vowel Hunt.** Fill in the missing vowels and write the spelling words.

a. r _ c _ ss
b. _ ngl _ sh
c. j _ ll _
d. h _ lpf _ l
e. sh _ lt _ r
f. p _ _ pl _
g. f _ _ rf _ l
h. m _ ss _ g _
i. dr _ ss _ r
j. r _ c _ rd

III. **Word Maze.** Fill in the missing letters to find the spelling words. Write the words in the blanks beside the numbers.

Across: 2. 4. 5. 6. 7. 10.

Down: 1. 3. 8. 9.



99

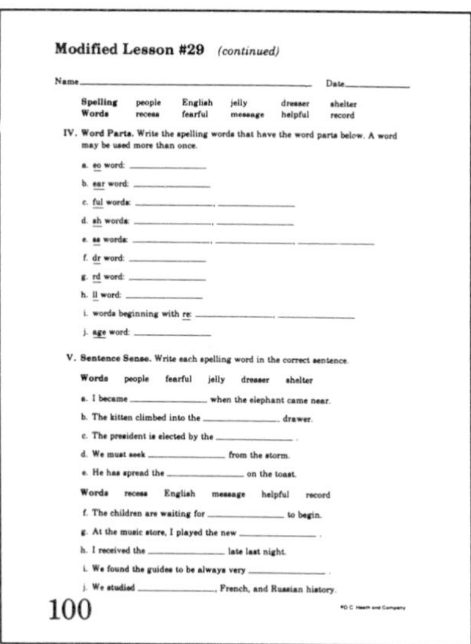

**Modified Lesson #29** *(continued)*

Name ______ Date ______

**Spelling Words** people recess English fearful jelly message dresser helpful shelter record

IV. **Word Parts.** Write the spelling words that have the word parts below. A word may be used more than once.

a. eo word:
b. ear word:
c. ful words:
d. sh words:
e. ss words:
f. dr word:
g. rd word:
h. ll word:
i. words beginning with re:
j. age word:

V. **Sentence Sense.** Write each spelling word in the correct sentence.

**Words** people fearful jelly dresser shelter

a. I became ______ when the elephant came near.
b. The kitten climbed into the ______ drawer.
c. The president is elected by the ______.
d. We must seek ______ from the storm.
e. He has spread the ______ on the toast.

**Words** recess English message helpful record

f. The children are waiting for ______ to begin.
g. At the music store, I played the new ______.
h. I received the ______ late last night.
i. We found the guides to be always very ______.
j. We studied ______, French, and Russian history.

100



### Home Activity

A weekly homework assignment

### Modified Lesson

An alternative lesson for limited spellers

*(The Answer Key can be found in the Teacher's Resource Book.)*

## LESSON 29 CONTINUED

### Challenge Exercise #29

Name____________________ Date________

**Word Watch.** Originally a cellar was an above-ground room, much like a pantry or granary, used to store foods. The word *cellar* is derived from the Latin word *cella*, meaning "small room." Over the years, the word has undergone several changes. Four hundred years ago, the English spoke of storing grain in the *celer*. Today the word *cellar* refers to a storage area that has moved from the above-ground level to below ground.

**Word Analogies.** Decide on the relationship that exists between the first pair of words. Using the Other Word Forms on page 116, find a word that completes the second pair of words and establishes the same relationship.

1. *potatoes* is to *gravy* as *salad* is to ________
2. *coffee breaks* is to *offices* as ________ is to *schools*
3. *book* is to *novel* as ________ is to *magazine*
4. *able* is to *capable* as *defenseless* is to ________
5. *umbrella* is to *protecting* as *tent* is to ________

**Challenge Words Student Activity**

Use the challenge words below to complete the statements an actor might say.

**energy dreadful elements gentlemen director**

1. My audition was a ________ experience.
2. The ________ shouted when I forgot my lines.
3. The drama contains several ________ of mystery.
4. Acting requires much ________ from the players.
5. I played the part of one of three elderly ________.

**Working With Words: Student Writing Activity**

Use as many Other Word Forms as you can from page 116 to write real or imaginary one-sentence reviews of a play. (Example: The actors were *helpless* to save the confusing drama.)





**Challenge Exercise**
Additional activities for advanced spellers

**Spelling Words**

| | | | | |
|---|---|---|---|---|
| elbow | jelly | begged | message | dresser |
| unless | attend | cellar | tennis | helpful |
| shelter | lemon | record | people | recess |
| secret | English | period | nearby | fearful |

**E. Not ______, But** Write a spelling word for each phrase below.

1. not faraway, but nearby
2. not useless, but helpful
3. not brave, but fearful
4. not a comma, but a period
5. not English, but French
6. not things, but people
7. not study period, but recess
8. not the cellar, but the attic
9. not known, but secret
10. not if, but unless
11. not attend, but be absent
12. not asked, but begged
13. not a knee, but an elbow
14. not a closet, but a dresser
15. not peanut butter, but jelly
16. not an orange, but a lemon
17. not uncover, but shelter
18. not golf, but tennis
19. not a code, but a message
20. not a record, but a tape



## CONTROLLED DICTATION (Optional)

These dictation sentences provide maintenance for spelling words previously taught and practice for words currently being studied. Dictation should be administered on Day 4. The teacher or another student may dictate the sentences. Be sure to dictate all marks of punctuation. Challenge Word sentences are preceded by an asterisk.

1. The **secret record** is sealed in an old **dresser** in the **cellar**.
2. I am **fearful** of adding bitter **lemon** to the **jelly**.
3. We will **attend** the **tennis** match **nearby**.
4. The **message** was left at the **shelter**.
5. During the **recess period**, we **begged** the children to be **helpful.**
6. Some **people** at headquarters do not speak the **English** language.
7. You could hurt your **elbow unless** you are careful.

*8. High winds and heavy rains were only two **elements** of our **dreadful** weekend.
*9. The **director** told the girls to save their **energy** for the hike back.
*10. The little boys were perfect **gentlemen**.

**F. Using Other Word Forms** Write the Other Word Form that fits each clue.

Base Words: periodical(ly) beg(ing) message(er) secret(ly) shelter(ed)

1. protected from the weather sheltered
2. a deliverer of messages messenger
3. every now and then periodically
4. asking for or pleading begging
5. not openly; privately secretly

**G. Challenge Words** Write the Challenge Word that completes each phrase.

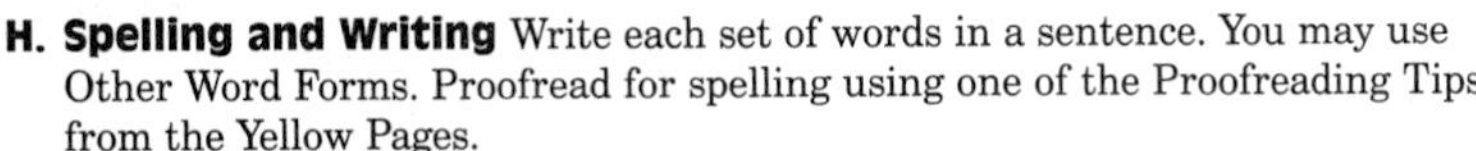

| director | dreadful | elements | energy | gentlemen |
|---|---|---|---|---|

1. ladies and gentlemen
2. actor and director
3. power and energy
4. terrible and dreadful
5. compound and elements

**H. Spelling and Writing** Write each set of words in a sentence. You may use Other Word Forms. Proofread for spelling using one of the Proofreading Tips from the Yellow Pages.

1. tennis, English, people
2. lemon, elbow, fearful
3. cellar, secret, jelly
4. shelter, message, attend
5. nearby, dresser, helpful
6. recess, period, unless
7. begged, record, secretly
8. director, dreadful, gentlemen
9. elements, energy, unless



## USING OTHER WORD FORMS

Vocabulary is expanded through the use of other forms of basic spelling words. Emphasis is on the relationship of syntax to suffix choices. The following generalization applies to the Other Word Forms used in Exercise F.

### Spelling Rule

Doubling the final consonant when adding suffixes

When adding a suffix that begins with a vowel to one-syllable words that end with one vowel and one consonant, double the final consonant. **(beg, begging)**

## POSTTEST AND PROOFREADING

Follow the same testing procedures used in the Pretest, although you may wish to correct the tests yourself. Have students write any misspelled words on the Words to Learn Sheet and record spelling success on the Progress Chart.

## THE SPELLING-WRITING LINK

**Purpose** This activity helps students effectively transfer lesson words into their daily writing. Students (a) determine a relationship among three given words and (b) write a complete sentence.

**Procedure** On the chalkboard, write the three words from line 1: **tennis, English, people,** and the Other Word Forms: **peoples, England, peopling.** Have students read the words and think of ways the three words might be related. Have them think of things or people the words suggest. Ask students to create sentences using some of their ideas. You can provide a sample sentence: **People from England love to watch tennis matches.**

**Practice** Tell students to write original sentences using the word sets and to proofread their work. You may want them to circle the lesson words.

![LESSON 30 REVIEW]

# LESSON 30 REVIEW

## OBJECTIVES

- to review the spelling of the 100 words studied in Lessons 25-29
- to promote the use of other forms of the 100 spelling words
- to apply high-utility generalizations for the addition of suffixes

| Summary of Skills | Exercises |
|---|---|
| Proofreading | A, D |
| Visual Discrimination | A, D |
| Context Usage | B |
| Vocabulary Development | C |

## REVIEW OF LESSONS 25-29

The goal of the review exercises is to expand each student's spelling power. The one hundred spelling words studied in the five preceding lessons are presented in challenging formats where the focus is shifted from the spelling words to the Other Word Forms.

## WORD REVIEW PROCEDURE

Students are encouraged to use this abbreviated version of the **S-H-A-R-P** procedure when reviewing the spelling words at the top of each review page.

**LOOK** at each word.
**SAY** the word to yourself.
**THINK** about the letters that spell the word.

# 30

## REVIEWING LESSONS 25-29

| | | | | |
|---|---|---|---|---|
| altered | canal | false | nearby | select |
| angry | deaf | fasten | palm | tennis |
| bought | direct | headquarters | quest | ugly |
| calm | eighteen | health | question | weigh |
| calves | English | lemon | secret | western |

**A. Word Search** Twenty-two Other Word Forms and three spelling words can be found in the word puzzle. The words appear down, diagonally, and across. Circle and write each word. Use the **Spelling Dictionary**.

```
c a l f p w e s t e r l y u q
a l n g a d i r e c t o r x u
l t m g i s b u y i n g y p e
m e t o r c t l v q u e s t s
l r v t s i l e m o n y p i t
y s k z q t e n n i s m o n i
e n g l a n d r h e u w t e o
u g l i n e s s e c r e t s n
p a l m s h r e a p n i b b e
r p o r l d x w l v a g i o d
w f a l s e l y t e b h a i c
m g r o o a u n h a c s t n a
l k j r m f u t y e o t z g n
e i g h t e e n t h p s e n a
v c r o t n d n e a r b y d l
l a m h e a d q u a r t e r s
```

**Down**

1. calmly
2. alters
3. deafen
4. healthy
5. weighs
6. questioned
7. canals

**Diagonally**

8. angrier
9. fastener
10. selected

**Across**

11. calf
12. westerly
13. director
14. buying
15. quests
16. lemony
17. tennis
18. England
19. ugliness
20. secrets
21. palms
22. falsely
23. eighteenth
24. nearby
25. headquarters

REVIEW



## MEETING INDIVIDUAL NEEDS / ASSIGNMENT GUIDE

| 5-Day Plan | 3-Day Plan | Limited Spellers | Average Spellers | Advanced Spellers |
|---|---|---|---|---|
| 1 and 2 | 1 | • Modified Lesson Visual Warm-up Word Parts | • Regular Lesson Spelling Activities<br>• Home Activity | • Regular Lesson Spelling Activities<br>• Home Activity |
| 3 and 4 | 2 | • Modified Lesson Vowel Puzzle Word Match Finish the Sentence | • Regular Lesson Spelling Activities<br>• Proofreading Exercise(s) | • Regular Lesson Spelling Activities<br>• Proofreading Exercise(s)<br>• Challenge Word Review |
| 5 | 3 | • Test Modified Lesson Words<br>• Words to Learn Sheet | • Review Test or Standardized-format Test<br>• Words to Learn Sheet | • Review Test or Standardized-format Test<br>• Words to Learn Sheet |

| ■ | ★ | ▲ | ◆ | ● |
|---|---|---|---|---|
| multiply | smaller | drawing | salty | thunder |
| eighty | mention | freckles | cherries | settle |
| heavy | remember | sweater | leather | meadow |
| engine | average | valentine | gasoline | answer |
| record | helpful | attend | shelter | cellar |

**B. Newspaper Headlines** Write Other Word Forms or the spelling words to complete the newspaper headlines. The shape tells you in what column you can find the spelling word. Write each word or its Other Word Form only once. Capitalize each word. If you need help, use the **Spelling Dictionary**.

1. Town Buys New Fire ■ Engines
2. Dogs ◆ Sheltered From Cold
3. ◆ Cherry Blossoms Bloom
4. New Skin Cream Removes ▲ Freckles
5. Pioneer ● Settles *or* Settled on Moon
6. ◆ Gasoline Explosion Causes Damage
7. World's ★ Smallest Dog Wins Award
8. Baseball Fan ▲ Attends World Series
9. ◆ Salt Mine Clue to Mystery
10. Candy ▲ Valentines Stolen From Van
11. Farmers Plow Old ● Meadows
12. Winner Breaks All ■ Records
13. Scouts' Wishes Are ● Answered
14. Thirty ● Cellars Damaged by Flood
15. Baseball ★ Averages Challenged
16. ● Thundering Herd Stampedes Village
17. Old Memories ★ Remembered
18. Town Celebrates ■ Eightieth Birthday
19. ◆ Leathery Hide Saves Circus Elephant
20. ■ Heaviest Snowfall in Years Blankets State
21. Firefighter ★ Helps Child to Safety
22. Artist ▲ Draws Self-Portrait
23. Speaker ★ Mentions New Plan
24. Flu Germs ■ Multiplying Daily
25. New Yarns Create New ▲ Sweaters

REVIEW



## CREATIVE WRITING

**(An optional writing activity)**

**Recipe for Writing:** This imaginative writing activity uses spelling words and Other Word Forms studied in Lessons 25-29.

COMBINE:
1 treasure in a nearby meadow
2 messages in a secret language
4 flashlights
4 small, but heavy kettles
1 feather machine

SEASON with your own original ideas and COOK UP a story with a unique FLAVOR. Proofread before SERVING.

The RECIPE words appear in the following lessons.

| Lesson | Words |
|---|---|
| 25 | small |
| 26 | flashlights, kettles |
| 27 | treasure, meadow, heavy, feather |
| 28 | language, machine |
| 29 | messages, secret, nearby |

REVIEW

### Optional Activity Masters

Those using the Hardcover Pupil Edition may wish to use the Optional Activity Masters in the Teacher's Resource Book for Exercises A and D.

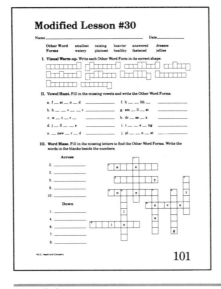

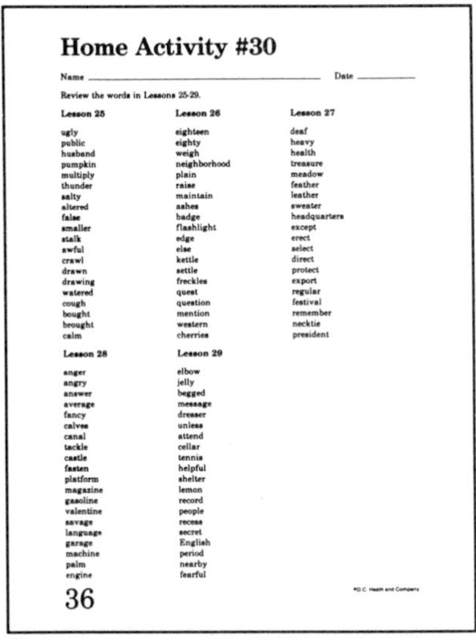

**Home Activity #30**

Name ______ Date ______

Review the words in Lessons 25-29.

| Lesson 25 | Lesson 26 | Lesson 27 |
|---|---|---|
| ugly | eighteen | deaf |
| public | eighty | heavy |
| husband | weigh | health |
| pumpkin | neighborhood | treasure |
| multiply | plain | meadow |
| thunder | raise | feather |
| salty | maintain | leather |
| altered | ashes | sweater |
| false | badge | headquarters |
| smaller | flashlight | except |
| stalk | edge | erect |
| awful | else | select |
| crawl | kettle | direct |
| drawn | settle | protect |
| drawing | freckles | export |
| watered | quest | regular |
| cough | question | festival |
| bought | mention | remember |
| brought | western | necktie |
| calm | cherries | president |

| Lesson 28 | Lesson 29 |
|---|---|
| anger | elbow |
| angry | jelly |
| answer | begged |
| average | message |
| fancy | dresser |
| calves | unless |
| canal | attend |
| tackle | cellar |
| castle | tennis |
| fasten | helpful |
| platform | shelter |
| magazine | lemon |
| gasoline | record |
| valentine | people |
| savage | recess |
| language | secret |
| garage | English |
| machine | period |
| palm | nearby |
| engine | fearful |

36



**Modified Lesson #30**

Name ______ Date ______

Other Word Forms: smallest, raising, heavier, answered, dresses, watery, plainest, healthy, fastened, jellies

I. **Visual Warm-up.** Write each Other Word Form in its correct shape.

II. **Vowel Hunt.** Fill in the missing vowels and write the Other Word Forms.

a. f __ st __ n __ d ______
b. h __ __ v __ __ r ______
c. w __ t __ r __ ______
d. j __ ll __ __ s ______
e. __ nsw __ r __ d ______
f. h __ __ lth __ ______
g. sm __ ll __ st ______
h. dr __ ss __ s ______
i. r __ __ s __ ng ______
j. pl __ __ n __ st ______

III. **Word Maze.** Fill in the missing letters to find the Other Word Forms. Write the words in the blanks beside the numbers.

Across
2. ______
3. ______
5. ______
9. ______
10. ______

Down
1. ______
4. ______
6. ______
7. ______
8. ______



101

**Modified Lesson #30** *(continued)*

Name ______ Date ______

Other Word Forms: smallest, raising, heavier, answered, dresses, watery, plainest, healthy, fastened, jellies

IV. **Word Parts.** Write the Other Word Forms that have the word parts below. A word may be used more than once.

a. dr word: ______
b. sm word: ______
c. est words: ______, ______
d. ing word: ______
e. words changing y to i before adding er or es: ______, ______
f. ll words: ______, ______
g. words ending in y: ______, ______
h. ed words: ______, ______
i. words ending in es: ______, ______
j. ai words: ______, ______
k. ea words: ______, ______

V. **Sentence Sense.** Write each Other Word Form in the correct sentence.

Words: smallest, raising, heavier, answered, dresses

a. She bought several new ______.
b. Who ______ the phone?
c. The stone is ______ than the log.
d. The students are ______ the flag.
e. Your puppy is the ______ of the litter.

Words: watery, plainest, healthy, fastened, jellies

f. The rope was ______ to the pole.
g. The soup was thin and ______.
h. Jams and ______ are made of fruit.
i. Choose the ______ wallpaper for the room.
j. Exercise will keep you fit and ______.

102



### Home Activity

A weekly homework assignment

### Modified Lesson

An alternative lesson for limited spellers

*(The Answer Key can be found in the Teacher's Resource Book.)*

# LESSON 30 CONTINUED

## Challenge Word Review

The Challenge Words from the previous five lessons are listed below if you wish to review the Challenge Words with your more advanced students.

1. cautious
2. vault
3. lawyer
4. lofty
5. awesome
6. understanding
7. projector
8. protection
9. reflected
10. refreshments
11. correctly
12. inspection
13. lecture
14. mentally
15. tension
16. commander
17. handicapped
18. data
19. mackerel
20. romantic
21. director
22. dreadful
23. elements
24. energy
25. gentlemen

| ■ | ★ | ▲ | ◆ | ● |
|---|---|---|---|---|
| husband | pumpkin | drawn | brought | cough |
| plain | raise | ashes | flashlight | kettle |
| treasure | feather | erect | necktie | export |
| machine | magazine | savage | tackle | platform |
| elbow | unless | dresser | period | recess |

REVIEW

**C. Words in a Series** Write Other Word Forms or the spelling words to complete each series. The shape tells you in what column you can find the spelling word. Use each word or its Other Word Form only once.

1. wildly, ferociously, ▲ **savagely**
2. bureaus, chests, ▲ **dressers**
3. stages, landings, ● **platforms**
4. shoulders, knees, ■ **elbows**
5. pans, pots, ● **kettles**
6. simply, commonly, ■ **plainly**
7. lifted, elevated, ★ **raised**
8. free times, breaks, ● **recesses**
9. squashes, gourds, ★ **pumpkins**
10. built, constructed, ▲ **erected**
11. beacons, lanterns, ◆ **flashlights**
12. sneezing, choking, ● **coughing**
13. sent out, shipped, ● **exported**
14. scarves, bow ties, ◆ **neckties**
15. pulleys, levers, ■ **machines**
16. commas, colons, ◆ **periods**
17. burned material, remains, ▲ **ashes**
18. mate, partner, ■ **husband**
19. pamphlets, journals, ★ **magazines**
20. if not, except if, ★ **unless**
21. soft, light, ★ **feathery**
22. stopped, tripped, ◆ **tackled**
23. valuables, jewels, ■ **treasures**
24. sketching, painting, ▲ **drawing**
25. carries, takes, ◆ **brings**

122 Review—Lesson 30

### Proofreading Exercise Lesson #30

Name __________ Date __________

**Proofreading the Spelling of Others**

Miguel and Maria wrote a gift list. They misspelled some of the words. Circle the errors. Write the correct words on the lines.

Gift List

1. two large fether pillows 1. ______
2. a leathar jacket 2. ______
3. a plain nektie for father 3. ______
4. a fancy swetter 4. ______
5. a toy cassel for the twins 5. ______
6. new fishing tackel 6. ______
7. a mower powered by gazoline 7. ______
8. a new engin for the electric train 8. ______
9. eighteen jars of strawberry jely 9. ______
10. a steel tenis racket 10. ______
11. an automatic washing mechine 11. ______
12. a book about world festivles 12. ______
13. a toy tresure chest 13. ______
14. a regular tea kettel 14. ______
15. a pair of westen jeans 15. ______
16. a frame for Teddy's drauing 16. ______
17. a book about good helth practices 17. ______
18. a shalter for camping 18. ______
19. a children's magasine 19. ______
20. a dictionary of the English languaje 20. ______

150



## Proofreading Exercise

| anger | crawl | fearful | maintain | protect |
|---|---|---|---|---|
| awful | edge | festival | message | public |
| badge | else | garage | neighborhood | regular |
| begged | except | jelly | people | stalk |
| castle | fancy | language | president | watered |

**D. Break the Code** Use the code to write twenty-four Other Word Forms and one spelling word. Write each word.

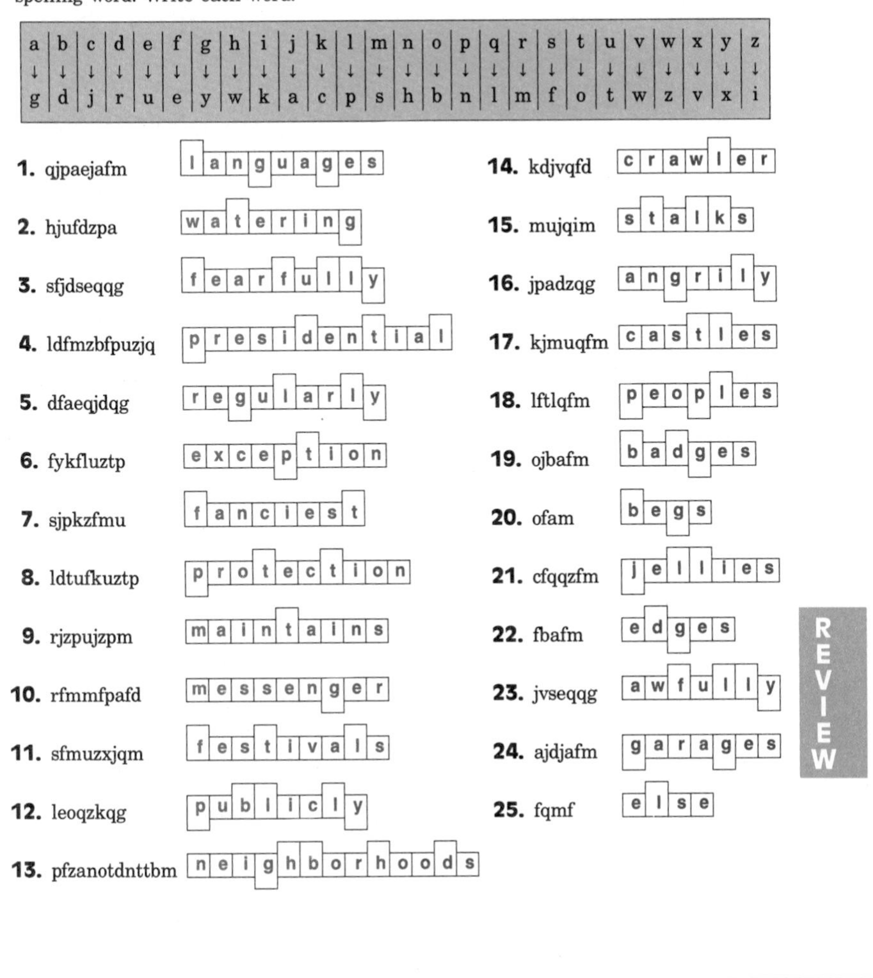

| a | b | c | d | e | f | g | h | i | j | k | l | m | n | o | p | q | r | s | t | u | v | w | x | y | z |
|---|---|---|---|---|---|---|---|---|---|---|---|---|---|---|---|---|---|---|---|---|---|---|---|---|---|
| ↓ | ↓ | ↓ | ↓ | ↓ | ↓ | ↓ | ↓ | ↓ | ↓ | ↓ | ↓ | ↓ | ↓ | ↓ | ↓ | ↓ | ↓ | ↓ | ↓ | ↓ | ↓ | ↓ | ↓ | ↓ | ↓ |
| g | d | j | r | u | e | y | w | k | a | c | p | s | h | b | n | l | m | f | o | t | w | z | v | x | i |

1. qjpaejafm languages
2. hjufdzpa watering
3. sfjdseqqg fearfully
4. ldfmzbfpuzjq presidential
5. dfaeqjdqg regularly
6. fykfluztp exception
7. sjpkzfmu fanciest
8. ldtufkuztp protection
9. rjzpujzpm maintains
10. rfmmfpafd messenger
11. sfmuzxjqm festivals
12. leoqzkqg publicly
13. pfzanotdnttbm neighborhoods
14. kdjvqfd crawler
15. mujqim stalks
16. jpadzqg angrily
17. kjmuqfm castles
18. lftlqfm peoples
19. ojbafm badges
20. ofam begs
21. cfqqzfm jellies
22. fbafm edges
23. jvseqqg awfully
24. ajdjafm garages
25. fqmf else

REVIEW



## REVIEW TEST

Twenty-five words, selected randomly from the five spelling lists, constitute the test and are listed with the appropriate phrases. Follow the same testing procedure used to administer the weekly Pretest and Posttest. Have students write any misspelled words on the Words to Learn Sheet. As an alternative testing option, you may wish to use the Standardized-format Test for this Review Lesson, found in the Teacher's Resource Book.

REVIEW

### Test Words and Phrases

| | |
|---|---|
| 1. husband | **husband** and wife |
| 2. salty | too **salty** to eat |
| 3. stalk | a **stalk** of corn |
| 4. drawing | tore the **drawing** paper |
| 5. brought | **brought** our friend |
| 6. weigh | to **weigh** and measure |
| 7. maintain | to **maintain** order |
| 8. edge | at the **edge** of the wharf |
| 9. freckles | covered with **freckles** |
| 10. western | wore **western** clothes |
| 11. health | in good **health** |
| 12. leather | dressed in **leather** |
| 13. erect | will **erect** a building |
| 14. export | the **export** of wheat |
| 15. necktie | struggled with my **necktie** |
| 16. answer | did not **answer** |
| 17. canal | dug the **canal** |
| 18. platform | stood on the **platform** |
| 19. savage | the lion's **savage** roar |
| 20. palm | in the **palm** of my hand |
| 21. jelly | spread the **jelly** |
| 22. attend | will **attend** together |
| 23. shelter | **shelter** from the storm |
| 24. recess | waiting for **recess** |
| 25. nearby | **nearby** field |

**Review Test: Lesson 30**

Name________ Date______

**Directions:** Read each sentence. Select the word with the correct spelling to complete each sentence. Fill in the correct letter in the answer column.

1. We met both ____ and wife. A. husband C. huzband B. husbend D. huzbend
2. The nuts are too ____ to eat. A. sawlty C. salty B. saulty D. saltey
3. She cut down a ____ of corn. A. stork C. stalk B. stolk D. stauk
4. Who ____ the drawing paper? A. tor C. toer B. taur D. tore
5. We ____ our friend to school. A. brout C. braught B. brought D. braut
6. We need to ____ and measure it. A. waigh C. weigh B. waye D. waiye
7. Police need to ____ order. A. manetane C. maintane B. manetain D. maintain
8. I sat at the ____ of the wharf. A. eged C. edge B. egge D. edje
9. Each face was covered with ____ . A. freckles C. frekels B. freckels D. freckals
10. The rider wore ____ clothes. A. westirn C. western B. westurn D. westorn
11. I am in good ____ . A. helth C. health B. hellth D. healthe
12. The models were dressed in ____ . A. lether C. leathar B. lethar D. leather
13. They will ____ a building. A. erect C. errect B. erekt D. errekt
14. The ____ of wheat was halted. A. exsport C. ecksport B. export D. expote
15. I struggled with my ____ . A. nektie C. necktie B. neckty D. kneckty
16. We did not ____ the phone. A. anser C. answer B. anwser D. answur
17. Many workers dug the ____ . A. cannel C. cannal B. canel D. canal
18. Everyone stood on the ____ . A. platform C. platfrom B. pletform D. plateform
19. We heard the lion's ____ roar. A. savege C. savaje B. savije D. savage
20. It's in the ____ of my hand. A. parm C. palm B. pam D. palme
21. Who has spread the ____ ? A. jilly C. jelley B. gelly D. jelly
22. We will ____ together. A. attind C. attend B. atand D. atend
23. They sought ____ from the storm. A. shallter C. shellter B. shalter D. shelter
24. The children are waiting for ____ . A. recess C. reccess B. reccess D. reces
25. We played on a ____ field. A. nereby C. nerebey B. nearbie D. nearby

Answer Column

1.–25. A B C D



159

**Standardized-format Test**

LESSON

# 31

### OBJECTIVES

- to spell 20 high-frequency words with the /ă/ and variant sounds of the vowel "a"
- to proofread these words in daily writing
- to become familiar with 26 other forms of the spelling words

| Summary of Skills | Exercises |
|---|---|
| Auditory Discrimination | A |
| Proofreading | A, C, E, I |
| Visual Discrimination | C, E |
| Context Usage | D |
| Word Analysis | D |
| Vocabulary Development | F, G, H |
| Dictionary Skills | F |
| Original Writing | I |

### PRETEST AND PROOFREADING

The Pretest identifies the words students are able to spell, as well as the words they need to learn. You may wish to use Other Word Forms when giving the Pretest. Five suggested Other Word Forms are underlined on this page.

To administer the Pretest:

**READ** each word aloud.
**SAY** the phrase containing the word.
**REPEAT** the word.

Have students correct the Pretest using the Corrected-test Procedure. They may record their scores on a personal Progress Chart (see the Teacher's Resource Book) and study misspelled words using the **S-H-A-R-P** procedure.

### OTHER WORD FORMS

This section presents related forms of the spelling words to strengthen spelling power and vocabulary knowledge.

**Enrichment Activity**

Have students write synonyms or related phrases for these Other Word Forms. Be sure they write the Other Word Form with its synonym next to it.

**gathered, avenues, pastures, shadowing**

**A. Pretest and Proofreading**

**B. Spelling Words and Phrases**

1. **avenue** — the tree-lined avenue
2. **afterward*** — joined them afterward
3. **captain*** — talked with the captain
4. **tablet*** — writing tablet
5. **grandfather*** — went with my grandfather
6. **handsome*** — handsome animal
7. **handful** — a handful for each of us
8. **palace** — behind the palace wall
9. **factory*** — the new factory
10. **families** — several families
11. **pasture*** — cows grazing in the pasture
12. **plastic** — made of plastic
13. **gravel** — played in the gravel pit
14. **shadow*** — will cast a long shadow
15. **piano** — could play the piano
16. **gathering*** — were gathering there
17. **practicing** — practicing each day
18. **pajamas** — red-striped pajamas
19. **altogether*** — altogether satisfied
20. **although** — although we tried

*Other Word Forms*

| | |
|---|---|
| avenues | pastures, pastured |
| afterwards | plastics |
| captains | gravels, gravelly |
| tablets | shadows, shadowed, shadowing |
| grandfathers | pianos, pianist |
| handsomely | gather, gathers, gathered |
| handfuls | practice, practices, practiced |
| palaces | |
| factories | |
| family | |

**C. Visual Warm-up** Write each word in its correct shape.

a. gathering
b. captain
c. pajamas
d. avenue
e. tablet
f. although
g. handsome
h. pasture
i. families
j. altogether
k. handful
l. practicing
m. shadow
n. piano
o. factory
p. palace
q. grandfather
r. plastic
s. gravel
t. afterward



*Modified Lesson words are asterisked.
The Modified Lesson is found in the Teacher's Resource Book.

### MEETING INDIVIDUAL NEEDS / ASSIGNMENT GUIDE

| 5-Day Plan | 3-Day Plan | Limited Spellers | Average Spellers | Advanced Spellers |
|---|---|---|---|---|
| 1 | 1 | • Pretest<br>• Progress Chart | • Pretest<br>• Progress Chart<br>• Home Activity | • Pretest<br>• Progress Chart<br>• Home Activity |
| 2 | | • Modified Lesson Visual Warm-up Ending Sounds | • Regular Lesson Visual Warm-up | • Regular Lesson Visual Warm-up |
| 3 and 4 | 2 | • Modified Lesson Vowel Puzzle Word Match Finish the Sentence | Spelling Activities | Spelling Activities<br>• Challenge Exercise |
| 5 | 3 | • Posttest<br>• Words to Learn Sheet<br>• Progress Chart | • Posttest<br>• Words to Learn Sheet<br>• Progress Chart | • Posttest<br>• Words to Learn Sheet<br>• Progress Chart |

**D. Noun or Verb** Sometimes a word may be a noun or a verb, depending on how it is used in a sentence. Find a spelling word or Other Word Form (p. 124) that fits in each pair of sentences. Circle *N* or *V* beside each sentence.

1. a. My shadow follows me everywhere. (N) V
   b. The trees will shadow him from the sun. N (V)
2. a. You must practice your tennis serve. N (V)
   b. Choir practice will be held this morning. (N) V
3. a. A crowd was gathering in the park for the concert. N (V)
   b. Sixteen grandchildren attended the family gathering. (N) V
4. a. The cows will pasture in the upper meadow. N (V)
   b. Wild flowers grew abundantly in the pasture. (N) V

**E. Twenty Words** The twenty spelling words can be found in the word puzzle. The words appear across, down, and diagonally. Circle and write the words.

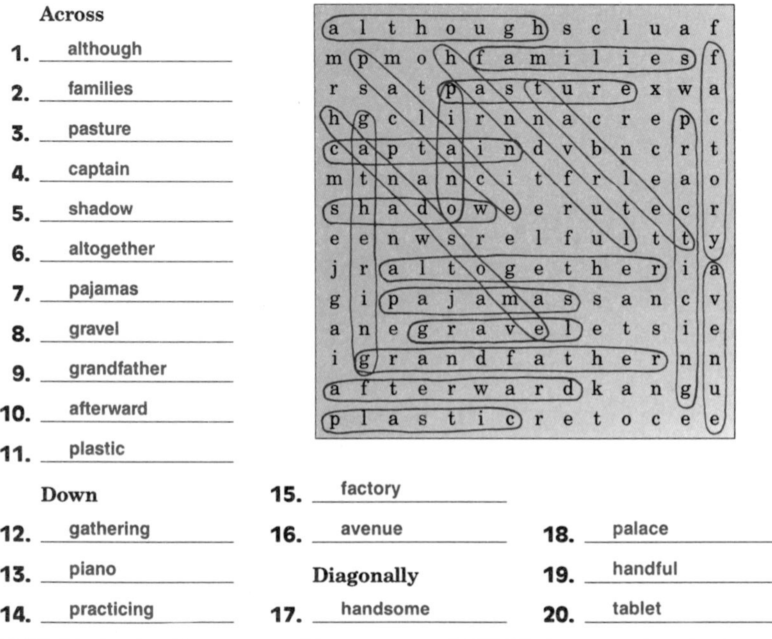


Across

1. although
2. families
3. pasture
4. captain
5. shadow
6. altogether
7. pajamas
8. gravel
9. grandfather
10. afterward
11. plastic

Down

12. gathering
13. piano
14. practicing
15. factory
16. avenue

Diagonally

17. handsome
18. palace
19. handful
20. tablet



## OPTIONAL TEACHING PLAN

Write the three Word Group headings on the chalkboard. Ask the students to name the seventeen spelling words with the short **a** sound. Write the words as the students say them. Continue identifying the other Word Groups. Note the short **a** sound of **a** in **avenue**, the /ə/ (schwa) and /ä/ sounds of **a** in **pajamas**, and the /ô/ sound of **a** in **altogether**.

| Word Groups | | |
|---|---|---|
| /ă/ words | avenue<br>afterward<br>captain<br>tablet<br>grand-father<br>handsome<br>handful<br>palace<br>factory<br>families<br>pasture | plastic<br>gravel<br>shadow<br>piano<br>gathering<br>practicing<br>**agony**<br>**baggage**<br>**adverb**<br>**manuscript**<br>**Massa-chusetts** |
| /ə/ and /ä/: **a** word | pajamas | |
| /ô/: **a** words | altogether | although |

*Challenge Words are boldfaced.*

### Optional Activity Masters

Those using the Hardcover Pupil Edition may wish to use the Optional Activity Masters in the Teacher's Resource Book for Exercises C and E.

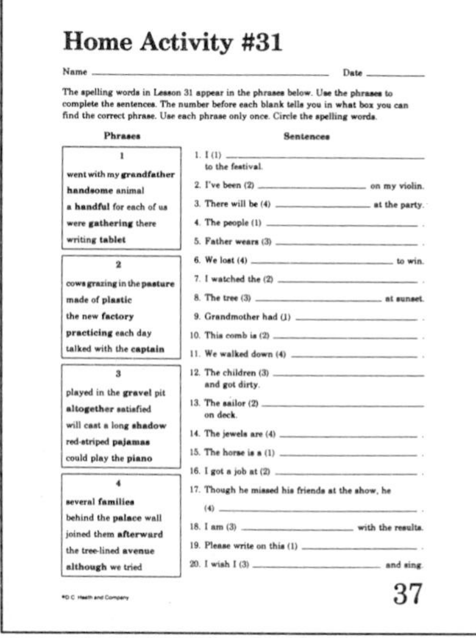
Home Activity #31

The spelling words in Lesson 31 appear in the phrases below. Use the phrases to complete the sentences. The number before each blank tells you in what box you can find the correct phrase. Use each phrase only once. Circle the spelling words.

37

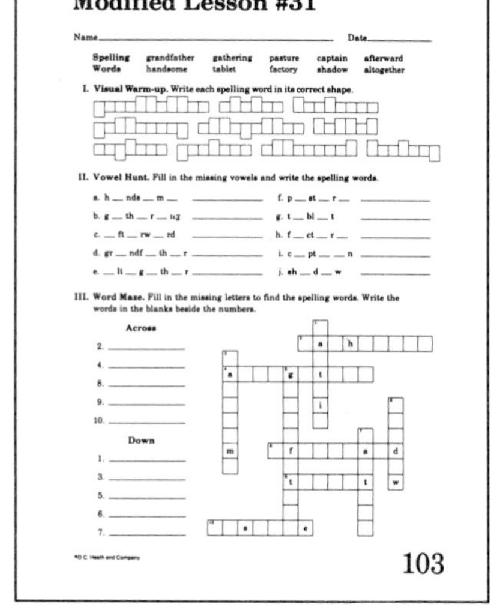
Modified Lesson #31

I. Visual Warm-up. Write each spelling word in its correct shape.

II. Vowel Hunt. Fill in the missing vowels and write the spelling words.

III. Word Maze. Fill in the missing letters to find the spelling words. Write the words in the blanks beside the numbers.

103

Modified Lesson #31 *(continued)*

IV. Word Parts.

V. Sentence Sense. Write each spelling word in the correct sentence.

104

### Home Activity

A weekly homework assignment

### Modified Lesson

An alternative lesson for limited spellers

*(The Answer Key can be found in the Teacher's Resource Book.)*

LESSON

# 31

CONTINUED

### Challenge Exercise #31

Name____________________ Date________

**Word Watch.** Around 1450 in England, the word *handsome* was reserved for tools and implements. An ax that felt pleasing to the grip was handsome. Most workers preferred handsome tools because of the better results that these tools produced. In time, *handsome* was broadened to include men who were skilled horsemen. The most able riders were considered handsome riders. Today the word *handsome* is usually reserved for any man who is pleasing to look at. However, people also speak of handsome animals and handsome rewards.

**Word Analogies.** Decide on the relationship that exists between the first pair of words. Using the Other Word Forms on page 124, find a word that completes the second pair of words and establishes the same relationship.

1. *sand* is to *beaches* as *grass* is to ________
2. *mansions* is to *shacks* as ________ is to *huts*
3. *pedals* is to *bicycles* as *keys* is to ________
4. *spools* is to *thread* as ________ is to *paper*
5. *disbands* is to *scatters* as *convenes* is to ________

**Challenge Words Student Activity**
Use the challenge words below to complete the relationships.

**adverb** **agony** **manuscript** **baggage** **Massachusetts**

1. misery, pain, ________
2. noun, adjective, ________
3. luggage, suitcases, ________
4. paper, scroll, ________
5. Rhode Island, Colorado, ________

**Working With Words: Student Writing Activity**
Use as many Other Word Forms as you can from page 124 to write tongue twisters, sentences with words that all begin with the same sound. (Example: Shane seldom *shadows* shameful sharks.)

140



## Challenge Exercise

Additional activities for advanced spellers

### Spelling Words

| | | | |
|---|---|---|---|
| avenue | afterward | captain | tablet |
| grandfather | handsome | handful | palace |
| factory | families | pasture | plastic |
| gravel | shadow | piano | gathering |
| practicing | pajamas | altogether | although |

**F. Words and Meanings** Write a spelling word for each meaning. Check your answers in the **Spelling Dictionary**.

1. a wide street **avenue**
2. the leader of a group **captain**
3. even though **although**
4. a keyboard musical instrument **piano**
5. coming together in a group **gathering**
6. a building where goods are made **factory**
7. the home of a king or queen **palace**
8. several sets of parents and their children **families**
9. later **afterward**
10. the father of a person's father or mother **grandfather**
11. pebbles and small pieces of rock **gravel**
12. totally or completely **altogether**
13. clothing for sleeping **pajamas**
14. the amount that can be held in a person's hand **handful**
15. a substance that can be easily shaped **plastic**
16. shade made by a person, animal, or object **shadow**
17. grassland where animals graze **pasture**
18. pad of paper **tablet**
19. good-looking **handsome**
20. doing many times over to gain skill **practicing**



## CONTROLLED DICTATION (Optional)

These dictation sentences provide maintenance for spelling words previously taught and practice for words currently being studied. Dictation should be administered on Day 4. The teacher or another student may dictate the sentences. Be sure to dictate all marks of punctuation. Challenge Word sentences are preceded by an asterisk.

1. I wrote my **piano** appointments on the yellow **tablet**.
2. **Afterward**, **grandfather** picked up a **handful** of **gravel**.
3. There were **altogether** too many **families** at the **gathering**.
4. The **factory** on the next **avenue** makes **plastic** knives and forks.
5. A **handsome captain** visited the **palace**.
6. **Although** it is odd, the band is **practicing** in the **pasture**.
7. Drying on the line, the **pajamas** cast a long **shadow**.

*8. The **manuscript** was sent to a printer in **Massachusetts**.
*9. The man was in **agony** when his **baggage** was lost.
*10. An **adverb** is used to tell more about a verb.

**G. Using Other Word Forms** Write the Other Word Form that replaces each underlined word or phrase.

Base Words: piano(s) practice(ed) afterward(s) palace(s) gather(ed)

1. Later, we decided to attend the concert. afterwards
2. A large crowd came together in the hall. gathered
3. Two grand instruments were on the stage. pianos
4. The musicians had rehearsed for weeks. practiced
5. They had performed in the finest castles of Europe. palaces

**H. Challenge Words** Write the Challenge Word that fits each clue.

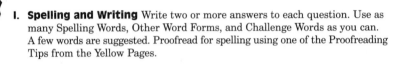

| agony | baggage | adverb | manuscript | Massachusetts |
|---|---|---|---|---|

1. gear packed for a trip baggage
2. story submitted to a publisher manuscript
3. a New England state Massachusetts
4. a part of speech adverb
5. great pain agony

**I. Spelling and Writing** Write two or more answers to each question. Use as many Spelling Words, Other Word Forms, and Challenge Words as you can. A few words are suggested. Proofread for spelling using one of the Proofreading Tips from the Yellow Pages.

1. What business was his father's father in?
   factories grandfather pajamas avenue plastic Massachusetts
2. When will the crew meet the captain?
   handsome palace gathering shadow afterward captain
3. Where were the girls before they went to the gym?
   pasture piano altogether families practicing baggage



## THE SPELLING-WRITING LINK

**Purpose** This activity helps students retain the correct spelling of words and transfer the words to their daily writing. Students use lesson words to answer questions.

**Procedure** Read the first question and write the suggested words on the chalkboard: **factories, grandfather, pajamas, avenue, plastic, Massachusetts.** Have students list some Other Word Forms of the lesson words. Brainstorm with the class possible answers to question 1. Remind students to look at all the lesson words for ideas. Write the answers on the chalkboard, noting any lesson words.

**Practice** Tell students to finish the activity by writing two or more answers to each question. Remind them to proofread their work for spelling.

## USING OTHER WORD FORMS

Vocabulary is expanded through the use of other forms of basic spelling words. Emphasis is on the relationship of syntax to suffix choices. The following generalizations apply to the Other Word Forms used in Exercise G.

### Spelling Rule

Adding suffixes to words ending in silent **e**

When adding a suffix that begins with a vowel to words that end with silent **e**, drop the final **e**.
**(practice, practiced)**

Forming plurals

Add **s** to most nouns to form plurals.
**(palace, palaces)**

## POSTTEST AND PROOFREADING

Follow the same testing procedures used in the Pretest, although you may wish to correct the tests yourself. Have students write any misspelled words on the Words to Learn Sheet and record spelling success on the Progress Chart.

# LESSON 32

## OBJECTIVES

- to spell 20 high-frequency words with the /ĕ/, /ĭ/, and /ă/
- to proofread these words in daily writing
- to become familiar with 32 other forms of the spelling words

| Summary of Skills | Exercises |
|---|---|
| Auditory Discrimination | A |
| Proofreading | A, C, J |
| Visual Discrimination | C |
| Word Analysis | D, F |
| Vocabulary Development | E, H, I |
| Dictionary Skills | G |
| Original Writing | J |

## PRETEST AND PROOFREADING

The Pretest identifies the words students are able to spell, as well as the words they need to learn. You may wish to use Other Word Forms when giving the Pretest. Five suggested Other Word Forms are underlined on this page.

To administer the Pretest:

**READ** each word aloud.
**SAY** the phrase containing the word.
**REPEAT** the word.

Have students correct the Pretest using the Corrected-test Procedure. They may record their scores on a personal Progress Chart (see the Teacher's Resource Book) and study misspelled words using the **S-H-A-R-P** procedure.

## OTHER WORD FORMS

This section presents related forms of the spelling words to strengthen spelling power and vocabulary knowledge.

### Enrichment Activity

Have students write Other Word Forms under the appropriate vowel sound.

**short e   short i   short a**

# 32

**A. Pretest and Proofreading**

**B. Spelling Words and Phrases**

1. **nephew** — niece and nephew
2. **everywhere*** — everywhere they go
3. **entire** — the entire day
4. **elephant*** — circus elephant
5. **lemonade** — another lemonade stand
6. **anyhow*** — will do it anyhow
7. **anyone*** — if anyone cares
8. **anywhere*** — fits anywhere
9. **anyway*** — didn't want it anyway
10. **friendly*** — a friendly wave
11. **weather** — stormy weather
12. **breakfast*** — late for breakfast
13. **liberty** — liberty or death
14. **visitor*** — greeted the visitor
15. **wilderness** — a wilderness trail
16. **withdraw** — will withdraw your name
17. **industry** — the steel industry
18. **interest*** — a great deal of interest
19. **install** — will install the phone
20. **talent** — a talent for singing

*Other Word Forms*

nephews
entirely
elephants
friend, friendlier, friendliest, friendliness
weathered
breakfasts, breakfasted, breakfasting
liberties, liberate
visitors, visit, visits, visited, visiting
wild, wildness
withdraws, withdrew, withdrawing
industries, industrial
interests, interested, interesting
installs, installed, installing
talented

**C. Visual Warm-up** Write each word in its correct shape.

a. nephew
b. anyhow
c. elephant
d. weather
e. withdraw
f. anyone
g. entire
h. interest
i. wilderness
j. friendly
k. anyway
l. visitor
m. anywhere
n. everywhere
o. breakfast
p. install
q. industry
r. lemonade
s. liberty
t. talent



*Modified Lesson words are asterisked.
The Modified Lesson is found in the Teacher's Resource Book.

## MEETING INDIVIDUAL NEEDS / ASSIGNMENT GUIDE

| 5-Day Plan | 3-Day Plan | Limited Spellers | Average Spellers | Advanced Spellers |
|---|---|---|---|---|
| 1 | 1 | • Pretest<br>• Progress Chart | • Pretest<br>• Progress Chart<br>• Home Activity | • Pretest<br>• Progress Chart<br>• Home Activity |
| 2 | | • Modified Lesson Visual Warm-up Ending Sounds | • Regular Lesson Visual Warm-up | • Regular Lesson Visual Warm-up |
| 3 and 4 | 2 | • Modified Lesson Vowel Puzzle Word Match Finish the Sentence | Spelling Activities | Spelling Activities<br>• Challenge Exercise |
| 5 | 3 | • Posttest<br>• Words to Learn Sheet<br>• Progress Chart | • Posttest<br>• Words to Learn Sheet<br>• Progress Chart | • Posttest<br>• Words to Learn Sheet<br>• Progress Chart |

**D. Be a Word Detective** The same two letters are missing from each of the words below. Write the words.

1. interest
2. visitor
3. liberty
4. entire
5. friendly
6. wilderness
7. industry
8. withdraw

| | | | | | | | | | |
|---|---|---|---|---|---|---|---|---|---|
| | i | n | t | e | r | e | s | t | |
| | | v | i | s | i | t | o | r | |
| | | l | i | b | e | r | t | y | |
| | | e | n | t | i | r | e | | |
| | | f | r | i | e | n | d | l | y |
| w | i | l | d | e | r | n | e | s | s |
| | i | n | d | u | s | t | r | y | |
| | w | i | t | h | d | r | a | w | |

**E. Generally Speaking** Write a spelling word for the group it best fits.

1. lion, tiger, elephant
2. ability, skill, talent
3. rain, snow, weather
4. breakfast, lunch, dinner
5. set, adjust install
6. uncle, niece, nephew
7. punch, juice, lemonade

**F. Circles and Squares** Match the circles and squares to form five words from the spelling list. Write the words.

1. everywhere
2. anyhow
3. anyone
4. anywhere
5. anyway

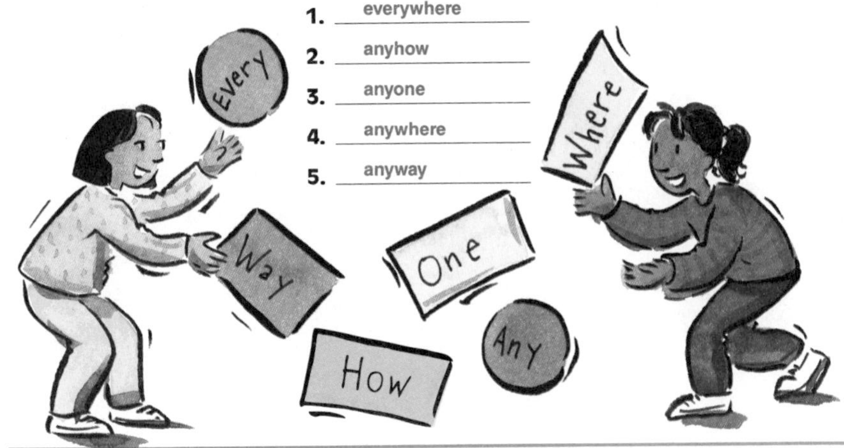




## OPTIONAL TEACHING PLAN

Write the six Word Group headings on the chalkboard. Ask the students to name the five spelling words with the short **e** sound spelled with **e**. Write the words as the students say them. Continue identifying the other Word Groups. Note that the short **e** sound is spelled with **e** in **nephew**, with **a** in **anyhow**, with **ie** in **friendly**, and with **ea** in **weather**.

| Word Groups | | |
|---|---|---|
| /ĕ/: **e** words | nephew<br>entire<br>elephant<br>lemonade<br>everywhere | **central**<br>**distress**<br>**extended**<br>**rebellion**<br>**tenderly** |
| /ĕ/: **a** words | anyhow<br>anyone | anywhere<br>anyway |
| /ĕ/: **ie** word | friendly | |
| /ĕ/: **ea** words | weather | breakfast |
| /ĭ/ words | liberty<br>visitor<br>withdraw<br>wilderness | industry<br>interest<br>install |
| /ă/ word | talent | |

*Challenge Words are boldfaced.*

### Optional Activity Masters

Those using the Hardcover Pupil Edition may wish to use the Optional Activity Masters in the Teacher's Resource Book for Exercises C and D.

**Home Activity #32**

Name ______ Date ______

The spelling words in Lesson 32 appear in the phrases below. Write each phrase in a sentence and circle the spelling word.

| Phrases | Sentences |
|---|---|
| 1. niece and nephew | 1. |
| 2. will do it anyhow | 2. |
| 3. everywhere they go | 3. |
| 4. if anyone cares | 4. |
| 5. fits anywhere | 5. |
| 6. didn't want it anyway | 6. |
| 7. a talent for singing | 7. |
| 8. late for breakfast | 8. |
| 9. the entire day | 9. |
| 10. circus elephant | 10. |
| 11. another lemonade stand | 11. |
| 12. a friendly wave | 12. |
| 13. stormy weather | 13. |
| 14. liberty or death | 14. |
| 15. greeted the visitor | 15. |
| 16. a great deal of interest | 16. |
| 17. will install the phone | 17. |
| 18. a wilderness trail | 18. |
| 19. will withdraw your name | 19. |
| 20. the steel industry | 20. |

38

**Modified Lesson #32**

Name ______ Date ______

Spelling Words: anyhow, everywhere, anyone, anywhere, anyway, breakfast, elephant, friendly, visitor, interest

I. Visual Warm-up. Write each spelling word in its correct shape.

II. Vowel Hunt. Fill in the missing vowels and write the spelling words.

III. Word Maze. Fill in the missing letters to find the spelling words. Write the words in the blanks beside the numbers.

105

**Modified Lesson #32** *(continued)*

Name ______ Date ______

Spelling Words: anyhow, everywhere, anyone, anywhere, anyway, breakfast, elephant, friendly, visitor, interest

IV. Word Parts. Write the spelling words that have the word parts below. A word may be used more than once.

V. Sentence Sense. Write each spelling word in the correct sentence.

106

### Home Activity

A weekly homework assignment

### Modified Lesson

An alternative lesson for limited spellers

*(The Answer Key can be found in the Teacher's Resource Book.)*

# LESSON 32 CONTINUED

Challenge Exercise #32

Name________________ Date________

**Word Watch.** The word *breakfast* has firm roots in Old England. Derived from the two words *brecan*, meaning "break," and *faestan*, meaning "fast," the word literally means "to break the fast." The long period between supper and the first meal of the next day, when no food was taken, was considered a fast. In the morning, the English would break the fast when they ate *brekfast*. In time the word changed to *breakfast*.

**Word Analogies.** Decide on the relationship that exists between the first pair of words. Using the Other Word Forms on page 128, find a word that completes the second pair of words and establishes the same relationship.

1. *agricultural* is to *farms* as ________ is to *factories*
2. *roasts* is to *dinners* as *cereals* is to ________
3. *foe* is to *ally* as *enemy* is to ________
4. *anteater* is to *snouts* as ________ is to *trunks*
5. *imprison* is to *caged* as ________ is to *freed*

**Challenge Words Student Activity**

Use the challenge words below to complete the series.

**distress** **central** **rebellion** **extended** **tenderly**

1. struggle, uprising, ________
2. gently, carefully, ________
3. stretched, lengthened, ________
4. misery, discomfort, ________
5. middle, inner, ________

**Working With Words: Student Writing Activity**

Use as many Other Word Forms as you can from page 128 to write catchy slogans for radio or television commercials. (Example: Friends become *friendlier* when you use *industrial*-strength mouthwash!)



141

## Challenge Exercise

Additional activities for advanced spellers

**Spelling Words**

| | | | |
|---|---|---|---|
| nephew | everywhere | entire | elephant |
| lemonade | anyhow | anyone | anywhere |
| anyway | friendly | weather | breakfast |
| liberty | visitor | wilderness | withdraw |
| industry | interest | install | talent |

**G. Guide Words** These word pairs are guide words that might appear in a dictionary. Write the words from the spelling list that would appear on the same page as each pair of guide words.

**act - apartment**

1. anyhow
2. anyone
3. anywhere
4. anyway

**bought - canyon**

5. breakfast

**dry - escape**

6. entire
7. elephant

**everywhere - festive**

8. everywhere

**freeze - graze**

9. friendly

**help - ironing**

10. industry
11. install
12. interest

**known - machine**

13. liberty
14. lemonade

**mud - offer**

15. nephew

**stray - talent**

16. talent

**uncle - west**

17. visitor
18. weather

**western - wrist**

19. wilderness
20. withdraw



## CONTROLLED DICTATION (Optional)

These dictation sentences provide maintenance for spelling words previously taught and practice for words currently being studied. Dictation should be administered on Day 4. The teacher or another student may dictate the sentences. Be sure to dictate all marks of punctuation. Challenge Word sentences are preceded by an asterisk.

1. Do you know **anyone** who can **install** the heater before the cold **weather** starts?
2. That **elephant** is so **friendly** that it drinks **lemonade**.
3. Our **nephew** wouldn't go **anywhere** before **breakfast**.
4. **Everywhere** the **visitor** went on his trip, he took an **interest** in what he viewed.
5. **Anyway**, the **entire** company has enough **talent** so that I can **withdraw** from the show.
6. Pilgrims in quest of **liberty** settled in the **wilderness**.
7. The public doesn't know much about **industry anyhow**.

*8. We'll meet at a **central** point.
*9. A **rebellion** will cause **distress**.
*10. She **extended** her hand very **tenderly** to the child.

**H. Using Other Word Forms** Write the Other Word Form that fits each group of words.

Base Words: industry(es) interest(ed) friendly(er) withdraw(ew) visit(ing)

1. took away, removed, withdrew
2. calling on, attending, visiting
3. curious about, concerned, interested
4. businesses, trades, industries
5. kinder, more favorable, friendlier

**I. Challenge Words** Write the Challenge Word that fits each clue.

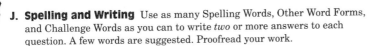

| central | distress | extended | rebellion | tenderly |
|---|---|---|---|---|

1. toward the middle central
2. in a gentle manner tenderly
3. stretched extended
4. a revolt rebellion
5. danger distress

**J. Spelling and Writing** Use as many Spelling Words, Other Word Forms, and Challenge Words as you can to write *two* or more answers to each question. A few words are suggested. Proofread your work.

1. What might you see and do if you were on a safari?

   everywhere – weather – wilderness – elephant – anywhere – rebellion

2. What are some things you might talk about with a bank employee?

   industry – interest – install – withdraw – central – extended

3. What would you say after you watched gymnasts from the United States Olympic team perform at your school?

   anyhow – friendly – visitor – entire – anyone – talent



## USING OTHER WORD FORMS

Vocabulary is expanded through the use of other forms of basic spelling words. Emphasis is on the relationship of syntax to suffix choices. The following generalizations apply to the Other Word Forms used in Exercise H.

### Spelling Rule

Forming plurals

To form the plurals of nouns ending with consonant-**y**, change the **y** to **i** and add **es**. (**industry, industries**)

Adding suffixes to words ending in **y**

When adding a suffix to words ending with consonant-**y**, change the **y** to **i**, unless the suffix begins with **i**. (**friendly, friendlier**)

## POSTTEST AND PROOFREADING

Follow the same testing procedures used in the Pretest, although you may wish to correct the tests yourself. Have students write any misspelled words on the Words to Learn Sheet and record spelling success on the Progress Chart.

## THE SPELLING-WRITING LINK

**Purpose** This activity helps students retain the correct spelling of words and transfer the words to their daily writing. Students use lesson words to answer questions promoting higher-order thinking skills.

**Procedure** Read the first question and write the suggested words on the chalkboard: **everywhere, weather, wilderness, elephant, anywhere, rebellion.** Have students list some Other Word Forms of the lesson words. Brainstorm with the class possible answers to question 1. Remind students to look at all the lesson words for ideas. Write the answers on the chalkboard, noting any lesson words.

**Practice** Tell students to finish the activity by writing two or more answers to each question. Remind them to proofread their work.

# LESSON 33

## OBJECTIVES

- to spell 20 high-frequency **ar** words with the /är/ and /âr/
- to proofread these words in daily writing
- to become familiar with 39 other forms of the spelling words

| Summary of Skills | Exercises |
|---|---|
| Auditory Discrimination | A |
| Proofreading | A, C, I |
| Visual Discrimination | C |
| Word Analysis | D, E |
| Vocabulary Development | F |
| Context Usage | G, H |
| Original Writing | I |

## PRETEST AND PROOFREADING

The Pretest identifies the words students are able to spell, as well as the words they need to learn. You may wish to use Other Word Forms when giving the Pretest. Five suggested Other Word Forms are underlined on this page.

To administer the Pretest:

**READ** each word aloud.
**SAY** the phrase containing the word.
**REPEAT** the word.

Have students correct the Pretest using the Corrected-test Procedure. They may record their scores on a personal Progress Chart (see the Teacher's Resource Book) and study misspelled words using the **S-H-A-R-P** procedure.

## OTHER WORD FORMS

This section presents related forms of the spelling words to strengthen spelling power and vocabulary knowledge.

### Enrichment Activity

Have students write Other Word Forms under the appropriate ending.

-ing    -ed    -s    -est    -er

**A. Pretest and Proofreading**

**B. Spelling Words and Phrases**

1. **scar** — will leave a scar
2. **scarf** — tightened my scarf
3. **guard** — the guard at the gate
4. **charge*** — to charge forward
5. **largely** — largely to blame
6. **carpet*** — sat on the carpet
7. **darkness*** — the darkness of night
8. **pardon** — to beg your pardon
9. **harvest*** — completed the harvest
10. **harbor** — headed for the harbor
11. **artist** — the artist at work
12. **parties*** — some birthday parties
13. **partner*** — worked with a partner
14. **hardware*** — at the hardware store
15. **carloads** — carloads of spectators
16. **alarm*** — sounded the alarm
17. **apartment*** — a five-room apartment
18. **depart*** — will depart on schedule
19. **remarkable** — a remarkable stunt
20. **parents** — for our parents

*Other Word Forms*

| | |
|---|---|
| scars, scarred, scarring | party |
| scarves | partnership |
| guarded | hardwares |
| charges, charged, charging | carload |
| large, larger, largest | alarmed, alarming |
| carpeted, carpeting | apartments |
| dark, darkest, darkening | departs, departing, departure |
| pardoned, pardonable | remark, remarked |
| harvester, harvesting | parent, parental |
| harboring, harbored | |
| artists, artistic, art | |

**C. Visual Warm-up** Write each word in its correct shape.

a. parties
b. partner
c. harbor
d. pardon
e. largely
f. scar
g. charge
h. parents
i. depart
j. artist
k. apartment
l. carloads
m. harvest
n. carpet
o. hardware
p. guard
q. darkness
r. remarkable
s. alarm
t. scarf



*Modified Lesson words are asterisked.
The Modified Lesson is found in the Teacher's Resource Book.

## MEETING INDIVIDUAL NEEDS / ASSIGNMENT GUIDE

| 5-Day Plan | 3-Day Plan | Limited Spellers | Average Spellers | Advanced Spellers |
|---|---|---|---|---|
| 1 | 1 | • Pretest<br>• Progress Chart | • Pretest<br>• Progress Chart<br>• Home Activity | • Pretest<br>• Progress Chart<br>• Home Activity |
| 2 | | • Modified Lesson<br>Visual Warm-up<br>Ending Sounds | • Regular Lesson<br>Visual Warm-up | • Regular Lesson<br>Visual Warm-up |
| 3 and 4 | 2 | • Modified Lesson<br>Vowel Puzzle<br>Word Match<br>Finish the Sentence | Spelling Activities | Spelling Activities<br>• Challenge Exercise |
| 5 | 3 | • Posttest<br>• Words to Learn Sheet<br>• Progress Chart | • Posttest<br>• Words to Learn Sheet<br>• Progress Chart | • Posttest<br>• Words to Learn Sheet<br>• Progress Chart |

**D. Little Word—Big Word** Write the big word or words from the spelling list that include each little word below.

1. You find a part in parties, partner, apartment, and depart.
2. See the car in scar, scarf, carpet, and carloads.
3. You find hard in hardware.
4. There is an arm in alarm.
5. You find rents in parents.
6. See the or in harbor.
7. There is a vest in harvest.
8. You find a mark in remarkable.
9. There is dark in darkness.
10. You find large in largely.

**E. Bases and Suffixes** The spelling list contains thirteen base words and seven words with suffixes. Write each spelling word.

| | Words with Suffixes | Base Words | | Words with Suffixes | Base Words |
|---|---|---|---|---|---|
| 1. | partnership | partner | 11. | pardonable | pardon |
| 2. | hardwares | hardware | 12. | scarred | scar |
| 3. | alarming | alarm | 13. | scarves | scarf |
| 4. | apartments | apartment | 14. | remarkable | remark |
| 5. | departing | depart | 15. | parents | parent |
| 6. | harvesting | harvest | 16. | carloads | carload |
| 7. | harbored | harbor | 17. | artist | art |
| 8. | guarded | guard | 18. | parties | party |
| 9. | charging | charge | 19. | largely | large |
| 10. | carpeted | carpet | 20. | darkness | dark |



## OPTIONAL TEACHING PLAN

Write the two Word Group headings on the chalkboard. Ask the students to name the nineteen spelling words with the /är/ sound. Write the words as the students say them. Continue identifying the other Word Group. Note the /är/ sound of **ar** in words such as **scar** and the /âr/ sound of **ar** in **parents**. Point out the compound words **hardware** and **carloads**.

| Word Groups | | |
|---|---|---|
| /är/ words | scar | partner |
| | scarf | hardware |
| | guard | carloads |
| | charge | alarm |
| | largely | apartment |
| | carpet | depart |
| | darkness | remarkable |
| | pardon | **carbon** |
| | harvest | **carpenter** |
| | harbor | **parlor** |
| | artist | **parchment** |
| | parties | |
| /âr/ words | parents | **narrowly** |

*Challenge Words are boldfaced.*

### Optional Activity Masters

Those using the Hardcover Pupil Edition may wish to use the Optional Activity Master in the Teacher's Resource Book for Exercise C.

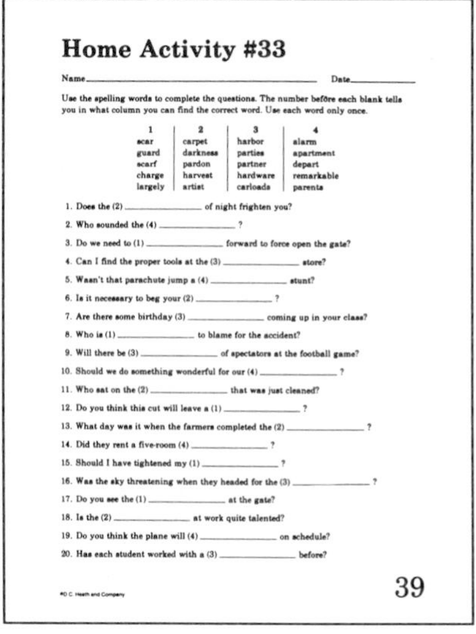

## Home Activity #33

Name________________ Date__________

Use the spelling words to complete the questions. The number before each blank tells you in what column you can find the correct word. Use each word only once.

| 1 | 2 | 3 | 4 |
|---|---|---|---|
| scar | carpet | harbor | alarm |
| guard | darkness | parties | apartment |
| scarf | pardon | partner | depart |
| charge | harvest | hardware | remarkable |
| largely | artist | carloads | parents |

1. Does the (2) ________ of night frighten you?
2. Who sounded the (4) ________ ?
3. Do we need to (1) ________ forward to force open the gate?
4. Can I find the proper tools at the (3) ________ store?
5. Wasn't that parachute jump a (4) ________ stunt?
6. Is it necessary to beg your (2) ________ ?
7. Are there some birthday (3) ________ coming up in your class?
8. Who is (1) ________ to blame for the accident?
9. Will there be (3) ________ of spectators at the football game?
10. Should we do something wonderful for our (4) ________ ?
11. Who sat on the (2) ________ that was just cleaned?
12. Do you think this cut will leave a (1) ________ ?
13. What day was it when the farmers completed the (2) ________ ?
14. Did they rent a five-room (4) ________ ?
15. Should I have tightened my (1) ________ ?
16. Was the sky threatening when they headed for the (3) ________ ?
17. Do you see the (1) ________ at the gate?
18. Is the (2) ________ at work quite talented?
19. Do you think the plane will (4) ________ on schedule?
20. Has each student worked with a (3) ________ before?



39

## Modified Lesson #33

Name________________ Date__________

| Spelling Words | charge | darkness | parties | hardware | apartment |
|---|---|---|---|---|---|
| | carpet | harvest | partner | alarm | depart |

I. **Visual Warm-up.** Write each spelling word in its correct shape.

II. **Vowel Hunt.** Fill in the missing vowels and write the spelling words.

a. ch __ rg __ ________ f. c __ rp __ t ________
b. h __ rv __ st ________ g. d __ rkn __ ss ________
c. p __ rt __ __ s ________ h. p __ rtn __ r ________
d. __ l __ rm ________ i. h __ rdw __ r __ ________
e. d __ p __ rt ________ j. __ p __ rtm __ nt ________

III. **Word Maze.** Fill in the missing letters to find the spelling words. Write the words in the blanks beside the numbers.

Across
2. ________
3. ________
4. ________
6. ________
8. ________
9. ________

Down
1. ________
3. ________
5. ________
7. ________



107

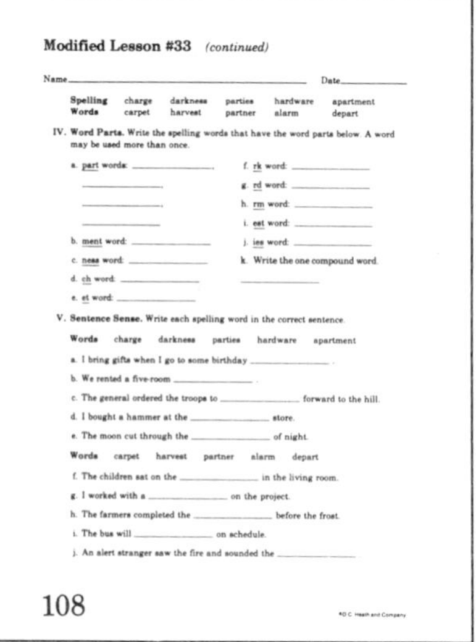

## Modified Lesson #33 *(continued)*

Name________________ Date__________

| Spelling Words | charge | darkness | parties | hardware | apartment |
|---|---|---|---|---|---|
| | carpet | harvest | partner | alarm | depart |

IV. **Word Parts.** Write the spelling words that have the word parts below. A word may be used more than once.

a. part words: ________, ________, ________, ________
b. ment word: ________
c. ness word: ________
d. ch word: ________
e. et word: ________
f. rk word: ________
g. rd word: ________
h. rm word: ________
i. est word: ________
j. ies word: ________
k. Write the one compound word. ________

V. **Sentence Sense.** Write each spelling word in the correct sentence.

**Words** charge darkness parties hardware apartment

a. I bring gifts when I go to some birthday ________ .
b. We rented a five-room ________ .
c. The general ordered the troops to ________ forward to the hill.
d. I bought a hammer at the ________ store.
e. The moon cut through the ________ of night.

**Words** carpet harvest partner alarm depart

f. The children sat on the ________ in the living room.
g. I worked with a ________ on the project.
h. The farmers completed the ________ before the frost.
i. The bus will ________ on schedule.
j. An alert stranger saw the fire and sounded the ________

108



### Home Activity

A weekly homework assignment

### Modified Lesson

An alternative lesson for limited spellers

*(The Answer Key can be found in the Teacher's Resource Book.)*

### Challenge Exercise #33

Name________________________ Date__________

**Word Watch.** A thousand years ago, the English referred to the third season of the year as the *haerfest*, the season to bring in the crops. Later the word *fall* took over with its reference to the "fall of the leaf." Though the name of the season changed, the word *haerfest* remained to refer, particularly, to the picking of the wheat crop. By 1526, English writers were using the word *harvest* to refer to the picking of all crops during the fall of the year.

**Word Analogies.** Decide on the relationship that exists between the first pair of words. Using the Other Word Forms on page 132, find a word that completes the second pair of words and establishes the same relationship.

1. *painted* is to *wall* as __________ is to *floor*
2. *planting* is to *sowing* as *reaping* is to __________
3. *tallest* is to *shortest* as __________ is to *smallest*
4. *arrives* is to *comes* as *leaves* is to __________
5. *sunny* is to *brightening* as *cloudy* is to __________

**Challenge Words Student Activity**
Use the challenge words below to complete each definition.

**narrowly  carpenter  parlor  carbon  parchment**

1. used for important documents: __________
2. found in a house: __________
3. missed by only a little __________
4. substance found in diamonds: __________
5. works with woodworking tools: __________

**Working With Words: Student Writing Activity**
Use as many Other Word Forms as you can from page 132 to write classified ads for workers for your business. (Example of a farmer's ad: Help Wanted—*harvesting* experience essential)

142



## Challenge Exercise

Additional activities for advanced spellers

**Spelling Words**

| | | | | |
|---|---|---|---|---|
| scar | scarf | guard | charge | largely |
| carpet | darkness | pardon | harvest | harbor |
| artist | parties | partner | hardware | carloads |
| alarm | apartment | depart | remarkable | parents |

**F. Word Parts** Answer each question with an ar word from the spelling list. Write the word.

1. What ar likes to paint? artist
2. What ar will leave? depart
3. What ar needs someone else? partner
4. What ar happens on birthdays? parties
5. What ar is a place to live? apartment
6. What ar is nails and tools? hardware
7. What ar excuses someone? pardon
8. What ar rings a warning? alarm
9. What ar provides protection? guard
10. What ar is not light? darkness
11. What ar happens mostly? largely
12. What ar means you will pay later? charge
13. What ar is usually done in the fall? harvest
14. What ar is found underfoot? carpet
15. What ar is a safe home for your boat? harbor
16. What ar keeps your neck warm? scarf
17. What ar feeds you and cares for you? parents
18. What ar is amazing? remarkable
19. What ar was a wound? scar
20. What ar fills automobiles? carloads

134 Lesson 33

## CONTROLLED DICTATION (Optional)

These dictation sentences provide maintenance for spelling words previously taught and practice for words currently being studied. Dictation should be administered on Day 4. The teacher or another student may dictate the sentences. Be sure to dictate all marks of punctuation. Challenge Word sentences are preceded by an asterisk.

1. My **partner** helped me choose the **carpet** for the **apartment**.
2. The **artist** stored **carloads** of paint and **hardware** in the trunks.
3. Ships **depart** from the **harbor** in the **darkness** of night.
4. My **parents** offered to pay the **charge** for the birthday **parties**.
5. The awful **scar** was **largely** covered by a **scarf**.
6. The grain **harvest** this year was **remarkable**.
7. The general may **pardon** the **guard** for touching off the **alarm**.

*8. The writing on the **parchment** was hard to read.
*9. The **carpenter** **narrowly** missed hitting the **parlor** window.
*10. They used **carbon** paper to copy the letter.

**G. Using Other Word Forms** Write the Other Word Form that completes each sentence.

Base Words: guard(ed) alarm(ing) artist(ic) scarf(es) darken(ing)

1. They wore ___scarves___ and hats to keep warm.
2. The ferocious dog ___guarded___ the entrance.
3. The sky is ___darkening___, meaning a storm is on the way.
4. She has true ___artistic___ talent.
5. The loud, honking noise was ___alarming___.

**H. Challenge Words** Write the Challenge Word that completes each sentence.

| narrowly | carbon | carpenter | parlor | parchment |
|---|---|---|---|---|

1. A ___carpenter___ may use a hammer.
2. Someone who ___narrowly___ escapes injury is lucky.
3. Coal is made up of ___carbon___.
4. A sitting room may be called a ___parlor___.
5. A scribe may write on ___parchment___.

**I. Spelling and Writing** Use as many Spelling Words, Other Word Forms, and Challenge Words as you can to write *two* or more answers to each question. A few words are suggested. Proofread your work.

1. What might a ship's captain do to protect a valuable cargo?

   guard – charge – darkness – alarm – harbor

2. What would you say to friends who are about to leave your home without cleaning up a mess they made?

   carpet – parents – depart – apartment – parties – parlor

3. What would you like to know before you start a project for the annual science fair?

   hardware – partner – artist – largely – carbon



## THE SPELLING-WRITING LINK

**Purpose** This activity helps students retain the correct spelling of words and transfer the words to their daily writing. Students use lesson words to answer questions promoting higher-order thinking skills.

**Procedure** Read the first question and write the suggested words on the chalkboard: **guard, charge, darkness, alarm, harbor.** Have students list some Other Word Forms of the lesson words. Brainstorm with the class possible answers to question 1. Remind students to look at all the lesson words for ideas. Write the answers on the chalkboard, noting any lesson words.

**Practice** Tell students to finish the activity by writing two or more answers to each question. Remind them to proofread their work.

## USING OTHER WORD FORMS

Vocabulary is expanded through the use of other forms of basic spelling words. Emphasis is on the relationship of syntax to suffix choices. The following generalization applies to the Other Word Forms used in Exercise G.

### Spelling Rule

Forming plurals

To form the plurals of nouns ending with **f**, or **fe**, change the **f** or **fe** to **v** and add **es**. (**scarf, scarves**)

## POSTTEST AND PROOFREADING

Follow the same testing procedures used in the Pretest, although you may wish to correct the tests yourself. Have students write any misspelled words on the Words to Learn Sheet and record spelling success on the Progress Chart.

LESSON

# 34

## OBJECTIVES

- to spell 20 high-frequency words with the /o͞o/ and /ō/
- to proofread these words in daily writing
- to become familiar with 45 other forms of the spelling words

| Summary of Skills | Exercises |
|---|---|
| Auditory Discrimination | A |
| Proofreading | A, C, D, I |
| Visual Discrimination | C, D |
| Vocabulary Development | E, F, G |
| Context Usage | G |
| Original Writing | I |

## PRETEST AND PROOFREADING

The Pretest identifies the words students are able to spell, as well as the words they need to learn. You may wish to use Other Word Forms when giving the Pretest. Five suggested Other Word Forms are underlined on this page.

To administer the Pretest:

**READ** each word aloud.
**SAY** the phrase containing the word.
**REPEAT** the word.

Have students correct the Pretest using the Corrected-test Procedure. They may record their scores on a personal Progress Chart (see the Teacher's Resource Book) and study misspelled words using the **S-H-A-R-P** procedure.

## OTHER WORD FORMS

This section presents related forms of the spelling words to strengthen spelling power and vocabulary knowledge.

### Enrichment Activity

Have students write variations of the same sentence using each of the Other Word Forms for a spelling word.

The student **improved** his grades remarkably. **improve, improving, improvement**

**A. Pretest and Proofreading**

**B. Spelling Words and Phrases**

1. **schoolmate*** — introducing a schoolmate
2. **rooster** — when the rooster overslept
3. **proving*** — proving you to be correct
4. **improved** — improved quickly
5. **whose** — whose lost kitten
6. **due** — if the book is due
7. **duties** — duties of the principal
8. **rulers*** — metal rulers
9. **student** — elected the student
10. **truth*** — to tell the truth
11. **suits*** — wet bathing suits
12. **ruin** — will ruin the story
13. **groups*** — several groups
14. **route** — changed their route
15. **flew*** — flew south for the winter
16. **blew*** — blew up the balloons
17. **chewing** — chewing the gum
18. **threw** — threw it to the ground
19. **newspapers*** — has read two newspapers
20. **sew*** — will sew on a patch

*Other Word Forms*

schoolmates
roosters
prove, proved, proof
improve, improving, improvement
who, whom
dues
duty, dutiful, dutifully
rule, rules, ruled, ruler
students
truths, truthful
suit, suited
ruined, ruining
group, grouped, grouping
routed, routing
fly, flies, flying
blow, blows, blowing
chew, chews, chewed
throw, throwing, thrown
newspaper
sewn, sewed

**C. Visual Warm-up** Write each word in its correct shape.

a. flew
b. chewing
c. whose
d. blew
e. sew
f. route
g. improved
h. threw
i. duties
j. rooster
k. groups
l. due
m. student
n. newspapers
o. suits
p. proving
q. truth
r. rulers
s. ruin
t. schoolmate



*Modified Lesson words are asterisked.
The Modified Lesson is found in the Teacher's Resource Book.

## MEETING INDIVIDUAL NEEDS / ASSIGNMENT GUIDE

| 5-Day Plan | 3-Day Plan | Limited Spellers | Average Spellers | Advanced Spellers |
|---|---|---|---|---|
| 1 | 1 | • Pretest • Progress Chart | • Pretest • Progress Chart • Home Activity | • Pretest • Progress Chart • Home Activity |
| 2 | | • Modified Lesson Visual Warm-up Ending Sounds | • Regular Lesson Visual Warm-up | • Regular Lesson Visual Warm-up |
| 3 and 4 | 2 | • Modified Lesson Vowel Puzzle Word Match Finish the Sentence | Spelling Activities | Spelling Activities • Challenge Exercise |
| 5 | 3 | • Posttest • Words to Learn Sheet • Progress Chart | • Posttest • Words to Learn Sheet • Progress Chart | • Posttest • Words to Learn Sheet • Progress Chart |

**D. Break the Code** Use the code to write the spelling words. Next to each spelling word, write an Other Word Form (p. 136).

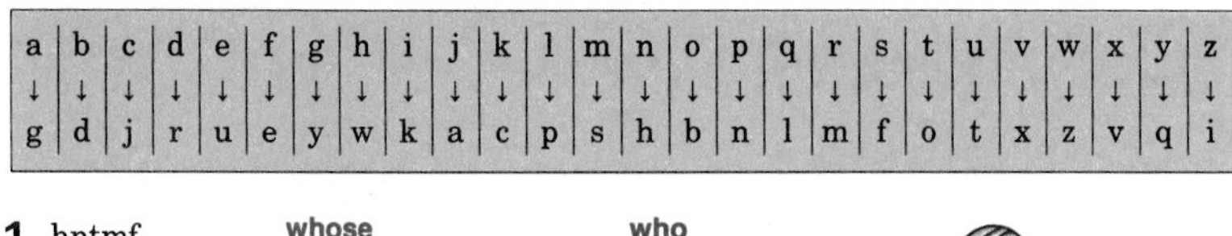

| a | b | c | d | e | f | g | h | i | j | k | l | m | n | o | p | q | r | s | t | u | v | w | x | y | z |
|---|---|---|---|---|---|---|---|---|---|---|---|---|---|---|---|---|---|---|---|---|---|---|---|---|---|
| ↓ | ↓ | ↓ | ↓ | ↓ | ↓ | ↓ | ↓ | ↓ | ↓ | ↓ | ↓ | ↓ | ↓ | ↓ | ↓ | ↓ | ↓ | ↓ | ↓ | ↓ | ↓ | ↓ | ↓ | ↓ | ↓ |
| g | d | j | r | u | e | y | w | k | a | c | p | s | h | b | n | l | m | f | o | t | x | z | v | q | i |

1. hntmf — whose — who
2. mfh — sew — sewn
3. deqfdm — rulers — rule
4. undfh — threw — throw
5. knfhzpa — chewing — chew
6. oqfh — blew — blow
7. pfhmljlfdm — newspapers — newspaper
8. dttmufd — rooster — roosters
9. mknttqrjuf — schoolmate — schoolmates
10. ldtxzpa — proving — prove
11. sqfh — flew — fly
12. zrldtxfb — improved — improve
13. udeun — truth — truths
14. beuzfm — duties — duty
15. muebfpu — student — students
16. adtelm — groups — group
17. dteuf — route — routed
18. dezp — ruin — ruined
19. mezum — suits — suit
20. bef — due — dues

Accept any Other Word Form that appears in the Spelling Dictionary.

**E. Homophones** Write the spelling word or Other Word Form (p. 136) that is a homophone for each word below.

1. so — sew
2. through — threw
3. root — route
4. dew — due

Working Words in Spelling **137**



## OPTIONAL TEACHING PLAN

Write the six Word Group headings on the chalkboard. Ask the students to name the two spelling words with the /o͞o/ sound that are spelled with **oo**. Continue identifying the other Word Groups. Note the different spellings of the /o͞o/ sound: **oo, o, u, ou,** and **ew.**

| Word Groups | | |
|---|---|---|
| /o͞o/: **oo** words | schoolmate<br>rooster | **proofread**<br>**drooping** |
| /o͞o/: **o** words | proving<br>improved | whose |
| /o͞o/: **u** words | due<br>duties<br>rulers<br>student<br>truth<br>suits | ruin<br>**lunar**<br>**superior**<br>**supermarket** |
| /o͞o/: **ou** words | groups | route |
| /o͞o/: **ew** words | flew<br>blew<br>chewing | threw<br>newspapers |
| /ō/: **ew** word | | sew |

*Challenge Words are boldfaced.*

### Optional Activity Masters

Those using the Hardcover Pupil Edition may wish to use the Optional Activity Masters in the Teacher's Resource Book for Exercises C and F.

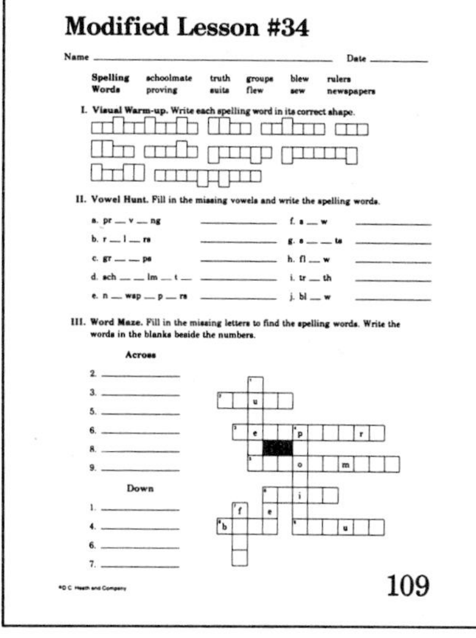

Home Activity #34 — 40

Name _____ Date _____

Use the spelling words to complete the questions. The number before each blank tells you in what column you can find the correct word. Use each word only once.

| 1 | 2 | 3 | 4 |
|---|---|---|---|
| blew | due | ruin | sew |
| rooster | truth | groups | chewing |
| proving | duties | route | rulers |
| improved | student | flew | threw |
| whose | suits | schoolmate | newspapers |

1. The class elected the (2) _____ for Student Council president.
2. A sad ending will (3) _____ the story.
3. The clown (1) _____ up the balloons for the children.
4. He is (4) _____ the gum and blowing a bubble.
5. The hikers changed their (3) _____ from north to south.
6. I wonder (1) _____ lost kitten this is.
7. Use the metal (4) _____ to measure the window frame.
8. Each witness is expected to tell the (2) _____.
9. The principal is introducing a (3) _____ of mine to the PTA.
10. Don't bring those wet bathing (2) _____ into the house.
11. The editor has read two (4) _____, each expressing a different view.
12. I didn't wake when the (1) _____ overslept.
13. The boy grew tired of eating the apple and (4) _____ it to the ground.
14. Preparing budgets is one of the (2) _____ of the principal.
15. There were several (3) _____ marching in the parade.
16. The test results are (1) _____ you to be correct.
17. I will (4) _____ on a patch to mend my sleeve.
18. Her health (1) _____ quickly with time.
19. You should go to the library if the book is (2) _____.
20. The geese (3) _____ south for the winter.

Modified Lesson #34 — 109

Name _____ Date _____

Spelling Words: schoolmate truth groups blew rulers proving suits flew sew newspapers

**I. Visual Warm-up.** Write each spelling word in its correct shape.

**II. Vowel Hunt.** Fill in the missing vowels and write the spelling words.

a. pr __ v __ ng _____
b. r __ l __ rs _____
c. gr __ __ ps _____
d. sch __ __ lm __ t __ _____
e. n __ wsp __ p __ rs _____
f. s __ w _____
g. s __ __ ts _____
h. fl __ w _____
i. tr __ th _____
j. bl __ w _____

**III. Word Maze.** Fill in the missing letters to find the spelling words. Write the words in the blanks beside the numbers.

Across
Down

Modified Lesson #34 (continued) — 110

Name _____ Date _____

Spelling Words: schoolmate truth groups blew rulers proving suits flew sew newspapers

**IV. Word Parts.** Write the spelling words that have the word parts below. A word may be used more than once.

a. _ew_ word with the sound of long u: _____
b. other _ew_ words: _____ _____
c. word ending in _th_: _____
d. _ing_ word: _____
e. _oo_ word: _____
f. _ui_ word: _____
g. _oo_ word: _____
h. _sch_ word: _____
i. words ending in _s_: _____ _____ _____ _____
j. Write the two compound words. _____ _____

**V. Sentence Sense.** Write each spelling word in the correct sentence.

Words: schoolmate truth groups blew rulers
a. I was introducing a _____ to my parents.
b. We used metal _____ to draw the margins.
c. It's my duty to tell you the _____.
d. Who _____ up the balloons?
e. Several _____ of children entered the zoo.

Words: proving suits flew sew newspapers
f. The birds _____ south for the winter.
g. Each student has read two _____.
h. The tailor will _____ on a patch.
i. The detective is _____ you to be correct.
j. The swimmers wore wet bathing _____.

**Home Activity**
A weekly homework assignment

**Modified Lesson**
An alternative lesson for limited spellers

Working Words in Spelling **137**

*(The Answer Key can be found in the Teacher's Resource Book.)*

LESSON

# 34

CONTINUED

### Challenge Exercise #34

Name__________ Date__________

**Word Watch.** The word *duty* was born in France as *duete*, a form of the word *due*. *Duete* meant "the respectful and obedient conduct owed one's parents and superiors." Without question, it was a child's *duete* always to obey parents and persons of authority. The English also spoke of this responsibility but called it *dewte*. Today the word is written as *duty* and refers to any task or responsibility a person is expected to accomplish.

**Word Analogies.** Decide on the relationship that exists between the first pair of words. Using the Other Word Forms on page 136, find a word that completes the second pair of words and establishes the same relationship.

1. *does* is to *stags* as *hens* is to ________
2. *touches* is to *fingers* as ________ is to *teeth*
3. *clutched* is to *grasped* as *tossed* is to ________
4. *drives* is to *automobiles* as ________ is to *planes*
5. *hammered* is to *carpenter* as ________ is to *tailor*

**Challenge Words Student Activity**

Write the challenge words below to complete the sentences.

**lunar proofread superior drooping supermarket**

1. Last night we saw a ________ eclipse.
2. Please ________ your paper for spelling errors.
3. I am so sleepy that my eyelids are ________ .
4. Please get the groceries at the ________ .
5. That bike is ________ to mine in every way.

**Working With Words: Student Writing Activity**

Use as many Other Word Forms as you can from page 136 to write a plan for your teacher on how to get more students involved in classroom projects. Use the format of a friendly letter.



143

## Challenge Exercise

Additional activities for advanced spellers

**Spelling Words**

| | | | | |
|---|---|---|---|---|
| schoolmate | rooster | proving | improved | whose |
| due | duties | rulers | student | truth |
| suits | ruin | groups | route | flew |
| blew | chewing | threw | newspapers | sew |

**F. Crossword Puzzle** Solve the puzzle by using all the words from the spelling list. Write each word. Check your answers in the **Spelling Dictionary**.

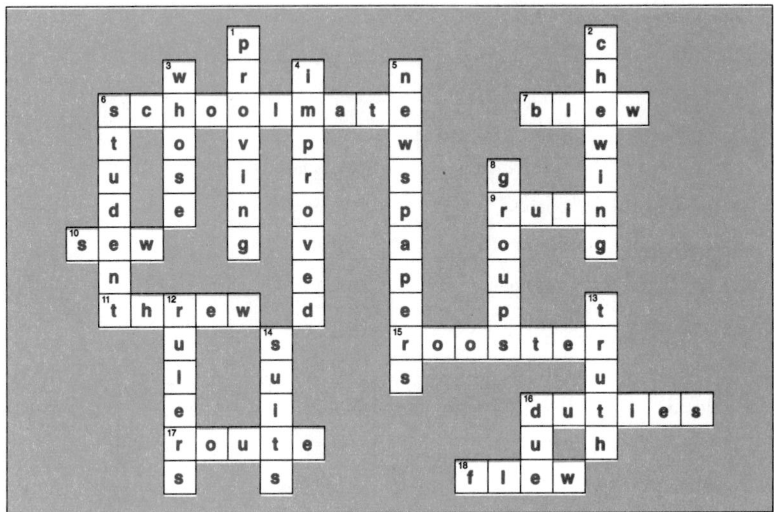

**Across**

**6.** a pal in your class
**7.** did to put out candles
**9.** to wreck
**10.** to connect with thread
**11.** did to a ball
**15.** a male chicken
**16.** responsibilities
**17.** the road to take
**18.** how birds got south

**Down**

**1.** showing to be true
**2.** crushing with teeth
**3.** possessive of *who*
**4.** did better
**5.** reading materials printed daily
**6.** a learner in school
**8.** several sets of people
**12.** kings
**13.** a true statement
**14.** sets of clothing
**16.** expected

**138** Lesson 34

## CONTROLLED DICTATION (Optional)

These dictation sentences provide maintenance for spelling words previously taught and practice for words currently being studied. Dictation should be administered on Day 4. The teacher or another student may dictate the sentences. Be sure to dictate all marks of punctuation. Challenge Word sentences are preceded by an asterisk.

1. My **schoolmate** is one **student whose** English has **improved.**
2. **Groups** of swallows **flew** the same **route.**
3. Use only straight **rulers** to line the **newspapers.**
4. In **truth,** workers at this factory were once asked to **sew** buttons on **suits** by hand.
5. In the story, the **rooster** was **chewing** grain while the winds **blew.**
6. Regular **duties** are **due** to **ruin** their golf game.
7. **Proving** his talent as a pitcher, he **threw** a fast ball.

*8. The **supermarket** in our town is **superior** to all others.
*9. Will you **proofread** my report about the **lunar** landing.
*10. The **drooping** plants need water.

**G. Using Other Word Forms** Write the Other Word Form that completes each sentence.

Base Words: ruin(ed) throw(n) group(ed) sew(n) improve(ment)

1. Something that made it better is an improvement.
2. Something that has been mended has been sewn.
3. Something that is tossed is thrown.
4. Something that is spoiled is ruined.
5. Something that has been sorted has been grouped.

**H. Challenge Words** Write the Challenge Word that completes each analogy.

| proofread | drooping | lunar | superior | supermarket |
|---|---|---|---|---|

1. **budding** is to **blossoming** as **wilting** is to drooping
2. **write** is to **compose** as **edit** is to proofread
3. **clothing** is to **department store** as **food** is to supermarket
4. **sun** is to **solar** as **moon** is to lunar
5. **bad** is to **good** as **inferior** is to superior

**I. Spelling and Writing** Write each set of words in a sentence. You may use Other Word Forms. Proofread for spelling using one of the Proofreading Tips from the Yellow Pages.

1. student, newspaper, schoolmate
2. truth, chewing, blew
3. flew, route, groups
4. duties, whose, throw
5. rulers, improved, ruin
6. rooster, suits, flying
7. proving, due, sews
8. proofread, superior, supermarket
9. drooping, lunar, ruin



## USING OTHER WORD FORMS

Vocabulary is expanded through the use of other forms of basic spelling words. Emphasis is on the relationship of syntax to suffix choices. The following generalization applies to the Other Word Forms used in Exercise G.

### Spelling Rule

Adding suffixes to words ending in silent **e**

> When adding a suffix that begins with a consonant to words that end with silent **e**, keep the final **e**. **(improve, improvement)**

## POSTTEST AND PROOFREADING

Follow the same testing procedures used in the Pretest, although you may wish to correct the tests yourself. Have students write any misspelled words on the Words to Learn Sheet and record spelling success on the Progress Chart.

## THE SPELLING-WRITING LINK

**Purpose** This activity helps students effectively transfer lesson words into their daily writing. Students (a) determine a relationship among three given words and (b) write a complete sentence.

**Procedure** On the chalkboard, write the three words from line 1: **student, newspaper, schoolmate,** and the Other Word Forms: **students, newspapers, schoolmates.** Have students read the words and think of ways the three words might be related. Have them think of things or people the words suggest. Ask students to create sentences using some of their ideas. You can provide a sample sentence: **Three students wrote a newspaper for their schoolmates.**

**Practice** Tell students to write original sentences using the word sets and to proofread their work. You may want them to circle the lesson words.

# LESSON 35

## OBJECTIVES

- to spell 20 high-frequency words with the /yo͞o/, /ûr/, /ə/, /ŏ/, and /ĭ/
- to proofread these words in daily writing
- to become familiar with 38 other forms of the spelling words

| Summary of Skills | Exercises |
|---|---|
| Auditory Discrimination | A |
| Proofreading | A, C, D, I |
| Visual Discrimination | C, D |
| Dictionary Skills | E |
| Vocabulary Development | F |
| Context Usage | G, H |
| Original Writing | I |

## PRETEST AND PROOFREADING

The Pretest identifies the words students are able to spell, as well as the words they need to learn. You may wish to use Other Word Forms when giving the Pretest. Five suggested Other Word Forms are underlined on this page.

To administer the Pretest:

**READ** each word aloud.
**SAY** the phrase containing the word.
**REPEAT** the word.

Have students correct the Pretest using the Corrected-test Procedure. They may record their scores on a personal Progress Chart (see the Teacher's Resource Book) and study misspelled words using the **S-H-A-R-P** procedure.

## OTHER WORD FORMS

This section presents related forms of the spelling words to strengthen spelling power and vocabulary knowledge.

### Enrichment Activity

Have students write opposite words or phrases for these Other Word Forms. Be sure they write the Other Word Form with its opposite next to it.

**probable, beauty, doctoring, connects**

**A. Pretest and Proofreading**

**B. Spelling Words and Phrases**

1. **beautiful*** — a beautiful city
2. **musician** — a lonely musician
3. **fir*** — a forest of fir trees
4. **skirt*** — a skirt and sweater
5. **circle*** — joined the circle
6. **squirrel** — a chipmunk or a squirrel
7. **concern** — had no concern
8. **connect** — to connect the wires
9. **congress*** — a congress of delegates
10. **doctor*** — called the doctor
11. **beyond** — beyond their control
12. **closet*** — locked in the closet
13. **promise*** — kept their promise
14. **costume*** — will put on the costume
15. **products** — several new products
16. **probably** — probably will win
17. **popular** — not a popular idea
18. **horizontal** — onto the horizontal bar
19. **electricity** — the hum of electricity
20. **addition*** — in addition to

*Other Word Forms*

| | |
|---|---|
| beautifully, beauty | promises, promised, promising |
| music, musical, musically | costumed |
| firs | production, produce, produces, produced, producing |
| skirted, skirting | |
| circled, circling | |
| squirrels | probable, probability |
| concerned, concerning | popularly, popularity |
| connector, connects | horizontally |
| congresses, congressional | electric, electrify, electrician |
| doctoring | |
| closets | additional, additionally |

**C. Visual Warm-up** Write each word in its correct shape.

a. addition
b. congress
c. circle
d. products
e. musician
f. closet
g. fir
h. costume
i. popular
j. doctor
k. probably
l. squirrel
m. connect
n. electricity
o. promise
p. skirt
q. beyond
r. horizontal
s. concern
t. beautiful

140 Lesson 35

*Modified Lesson words are asterisked.
The Modified Lesson is found in the Teacher's Resource Book.

## MEETING INDIVIDUAL NEEDS / ASSIGNMENT GUIDE

| 5-Day Plan | 3-Day Plan | Limited Spellers | Average Spellers | Advanced Spellers |
|---|---|---|---|---|
| 1 | 1 | • Pretest<br>• Progress Chart | • Pretest<br>• Progress Chart<br>• Home Activity | • Pretest<br>• Progress Chart<br>• Home Activity |
| 2 | | • Modified Lesson Visual Warm-up Ending Sounds | • Regular Lesson Visual Warm-up | • Regular Lesson Visual Warm-up |
| 3 and 4 | 2 | • Modified Lesson Vowel Puzzle Word Match Finish the Sentence | Spelling Activities | Spelling Activities<br>• Challenge Exercise |
| 5 | 3 | • Posttest<br>• Words to Learn Sheet<br>• Progress Chart | • Posttest<br>• Words to Learn Sheet<br>• Progress Chart | • Posttest<br>• Words to Learn Sheet<br>• Progress Chart |

**D. Break the Code** Use the code to write the spelling words.

| a | b | c | d | e | f | g | h | i | j | k | l | m |
|---|---|---|---|---|---|---|---|---|---|---|---|---|
| ↕ | ↕ | ↕ | ↕ | ↕ | ↕ | ↕ | ↕ | ↕ | ↕ | ↕ | ↕ | ↕ |
| z | y | x | w | v | u | t | s | r | q | p | o | n |

1. xlmxvim concern
2. xlmtivhh congress
3. zwwrgrlm addition
4. yvzfgrufo beautiful
5. vovxgirxrgb electricity
6. yvblmw beyond
7. uri fir
8. hprig skirt
9. klkfozi popular
10. nfhrxrzm musician
11. xrixov circle
12. xolhvg closet
13. xlhgfnv costume
14. sliralmgzo horizontal
15. kilnrhv promise
16. kilwfxgh products
17. kilyzyob probably
18. hjfriivo squirrel
19. wlxgli doctor
20. xlmmvxg connect

**E. Guide Words** These word pairs are guide words that might appear in a dictionary. Write the words from the spelling list that would appear on the same page as each pair of guide words.

**act – apartment**
1. addition

**balloon – bottom**
2. beautiful
3. beyond

**circle – copper**
4. circle
5. concern
6. connect
7. congress
8. closet

**copy – daughter**
9. costume

**day – dropped**
10. doctor

**dry – escape**
11. electricity

**fifteen – freedom**
12. fir

**helping – ironing**
13. horizontal

**mud – offer**
14. musician

**patch – preparing**
15. popular

**president – quart**
16. promise
17. products
18. probably

**skirt – strain**
19. skirt
20. squirrel

Working Words in Spelling **141**

## OPTIONAL TEACHING PLAN

Write the five Word Group headings on the chalkboard. Ask the students to name the two spelling words with the /yo͞o/ sound. Note that the /yo͞o/ sound is spelled with **eau** in **beautiful** and with **u** in **musician**. Write the words as the students say them. Continue identifying the other Word Groups. Compare the /ə/ (schwa) sound in **concern** with the short **o** sound in **congress**.

| Word Groups | | |
|---|---|---|
| /yo͞o/ words | beautiful | musician |
| /ûr/ words | fir<br>skirt<br>circle<br>squirrel | **squirmed**<br>**perfect**<br>**burden** |
| /ə/ words | concern<br>connect | **cathedral** |
| /ŏ/: **o** words | congress<br>doctor<br>beyond<br>closet<br>promise | costume<br>products<br>probably<br>popular<br>horizontal |
| /ĭ/ words | electricity<br>addition | **discount** |

*Challenge Words are boldfaced.*

### Optional Activity Masters

Those using the Hardcover Pupil Edition may wish to use the Optional Activity Master in the Teacher's Resource Book for Exercise C.

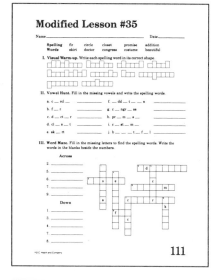

Home Activity #35 — 41

Modified Lesson #35 — 111

Modified Lesson #35 (continued) — 112

### Home Activity

A weekly homework assignment

### Modified Lesson

An alternative lesson for limited spellers

*(The Answer Key can be found in the Teacher's Resource Book.)*

LESSON

# 35

CONTINUED

### Challenge Exercise #35

Name____________________ Date__________

**Word Watch.** The ancient Greeks had a special name for the little creature we call *squirrel*. Living in a land where the midday sun is unusually warm, the Greeks were fascinated by the nut-eating creature that carried its own furry-tailed umbrella around to protect itself from the sun. The Greeks called it *skiuros*, building the word from *skia*, meaning "shade," and *ouva*, meaning "tail." To the Greeks the creature was the "shady-tail." The word passed through the Latin language and eventually traveled to England where it became *squirrel*. In 1624 Captain John Smith wrote about the "amazing Virginia squirrels that grew to be the size of rabbits."

**Word Analogies.** Decide on the relationship that exists between the first pair of words. Using the Other Word Forms on page 140, find a word that completes the second pair of words and establishes the same relationship.

1. *untruths* is to *lies* as *vows* is to ________
2. *coconuts* is to *palms* as *cones* is to ________
3. *pantries* is to *food* as ________ is to *clothing*
4. *boxed* is to *squared* as *ringed* is to ________
5. *pipes* is to *plumber* as *wires* is to ________

**Challenge Words Student Activity**

Use the challenge words below to complete the sentences.

**discount** **perfect** **cathedral** **squirmed** **burden**

1. That room has a high ________ ceiling.
2. The donkey carried a heavy ________.
3. That store gives a ________ if you pay cash.
4. You can use a compass to draw a ________ circle.
5. The new little puppies ________ and squealed.

**Working With Words: Student Writing Activity**

Use as many Other Word Forms as you can from page 140 to write a letter asking the President of the United States to visit your school to view a musical play about great American leaders. Use the format of a friendly letter.

144



## Challenge Exercise

Additional activities for advanced spellers

**Spelling Words**

| | | | |
|---|---|---|---|
| beautiful | musician | fir | skirt |
| circle | squirrel | concern | connect |
| congress | doctor | beyond | closet |
| promise | costume | products | probably |
| popular | horizontal | electricity | addition |

**F. Private Eye** Find the spelling word to solve each clue. Write the word.

1. She works in a hospital. doctor
2. You'll find clothing stored here. closet
3. It likes acorns. squirrel
4. This is not vertical. horizontal
5. Most stage actors wear one. costume
6. A kilt is similar to this. skirt
7. A violinist is certainly one. musician
8. Sometimes this can be shocking. electricity
9. This can never be square. circle
10. Representatives and senators form this. congress
11. The spruce is definitely one. fir
12. Math students do well at this. addition
13. A vow is one that can't be broken. promise
14. Bridges do this very well. connect
15. This is outside the limits. beyond
16. This is most likely. probably
17. Successful rock groups are always so. popular
18. These are answers in multiplication. products
19. Magnificent sunsets are always this. beautiful
20. If you worry, you have lots of this. concern

142 Lesson 35

## CONTROLLED DICTATION (Optional)

These dictation sentences provide maintenance for spelling words previously taught and practice for words currently being studied. Dictation should be administered on Day 4. The teacher or another student may dictate the sentences. Be sure to dictate all marks of punctuation. Challenge Word sentences are preceded by an asterisk.

1. She will **probably** choose that ragged **skirt** for her **costume**.
2. **Congress** must show **concern** for the safe use of **popular products**.
3. Will someone offer to **connect** the **electricity** for the **doctor**?
4. In **addition** to the **musician**, my cousin and I joined the **circle**.
5. A **beautiful** red **squirrel** was seen **beyond** the **fir** trees.
6. Did you **promise** to put a new **horizontal** bar in my **closet**?

*7. Isn't this a **perfect** setting for a **cathedral**!
*8. We **squirmed** under the **burden** of the heavy load.
*9. We bought it at a **discount** store.

**G. Using Other Word Forms** Write the Other Word Form that completes each sentence.

Base Words: produce(tion) music(al) beautiful(ly) popular(ity) promise(ing)

1. The play was full of music. It was a musical.
2. Everybody likes the actor. His popularity is universal.
3. The young actress will be successful. She has a promising future.
4. She dances beautifully and is a pleasure to watch.
5. The musical was a great success. The whole production was splendid.

**H. Challenge Words** Write the Challenge Word that completes each sentence.

| burden | cathedral | perfect | squirmed | discount |
|---|---|---|---|---|

1. One hundred is a perfect score.
2. I don't want to burden you with extra work.
3. The restless child squirmed in his seat.
4. We got the best price at a discount store.
5. Notre Dame is a historic cathedral in France.

**I. Spelling and Writing** Use each phrase in a sentence. You may want to use the words in a different order or use Other Word Forms. Proofread for spelling using one of the Proofreading Tips from the Yellow Pages.

1. a beautiful costume
2. a popular musician
3. needles of the fir tree
4. skirt the issue
5. circle of friends
6. fed the hungry squirrel
7. showed concern
8. connect the pipes
9. members of the congress
10. an eye doctor
11. the space beyond
12. stored in the closet
13. promise to return
14. sells food products
15. will probably win
16. horizontal lines
17. the energy from electricity
18. addition of numbers



## USING OTHER WORD FORMS

Vocabulary is expanded through the use of other forms of basic spelling words. Emphasis is on the relationship of syntax to suffix choices. The following generalization applies to the Other Word Forms used in Exercise G.

### Spelling Rule

Adding suffixes to words ending in silent **e**

When adding a suffix that begins with a vowel to words that end with silent **e**, drop the final **e**.
**(promise, promising)**

## POSTTEST AND PROOFREADING

Follow the same testing procedures used in the Pretest, although you may wish to correct the tests yourself. Have students write any misspelled words on the Words to Learn Sheet and record spelling success on the Progress Chart.

## THE SPELLING-WRITING LINK

**Purpose** This activity helps students transfer lesson words into their daily writing. Students write complete sentences using the listed phrases.

**Procedure** On the chalkboard write the phrase from line one: **a beautiful sunset.** Have the students read the phrase and note how it could be used in a sentence. Have them think about things or people the phrase suggests. You can provide a sample sentence: **A beautiful sunset greeted us as we left the canyon.**

**Practice** Tell the students to write original sentences using the phrases. Remind them they can use Other Word Forms or change the phrases around if it will improve the sentences.

# LESSON 36 REVIEW

## OBJECTIVES

- to review the spelling of the 100 words studied in Lessons 31-35
- to promote the use of other forms of the 100 spelling words
- to apply high-utility generalizations for the addition of suffixes

| Summary of Skills | Exercises |
|---|---|
| Word Analysis | A |
| Vocabulary Development | B, D |
| Dictionary Skills | C |
| Context Usage | D |

## REVIEW OF LESSONS 31-35

The goal of the review exercises is to expand each student's spelling power. The one hundred spelling words studied in the five preceding lessons are presented in challenging formats where the focus is shifted from the spelling words to the Other Word Forms.

## WORD REVIEW PROCEDURE

Students are encouraged to use this abbreviated version of the **S-H-A-R-P** procedure when reviewing the spelling words at the top of each review page.

**LOOK** at each word.
**SAY** the word to yourself.
**THINK** about the letters that spell the word.

---

# 36

**REVIEWING LESSONS 31-36**

| | | | | |
|---|---|---|---|---|
| gravel | gathering | practicing | shadow | captain |
| visitor | interest | elephant | talent | breakfast |
| scar | pardon | harvest | alarm | remarkable |
| ruin | proving | improved | rulers | sew |
| skirt | connect | concern | promise | circle |

**A. Word Building** Add word parts to each spelling word or its base word to make Other Word Forms. Write the words.

| Spelling Words | *s* or *es* | *ed* | *ing* |
|---|---|---|---|
| Example: **walk** | *walks* | *walked* | *walking* |
| **1.** practicing | practices | practiced | |
| **2.** proving | proves | proved | |
| **3.** ruin | ruins | ruined | ruining |
| **4.** visitor | visits | visited | visiting |
| **5.** pardon | pardons | pardoned | pardoning |
| **6.** improved | improves | | improving |
| **7.** alarm | alarms | alarmed | alarming |
| **8.** breakfast | breakfasts | breakfasted | breakfasting |
| **9.** shadow | shadows | shadowed | shadowing |
| **10.** interest | interests | interested | interesting |
| **11.** promise | promises | promised | promising |
| **12.** captain | captains | captained | captaining |
| **13.** sew | sews | sewed | sewing |
| **14.** elephant | elephants | | |
| **15.** talent | talents | talented | |
| **16.** gravel | gravels | graveled | graveling |
| **17.** remarkable | remarks | remarked | remarking |
| **18.** rulers | rules | ruled | ruling |
| **19.** concern | concerns | concerned | concerning |
| **20.** connect | connects | connected | connecting |
| **21.** harvest | harvests | harvested | harvesting |
| **22.** skirt | skirts | skirted | skirting |
| **23.** scar | scars | scarred | scarring |
| **24.** circle | circles | circled | circling |
| **25.** gathering | gathers | gathered | |

REVIEW



## MEETING INDIVIDUAL NEEDS / ASSIGNMENT GUIDE

| 5-Day Plan | 3-Day Plan | Limited Spellers | Average Spellers | Advanced Spellers |
|---|---|---|---|---|
| 1 and 2 | 1 | • Modified Lesson Visual Warm-up Word Parts | • Regular Lesson Spelling Activities • Home Activity | • Regular Lesson Spelling Activities • Home Activity |
| 3 and 4 | 2 | • Modified Lesson Vowel Puzzle Word Match Finish the Sentence | • Regular Lesson Spelling Activities • Proofreading Exercise(s) | • Regular Lesson Spelling Activities • Proofreading Exercise(s) • Challenge Word Review |
| 5 | 3 | • Test Modified Lesson Words • Words to Learn Sheet | • Review Test or Standardized-format Test • Words to Learn Sheet | • Review Test or Standardized-format Test • Words to Learn Sheet |

| ■ | ★ | ▲ | ◆ | ● |
|---|---|---|---|---|
| altogether | palace | piano | pajamas | handful |
| wilderness | lemonade | friendly | nephew | install |
| apartment | parties | carpet | scarf | guard |
| groups | due | whose | blew | chewing |
| beautiful | beyond | probably | costume | squirrel |

**B. Puzzling Clues** Write Other Word Forms or the spelling words to complete each clue. The shape before each group of spaces tells you in what column you can find the spelling word. Use each word or its Other Word Form only once.

1. Never incompletely ■ a l t o g e t h e r
2. Its opposite is never "friendmore." ▲ f r i e n d l e s s
3. Putting in the telephone lines ● i n s t a l l i n g
4. Furry nut gatherers ● s q u i r r e l s
5. Its opposite is never "feetfuls." ● h a n d f u l s
6. Clothing for trick-or-treaters ◆ c o s t u m e s
7. A summertime pick-me-up ★ l e m o n a d e
8. Nieces are never these. ◆ n e p h e w s
9. People walk all over them. ▲ c a r p e t s
10. Small blankets for the neck ◆ s c a r v e s
11. Homes for queens and kings ★ p a l a c e s
12. Night clothing ◆ p a j a m a s
13. Their keys fit no locks. ▲ p i a n o s
14. They keep an eye on things. ● g u a r d s
15. Far out! ★ b e y o n d
16. What the north wind does ◆ b l o w s
17. Describes some animals and some playing cards ■ w i l d
18. Your teeth do this best. ● c h e w
19. Describes what your library books could be ★ d u e
20. The mystery person? ▲ w h o

REVIEW



## CREATIVE WRITING

**(An optional writing activity)**

**Recipe for Writing:** This imaginative writing activity uses spelling words and Other Word Forms studied in Lessons 31-35.

COMBINE:

1 breakfast party at a beautiful palace
1 talented musician
9 guarded the group dutifully
5 carloads of friendly visitors
1 alarm

SEASON with your own original ideas and COOK UP a story with a unique FLAVOR. Proofread before SERVING.

The RECIPE words appear in the following lessons.

| Lesson | Words |
|---|---|
| 31 | palace |
| 32 | breakfast, talented, friendly, visitors |
| 33 | party, guarded, carloads, alarm |
| 34 | group, dutifully |
| 35 | beautiful, musician |

REVIEW

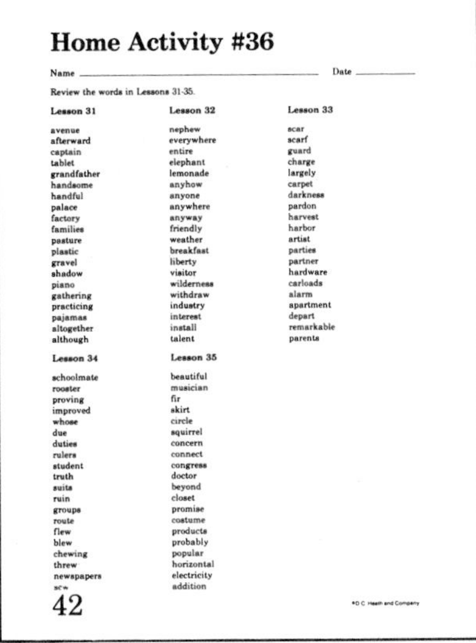

**Home Activity #36**

Name ______ Date ______

Review the words in Lessons 31-35.

| Lesson 31 | Lesson 32 | Lesson 33 |
|---|---|---|
| avenue | nephew | scar |
| afterward | everywhere | scarf |
| captain | entire | guard |
| tablet | elephant | charge |
| grandfather | lemonade | largely |
| handsome | anyhow | carpet |
| handful | anyone | darkness |
| palace | anywhere | pardon |
| factory | anyway | harvest |
| families | friendly | harbor |
| pasture | weather | artist |
| plastic | breakfast | parties |
| gravel | liberty | partner |
| shadow | visitor | hardware |
| piano | wilderness | carloads |
| gathering | withdraw | alarm |
| practicing | industry | apartment |
| pajamas | interest | depart |
| altogether | install | remarkable |
| although | talent | parents |

| Lesson 34 | Lesson 35 |
|---|---|
| schoolmate | beautiful |
| rooster | musician |
| proving | fir |
| improved | skirt |
| whose | circle |
| due | squirrel |
| duties | concern |
| rulers | connect |
| student | congress |
| truth | doctor |
| suits | beyond |
| ruin | closet |
| groups | promise |
| route | costume |
| flew | products |
| blew | probably |
| chewing | popular |
| threw | horizontal |
| newspapers | electricity |
| sew | addition |

42 ©D.C. Heath and Company

**Modified Lesson #36**

Name ______ Date ______

**Other Word Forms** pastures tablets visited friendlier charged harvested sewing proof doctors circled

I. **Visual Warm-up.** Write each Other Word Form in its correct shape.

II. **Vowel Hunt.** Fill in the missing vowels and write the Other Words Forms.

a. v__s__t__d ______ f. pr__ __f ______
b. h__rv__st__d ______ g. s__w__ng ______
c. p__st__r__s ______ h. t__bl__ts ______
d. c__rcl__d ______ i. d__ct__rs ______
e. fr__ __ndl__ __r ______ j. ch__rg__d ______

III. **Word Maze.** Fill in the missing letters to find the Other Word Forms. Write the words in the blanks beside the numbers.

Across: 4. ______ 6. ______ 7. ______ 9. ______ 10. ______

Down: 1. ______ 2. ______ 3. ______ 5. ______ 8. ______

©D.C. Heath and Company 113

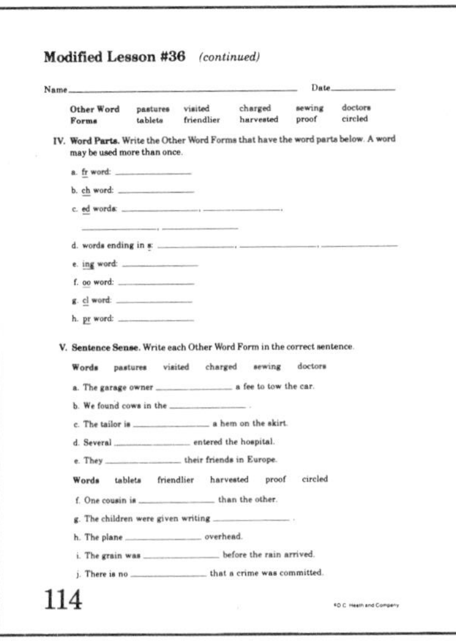

**Modified Lesson #36** *(continued)*

Name ______ Date ______

**Other Word Forms** pastures tablets visited friendlier charged harvested sewing proof doctors circled

IV. **Word Parts.** Write the Other Word Forms that have the word parts below. A word may be used more than once.

a. fr word: ______
b. ch word: ______
c. ed words: ______, ______, ______, ______
d. words ending in s: ______, ______, ______
e. ing word: ______
f. oo word: ______
g. cl word: ______
h. pr word: ______

V. **Sentence Sense.** Write each Other Word Form in the correct sentence.

**Words** pastures visited charged sewing doctors

a. The garage owner ______ a fee to tow the car.
b. We found cows in the ______ .
c. The tailor is ______ a hem on the skirt.
d. Several ______ entered the hospital.
e. They ______ their friends in Europe.

**Words** tablets friendlier harvested proof circled

f. One cousin is ______ than the other.
g. The children were given writing ______ .
h. The plane ______ overhead.
i. The grain was ______ before the rain arrived.
j. There is no ______ that a crime was committed.

114 ©D.C. Heath and Company

**Home Activity**
A weekly homework assignment

**Modified Lesson**
An alternative lesson for limited spellers

*(The Answer Key can be found in the Teacher's Resource Book.)*

### Challenge Word Review

The Challenge Words from the previous five lessons are listed below if you wish to review the Challenge Words with your more advanced students.

1. agony
2. baggage
3. adverb
4. manuscript
5. Massachusetts
6. central
7. distress
8. extended
9. rebellion
10. tenderly
11. narrowly
12. carbon
13. carpenter
14. parlor
15. parchment
16. proofread
17. drooping
18. lunar
19. superior
20. supermarket
21. burden
22. cathedral
23. perfect
24. squirmed
25. discount

| | | | | |
|---|---|---|---|---|
| afterward | charge | factory | horizontal | products |
| anyhow | congress | flew | musician | rooster |
| anyone | depart | grandfather | parents | schoolmate |
| anyway | duties | harbor | plastic | tablet |
| anywhere | everywhere | hardware | popular | threw |

**C. Alphabetical Order** Find the spelling word that comes alphabetically right *before* each word below. Write the spelling word and an Other Word Form for each spelling word.

| | Before | Spelling Words | Other Word Forms |
|---|---|---|---|
| 1. | aim | afterward | afterwards |
| 2. | rough | rooster | roosters |
| 3. | harvest | hardware | hardwares |
| 4. | grape | grandfather | grandfathers |
| 5. | cheat | charge | charges |
| 6. | flight | flew | fly |
| 7. | tackle | tablet | tablets |
| 8. | hose | horizontal | horizontally |
| 9. | scorn | schoolmate | schoolmates |
| 10. | thrill | threw | throw |
| 11. | depend | depart | departs |
| 12. | color | congress | congresses |
| 13. | each | duties | duty |
| 14. | park | parents | parent |
| 15. | harmful | harbor | harboring |
| 16. | program | products | production |
| 17. | porch | popular | popularly |
| 18. | favor | factory | factories |
| 19. | mystery | musician | music |
| 20. | plenty | plastic | plastics |

Accept any Other Word Form that appears in the Spelling Dictionary.

REVIEW

21. Write the five words that appear in the spelling list but have no Other Word Forms.

a. anyhow
b. anywhere
c. anyone
d. everywhere
e. anyway

146 Review—Lesson 36

### Proofreading Exercise Lesson #36

Name ______ Date ______

**Proofreading the Spelling of Others**

The fifth graders wrote safety slogans for bumper stickers. They made some spelling errors. Circle the misspelled words. Write the correct words on the lines.

1. Drive slowly. Stay alive and handsum. 1. ______
2. If you can read this, you're too frendly. 2. ______
3. Be an artest behind the wheel. 3. ______
4. Please pardun my dents. 4. ______
5. Safety siutes my driving style. 5. ______
6. Don't drive beyawned the limits. 6. ______
7. Bad drivers ruen good cars. 7. ______
8. Speed is never the avenew to take. 8. ______
9. Make careful driving a populer idea! 9. ______
10. If the alorm rings, I'm in trouble. 10. ______
11. A parking lot is never a safe harber. 11. ______
12. The careful driver has "wheel talant". 12. ______
13. We drive everyware with care. 13. ______
14. With "safety first" your new car becomes a palice on wheels. 14. ______
15. Drive as if you have an intrest in living. 15. ______
16. Careful drivers always react to the whether. 16. ______
17. Courtesy is the safe roote to travel. 17. ______
18. Let safety be your first consern. 18. ______
19. Keep your partys off the road! 19. ______
20. Common sense is my riding partnor. 20. ______



151

### End-of-year Proofreading Review

Name ______ Date ______

**Directions:** Circle the misspelled word in each group. Write each word correctly on the line.

| | | | | | |
|---|---|---|---|---|---|
| 1. cellar | hardware | nefew | cabbage | 1. ______ |
| 2. helmit | cutting | tablet | guide | 2. ______ |
| 3. lonely | sentance | palm | eighteen | 3. ______ |
| 4. stubborn | charge | ashamed | avenew | 4. ______ |
| 5. unload | cherries | skurt | husband | 5. ______ |
| 6. overturn | entire | village | averige | 6. ______ |
| 7. shelter | chimeny | elephant | select | 7. ______ |
| 8. plastic | safely | message | bundel | 8. ______ |
| 9. however | pumpkin | arrow | finel | 9. ______ |
| 10. differant | export | parents | harvest | 10. ______ |
| 11. foolish | split | valintine | calm | 11. ______ |
| 12. safety | thum | whale | cocoa | 12. ______ |
| 13. protest | pejamas | altered | sew | 13. ______ |
| 14. beautiful | secret | praize | passenger | 14. ______ |
| 15. kettle | choice | anyhow | nothern | 15. ______ |
| 16. ketchin | carried | company | stalk | 16. ______ |
| 17. loose | remember | squrel | ladies | 17. ______ |
| 18. bitter | colored | listen | dooties | 18. ______ |
| 19. doller | regular | English | finger | 19. ______ |
| 20. savings | threw | calves | clozet | 20. ______ |
| 21. payment | savige | current | recess | 21. ______ |
| 22. copies | flight | guard | groath | 22. ______ |
| 23. carpet | betray | maintane | tackle | 23. ______ |
| 24. freedom | heavey | gathering | voices | 24. ______ |
| 25. question | brook | potatoe | promise | 25. ______ |
| 26. cousin | student | cheet | swallow | 26. ______ |
| 27. caugh | sample | treasure | rooster | 27. ______ |
| 28. August | canyan | wilderness | raise | 28. ______ |
| 29. automobile | compass | docter | dealing | 29. ______ |
| 30. liberty | fammilies | whose | station | 30. ______ |

152



**Proofreading Exercise**

**End-of-year Proofreading Review**

| ■ | ★ | ▲ | ◆ | ● |
|---|---|---|---|---|
| avenue | weather | handsome | families | pasture |
| industry | entire | although | liberty | withdraw |
| largely | darkness | artist | carloads | partner |
| newspapers | route | suits | student | duties |
| fir | doctor | closet | electricity | addition |

**D. S-t-r-e-t-c-h the Meaning** Write Other Word Forms or the spelling words to stretch the words and their meanings. The shape tells you in what column you can find the spelling word. Write each word or its Other Word Form only once. If you need help, use the **Spelling Dictionary**.

1. ▲ closets : places where shirts and ▲ suits hang
2. ★ doctors : persons sometimes thought of as ▲ artists in the operating room
3. ■ avenues : ★ routes for city drivers
4. daily ■ newspapers : important products of printing ■ industries
5. ■ fir trees: evergreens often found in very ■ large forests
6. ◆ carloads : describes autos stuffed with ◆ family members
7. ● pastures : places where cows graze
8. ◆ electric bulbs: things that bring light to ★ dark places
9. ◆ liberty : a freedom that is everyone's ● duty to keep alive
10. your ● partners : members of your team
11. total: the ★ entire amount in ● addition
12. fewer ◆ students : what results when some classmates are ● withdrawn from your group
13. fair ★ weather : a time for a picnic, ▲ although there could be some rain
14. ▲ handsome : good looking

REVIEW



## REVIEW TEST

Twenty-five words, selected randomly from the five spelling lists, constitute the test and are listed with the appropriate phrases. Follow the same testing procedure used to administer the weekly Pretest and Posttest. Have students write any misspelled words on the Words to Learn Sheet. As an alternative testing option, you may wish to use the Standardized-format Test for this Review Lesson, found in the Teacher's Resource Book.

REVIEW

### Test Words and Phrases

| | |
|---|---|
| 1. afterward | joined them **afterward** |
| 2. handsome | **handsome** animal |
| 3. families | several **families** |
| 4. shadow | will cast a long **shadow** |
| 5. pajamas | red-striped **pajamas** |
| 6. nephew | niece and **nephew** |
| 7. lemonade | another **lemonade** stand |
| 8. anyway | didn't want it **anyway** |
| 9. visitor | greeted the **visitor** |
| 10. install | will **install** the phone |
| 11. guard | the **guard** at the gate |
| 12. darkness | the **darkness** of night |
| 13. artist | the **artist** at work |
| 14. carloads | **carloads** of spectators |
| 15. remarkable | a **remarkable** stunt |
| 16. proving | **proving** you to be correct |
| 17. truth | to tell the **truth** |
| 18. suits | wet bathing **suits** |
| 19. flew | **flew** south for the winter |
| 20. newspapers | has read two **newspapers** |
| 21. fir | a forest of **fir** trees |
| 22. concern | had no **concern** |
| 23. beyond | **beyond** their control |
| 24. products | several new **products** |
| 25. electricity | the hum of **electricity** |

**Review Test: Lesson #36**

Name________________ Date________

**Directions:** Read each sentence. Select the word with the correct spelling to complete each sentence. Fill in the correct letter in the answer column.

1. We joined them ____ . A. afterwood B. afterward C. afterwad D. aftreward
2. That horse is a ____ animal. A. hansome B. handsome C. handsum D. hansum
3. Several ____ camped there. A. families B. fammilies C. familys D. famalies
4. The pole will cast a long ____ . A. shaddo B. shaddow C. shadow D. shedow
5. I wore red-striped ____ . A. pagamas B. pajamas C. pajarmas D. pajames
6. Our niece and ____ visited us. A. nepew B. neffew C. nephyou D. nephew
7. Do we need another ____ stand? A. lemonaid B. lemmonaid C. lemonade D. lemmonade
8. I didn't want it ____ . A. annyway B. anyway C. anyweigh D. enyway
9. Who greeted the ____ ? A. visitor B. visiter C. vissitor D. vissiter
10. We will ____ the phone. A. instal B. install C. enstall D. enstal
11. The ____ at the gate stopped us. A. gard B. garde C. gaurd D. guard
12. They fear the ____ of night. A. dakness B. dakniss C. darknes D. darkness
13. We watched the ____ at work. A. arteste B. artest C. artist D. artiss
14. Ten ____ of spectators arrived. A. carlods B. carlodes C. carloads D. calloads
15. She performed a ____ stunt. A. remakible B. remarkible C. remarckable D. remarkable
16. I am ____ you to be correct. A. proving B. proveing C. proofing D. prooving
17. He speaks the ____ . A. trooth B. truth C. troth D. trouth
18. We wore the wet bathing ____ . A. suits B. suts C. suets D. soots
19. I ____ south for the winter. A. flu B. floo C. flue D. flew
20. He has read two ____ . A. newspappers B. newspapars C. noospapers D. newspapers
21. We saw a forest of ____ trees. A. fur B. fir C. fer D. ferr
22. They had no ____ . A. consurn B. concirn C. concern D. consern
23. The fire is ____ their control. A. beyon B. beyond C. beyonde D. beyawn
24. We bought several new ____ . A. prauducts B. producks C. products D. porducts
25. Do you hear the hum of ____ ? A. electricity B. electrisity C. elecktrisity D. electircity

Answer Column: 1.–25. A B C D

160

©D.C. Heath and Company

**Standardized-format Test**

**End-of-year Test**

Name________________ Date________

**Directions:** Look at each group of words. Find the one word that is spelled correctly. Fill in the correct space in the answer column.

| | A | B | C | D |
|---|---|---|---|---|
| 1. | compair | cumpair | compare | cumpare |
| 2. | eastern | easton | eastin | eastirn |
| 3. | deside | decied | decide | desied |
| 4. | chozen | chozin | chosin | chosen |
| 5. | succure | secure | sucure | secur |
| 6. | delade | dilayed | delaid | delayed |
| 7. | sleeve | sleve | sleave | sleive |
| 8. | ovaturn | overton | overturn | overtern |
| 9. | groul | growl | growel | growle |
| 10. | American | Amercan | Amerecan | Amerrican |
| 11. | begining | beginning | bigening | beggining |
| 12. | problim | probblem | proublem | problem |
| 13. | fontin | fountin | fountain | fontaine |
| 14. | cacher | catcher | catsher | catchar |
| 15. | nauty | noughty | naughty | notty |
| 16. | information | infromation | infomation | infamation |
| 17. | stubbon | stuborn | stubon | stubborn |
| 18. | passanger | passenger | pasenger | passengar |
| 19. | chimney | chimnee | chimmey | chemney |
| 20. | apointment | apointmint | appointment | appointmint |
| 21. | brot | braut | broght | brought |
| 22. | frekles | freakles | freckles | frecles |
| 23. | prezident | president | presidant | priesdent |
| 24. | average | avirage | avrage | avrige |
| 25. | shellter | shalter | shelter | sheltor |
| 26. | altogather | alltogether | altogethor | altogether |
| 27. | nephue | nephew | nefew | knephew |
| 28. | harvist | havist | harvest | havest |
| 29. | rooster | ruster | rouster | roostir |
| 30. | horizontle | horisontal | horizontal | horisontle |

Answer Column: 1.–30. A B C D

©D.C. Heath and Company

161

**End-of-year Standardized-format Test**

## Spelling Dictionary/WORDFINDER

Your Spelling Dictionary/WORDFINDER lists all the basic spelling words and Other Word Forms in your spelling book. If the entry word is a spelling word, it is listed in **dark type**. If the entry word is not in dark type, then the spelling word is listed with the Other Word Forms at the end of the definition.

The Spelling Dictionary/WORDFINDER gives you a quick way to check the spelling and meanings of your spelling words. Because the Spelling Dictionary/WORDFINDER includes many of the words you will need in daily writing, you will find it useful for other schoolwork too.

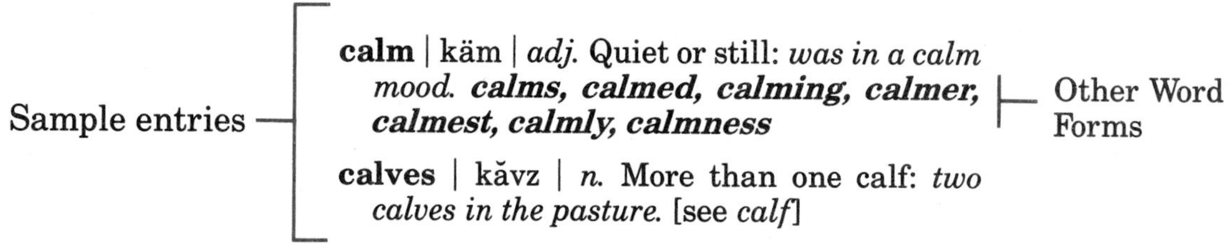

Sample entries
**calm** | käm | *adj.* Quiet or still: *was in a calm mood.* ***calms, calmed, calming, calmer, calmest, calmly, calmness***
**calves** | kăvz | *n.* More than one calf: *two calves in the pasture.* [see *calf*]
Other Word Forms


### PRONUNCIATION KEY

| | | | | | |
|---|---|---|---|---|---|
| ă | pat | j | judge | sh | dish, ship |
| ā | aid, fey, pay | k | cat, kick, pique | t | tight |
| â | air, care, wear | l | lid, needle | th | path, thin |
| ä | father | m | am, man, mum | *th* | bathe, this |
| b | bib | n | no, sudden | ŭ | cut, rough |
| ch | church | ng | thing | û | circle, firm, heard, |
| d | deed | ŏ | horrible, pot | | term, turn, urge, word |
| ĕ | pet, pleasure | ō | go, hoarse, row, toe | v | cave, valve, vine |
| ē | be, bee, easy, leisure | ô | alter, caught, for, paw | w | with |
| f | fast, fife, off, phase, rough | oi | boy, noise, oil | y | yes |
| g | gag | ou | cow, out | yōō | abuse, use |
| h | hat | ŏŏ | took | z | rose, size, xylophone, zebra |
| hw | which | ōō | boot, fruit | zh | garage, pleasure, vision |
| ĭ | pit | p | pop | ə | about, silent, pencil |
| ī | by, guy, pie | r | roar | | lemon, circus |
| î | dear, deer, fierce, mere | s | miss, sauce, see | ər | butter |

STRESS
Primary stress ′ **bi•ol′o•gy** |bī ŏl′ə jē| Secondary stress ′ **bi′o•log′i•cal** |bī′ə lŏj′ĭ kəl|

# A

act | ăkt | *n.* One of the main divisions of a play or opera: *a long first act.* ***acts, acted, acting, action, actor, actress***

**acts** | ăkts | *n.* More than one act: *a play with three acts.* [see *act*]

add | ăd | *v.* To find the sum of two or more numbers: *will add these numbers.* ***adds, added, adding, addition, additions, additional, additionally***

**addition** | ə **dĭsh**′ən | *n.* The adding of two or more numbers: *correct addition.* – **In addition to** – Besides. [see *add*]

**afterward** | **ăf**′tər wərd | *adv.* Later: *will sign up afterward.* ***afterwards***

**aim** | ām | *n.* **1.** The act of pointing something, usually a weapon, at an object: *took aim at the target.* **2.** A purpose or goal: *the aim of the meeting.* ***aims, aimed, aiming, aimless, aimlessly, aimlessness***

**alarm** | ə **lärm**′ | *n.* A device that, when sounded, warns people: *a burglar alarm.* ***alarms, alarmed, alarming, alarmingly***

**allow** | ə **lou**′ | *v.* To let happen or be done: *will allow them to play.* ***allows, allowed, allowing, allowable, allowance***

**all right** | **ôl**′**rīt**′ | Correct: *if the answers were all right.*

alter | **ôl**′tər | *v.* **1.** To change in some way: *will alter her way of dressing.* **2.** To change the fit of clothing: *to alter the hem on a skirt.* ***alters, altered, altering, alteration***

**altered** | **ôl**′tərd | *v.* **1.** Changed in some way: *altered the schedule.* **2.** Changed the fit of clothing: *altered the coat sleeves.* [see *alter*]

**although** | ôl *th***ō**′ | *conj.* Even though: *although you helped.*

**altogether** | ôl′tə **gĕ***th*′ər | *adv.* Completely; totally: *altogether pleased with the results.*

America | ə **mĕr**′ĭ kə | *n.* The United States: *born in America.* ***Americas, American, Americans, Americanize, Americanism***

**American** | ə **mĕr**′ĭ kən | *adj.* Of the United States: *American cities.* *n.* A citizen of the United States: *an American living in Europe.* [see *America*]

**amuse** | ə **myo͞oz**′ | *v.* To give pleasure by making someone laugh or smile: *will amuse us with jokes.* ***amuses, amused, amusing, amusingly, amusement***

**anger** | **ăng**′gər | *n.* A feeling of rage against someone or something that has caused injury or wrong: *a shout of anger.* ***angers, angered, angering, angry, angrier, angriest, angrily***

**angle** | **ăng**′gəl | *n.* The space formed between two straight lines when they meet: *the angle formed by the hands of a clock.* ***angles, angled, angling***

**angry** | **ăng**′grē | *adj.* Feeling or showing anger: *in an angry mood.* [see *anger*]

**ankle** | **ăng**′kəl | *n.* The joint attaching the foot to the leg: *sprained her ankle.* ***ankles***

**answer** | **ăn**′sər | *v.* To respond to a question: *to answer correctly.* ***answers, answered, answering***

**anyhow** | **ĕn**′ē hou′ | *adv.* In any case; nevertheless: *will worry anyhow.*

**anyone** | **ĕn**′ē wŭn′ | *pron.* Any person; anybody: *if anyone knows.*

**anyway** | **ĕn**′ē wā′ | *adv.* In any case: *will rain anyway.*

**anywhere** | **ĕn**′ē hwâr′ | *adv.* At, in, or to any place: *will go anywhere in the United States.*

**apartment** | ə **pärt**′mənt | *n.* A room or group of rooms rented as a home: *the apartment on the fifth floor.* ***apartments***

appoint | ə **point**′ | *v.* To select a time or place: *to appoint the gym for the school fair.* ***appoints, appointed, appointing, appointment, appointments***

**appointment** | ə **point**′ mənt | *n.* A prearranged meeting: *an appointment at three o'clock.* [see *appoint*]

**April** | **ā**′prəl | *adj.* Of April: *April flowers.* *n.* The fourth month: *a birthday in April.* ***Apr.***

**apron** | a′prən | *n.* A garment tied around the waist to protect the clothes on the front of the body: *an apron worn to do dishes.* ***aprons, aproned***

**aren't** | ärnt | Contraction for *are not: because we aren't going.*

**arrow** | ăr′ō | *n.* A thin, pointed shaft that is shot from a bow: *bow and arrow.* ***arrows***

art | ärt | *n.* Drawing, painting, and sculpture: *courses in art and poetry.* ***arts, artist, artists, artistic, artistically, artistry***

**artist** | **är**′ tĭst | *n.* A person who draws, paints, or sculpts: *the artist who is carving the sculpture.* [see *art*]

ash | ăsh | *n.* The remains of something that has been completely burned: *ash in the fireplace.* ***ashes, ashy***

**ashamed** | ə **shāmd**′ | *adj.* Feeling uncomfortable for having done something wrong: *ashamed of his actions.* [see *shame*]

**ashes** | **ăsh**′ĭz | *n.* The remains of something that has been completely burned: *swept the ashes.* [see *ash*]

**astronaut** | **ăs**′ trə nŏt′ | *n.* A member of the crew of a spacecraft: *the astronaut in the control room.* ***astronauts, astronautic, astronautics, astronautical***

attach | ə **tăch**′ | *v.* To join together: *to attach a stamp to an envelope.* ***attaches, attached, attaching, attachable, attachment***

**attached** | ə **tăcht**′ | *v.* Joined together: *attached a hook to a fishing rod.* [see *attach*]

**attack** | ə **tăk**′ | *n.* The act of using force or weapons against: *a surprise attack. v.* To begin a fight: *to attack without warning.* ***attacks, attacked, attacking, attacker***

**attend** | ə **tĕnd**′ | *v.* To go to; be present at: *will attend the party.* ***attends, attended, attending, attendance, attendant***

**audience** | **ô**′ dē əns | *n.* The people gathered to see or hear something: *large audience in the theater.* ***audiences***

**August** | ô′ gəst | *adj.* Of August: *August weather. n.* The eighth month of the year: *the first week in August.* ***Aug.***

**aunt** | ănt | *n.* The sister of one's mother or father: *my father's aunt.* ***aunts***

**automobile** | ô′tə mə **bēl**′ | *n.* A passenger vehicle with an engine, driven on land: *an automobile with front-wheel drive.* ***automobiles, auto***

**autumn** | **ô**′təm | *adj.* Related to autumn: *autumn harvest. n.* The season between summer and winter: *a rainy autumn.* ***autumns, autumnal***

**avenue** | **ăv**′ə nōō′ | *n.* A wide street: *cars along the avenue.* ***avenues, Ave.***

**average** | **ăv**′ər ĭj | *n.* The number that is typical or representative of a group of numbers: *5 is the average of 3 and 7. adj.* Usual: *an average amount of rain in the month of September.* ***averages, averaged, averaging***

**awful** | **ô**′fəl | *adj.* Terrible: *awful temper.* ***awfully***

## B

bad | băd | *adj.* Not good: *bad behavior.* ***worse, worst***

**badge** | băj | *n.* Something worn to show rank, membership, occupation, etc.: *the officer's badge.* ***badges***

**bait** | bāt | *n.* Anything used to attract animals or fish to be caught: *bait for trout.* ***baits, baited, baiting***

**balloon** | bə **lōōn**′ | *n.* An elastic rubber bag made to be filled with air or other gases: *bought a balloon at the parade.* ***balloons, ballooned, ballooning***

**bare** | bâr | *adj.* Unclothed: *bare shoulders.* ***bares, bared, baring, barer, barest, barely***

ă pat / ā pay / â care / ä father / ĕ pet / ē be / ĭ pit / ī pie / î fierce / ŏ pot / ō go / ô paw, for / oi oil / ŏŏ book / ōō boot / ou out / ŭ cut / û fur / *th* the / th thin / hw which / zh vision / ə ago, item, pencil, atom, circus

**barrel** | **bâr**′əl | *n.* A large wooden container with round, flat ends and sides that curve out: *a barrel for water.* ***barrels, barreled, barreling, barrelful***

**basement** | **bās**′mənt | *n.* The lowest story of a building, usually below ground: *boxes in the basement.* ***basements***

**beam** | bēm | *n.* A ray of light: *the beam from the lighthouse.* ***beams, beamed, beaming***

beat | bēt | *v.* **1.** To cause to lose: *will beat him at golf.* **2.** To mix by stirring quickly: *will beat the eggs.* ***beats, beaten, beating, beater***

**beaten** | **bēt**′n | *adj.* **1.** Defeated: *the beaten enemy.* **2.** Mixed by stirring quickly: *has beaten the cake batter.* [see *beat*]

**beautiful** | **byōō**′tə fəl | *adj.* Pleasing to the senses: *a beautiful painting.* [see *beauty*]

beauty | **byōō**′tē | *n.* A quality that pleases the senses: *the beauty of music.* ***beautiful, beautifully, beautify, beautified, beautifying, beautification***

beg | bĕg | *v.* To plead; ask for earnestly: *to beg forgiveness.* ***begs, begged, begging, beggar***

**begged** | bĕgd | *v.* Pleaded; asked for earnestly: *begged for some help.* [see *beg*]

begin | bĭ **gĭn**′ | *v.* To start: *will begin the puzzle.* ***begins, began, begun, beginning***

**beginning** | bĭ **gĭn**′ĭng | *v.* Starting: *beginning to heal.* [see *begin*]

**betray** | bĭ **trā**′ | *v.* To be a traitor to; double-cross: *to betray the soldiers to the enemy.* ***betrays, betrayed, betraying, betrayer, betrayal***

**beyond** | bē **ŏnd**′ | *prep.* Outside the reach or understanding of: *beyond my ability.*

**bitter** | **bĭt**′ər | *adj.* Sharp or unpleasant in flavor: *the bitter fruit.* ***bitterly, bitterness***

bleed | blēd | *v.* To lose blood: *did bleed from the wound.* ***bleeds, bled, bleeding, blood, bloody, bloodier, bloodiest, bloodiness***

**bleeding** | **blē**′dĭng | *n.* The losing of blood: *slow bleeding from the cut.* [see *bleed*]

**blew** | blōō | *v.* Sent out a strong current of air: *blew on the hot soup.* [see *blow*]

**blood** | blŭd | *n.* The red fluid that moves through the body, carrying oxygen, digested food, and waste: *blood from a vein.* [see *bleed*]

**blossom** | **blŏs**′əm | *n.* A flower: *the blossom on the plant.* ***blossoms, blossomed, blossoming, blossomless***

**blouse** | blous | *n.* A loose shirt worn by women: *cotton blouse.* ***blouses, bloused***

blow | blō | *v.* To send out a strong current of air: *to blow air into the balloon.* –**Blow up**– To fill with air. ***blows, blew, blown, blowing, blower***

**bodies** | **bŏd**′ēz | *n.* More than one body: *heavenly bodies of stars.* [see *body*]

body | **bŏd**′ē | *n.* A mass or portion of matter: *body of water.* ***bodies, bodily***

**bond** | bŏnd | *n.* Something that ties or unites: *a bond between sisters.* ***bonds, bonded, bonding, bondage***

**border** | **bôr**′dər | *n.* An outer part or edge of anything: *the county border.* ***borders, bordered, bordering***

**bore** | bôr | *v.* **1.** To make a hole by using a tool that turns: *will bore through the wall.* **2.** To make weary by being dull or uninteresting: *movies that bore me.* ***bores, bored, boring, boredom, borer***

**bottom** | **bŏt**′əm | *n.* The lowest part or edge: *the bottom of a box.* ***bottoms, bottomless***

**bought** | bôt | *v.* Purchased: *bought new shoes.* [see *buy*]

**braid** | brād | *n.* A length of three or more strands of ribbon or hair woven together: *long blond braid.* *v.* To weave three or more strands together: *will braid her hair.* ***braids, braided, braiding***

**brain** | brān | *n.* The part of the central nervous system in vertebrates that is enclosed in the skull and consists of nerve cells and fibers for controlling almost all bodily functions. *X ray of the brain.* ***brains, brainy, brainier, brainiest, brainless***

**brake** | brāk | *n.* Something used to slow down or stop the motion of a wheeled vehicle by rubbing against or pressing: *the brake on the bicycle.* ***brakes, braked, braking***

branch | brănch | *n.* Any wood part growing out from the trunk of a tree: *a fallen tree branch.* ***branches, branched, branching***

**branches** | **brăn**′ chĭz | *n.* More than one branch: *branches of a redwood.* [see *branch*]

**brass** | brăs | *n.* An alloy that contains copper and zinc: *polished the brass.* ***brasses, brassy***

**break** | brāk | *v.* To come apart by force: *will break on the tile floor. n.* A brief interruption in work: *a morning break.* ***breaks, broke, breaking, broken, breakable***

**breakfast** | **brĕk**′fəst | *n.* The first meal of the day: *eggs for breakfast.* ***breakfasts, breakfasted, breakfasting***

**bridge** | brĭj | *n.* A structure that provides a way over a river, road, or other obstacle: *steel bridge.* ***bridges, bridged, bridging***

bring | brĭng | *v.* To come with someone or something: *will bring a guest.* ***brings, brought, bringing***

**brook** | bro͝ok | *n.* A small natural stream of water: *fishing in the brook.* ***brooks***

**brought** | brôt | *v.* Came with someone or something: *brought a gift for you.* [see *bring*]

build | bĭld | *v.* To make or construct by putting materials or parts together: *to build toys.* ***builds, built, building, buildings, builder***

**building** | **bĭl**′dĭng | *adj.* Related to building: *the building renovation. n.* A structure like a house or store; something built: *brick building. v.* Making or constructing: *building a garage.* [see *build*]

**bundle** | **bŭn**′dl | n. Several things tied or wrapped together: *a bundle of old clothes.* ***bundles, bundled, bundling, bundler***

**burglar** | **bûr**′glər | *n.* A person who breaks into a building to steal: *arrested the burglar inside the bank.* ***burglars, burglary, burglarize, burglarized***

**burst** | bûrst | *v.* To go, come, or do suddenly or by force: *as water burst from the hose.* ***bursts, bursting***

**button** | **bŭt**′n | *n.* A disk of plastic, metal, etc., sewn on garments to hold them together or to decorate them: *a button on the cuff.* ***buttons, buttoned, buttoning***

buy | **bī** | *v.* To get something by paying money: *to buy milk.* ***buys, bought, buying, buyer***

## C

**cabbage** | **kăb**′ĭj | *n.* A vegetable with leaves that overlap to form a round head: *soup made from cabbage.* ***cabbages***

calf | kăf | *n.* A young cow or bull: *a calf in the barn.* ***calves***

**calm** | käm | *adj.* Quiet or still: *was in a calm mood.* ***calms, calmed, calming, calmer, calmest, calmly, calmness***

**calves** | kăvz | *n.* More than one calf: *two calves in the pasture.* [see *calf*]

**canal** | kə **năl**′ | *n.* A waterway dug for irrigation or navigation: *digging a canal.* ***canals***

**canyon** | **kăn**′yən | *n.* A deep hollow in the earth's surface, carved by a river: *the steep walls of the canyon.* ***canyons***

**captain** | **kăp**′tən | *n.* The leader of a group: *captain of the team.* ***captains, captained, captaining, captainship***

carload | **kär**′lōd′ | *n.* As much as a car can hold: *carload of groceries.* ***carloads***

**carloads** | **kär**′lōdz′ | *n.* More than one carload: *carloads of students.* [see *carload*]

ă pat / ā pay / â care / ä father / ĕ pet / ē be / ĭ pit / ī pie / î fierce / ŏ pot / ō go / ô paw, for / oi oil / o͝o book / o͞o boot / ou out / ŭ cut / û fur / *th* the / th thin / hw which / zh vision / ə ago, item, pencil, atom, circus

**carpet** | kär′pĭt | *n.* A woven covering for floors: *worn gray carpet.* ***carpets, carpeted, carpeting***

**carried** | kăr′ēd | *v.* Taken from one place to another: *was carried on his back.* [see *carry*]

**carries** | kăr′ēz | *v.* Takes something from one place to another: *carries the small packages.* [see *carry*]

carry | **kăr′ē** | *v.* To take something from one place to another: *to carry a box.* ***carries, carried, carrying, carrier, carriage***

**castle** | **kăs′**əl | *n.* A large building or group of buildings with thick walls and other protections against attack; fort: *built a sand castle.* ***castles***

catch | kăch | *v.* **1.** To become sick with: *to catch the flu.* **2.** To capture or seize: *to catch the prisoner.* **3.** To grab hold of something moving: *to catch a ball.* ***catches, caught, catching, catcher, catchers***

**catcher** | **kăch′**ər | *n.* The player behind home plate who catches the ball from the pitcher: *the foul ball caught by the catcher.* [see *catch*]

**caught** | kôt | *v.* **1.** Become sick with: *caught the measles.* **2.** Captured or seized: *caught the thief.* [see *catch*]

cause | kôz | *v.* To make happen: *to cause the fight.* ***causes, caused, causing, causable***

**caused** | kôzd | *v.* Made happen: *caused the bad weather.* [see *cause*]

**cellar** | **sĕl′**ər | *n.* An underground room used for storage: *firewood in the cellar.* ***cellars***

change | chānj | *v.* To substitute or make different: *to change the record.* ***changes, changed, changing, changeable, changeably, changeless, changer***

**changing** | **chānj′***ĭng* | *v.* Substituting or making different: *is changing the sheets on the bed.* [see *change*]

**charge** | chärj | *v.* **1.** To rush ahead: *to charge up the hill.* **2.** To delay payment by recording the amount owed: *will charge the coat.* ***charges, charged, charging, charger, chargeable***

**cheat** | chēt | *n.* A dishonest person who tricks others: *found him to be a cheat.* ***cheats, cheated, cheating, cheater***

**cherries** | **chĕr′**ēz | *n.* More than one cherry: *a bowl of cherries.* [see *cherry*]

cherry | **chĕr′**ē | *n.* A small, round fruit with a pit: *one cherry in the bowl.* ***cherries***

chew | cho͞o | *v.* To grind or crush with the teeth: *will chew slowly.* ***chews, chewed, chewing, chewy, chewier, chewiest, chewer***

**chewing** | **cho͞o′**ĭng | *v.* Grinding or crushing with the teeth: *chewing on a piece of string.* [see *chew*]

**chief** | chēf | *n.* The leader: *chief of police.* ***chiefs, chiefly, chieftain***

**chimney** | **chĭm′**nē | *n.* A hollow, upright brick or stone structure for carrying smoke from a fireplace, furnace, etc.: *a 30-foot chimney.* ***chimneys***

**choice** | chois | *n.* **1.** The power to choose: *no choice in the matter.* **2.** Something to be chosen among several: *choice of three colors.* ***choices, choicer, choicest***

**choose** | cho͞oz | *v.* To decide or select: *to choose each piece of fruit.* ***chooses, chose, chosen, choosing, choosy, choice, choices***

**chosen** | **chō′**zən | *v.* Decided or selected: *had chosen the right answer.* [see *choose*]

**circle** | **sûr′**kəl | *n.* A closed round line whose every point is at the same distance from the center: *drew a circle. v.* To enclose in a round line: *to circle the right answer.* ***circles, circled, circling, circular***

**cities** | **sĭt′**ēz | *n.* More than one city: *cities along the coast.* [see *city*]

city | **sĭt′**ē | *n.* A large, important town: *the city of Dallas.* ***cities***

**clerk** | klûrk | *n.* **1.** A person who sells goods in a store: *the clerk in the shoe department.* **2.** An office worker who types, files, or keeps records: *a clerk in an insurance company.* ***clerks, clerked, clerking, clerical***

**cliff** | klĭf | *n.* A steep face of rock: *the cliff above the valley.* ***cliffs***

**climate** | **klī**'mĭt | *n.* The particular kind of weather of a place: *cold climate.* ***climates, climatic***

**closet** | **klŏz**'ĭt | *n.* A small room for hanging clothes or storing supplies: *five suits in the closet.* ***closets***

**cloth** | klôth | *n.* A material made by weaving, knitting, or matting fibers together: *wool cloth.* ***cloths, clothe, clothes, clothed, clothing***

**cocoa** | **kō**'kō | *n.* A hot drink made with milk or water and the powder of cacao seeds: *cocoa on a cold day.*

**collar** | **kŏl**'ər | *n.* The part of a garment that makes a band around the neck: *a starched shirt collar.* ***collars, collared, collaring***

color | **kŭl**'ər | *v.* To put on a shade, hue, or tint: *will color with crayons.* ***colors, colored, coloring, colorful, colorfully***

**colored** | **kŭl**'ərd | *adj.* Having color, especially other than black or white: *a colored pattern.* [see *color*]

**colt** | kōlt | *n.* A young male horse: *colt in the barn.* ***colts***

**comfort** | **kŭm**'fərt | *n.* Something or someone that gives relief from grief or fear: *the comfort of friendship. v.* To make feel better: *to comfort when sad.* ***comforts, comforted, comforting, comfortable, comfortably, comfortableness, comforter***

**company** | **kŭm**'pə nē | *n.* **1.** One or more guests: *having company tonight.* **2.** A business: *the computer company.* ***companies, companion***

**compare** | kəm **păr**' | *v.* To study the similarities or differences of: *will compare their heights.* ***compares, compared, comparing, comparable, comparison***

**compass** | **kŭm**'pəs | *n.* A device containing a magnetic needle, used to show geographic direction: *when the needle of the compass pointed north.* ***compasses***

**concern** | kən **sûrn**' | *n.* Serious interest or worry: *a concern about her health.* ***concerns, concerned, concerning***

**conduct** | kən **dŭkt**' | *v.* **1.** To direct musicians: *will conduct the choir.* **2.** To lead: *to conduct the club meeting.* ***conducts, conducted, conducting, conductible, conduction, conductor***

**congress** | **kŏng**' grĭs | *n.* A meeting of representatives to discuss a subject: *a congress of doctors.* ***congresses, congressional***

**connect** | kə **nĕkt**' | *v.* To join: *will connect the parts.* ***connects, connected, connecting, connective, connection, connector***

**consent** | kən **sĕnt**' | *n.* Approval or agreement: *has her consent to leave. v.* To give approval or permission: *will consent to the plan.* ***consents, consented, consenting***

**content** | kən **tĕnt**' | *adj.* Pleased: *to be content to wait here.* ***contents, contented, contentedly, contentment***

**contract** | **kŏn**'trăckt | *n.* An agreement between two or more people, often involving an exchange of work or goods: *agreed to the new contract.* ***contracts, contracted, contracting, contractor, contraction***

**control** | kən **trōl**' | *n.* The power to guide: *has control of the car.* ***controls, controlled, controlling, controllable, controller***

**copies** | **kŏp**'ēz | *n.* More than one copy: *five copies of the report.* [see *copy*]

**copper** | **kŏp**'ər | *n.* A reddish-brown element found in various ores: *a ring made of copper.* ***coppered, coppery***

copy | **cŏp**'ē | *n.* A thing that is made just like another: *a copy of the letter.* ***copies, copied, copying, copier***

**costume** | **kŏs**'to͞om' | *n.* The clothes a person wears for disguise or when playing a part: *a costume for the actor.* ***costumes, costumed, costuming***

ă pat / ā pay / â care / ä father / ĕ pet / ē **be** / ĭ pit / ī pie / î fierce / ŏ pot / ō go / ô paw, for / oi oil / o͝o book / o͞o boot / ou out / ŭ cut / û fur / *th* the / th thin / hw which / zh vision / ə ago, item, pencil, atom, circus

**cough** | kôf | *n.* The act of air being forced from the lungs suddenly: *a cough and a sneeze.* ***coughs, coughed, coughing***

**couldn't** | **kŏŏd**′nt | Contraction for *could not: couldn't sing.*

**county** | **koun**′tē | *n.* In the United States, one of the divisions of a state: *the sheriff of the county.* ***counties***

**course** | kôrs | *n.* **1.** The direction taken: *strayed from their course.* **2.** An area for sports: *racing course.* ***courses, coursed***

**court** | kôrt | *n.* A place where decisions on legal cases are made: *if the court rules favorably.* ***courts, courted, courting***

**cousin** | **kŭz**′ən | *n.* The child of one's aunt or uncle: *a younger cousin.* ***cousins***

**coward** | **kou**′ərd | *n.* A person who has no courage or is easily frightened: *ran away like a coward.* ***cowards, cowardly, cowardliness***

**crawl** | krôl | *v.* To move on hands and knees: *will crawl into the cave.* ***crawls, crawled, crawling, crawler***

**crazy** | **krā**′zē | *adj.* Unusual, foolish, or insane: *a crazy way to drive.* ***crazier, craziest, crazily, craziness***

**creek** | krēk | *n.* A small stream of water that usually leads to a river: *swimming in the creek.* ***creeks***

**crop** | krŏp | *n.* The amount of plants grown for use as food in a single season: *this year's wheat crop.* ***crops, cropped, cropping***

**crops** | krŏps | *n.* A variety of plants grown for use as food: *crops of rye and corn.* [see *crop*]

**crouch** | krouch | *v.* To bend deeply at the knees: *to crouch under the low beam.* ***crouches, crouched, crouching***

**crowd** | kroud | *n.* A large number of people gathered together: *a crowd of football fans.* ***crowds, crowded, crowding***

**crowded** | **kroud**′ĭd | *adj.* Filled with many people: *crowded store.* [see *crowd*]

**crush** | krŭsh | *v.* To press with enough force to break: *will crush the old boxes.* ***crushes, crushed, crushing, crushable, crusher***

**current** | **kûr**′ənt | *n.* A flow of air or liquid: *a swift current of water.* ***currents, currently***

**cut** | kŭt | *v.* To form, divide, or open with a sharp tool: *will cut the bread.* ***cuts, cutting, cutter***

**cute** | kyōōt | *adj.* Pretty: *a cute child.* ***cuter, cutest, cutely, cuteness***

**cutting** | **kŭt**′ĭng | *v.* Forming, dividing, or opening with a sharp tool: *is cutting the cake.* [see *cut*]

## D

**daily** | **dā**′lē | *adj.* Done or appearing every day or weekday: *daily newspaper.* [see *day*]

**dark** | därk | *adj.* With very little or no light: *the dark cave.* ***darker, darkest, darken, darkens, darkened, darkening, darkness***

**darkness** | **därk**′nĭs | *n.* Very little or no light: *the darkness before dawn.* [see *dark*]

**daughter** | **dô**′tər | *n.* One's female child: *son and daughter.* ***daughters***

**day** | dā | *n.* The time of light between one night and the next: *a long summer day.* ***days, daily, dailies***

**deaf** | dĕf | *adj.* Unable to hear: *deaf person.* ***deafen, deafens, deafening, deafness***

**deal** | dēl | *v.* To give out playing cards: *to deal the entire deck.* ***deals, dealt, dealing, dealings, dealer***

**dealing** | **dē**′lĭng | *v.* Giving out playing cards: *dealing eight cards to a player.* [see *deal*]

**decide** | dĭ **sīd**′ | *v.* To make up one's mind; make a decision: *to decide on the answer.* ***decides, decided, deciding, decision***

**deed** | dēd | *n.* An act or a thing done: *a deed for charity.* ***deeds, deeded***

**delay** | dĭ **lā**′ | *v.* To put off until a later time: *to delay the game.* ***delays, delayed, delaying***

**delayed** | dĭ **lād**′ | *v.* Put off until a later time: *delayed his arrival by two hours.* [see *delay*]

**depart** | dĭ **pärt**′ | *v.* To leave: *will depart at noon.* ***departs, departed, departing, departure***

**depend** | dĭ **pĕnd′** | *v.* To rely on or trust: *will depend on the coach for help.* ***depends, depended, depending, dependable, dependably, dependence, dependency, dependent***

**desert** | **dĕz′**ərt | *n.* A dry, sandy region without trees: *camels on the desert.* ***deserts, deserted, deserting, deserter, desertion***

differ | **dĭf′**ər | *v.* To be unlike: *to differ in opinion.* ***differs, differed, differing, different, differently, difference***

**different** | **dĭf′**ər ənt | *adj.* Unlike or separate: *different from other animals.* [see *differ*]

**direct** | dĭ **rĕkt′** | *v.* To conduct, manage, or guide: *can direct the orchestra.* ***directs, directed, directing, director, directly, direction, directional, directness***

**ditch** | dĭch | *n.* A long, narrow trench dug in the earth: *filled the ditch.* ***ditches, ditched, ditching***

**divide** | dĭ **vīd′** | *v.* **1.** To perform the mathematical operation of division on a number: *will divide 20 by 5.* **2.** To split up and give out: *to divide the pencils among the fifth-grade students.* ***divides, divided, dividing, dividend, divider, division, divisor***

**doctor** | **dŏk′**tər | *n.* A person who treats the sick: *the doctor who treated my cold.* ***doctors, doctored, doctoring***

**doesn't** | **dŭz′**ənt | Contraction for *does not: doesn't need help.*

**dollar** | **dŏl′**ər | *n.* A unit of money in the United States, equal to 100 cents: *a dollar for the pen.* ***dollars***

**don't** | dōnt | Contraction for *do not: if you don't leave now.*

**double** | **dŭb′**əl | *adv.* Two together: *rode double on the ski lift. adj.* Twice as much: *double amount.* ***doubles, doubled, doubling, doubly***

**downstairs** | doun′**stârz′** | *adv.* To or on a lower floor: *will go downstairs.*

**dozen** | **dŭz′**ən | *n.* Twelve: *will buy a dozen.* ***dozens***

draw | drô | *v.* To sketch or paint: *will draw a picture.* ***draws, drew, drawn, drawing, drawer***

**drawing** | **drô′**ĭng | *adj.* For drawing: *the drawing markers. v.* Sketching or painting: *is drawing your portrait.* [see *draw*]

**drawn** | drôn | *v.* Sketched or painted: *has drawn several trees.* [see *draw*]

dress | drĕs | *n.* Clothes: *in warm dress.* ***dresses, dressed, dressing, dresser, dressers***

**dresser** | **drĕs′**ər | *n.* A chest of drawers for clothes: *shirts in the dresser.* [see *dress*]

**dried** | drīd | *adj.* Without wetness: *a dried grape. v.* Got rid of wetness: *dried the clothes outside.* [see *dry*]

drop | drŏp | *v.* To fall or let fall: *will drop the hot potato.* ***drops, dropped, dropping, dropper***

**dropped** | drŏpt | *v.* Let fall: *dropped the eggs.* [see *drop*]

dry | drī | *adj.* Not wet or damp: *dry clothes. v.* To get rid of wetness: *to dry the dishes.* ***dries, dried, drying, drier, driest, dryly, dryness***

**due** | do͞o | *adj.* Expected: *if the plane is due soon.* ***dues***

**duties** | **do͞o′**tēz | *n.* Tasks: *duties of the job.* [see *duty*]

duty | **do͞o′**tē | *n.* What a person should do: *your duty to help with the housework.* ***duties, dutiful, dutifully***

## E

east | ēst | *n.* The direction of the sunrise: *toward the east.* ***eastern, Easterner, eastward, easterly***

ă pat / ā pay / â care / ä father / ĕ pet / ē be / ĭ pit / ī pie / î fierce / ŏ pot / ō go / ô paw, for / oi oil / o͝o book / o͞o boot / ou out / ŭ cut / û fur / *th* the / th thin / hw which / zh vision / ə ago, item, pencil, atom, circus

**eastern** | ē′stərn | *adj.* Of, in, toward, or from the east: *eastern border.* [see *east*]

**easy** | ē′ zē | *adj.* Not needing much effort: *easy task to complete.* ***easier, easiest, easily, easiness***

**edge** | ĕj | *n.* The point where something begins or ends: *the edge of the cliff.* ***edges, edged, edging, edgy***

**eighteen** | ā′tēn′ | *adj.* Eight more than ten: *eighteen roses.* ***eighteenth, eighteenths***

**eighty** | ā′tē | *adj.* Eight times ten: *eighty days.* ***eighties, eightieth***

**elbow** | ĕl′ bō | *n.* The joint between the lower and the upper arm: *scraped my elbow.* ***elbows***

**electricity** | ĭ lĕk trĭs′ĭ tē | *n.* A form of energy in subatomic particles, able to produce light, motion, and heat: *a car run by electricity.* ***electric, electrical, electrify, electrifies, electrified, electrifying, electrocute, electrician***

**elephant** | ĕl′ə fənt | *n.* A large mammal with a long trunk and ivory tusks: *the tusks on an elephant.* ***elephants***

**else** | ĕls | *adj.* More; besides: *someone else to help.*

**empty** | ĕmp′tē | *adj.* Containing nothing: *an empty glass.* ***empties, emptied, emptying, emptiness***

**engine** | ĕn′jən | *n.* A machine that turns energy into motion: *car engine.* ***engines, engineer, engineers, engineered, engineering***

England | ĭng′glənd | *n.* The largest part of Great Britain: *a large stone castle in England.* ***English***

**English** | ĭng′glĭsh | *n.* The language spoken in England, the United States, Canada, and many other countries: *learned to speak English.* [see *England*]

**enough** | ĭ nŭf′ | *n.* The amount needed or wanted: *more than enough for me.*

enter | ĕn′tər | *v.* To go or come into: *will enter the room.* ***enters, entered, entering, entrance***

**entered** | ĕn′tərd | *v.* Went or came into: *entered the cave.* [see *enter*]

**entire** | ĕn tīr′ | *adj.* Whole or total: *raining the entire day.* ***entirely, entirety***

**envied** | ĕn′vēd | *v.* Desired what someone else has: *envied his artistic talent.* [see *envy*]

envy | ĕn′vē | *v.* To desire what someone else has: *to envy her basketball skill.* ***envies, envied, envying, envious, enviously***

**erect** | ĭ rĕkt′ | *v.* To build: *will erect a home.* *adj.* Up straight: *erect posture.* ***erects, erected, erecting, erectly***

**escape** | ĭ skāp′ | *v.* To get away from a place of imprisonment or danger: *to escape from jail.* *n.* The act of leaving a place of imprisonment or danger: *the daring escape from the castle.* ***escapes, escaped, escaping, escapee, escapist***

**everywhere** | ĕv′rē hwâr′ | *adv.* In all places: *searched everywhere.*

**except** | ĕk sĕpt′ | *prep.* Other than: *everyone except me.* ***excepts, excepted, excepting, exception, exceptional, exceptionally***

**excite** | ĭk sīt′ | *v.* To stir up the feelings of: *will excite her curiosity.* ***excites, excited, exciting, excitedly, excitement, excitable***

**exciting** | ĭk sī′tĭng | *adj.* Stirring or creating excitement: *an exciting adventure.* [see *excite*]

**excuse** | ĭk skyōōs′ | *n.* A true or untrue reason that is given: *an excuse for leaving school early.* ***excuses, excused, excusing, excusable***

**export** | ĕk′spôrt | *n.* Articles sent out of a country for sale in another country: *an export of beef.* *v.* To send articles out of a country for sale in another country: *will export a ton of grain.* ***exports, exported, exporting, exporter, exportation***

## F

**fact** | făkt | *n.* Something known to be true: *proved this to be a fact.* ***facts, factual, factually***

**factory** | **făk**'tə rē | *n.* A building where goods are made: *clothing factory.* ***factories***

**faint** | fānt | *v.* To lose consciousness for a short time: *will faint from the heat.* ***faints, fainted, fainting, fainter, faintest, faintly***

fair |fâr | *adj.* Honest and just: *a fair decision.* ***fairs, fairer, fairest, fairly, fairness***

**fairly** | **fâr**'lē | *adv.* Honestly and justly: *spoke fairly of her.* [see *fair*]

**false** | fôls | *adj.* Not true: *a false statement.* ***falsely, falsify, falsified, falsifying, falsehood***

fame | fām | *n.* The fact of being well-known: *the actor's fame.* ***famed, famous, famously***

**families** | **făm**'ə lēz | *n.* More than one family: *two new families on the street.* [see *family*]

family | **făm**'ə lē | *n.* Parents and their children: *large family.* ***families***

**famous** | **fā**'məs | *adj.* Well-known: *a famous author.* [see *fame*]

**fancy** | **făn**'sē | *adj.* Decorated; not plain: *fancy clothes.* ***fancies, fancied, fancying, fancier, fanciest, fanciful***

**fare** | fâr | *n.* The price charged to ride a bus, train, airplanc, etc.: *money for cab fare.* ***fares, fared, faring***

**fasten** | **făs**'ən | *v.* To join, connect, or tie together: *will fasten the shoelaces.* ***fastens, fastened, fastening, fastener***

**favor** | **fā**'vər | *n.* An act of kindness: *returned the favor.* ***favors, favored, favoring, favorable, favorably, favoritism, favorite***

fear | fîr | *v.* To be afraid of: *to fear snakes.* ***fears, feared, fearing, fearful, fearfully, fearless***

**fearful** | **fîr**'fəl | *adj.* Frightened or scared: *fearful of thunder and lightning.* [see *fear*]

**feather** | **fĕ*th***'ər | *n.* One of the light growths that cover a bird's skin: *a pigeon feather.* ***feathers, feathered, feathering, feathery***

**festival** | **fĕs**'tə vəl | *n.* A time of merriment, rejoicing, and feasting, in memory of an important event: *a spring festival.* [see *festive*]

festive | **fĕs**'tĭv | *adj.* Happy or merry: *a festive occasion.* ***festively, festivity, festival, festivals***

fifteen | fĭf **tēn**' | *n.* The number after fourteen: *a box of fifteen.* ***fifteenth, fifteenths***

**fifteenth** | fĭf **tēnth**' | *n.* One of fifteen equal parts: *fifteenth in line.* *adj.* Next after the fourteenth: *the fifteenth time.* [see *fifteen*]

**fifth** | fĭfth | *n.* One of five equal parts: *a fifth of the pie.* *adj.* Next after the fourth: *their fifth pet.* [see *five*]

file | fīl | *v.* To sort books, papers, etc., in a useful order: *will file the accident reports.* ***files, filed, filing, filer***

**filing** | **fī**'lĭng | *v.* Sorting books, papers, etc., in a useful order: *filing the letters.* [see *file*]

**final** | **fī**'nəl | *adj.* Last in a series: *the final chapter.* ***finals, finally, finalize, finalist***

fine | fīn | *adj.* Excellent; very good: *a fine job.* ***fines, fined, fining, finer, finest***

**finest** | **fī**'nĭst | *adj.* The best or the most excellent: *the finest china.* [see *fine*]

**finger** | **fĭng**'gər | *n.* One of the five body parts that extend from the hand: *a ring for your finger.* ***fingers, fingered, fingering***

**finish** | **fĭn**'ĭsh | *n.* An end: *reached the finish last.* *v.* To reach the end of: *will finish the book tomorrow.* ***finishes, finished, finishing, finisher***

**fir** | fûr | *adj.* Of firs: *fir forest.* *n.* An evergreen tree: *planted a fir.* ***firs***

five | fīv | *n.* The number after four: *a group of five.* ***fifth, fifths***

ă pat / ā pay / â care / ä father / ĕ pet / ē be / ĭ pit / ī pie / î fierce / ŏ pot / ō go / ô paw, for / oi oil / ŏŏ book / ōō boot / ou out / ŭ cut / û fur / *th* the / th thin / hw which / zh vision / ə ago, item, pencil, atom, circus

**flashlight** | **flăsh**′līt′ | *n.* A small, portable lamp, operated by batteries: *flashlight in the tent.* ***flashlights***

**flew** | flo͞o | *v.* Moved through air with wings: *flew to Denver.* [see *fly*]

**flight** | flīt | *n.* **1.** An airplane that makes scheduled trips: *will board the next flight.* **2.** A set of steps or stairs leading from one floor or landing to the next: *one flight up.* ***flights***

**flood** | flŭd | *n.* A great flow of water over what is usually dry: *a flood near the river.* ***floods, flooded, flooding***

fly | flī | *v.* To move through air with wings: *geese fly.* ***flies, flew, flown, flying, flier***

fool | fo͞ol | *n.* A person who acts in a silly manner or without sense: *a fool to drive so fast.* ***fools, fooled, fooling, foolish, foolishly, foolishness***

**foolish** | **fo͞o**′lĭsh | *adj.* In a silly manner; without sense: *foolish action.* [see *fool*]

**forbid** | fər **bĭd**′ | *v.* To order not to do: *to forbid me from staying up late.* ***forbids, forbade, forbidding, forbidden***

**forever** | fôr **ĕv**′ər | *n.* A length of time that never ends: *strong enough to last forever.*

form | fôrm | *v.* To make or shape: *will form the clay.* ***forms, formed, forming, formal, formally, formalize, formality, formation***

**formed** | fôrmd | *v.* Made or shaped: *formed the cans into a pyramid.* [see *form*]

**forward** | **fôr**′wərd | *adv.* Ahead: *moving forward.* ***forwards, forwarded, forwarding, forwardness***

**foul** | foul | *n.* An unfair play in sports: *a foul in left field. adj.* In sports, against the rules of the game: *foul ball.* ***fouls, fouled, fouling, foulest***

**fountain** | **foun**′tən | *n.* An upward jet of water: *threw coins into the fountain.* ***fountains***

freckle | **frĕk**′əl | *n.* A small brown spot on the skin: *one freckle on her nose.* ***freckles, freckled, freckling***

**freckles** | **frĕk**′əlz | *n.* More than one freckle: *freckles on my arms.* [see *freckle*]

free | frē | *adj.* Not under control of another: *free country.* ***frees, freed, freeing, freely, freedom***

**freedom** | **frē**′dəm | *n.* The state of being free: *freedom from fear.* [see *free*]

**freeze** | frēz | *v.* **1.** To become solid by cold: *since water will freeze quickly.* **2.** To become perfectly still: *will freeze in your tracks.* ***freezes, froze, freezing, frozen, freezer***

friend | frĕnd | *n.* A person one knows or likes: *a kind, helpful friend.* ***friends, friendly, friendlier, friendliest, friendliness, friendless, friendship***

**friendly** | **frĕnd**′lē | *adj.* Kind; of a friend: *a friendly smile.* [see *friend*]

**fright** | frīt | *n.* Sudden terror or fear: *frozen in fright.* ***frights, frighten, frightens, frightened, frightening, frightful***

**frozen** | **frō**′zən | *adj.* Turned solid by cold: *frozen vegetables.* [see *freeze*]

**further** | **fûr**′*th*ər | *adv.* At or to a greater amount or extent: *won't speak further.* ***furthers, furthered, furthering, furthest, furthermore***

## G

**gain** | gān | *v.* To increase in weight: *did gain five pounds. n.* An increase: *a gain of ten points.* ***gains, gained, gaining, gainful, gainfully***

**gallon** | **găl**′ən | *n.* A liquid measure equal to four quarts: *a gallon of milk.* ***gallons***

**garage** | gə **räzh**′ | *n.* A building where cars are parked: *two cars in the garage.* ***garages, garaged, garaging***

**gasoline** | **găs**′ə lēn′ | *n.* A fuel made from petroleum or from gas in the earth: *gasoline for the engine.*

gather | **găth**′ər | *v.* To come together in a group: *will gather in the gym for the basketball game.* ***gathers, gathered, gathering, gatherings, gatherer***

**gathering** | găth′ər ĭng | *v.* Coming together in a group: *gathering in a park. n.* A group of people: *a gathering of students.* [see *gather*]

**general** | jĕn′ər əl | *adj.* Not detailed or precise: *only a general plan. n.* The highest ranking army officer: *a general reviewing the troops.* ***generals, generally, generality, generalization***

**golf** | gŏlf | *n.* An outdoor game played on a course having nine or eighteen holes spaced far apart. The player uses clubs to hit a ball into one hole after another, taking as few strokes as possible: *clubs for playing golf.* ***golfs, golfing, golfer***

good | go͝od | *adj.* Kind: *a good person.* ***goodness***

**goodness** | go͝od′ nĭs | *interj.* An exclamation that shows surprise: *Oh my goodness! n.* Kindness: *from the goodness of my heart.* [see *good*]

**govern** | gŭv′ərn | *v.* To rule through accepted laws: *to govern the people.* ***governs, governed, governing, government, governor, governors***

**grace** | grās | *n.* Ease and beauty of manner or movement: *dances with grace.* ***graces, graced, gracing, graceful, gracefulness, gracefully, graceless, gracelessly***

**grandfather** | grănd′fä′thər | *n.* The father of one's father or mother: *worked with my grandfather.* ***grandfathers***

grape | grāp | *n.* A berrylike fruit that grows in bunches on vines: *ripe grapes.* ***grapes***

**grapefruit** | grāp′fro͞ot′ | *n.* A round yellow citrus fruit: *ate grapefruit.* ***grapefruits***

**grapes** | grāps | *n.* More than one grape: *purple grapes.* [see *grape*]

**grasp** | grăsp | *n.* A strong, firm hold: *a grasp on the handle.* ***grasps, grasped, grasping***

**gravel** | grăv′əl | *adj.* Made of gravel: *gravel path. n.* Pebbles and small pieces of rock: *a driveway of gravel.* ***gravels, graveled, graveling, gravelly***

**graze** | grāz | *v.* To feed on live grass: *will graze in the meadow.* ***grazes, grazed, grazing***

great | grāt | *adj.* Big in size, amount, or extent: *the great lion.* ***greater, greatest, greatly, greatness***

**greatest** | grā′tĭst | *adj.* Biggest in size, amount, or extent: *picked the greatest watermelon.* [see *great*]

group | gro͞op | *n.* A number of persons or things gathered together: *a group of men.* ***groups, grouped, grouping***

**groups** | gro͞ops | *n.* More than one group: *groups of numbers.* [see *group*]

grow | grō | *v.* To become larger: *will grow from the bud.* ***grows, grew, growing, grown, growth, grower***

**growl** | groul | *n.* An angry rumbling sound: *the lion's growl of pain.* ***growls, growled, growling, growler***

**growth** | grōth | *n.* The amount that has become bigger: *growth of two inches since last week.* [see *grow*]

**guard** | gärd | *n.* A person who watches over or protects another person or a place: *the king's trusted guard.* ***guards, guarded, guarding***

**guide** | gīd | *v.* To direct or show the way: *will guide the campers. n.* Someone who leads the way: *the museum guide.* ***guides, guided, guiding, guidance***

**gulf** | gŭlf | *n.* An arm of an ocean or sea that is partly surrounded by land: *a cool breeze from the gulf.* ***gulfs***

**hadn't** | hăd′nt | Contraction for *had not: hadn't a chance of winning.*

ă pat / ā pay / â care / ä father / ĕ pet / ē be / ĭ pit / ī pie / î fierce / ŏ pot / ō go / ô paw, for / oi oil / o͝o book / o͞o boot / ou out / ŭ cut / û fur / *th* the / th thin / hw which / zh vision / ə ago, item, pencil, atom, circus

**Halloween** | hăl′ō **ēn**′ | *adj.* Of or for Halloween: *Halloween treats. n.* The evening of October 31, observed by children playing pranks and asking for treats: *costume for Halloween.*

**handful** | **hănd**′fo͝ol′ | *n.* The amount that can be held in one's hand: *handful of raisins and nuts.* ***handfuls***

**handsome** | **hăn**′səm | *adj.* Good-looking: *a handsome suit.* ***handsomer, handsomest, handsomely, handsomeness***

**harbor** | **här**′bər | *n.* A coastal area of water used to shelter boats: *sailed into the crowded harbor.* ***harbors, harbored, harboring***

**hardware** | **härd**′wâr′ | *adj.* Of or related to hardware: *hardware supplies. n.* Articles made of metal: *hardware in the toolbox.* ***hardwares***

**harvest** | **här**′vĭst | *n.* The gathering of crops: *a harvest of grain.* ***harvests, harvested, harvesting, harvester***

**hasn't** | **hăz**′nt | Contraction for *has not: hasn't any idea.*

**hatch** | hăch | *n.* A group of young brought forth from eggs: *a hatch of turtles. v.* To come out of an egg at birth: *will hatch from the eggs soon.* ***hatches, hatched, hatching, hatchery***

**headquarters** | **hĕd**′kwôr′tərz | *n.* An office from which a commander sends orders: *police headquarters.*

**health** | hĕlth | *n.* A person's physical condition: *in good health.* ***healthy, healthier, healthiest, healthful, healthiness***

**heap** | hēp | *n.* A large pile of things thrown one on another: *a heap of clothes.* ***heaps, heaped, heaping***

**heavy** | **hĕv**′ē | *adj.* Difficult to lift; not light: *carried the heavy suitcase.* ***heavier, heaviest, heavily, heaviness***

**helmet** | **hĕl**′mĭt | *n.* A covering of sturdy material worn to protect the head: *put on an astronaut's space helmet.* ***helmets, helmeted***

help | hĕlp | *v.* To aid; do what is useful: *will help me clean.* ***helps, helped, helping, helpful, helpfully, helpfulness, helpless***

**helpful** | **hĕlp**′fəl | *adj.* Providing aid; useful: *a helpful worker.* [see *help*]

**herd** | hûrd | *n.* A group of one kind of animal that stays or is kept together: *a herd of cows.* ***herds, herded, herding, herder***

**holiday** | **hŏl**′ĭ dā′ | *n.* A day when one does not work: a day to celebrate an event, person, etc.: *a holiday at the ocean.* ***holidays***

**honest** | **ŏn**′ĭst | *adj.* Truthful and fair: *an honest judge.* ***honestly, honesty***

horizon | hə **rī**′zən | *n.* The line where the earth and sky appear to meet: *the sun sinking below the horizon.* ***horizons, horizontal, horizontally***

**horizontal** | hôr′ĭ **zŏn**′tl | *adj.* Flat or level: *a horizontal sheet of rock.* [see *horizon*]

**hose** | hōz | *n.* A tube of flexible material used for carrying liquid over short distances: *the garden hose.* ***hoses, hosed, hosing***

**household** | **hous**′hōld′ | *adj.* Of a household: *household chores. n.* All the people living together in a house or residence: *a happy household.* ***households, householder***

**however** | hou **ĕv**′ər | *adv.* No matter how: *however busy you are.*

**howl** | houl | *n.* A shout or a long, loud cry: *a howl of pain.* ***howls, howled, howling, howler***

**husband** | **hŭz**′bənd | *n.* A man who is married: *the husband of that woman.* ***husbands***

## I

**I'd** | īd | Contraction for *I should, I would, or I had: if I'd wait.*

**ideal** | ī **dē**′əl | *adj.* Perfect: *an ideal day for tennis.* ***ideals, ideally, idealism, idealist, idealistic***

**I'll** | īl | Contraction for *I will* or *I shall: when I'll leave.*

improve | ĭm **pro͞ov′** | *v.* To make or do better: *to improve your chances of winning.* ***improves, improved, improving, improvement***

**improved** | ĭm **pro͞ovd′** | *v.* Made or did better: *improved her skill.* [see *improve*]

**industry** | **ĭn′**də strē | *n.* All of manufacturing, business, and trade: *a city with declining industry.* ***industries, industrious, industrial, industrialist, industrialism***

inform | ĭn **fôrm′** | *v.* To give facts or knowledge to: *will inform us of your plans.* ***informs, informed, informing, informative, information, informational, informer***

**information** | ĭn′fər **mā′**shən | *n.* Facts or knowledge received or given: *information on farming.* [see *inform*]

**install** | ĭn **stôl′** | *v.* To set in place or adjust for use: *will install the washing machine.* ***installs, installed, installing, installation, installment***

**intend** | ĭn **tĕnd′** | *v.* To plan or have in mind: *to intend to start early.* ***intends, intended, intending***

**intent** | ĭn **tĕnt′** | *n.* An aim or purpose: *good intent.* ***intents, intently, intention, intentional, intentionally***

**interest** | **ĭn′**tər ĭst | *n.* Curiosity: *an interest in whales.* ***interests, interested, interesting, interestingly***

**invent** | ĭn **vĕnt′** | *v.* To make up or discover for the first time: *to invent a gasless car.* ***invents, invented, inventing, inventive, inventiveness, inventor, invention***

**invite** | ĭn **vīt′** | *v.* To ask someone to take part in something: *to invite friends to a special birthday party.* ***invites, invited, inviting, invitation***

iron | **ī′**ərn | *v.* To smooth clothing with a heated iron: *will iron the shirt.* ***irons, ironed, ironing***

**ironing** | **ī′**ər nĭng | *n.* Clothing to be ironed: *a stack of ironing. v.* Smoothing clothing with a heated iron: *ironing a dress.* [see *iron*]

**item** | **ī′**təm | *n.* A single object or piece: *selected each item very carefully.* ***items, itemize, itemized, itemizing***

**I've** | īv | Contraction for *I have: when I've gone to the store.*

## J

**jacket** | **jăk′**ĭt | *n.* A short coat: *fur jacket.* ***jackets***

**jelly** | **jĕl′**ē | *n.* A soft, clear food made by boiling fruit juice and sugar with a thickener: *toast with jelly.* ***jellies, jellied, jell, jells, jelled, jelling***

joke | jōk | *n.* Something done or said to cause laughter: *a silly joke.* ***jokes, joked, joking, jokingly, joker***

**jokes** | jōks | *n.* More than one joke: *laughed at all her jokes.* [see *joke*]

**judge** | jŭj | *v.* To decide or settle a contest or issue: *to judge the tennis match. n.* A person who watches over a contest and decides the winner: *the judge on the game show.* ***judges, judged, judging, judgment***

juice | jo͞os | *n.* The liquid in meat, vegetables, or fruits: *orange juice.* ***juices, juicy, juicier, juiciest, juiciness***

**juicy** | **jo͞o′** sē | *adj.* Full of juice: *juicy peach.* [see *juice*]

**jungle** | **jŭng′**gəl | *n.* An area thickly overgrown with tropical trees and plants: *tigers in the jungle.* ***jungles***

**junior** | **jo͞o′**nyər | *n.* A student in the next-to-last year of high school or college: *a junior in our school. adj.* Made up of or for younger people: *junior membership.* ***Jr., juniors***

ă **pat** / ā **pay** / â **care** / ä **father** / ĕ **pet** / ē **be** / ĭ **pit** / ī **pie** / î **fierce** / ŏ **pot** / ō **go** / ô **paw**, **for** / oi **oil** / o͝o **book** / o͞o **boot** / ou **out** / ŭ **cut** / û **fur** / *th* **the** / th **thin** / hw **which** / zh vi**s**ion / ə **a**go, it**e**m, penc**i**l, at**o**m, circ**u**s

# K

**kettle** | kĕt′l | *n.* A metal pot for boiling liquids: *kettle of soup.* ***kettles***

**kitchen** | kĭch′ən | *adj.* Related to a kitchen: *kitchen stove. n.* A room where food is cooked: *the stove in the kitchen.* ***kitchens***

knife | nīf | *n.* A flat metal blade fastened to a handle and used for spreading or cutting: *the butter knife.* ***knives, knifed, knifing***

**knives** | nīvz | *n.* More than one knife: *steak knives.* [see *knife*]

**knock** | nŏk | *n.* A noise made by a hit: *a light knock on the door.* ***knocks, knocked, knocking, knocker***

know | nō | *v.* **1.** To have the facts about: *to know the problem.* **2.** To be aware of: *does know the danger of fire.* ***knows, knew, knowing, knowingly, known, knowledge***

**knowing** | nō′ĭng | *n.* Awareness: *because knowing isn't always believing. adj.* Having awareness or knowledge: *a knowing scholar.* [see *know*]

**known** | nōn | *v.* Been aware of: *had known the outcome. adj.* Accepted in general: *known for his honesty.* [see *know*]

# L

**ladies** | lā′dēz | *n.* More than one lady: *the ladies on the committee.* [see *lady*]

lady | lā′dē | *n.* Any woman referred to in a polite way: *the lady in charge.* ***ladies***

**language** | lăng′gwĭj | *adj.* Of languages: *language class. n.* The speech and writing that a nation or a particular group uses to communicate: *learned a new language.* ***languages***

large | lärj | *adj.* Big: *a large apple.* ***larger, largest, largely, largeness***

**largely** | lärj′lē | *adv.* Mostly: *largely to blame.* [see *large*]

**leather** | lĕth′ər | *n.* The cleaned, tanned skin of an animal: *leather for shoes.* ***leathers, leathered, leathery***

**lemon** | lĕm′ən | *adj.* Flavored with lemon: *lemon cookies. n.* A yellow citrus fruit: *lemon for the tea.* ***lemons, lemony***

**lemonade** | lĕm′ə nād′ | *n.* A drink made by mixing lemon juice, water, and sugar: *lemonade on a hot day.*

**liberty** | lĭb′ər tē | *n.* Freedom; independence: *fought for our country's liberty and justice.* ***liberties, liberate, liberates, liberated, liberating, liberation, liberator***

**limb** | lĭm | *n.* A large branch of a tree: *the limb that broke.* ***limbs, limber***

**limp** | lĭmp | *n.* An irregular way of walking that results from an injured leg: *the patient's limp.* ***limps, limped, limping, limper***

line | līn | *v.* To sew a layer of cloth inside a jacket, dress, etc.: *will line the wool coat.* ***lines, lined, lining, liner***

**lining** | lī′nĭng | *n.* The layer of cloth inside a jacket, dress, etc.: *a jacket's lining.* [see *line*]

**listen** | lĭs′ən | *v.* To try to hear something: *will listen to the speech.* ***listens, listened, listening, listener***

live | lĭv | *adj.* Alive: *live plant.* ***lively, livelier, liveliest, lives, lived, living, livable, lifeless, life***

**lively** | līv′lē | *adj.* Filled with life or action: *a lively crowd.* [see *live*]

load | lōd | *v.* To put cargo in or on: *will load ten boxes onto the truck.* ***unload, unloads, unloaded, unloading***

loaf | lōf | *v.* To spend time doing nothing: *to loaf all day.* ***loafs, loafed, loafing, loafer***

**loafing** | lō′fĭng | *n.* The act of spending time doing nothing: *a day for loafing.* [see *loaf*]

**loan** | lōn | *n.* Money lent to be paid back with interest: *a loan to make home repairs.* ***loans, loaned, loaning***

**lodge** | lŏj | *n.* A countrylike house where people stay for short periods of time: *a ski lodge.* ***lodges, lodged, lodging, lodger***

lone | lōn | *adj.* Being without others: *a lone star in the sky.* ***lonely, lonelier, loneliest, loneliness, loner, lonesome***

**lonely** | **lōn**'lē | *adj.* Sad at being without others: *lonely child at camp.* [see *lone*]

**lonesome** | **lōn**'səm | *adj.* Sad at being without others: *lonesome man.*[see *lone*]

**loose** | lo͞os | *adj.* Not tight or fastened: *loose sweater.* ***looses, loosed, loosing, loosen, loosens, loosened, loosening, looser, loosest, loosely, looseness***

# M

**machine** | mə **shēn**' | *n.* A device that uses energy to perform a task: *sewing machine.* ***machines, machinery, machinist***

**magazine** | **măg**'ə zēn | *adj.* Of or for magazines: *magazine stand. n.* A publication of stories and articles, issued regularly: *sports magazine.* ***magazines***

**maintain** | mān **tān**' | *v.* To keep up: *to maintain a friendship.* ***maintains, maintained, maintaining, maintenance***

**married** | **măr**'ēd | *v.* Brought together as wife and husband: *married today.* [see *marry*]

marry | **măr**'ē | *v.* To bring together as wife and husband: *will marry the couple.* ***marries, married, marrying, marriage***

match | măch | *n.* A piece of wood or cardboard coated at one end with a mixture that catches fire when rubbed on a rough or special surface: *a match to light the oven.* ***matches, matched, matching, matchless***

**matches** | **măch**'ĭz | *n.* More than one match: *box of kitchen matches.* [see *match*]

**mayor** | **mā**'ər | *n.* The person who heads the government of a city or town: *was elected mayor.* ***mayors, mayoral***

**meadow** | **mĕd**'ō | *n.* Grassy land, usually used for growing hay or as pasture: *cows in the meadow.* ***meadows***

**meantime** | **mēn**'tīm' | *n.* The same time: *in the meantime. adv.* At the same time: *Meantime, listen carefully.*

**meanwhile** | **mēn**'hwīl' | *n.* The same time: *in the meanwhile. adv.* At the same time: *Meanwhile, rest here.*

**member** | **mĕm**'bər | *n.* A person who belongs to a group: *member of the club.* ***members, membership***

**mention** | **mĕn**'shən | *n.* The act of speaking about or referring to: *a mention of your work. v.* To speak about or refer to: *will mention my name.* ***mentions, mentioned, mentioning, mentionable***

**merchant** | **mûr**'chənt | *n.* A person who buys and sells to make a profit: *goods from the local merchant.* ***merchants, merchandise***

**message** | **mĕs**'ĭj | *n.* Spoken or written words sent from one person to another: *a message to call home.* ***messages, messenger, messengers***

**midnight** | **mĭd**'nīt' | *n.* Twelve o'clock at night: *arrived at midnight.* [see *night*]

**million** | **mĭl**'yən | *adj.* One thousand thousand: *a million people. n.* A number equal to one thousand thousand: *counted to a million.* ***millions, millionth, millionaire***

**minute** | **mĭn**'ĭt | *n.* Sixty seconds: *one minute ago.* ***minutes***

**mirror** | **mĭr**'ər | *n.* A glass surface that reflects images clearly: *saw himself in the mirror.* ***mirrors, mirrored, mirroring***

**mistake** | mĭ **stāk**' | *n.* An error: *a mistake on the test.* ***mistakes, mistook, mistaking, mistaken, mistakenly, mistakable***

**model** | **mŏd**'l | *adj.* Built as a small-scale copy: *a model plane. n.* A small-scale copy of something: *a model of a sailboat.* ***models, modeled, modeling***

ă **pat** / ā **pay** / â **care** / ä **father** / ĕ **pet** / ē **be** / ĭ **pit** / ī **pie** / î **fierce** / ŏ **pot** / ō **go** / ô **paw**, **for** / oi **oil** / o͝o **book** / o͞o **boot** / ou **out** / ŭ **cut** / û **fur** / *th* **the** / th **thin** / hw **which** / zh **vision** / ə **ago, item, pencil, atom, circus**

**moment** | **mō**'mənt | *n.* A very brief space of time: *will wait a moment.* ***moments, momentary***

month | **mŭnth** | *n.* One of the twelve divisions of a year: *month of May.* ***months, monthly***

**monthly** | **mŭnth**'lē | *adv.* Every month: *visited monthly.* [see *month*]

**mood** | mo͞od | *n.* A general state of mind or feeling: *in a good mood.* ***moods, moody, moodiness***

**moss** | môs | *n.* Small green plants that form a dense growth on ground, trees, or rocks: *moss on the forest trees.* ***mosses, mossy***

**motor** | **mō**'tər | *n.* An engine that produces motion: *a motor on the boat.* ***motors, motored, motoring, motorize, motorist***

**mountain** | **moun**'tən | *adj.* Of mountains: *mountain air.* *n.* A steep hill: *climbed the mountain.* ***mountains, mountainous, mountaineer, mountainside***

mud | mŭd | *n.* Wet earth that is soft and sticky: *stuck in the mud.* ***muddy, muddies, muddied, muddying, muddier, muddiest***

**muddy** | **mŭd**'ē | *adj.* Covered with mud: *muddy floor.* [see *mud*]

**multiply** | **mŭl**'tə plī | *v.* To add a number to itself a certain number of times: *will multiply 16 by 20.* ***multiplies, multiplied, multiplying, multiple, multiplication, multiplier***

music | **myo͞o**'zĭk | *n.* The art of combining sounds that are pleasing or meaningful to a listener: *the loud music of the band.* ***musical, musically, musician***

**musician** | myo͞o **zĭsh**'ən | *n.* A person skilled in the performance or composition of music: *the musician at the piano.* [see *music*]

# N

**nation** | **nā**'shən | *n.* The land occupied by a country: *a small nation in Europe.* ***nations, national, nationally, nationalist, nationality***

**nature** | **nā**'chər | *n.* Everything except anything made by human beings: *the beauties of nature.* ***natures, natured, natural, naturally, naturalness***

**naughty** | **nô**'tē | *adj.* Bad: *a naughty way to act.* ***naughtier, naughtiest, naughtily, naughtiness***

**navy** | **nā**'vē | *n.* **1.** A dark-blue color: *a dress of navy.* **2.** The branch of a nation's armed forces organized for sea warfare: *trained in a navy.* ***navies, naval***

**nearby** | **nîr**'bī' | *adj.* Close by: *nearby forest.*

**necktie** | **nĕk**'tī | *n.* A narrow piece of cloth worn under a shirt collar and tied in front: *silk necktie.* ***neckties***

**needle** | **nē**'dl | *n.* **1.** A slender sewing tool, pointed at one end and with a hole in the other end to pass a thread through: *sewing needle.* **2.** A slender rod, usually, used in pairs, for knitting: *plastic knitting needle.* ***needles, needled, needling***

neighbor | **nā**'bər | *n.* A person who lives next door or nearby: *the neighbor to the left.* ***neighbors, neighboring, neighborly, neighborliness, neighborhood, neighborhoods***

**neighborhood** | **nā**'bər ho͝od' | *n.* The people living in a particular area: *a neighborhood of adults.* [see *neighbor*]

**nephew** | **nĕf**'yo͞o | *n.* The son of a person's brother or sister: *his oldest nephew.* ***nephews***

newspaper | **no͞oz**'pā'pər | *n.* A daily or weekly publication printed on large paper and containing articles, pictures, advertisements, etc.: *the newspaper lying on the front porch.* ***newspapers***

**newspapers** | **no͞oz**'pā pərz | *n.* More than one newspaper: *five different newspapers.* [see *newspaper*]

night | nīt | *n.* The hours of darkness between sunset and sunrise: *a rainy night.* ***nights, nightly, midnight, midnights***

nine | nīn | *n.* The number after eight: *a total of nine.* ***nines, ninth, ninths***

**ninth** | nīnth | *adj.* After the eighth: *the ninth child.* [see *nine*]

north | nôrth | *n.* The direction to the right of the setting sun: *snow to the north.* ***northern, Northerner, northerly, northward***

**northern** | **nôr**′*th*ərn | *adj.* Of, in, toward, or from the north: *traveled to the northern district.* [see *north*]

## O

**odd** | ŏd | *adj.* Of whole numbers that cannot be evenly divided by 2: *the odd numbers 33 and 11.* ***odds, odder, oddest, oddly, oddness, oddity***

**offer** | **ô**′fər | *n.* Something presented as a suggestion, plan, or proposal: *an offer of advice.* ***offers, offered, offering***

**often** | **ô**′fən | *adv.* Frequently: *went there often.* ***oftener, oftenest***

**operate** | **ŏp**′ə rāt′ | *v.* **1.** To control the running of a machine: *can operate the bulldozer.* **2.** To perform surgery: *will operate on the patient.* ***operates, operated, operating, operator, operation, operational***

**orchard** | **ôr**′chərd | *n.* An area in which fruit trees are grown: *an apple orchard.* ***orchards***

order | **ôr**′dər | *v.* To command or tell what to do: *will order you to leave.* ***orders, ordered, ordering, orderly***

**ordered** | **ôr**′dərd | *v.* Commanded or told what to do: *ordered the carpenters to keep working.* [see *order*]

**ore** | ôr | *n.* A mineral containing metal for which it is mined: *ore in the mine.* ***ores***

**organ** | **ôr**′gən | *n.* A musical instrument whose sound is produced by air blown through pipes when keys are struck: *played the organ.* ***organs, organist***

**outline** | **out**′līn′ | *n.* A drawing of only the outer edge of something: *drew an outline of the house.* ***outlines, outlined, outlining***

**overcome** | ō′vər **kŭm**′ | *adj.* Exhausted or made helpless: *was overcome with much sadness.* ***overcomes, overcame, overcoming***

**overturn** | ō′vər **tûrn**′ | *v.* To turn upside down: *if the boat will overturn.* ***overturns, overturned, overturning***

**owe** | ō | *v.* **1.** To have to give a sum of: *to owe money.* **2.** To have a duty to give: *does owe us an explanation.* ***owes, owed, owing***

## P

**pajamas** | pə **jä**′məz | *n.* A loose shirt and trousers worn for sleeping: *flannel pajamas.*

**palace** | **păl**′ĭs | *adj.* Related to a palace: *the palace guard. n.* The official home of a royal person: *the queen's palace.* ***palaces***

**palm** | päm | *n.* **1.** The inside surface of the hand, between the fingers and the wrist: *many lines on your palm.* **2.** A tree with a tall trunk, leaves at the top, and no branches: *grow a palm in the yard.* ***palms, palmed, palming, palmist, palmistry***

**parade** | pə **rād**′ | *n.* A march or procession: *a parade on the Fourth of July.* ***parades, paraded, parading***

**pardon** | **pär**′dn | *n.* Forgiveness: *begged his pardon.* ***pardons, pardoned, pardoning, pardonable***

parent | **pâr**′ənt | *n.* A father or mother: *a hug from her parent.* ***parents, parental***

**parents** | **pâr**′ənts | *n.* One's father and mother: *the parents of that child.* [see *parent*]

**parties** | **pär**′tēz | *n.* More than one party: *several holiday parties.* [see *party*]

**partner** | **pärt**′nər | *n.* One of two or more persons involved in an activity: *my skating partner.* ***partners, partnership***

ă pat / ā pay / â care / ä father / ĕ pet / ē be / ĭ pit / ī pie / î fierce / ŏ pot / ō go / ô paw, for / oi oil / o͝o book / o͞o boot / ou out / ŭ cut / û fur / *th* the / th thin / hw which / zh vision / ə ago, item, pencil, atom, circus

party | **pär'tē** | *n.* An event for which a group of people are gathered together to have fun: *a party for the new graduates.* ***parties, partied, partying***

**passenger** | **păs'**ən jər | *n.* One who rides in, but does not drive, a vehicle: *passenger on a bus.* ***passengers***

**pasture** | **păs'**chər | *n.* Grassland on which animals graze: *pasture for the farm animals.* *v.* To graze on grassland: *if the sheep pasture until the sun sets.* ***pastures, pastured, pasturing***

**patch** | păch | *n.* A small area that is different from the area around it: *a patch of burned grass.* *v.* To cover and repair a hole in something with something else: *will patch the potholes.* ***patches, patched, patching***

pay | pā | *v.* To give money to for goods or for work done: *will pay their grocery bills.* ***pays, paid, paying, payable, payment, payments***

**payment** | **pā'**mənt | *n.* An amount paid: *made a weekly payment.* [see *pay*]

**peace** | pēs | *n.* Freedom from war or disorder: *peace after war.* ***peaceful, peacefully, peacefulness***

**people** | **pē'**pəl | *n.* Human beings: *friendly people.* ***peoples, peopled, peopling***

**perfume** | **pûr'**fyo͞om' | *n.* A liquid with a sweet smell: *perfume that smells like roses.* ***perfumes, perfumed, perfumer***

**perhaps** | pər **hăps'** | *adv.* Possibly; maybe: *will perhaps win.*

**period** | **pîr'**ē əd | *n.* The punctuation mark used at the end of some sentences and after most abbreviations: *a period or a question mark.* ***periods, periodical, periodically***

**person** | **pûr'**sən | *n.* A human being: *a friendly person.* ***persons, personal, personally, personalize, personable, personality***

**piano** | pē **ăn'**ō | *n.* A keyboard musical instrument sounded by a hammer striking a wire when a key is struck: *sat at the piano.* ***pianos, pianist***

**piece** | pēs | *n.* A part of something that has been broken or divided: *piece of apple pie.* ***pieces, pieced, piecing***

pilgrim | **pĭl'**grĭm | *n.* A traveler: *pilgrim on a journey.* ***pilgrims, pilgrimage***

**pilgrims** | **pĭl'**grĭmz | *n.* Travelers: *pilgrims heading east.* [see *pilgrim*]

pitch | pĭch | *v.* To throw or toss: *to pitch to the batter.* ***pitches, pitched, pitching, pitcher, pitchers***

**pitcher** | **pĭch'**ər | *n.* The baseball player who throws, or pitches, the ball to the batter: *our team's pitcher.* [see *pitch*]

**plain** | plān | *adj.* Simple; not fancy: *plain clothing.* ***plainer, plainest, plainly, plainness***

plan | plăn | *v.* To think out ahead of time what is to be made or done: *will plan a fun vacation.* ***plans, planned, planning, planner***

**planning** | **plăn'**ĭng | *v.* Thinking out ahead of time what is to be made or done: *planning a cookout for Saturday.* [see *plan*]

**plantation** | plăn **tā'**shən | *n.* A large farm or estate on which workers tend the crops and often live on the same property: *a cotton plantation.* ***plantations***

**plastic** | **plăs'**tĭk | *n.* A chemically made substance that is easily molded or shaped: *a car made of plastic.* ***plastics***

**platform** | **plăt'**fôrm | *n.* A raised, horizontal surface: *platform for the musicians.* ***platforms***

**popular** | **pŏp'**yə lər | *adj.* Liked by many: *a popular book.* ***popularly, popularity***

**potato** | pə **tā'**tō | *n.* An oval, starchy vegetable with a thin skin: *a boiled potato.* ***potatoes***

**powder** | **pou'**dər | *n.* A substance of very tiny particles: *a box of talcum powder.* ***powders, powdered, powdering***

practice | **prăk'**tĭs | *v.* To do many times over to gain skill: *will practice piano lessons daily.* ***practices, practiced, practicing***

**practicing** | **prăk**′tĭs ĭng | *v.* Doing many times over to gain skill: *was practicing my pitching.* [see *practice*]

**praise** | prāz | *n.* Words that express admiration; a compliment: *won praise for her piano playing.* ***praises, praised, praising***

**preach** | prēch | *v.* To lecture or speak to: *will preach about good health.* ***preaches, preached, preaching, preacher***

prepare | prĭ **pâr**′ | *v.* To make or get ready: *to prepare the dinner.* ***prepares, prepared, preparing, preparation***

**preparing** | prĭ **pâr**′ĭng | *v.* Making or getting ready: *preparing to leave.* [see *prepare*]

**president** | **prĕz**′ĭ dənt | *n.* The chief executive of a republic: *was president for four years.* ***presidents, presidential, presidency***

**prince** | prĭns | *n.* The son of a king or queen: *prince of this country.* ***princes, princely, princess***

print | prĭnt | *v.* To form letters or words as they are in printed material: *should print the two messages on white paper.* ***prints, printed, printing, printer***

**printing** | **prĭn**′tĭng | *n.* Letters or words as they are in printed material: *neat and even printing.* –**Printing press**– A machine for rapidly printing the same material onto many sheets of paper. [see *print*]

probable | **prŏb**′ə bəl | *adj.* Likely to occur: *a probable result.* ***probably, probability***

**probably** | **prŏb**′ə blē | *adv.* Most likely: *is probably correct.* [see *probable*]

**problem** | **prŏb**′ləm | *n.* **1.** A troubling question or situation: *the problem of always being late.* **2.** A question to be solved by mathematics: *a hard problem on the math test.* ***problems, problematic***

**product** | **prŏd**′əkt | *n.* **1.** Something made to be sold: *sold the product to a customer.* **2.** An answer from multiplying: *the product of 10 times 20.* ***products, produce, produces, produced, producing, productive, production***

**products** | **prŏd**′əkts | *n.* **1.** Things made to be sold: *farm products.* **2.** Answers from multiplying: *the products of 2 times 4 and 3 times 8.* [see *product*]

**program** | **prō**′grăm | *n.* A plan of what will be done or presented: *followed a program of daily exercise.* ***programs, programmed, programming, programmer***

**promise** | **prŏm**′ĭs | *n.* A declaration binding a person to do or not to do something; a vow: *a promise to be on time.* ***promises, promised, promising***

**pronounce** | prə **nouns**′ | *v.* To make the sounds of by speech: *to pronounce French perfectly.* ***pronounces, pronounced, pronouncing, pronunciation***

**protect** | prə **tĕkt**′ | *v.* To shelter from harm or danger: *seat belts to protect you.* ***protects, protected, protecting, protective, protection, protector***

**protest** | prə **tĕst**′ | *v.* To express objection to something: *to protest the lawyer's comment on the robbery case.* ***protests, protested, protesting, protester***

prove | pro͞ov | *v.* To show that something is true: *will prove I am right.* ***proves, proved, proving, proven, proof***

**proving** | **pro͞o**′vĭng | *v.* Showing that something is true: *is proving the idea.* [see *prove*]

**public** | **pŭb**′lĭk | *n.* The people as a whole: *for the public to decide.* ***publicly, publicize, publicity***

**pumpkin** | **pŭmp**′kĭn | *n.* A large, round fruit used as a vegetable or for pies: *12-pound pumpkin.* ***pumpkins***

ă **pat** / ā **pay** / â **care** / ä **father** / ĕ **pet** / ē **be** / ĭ **pit** / ī **pie** / î **fierce** / ŏ **pot** / ō **go** / ô **paw**, **for** / oi **oil** / o͝o **book** / o͞o **boot** / ou **out** / ŭ **cut** / û **fur** / *th* **the** / th **thin** / hw **which** / zh **vision** / ə **ago**, **item**, **pencil**, **atom**, **circus**

**pupil** | **pyōō**'pəl | *n.* A student: *the kindergarten pupil.* ***pupils***

put | pŏŏt | *v.* To set or place: *will put the dishes on the table.* **–Put on–** To clothe oneself with. ***puts, putting***

**putting** | **pŏŏt**'ĭng | *v.* Setting or placing: *is putting books in a stack.* [see *put*]

**puzzle** | **pŭz**'əl | *n.* A problem or task to be solved for fun: *a wooden puzzle.* ***puzzles, puzzled, puzzling, puzzler***

# Q

**quart** | kwôrt | *n.* A liquid measure equal to one fourth of a gallon: *quart of milk.* ***quarts***

**quarter** | **kwôr**'tər | *n.* A coin worth 25 cents: *a quarter for the bus ride home.* ***quarters, quartered, quartering, quarterly***

**quest** | kwĕst | *n.* A search: *a quest for truth.* ***quests, quested, questing***

**question** | **kwĕs**'chən | *n.* Something asked in order to get information: *a difficult question to answer.* ***questions, questioned, questioning, questionable, questionably, questionnaire, questioner***

quick | kwĭk | *adj.* Fast: *a quick walk.* ***quicker, quickest, quickly, quickness***

**quickly** | **kwĭk**'lē | *adv.* Rapidly: *moving quickly toward us.* [see *quick*]

# R

**racket** | **răk**'ĭt | *n.* An oval frame with interlaced strings and a handle, used in sports to strike a ball: *squash racket.* ***rackets***

rag | răg | *n.* A piece of old, torn, or leftover cloth: *a rag for cleaning.* ***rags, ragged, raggedly, raggedness***

**ragged** | **răg**'ĭd | *adj.* **1.** Rough or uneven: *ragged piece of metal.* **2.** Tattered or worn: *ragged clothes.* [see *rag*]

**raise** | rāz | *v.* To lift to a higher place: *will raise the shelf one foot above the table.* ***raises, raised, raising***

**rank** | răngk | *n.* A position or class: *in the third rank. v.* To put in an order; rate: *to rank the students' grades.* ***ranks, ranked, ranking***

**rare** | râr | *adj.* **1.** Not usual: *a rare butterfly.* **2.** Cooked so the inside is still red: *barbecuing rare steak for dinner.* ***rarer, rarest, rarely, rareness, rarity***

reach | rēch | *v.* **1.** To arrive at: *will reach the top of a hill.* **2.** To stretch out a hand for something: *can reach the glass of milk.* ***reaches, reached, reaching, reachable***

**reached** | rēcht | *v.* **1.** Stretched out a hand for something: *reached for his coat.* **2.** Arrived at: *reached our destination.* [see *reach*]

**reaches** | **rē**'chĭz | *v.* **1.** Arrives at: *reaches the top of the stairs.* **2.** Stretches out a hand for something: *reaches for the ball.* [see *reach*]

real | **rē**'əl | *adj.* True or actual: *the real story.* ***really, realistic, realize, reality, realist, realization***

**really** | **rē**'ə lē | *adv.* Truly or actually: *is really happening.* [see *real*]

**reason** | **rē**'zən | *n.* **1.** An explanation: *your reason for being late.* **2.** A cause for an action or feeling: *the reason for your happiness.* ***reasons, reasoned, reasoning, reasonable, reasonably***

**recess** | **rē**'sĕs' | *n.* A period of time when normal activity is stopped: *an hour's recess from working.* ***recesses, recessed, recessing, recession***

**record** | **rĕk**'ərd | *n.* **1.** A flat, grooved vinyl disk to be played on a phonograph: *a record of piano music.* **2.** The best rate, amount, speed, etc., that has been reached: *broke the record for the 100-yard dash.* ***records, recorded, recording, recorder***

**regular** | **rĕg**'yə lər | *adj.* Usual or normal: *regular visit.* ***regularly, regularity, regulate, regulates, regulated, regulating, regulation***

**remain** | rĭ **mān**' | *v.* To stay or continue to stay in a place: *will remain in your seats during the test.* ***remains, remained, remaining, remainder***

remark | rĭ **märk′** | *n.* A short statement; comment: *a funny remark.* ***remarks, remarked, remarking, remarkable, remarkably***

**remarkable** | rĭ **mär′**kə bəl | *adj.* Worthy of comment; astounding: *a remarkable meteor shower.* [see *remark*]

**remember** | rĭ **mem′**bər | *v.* To recall or think of again: *will remember the appointment.* ***remembers, remembered, remembering, remembrance***

**replied** | rĭ **plīd′** | *v.* Answered: *replied too late.* [see *reply*]

reply | rĭ **plī′** | *v.* To answer: *to reply to a question.* ***replies, replied, replying***

**ribbon** | **rĭb′**ən | *n.* A strip of satin, velvet, etc., used for tying or decorating things: *a ribbon in her hair.* ***ribbons***

**rifle** | **rī′**fəl | *n.* A gun, fired from the shoulder, having spiral grooves in the barrel: *officer's rifle.* ***rifles, rifled, rifling, rifler, riflery***

**rise** | rīz | *v.* To go or move upward: *watched the kite rise.* ***rises, rose, rising, risen***

**risk** | rĭsk | *n.* The chance of harm or danger: *to swim at your own risk.* *v.* To take a dangerous chance: *to risk her safety.* ***risks, risked, risking, risky, riskier, riskiest***

**rooster** | **rōō′**stər | *n.* A full-grown male chicken: *rooster in the barn.* ***roosters***

**rough** | rŭf | *adj.* **1.** Not smooth or even: *rough pavement.* **2.** Without details; incomplete: *a rough idea.* ***roughs, roughed, roughing, rougher, roughest, roughly, roughness***

**route** | rōōt | *n.* A road or course: *the route along the river.* ***routes, routed, routing***

**ruin** | **rōō′**ĭn | *v.* To destroy or spoil: *will ruin your shirt.* *n.* One or more ancient buildings in terrible condition: *the ruin of the stone bridge.* ***ruins, ruined, ruining, ruinous***

rule | rōōl | *v.* **1.** To draw straight lines: *will rule the paper.* **2.** To govern a country: *will be the next king to rule.* ***rules, ruled, ruling, ruler, rulers***

**rulers** | **rōō′**lərz | *n.* **1.** Straight-edged strips used for measuring or drawing: *used rulers to measure the room.* **2.** People who govern countries: *rulers of many nations.* [see *rule*]

# S

safe | sāf | *adj.* Free from harm, risk, or danger: *in a safe place.* ***safes, safer, safest, safely, safeness, safety***

**safely** | **sāf′**lē | *adv.* With care to avoid harm: *was safely crossing the street.* [see *safe*]

**safety** | **sāf′**tē | *adj.* Of or for safety: *safety helmet.* *n.* Freedom from harm, risk, or danger: *stayed back for safety.* [see *safe*]

sail | sāl | *v.* To travel on water in a boat that moves by the wind's action on sails: *to sail the Atlantic.* ***sails, sailed, sailing, sailor, sailors***

**sailor** | **sā′**lər | *n.* A person who is a member of a ship's crew: *more than one sailor on the yacht.* [see *sail*]

salt | sôlt | *n.* A white substance used for food, found in the earth and the sea: *salt for the meat.* ***salts, salted, salting, salty, saltier, saltiest***

**salty** | **sôl′**tē | *adj.* Full of salt: *salty ham.* [see *salt*]

**sample** | **săm′**pəl | *n.* An example from a group that shows what the group is like: *a sample of cloth.* ***samples, sampled, sampling, sampler***

**savage** | **săv′**ĭj | *adj.* Fierce, brutal, or cruel: *the dog's savage growl.* ***savages, savagely, savageness***

ă pat / ā pay / â care / ä father / ĕ pet / ē be / ĭ pit / ī pie / î fierce / ŏ pot / ō go / ô paw, for / oi oil / ŏŏ book / ōō boot / ou out / ŭ cut / û fur / *th* the / th thin / hw which / zh vision / ə ago, item, pencil, atom, circus

save | sāv | *v.* To prevent loss or waste of: *will save money for groceries.* ***saves, saved, saving, savings, saver***

**savings** | sā′vĭngz | *n.* Money saved: *a small savings in the bank.* [see *save*]

**scar** | skär | *n.* The mark left after a wound has healed: *a scar on my leg.* ***scars, scarred, scarring***

**scarce** | skârs | *adj.* Not in great supply: *scarce water supply.* ***scarcer, scarcest, scarcely, scarcity, scarceness***

**scare** | skâr | *v.* To frighten: *will scare the mouse.* ***scares, scared, scaring, scary, scarier, scariest, scarer, scariness***

**scarf** | skârf | *n.* A piece of fabric worn around the head or neck: *silk scarf.* ***scarves***

**schoolmate** | **sko͞ol′māt′** | *n.* A companion at school: *library books for my schoolmate.* ***schoolmates***

**scorn** | skôrn | *v.* To look down on: *To scorn their advice.* ***scorns, scorned, scorning, scornful, scornfully, scornfulness***

**scowl** | skoul | *n.* An angry look or frown: *directed a scowl at the noisy audience.* ***scowls, scowled, scowling, scowler***

**seal** | sēl | *v.* To close tight, as with glue or wax: *to seal the package. n.* A sea mammal with flippers: *the trained seal.* ***seals, sealed, sealing, sealer***

**seashore** | **sē′**shôr′ | *n.* The land near the edge of the sea: *shells along the seashore.* ***seashores***

**secret** | **sē′**krĭt | *n.* Something kept hidden from others: *knows a secret. adj.* Hidden from others: *a secret hiding place.* ***secrets, secretive, secretly, secrecy***

**secure** | sĭ **kyo͝or′** | *v.* To fasten firmly: *will secure all the doors.* ***secures, secured, securing, securely, security***

**select** | sĭ **lĕkt′** | *v.* To choose: *will select a book to buy.* ***selects, selected, selecting, selective, selection***

**sentence** | **sĕn′**təns | *n.* A group of words, containing a subject and a predicate, that express a complete thought: *to punctuate the sentence.* ***sentences, sentenced, sentencing***

**settle** | **sĕt′**l | *v.* To choose a place to live and make a home there: *to settle in a new city.* ***settles, settled, settling, settlement, settler***

**sew** | sō | *v.* To use a needle and thread: *will sew a button on the shirt.* ***sews, sewed, sewn, sewing***

**shack** | shăk | *n.* A small, roughly built cabin: *an old shack in the woods.* ***shacks***

**shadow** | **shăd′**ō | *n.* Shade made by a person, animal, or object: *a long shadow at dusk. v.* To throw shade on: *trees that shadow the house.* ***shadows, shadowed, shadowing, shadowy***

shake | shāk | *v.* **1.** To move or cause to move quickly to and fro, back and forth, or up and down: *will shake the juice.* **2.** To clasp hands to greet, congratulate, etc.: *will shake your hand if you win.* ***shakes, shook, shaking, shaken, shaky, shaker***

shame | shām | *n.* An uncomfortable feeling for having done something wrong: *felt shame when lying.* ***shames, shamed, shaming, shameless, shameful, ashamed, ashamedly***

**shelter** | **shĕl′**tər | *n.* Protection: *a shelter from the cold. v.* To protect: *to shelter your eyes from the bright sun.* ***shelters, sheltered, sheltering***

**shook** | sho͝ok | *v.* Moved or caused to move quickly: *shook out the rugs.* [see *shake*]

shop | shŏp | *v.* To look at or buy things in a store: *to shop for food.* ***shops, shopped, shopping, shopper***

**shopping** | **shŏp′**ĭng | *adj.* Of looking at or buying things in a store: *a shopping spree. v.* Looking at or buying things in a store: *was shopping for clothes.* [see *shop*]

**shovel** | **shŭv′**əl | *n.* A tool with a long handle and a flattened scoop, used to lift and throw matter: *a snow shovel.* ***shovels, shoveled, shoveling, shoveler***

**signal** | sĭg′nəl | *n.* A sign that gives notice or warning: *a signal to stop.* ***signals, signaled, signaling, signaler***

**silly** | sĭl′ē | *adj.* Senseless or foolish: *a silly joke.* ***sillier, silliest, silliness***

**skim** | skĭm | *v.* To read hastily for only the most obvious: *will skim the book by tomorrow afternoon.* ***skims, skimmed, skimming, skimmer***

skin | **skĭn** | *v.* To injure by scraping: *will skin my legs if I fall on the sidewalk.* ***skins, skinned, skinning***

**skinned** | skĭnd | *v.* Injured by scraping: *skinned his knee on the ice.* [see *skin*]

**skirt** | skûrt | *n.* A piece of clothing that hangs from the waist but is not divided between the legs: *the plaid skirt.* ***skirts, skirted, skirting***

**sleeve** | slēv | *n.* The part of a garment covering the arm: *sleeve of the jacket.* ***sleeves, sleeved, sleeveless***

slip | slĭp | *v.* To lose balance or footing on a slippery surface: *might slip on the ice.* ***slips, slipped, slipping, slippery, slipperiness, slipper, slippers***

**slipped** | slĭpt | *v.* Lost balance or footing on a slippery surface: *slipped on the wet leaves.* [see *slip*]

small | smôl | *adj.* Little: *small building.* ***smaller, smallest, smallness***

**smaller** | **smôl**′ər | *adj.* Littler: *the smaller child.* [see *small*]

**smooth** | smo͞o*th* | *v.* To make something flat or level: *will smooth the covers.* ***smooths, smoothed,' smoothing, smoothness, smoother, smoothest, smoothly***

**soak** | sōk | *v.* To let remain in liquid until wet through: *will soak in soapy water.* ***soaks, soaked, soaking***

**somehow** | **sŭm**′hou′ | *adv.* In one way or another: *will begin somehow.*

**someone** | **sŭm**′wŭn′ | *pron.* Some person: *told someone the story.*

**somewhat** | **sŭm**′hwät′ | *adv.* Rather; slightly: *is somewhat peculiar.*

**somewhere** | **sŭm**′hwĕr′ | *adv.* At, in, or to one place or another: *is resting somewhere.* *n.* An unknown place: *somewhere to rest for the night.*

**sour** | sour | *adj.* Having a sharp taste: *sour lemon.* ***sours, soured, souring, sourest, sourly, sourness***

south | south | *n.* The direction to the left of the setting sun: *warmer to the south.* ***southern, Southerner, southerly, southward***

**southern** | **sŭ***th*′ərn | *adj.* Of, in, toward, or from the south: *pink clouds in the southern sky.* [see *south*]

**sparrow** | **spăr**′ō | *n.* A small gray or brown songbird: *a sparrow on the feeder.* ***sparrows***

**split** | splĭt | *n.* An acrobatic trick in which the legs are spread far apart in opposite directions: *the ballerina who did a split.* ***splits, splitting, splitter***

**spoon** | spo͞on | *n.* An eating utensil consisting of a small shallow bowl and a handle: *spoon for the soup.* ***spoons, spooned, spooning***

**spray** | sprā | *n.* A moving group of water droplets: *the spray of an ocean wave.* ***sprays, sprayed, spraying, sprayer***

**square** | skwâr | *n.* A rectangle with four equal sides: *a four-inch square.* ***squares, squared, squaring, squarely, squareness, squarer, squarest, squarish***

**squirrel** | **skwûr**′əl | *n.* A gray or reddish-brown rodent with a bushy tail: *the furry squirrel.* ***squirrels, squirreled, squirreling***

**stack** | stăk | *n.* A large pile of something: *a stack of dishes.* ***stacks, stacked, stacking***

**stalk** | stôk | *n.* The main stem of a plant: *a stalk of wheat.* ***stalks, stalked, stalking***

ă pat / ā pay / â care / ä father / ĕ pet / ē be / ĭ pit / ī pie / î fierce / ŏ pot / ō go / ô paw, for / oi oil / o͝o book / o͞o boot / ou out / ŭ cut / û fur / *th* the / th thin / hw which / zh vision / ə ago, item, pencil, atom, circus

**station** | **stā**′shən | *n.* **1.** A place that transmits radio or television signals: *a radio station.* **2.** A regular stopping place along a route: *boarded at the last station.* ***stations, stationed, stationing, stationary***

**stoop** | stōōp | *v.* To bend forward and downward: *will stoop to get into the cave.* ***stoops, stooped, stooping***

**straight** | strāt | *adj.* Free from bends or curves: *straight road.* ***straighter, straightest, straighten, straightens, straightened, straightening, straightener***

**strain** | strān | *v.* **1.** To pull hard: *to strain in the tug-of-war.* **2.** To push through a strainer: *will strain the orange juice.* ***strains, strained, straining, strainer***

**stray** | strā | *v.* To wander from the right course: *to stray from the marked path.* ***strays, strayed, straying***

strike | strīk | *v.* To hit hard: *to strike the nail with a hammer.* ***strikes, struck, striking, striker***

**strip** | strĭp | *n.* A narrow, flat piece of something: *a strip of paper for a bookmark.* *v.* To pull off; remove: *will strip the sheets from the bed.* ***strips, stripped, stripping***

**struck** | strŭk | *v.* Hit hard: *struck by a hurricane.* [see *strike*]

**stubborn** | **stŭb**′ərn | *adj.* Difficult to deal with or manage: *a stubborn knot.* ***stubborner, stubbornest, stubbornly, stubbornness***

**student** | **stōōd**′nt | *n.* A person who attends a school: *new student in our class.* ***students***

**studies** | **stŭd**′ēz | *v.* Learns facts or ideas about a subject: *studies math.* [see *study*]

study | **stŭd**′ē | *v.* To learn facts or ideas about a subject: *to study for the test.* ***studies, studied, studying, studious***

**stuff** | stŭf | *v.* To pack too fully: *to stuff the red suitcase with clothes.* ***stuffs, stuffed, stuffing, stuffy***

**stump** | stŭmp | *n.* The lower part of a tree, left after the main part is cut off: *a stump that is covered with moss.* ***stumps, stumped, stumping, stumpy***

suit | sōōt | *n.* A set of clothing, usually a jacket and trousers or skirt, to be worn together: *gray wool suit.* **–Bathing suit–** A garment worn for swimming. ***suits, suited, suiting, suitable***

**suits** | sōōts | *n.* More than one suit: *two striped suits.* [see *suit*]

sun | sŭn | *n.* The star around which all the planets in the solar system revolve: *the planet nearest to the sun.* ***suns, sunned, sunning, sunny, sunnier, sunniest, sunniness***

**sunny** | **sŭn**′ē | *adj.* **1.** Filled with sunshine: *sunny room.* **2.** Cheerful: *has a sunny personality.* [see *sun*]

sure | shōōr | *adj.* Certain: *sure of the answer.* ***surer, surest, surely, sureness***

**surely** | **shōōr**′lē | *adv.* Certainly: *surely knows the way.* [see *sure*]

surprise | sər **prīz**′ | *n.* Something not expected: *a surprise for my birthday.* ***surprises, surprised, surprising, surprisingly***

**surprises** | sər **prī**′ zĭz | *n.* More than one surprise: *surprises for the party.* [see *surprise*]

**swallow** | **swŏl**′ō | *v.* To cause food or drink to pass down the throat: *to swallow a peanut.* *n.* Any of several birds with long wings and a forked tail: *the swallow in the barn.* ***swallows, swallowed, swallowing***

**sway** | swā | *v.* To move back and forth: *to sway in the breeze.* ***sways, swayed, swaying***

**sweater** | **swĕt**′ər | *n.* A knitted garment for the upper part of the body: *wool sweater.* ***sweaters***

swim | swĭm | *v.* To move through water by using arms, legs, fins, etc.: *to swim in the lake.* ***swims, swam, swum, swimming, swimmer***

**swimming** | **swĭm**′ĭng | *v.* Moving through water by using arms, legs, fins, etc.: *is swimming to shore.* [see *swim*]

# T

**tablet** | tăb'lĭt | *n.* A pad of paper: *a small tablet for notes.* ***tablets***

**tackle** | tăk'əl | *n.* In football, the act of stopping and throwing to the ground an opponent who has the ball: *a tackle of the quarterback.* *v.* **1.** To seize: *will tackle him if he tries to escape.* **2.** To undertake or try to deal with: *will tackle the problem later.* ***tackles, tackled, tackling, tackler***

**talent** | tăl'ənt | *n.* A special ability: *a talent for drawing.* ***talents, talented***

**taught** | tôt | *v.* Gave lessons in: *taught French.* [see *teach*]

teach | tēch | *v.* To give lessons in: *will teach science and English.* ***teaches, taught, teaching, teacher***

**temper** | tĕm'pər | *n.* **1.** A mood; state of mind: *an even temper.* **2.** An angry state of mind: *in a bad temper.* ***tempers, tempered, tempering***

**tennis** | tĕn'ĭs | *n.* A sport played by two or four players on a court with a net. The players hit a ball back and forth over the net with a racket: *a three-hour game of tennis.*

thank | thăngk | *v.* To say that one is grateful for something: *will thank them for helping.* ***thanks, thanked, thanking, thankful, thankfully, thankless, thanksgiving***

**thankful** | thăngk'fəl | *adj.* Grateful: *thankful for the meal.*

**threw** | thrōō | *v.* Tossed: *threw the ball to first base.* [see *throw*]

**thrill** | thrĭl | *n.* A sudden, exciting feeling: *a thrill at seeing the tallest building.* ***thrills, thrilled, thrilling, thrillingly, thriller***

**throat** | thrōt | *n.* The passage leading from the mouth to the stomach or lungs: *a sore throat.* ***throats, throaty***

throw | thrō | *v.* To toss: *to throw a ball.* ***throws, threw, thrown, throwing, thrower***

**thumb** | thŭm | *n.* The short, thick first finger of the hand: *a cut on her thumb.* ***thumbs, thumbed, thumbing***

**thunder** | thŭn'dər | *n.* The loud noise that follows lightning: *the thunder during the storm.* *v.* To make a noise like thunder: *to thunder through the halls.* ***thunders, thundered, thundering***

tie | tī | *v.* To fasten with string, rope, etc.: *will tie the boat to the dock.* ***ties, tied, tying***

**tied** | tīd | *v.* Fastened with string, rope, etc.: *tied his shoes.* [see *tie*]

**tomato** | tə mā'tō | *n.* A fleshy reddish fruit eaten as a vegetable: *ripe tomato.* ***tomatoes***

tone | tōn | *n.* **1.** A sound of a certain quality: *the deep tone of the foghorn.* **2.** A shade of color: *a blue tone in the painting.* ***tones, toned, toning, toneless, toner***

**tones** | tōnz | *n.* **1.** Sounds of a certain quality: *tones of the choir.* **2.** Shades of color: *many red tones in the rug.* [see *tone*]

**topic** | tŏp'ĭk | *n.* A subject: *the topic for the lecture.* ***topics***

**toss** | tôs | *v.* To move oneself about with force or intensity: *to toss all night while trying to sleep.* ***tosses, tossed, tossing***

**touch** | tŭch | *v.* To feel with part of the body: *to touch the rough rock.* ***touches, touched, touching, touchable, touchy***

**toward** | tôrd | *prep.* In the direction of: *toward the sunset.* ***towards***

**treasure** | trĕzh'ər | *n.* Riches or valuable items: *the treasure in the sunken ship.* ***treasures, treasured, treasuring, treasurer, treasury***

**troop** | trōōp | *v.* To move together in large numbers: *will troop around the flagpole.* ***troops, trooped, trooping, trooper***

ă pat / ā pay / â care / ä father / ĕ pet / ē **be** / ĭ pit / ī pie / î fierce / ŏ pot / ō **go** / ô paw, for / oi oil / ŏŏ book / ōō **boot** / ou **out** / ŭ cut / û fur / *th* **the** / th **thin** / hw **which** / zh vision / ə ago, item, pencil, atom, circus

**trouble** | **trŭb**′əl | *n.* Difficulty, pain, or worry: *caused trouble in class.* ***troubles, troubled, troubling, troublesome***

**trout** | trout | *n.* A freshwater fish: *to fish for trout.* ***trouts***

**truth** | trōōth | *n.* A statement proven to be accepted as true: *a scientific truth.* ***truths, truthful, truthfully, truthfulness***

# U

**ugly** | **ŭg**′lē | *adj.* **1.** Dangerous: *ugly fire.* **2.** Unpleasant to look at: *ugly picture.* ***uglier, ugliest, ugliness***

**uncle** | **ŭng**′kəl | *n.* The brother of one's mother or father: *the son of my uncle.* ***uncles***

**uniform** | **yōō**′nə fôrm′ | *n.* The outfit worn by group members on duty, by which they may be known as belonging to that group: *the guard's uniform.* ***uniforms, uniformed, uniformly***

**unit** | **yōō**′nĭt | *n.* One thing or person: *a unit of weight.* ***units, unite, unites, united, uniting, unity***

**unless** | ŭn **lĕs**′ | *conj.* If not; except if: *unless you leave.*

**unload** | ŭn **lōd**′ | *v.* To remove cargo from: *to unload the trunk.* [see *load*]

**unwilling** | ŭn **wĭl**′ĭng | *adj.* Not wishing or desiring: *unwilling to change.* [see *will*]

up | ŭp | *adv.* To a higher place: *when the plane flew up.* ***upper***

**upper** | **ŭp**′ər | *adj.* Higher: *on the upper shelf.* [see *up*]

usual | **yōō**′zhōō əl | *adj.* Common or ordinary: *meet at the usual place.* ***usually, usualness***

**usually** | **yōō**′zhōō ə lē | *adv.* Commonly or ordinarily: *usually happy.* [see *usual*]

# V

**valentine** | **văl**′ən tīn′ | *n.* A card or gift given on Valentine's Day: *sent him a valentine.* ***valentines***

**valley** | **văl**′ē | *n.* A narrow, low land between mountains or hills: *rode into the valley.* ***valleys***

**view** | vyōō | *n.* A scene or something seen: *a view from the roof.* ***views, viewed, viewing, viewer***

**village** | **vĭl**′ĭj | *adj.* Of or related to a village: *village residents. n.* A group of houses and other buildings that form a community smaller than a town: *in the center of the village.* ***villages, villager***

visit | **vĭz**′ĭt | *v.* To go or come to see: *will visit some friends.* ***visits, visited, visiting, visitor, visitors***

**visitor** | **vĭz**′ĭ tər | *n.* A person who visits; guest: *welcomed the visitor from another country.* [see *visit*]

voice | vois | *n.* The sound made through a person's mouth: *strange voice.* ***voices, voiced, voicing, voiceless***

**voices** | **vois**′ĭz | *n.* More than one voice: *voices from the audience.* [see *voice*]

vote | vōt | *n.* One's choice in an election: *placing a vote in the ballot box.* ***votes, voted, voting, voter***

**votes** | vōts | *n.* More than one vote: *totaled the votes.* [see *vote*]

# W

**waist** | wāst | *n.* The part of a person's body between the ribs and the hips: *above the waist.* ***waists***

water | **wô**′tər | *v.* To moisten or supply with water: *will water the roses.* ***waters, watered, watering, watery***

**watered** | **wô**′tərd | *v.* Moistened or supplied with water: *watered the lawn with the sprinkler.* [see *water*]

**weather** | **wĕ*th***′ər | *n.* The condition of air at a certain time and place: *hot summer weather.*

**weigh** | wā | *v.* To find out how heavy something is: *will weigh the bag of apples.* ***weighs, weighed, weighing, weight, weights, weightless***

**we're** | wîr | Contraction for *we are: when we're ready.*

**weren't** | wûrnt | Contraction for *were not: because we weren't prepared.*

west | wĕst | *n.* The direction of the sunset: *headed toward the west.* ***western, Westerner, westerly, westward***

**western** | **wĕs**′tərn | *adj.* Of, in, toward, or from the west: *the western sky.* [see *west*]

**we've** | wēv | Contraction for *we have: when we've arrived.*

**whale** | hwāl | *n.* A mammal that lives in the sea and looks like a large fish: *a whale near the ship.* ***whales, whaling, whaler, whalers***

who | ho͞o | *pron.* That: *the man who knows you.* ***whom, whose***

**whole** | hōl | *adj.* Complete or entire: *a whole box of books.* ***wholes, wholesome, wholly***

**whose** | ho͞oz | *adj.* Of whom or which: *whose bike I borrowed.* [see *who*]

**wicked** | **wĭk**′ĭd | *adj.* Evil or bad: *wicked thoughts.* ***wickedly, wickedness***

wild | wīld | *adj.* Untamed; growing or found in a natural state: *wild blueberries.* ***wilder, wildest, wildly, wilds, wilderness, wildness***

**wilderness** | **wĭl**′dər nĭs | *n.* An unpopulated region in its natural condition: *hiked into the wilderness.* [see *wild*]

will | wĭl | *v.* To desire or wish: *as you will.* ***unwilling, unwillingly, unwillingness***

**withdraw** | wĭ*th* **drô**′ | *v.* To take away; remove: *will withdraw my vote.* ***withdraws, withdrew, withdrawn, withdrawing, withdrawal***

**wonder** | **wŭn**′dər | *v.* To feel awe, doubt, or surprise: *will wonder at the beautiful sight.* *n.* Something that creates awe or admiration: *a wonder to see.* ***wonders, wondered, wondering, wonderful, wonderfully, wondrous***

**worse** | wûrs | *adj.* Less good: *worse storm than yesterday's.* [see *bad*]

**wouldn't** | **wo͝od**′nt | Contraction for *would not: wouldn't want any.*

**wrist** |rĭst | *n.* The joint where the hand and forearm meet: *broke her wrist playing tennis.* ***wrists***

ă pat / ā pay / â care / ä father / ĕ pet / ē be / ĭ pit / ī pie / î fierce / ŏ pot / ō go / ô paw, for / oi oil / o͝o book / o͞o boot / ou out / ŭ cut / û fur / *th* the / th thin / hw which / zh vision / ə ago, item, pencil, atom, circus

# Yellow Pages

# Proofreading Tips

**Finding and correcting the spelling errors in your own writing is an important skill. Try these different ways to check your spelling.**

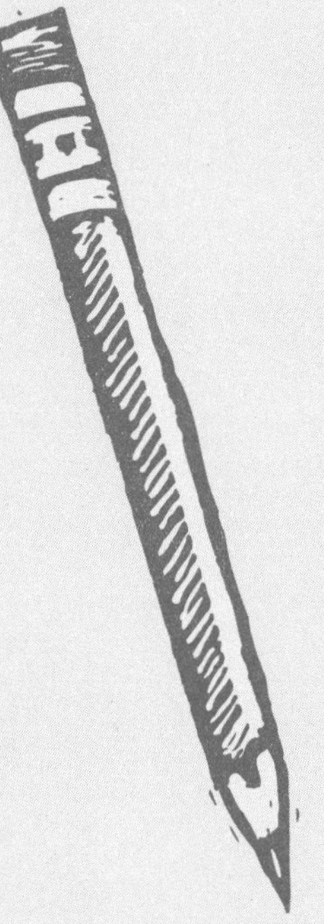

1. Read each word letter by letter, touching every letter with a pencil or pen.
2. Read each word letter by letter, putting a dot under every letter.
3. Have a partner read your work aloud while you check it silently.
4. Read your work out loud to yourself.
5. Read your work backwards, word by word, to yourself.
6. Read through your work. Circle any words that look wrong.
7. Look for words and word parts you often misspell. Double-check their spellings.
8. Check for words that are easy to mix up—*too* instead of *two*, *your* instead of *you're*.
9. Type your work on a computer and use the spell checker. Remember that a spell checker only recognizes that a word is correctly spelled, not that it is correctly used.
10. Find correct spellings wherever you can. Here are some ideas:
    - Try writing the word different ways until it looks right.
    - Say the word slowly. Spell all its syllables.
    - Use what you know about spelling rules, letter sounds, and word shapes.
    - Look for the word on your Personal Spelling List.
    - Have you seen the word somewhere? in a book? on the wall? Find it again.
    - Check the lists in these Yellow Pages.
    - Check a dictionary.
    - Ask someone.

**Now make up your own ways to find correct spellings!**

# Spelling Rules

**There are many spelling rules, but only a few of them do most of the work. Nearly all the rules here tell how to add endings to words.** *(See pages 190–191 for some of these endings.)* **Unlike some spelling "rules," these work most of the time!**

**FORMING PLURALS ("more than one")**

**Add *s* to most words:**

aprons
operas
exhibits

**Add *es* to words ending with *s, ss, sh, ch, x*:**

buses
dresses
wishes
patches
boxes

**Change the *f* or *fe* at the end of some words to *v* and add *es*:**

calf, calves
wolf, wolves
life, lives
shelf, shelves
self, selves
knife, knives

**Know the few nouns that change their spellings:**

child, children
foot, feet
mouse, mice
man, men
woman, women
tooth, teeth

## ADDING ENDINGS BEGINNING WITH A VOWEL TO...

### *...Words Ending with a Vowel Plus a Consonant*

**Double the final consonant of a one-syllable word:**

bag, bagged
grip, gripper
get, getting
rot, rotten

**Double the final consonant of words with more than one syllable when the last syllable is accented:**

permit, permitted
regret, regretting

**Don't double the final consonant when the last syllable is not accented:**

model, modeling
travel, traveler

## ADDING ENDINGS TO...

### *...Words Ending with Silent* E

**Drop the final *e* when adding an ending that begins with a vowel:**

hurdle, hurdling
hostile, hostility
scrape, scraper
nerve, nervous

**Keep the final *e* when adding an ending that begins with a consonant:**

active, actively
resource, resourceful
gentle, gentleness

## ADDING ENDINGS TO...

### *...Words Ending with* Y

**Add the ending right onto the root when the word ends with a vowel + *y*:**

joy, joyous
journey, journeyed
employ, employment
betray, betraying

**Change the *y* to *i* before adding the ending when a word ends with a consonant + *y*:**

lady, ladies
shiny, shiniest
lucky, luckily
try, tried

## *I* BEFORE *E*

**Remember the rule:**
***i* before *e*, except after *c*, or when rhyming with *say*, as in *neighbor* and *weigh*:**

believe
ceiling
sleigh

**but learn the exceptions, too:**

seize
either
their
neither
weird
height
leisure

# Spelling Strategies

**Perfect spellers are hard to find, but almost anyone can be a good speller. The differences between good spellers and bad spellers are:**

> **Good spellers know when words are spelled incorrectly. Bad spellers don't.**
>
> **Good spellers proofread and correct themselves. Bad spellers don't.**

**Following are some strategies for improving your spelling. Try them all. Then think of your own.**

## PERSONAL WORD LISTS

Make lists—or a personal dictionary—of words you use in your writing. Use them as your own personal references.

1. **Difficult Words.** Collect words that are difficult for you to spell. Write them in alphabetical order so they're easy to find. Study them. Write them. Have a partner test you, and use the Proofreading Tips on page 178 to check your spelling. When you can spell and write a word with ease, cross it out and add a new one. Keep changing your list, and don't let it get too long.

2. **Writing Bank.** The best stories you will write are about what you know. Collect the correct spellings of words that name:

   - family, friends, classmates, people you see and do things with
   - places you go, where they are, what they look like, what you do there, where you live
   - things you do, what interests you, what you wish for, your hobbies, your collections
   - sports, movies, video games you enjoy

   The personal words in your Writing Bank can give you ideas for writing.

3. **Personal Computer File.** If you use a computer, dedicate a file to your personal word lists. Be sure to proofread your word list even if you spell check it. *Sum thymes the spell check excepts a word as write, butt its knot the word yew mien two ewes.*

## STUDY TIPS

The list of words you can spell easily gets longer as you study and use words from your regular spelling lists and your daily writing. Here are some ways to learn new words for your list.

1. **S-H-A-R-P.** Use the S-H-A-R-P study procedure on page 3 in your spelling book to study spelling words, difficult words, personal words, or any other words you use in your writing.
2. **Hard Spots.** Pay special attention to parts of a word that give you trouble. Study them extra hard. Be on the lookout for these every time you write.
3. **Memory Tricks.** If all else fails, try a memory trick to remember difficult spellings.
   - Make up a spelling-helper pronunciation: princi**pal**, choc-**o**-late.
   - Use meaning-helper word parts: the **real** in **real**ity; the **ear** in h**ear**.
   - Make up your own memory-helper saying. For example,

     A fri**end** is a fri**end** to the **end**.

     There's one ***s*** in **s**and in the de**s**ert, and two ***s***'s in **s**trawberry **s**hortcake for de**ss**ert.

## APPROXIMATION

When you are writing a first draft, you sometimes want to use an exact word, a great word, but you haven't yet learned to spell it. Instead of stopping to make sure you get it right the first time, try this:

1. **Spell the word as best you can.** (This is called "approximation." It means "close, but maybe not quite right.")
2. **Circle the word and continue with your writing.**
3. **After you have finished the first draft, go back and correct the circled word.**

Then add the word to your Personal Word List, study it, and use it the next time you are writing.

# 240 Most Useful Words

**If you can spell these words, more than half of what you write will be correctly spelled. (Words marked * are often misspelled.)**

| A | B | C | D | E | F | G | H | I |
|---|---|---|---|---|---|---|---|---|
| *about | back | called | day | eat | family | game | had | if |
| after | be | came | did | end | father | gave | happy | I'm |
| *again | bear | can | *didn't | even | fell | get | has | in |
| all | *because | car | do | ever | find | girl | have | into |
| also | bed | cat | dog | *every | fire | give | he | is |
| *always | *been | *come | *don't | | *first | go | head | it |
| am | *before | *could | door | | fish | *going | *heard | *its |
| an | best | | down | | five | gone | help | *it's |
| and | big | | | | food | good | her | |
| another | black | | | | for | got | here | |
| any | book | | | | form | | him | |
| are | boy | | | | found | | his | |
| around | brother | | | | *four | | home | |
| as | but | | | | *friend | | horse | |
| asked | *by | | | | fun | | *house | |
| at | | | | | | | how | |
| away | | | | | | | | |

### J

just

### K

*knew
*know

### L

land
last
left
like
*little
live
long
look
*lot
love

### M

mad
made
man
*many
may
me
men
money
more
*morning
most
*mother
much
my

### N

name
need
never
new
next
nice
*night
no
not
now

### O

of
*off
oh
old
on
*once
one
only
or
other
our
out
over

### P

*people
place
*play
put

### R

ran
*really
red
ride
*right
room
run

### S

*said
saw
say
school
see
she
should
sister
small
so
*some
*something
*sometimes
*soon
spring
started
still
*summer
*swimming

### T

take
tell
ten
*than
that
the
*their
them
*then
*there
these
*they
thing
think
this
three
*through
time
to
told
*too
took
tree
tried
two

### V

*very

### W

walk
want
wanted
was
water
way
we
well
went
*were
what
*when
*where
*which
while
*white
who
why
will
with
woods
work
*would

### Y

year
yes
you
*your

# Homonyms and Other Troublesome Words

**Some words sound alike but have different spellings and meanings. They are easy to confuse when you write.**

**accept, except**

Please **accept** my invitation.

Everyone was invited **except** me.

**allowed, aloud**

Smoking is not **allowed**.

The teacher reads **aloud** to the class.

**a lot** (2 words)

I have **a lot** of homework today.

**already, all ready**

He's **already** finished.

Now he's **all ready** to leave.

**ant, aunt**

An **ant** was on my sandwich.

My **aunt** and uncle are here!

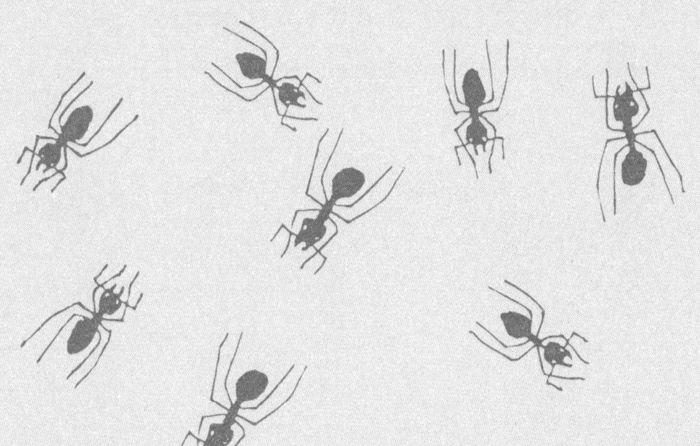

**ate, eight**

Who **ate** the last piece?

We hiked for nearly **eight** hours.

**been, bin**

Where have you **been**?

She stored the vegetables in a **bin**.

**blew, blue**

Everyone **blew** whistles at the same time.

I'm black and **blue** from the scrimmage.

**by, buy**

Come **by** when you're finished.

You can **buy** whatever you want.

**capital, capitol**

Begin each sentence with a **capital**.

The state **capitol** is a beautiful building.

**cent, sent, scent**

It didn't cost a **cent**.

Someone **sent** it to her.

The perfume has the **scent** of roses.

**chews, choose**

He **chews** each bite slowly.

Let's **choose** up teams!

### close, clothes

Did you remember to **close** the door?

I have to hang up my **clothes**.

### do, dew, due

**Do** you remember what you did?

The grass was still wet with morning **dew**.

When is our science report **due**?

### for, four

I'll buy something **for** you.

I need **four** pencils for school.

### hear, here

Did you **hear** a scraping sound?

We're the only ones **here**.

### heard, herd

He **heard** the soft lowing of the cattle.

The **herd** was a bit restless.

### hole, whole

Put the round peg in the round **hole**.

You have to finish the **whole** puzzle.

### hour, our

It'll take at least an **hour**.

We'll do **our** best.

### its, it's

The ball has lost **its** bounce.

Maybe **it's** time to get another one.

### know, no

Does he **know** her?

I have **no** idea.

### knows, nose

Nobody **knows** the way.

His sensitive **nose** will find the way.

### lay, lie

**Lay** the boxes on the floor.

Now go and **lie** down for a while.

### lets, let's

Everyone **lets** him do what he wants.

**Let's** wait and see what happens.

### new, knew

Is that a **new** shirt you're wearing?

I **knew**, because it was so smooth.

### not, knot

We're **not** going to be able to go yet.

Can you untie this **knot**?

### past, passed

It's half **past** nine and I'm finished.

We **passed** the slow-moving truck.

### peace, piece

Everyone prefers **peace** to war.

My favorite **piece** is the crusty corner.

### plain, plane

He wore a **plain** green sweater.

The **plane** prepared for takeoff.

### presents, presence

The **presents** were wrapped in white paper.

Her **presence** in the room quieted the class.

### principle, principal

He is a person of high **principles**.

"The **principal** is your pal" is a mnemonic device.

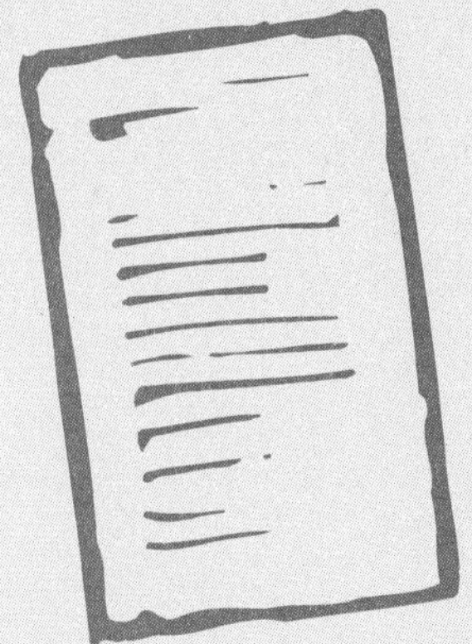

**quit, quite, quiet**

I wish he'd **quit** talking.

I'm not **quite** ready to go yet.

The baby's sleeping so try to be **quiet**.

**right, write**

Do we turn left, or **right**?

Why don't you **write** yourself a letter?

**some, sum**

Don't you have **some** homework?

The **sum** of 3456 + 6543 is 9999.

**stationary, stationery**

The fort was a **stationary** target.

The letter was written on pink **stationery**.

**than, then**

No one can run faster **than** you!

She sang one song, **then** she sang another.

**there, their, they're**

Put it over **there** by the sink.

Are the campers in **their** cabins?

They said **they're** going to help us.

**theirs, there's**

Are these jackets **theirs** or yours?

Where **there's** smoke, **there's** fire.

**through, threw**

She walked **through** the gate.

You **threw** away a perfectly good boot!

**to, too, two**

Go **to** jail.

Go there directly, **too**.

Do not collect **two** hundred dollars.

**way, weigh**

Show me the **way** to go home.

That must **weigh** a ton!

**weak, week**

I'm not as **weak** as I look.

In a **week**, they're going on vacation.

**wear, where**

What are you going to **wear**?

If I knew **where** we're going, I'd tell you.

**weather, whether**

We're having mild **weather**.

We'll go **whether** it rains or not.

**which, witch**

I don't know **which** book to read first.

Is she the good **witch** or the bad one?

**who's, whose**

**Who's** ready for dessert?

Do you know **whose** hat is on the chair?

**wood, would**

The ship model is carved from **wood**.

He said he **would** probably sell it.

**your, you're**

Is this **your** book?

Thanks, **you're** a good friend to return it.

# Common Contractions

**A contraction is a word made by joining two words. An apostrophe is used to take the place of the letter(s) left out.**

**is + not = isn't** **it + is = it's**

**Contractions are not difficult to spell once you understand the way they are formed.**

**VERB + *not***

| | |
|---|---|
| is | isn't |
| are | aren't |
| was | wasn't |
| were | weren't |
| have | haven't |
| has | hasn't |
| had | hadn't |
| do | don't |
| does | doesn't |
| did | didn't |
| can | can't |
| could | couldn't |
| must | mustn't |
| will | won't |
| would | wouldn't |
| shall | shan't |
| should | shouldn't |

**PRONOUN + VERB**

| | | | | |
|---|---|---|---|---|
| | | am | | I'm |
| | | will | | I'll |
| **I** | **+** | have | **=** | I've |
| | | had | | I'd |
| | | would | | I'd |
| | | are | | you're, we're, they're |
| **you** | | will | | you'll, we'll, they'll |
| **we** | **+** | have | **=** | you've, we've, they've |
| **they** | | had | | you'd, we'd, they'd |
| | | would | | you'd, we'd, they'd |
| | | is | | he's, she's, it's |
| **he** | | will | | he'll, she'll, it'll |
| **she** | **+** | has | **=** | he's, she's, it's |
| **it** | | had | | he'd, she'd, it'd |
| | | would | | he'd, she'd, it'd |

**OTHER CONTRACTIONS**

In talk, informal writing, and written dialog, contracted words are common. Each word in column 1, for example, can form a contraction with most words in column 2.

| **1** | | **2** | | |
|---|---|---|---|---|
| who | | is | | ________'s |
| what | | are | | ________'re |
| when | | will | | ________'ll |
| where | **+** | has | **=** | ________'s |
| why | | have | | ________'ve |
| here | | had | | ________'d |
| there | | would | | ________'d |

# Roots and Affixes

**A root is a word or word part without additions. You can often add affixes to roots to make new words. A prefix is an affix at the beginning of a word. A suffix is an affix at the end of a word.**

| | |
|---|---|
| **danger** | **root word** |
| en**danger** | prefix + **root** |
| **danger**ous | **root** + suffix |
| en**danger**ed | prefix + **root** + suffix |
| unen**danger**ed | prefix + prefix + **root** + suffix |
| **danger**ously | **root** + suffix + suffix |

**If you know how to spell the root, how to spell common affixes, and the spelling rules for adding suffixes** *(See pages 179–180)*, **you know how to spell thousands and thousands of words.**

Here are some of the extra words you can spell just by adding prefixes and suffixes to the words **person** and **simple**. Notice that adding a suffix sometimes changes the spelling of the root word.

| | | | |
|---|---|---|---|
| **person**ify | **person**able | **simpl**er | **simpl**ification |
| **person**al | **person**age | **simpl**est | un**simpl**ifed |
| im**person**al | **person**alize | **simpl**y | over**simpl**ification |
| inter**person**al | de**person**alize | **simpl**ify | **simple**ton |
| **person**ality | im**person**ation | **simpl**icity | |

The Other Word Forms in your spelling lessons and the following lists will help you multiply the number of words you know how to spell.

### PREFIXES

Many of your spelling words are root words that can become new words with new meanings when a prefix is added. Adding a prefix does not usually change the spelling of the root word. In addition, many English words are made of prefixes combined with ancient Greek and Latin root words.

| | Prefix | Meaning | Examples |
|---|---|---|---|
| **how much,** | semi- | half, twice | semifinal, semicircle |
| **how many** | tri- | three | triangle, tricycle |
| | kilo- | thousand | kilogram, kilometer |

| | Prefix | Meaning | Examples |
|---|---|---|---|
| | micro- | very small | microscopic, microfilm |
| | dec- | ten | decade, decimal |
| | mono- | one, single | monorail, monologue |
| | multi- | much, many | multimillionaire, multipurpose |
| | bi- | two | bicycle, bilingual |
| **where** | sub- | under, below | submarine, submerge |
| | geo- | earth, of the earth | geography, geologist |
| | by- | near | bypass, bystander |
| | circum- | round | circumpolar, circumscribe |
| | in- | into | inhale, inflate |
| | inter- | between | interrupt, intercom |
| | trans- | across, elsewhere | transatlantic, transplant |
| | under- | below | underpass, underground |
| | tele- | distant | telephone, telescope |
| | de- | from | decaf, detour |
| | mid- | middle | midsummer, midday |
| | en- | cause to be, in | endangered, enclose |
| | off- | from | off-line, offshore |
| | extra- | outside | extraterrestrial, extraordinary |
| | on- | on | onlooker, onshore |
| **not** | im- | not | impatient, immobile |
| | anti- | opposite of, against | antifreeze, antisocial |
| | ir- | opposite, not | irresponsible, irresistible |
| | non- | opposite of, not | nonstop, nonfiction |
| **when** | pre- | before | preheat, prefix |
| | fore- | before, in front of | forefather, forecast |
| | post- | later, after (in time) | postscript, postwar |
| | pro- | forward | proceed, progress |
| **extent** | super- | over, above, greater | superhighway, superhuman |
| | over- | too much | overcrowd, overcome |
| | out- | more | outran, outnumber |
| **who** | co- | together | co-author, copilot |
| | auto- | self, by itself | autograph, autobiography |
| | self- | self | self-respect, self-taught |

## SUFFIXES

You can make many new words by adding suffixes to the ends of root words. The Other Word Forms of your spelling lessons show the many new words you can spell simply by adding a few endings to the spelling words.

Remember that the spelling of the root word may change when you add a suffix: **marry/marri**age, **excel/excell**ent, **nerve/nerv**ous. (See the Spelling Rules on page 180.)

| Suffix | Meaning | Examples |
|---|---|---|
| -able | able to be | enjoyable, favorable, comfortable, acceptable |
| -ade | action of | blockade, escapade, barricade, promenade |
| -age | action of | postage, marriage, package, pilgrimage |
| -al | relating to | natural, musical, maternal, trial |
| -ance | state of | allegiance, annoyance, repentance, resistance |
| -ation | state of | starvation, fascination, inspiration, admiration |
| -ence | state of being | confidence, dependence, difference, absence |
| -ent | being or condition | excellent, confident, president, provident |
| -er | one who, more | teacher, printer, buyer; smaller, larger, faster |
| -ese | language, native of | Japanese, Chinese, Vietnamese, Portuguese |
| -hood | state of | childhood, adulthood, falsehood, statehood |
| -ian | relating to | barbarian, librarian, Houstonian, physician |
| -ible | causing, able to be | contemptible, terrible, gullible, eligible |
| -ic | relating to | aquatic, comic, public, historic, lunatic |
| -ify | to make | simplify, clarify, beautify, mummify, purify |
| -ing | material that | bedding, frosting, roofing, stuffing, lining |
| -ion | state of | admission, action, suspicion, companion |
| -ism | action or condition | enthusiasm, patriotism, baptism, heroism |
| -ist | one who | dentist, geologist, physicist, aerialist, cyclist |
| -ity | state of | ability, activity, electricity, locality, vanity |
| -ive | tending to | adhesive, active, evasive, captive, creative |
| -ize | to make or do | monopolize, specialize, vaporize, magnetize |
| -less | without | needless, careless, useless, regardless |
| -logy | subject of study | mineralogy, biology, phrenology, astrology |
| -ly | quality of | motherly, hourly, boldly, patiently, dryly |
| -ment | quality of | agreement, amusement, argument, amazement |
| -ness | state of | kindness, happiness, quickness, firmness |
| -or | action or work | governor, inventor, escalator, doctor, actor |
| -ous | nature of | mountainous, envious, ambitious, generous |
| -ship | state of | friendship, statesmanship, hardship, ownership |
| -some | action or state | awesome, tiresome, quarrelsome, burdensome |
| -teen | number 10 | thirteen, fifteen, seventeen, nineteen |
| -th | number | fourth, tenth, hundredth, thousandth, millionth |
| -ty | state or condition | priority, loyalty, honesty, unity, conformity |
| -ure | action | failure, censure, exposure, enclosure, signature |

**CREDITS**

**Cover Design:** Design Five

**Photography:** Joseph Sachs

**Text Illustrations:**

Lamberto Alvarez
page 122

Ruth Flanigan
pages 3, 15, 105, 106

Shana Greger
pages 29, 30, 137

Jennifer Hewitson
page 5

Judy Love
pages 38, 134

Claude Martinot
pages 59, 61, 77, 126

Jennifer D. Paley
pages 21, 33, 58

Lauren Scheuer
page 129

Brad Teare
pages 53, 70, 71

# Resources

## Skills



## Word Lists

# Summary of Spelling Skills

Exercises in every lesson reinforce eight vital skill areas in the language arts.

| Summary of Skills |
| --- |
| Auditory Discrimination |
| Visual Discrimination |
| Vocabulary Development |
| Proofreading |
| Word Analysis |
| Dictionary Skills |
| Context Usage |
| Original Writing |

- **Auditory Discrimination**
  This skill is practiced during every dictated test and in exercises that ask students to match spelling words with rhyming words.
- **Visual Discrimination**
  Visual Warm-ups, word searches, word scrambles, and codes ensure that students develop a strong visual image of each word.
- **Vocabulary Development**
  Numerous exercises involving word comparisons, analogies, anagrams, word associations, and etymologies, as well as synonyms, antonyms, and homophones, strengthen word meanings and relationships while promoting vocabulary development.
- **Proofreading**
  The Pretest, Visual Warm-up, and Spelling and Writing exercise, which occur in every developmental lesson, ensure familiarity with the Corrected-test Procedure, a research-validated method for developing student ability to proofread their own spelling.
- **Word Analysis**
  Missing letter and classification exercises, as well as numerous exercises dealing with base words, affixes, and syllables, help students analyze sound/symbol relationships and the structure of words.
- **Dictionary Skills**
  Dictionary skills are continually practiced in exercises featuring alphabetization and guide word referencing.
- **Context Usage**
  Using a modified CLOZE procedure, students get regular reinforcement of word meaning in context, which in turn assists in the transfer of their spelling words to daily writing.
- **Original Writing**
  Every developmental lesson ends with Spelling and Writing, an exercise designed to promote the transfer of newly mastered spelling words to meaningful writing situations.

# Useful Spelling Rules

Very few spelling generalizations are presented in WORKING WORDS IN SPELLING. The only rules that should be taught are those that apply to large numbers of words, have few exceptions, and can be easily remembered. A limited number of spelling generalizations for adding suffixes to words are particularly useful.

Familiarity with the rules for forming suffixes can help students extend their spelling storehouse of words. These carefully-selected generalizations, which also appear in the annotated lessons when applicable, may be emphasized when discussing structural analysis skills.

### Doubling the Final Consonant When Adding Suffixes

1. When adding a suffix that begins with a vowel to one-syllable words that end with one vowel and one consonant, double the final consonant.
   **plan + ing = planning**
2. When adding a suffix that begins with a vowel to multisyllable words that are accented on the final syllable and end with one vowel and one consonant, double the final consonant.
   **permit + ed = permitted**

### Adding Suffixes to Words Ending in Silent *e*

1. When adding a suffix that begins with a vowel to words that end with silent *e*, drop the final *e*.
   **have + ing = having**
2. When adding a suffix that begins with a consonant to words that end with silent *e*, keep the final *e*.
   **close + ly = closely**

### Adding Suffixes to Words Ending in *y*

1. When adding a suffix to words ending with consonant-*y*, change the *y* to *i* unless the suffix begins with *i*.
   **cry + ed = cried**
   **cry + ing = crying**
2. When adding a suffix to words ending with vowel-*y*, do not change the *y* to *i*.
   **play + ing = playing**

### Forming Plurals

1. Add *s* to most nouns to form plurals.
   *flag* → *flags*
2. To form plurals of nouns ending with *s*, *ss*, *sh*, *ch*, or *x*, add *es*.
   *gas* → *gases*
   *dish* → *dishes*
   *ax* → *axes*
   *glass* → *glasses*
   *match* → *matches*
3. To form the plurals of nouns ending with consonant-*y*, change the *y* to *i* and add *es*.
   *baby* → *babies*
4. To form the plurals of nouns ending with vowel-*y*, add *s*.
   *monkey* → *monkeys*
5. To form the plurals of some nouns ending with *f* or *fe*, change the *f* or *fe* to *v* and add *es*.
   *calf* → *calves*
   *knife* → *knives*
6. A few nouns change their spellings to make the plural form.
   *child* → *children*
   *foot* → *feet*
   *man* → *men*
   *goose* → *geese*
   *mouse* → *mice*
   *tooth* → *teeth*
   *woman* → *women*
7. A few nouns are spelled the same in the singular and plural forms.
   *sheep*
   *moose*
   *deer*

# Scope and Sequence Chart

## PHONETIC ANALYSIS

| | LESSON |
|---|---|
| **Vowel Spelling /ă/** | |
| a | 16, 18, 21, 24, 26, 28, 30, 31, 32, 36 |
| au | 17, 18 |
| **Vowel Spelling /ā/** | |
| a | 1, 6, 19, 21, 24 |
| a-e | 1, 6, 19, 24 |
| ai | 7, 12, 26, 30 |
| ay | 7, 12, 19, 24 |
| ea | 1, 6 |
| ei | 26, 30 |
| **Vowel Spelling /ĕ/** | |
| a | 32, 36 |
| e | 11, 12, 21, 24, 26, 27, 28, 29, 30, 32, 36 |
| ea | 27, 30, 32, 36 |
| **Vowel Spelling /ē/** | |
| e | 2, 6, 29, 30 |
| ee | 8, 12 |
| ie | 8, 12, 21, 24 |
| **Vowel Spelling /ĭ/** | |
| i | 13, 18, 21, 22, 24, 32, 35, 36 |
| **Vowel Spelling /ī/** | |
| i | 3, 6, 8, 12 |
| ie | 3, 6, 8, 12 |
| i-e | 3, 6, 8, 12 |
| **Vowel Spelling /ŏ/** | |
| o | 9, 12, 14, 15, 17, 18, 35, 36 |
| **Vowel Spelling /ō/** | |
| o | 4, 6, 9, 12, 21, 23, 24 |
| oa | 10, 12, 23, 24 |
| o-e | 4, 6 |
| **Vowel Spelling /ô/** | |
| a | 25, 30, 31, 36 |
| au | 17, 18 |
| aw | 25, 30 |
| ou | 25, 30 |
| **Vowel Spelling /*oi*/** | |
| oi | 23, 24 |
| **Vowel Spelling /*ou*/** | |
| ou | 10, 12, 15, 18 |
| ow | 10, 12, 21, 24 |
| **Vowel Spelling /o͝o/** | |
| oo | 15, 18 |
| ou | 15, 18 |

| | LESSON |
|---|---|
| **Vowel Spelling /o͞o/** | |
| ew | 34, 36 |
| o | 34, 36 |
| oo | 5, 6, 14, 18, 34, 36 |
| ou | 34, 36 |
| u | 5, 6, 34, 36 |
| **Vowel Spelling /ŭ/** | |
| o | 14, 15, 18, 22, 23, 24 |
| ou | 15, 18 |
| u | 20, 24, 25, 30 |
| **Vowel Spelling /*yo͞o*/** | |
| u | 5, 6, 35, 36 |
| eau | 35, 36 |
| u-e | 5, 6 |
| **Vowel Spelling /ə/** | |
| a | 28, 30, 31, 36 |
| o | 17, 18, 35, 36 |
| **Vowel-*r* Spelling /âr/** | |
| ar | 1, 6, 33, 36 |
| air | 7, 12 |
| **Vowel-*r* Spelling /ăr/** | |
| ar | 21, 24 |
| **Vowel-*r* Spelling /är/** | |
| ar | 5, 6, 33, 36 |
| **Vowel-*r* Spelling /ĕr/** | |
| er | 26, 30 |
| **Vowel-*r* Spelling /ĭr/** | |
| ir | 21, 24 |
| **Vowel-*r* Spelling /îr/** | |
| er | 2, 6, 29, 30 |
| ear | 29, 30 |
| **Vowel-*r* Spelling /īr/** | |
| ir | 8, 12 |
| **Vowel-*r* Spelling /ôr/** | |
| ar | 14, 18 |
| or | 4, 6, 23, 24 |
| our | 14, 18 |
| **Vowel-*r* Spelling /*our*/** | |
| our | 10, 12 |
| **Vowel-*r* Spelling /ûr/** | |
| er | 11, 12 |
| ir | 35, 36 |
| or | 19, 24 |
| ur | 9, 12, 20, 24 |
| **Vowel-*r* Spelling /*yo͝or*/** | |
| ur | 5, 6 |
| **Vowel-*r* Spelling /ər/** | |
| er | 9, 11, 12 |

## STRUCTURAL ANALYSIS

| | LESSON |
|---|---|
| **Base Words** | 3, 12, 13, 18, 22, 24, 25, 32, 33, 36 |
| **Compound Words** | 2, 6, 8, 9, 10, 12, 15, 18, 19, 23, 24, 26, 27, 29, 30, 31, 33, 34, 36 |
| **Suffixes — No base change** | |
| -ed | 2, 4, 6, 7, 10, 11, 12, 13, 14, 16, 18, 19, 21, 22, 23, 24, 25, 26, 27, 29, 30, 31, 33, 34, 36 |
| -er | 2, 4, 9, 12, 13, 16, 17, 18, 25, 28, 29, 30 |
| -es | 2, 6, 12, 13, 15, 16, 18, 21, 26, 30 |
| -est | 1, 6, 30 |
| -ing | 2, 3, 6, 7, 8, 10, 11, 12, 13, 15, 18, 20, 21, 22, 23, 24, 25, 30, 31, 32, 33, 34, 36 |
| -s | 1, 4, 6, 8, 9, 10, 12, 13, 14, 16, 17, 18, 19, 22, 23, 24, 26, 28, 30, 31, 33, 34, 35, 36 |
| **Suffixes — Changing *f* to *v*** | |
| -es | 3, 6, 28, 30, 33, 36 |
| **Suffixes — Changing *y* to *i*** | |
| -ed | 3, 6, 8, 12, 21. 24 |
| -es | 8, 12, 14, 18, 19, 20, 21, 22, 23, 24, 25, 26, 30, 31, 33, 34, 36 |
| -est | 1, 2, 3, 17, 20, 22, 24, 30 |
| **Suffixes — Doubling final consonant** | |
| -ed | 13, 14, 18, 21, 24, 29, 30, 36 |
| -ing | 13, 14, 18, 20, 21, 24, 29, 36 |

| | LESSON |
|---|---|
| **Suffixes — Dropping final *e*** | |
| -ed | 3, 6, 17, 18, 19, 24, 30, 31, 34, 36 |
| -er | 4, 5, 6, 9 |
| -est | 1, 3, 6 |
| -ing | 1, 3, 4, 6, 7, 8, 12, 15, 19, 20, 23, 24, 26, 28, 31, 34, 36 |
| **Other suffix forms** | |
| -able | 2, 23, 33, 36 |
| -dom | 8, 12 |
| -ern | 4, 6, 15, 18, 26, 30 |
| -ful | 2, 6, 16, 18, 23, 29, 30, 31, 35, 36 |
| -ian | 35, 36 |
| -ish | 5, 6 |
| -ity | 35, 36 |
| -ly | 1, 2, 3, 4, 5, 6, 7, 11, 12, 13, 18, 23, 24, 26, 27, 28, 29, 30, 31, 33, 35, 36 |
| -ment | 7, 12, 19, 23, 24, 33, 34 |
| -ness | 15, 18, 24, 30, 31, 32, 33, 36 |
| -or | 7, 11, 12, 17, 30, 31, 32, 36 |
| -ous | 12, 19, 24 |
| -some | 4, 6, 31, 36 |
| -teen | 13, 18, 26, 30 |
| -th | 3, 6, 13, 18, 23, 24, 26, 30 |
| -ty | 19, 24 |
| -y | 5, 9, 18, 25, 26, 27, 30 |
| **Syllabication** | 4, 6, 20 |

## AUDITORY DISCRIMINATION

| | |
|---|---|
| **Rhyming Words** | 8, 20 |

## VISUAL DISCRIMINATION

| | |
|---|---|
| **Letter Sequencing** | 1, 2, 3, 4, 5, 6, 7, 8, 9, 10, 11, 12, 13, 14, 15, 16, 17, 19, 20, 21, 22, 23, 25, 26, 27, 28, 29, 30, 31, 32, 33, 34, 35, 36 |
| **Word Parts** | 4, 5, 7, 9, 10, 14, 16, 17, 20, 22, 24, 26, 32, 33 |
| **Word Recognition** | 1, 2, 3, 4, 5, 6, 7, 8, 9, 10, 11, 12, 13, 15, 16, 19, 20, 21, 22, 23, 25, 26, 27, 28, 29, 30, 31, 32, 33, 34, 35 |

## Scope and Sequence Chart Continued

### VOCABULARY

| | LESSON | | LESSON |
|---|---|---|---|
| **Analogies** | 2, 10, 17, 22 | **Homophones** | 1, 34 |
| **Antonyms** | 4, 5, 9, 10, 11, 15, 17, 22, 26, 29, 34, 35, 36 | **Synonyms** | 1, 2, 4, 5, 8, 9, 10, 11, 13, 14, 16, 17, 18, 19, 20, 21, 23, 25, 26, 27, 28, 29, 30, 31, 32, 33, 34, 35 |
| **Compound Words** | 2, 6, 8, 10, 12, 19, 23, 24, 26, 27, 29, 30, 31, 33, 34, 36 | **Word Relationships** | 1, 4, 8, 11, 14, 17, 20, 21, 22, 25, 26, 28, 29, 30, 32, 35, 36 |
| **Content Area Words** | Teacher Resources | | |
| **Contractions** | 2, 3, 4, 5, 6, 11, 12, 15, 16, 18 | | |

### CONTEXT CLUES

| | | | |
|---|---|---|---|
| **Phrase Clue** | 1, 2, 3, 4, 5, 7, 8, 9, 10, 11, 13, 14, 15, 16, 17, 19, 20, 21, 22, 23, 25, 26, 27, 28, 29, 31, 32, 33, 34, 35 | **Sentence Completion** | 1, 2, 3, 4, 5, 6, 9, 10, 11, 13, 14, 17, 18, 19, 21, 23, 24, 25, 27, 33, 34, 35 |
| **Phrase Completion** | 4, 8, 9, 11, 15, 22, 23, 27, 29, 30, 36 | **Story Completion** | 6, 12 |

### DICTIONARY SKILLS

| | | | |
|---|---|---|---|
| **Alphabetizing** | 3, 9, 16, 17, 18, 20, 23, 36 | **Multiple Meanings** | 23, 28 |
| **Base Words** | 6, 12, 13, 18, 22, 24, 30, 33, 36 | **Parts of a Dictionary** | 5, 8, 10 |
| **Finding Other Word Forms** | 6, 12, 18, 24, 30, 36 | **Using Guide Words** | 15, 19, 27, 32, 35 |
| | | **Word Meanings** | 1, 4, 5, 8, 9, 11, 14, 16, 23, 27, 29, 31, 34 |

### MECHANICS

| | | | |
|---|---|---|---|
| **Capitalization** | 1, 2, 3, 4, 5, 7, 8, 9, 10, 11, 12, 13, 14, 15, 16, 17, 18, 19, 20, 21, 22, 23, 24, 25, 26, 27, 28, 29, 30, 31, 32, 33, 34, 35, 36 | **Punctuation** | 1, 2, 3, 4, 5, 7, 8, 9, 10, 11, 13, 14, 15, 16, 17, 18, 19, 20, 21, 22, 23, 25, 26, 27, 28, 29, 30, 31, 32, 33, 34, 35, 36 |
| **Contractions** | 2, 3, 4, 5, 6, 11, 12, 15, 16, 18 | | |

### PROOFREADING PERSONAL SPELLING

| | |
|---|---|
| **Proofreading** | 1, 2, 3, 4, 5, 7, 8, 9, 10, 11, 13, 14, 15, 16, 17, 19, 20, 21, 22, 23, 25, 26, 27, 28, 29, 31, 32, 33, 34, 35 |

## WRITING

| | LESSON | | LESSONS |
|---|---|---|---|
| | | Creating Sentences with Spelling Words | 1, 2, 3, 4, 5, 7, 8, 9, 10, 11, 13, 14, 15, 16, 17, 19, 20, 21, 22, 23, 25, 26, 27, 28, 29, 31, 32, 33, 34, 35. |

## PROOFREADING THE SPELLING OF OTHERS *(from Proofreading Exercises)*

| | |
|---|---|
| **Proofreading** | 6, 12, 18, 24, 30, 36 |

## AUDITORY DISCRIMINATION *(from Teacher Annotated Lessons)*

| | | | |
|---|---|---|---|
| **Sentence Dictation** | 1, 2, 3, 4, 5, 7, 8, 9, 10, 11, 13, 14, 15, 16, 17, 19, 20, 21, 22, 23, 25, 26, 27, 28, 29, 31, 32, 33, 34, 35 | **Word Dictation** | 1, 2, 3, 4, 5, 6, 7, 8, 9, 10, 11, 12, 13, 14, 15, 16, 17, 18, 19, 20, 21, 22, 23, 24, 25, 26, 27, 28, 29, 30, 31, 32, 33, 34, 35, 36 |

## VOCABULARY *(from Challenge Exercises)*

| | | | |
|---|---|---|---|
| **Analogies** | 1, 2, 3, 4, 5, 7, 8, 9, 10, 11, 13, 14, 15, 16, 17, 19, 20, 21, 22, 23, 25, 26, 27, 28, 29, 31, 32, 33, 34, 35 | **Etymologies** | 1, 2, 3, 4, 5, 7, 8, 9, 10, 11, 13, 14, 15, 16, 17, 19, 20, 21, 22, 23, 25, 26, 27, 28, 29, 31, 32, 33, 34, 35 |
| **Challenge Words** | 1, 2, 3, 4, 5, 7, 8, 9, 10, 11, 13, 14, 15, 16, 17, 19, 20, 21, 22, 23, 25, 26, 27, 28, 29, 31, 32, 33, 34, 35 | | |

## WRITING *(from Challenge Exercises)*

| | |
|---|---|
| **Ads** | 10, 22, 32, 33 |
| **Letters** | 1, 16, 34, 35 |
| **Paragraphs** | 11, 17, 19, 20 |
| **Phrases** | 3, 9, 13, 23, 26 |
| **Rhymes** | 15, 27 |
| **Sentences** | 2, 4, 5, 7, 8, 14, 21, 25, 28, 29, 31 |

# About the Word Lists

Students using WORKING WORDS IN SPELLING are better equipped to spell correctly in their daily writing because they study and practice the high-frequency writing words they are most likely to use. There are nearly 4,000 high-frequency writing words in the overall program and over 13,000 of their related forms (Other Word Forms). These spelling words constitute over 99% of the most commonly used words in both student and adult writing.

| NUMBER OF WORDS PER LEVEL | | | | |
|---|---|---|---|---|
| Level/Grade | Initial Core Words | Other Word Forms | Challenge Words | Content Words |
| A / 1 | 120 | 155 | | |
| B / 2 | 316 | 650 | 120 | 279 (A, B, C) |
| C / 3 | 420 | 1086 | 150 | |
| D / 4 | 540 | 1600 | 150 | |
| E / 5 | 600 | 1908 | 150 | 721 (D, E, F) |
| F / 6 | 600 | 2534 | 150 | |
| G / 7 | 600 | 2329 | 150 | 333 (G, H) |
| H / 8 | 750 | 3341 | 150 | |
| TOTAL 1–8 | 3946 | 13,603 | 1020 | 1333 |
| GRAND TOTAL: 19,902 | | | | |

## Organizing the Spelling Words

The words for the program were allocated by level according to frequency of use, word difficulty, and complexity of meaning appropriate at each level. Each lesson contains a balance of easy, moderately difficult, and difficult words.

The words in each lesson are clustered by phonetic and structural patterns. Students then are able to categorize their spelling words in patterns that are meaningful *to them*. Never is an entire lesson devoted to a single vowel sound spelling or phonogram. This accords with the most recent research of how students develop in spelling awareness. They exercise their ability to generalize about spelling patterns in the words they encounter in a way they may not with precategorized spelling lists.

## References

The following resources were used to develop the WORKING WORDS IN SPELLING word list and divide the list by grade level:


Buckingham, B. R., and E. W. Dolch. *A Combined Word List*. Boston: Ginn and Company, 1936.

Carrol, J. B., Peter Davies, and Barry Richman. *Word Frequency Book*. New York: The American Heritage Publishing Co., 1971.

Dale, Edgar, and Joseph O'Rourke. *The Living Word Vocabulary*. Chicago: World Book-Childcraft International, Inc., 1981.

Fry, Edward, and Dona Fountoukidis. *The Reading Teacher's Book of Lists*. Englewood Cliffs, N.J.: Prentice-Hall, Inc., 1993.

Glazier, Stephen. *Word Menu*. New York: Random House, 1992.

Greene, Harry A., and Bradley M. Loomer. *The New Iowa Spelling Scale.* Iowa City: The University of Iowa, 1977.

Harris, Albert J., and Milton D. Jacobson. *Basic Reading Vocabularies.* New York: Macmillan Publishing Co., Inc., 1982.

Horn, Ernest. *A Basic Writing Vocabulary: 10,000 Frequently Used Words in Writing*. Monograph First Series, No. 4. Iowa City: The University of Iowa, 1926.

Rinsland, Harry. *A Basic Vocabulary of Elementary School Children*. New York: Macmillan Co., 1945.

Sitton, Rebecca. *Spelling Sourcebook 1: Your Guide for Developing Research-Based Spelling Instruction for the Writing-Rich Classroom*. Spokane, WA, 1993.

Thorndike, Edward L., and Irving Lorge. *The Teacher's Word Book of 30,000 Words*. New York: Columbia University, 1944.

# Word List For Level E

Challenge Words are in color.

| Lesson | Word |
|---|---|
| **A** | |
| 16 | acts |
| 35 | addition |
| 23 | adjusting |
| 31 | adverb |
| 3 | advised |
| 31 | afterward |
| 31 | agony |
| 2 | agreeable |
| 7 | aim |
| 33 | alarm |
| 21 | allow |
| 8 | all right |
| 25 | altered |
| 31 | although |
| 31 | altogether |
| 11 | American |
| 5 | amuse |
| 28 | anger |
| 16 | angle |
| 28 | angry |
| 16 | ankle |
| 28 | answer |
| 16 | antenna |
| 32 | anyhow |
| 32 | anyone |
| 32 | anyway |
| 32 | anywhere |
| 33 | apartment |
| 23 | appointment |
| 19 | April |
| 19 | apron |
| 5 | aren't |
| 21 | arrow |
| 33 | artist |
| 19 | ashamed |
| 26 | ashes |
| 16 | aspect |
| 17 | astronaut |
| 21 | atlas |
| 21 | attached |
| 16 | attaching |
| 21 | attack |
| 16 | attacking |
| 29 | attend |
| 17 | audience |
| 17 | August |
| 17 | aunt |
| 17 | automatic |
| 17 | automobile |
| 17 | autumn |
| 31 | avenue |
| 28 | average |
| 25 | awesome |
| 25 | awful |
| **B** | |
| 26 | badge |
| 31 | baggage |
| 7 | bait |
| 14 | balloon |
| 1 | bare |
| 21 | barrel |
| 19 | basement |
| 19 | bathing |
| 2 | beam |
| 2 | beaten |
| 35 | beautiful |
| 29 | begged |
| 13 | beginning |
| 19 | betray |
| 35 | beyond |
| 21 | bitter |
| 8 | bleachers |
| 8 | bleeding |
| 34 | blew |
| 15 | blood |
| 14 | blossom |
| 10 | blouse |
| 14 | bodies |
| 9 | bond |
| 4 | border |
| 4 | bore |
| 14 | bottom |
| 25 | bought |
| 7 | braid |
| 7 | brain |
| 1 | brake |
| 16 | branches |
| 16 | brass |
| 1 | break |
| 32 | breakfast |
| 8 | breezes |
| 22 | bridge |
| 3 | bridle |
| 15 | brook |
| 25 | brought |
| 22 | building |
| 20 | bundle |
| 35 | burden |
| 9 | burglar |
| 9 | burst |
| 20 | button |
| **C** | |
| 21 | cabbage |
| 16 | calendar |
| 25 | calm |
| 28 | calves |
| 28 | canal |
| 1 | canary |
| 16 | canyon |
| 31 | captain |
| 33 | carbon |
| 33 | carloads |
| 33 | carpenter |
| 33 | carpet |
| 21 | carried |
| 21 | carries |
| 28 | castle |
| 16 | catcher |
| 35 | cathedral |
| 17 | caught |
| 17 | caused |
| 25 | cautious |
| 29 | cellar |
| 32 | central |
| 19 | changing |
| 33 | charge |
| 2 | cheat |
| 26 | cherries |
| 34 | chewing |
| 8 | chief |
| 22 | chimney |
| 23 | choice |
| 5 | choose |
| 4 | chosen |
| 35 | circle |
| 22 | cities |
| 11 | clerk |
| 22 | cliff |
| 8 | climate |
| 35 | closet |
| 14 | cloth |
| 23 | cocoa |
| 14 | collar |
| 23 | colored |
| 23 | colt |
| 23 | comfort |
| 22 | comic |
| 28 | commander |
| 23 | company |
| 1 | compare |
| 22 | compass |
| 15 | compound |
| 35 | concern |
| 17 | conduct |
| 35 | congress |
| 35 | connect |
| 17 | consent |
| 20 | construct |
| 17 | content |
| 17 | contract |
| 17 | control |
| 14 | copies |
| 14 | copper |
| 27 | correctly |
| 35 | costume |
| 25 | cough |
| 15 | couldn't |
| 10 | county |
| 20 | couple |
| 14 | course |
| 14 | court |
| 15 | cousin |
| 10 | coward |
| 19 | crater |
| 25 | crawl |
| 1 | crazy |
| 8 | creek |
| 9 | crops |
| 10 | crouch |
| 10 | crowded |
| 20 | crush |
| 20 | current |
| 5 | cute |
| 20 | cutting |
| **D** | |
| 7 | daily |
| 21 | dandelion |
| 33 | darkness |
| 28 | data |
| 17 | daughter |
| 27 | deaf |
| 2 | dealing |
| 3 | decide |
| 19 | decoration |
| 2 | decrease |
| 8 | deed |
| 7 | delayed |
| 33 | depart |
| 11 | depend |
| 11 | desert |
| 22 | different |
| 22 | digits |
| 27 | direct |
| 29 | director |
| 35 | discount |
| 32 | distress |
| 13 | ditch |
| 3 | divide |
| 35 | doctor |
| 3 | doesn't |
| 14 | dollar |
| 4 | don't |
| 15 | double |
| 10 | downstairs |
| 15 | dozen |
| 25 | drawing |
| 25 | drawn |
| 29 | dreadful |
| 29 | dresser |
| 3 | dried |
| 34 | drooping |
| 14 | dropped |
| 34 | due |
| 20 | dumb |
| 34 | duties |
| **E** | |
| 2 | easier |
| 2 | eastern |
| 2 | easy |
| 26 | edge |
| 26 | eighteen |
| 26 | eighty |
| 29 | elbow |
| 35 | electricity |
| 29 | elements |
| 32 | elephant |
| 26 | else |
| 11 | empty |
| 29 | energy |
| 28 | engine |
| 29 | English |
| 15 | enough |
| 11 | entered |
| 32 | entire |
| 21 | envied |
| 27 | erect |
| 1 | escape |
| 32 | everywhere |
| 27 | except |
| 8 | excite |
| 8 | exciting |
| 5 | excuse |

| Lesson | Word |
|---|---|
| 27 | export |
| 32 | extended |

**F**

| Lesson | Word |
|---|---|
| 16 | fact |
| 31 | factory |
| 7 | faint |
| 7 | fairly |
| 7 | faithful |
| 25 | false |
| 31 | families |
| 19 | famous |
| 28 | fancy |
| 1 | fare |
| 21 | fashionable |
| 28 | fasten |
| 19 | favor |
| 29 | fearful |
| 27 | feather |
| 27 | festival |
| 13 | fifteenth |
| 13 | fifth |
| 3 | filing |
| 3 | final |
| 3 | finest |
| 22 | finger |
| 22 | finish |
| 35 | fir |
| 26 | flashlight |
| 34 | flew |
| 8 | flight |
| 15 | flood |
| 5 | foolish |
| 4 | forbid |
| 9 | forever |
| 14 | forgotten |
| 4 | formed |
| 4 | forward |
| 10 | foul |
| 15 | fountain |
| 26 | freckles |
| 8 | freedom |
| 8 | freeze |
| 32 | friendly |
| 8 | fright |
| 4 | frozen |
| 9 | further |

**G**

| Lesson | Word |
|---|---|
| 7 | gain |
| 21 | gallon |
| 28 | garage |
| 28 | gasoline |
| 31 | gathering |
| 11 | general |
| 29 | gentlemen |
| 8 | gleefully |
| 9 | golf |
| 15 | goodness |
| 15 | govern |
| 1 | grace |
| 31 | grandfather |
| 19 | grapefruit |
| 1 | grapes |
| 16 | grasp |
| 31 | gravel |
| 1 | graze |
| 1 | greatest |
| 34 | groups |
| 10 | growl |
| 23 | growth |
| 33 | guard |
| 3 | guidance |
| 3 | guide |
| 20 | gulf |

**H**

| Lesson | Word |
|---|---|
| 3 | hadn't |
| 8 | Halloween |
| 31 | handful |
| 28 | handicapped |
| 31 | handsome |
| 33 | harbor |
| 33 | hardware |
| 33 | harvest |
| 16 | hasn't |
| 16 | hatch |
| 27 | headquarters |
| 27 | health |
| 2 | heap |
| 27 | heavy |
| 11 | helmet |
| 29 | helpful |
| 11 | herd |
| 17 | holiday |
| 17 | honest |
| 35 | horizontal |
| 4 | hose |
| 15 | household |
| 10 | however |
| 10 | howl |
| 25 | husband |

**I**

| Lesson | Word |
|---|---|
| 3 | I'd |
| 2 | ideal |
| 3 | identify |
| 3 | I'll |
| 34 | improved |
| 32 | industry |
| 19 | information |
| 13 | innumerable |
| 27 | inspection |
| 32 | install |
| 20 | instructions |
| 23 | insult |
| 11 | intend |
| 11 | intent |
| 32 | interest |
| 11 | invent |
| 3 | invite |
| 8 | ironing |
| 3 | item |

**J**

| Lesson | Word |
|---|---|
| 16 | jacket |
| 29 | jelly |
| 4 | jokes |
| 20 | judge |
| 5 | juicy |
| 20 | jungle |
| 5 | junior |

**K**

| Lesson | Word |
|---|---|
| 26 | kettle |
| 13 | kitchen |
| 3 | knives |
| 17 | knock |
| 23 | knowing |
| 23 | known |

**L**

| Lesson | Word |
|---|---|
| 19 | ladies |
| 28 | language |
| 33 | largely |
| 7 | laser |
| 25 | lawyer |
| 27 | leather |
| 27 | lecture |
| 29 | lemon |
| 32 | lemonade |
| 32 | liberty |
| 13 | limb |
| 8 | limestone |
| 13 | limp |
| 3 | lining |
| 22 | listen |
| 3 | lively |
| 13 | lizards |
| 10 | loafing |
| 10 | loan |
| 17 | lobster |
| 9 | lodge |
| 25 | lofty |
| 4 | lonely |
| 4 | lonesome |
| 5 | loose |
| 15 | luckily |
| 34 | lunar |

**M**

| Lesson | Word |
|---|---|
| 28 | machine |
| 28 | mackerel |
| 28 | magazine |
| 26 | maintain |
| 31 | manuscript |
| 21 | married |
| 31 | Massachusetts |
| 16 | matches |
| 7 | mayor |
| 27 | meadow |
| 2 | meaningful |
| 2 | meantime |
| 2 | meanwhile |
| 11 | member |
| 27 | mentally |
| 26 | mention |
| 11 | merchant |
| 29 | message |
| 22 | midnight |
| 22 | military |
| 22 | million |
| 22 | minute |
| 21 | mirror |
| 3 | miser |
| 22 | miserable |
| 1 | mistake |
| 10 | moat |
| 14 | model |
| 9 | moment |
| 23 | monthly |
| 5 | mood |
| 9 | moss |
| 9 | motor |
| 10 | mountain |
| 20 | muddy |
| 25 | multiply |
| 15 | mumble |
| 35 | musician |

**N**

| Lesson | Word |
|---|---|
| 33 | narrowly |
| 19 | nation |
| 21 | nationally |
| 19 | nature |
| 17 | naughty |
| 19 | navy |
| 29 | nearby |
| 27 | necktie |
| 8 | needle |
| 26 | neighborhood |
| 32 | nephew |
| 34 | newspapers |
| 19 | nickname |
| 3 | ninth |
| 4 | northern |

**O**

| Lesson | Word |
|---|---|
| 9 | odd |
| 14 | offer |
| 17 | offered |
| 17 | often |
| 1 | operate |
| 14 | operated |
| 9 | operators |
| 9 | oppose |
| 4 | orchard |
| 4 | ordered |
| 4 | ore |
| 23 | organ |
| 15 | outline |
| 9 | overcome |
| 9 | overturn |
| 23 | owe |
| 23 | ownership |

**P**

| Lesson | Word |
|---|---|
| 31 | pajamas |
| 31 | palace |
| 28 | palm |
| 19 | parade |
| 33 | parchment |
| 33 | pardon |
| 33 | parents |
| 33 | parlor |
| 33 | parties |
| 33 | partner |
| 21 | passenger |
| 31 | pasture |
| 16 | patch |
| 7 | payment |
| 2 | peace |
| 2 | peacefully |
| 29 | people |
| 35 | perfect |
| 11 | perfume |
| 11 | perhaps |
| 29 | period |
| 11 | person |
| 31 | piano |
| 8 | piece |
| 22 | pilgrims |
| 13 | pitcher |
| 26 | plain |
| 21 | planning |
| 19 | plantation |
| 31 | plastic |
| 28 | platform |
| 23 | poetry |
| 4 | polar |
| 35 | popular |
| 7 | population |
| 4 | post office |
| 21 | potato |
| 10 | pounced |
| 10 | powder |
| 15 | powerfully |
| 31 | practicing |
| 7 | praise |
| 2 | preach |
| 1 | preparing |
| 27 | president |
| 19 | prey |
| 13 | prince |
| 13 | printing |
| 35 | probably |
| 14 | problem |
| 15 | product |
| 35 | products |
| 9 | program |
| 26 | projector |

# Previous Level Word List (Level D)

Lesson/Word

**A**

| Lesson | Word |
|---|---|
| 29 | above |
| 27 | absent |
| 2 | across |
| 31 | address |
| 28 | afraid |
| 9 | again |
| 20 | agree |
| 16 | ahead |
| 28 | aid |
| 1 | alike |
| 11 | almost |
| 23 | alone |
| 16 | already |
| 32 | always |
| 32 | among |
| 29 | amount |
| 32 | another |
| 32 | anybody |
| 26 | apiece |
| 4 | arithmetic |
| 29 | around |
| 31 | attic |
| 23 | awoke |
| 2 | ax |

**B**

| Lesson | Word |
|---|---|
| 2 | backward |
| 20 | banner |
| 33 | baseball |
| 27 | basket |
| 29 | basketball |
| 20 | battle |
| 31 | beast |
| 32 | beat |
| 20 | beef |
| 33 | before |
| 2 | began |
| 3 | begin |
| 3 | begun |
| 1 | being |
| 21 | belonged |
| 5 | bend |
| 22 | between |
| 13 | bid |
| 31 | bigger |
| 11 | bind |
| 17 | birthday |
| 5 | blade |
| 5 | blame |
| 19 | blanket |
| 27 | blast |
| 5 | blaze |
| 11 | blind |
| 5 | blocks |
| 31 | bloom |
| 28 | board |
| 14 | boil |
| 33 | born |
| 21 | bother |
| 29 | bound |
| 35 | branch |
| 5 | brave |
| 16 | breath |
| 9 | brick |
| 16 | broke |
| 7 | bruise |
| 7 | brush |
| 17 | bucket |
| 28 | build |
| 28 | built |
| 7 | bump |
| 21 | burn |
| 28 | busy |

**C**

| Lesson | Word |
|---|---|
| 27 | cabin |
| 31 | cable |
| 2 | camel |
| 20 | candle |
| 2 | can't |
| 1 | cape |
| 26 | careful |
| 26 | careless |
| 3 | cases |
| 29 | cash |
| 20 | cattle |
| 27 | center |
| 27 | cents |
| 28 | chain |
| 25 | chance |
| 25 | change |
| 13 | chart |
| 10 | chase |
| 8 | check |
| 20 | cheer |
| 21 | chop |
| 22 | chose |
| 23 | clever |
| 11 | climb |
| 35 | clothes |
| 35 | clothing |
| 10 | clown |
| 7 | club |
| 22 | coach |
| 22 | coal |
| 14 | coin |
| 32 | color |
| 21 | copy |
| 33 | corner |
| 33 | correct |
| 34 | count |
| 19 | crack |
| 19 | crash |
| 26 | cried |
| 8 | crime |
| 2 | crossing |
| 10 | crowd |

**D**

| Lesson | Word |
|---|---|
| 25 | dancing |
| 25 | danger |
| 1 | dare |
| 35 | dash |
| 15 | dawn |
| 16 | death |
| 27 | December |
| 5 | deck |
| 14 | deliver |
| 29 | demand |
| 3 | didn't |
| 13 | dim |
| 17 | dirty |
| 29 | discover |
| 1 | dive |
| 2 | draft |
| 7 | drag |
| 28 | drain |
| 19 | drank |
| 15 | draw |
| 31 | dream |
| 9 | drill |
| 14 | driving |
| 16 | during |

**E**

| Lesson | Word |
|---|---|
| 15 | early |
| 15 | earn |
| 15 | earth |
| 23 | eleven |
| 33 | enjoy |
| 3 | enter |
| 35 | evening |
| 23 | event |
| 35 | everybody |
| 35 | everyone |
| 35 | everything |

**F**

| Lesson | Word |
|---|---|
| 1 | fade |
| 32 | fallen |
| 13 | farther |
| 3 | fate |
| 15 | fears |
| 31 | feast |
| 26 | February |
| 22 | feeling |
| 27 | fence |
| 35 | fever |
| 16 | few |
| 26 | field |
| 33 | film |
| 27 | fireplace |
| 19 | flash |
| 19 | fled |
| 5 | flock |
| 28 | floor |
| 34 | flour |
| 25 | flow |
| 32 | follow |
| 21 | fond |
| 33 | fork |
| 33 | fort |
| 33 | forty |
| 33 | fourteen |
| 33 | fourth |
| 10 | frame |
| 8 | fresh |
| 19 | Friday |
| 26 | fried |
| 26 | friends |
| 29 | front |
| 16 | froze |

**G**

| Lesson | Word |
|---|---|
| 29 | gang |
| 19 | glasses |
| 16 | globe |
| 23 | glow |
| 23 | golden |
| 32 | gotten |
| 10 | gown |
| 29 | grandmother |
| 23 | greet |
| 21 | grind |
| 4 | grip |
| 25 | grown |

**H**

| Lesson | Word |
|---|---|
| 27 | habit |
| 15 | hammer |
| 20 | handle |
| 35 | handy |
| 31 | happening |
| 20 | harm |
| 26 | hate |
| 15 | heard |
| 15 | heart |
| 17 | heating |
| 20 | heel |
| 25 | hero |
| 1 | he's |
| 11 | higher |
| 11 | highest |
| 11 | highway |
| 1 | hire |
| 4 | history |
| 17 | holding |
| 2 | holes |
| 10 | homesick |
| 29 | honey |
| 23 | hoping |
| 35 | hotel |
| 34 | hour |
| 34 | huge |
| 7 | hundred |
| 7 | hung |
| 7 | hungry |
| 3 | hunter |

**I**

| Lesson | Word |
|---|---|
| 28 | inch |
| 34 | inches |
| 23 | indeed |
| 19 | iron |
| 19 | island |
| 3 | it's |
| 3 | itself |

**J**

| Lesson | Word |
|---|---|
| 9 | jail |
| 23 | January |
| 20 | jar |
| 21 | job |
| 14 | join |
| 34 | July |
| 34 | June |

**K**

| Lesson | Word |
|---|---|
| 8 | kept |
| 33 | kick |
| 4 | knee |
| 4 | knew |
| 4 | knife |
| 4 | know |
| 4 | knows |

**L**

| Lesson | Word |
|---|---|
| 3 | lace |
| 15 | ladder |
| 19 | lamb |
| 35 | landing |
| 26 | lately |
| 23 | laugh |
| 15 | lawn |
| 15 | laws |
| 26 | lazy |
| 17 | leading |
| 17 | leaf |
| 17 | leak |
| 15 | lean |
| 32 | leaving |
| 19 | led |
| 5 | lend |
| 26 | less |
| 26 | lessen |
| 26 | letting |
| 23 | level |
| 16 | lightly |
| 16 | lightning |
| 27 | likely |
| 28 | living |
| 28 | loads |
| 31 | loop |
| 9 | loud |
| 17 | lucky |
| 3 | lump |
| 3 | lung |
| 26 | lying |

**M**

| Lesson | Word |
|---|---|
| 15 | madder |
| 2 | madly |
| 27 | magic |
| 28 | mailed |
| 26 | making |
| 2 | mapping |
| 13 | marble |
| 13 | March |
| 13 | marker |
| 29 | mask |
| 15 | matter |
| 32 | May |
| 15 | meal |
| 32 | means |
| 1 | meet |
| 22 | meeting |
| 5 | melt |
| 31 | middle |
| 11 | mighty |
| 11 | mild |
| 1 | mile |
| 13 | mint |
| 13 | mist |

| Lesson | Word |
|---|---|
| 13 | mix |
| 29 | Monday |
| 19 | monster |
| 29 | month |
| 11 | mostly |
| 34 | mouse |
| 16 | music |

**N**

| Lesson | Word |
|---|---|
| 9 | nails |
| 32 | nearest |
| 26 | nineteen |
| 23 | nobody |
| 14 | noise |
| 29 | none |
| 10 | notebooks |
| 16 | November |
| 17 | number |
| 21 | nurse |

**O**

| Lesson | Word |
|---|---|
| 28 | oak |
| 35 | ocean |
| 7 | o'clock |
| 32 | October |
| 14 | oil |
| 17 | oldest |
| 35 | omit |
| 35 | only |
| 35 | opening |
| 32 | orange |
| 34 | ounce |
| 9 | outfits |
| 25 | owner |

**P**

| Lesson | Word |
|---|---|
| 35 | package |
| 35 | packed |
| 20 | paddle |
| 9 | pain |
| 20 | partly |
| 20 | party |
| 31 | paste |
| 25 | peek |
| 22 | phone |
| 34 | picnic |
| 34 | picture |
| 1 | pile |
| 31 | pillow |
| 13 | plane |
| 32 | playmate |
| 27 | plenty |
| 3 | plum |
| 5 | pocket |
| 35 | poem |
| 14 | point |
| 31 | pool |
| 16 | porch |
| 11 | post |
| 17 | poster |
| 34 | pound |
| 33 | pouring |
| 10 | power |
| 8 | press |
| 33 | pretend |
| 4 | prices |
| 8 | pride |
| 28 | print |
| 4 | prize |
| 9 | proud |
| 19 | provide |
| 21 | purse |

**Q**

| Lesson | Word |
|---|---|
| 25 | queen |
| 19 | quiet |
| 8 | quit |
| 8 | quite |

**R**

| Lesson | Word |
|---|---|
| 1 | races |
| 2 | rack |
| 28 | rainy |
| 35 | ranch |
| 25 | ranger |
| 32 | ray |
| 32 | reader |
| 22 | real |
| 29 | recover |
| 21 | remind |
| 28 | repair |
| 13 | replace |
| 21 | returning |
| 13 | reward |
| 33 | rich |
| 27 | ripe |
| 14 | river |
| 28 | roar |
| 23 | rolled |
| 31 | root |
| 34 | rules |

**S**

| Lesson | Word |
|---|---|
| 29 | sack |
| 20 | saddle |
| 9 | sail |
| 32 | sank |
| 23 | Saturday |
| 3 | saves |
| 5 | scale |
| 17 | scold |
| 16 | score |
| 7 | scrap |
| 10 | scrape |
| 34 | scream |
| 7 | scrub |
| 32 | season |
| 22 | seat |
| 33 | second |
| 1 | seemed |
| 27 | sense |
| 14 | September |
| 23 | seventh |
| 5 | shake |
| 10 | shame |
| 26 | shape |
| 10 | share |
| 26 | sharing |
| 19 | shed |
| 20 | sheep |
| 25 | sheet |
| 8 | shell |
| 1 | she's |
| 4 | shine |
| 14 | shining |
| 17 | shirt |
| 5 | shock |
| 22 | shore |
| 9 | shout |
| 10 | shower |
| 25 | shown |
| 27 | sidewalk |
| 27 | sideways |
| 33 | silk |
| 14 | silver |
| 34 | since |
| 34 | single |
| 33 | sink |
| 17 | sir |
| 31 | sitting |
| 13 | sixteen |
| 13 | sixth |
| 1 | size |
| 5 | skate |
| 13 | skating |
| 9 | skill |
| 25 | sleepy |
| 8 | slept |
| 14 | sliced |
| 4 | slid |
| 4 | slide |
| 14 | sliding |
| 4 | slip |
| 25 | slowly |
| 4 | smile |
| 22 | smoke |
| 7 | snap |
| 34 | sneakers |
| 21 | sob |
| 14 | soil |
| 10 | sore |
| 11 | sort |
| 10 | space |
| 31 | speak |
| 8 | spend |
| 4 | spin |
| 22 | spoke |
| 22 | sport |
| 31 | stable |
| 5 | stake |
| 34 | steam |
| 25 | steel |
| 20 | steep |
| 7 | stocking |
| 22 | stole |
| 22 | stories |
| 25 | strange |
| 15 | straw |
| 34 | stream |
| 8 | strike |
| 21 | strong |
| 17 | study |
| 3 | sum |
| 17 | Sunday |
| 21 | sure |
| 25 | sweep |
| 3 | swift |
| 9 | swim |
| 28 | swing |
| 11 | sword |

**T**

| Lesson | Word |
|---|---|
| 22 | team |
| 22 | tear |
| 23 | teeth |
| 26 | tend |
| 9 | thick |
| 29 | thousand |
| 16 | thread |
| 25 | throw |
| 13 | ticket |
| 13 | tin |
| 19 | tiny |
| 27 | tired |
| 21 | ton |
| 31 | tooth |
| 2 | tore |
| 10 | tower |
| 10 | trace |
| 7 | trap |
| 8 | tribe |
| 9 | trick |
| 8 | trim |
| 7 | trust |
| 16 | Tuesday |
| 21 | turtle |
| 27 | twenty |
| 27 | twenty-five |

**U**

| Lesson | Word |
|---|---|
| 7 | unlock |
| 17 | until |

**W**

| Lesson | Word |
|---|---|
| 1 | wade |
| 9 | wait |
| 28 | waiting |
| 31 | waste |
| 15 | weak |
| 16 | wear |
| 14 | Wednesday |
| 22 | weekend |
| 25 | wheel |
| 8 | whip |
| 33 | windy |
| 2 | woke |
| 34 | woman |
| 14 | women |
| 2 | won't |
| 2 | wore |
| 11 | worn |
| 11 | worry |
| 11 | worth |
| 29 | wound |
| 19 | wrap |
| 14 | writer |
| 21 | wrong |

**Y**

| Lesson | Word |
|---|---|
| 20 | yard |
| 8 | yellow |

# Next Level Word List (Level F)

Lesson/Word

**A**

27 abandon
32 ability
4 abroad
25 accent
26 accept
27 accident
4 according
34 account
1 ache
21 acid
13 acre
25 action
25 active
32 activity
23 adjust
9 admire
32 admission
28 admit
22 adopt
14 advance
27 advantage
11 adventure
27 advertise
9 advice
26 affect
35 against
8 agreement
35 amendment
5 amusement
1 anxious
15 appeal
34 approve
13 area
19 argument
19 armor
13 arrangement
31 arrest
9 arrive
19 article
35 assembly
34 assigned
28 assist
33 astonished
25 athlete
7 attain
35 attention
27 attractive
33 auction
33 author
25 avoid
33 awfully
33 awkward

**B**

14 balance
7 bargain
1 bathe
27 battery
1 behave
15 beneath
17 berry
16 bicycle
23 bluff
25 boiler
22 borrowed
15 breathe
8 brief
4 broad
29 burden
17 buried
34 bushel
32 business

**C**

27 cabinet
1 calendar
21 campus
13 capable
27 capital
5 capture
19 carefully
27 catalog
33 caution
31 cement
31 century
33 chalk
7 chamber
1 champion
25 channel
27 chapter
19 charity
19 charming
2 cheap
32 citizen
7 claims
4 coarse
26 collect
33 colonies
14 command
22 comment
22 common
22 companion
2 complete
17 computer
34 concerned
22 concert
5 confuse
34 connection
7 contain
22 contemplate
10 continent
32 continue
10 contribute
35 convention
8 convince
4 cooperate
29 countries
29 courage
15 creature
28 credit
8 creep
11 cruel
35 cultivate
23 cunning
5 curious
29 curtain
17 curve
34 cushion
29 customer

**D**

14 damage
13 dangerous
1 debate
20 debt
2 decent
19 declare
9 decline
35 decorate
15 defeat
26 defense
16 delightfully
32 delivery
28 dentist
19 department
28 deposit
20 depth
17 deserve
16 design
9 desire
17 dessert
25 destroy
16 diameter
3 diamond
32 dictionary
3 diet
34 differ
29 difficult
26 directed
35 direction
2 disappear
1 disaster
5 discontinue
23 discuss
15 disease
9 dislike
28 dismiss
5 dispute
3 distant
28 district
21 disturb
32 division
34 document
34 doubt

**E**

2 eager
13 echo
20 effort
35 election
31 element
31 elevator
20 empire
31 enemies
8 energy
4 enforce
7 entertain
9 entirely
31 envelope
2 equal
20 error
1 establish
1 estate
2 evil
7 exact
27 exactly
27 example
13 exchange
9 excitement
7 exclaim
31 exercise
28 exhibit
26 expect
26 expense
20 expensive
20 expert
7 explain
4 explore
34 expose
31 express
31 extent
20 extra

**F**

27 factories
34 familiar
19 farewell
33 fault
19 favorable
13 favorite
5 figure
3 finally
29 firm
13 flavor
21 forbidden
4 force
22 forehead
10 foreign
22 fortune
14 frankly
25 freight
16 frighten
34 fully
11 funeral
17 furnace
29 furniture
5 future

**G**

14 gallop
19 garbage
2 gear
26 gentle
4 ghost
14 glance
34 glitter
11 gloomy
10 glory
22 gossip
29 government
1 grateful
9 greater
8 grief
10 groceries

**H**

21 handkerchief
27 happiness
34 harmony
1 haste
1 headache
20 healthy
16 height
35 hesitate
16 highly
9 horizon
5 human
5 humor

**I**

3 idle
4 import
10 important
32 impossible
34 improvement
28 impulse
9 inclined
11 include
28 income
15 increase
31 independent
3 infant
5 injure
28 inning
9 inquire
26 insects
28 insist
35 inspection
3 instant
20 instead
29 instruction
5 insure
11 introduce
35 invention
13 invitation
5 issue

**J**

15 jealous
11 jewels
25 joint
10 journey
5 jury

**K**

16 knitting
33 knowledge

**L**

13 labor
14 landlord
21 landscape
25 lantern
14 lasting
33 launch
33 laundry
33 lawyers
15 league
2 lease
20 length
26 lettuce
28 limit
3 linen
21 liquid
1 locate
22 loss
25 loyal

**M**

8 machinery
13 major
14 manage
14 manner
11 manual
11 manufacturing

# Content Area Words for Levels D, E & F

The following list provides students with the opportunity to expand their spelling vocabularies into other content areas. For ease of teacher reference, some of the lists are organized by topic. The following ideas suggest ways to introduce and use the content area spelling lists.

- Select and then introduce the "word(s) of the day." Ask students to define the meaning(s) or use the word(s) in a sentence. Provide explanations when necessary.
- Introduce content words as they fit with topics of study across the curriculum.
- Introduce content words weekly that fit into similar word groups and generalizations from the spelling lesson under study.

Whichever strategies you use to present the words, you may wish to include them in the weekly pretests and posttests. Students may then include appropriate content words on the **Words to Learn Sheet** and record selected words in the **Personal Spelling Dictionary.**

**Computer**

access
array
automation
backup
character
computer
console
cursor
database
debug
delete
directory
diskette
display
document
edit
erase
execute
field
format
function
graphics
hardware
hookup
index
input
insert
interrupt
keyboard
label
macro
matrix
megabyte
memory
merge
micro
monitor
network
offline
online
operator
output
overflow
password
portable
printer
printout
processor
programmer
prompt
random
reset
retrieve
routine
scan
software
storage
symbol
system
terminal
text
time sharing
troubleshoot
update
variable
video

## Language Arts

### Dictionary
alphabetical
definition
entry
pronunciation
syllable

### Figures of Speech
alliteration
metaphor
onomatopoeia
personification
simile

### Letters
closing
greeting
heading
salutation
signature

### Parts of Speech
adjective
adverb
comparative
conjunction
determiner
grammar
irregular
modifier
plural
possessive
preposition
pronoun
singular
superlative
tense

### Poetry
haiku
jingle
limerick
poetry
rhyme
rhythm
stanza
verse

### Punctuation
apostrophe
capitalization
colon
hyphen
punctuation
quotation
underlining

### Reference Aids
almanac
bibliography
encyclopedia
footnote
glossary
index
reference
thesaurus

### Sentences
clause
declarative
diagraming
exclamatory
imperative
interrogative
phrase
predicate
run-on
subject

### Words
abbreviation
affix
antonym
compound
contraction
homograph
initials
prefix
suffix
synonym

### Writing
autobiography
biography
character
climax
composition
conclusion
cursive
detail
dialogue
editing
experience
fable
fantasy
fiction
image
indent
legend
manuscript
myth
narrator
nonfiction
novel
novelist
outlining
plot
proofreading
report
revise
saga
setting
subtopic
summary
suspense
symbol

## Math

### Consumer Math
budget
discount
installment
wages

### Geometry
acute
arc
axis
congruent
construction
coordinate
corresponding
cylinder
diagonal
equilateral
hexagon
horizontal
intersect
isosceles
obtuse
octagon
parallelogram
pentagon
polygon
prism
pyramid
quadrilateral
rhombus
segment
semicircle
sphere
symmetry
trapezoid
vertex
vertical

### Measurement
capacity
centimeter
circumference
diameter
dimension
distance
formula
kilogram
kiloliter
kilometer
metric
milligram
milliliter
millimeter
perimeter
protractor
radius

### Numbers/ Number Theory
associative
calculator
commutative
composite
decimal
denominator
difference
distributive
dividend
division
divisor
equality
equation
equivalent
estimate
exponent
factorization
fraction
invert
minuend
multiple
multiplicand
multiplication
multiplier
negative
numerator
positive
prime
product
quotient
regrouping
remainder
subtraction
subtrahend

### Using Data
average
median
range
statistics
ratio

## Science

### Anatomy
abdomen
anatomy
biceps
bladder
cartilage
digestion
esophagus
gland
hormone
intestine
kidney
ligament
lymph
marrow
pancreas
plasma
respiration
saliva
skeletal
spinal
spleen
tendon
thorax
tissue
triceps

### Animal Behavior
adapt
behavior
evolution
extinct
hibernate
imprinting
instinct
predator
prey
species
survival

### Animal Classifications
amphibian
invertebrate
mammal
parasite
primate
reptile
vertebrate

# Content Area Words for Levels D, E & F Continued

**Atomics**
atomic
axon
electron
fission
fusion
ion
molecule
neutron
nuclear
nucleus
proton
radioactive

**Chemistry**
alcohol
carbon
chemical
crystal
compound
formula
graphite
hydrogen
litmus
mercury
nitrogen
oxygen
ozone
substance
sulphur
uranium

**Circulatory**
aorta
artery
atrium
capillary
cardiac
circulation
coronary
plasma
pulse
valve
vein
ventricle

**Environment**
conservation
ecology
environment
erosion
habitat
landfill
pollution
recycle

**Genetics**
characteristics
chromosome
dominant
gene
heredity
inherit
mutation
trait

**Geology**
earthquake
fault
fossil
geology
geyser
granite
lava
layer
magma
pumice
sediment
silt
topsoil

**Insect Stages**
antenna
caterpillar
cocoon
larva
molt
pupa

**Life Cycle**
cycle
decay
decompose
embryo
fertilize
offspring
ovum
reproduce
spore
yolk

**Lower Life Forms**
algae
amoeba
bacteria
cilia
fungus
lichen
microscopic
organism
paramecium
plankton
protozoan
virus

**Marine Animals**
barnacle
coral
dolphin
mollusk
mussel
octopus
oyster
periwinkle
porpoise
quahog
scallop
shrimp
sponge
squid
walrus

**Nervous System**
cerebellum
cerebrum
electrodes
impulse
medulla
neuron
reflex
response
stimulus

**Nutrition**
calcium
calorie
carbohydrate
enzyme
glucose
lactose
metabolism
nutrition
protein
starches
sucrose
vitamin

**Optics**
bifocal
binocular
concave
convex
cornea
iris
lens
microscope
myopic
optical
photography
pupil
reflect
refraction
retina
spectrum
telescope

**Physical Science**
accelerator
ampere
circuit
compression
conduction
convection
current
density
dynamo
electrical
electromagnet
filament
friction
generator
gravity
hydroelectric
insulator
kinetic
magnetism
pulsar
pressure
quasar
static
turbine
vacuum
vibration
voltage

**Plants**
annual
botany
chlorophyll
coniferous
deciduous
hybrid
perennial
pistil
pollen
pulp
sepal
stalk
stamen
tuber
vegetation

**Reptiles**
alligator
chameleon
crocodile
dinosaur
lizard
tortoise

**Teeth**
canine
cavity
cuspid
dentine
incisor
molar

**Universe**
asteroid
astronaut
astronomy
constellation
cosmic
eclipse
galaxy
lunar
meteor
orbit
phase
rotation
satellite
solar
spacecraft
telescope
universe

**Water**
absorb
condensation
dew
dissolve
elevation
evaporate
humidity
moisture
precipitation
saturate
vapor

**Weather**
altitude
atmosphere
barometer
blizzard
chinook
cirrus
cumulus
cyclone
forecast
hail
hurricane
monsoon
smog
squall
stratus
temperature
tempest
tornado

Social Studies

**Agriculture**
agriculture
citrus
cultivation
dairy
drought
fertilizer
irrigation
livestock
silo

**Canada**
Canadian
caribou
dominion
intermontane
maritime
parliament
premier
provinces
separatist

**Civil Liberties**
equality
integration
justice
minority
pacifist
privilege
riot
segregation
suffrage

**Civil War**
abolish
blockade
boycott
carpetbagger
confederacy
reconstruction
secede
sharecropping
slavery

**Colonial Times**
ally
brigade
cargo
colonist
infantry
loyalist
massacre
militia
minuteman
musket
patriot
Puritan
revolution
tariff
truce

**Continents/ Oceans**
Africa
Antarctica
Asia
Atlantic
Australia
Europe
North America
Pacific
South America

**Culture and Heritage**
ancestor
bilingual
ceremony
civilization
community
culture
descendant
emigrate
ethnic
generation
ghetto
heritage
immigrant
migrant
migration
nationality
nomads
poverty
prosperity
refugee
reservation
society
tenement
tradition

**Geography**
basin
bayou
delta
dune
grasslands
highland
isthmus
landforms
levee
lowland
mesa
pampa
peninsula
plateau
prairie
reef
region
savanna
steppe
timberline
tundra

**Government**
allegiance
amendments
citizen
constitution
council
democrat
diplomat
federal
inaugurate
legislature
military
overthrow
political
ratify
repeal
representative
republican
senator
tourism
veto

**Industrialization**
barter
commerce
communication
consumer
economics
exporting
forge
importing
industrial
laborer
manufacture
monopoly
occupation
petroleum
pipeline
production
refinery
resource
skyscraper
technology
textile

**Latin America**
adobe
Amazon
Aztec
cacao
conquistador
coup
hacienda
mestizo
missionary
plaza
pueblo

**Maps**
atlas
axis
equator
hemisphere
latitude
legend
longitude
meridian
polar
scale
symbol

**Population**
census
population
rural
suburb
survey
urban

**Water**
cove
fiord
geyser
glacier
gulf
iceberg
inlet
lagoon
oasis
strait
tributary

**Westward Movement**
Conestoga
expedition
exploration
frontier
homestead
pioneer
stockade
territories

# 240 Most Useful Words

This word list contains more than 50% of the words students use in daily writing. Use this list to maintain a minimum competency standard for your students.

**A**
about
after
again
all
also
always
am
an
and
another
any
are
around
as
asked
at
away

**B**
back
be
bear
because
bed
been
before
best
big
black
book
boy
brother
but
by

**C**
called
came
can
car
cat
come
could

**D**
day
did
didn't
do
dog
don't
door
down

**E**
eat
end
even
ever
every

**F**
family
father
fell
find
fire
first
fish
five
food
for
form
found
four
friend
fun

**G**
game
gave
get
girl
give
go
going
gone
good
got

**H**
had
happy
has
have
he
head
heard
help
her
here
him
his
home
horse
house
how

**I**
if
I'm
in
into
is
it
its
it's

**J**
just

**K**
knew
know

**L**
land
last
left
let
like
little
live
long
look
lot
love

**M**
mad
made
man
many
may
me
men
money
more
morning
most
mother
much
my

**N**
name
need
never
new
next
nice
night
no
not
now

**O**
of
off
oh
old
on
once
one
only
or
other
our
out
over

**P**
people
place
play
put

**R**
ran
really
red
ride
right
room
run

**S**
said
saw
say
school
see
she
should
sister
small
so
some
something
sometimes
soon
spring
started
still
summer
swimming

**T**
take
tell
ten
than
that
the
their
them
then
there
these
they
thing
think
this
three
through
time
to
told
too
took
tree
tried
two

**U**
under
until
up
upon
us

**V**
very

**W**
walk
want
wanted
was
water
way
we
well
went
were
what
when
where
which
while
white
who
why
will
with
woods
work
would

**Y**
year
yes
you
your

# Meeting Individual Needs

## Providing for Limited Spellers

### Modified Lesson

For each lesson in the student's text is an alternative lesson found in blackline copymaster format in the Teacher's Resource Book. The Modified Lesson provides an adjusted spelling program for those who are not able to study successfully every word in the weekly word list. It parallels the lesson in the student's text, using half of the weekly spelling word list. The Modified Lesson always provides the same five exercises, creating a predictable format that makes it easier for these students to do the exercises independently.

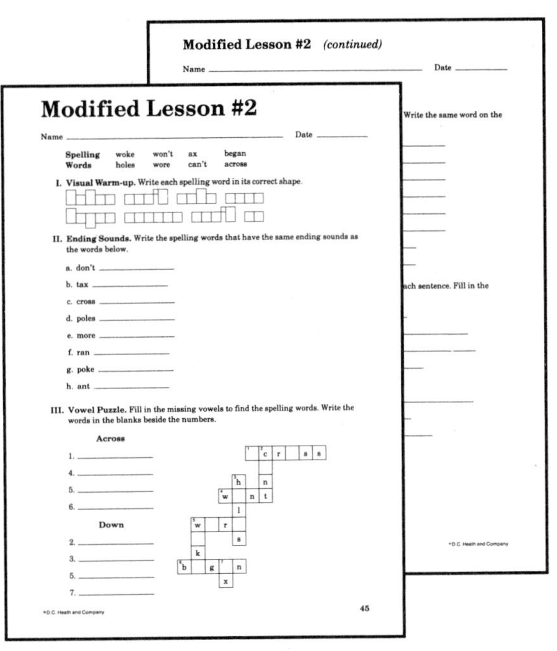

**Modified Lesson #2** *(continued)*

Name ______ Date ______

Write the same word on the

...ch sentence. Fill in the

©D.C. Heath and Company

**Modified Lesson #2**

Name ______ Date ______

**Spelling Words** woke won't ax began holes wore can't across

I. **Visual Warm-up.** Write each spelling word in its correct shape.

II. **Ending Sounds.** Write the spelling words that have the same ending sounds as the words below.

a. don't ______
b. tax ______
c. cross ______
d. poles ______
e. more ______
f. ran ______
g. poke ______
h. ant ______

III. **Vowel Puzzle.** Fill in the missing vowels to find the spelling words. Write the words in the blanks beside the numbers.

Across
1. ______
4. ______
5. ______
6. ______

Down
2. ______
3. ______
5. ______
7. ______

©D.C. Heath and Company 45

## Providing for Advanced Spellers

### Using Other Word Forms and Challenge Words

Students who demonstrate easy mastery and retention of the weekly spelling lists should still be required to complete all of the lesson exercises. The last three activities in each developmental lesson will challenge these advanced spellers.

The Using Other Word Forms activity provides practice with selected other forms of the spelling words that appear in the Other Word Forms box on the first page of the lesson. Getting advanced spellers in the habit of extending the base forms of the words they learn will give them an exceptional tool for vocabulary and spelling development.

The Challenge Words activity features challenging formats, such as word analogies. This activity presents new words that have sound/symbol patterns similar to the basic spelling words. Students are encouraged to extend what they have learned in the weekly lesson to these less familiar, more challenging words.

The Spelling and Writing activity in each developmental lesson provides practice with Other Word Forms and Challenge Words as well as the basic spelling words. Words are presented in meaningful contexts to enhance comprehension. The activity helps expand the writing vocabularies of advanced spellers.

### Challenge Exercise

This blackline copymaster, found in the Teacher's Resource Book, provides additional work with the challenge words introduced in the student's text. The formats remain challenging and include activities such as sentence completion, analogies, and etymologies. A creative writing idea focusing on the lesson's Other Word Forms is also provided.

**Challenge Exercise #3**

Name ______ Date ______

**Word Watch.** The Latin word for *book* was *liber*, and the word for *pamphlet* or *little book* was *libellus*. The contents of a *libellus* were always personal attacks on a prominent person. Later, the attacks appeared as single-page notices that could be nailed to the doors of public places. The written attacks were anonymous, but the results could still be damaging to a person's reputation. In time, the name of the leaflet was shortened to *libel*, and the word came to represent any published statement damaging to one's reputation. The word *libel* first appeared in England in the 14th century, and its spelling has remained unchanged for 600 years.

**Word Analogies.** Decide on the relationship that exists between one pair of words. Using the Other Word Forms on page 12, find a word that completes the other pair of words and establishes the same relationship.

1. disregard : ______ : : regard : notice
2. torrents : rain : : ______ : snow
3. cheer : shout : : secret : ______
4. students : instructed : : ______ : elected
5. departure : arrival : : ______ : returning

**Challenge Words Student Activity.** Use the Challenge Words below to solve the riddles.

**incredible invigorate cylindrical incision synthetic**

1. The shape of some containers: ______
2. Not the real thing: ______
3. An "unbelievable" word ______
4. A surgeon's claim to fame: ______
5. Give new vim and vitality to: ______

**Working With Words: Student Writing Activity**

Use as many Other Word Forms as you can from page 12 to write nonsense instructions for a tour guide at a National Park. (Example: To avoid sudden *crises*, step *precisely* and surely when climbing rocky surfaces.)

©D.C. Heath and Company 117

# Cooperative Team Learning

## An Alternative Teaching Approach

Research and classroom observation demonstrate that the majority of students learn very effectively from each other. Cooperative Learning taps into the learning power of students working together. Cooperative Team Learning, a formal cooperative procedure, groups students by two methods for two different purposes. One method groups students of like ability to do skills instruction. The other method groups students of mixed abilities to enhance planning or to stimulate a free flow of ideas through brainstorming and sharing. Both methods of Cooperative Team Learning can be used effectively to improve spelling power and promote the transfer of spelling words into daily writing.

A cooperative team—in this case, a pair of students—can learn to spell more effectively by identifying and correcting their own errors through the Corrected-test Procedure (see page T14) and other proofreading tasks. The steps below describe a useful procedure for cooperative teams to follow in studying, testing, and correcting their spelling words.

- **Step 1**
  Become familiar with the lesson word list and phrases. In a two-person team, one student reads the first word and phrase, the other the second word and phrase, and so on.
- **Step 2**
  The first student gives the test to the second student, reading aloud each word and phrase in the following fashion: "*cape*, a wool *cape; seemed, seemed* to know," and so on. The second student gives the test to the first student in the same manner.
- **Step 3**
  The first student spells each word correctly for the second student to begin team correcting. The correcting student touches each letter or puts a dot under each letter as the word is spelled. He or she immediately corrects the misspelled part of any word and writes it again correctly. Then the first student becomes the correcting student, and so on.
- **Step 4**
  Students record the words they missed on their **Words to Learn Sheets,** as described on page T 9. (Student Teams using the Spelling Manager, the optional computer software program, can use it to store and practice their difficult words.)

Cooperative Team Learning is also an effective alternative to the teaching strategies described in the Spelling-Writing Link for each developmental spelling lesson. Depending upon the type of activity that appears in the lesson, use the appropriate procedures outlined below.

- **Brainstorming Ideas to Answer Questions**
  Use this procedure when students need to answer questions about a story idea or questions that require higher-level thinking skills. Arrange students in pairs or small groups of mixed ability. Have each group brainstorm ideas for possible answers to the questions. Each student may record ideas and then write answers on his/her own sheet of paper.
- **Reading Passages to Answer Questions**
  Use this procedure when students are to read a passage and then answer questions. Arrange students in pairs or small groups of mixed ability. Have each group use the spelling words to brainstorm ideas for answers to the questions. Each student in a group may record ideas and then write answers on his/her own sheet of paper.
- **Writing Sentences with Spelling Words**
  Use this procedure when students must create sentences using two or more spelling words. Arrange students in pairs or small groups of mixed ability. Have each group brainstorm sentence ideas. Each student may record ideas and then write sentences on his/her own sheet of paper.
- **Proofreading Individual Work**
  Use this procedure for any activity type. Once students have completed their individual work, arrange them in pairs of like ability for proofreading. One student reads his/her work aloud while the partner looks on. As a team, students circle any word that either student suspects has an error. Partners switch roles and repeat this procedure. Next each student checks the suspected errors and makes any necessary corrections.
- **Sharing Literature**
  Use this procedure with story-idea or content-related activities. Refer to the Literature Links in the teacher notes. Assign student teams to read together the suggested stories or to research a topic using the suggested references.

### References

Durrell, Donald, ed. "Adapting Instruction to the Learning Needs of Children in the Intermediate Grades." *Boston University Journal of Education.* Boston University School of Education, 1959.

Kagan, Spencer. *Cooperative Learning.* San Juan Capistrano, CA: Resources for Teachers, Inc., 1992.

# ESL Chart for Spanish-speaking Students

Among the American school population, there is a growing segment of students learning English as a second language. Even those who are literate in their home languages—students who generally have an advantage when they learn to read and write in a second language—may have difficulty with English spellings. Spanish speakers, the largest group of these second language learners, have an added complication: spellings in their written language are regular and predictable; those of English are not.

Understanding the differences between Spanish and English sound and letter systems can provide insights into the spelling errors that Spanish speakers make when writing English. The chart below contrasts the two languages and identifies likely areas of spelling confusion, including several error categories that are common among even native English speakers (final sounds and endings, contractions, silent letters).

As an additional aid to teachers of Spanish-speaking students, WORKING WORDS IN SPELLING provides the Modified Lessons. The Modified Lessons simplify the learning of new spelling words–only half the words are practiced in five activities. Because students with limited English proficiency may not yet know the meanings of some words, the first four exercises provide practice writing the words rather than emphasizing meaning. The last exercise teaches meaning by encouraging students to use words in the context of sentences.

| ESL CHART FOR SPANISH-SPEAKING STUDENTS | |
|---|---|
| **b & v** | In Spanish the letters *b* and *v* are pronounced with the same sound – like the letter *b* in *balloon*. Students may have problems spelling words with the letter *v*. |
| **c, s, z** | In Spanish the following letters have the same sound – like the sound of the letter *s* in *sent:*<br>■ *c* preceding *e* or *i* ■ *s* ■ *z*<br>Students may be confused when spelling words with any of these three letters. |
| **ch & sh** | The *sh* digraph does not exist in Spanish. The *ch* combination is an actual letter in the Spanish alphabet and is less aspirated than the *ch* sound in English. *Ch* has the sound that is a cross between the *sh* in *shop* and the *ch* in *cheese*. Students may not recognize the sounds of *ch* and *sh* when spelling. |
| **h (initial position)** | The only silent letter in Spanish is *h*. Students may have difficulty spelling the letter *h* in the initial position of words. |
| **ge, gi, & j** | In Spanish, *ge, gi,* and *j* are strong guttural sounds with no equivalent in English. The English *h* has a sound that most closely approximates these Spanish sounds. Students may spell words such as *general* as *heneral, giraffe* as *hiraffe,* and *juvenile* as *huvenile*. These pronunciation differences can lead to spelling confusion. |
| **k** | In Spanish the letter *k* is found only in words of foreign origin and may, therefore, be unfamiliar to Spanish-speaking students. |
| **q** | The letter *q* always appears with *ue* or *ui* in Spanish and has the sound of *k* as in *kite*. |

| | |
|---|---|
| **w & wh** | The letter *w* and the digraph of *wh* do not exist in Spanish except in words of foreign origin. Spanish-speaking students may pronounce these with a *v* sound, which may cause confusion in spelling. |
| **cc, ll, rr** | There are only three double consonants in Spanish.<br>■ *cc*—pronounced like *ks* in *accent*<br>■ *ll*—pronounced like *y* in *yes*<br>■ *rr*—pronounced with a rolled-*r* sound<br>English words containing double consonants including those above may cause problems. |
| **s blends** | Because Spanish blends that begin with an *s* are always preceded by the vowels *a* or *e*, Spanish-speaking students may pronounce and spell English words with a vowel before the blends. For example, the word *scare* may become *escare*. The most common combinations that can create difficulties are *sc, sk, sl, sm, sn, sp, sq, st,* and *sw.* |
| **th** | The *th* digraph does not exist in Spanish. Students may spell *th* as *t*. For example, *that* might become *tat*. |
| **final consonant blends** | Because Spanish words do not usually end with final consonant blends, English words that do may cause confusion in spelling. Students will generally pronounce the first consonant and not the second. The most common combinations that can create difficulties are *ng, nd, st, nk, mp, nt, ft,* and *rl*. |
| **vowels** | In Spanish, vowels have a single sound:<br>■ *a* as in *spa*<br>■ *e* as in *weigh*<br>■ *i* as in *marine*<br>■ *o* as in *open*<br>■ *u* as in *tune*<br>Spanish-speaking students may have trouble with the various English vowel sounds and vowel combinations, substituting them with Spanish vowel sounds and combinations. |
| **ed** | In Spanish, the suffix *ed* is pronounced *aid*. This difference can cause problems, especially when *ed* has the soft *t* sound as in *wrapped*. |
| **plurals** | English plural words are likely to cause problems in both pronunciation and spelling for Spanish-speaking students. First of all, the pronunciation of the final *s* in English varies. It can have the *s* sound of *books* or the *z* sound of *roses*. Secondly, the rules in Spanish for adding plurals can create difficulty. These rules are:<br>■ For words ending in a vowel, add *s*.<br>Example: *casa* becomes *casas*<br>■ For words ending in a consonant, add *es*.<br>Example: *pared* becomes *paredes*<br>Spanish-speaking students may have problems with the plurals of English words ending with consonants, as most take *s*, and not *es*, for their plurals. For example, *chair* becomes *chairs*. |
| **contractions** | There are only two contractions in Spanish, and apostrophes do not exist. These contractions are:<br>■ a el = al<br>■ de el = del<br>Students may have a problem with apostrophes. |
| **silent letters** | The only silent letter in Spanish is *h*. Spanish-speaking students may omit silent letters in English words when spelling. For example, *comb* may become *com*. |

# Games

## Spelling Games and Activities

These spelling games and activities are provided for an occasional change-of-pace from the direct instruction in the core program. The purpose of the games and activities is to reinforce the basic spelling words.

## Spingo

**Players:** Small group or class.

**Materials:** A blank copy master and index cards.

**Procedure:** Create a Bingo-like game sheet with 25 one-inch squares. Draw a smaller square in the upper left-hand corner of each square. Make enough copies for every student. Then print the weekly spelling words and some Other Word Forms on 25 index cards and assign each card a number.

Provide each student with a copy of the game sheet. Have the students number the smaller squares 1 through 25 in random order. Have a student select an index card and read the number and word. The students write the word in the square with that number. The winner is the first student who fills a row across, down, or diagonally with correctly-spelled words.

## Tic-Tac-Toe

**Players:** Class.

**Materials:** Chalkboard and chalk or index cards.

**Procedure:** Put a tic-tac-toe grid on the chalkboard. Divide the class into Team X and Team 0. Have a student from each team come to the board. Read a spelling word from the weekly list (or from a previous lesson) to Player X. The student writes the word on the chalkboard. If the word is spelled correctly, the student places an X on the grid. If the word is misspelled, Player O tries to spell the word. Otherwise, a new word is read to Player 0. Continue the game with new pairs of students. When a team scores tic-tac-toe or the grid squares are filled, start a new game.

**Variation:** This game can also be played by two students, using paper and pencil. Have students write the spelling words on cards and take turns reading the words to each other.

# Games

## Word Block

**Players:** Two students.

**Materials:** A 14" x 22" sheet of oaktag, several sheets of construction paper in two different colors, a spelling book, paper, and a pencil.

**Procedure:** Prepare a game board out of the oaktag. Divide the game board into 70 two-inch squares (10 across and 7 down). Use the construction paper to create two sets of two-inch cards with 35 cards in each set.

Each player takes a set of cards. Player 1 selects a weekly spelling word or Other Word Form and asks Player 2 to spell it. Player 2 writes the word. Then Player 1 spells the word as Player 2 proofreads it, touching each letter. If correct, Player 2 places a square on the game board. Next Player 2 asks Player 1 to spell a word. Play continues until a player has 4 or 5 cards in a row across, down, or diagonally. The opposing player tries to prevent this from happening by blocking the other player's path.

## Team Spelling

**Players:** Class.

**Materials:** Index cards, a spelling book, chalkboard, and chalk.

**Procedure:** Write the weekly spelling words and some Other Word Forms on index cards. Divide the class into two teams and give each team half the cards. Teams alternate sending players on the opposing team to the chalkboard to write a spelling word. If the spelling word is written correctly, the word card is eliminated. If not, the word card remains in the game. The winner is the first team to eliminate the opposing team's word cards.

**Variation: Pitch** Write the weekly spelling words and some Other Word Forms on index cards as above. Then draw a baseball diamond on the board and a scoreboard with the number of innings to be played. Divide the class into two teams. Student pitchers from one team take turns reading words to opposing batters. Each team bats (spells a word) until three outs (misspellings) are made. Each correct spelling moves a player one base. As the players move around the bases, keep track of the runs for each team. Each run scores a point.

## Word-Search Puzzles

**Players:** Two students, small group, or class.

**Materials:** Graph paper, spelling books, and pencils.

**Procedure:** Give each student a sheet of graph paper. Ask the students to make their own word-search puzzles, using their weekly spelling words and some Other Word Forms. Tell the students to write the words across and down on the graph paper. Each letter in a word should fill one space. When all the words have been written, blank spaces should be filled with random letters. Later, have the students exchange and solve each other's puzzles. Make sure the students write the words as well as circle them.

# Games

## Codes

**Players:** Two students, small group, or class.

**Materials:** Spelling books, paper, and pencils.

**Procedure:** Give each student a sheet of paper. Ask the students to create their own special codes, using numbers or symbols to represent the letters of the alphabet. Then have the students use their codes to write each spelling word and some Other Word Forms. Later, have the students exchange and solve each other's codes.

## Write to Spell

**Players:** Small group or class.

**Materials:** Spelling books, paper, and pencils.

**Procedure:** Have a contest to see who can use the most spelling words or Other Word Forms in a sentence. Explain that although the sentence may be silly, it must be grammatical. Count only words that are spelled correctly.

## Build a Word

**Players:** Two students.

**Materials:** Index cards, a spelling book, paper, and pencil.

**Procedure:** Write selected words from the last several spelling lists on index cards. Indicate the page number in the spelling book on which each word first appears. Place the index cards face down in a pile.

Player 1 draws a card and writes as many Other Word Forms for the word as possible. Player 2 turns to the page number indicated on the index card and spells the Other Word Forms that Player 1 wrote. Player 1 touches each letter as a word is spelled and rewrites any misspelled word correctly. One point is awarded for each Other Word Form spelled correctly. Play continues with players taking turns and recording earned points on a score sheet. The winner is the player with the most points after all the word cards have been drawn.

## Dot-to-Dot Spelling

**Players:** Two students.

**Materials:** A blank duplicating master, a spelling book, paper, and a pencil.

**Procedure:** On the duplicating master, place 25 dots with 5 in each row. The dots should be about one inch apart. Provide the students with a copy of the game sheet, paper, and a pencil. Have the students alternate asking each other to spell a list word or Other Word Form. If the student spells a word correctly, two dots are connected with a line, across or down. The purpose is to form small squares. The student who closes up a square puts his or her initials in the square. The student with the greatest number of completed squares is the winner.

# Spelling Bibliography


Andrini, Beth. *Cooperative Learning: A Multi-Structural Approach.* San Juan Capistrano, CA: Resources for Teachers, Inc., 1991.

Baldwin, Ronald F. "The Effect of Teacher In-service Training and Knowledge of Research on Spelling Instruction and Achievement of Elementary School Children." Ph.D. Thesis, University of Iowa, 1975.

Barbe, Walter B., Azalia S. Francis, and Lois A. Braun, eds. *Spelling: Basic Skills for Effective Communication.* Columbus, OH: Zaner-Bloser, Inc., 1982.

Buchanan, Ethel. *Spelling for Whole Language Classrooms.* Winnepeg, Manitoba: Whole Language Consultants, 1989.

Carroll, J. B., Peter Davies, and Barry Richman. *Word Frequency Book.* New York: The American Heritage Publishing Co., 1971.

Chomsky, Carol. "Reading, Writing and Phonology." *Harvard Educational Review,* Vol. 40, May, 1970.

Chomsky, Noam, and Morris Halle. *The Sound Pattern of English.* New York: Harper and Row, 1968.

Cohen, Gloria Freeman. "A Developmental Study of Word Recognition Processes." Ed.D. Thesis, Rutgers, The State University of New Jersey, 1975.

Cohen, Leo A. "Evaluating Structural Analysis Methods Used in Spelling Books." Ed.D. Thesis, Boston University, 1969.

Culyer, Gail Blake. "A Synthesized Approach to Selecting Spelling Words and Generalizations." Ph.D. Thesis, The Florida State University, 1974.

Dale, Edgar, and Joseph O'Rourke. *The Living Word Vocabulary.* Chicago: World Book-Childcraft International, Inc., 1981.

Di Stefano, Philip, and Patricia Hagerty. "Teaching Spelling at the Elementary Level." *The Reading Teacher,* Vol. 38, January, 1985.

Durrell, Donald, ed. "Adapting Instruction to the Learning Needs of Children in the Intermediate Grades." *Boston University Journal of Education.* Boston University School of Education, 1959.

Fitzsimmons, Robert J., and Bradley M. Loomer. *Spelling: The Research Basis.* Iowa City: The University of Iowa, 1980.

Flood, James, and Peter H. Salus. *Language and the Language Arts.* Englewood Cliffs, NJ: Prentice-Hall, Inc., 1984.

Frith, Uta, ed. *Cognitive Processes in Spelling.* London: Academic Press, 1980.

Fry, Edward, and Dona Fountoukidis. *The Reading Teacher's Book of Lists.* Englewood Cliffs, NJ: Prentice-Hall, Inc., 1993.

Gates, Arthur I. *Generalization and Transfer in Spelling.* New York: Columbia University, 1935.

Gentry, J. Richard, and Jean Wallace Gillet. *Teaching Kids to Spell.* Portsmouth, NH: Heinemann, 1993.

Gentry, J. Richard, and Edmund H. Henderson. "Three Steps to Teaching Beginning Readers to Spell." *The Reading Teacher,* Vol. 31, March, 1978.

Glazier, Stephen. *Word Menu.* New York: Random House, 1992.

Graves, Donald H. "Research Update of Spelling Texts and Structural Analysis Methods." *Language Arts,* Vol. 54, No. 1. Urbana, IL: National Council of Teachers of English, 1977.

Greene, Henry A., and Bradley M. Loomer. *The New Iowa Spelling Scale.* Iowa City: The University of Iowa, 1977.

Haber, Ralph Norman, and Lyn R. Haber. "The Shape of a Word Can Specify Its Meaning." *Reading Research Quarterly,* Vol. XVI, No. 3. Newark, DE: International Reading Association, Inc., 1981.

Hagerty, Patricia. "Comparative Analysis of High Frequency Words Found in Commercial Spelling Series and Misspelled in Students' Writing to a Standard Measure of Word Frequency." Ed.D. Thesis, University of Colorado, 1981.

Hakanson, Edward Eric. "The Relationship Between Selected Visual and Auditory Perception Capacities and Spelling Capability as Measured by Tests Requiring Spelling Recognition and Spelling Recall." Ph.D. Thesis, University of Minnesota, 1966.

Hanna, Paul R., et al. *Phoneme-Grapheme Correspondences as Cues to Spelling Improvement.* Washington, DC: Government Printing Office, U.S. Office of Education, 1966.

Hanna, Paul R., Richard E. Hodges, and Jean S. Hanna. *Spelling: Structures and Strategies.* Boston: Houghton Mifflin Co., 1971.

Harp, Bill. "When the Principal Asks, 'Why Are Your Kids Giving Each Other Spelling Tests?'" *Reading Teacher,* Vol. 41, No. 7, March, 1988.

Henderson, Edmund H. *Teaching Spelling.* Boston: Houghton Mifflin Company, 1990.

Henderson, Edmund H. *Learning to Read and Spell.* DeKalb, IL: Northern Illinois University Press, 1981.

Henderson, Edmund H., and James W. Beers, eds. *Developmental and Cognitive Aspects of Learning to Spell: A Reflection of Word Knowledge.* Newark, DE: International Reading Association, Inc., 1980.

Henderson, Edmund H., and Shane Templeton. "A Developmental Perspective of Formal Spelling Instruction through Alphabet, Pattern, and Meaning." *The Elementary School Journal,* Vol. 66, No. 3, 1986.

Hillerich, Robert L. *Spelling: An Element of Written Expression.* Columbus, OH: Charles E. Merrill, Co., 1976.

Hillerich, Robert L. "Spelling: To Teach Not Just to Observe." *Illinois Schools Journal,* Vol. 66, No. 2, 1987.

Hodges, Richard E. "The Conventions of Writing." *Handbook of Research on Teaching the English Language Arts.* New York: Macmillan, 1991.

Horn, Ernest. *A Basic Writing Vocabulary: 10,000 Frequently Used Words in Writing.* Monograph First Series, No 4. Iowa City: The University of Iowa, 1926.

Horn, Ernest. "Spelling." *Encyclopedia of Educational Research,* 3rd ed. New York: Macmillan, 1960.

Horn, Thomas. "The Effect of the Corrected Test on Learning to Spell." Master's Thesis, The University of Iowa, 1946.

Horn, Thomas. "The Effect of Syllable Presentation of Words Upon Learning to Spell." Ph.D. Thesis, The University of Iowa, 1947.

Horn, Thomas. "Spelling." *Encyclopedia of Educational Research,* 4th ed. New York: Macmillan, 1969.

Horn, Thomas, and H. J. Otto. *Spelling Instruction: A Curriculum-Wide Approach.* Austin, TX: University of Texas, 1954.

Horsky, Gregory Alexander. "A Study of the Perception of Letters and Basic Sight Vocabulary Words of Fourth and Fifth Grade Children." Ph.D. Thesis, The University of Iowa, 1974.

Humphry, M. O. "The Effect of a Syllabic Presentation of Words Upon Learning to Spell." Master's Thesis, University of Texas, 1954.
Kagan, Spencer. *Cooperative Learning.* San Juan Capistrano, CA: Resources for Teachers, Inc., 1992.
Kingsley, J. H. "The Test-Study Method Versus Study-Test Method in Spelling." *Elementary School Journal,* Vol. 24. Chicago: The University of Chicago Press, 1923.
Larson, I. M. "Time Allotment in the Teaching of Spelling." Master's Thesis, University of Iowa, 1945.
Loomer, Bradley M. *Educator's Guide to Spelling Research and Practice.* Iowa City: The University of Iowa, Project Spelling, 1978.
Loomer, Bradley M. *The Most Commonly Asked Questions About Spelling . . . and What the Research Says.* North Billerica, MA: Curriculum Associates, 1982.
Lutz, Elaine. "ERIC/RCS Report: Invented Spelling and Spelling Development." *Language Arts,* Vol. 63, No. 7. November, 1986.
Lyman, Lawrence, and Harvey C. Foyle. *Cooperative Grouping for Interactive Learning: Students, Teachers, and Administrators.* Washington, DC: National Education Association, 1990.
MacGregor, Sister Marilyn. "Multiple Regression Analysis of Essential Variables Contributing to Spelling Achievement." Ed.D. Thesis, Boston University School of Education, 1976.
Maheady, Larry, and George F. Harper. "A Class-Wide Peer Tutoring Program to Improve the Spelling Test Performance of Low- Income, Third- and Fourth-Grade Students." *Education and Treatment of Children,* Vol. 10, No. 2. May, 1987.
Marino, Jacqueline L. "Children's Use of Phonetic, Graphemic, and Morphophonemic Cues in a Spelling Task." Ed.D. Thesis, State University of New York at Albany, 1978.
McSweeney, Miriam J. "Word Usage Techniques in Spelling." Ed.D. Thesis, Boston University, 1959.
Morris, Darrell. "Meeting the Needs of Poor Spellers in Elementary School: A Developmental Prospective." *Illinois Schools Journal,* Vol. 66, No. 2. 1987.
Petty, Walter T. "An Analysis of Certain Phonetic Elements in a Selected List of Persistently Difficult Spelling Words." Ph.D. Thesis, University of Iowa, 1955.
Read, Charles. *Children's Categorization of Speech Sounds in English Research.* Report No. 17. Urbana, IL: National Council of Teachers of English, 1975.
Read, Charles. *Children's Creative Spelling.* London: Routledge & Kegan Paul, 1986.
Read, Charles, and Richard Hodges. "Spelling." *Encyclopedia of Educational Research.* 5th Ed. New York: Macmillan, 1982.
Rinsland, Harry. *A Basic Vocabulary of Elementary School Children.* New York: Macmillan Co., 1945.
Schroeder, Howard H. "An Analysis of the Use of Visual and Auditory Perception in Spelling Instruction." Ph.D. Thesis, University of Iowa, 1968.
Simmons, Janice Louise. "The Relationship Between an Instructional Level in Spelling and the Instructional Level in Reading Among Elementary School Children," Ed.D. Thesis, University of Northern Colorado, 1978.
Sitton, Rebecca. *Increasing Student Spelling Achievement: Not Just on Tests, But in Daily Writing Across the Curriculum.* Bellevue, WA: Bureau of Education & Research, 1992.
Sitton, Rebecca. *Spelling Sourcebook 1: Your Guide for Developing Research-Based Spelling Instruction for the Writing-Rich Classroom.* Spokane, WA, 1993.
Sowers, Susan. "Six Questions Teachers Ask About Invented Spellings." *Understanding Writing: Ways of Observing, Learning & Thinking.* Eds. Thomas Newkirk and Nancie Atwell. Portsmouth, NH: Heinemann, 1986. 47–56.
Stetson, Elton, and Cheryl Laurent, eds. *Training Teachers to Use Research-Based Strategies Improves Student Achievement in Spelling.* Region V Education Service Center, 1984.
Stetson, Elton, Wendy Taylor, and Frances J. Boutin. *Eighty Years of Theory and Practice in Spelling: Those Who Wrote the Programs Forgot to Read the Literature.* Clearwater, FL: National Reading Conference, 1982.
Tarasoff, Mary. *Spelling Strategies You Can Teach.* Victoria, British Columbia: Pixelart Graphics, 1990.
Templeton, Shane. "Synthesis of Research on the Learning and Teaching of Spelling." *Educational Leadership,* Vol. 43, March, 1986.
Templeton, Shane. *Teaching the Integrated Language Arts.* Boston: Houghton Mifflin, Co., 1991.
Thomas, Ves. *Teaching Spelling.* Agincourt, Ontario: Gage Educational Publishing, Limited, 1979.
Thompson, Murray Daniel Jr. "The Effects of Spelling Patterns Training on the Spelling Behavior of Primary Elementary Students: An Evaluative Study." Ph.D. Thesis, University of Pittsburgh, 1977.
Thorndike, Edward L., and Irving Lorge. *The Teacher's Word Book of 30,000 Words.* New York: Columbia University, 1944.
Tireman, L. S. "The Value of Marking Hard Spots in Spelling." Master's Thesis, University of Iowa, 1927.
Wilde, Sandra. "A Proposal for a New Spelling Curriculum." *The Elementary School Journal,* Vol. 90, No. 3, 1990.
Wilde, Sandra. *You Kan Red This! Spelling and Punctuation for Whole Language Classrooms, K–6.* Portsmouth, NH: Heinemann, 1992.
Zutell, Jerry. "Spelling Strategies of Primary School Children and Their Relationship to Piaget's Concept of Decentration." *Research in the Teaching of English,* Vol. 13, February, 1979.

**Recent Publications**

Bolton, F., and D. Snowball. *Ideas for Spelling.* Portsmouth, NH: Heinemann, 1993.
Routman, Regie. "Reclaiming the Basics." *Instructor,* May/June 1996.
Stowe, Cynthia. *Spelling Smart!.* Englewood Cliffs, NJ: Center for Applied Research in Education, 1996.

***On the Internet***

*Spelling Instruction, A Bibliography of Spelling Research.* Bloomington, IN: ERIC Clearinghouse on Reading, English and Communications, Smith Research Center, User Service Division. E-mail address: ERICCS@indiana.edu

# Acknowledgments

## Readers

Dr. Marie Carducci Bolchazy
Reading/Language Arts Coordinator
Barrington School District 220
Barrington, IL

Dr. Rose M. Feinburg
Curriculum Coordinator K–8/ Director of Reading K–12
Needham Public Schools
Needham, MA

Lawrence G. Mickel
Principal
Orchard Hill Elementary School
South Windsor, CT

Maurice Poe
Associate Dean and Professor of Education
California State University
School of Education
Sacramento, CA

Rosemarie Wilkinson, Ed. D.
Language Arts Consultant
LaPorte ISD
La Porte, TX

## Field-test Coordinators

Martha Anderson
Principal
Crest View Elementary School
Waco, TX

Dr. Marie Carducci Bolchazy
Reading/Language Arts Coordinator
Barrington School District 220
Barrington, IL

C. Kenneth Delani
Principal
Josiah Haynes Elementary School
Sudbury, MA

Marsha Dolkas
Resource Specialist
E. V. Cain Middle School and Rock Creek School
Auburn, CA

Maureen Hagar
Language Arts Consultant
Arlington Heights District 25
Arlington Heights, IL

Beulah M. Johnson
Principal
South Waco Elementary School
Waco, TX

Leo J. LaMontagne
Principal
Ibn Khuldoon National School
Manama, Bahrain

Lawrence G. Mickel
Principal
Orchard Hill Elementary School
South Windsor, Connecticut

## Field-test Participants

### California

Fresno

- Kurt Watson
  Rowell Elementary School

Los Gatos

- Carol Burt
  Daves Avenue School
- Marianne Coveney
  Eileen Perkins
  Fisher Middle School

Monterey

- Rose DeBerry
  La Mesa Elementary School

Willits

- Douglas F. Case
  Baechtel Grove Middle School

### Connecticut

South Windsor

- Audrey Longo
  Fay Maguire
  Orchard Hill Elementary School

West Simsbury

- Edwin Boiczyk
  Tootin' Hills Elementary School

### Massachusetts

Lexington

- Laurie Fales
  Joseph Josiassen
  Harrington School

Sudbury

- Maria M. Papetti
  Josiah Haynes Elementary School

### Texas

Corpus Christi

- Ada Besinaiz
  Sara Dennis
  Sharon Flinn
  Magee Elementary School
- Anita Danaher
  Wood River Elementary School

New Brauntfels

- Joe Falsone
  Janice Gandy
  Susan Ott
  Deborah Smith
  Seele Elementary School

Waco

- Linda Taylor
  Alta Vista Elementary School